Tallest mohican

Kazuhiro Watanabe (Japan) boasts a truly hair-raising pompadour, in the shape of a 113.5-cm-tall (44.6-in) mohican. The height was verified at the Bloc de l'art hair salon in Tokyo, Japan, on 28 October 2011. It took a team of hair stylists four hours to sculpt Kazuhiro's gravity-defying coiffure.

TO THE LIMITS

Exploring the extremes of record-breaking

It took 50,000 years of evolution for a human to run a mile in less than four minutes; within two months, the record had been beaten... twice!

Do world records have their limits? Is there a point beyond which a record cannot be broken? This is a key question here at Guinness World Records because one of the fundamental criteria for us is that a record is breakable (apart from significant "firsts", of course). Yet surely there is an upper limit to every record...

For this year's book, we have asked our consultants, advisers and records managers to explore the outer limits of some popular categories. The question, each time, is how far can a record be pushed? So, what's the greatest age to which a human can live? Or the heaviest weight an athlete can lift in competition? Or the tallest tower we can build?

You'll find these features at the beginning of each chapter. What you may not find is a definitive answer to each question – some extremes are impossible to predict, of course, but we can at least explore the fascinating factors that define their limits.

FACT: The speed of light is considered the absolute speed limit in the universe; in theory, nothing is faster...

Can you live to 130 years?

Gerontology is the study of ageing (the word comes from the Greek for "old man" and "study"). To help us assess claims from the world's oldest people, we enlist the help of gerontologist Robert Young. His task is to ensure that claimants provide all the required documentation to support their stories.

In "How Long Can We Live?" on pp.66–67, Robert looks at the limits to old age. Will a man ever live longer than Christian Mortensen (right), the **oldest man ever** at 115 years 252 days? Will *anyone* ever exceed the 122 years 164 days of Jeanne Calment (below), the **oldest person ever**. And crucially, will they be able to prove it?!

HOW FAST CAN WE RUN?

How quickly can a human run 100 metres?

When Usain Bolt (Jamaica) ran the 100 m in 9.58 seconds, he smashed not only the world record but also the mathematical theories about athletic ability. Scientists did not expect anyone to go that fast until 2060. Can he go faster? If so, what's the fastest speed that it is physically possible to reach?

Sports scientist John Brenkus has written about this very subject in his book *The Perfection Point*. The perfect athlete would benefit from the ultimate in genetics, nutrition and training. But how much faster than Usain Bolt could this perfect athlete travel all if he were to make a flawless run in ideal conditions?

As Brenkus explains, the 100 m is a simple concept – you run from A to B as quickly as possible – but this involves four key stages:

1. Reacting to the gun: Starting pistols are a thing of the past. Why? The sound takes 0.025 seconds to travel the 9 m (36 ft) from lane 1 to lane 9, giving the first athlete an advantage. Today, the race starts with a beep from a speaker placed behind each runner. The key is to react quickly, but not too quickly. The perfect start is one-tenth of a second (100 milliseconds) after the beep. Moving off the blocks sooner than this will trigger a false start. If Usain Bolt had managed to get away in one-tenth of a second for his record-breaking run in 2009, he would have finished in 9.51 seconds.

2. Getting out of the blocks: While it's good to have strong calf and thigh muscles to get that explosive start, if they're too powerful, they'll be too heavy for a record-worthy sprint.

FACT: John D Rockefeller was the richest man who ever lived. Can anyone else ever beat his billions?

4. Slowing down as challenge is not possible: The final decelerating too quickly. Air resistance continues to act on runners, but by now their muscles will start to tire too and they won't be able to speed up the rate at which they are taking individual steps. Instead, they should increase their stride length – so that they can cover as great a distance as possible with each pace.

So, taking Usain Bolt's record time of 9.58 seconds and adjusting for what we've learned from the four stages, the result is a potential time of 9.01 seconds. But just think. It took humanity 190,000 years of development to run a mile in under 4 minutes. Once this barrier was breached – a barrier more psychological than physical – it took just 46 days for someone else to do it. 10 years later, 336 people had achieved it! So if 9.01 seconds seems an absolute scientific limit, then breaking the 9-second barrier will become the new holy grail of athletics. And as humans seem to have an inbuilt desire to overcome apparently insurmountable obstacles, it is surely conceivable that the barrier will be broken. Therefore, the real limit is 8.99 seconds.

THE PERFECT 100 M ATHLETE

Height: 1.87 m (6 ft 2 in)

Reaction time: 100 millisec

Head: shaved, with aerodynamic sunglasses

Altitude: 1,000 m (3,280 ft)

Tailwind: 2 m/sec (4.4 mi/h)

Leg inseam: 1 m (40 in)

Muscles: ideal balance of muscle fibres: 55–65% fast-twitch; 35–45% slow-twitch; 30.4 cm wide (12 in) thighs

Climate: barometric pressure of 986.78 millibars (29.14 in), 15% humidity, 27.7˚C (82˚F)

Running suit: skin-tight material to make air flow smoothly around body

Top speed: 41.3 km/h (29.4 mi/h)

Weight: 87 kg (192 lb) – only 4% fat

Shoes: lightest possible

ASAFA POWELL

CARL LEWIS

POWELL

FACT: Hossein Rezazadeh's over-105 kg weightlifting record has stood for 12 years. Is it unbeatable?

1895 (20 YEARS)   **1915 (40 YEARS)**   **1935 (60 YEARS)**   **1988 (113 YEARS)**   **1997 (122 YEARS)**

FEARSOME FLIERS · MASSIVE MAMMALS

IG CAN ANIMALS GET?

mit to animal life?

e, dinosaurs were not the largest creatures
e don't need to look into prehistory to find
holder: we currently share our planet with the
ver lived – the blue whale (see below). But
represent the absolute in animal size? What
tures, or birds? Here, GWR zoologist Dr Karl
Shuker sizes up the planet's largest inhabitants.

Size comparison Here we see the relative sizes of the mightiest creatures on Earth. Nothing on land has ever exceeded c.100 tonnes (220,000 lb) in the oceans, the upper limit is a 160-tonne (352,000-lb) whale.

Key
1. Blue whale
2. Argentinosaurus
3. Paralaxesatenean
4. Giganotosaurus
5. Quetzalcoatlus
6. African elephant
7. Human

African elephant (Loxodonta africana) – **largest ungulate and largest land mammal** 3–3.7 m (9 ft 10 in–12 ft 1 in) to shoulder; 4–7 tonnes (8,800–15,400 lb)

Alaskan moose (Alces alces gigas) – **largest deer** 2.34 m (7 ft 8 in) to shoulder

Quetzalcoatlus (Quetzalcoatlus northropi) – **largest flying creature** 12 m (39 ft) wingspan; 113 kg (250 lb)

A 160-tonne blue whale can **exist because of the support it receives from the water.** But on land, the upper weight limit – based on fossil evidence – is around 70–100 tonnes (154,000–220,000 lb), in the case of the herbivorous Argentinosaurus, which existed 95 million years ago.

A figure of about 100 tonnes is also the limit reached theoretically when examining the stress limits of bones – and the corresponding increase in muscle size – in terrestrial animals. Such a creature is feasible but would be limited by gravity, the availability of resources, the turnaround of offspring (larger animals produce fewer babies) and a lack of adaptability in times of crisis (such as a food shortage).

So if we were going to find an animal bigger than the blue whale, it would have to be in the oceans. Could the mysterious "Bloop" (see p.206) be a contender?

FACT: Argentinosaurus is known only from a few fragments found in the 1980s. Its skeleton towered some 7.3 m (24 ft).

Theropods ("beast-footed" dinosaurs) – largest ever land carnivores: up to 13 m (43 ft) long; 6 tonnes (13,230 lb)

Aldabra giant tortoise (Aldabrachelys gigantea) – **largest tortoise** 1.22 m (48 in) wide

Eastern lowland Gorilla (Gorilla beringei graueri) – **largest primate**, 163 kg (360 lb)

American bison (Bison bison) – **largest migrant on land** 2 m (6 ft 5 in) to shoulder; c.1 tonne (2,200 lb)

Red kangaroo (Macropus rufus) – **largest kangaroo** 1.8 m (5 ft 11 in) tall; 90 kg (198 lb)

Hippopotamus (Hippopotamus amphibius) – **heaviest artiodactyl**: up to 3,630 kg (8,000 lb); 1.4 m (4 ft 7 in) to shoulder

Southern white rhinoceros (Ceratotherium simum simum) – **largest rhino**: 1.5–4.6 m long; 3,500 kg (7,700 lb)

Wolf (Canis lupus) – **largest canid**: 1–1.6 m (39.5–63 in) long; weight: 16–80 kg

Saltwater crocodile (Crocodylus porosus) – **largest crocodilian**: 7 m (23 ft) long; 520 kg (1,150 lb)

Whale shark (Rhincodon typus) – **largest fish**: 12.65 m (41 ft 6 in) long; 15–21 tonnes (33,000–46,200 lb)

African ostrich

TO THE LIMITS

INTO THE ABYSS · MINING THE DEPTHS · FEELING THE PRESSURE

HOW DEEP CAN WE GO?

What's the greatest depth we can reach?

With his Virgin Oceanic project, Richard Branson (UK) hopes to achieve a solo trip to the deepest points in every ocean. But just how far will he be able to descend in his Deep Flight Challenger submersible? What's the absolute limit when it comes to plumbing the depths of our planet?

318.2 m (1,044 ft) Deepest scuba dive: Nuno Gomes (South Africa) descended a limb of a mine in the Red Sea off Dahab, Egypt, on 10 June 2005.

212 m (695 ft) Deepest half marathon: A competition between 11 racers in the Bochnia salt mine in Poland on 3 March 2004.

1.3 km (4,166 ft) Deepest concert: Agonizer (Finland) played in the Pyhäsalmi Mine Oy at Pyhäjärvi, Finland, on 4 August 2007.

1 km (3,345 ft) Deepest operational combat submarine: No military sub has gone deeper than the Russian K-278.

2 km (1.2 miles) Deepest dive by a mammal: A bull sperm whale (Physeter macrocephalus) studied off the coast of Dominica in the Caribbean in 1991.

2.4 km (1.5 miles) Deepest live TV broadcast by a presenter: Alastair Fothergill (UK) relayed Abyss Live for the BBC on 29 September 2002 from inside a Mir submersible, along the Mid-Atlantic Ridge off the east coast of the USA.

2.191 km (1.3 miles) Deepest cave: In September 2007, Ukrainian cavers (speleologists) reached a new record depth at the Krubera Cave in the Arabika Massif of Georgia.

4 km (2.5 miles) Wreck of RMS Titanic The pride of the White Star Line (UK) was sunk on 15 April 1912 off Newfoundland, Canada, with the loss of 1,522 lives. **The youngest person to dive to the Titanic** is Sebastian Harris (UK), who was 13 years old when he visited the site in the Mir 2 submersible on 2 August 2005.

3.6 km (2.2 miles) Deepest land-dwelling creature The 0.5-mm-long (0.02-in) nematode worm Halicephalobus mephisto – aka the "worm from Hell" – was found in a South African goldmine in 2011.

3.9 km (2.4 miles) Deepest mine: The TauTona gold mine near Carletonville, South Africa, began operation in 1962 and by 2008, had reached 3.9 km (2.4 miles) deep. It can take one hour to descend in the lift cage.

6.5 km (4 miles) Deepest submersible in service Built in 1990, the Shinkai 6500 is a Japanese three-man research submarine with a 7.35-cm-thick (2.9-in) hull. It made its 1,000th dive in 2007.

5.8 km (3.6 miles) Deepest shipwreck: World War II German blockade runner SS Rio Grande, discovered in 1996 at the bottom of the South Atlantic Ocean, on 30 November 1996.

..5.2 miles)
..fish: A 20-cm-long (8-in) ..of cusk-eel (Pseudoliparis ...el found in the Puerto Rico ..of the Atlantic Ocean.

10.9 km (6.7 miles) Deepest descent by a manned vessel Jacques Piccard (Switzerland) and Donald Walsh (USA) piloted the bathyscaphe Trieste to the "Challenger Deep" section of the Mariana Trench (see below) on 23 January 1960. On 25 March 2012, James Cameron (USA) made the same journey alone – the **deepest solo descent** – in the DEEPSEA CHALLENGER.

10.1 km (6.2 miles) Deepest oil well: The Deepwater Horizon semi-submersible drilling rig operated to this depth in the Tiber oil field in the Gulf of Mexico.

12.3 km (7.6 miles) Deepest penetration into Earth's crust: A geological exploratory borehole near Zapolyarny on the Kola peninsula of Arctic Russia. It was begun on 24 May 1970 and had reached this record depth in 1983, when work stopped because of a lack of funds.

FACT: To reach the Earth's centre of the crust, you'd have to drill 6,370 km (3,958 miles)

Deepest points in each ocean: Pacific: 10.9 km; Indian: 8.05 km; Southern: 7.24 km; Arctic: 5.45 km; Atlantic: 8.38 km

Tallest towers At 828 m (2,716 ft 6 in) to the top of its spire, the Burj Khalifa is currently the **tallest building** on Earth. Is the 1-km-tall (3,280-ft) tower planned for Saudi Arabia even possible?

On land: Even at 12.2 km (7.6 miles), the deepest bore hole (see below) is barely a scratch on Earth's surface. The planet's outer crust comprises 35 km (21.5 miles) of solid rock. Assuming we could stop water seeping into our hole – a constant problem in mines – we'd also have to contend with temperatures that rise the deeper we go; at the bottom of the 3,900-m-deep (2.4-mile) TauTona mineshaft (above), the heat rises to 55°C (131°F).

On breaking through the crust, we'd then face the challenge of the mantle: some 3,000 km (1,864 miles) of super-heated rock at 400–900°C (752–1,652°F) – depending on depth. Temperatures here are far beyond the operational limits of any heatproof suit known to man. Still want to keep digging?

In the ocean: Human beings evolved to live on land. Under the water, we soon discover the limits this places on us. We can't breathe, our senses become dulled, and the pressure exerted by the water as we travel deeper becomes increasingly dangerous. Here, we are little more than ill-equipped cavemen, using technology to plunge our Stone Age bodies into the abyss.

However, by shielding our fragile bodies from the effects of pressure, nitrogen narcosis and oxygen toxicity, we can voyage to the deepest, darkest crevices on our planet. As humans have already travelled to the deepest known point in the ocean, this is one record that has already been broken. The Virgin team now faces the added challenge of making the first solo dives to the deepest points in the oceans. Good luck!

FACT: The last 11 years are among the top 12 warmest years on record. Can we survive global warming?

How low can you go?

In March 2012, moviemaker James Cameron (Canada, inset) made the **deepest solo dive**, reaching the bottom of the Mariana Trench in the Pacific Ocean. Now, Richard Branson (UK, bottom right) hopes to visit the deepest points in each ocean. But what is the absolute limit to our deepest desires? GWR's adventure advisor Mike Flynn takes us in search of Earth's final frontiers on pp.114–115.

Virgin Oceanic

British Library Cataloguing-in-Publication Data:
A catalogue record for this book is available from the British Library

ISBN: 978-1-904994-86-2

Special thanks: Matthew White; Nigel Wright and Janice Browne at XAB Design.

For a complete list of credits and acknowledgements, turn to p.284.

If you wish to make a record claim, find out how on p.14. Always contact us before making a record attempt.

Check the official website – www.guinnessworldrecords.com – regularly for record-breaking news, plus video footage of record attempts. You can also join and interact with the GWR online community.

Sustainability
The trees that are harvested to print *Guinness World Records* are carefully selected from managed forests to avoid the devastation of the landscape.

The paper contained within this edition is manufactured by Stora Enso Veitsiluoto, Finland. The production site is Chain-of-Custody certified and operates within environmental systems certificated to ISO 14001 to ensure sustainable production.

Typefaces
This edition of *Guinness World Records* is set in Locator, a beautifully proportioned and highly readable sans serif typeface designed in the early 1990s by Robert Slimbach and Carol Twombly (both USA).

The display typeface is the sans serif font **Fargon**, which was designed in 2001 by Robby Woodard (USA). It was selected for its sci-fi feel, resonating with this year's theme of scientific exploration and discovery.

Pictured on the opposite page is the world's **biggest skateboard**. You'll find more about this behemoth of a board on p.103.

OFFICIALLY AMAZING

GUINNESS WORLD RECORDS 2013

CONTENTS

New design: Easy to read, clean-cut layout organized into colour-coded sections

Trip of a lifetime: Pay a visit to the new "World Tour" chapter on pp.126–39 and discover some record-breaking tourist hot spots

Actual size: Look out for this icon – it means you're seeing record holders at 100%

LEGO: Why is the Toy of the 20th century a record-breaker? See pp.176–77, 196–97 and 226–27.

Infographics: At-a-glance stats and figures fully illustrated down the right-hand page

4,000 entries: Fully revised with 3,000 new and updated superlative achievements

Trivia: Dizzying data, fun facts and awesome accomplishments in bite-sized chunks

Fantastic photography: More than 1,500 amazing images, including many seen here for the first time

BONUS CHAPTER

Find out more about how this year's book was created in the GWR 2013 Bonus Chapter – available exclusively in digital form. As well as going behind the scenes at the GWR offices, and presenting you with some never-before-seen photographs and records, we introduce you to our sports advisors and record managers, who will take the chance to update you on all the records broken at the 2012 London Olympics. To access this unique feature, visit **www.guinnessworldrecords.com/bonuschapter** – or if you've got access to a QR reader, scan the code above.

AUGMENTED REALITY

This year, the records are virtually exploding off the page thanks to our new Augmented Reality (AR) feature. It's a FREE app available to anyone with an iPhone/iTouch/iPad or Android device with a camera. Download the app using the QR code below or visit **www.guinnessworldrecords.com/seeit3d**. Then, when you see the **SEE IT 3D** logo in the book, point your device at the page and see records come to life in full 3D animation.

We're going to need a bigger book...
Check out the AR features:
Great white shark: 48–49
Bird-eating spider: 54–55
Slam-dunking parrot: 62–63
Shortest man: 64–65
Shortest dog: 144–45
Smallest helicopter: 182–183

SEE IT 3D

LOOK OUT FOR CROSS-REFERENCES TO RELATED RECORDS

EDITOR'S LETTER

A big thank you to everyone who's helped to make Guinness World Records a superlative success over the past year...

In the last 12 months, we've received 7,896 record applications from the UK and Ireland. Of these, just 261 made it through our rigorous ratification process, ranging from the **largest sticky toffee pudding** (334 kg; 736 lb 5 oz) in Lancashire and **longest cucumber** (107 cm; 42.1 in) in Gwent to the **oldest living female twins** (103-year-olds) in Aberdeenshire and the **largest human beatbox ensemble** (2,081), from Dublin, Ireland.

Globally, GWR records managers processed around 50,000 applications over the past year, and the British Isles' contribution to record-breaking places it second in the world, just behind the (rather larger) USA. So thank you to everyone who's made a claim – keep them coming!

One of the most exciting and gratifying aspects of working with this extraordinary organization is that there is no let-up in the enthusiasm for record-breaking. This year I am marking a decade with Guinness World Records, and I can say with authority that inspiring accomplishments continue to flood in, pushing the boundaries of what's humanly possible.

A newspaper journalist once asked me why we bother to continue monitoring record-breaking, given that every record worth breaking has been broken. Well, ask that question to the likes of film-maker/explorer James Cameron (Canada), who, at the time of writing, has just made the **first solo dive to the deepest point in the ocean** (see p.114), or the crew of the *Tûranor PlanetSolar*, the **first ship to circumnavigate the globe on solar power** (p.117), or 12-year-old Tom Schaar (USA), who managed to pull off the **first 1080 on a skateboard** – a trick that has defied even the most experienced skaters (p.287).

It's been 100 years since Roald Amundsen (Norway) made the **first visit to the South Pole** (p.116), but the desire for exploration and discovery is as healthy as it has always been, as our Adventure chapter (pp.112–25) proves.

There, you'll find a timeline of pioneering, plus an awe-inspiring collection of the recent records from explorers and globetrotters who personify the spirit of adventure and continue to widen our horizons.

Inspired by this question of the limits of record-breaking, we've included a feature at the start of each chapter that explores the absolutes of human accomplishment. The questions are simple – How fast can an athlete run? How tall can we build? How long can we live? – but the answers are less straightforward. You'll find an explanation of these "To the Limits" features on pp.2–3.

Vertical visitor: Being the **tallest man alive**, Sultan Kösen (Turkey) makes friends wherever he goes. Here he is visiting a school in the UK in March 2012, reassuring the students that it's good to be different. Turn to pp.78–79 to see how tall Sultan is and discover how the nations of the world size up against each other.

Chocoholics beware

GWR's Jacqui Fitt measures the **most expensive non-jewelled chocolate egg**, filled with couture chocolate and truffles and boasting edible gold leaf. It sold for £7,000 ($11,107) at a charity auction held on 20 March 2012 as part of World Record London, a series of record attempts organized by London & Partners (UK) in the run-up to the 2012 Olympics.

Botafogo-a-go-go: Artem Chigvintsev (Russia, above with TV star Kara Tointon) performed the **most botafogo dance steps in 30 seconds** on the set of *Strictly Come Dancing: It Takes Two* at BBC Television Centre in London, on 25 November 2011. This year's Entertainment chapter starts on p.208.

Many-faced monarch

A montage of 201,948 self-portraits formed gigantic artworks of Queen Elizabeth II when projected on to Buckingham Palace, London, from 19 to 21 April 2012. Designed by Ross Ashton (UK) for the Prince's Foundation for Children and the Arts, it set a new record for the **most artists working on a single art installation**. The montage helped celebrate the Queen's Diamond Jubilee – but does reaching that milestone make Her Majesty the longest-serving current head of state? Find out on pp.158–59.

FACT: The protective clothing worn by firemen is known as "turnout gear".

Fastest time to dress a fireman

Thanks to *Loose Women* (ITV) for being so enthusiastic about record-breaking over the year. In their latest feat, on 15 May 2012, Denise Welch (UK) dressed a strapping fireman in full uniform in a record 75 seconds.

FACT: Sofas, bathrooms, sheds... Is there anything Edd can't motorize? See for yourself on p.185.

And talking of the limits of human abilities, we've all been gripped by Olympic fever here at GWR. London is the home of Guinness World Records, of course, so we were particularly excited to see the city host the event for a third time – the **most times to host the Olympic Games**. For the first time ever, we've issued a digital update to our sports chapter that collates every new world record set at the Olympics – find out more at www.guinnessworldrecords.com/bonuschapter.

If you're a sports fan who enjoys the quirkier side of life, and you've not yet downloaded our *Wacky Sporting Champions* ebook, visit www.guinnessworldrecords.com/sport and take a look at our sideways glance at sporting superlatives. Breaking the record for the 100-m dash is one thing, but how fast would Usain Bolt be in a pair of high heels? Or a pair of swim fins? (continued on p.10)

Most people dressed as nurses

GWR's Damian Field was on call in Birmingham on 21 February 2012 to witness 201 participants at the BBC's "Red Alert Appeal" assemble the **largest gathering of people dressed as nurses**. Millions of pounds are raised for charity each year by record-breakers – see pp.256–57 for more.

Thanks to the mummy bloggers: Another first for GWR this year was our "mummy blogger" event, in which we invited parenting bloggers and their children to the office to meet some record holders and attempt a few records – congratulations to Kate Sutton for setting the standard for the **most dominoes stacked in 30 seconds** (19). As a final treat, Edd China (UK), creator of the **fastest sofa** in 2007, ferried everyone to the train station on his speedy settee.

Most heads of hair dyed in 24 hours

Damien Bennett (Ireland) was dyeing to be a record breaker and got his wish when he coloured the hair of 62 volunteers at The Style Club in Dublin on 16–17 February 2012. Damien dyed for the Shave or Dye 2012 charity campaign on Ray D'Arcy's Today FM radio show.

Hoffice visit

We've had many high-profile visitors to our offices over the years – Michael Jackson, for example, and even Her Majesty the Queen – and in November, we added to that list the **most watched man on TV**, David Hasselhoff (USA). "The Hoff" is just one of the TV stars in this year's book – you'll find more on pp.210–11 and pp.224–25.

EDITOR'S LETTER

In addition to the hundreds of claims we deal with on a daily basis, we acquire thousands of new and updated records from a team of consultants and advisers. We are particularly indebted this year to our science consultant David Hawksett for his contribution to our Green Earth chapter (pp.32–43). This ecological theme looks at the good, the bad and the ugly aspects of our treatment of the planet and takes as balanced a view as possible, based on our current understanding of this potentially controversial topic.

We also welcome aboard some new consultants for this year's book, including railway expert Martyn Chapman (check out his trains update, pp.174–75), science journalist Paul Parsons (who tackles the brain-itching topic of numbers, pp.198–99), and Rob Cave, whose enthusiasm for pop culture was invaluable for features on comics and graphic novels (pp.212–13) and video games (pp.228–29).

Thanks, too, to Dan Barrett, GWR's online Community Manager, for his indispensable help with the new social media feature (pp.164–65). We're living through an incredible digital revolution these days, in which records are being broken every second. Luckily, Dan gets to spend all day in conversation with our vast online community, helping us stay up to date with the latest traffic figures.

Blue (with cold) Peter

BBC *Blue Peter* presenter Helen Skelton (UK) travelled 805 km (500 miles) to the freezing environs of the South Pole. The Polar Challenge was in aid of Sport Relief and took 18 days. This adds to Helen's other Sport Relief record for the **longest solo journey by canoe**: she paddled 3234.79 km (2010 miles), from 20 January to 28 February 2010, through Peru and Brazil.

Bicycle fan

A delighted Ortis Deley (UK) from *The Gadget Show* (Channel 5) shows off the certificate he received for the **fastest bicycle powered by electric-ducted fans** (see p.185). Other marvels of design and industry can be found in our Engineering chapter, pp.166–89.

Pasta master Congratulations to TV chef Gino D'Acampo (Italy) for making the **most ravioli in two minutes** – he produced 22 GWR-approved pasta parcels on the set of *Let's Do Lunch... With Gino and Mel* (ITV) in London on 2 September 2011. Thanks to Gino and everyone on the show – here's to the next record attempt!

Frenetic Freddie

This year, GWR was proud to support Sport Relief and to cheer as Andrew "Freddie" Flintoff became a celebrated record-breaker in less than a day, on 19 March 2012. You can read about a couple of Freddie's feats on p.268 – they're not what you might expect from a cricketing legend! Above left, Freddie records the **fastest 100 m in a pedalo** – 1 min 58 sec, with fellow cricketer Steve Harmison. Below, as GWR's Rob Molloy looks on, he celebrates having faced the **most cricket deliveries in one minute**, with 19 from the likes of Harry Judd and Gary Lineker (all UK).

Leading at reading

Pupils and staff at St Mary's Primary School, Battersea in London were among 2,928 participants in the "Get London Reading" campaign. The 26 March 2012 event was the **largest reading lesson**, in which *Born to Run* (2007) by Michael Morpurgo (UK) provided the source for the eager readers' extract. If you want to read more, squeeze into pp.88–89 for other outsized teams.

Sign of success

More than 114,000 people in schools all over the world came together on 8 February 2012 to break the record for the most people performing sign language simultaneously to the same song in different locations. The event was organized by SignHealth (UK), who work on behalf of deaf people.

The **largest St Patrick's Day celebration at multiple venues** was organized by the Guinness brewery, and attended by 361,077 individuals globally on 17 March 2012. It was the climax of the brewery's "Friendliest Day of the Year" campaign, which saw 74,379 people pledging to celebrate St Patrick's Day with their friends – the **most pledges received for a campaign**. The two campaigns attracted an amazing 435,456 people!

This year's book has one foot in the digital realm in the shape of an exciting new "augmented reality" (AR) feature that really brings the records to life. First, download the free app at www.guinnessworldrecords.com/seeit3d (or use the QR code on p.7), then look out for the **SEE IT 3D** icon dotted around the book. Hold your device up to the page and it will trigger a 3D animation relating to a record on that page.

And don't worry if you don't own a smartphone or tablet – the book is bursting with the usual array of spectacular original photographs that you'll not find anywhere else. Picture Editor Michael Whitty has been touring the globe with his team to bring you the best in new photography. Among his favourite record-holders this year are Abbie Girl (**longest wave surfed by a dog**, p.62), the giant Westech truck (**largest mining truck**, pp.166–67) and Darlene Flynn (**largest collection of shoes**, p.100). Look out for Michael's behind-the-scenes accounts in the Snap Shot features included alongside some of the photos.

As ever, there's so much more to introduce: our *Star Wars* feature celebrates the 30th anniversary of *Return of the Jedi* (USA, 1983), on pp.226–27; a snapshot of the global economy marks another year of recession and austerity (pp.150–51); and, to take your mind off the economic gloom, a fun exploration of the weirder side of record-breaking with consultant Dr Karl Shuker's "mysterious world" (pp.154–55), which encompasses spontaneous human combustion, the Loch Ness Monster and a vast collection of "haunted" dolls!

I hope you'll agree that the records in this year's book are more exciting, more inspiring and more spectacular than ever. Of course, if you think you can do better, then please do get in touch. There are plenty of ways to get your name in the pages of the world's **best-selling copyright book** (see pp.14–15) and, with your help, the next 10 years of record-breaking will be as fruitful as the last.

Craig Glenday,
Editor-in-Chief
Follow me at twitter.com/craigglenday

Royal Mail delivers

GWR gave its stamp of approval to the Royal Mail Group (UK) for the **most charities supported by a payroll giving scheme**. From 2001 to 2011, Royal Mail employees gave to a total of 975 charities via donations from staff pay on a weekly or monthly basis. Up to December 2011, £28,915,950 had been distributed to the 975 charities by the Charities Trust.

Just the ticket
Comedian Peter Kay (UK) sold 1,140,798 tickets for his "Tour That Doesn't Tour Tour" of the UK and Ireland from 23 February 2010 to 25 November 2011 – the **most tickets sold for a stand-up comedy tour**. For comics of a different sort, turn to pp.212–13.

GWR DAY

Every year in mid-November, thousands of people around the world try to set or break records for Guinness World Records Day. It's a celebration of determination, ingenuity, craziness... and it's a lot of fun! You too can help raise money and awareness for your favourite charity. If you've got a special record you'd like to achieve, visit www.guinnessworldrecords.com to find out how to start. Who knows – you could be on these pages next year!

03

01

02

07

FACT:
More than 300,000 people attempted to break records on GWR Day in 2011.

09

10

FACT:
You don't need any particular skills to take part. Pants to Poverty enrolled commuters for their record.

08

13

14

15

18

FACT:
All records set on GWR Day are short-listed for inclusion in the next year's edition of GWR.

FACT:
GWR Day 2011 was the seventh year of this global celebration of record-breaking.

HIGHLIGHTS FROM OUR GWR DAY 2011...

Country	Record/event	Description
1. Ireland	Largest gathering of leprechauns	262, on *The Mooney Show* (RTE1)
2. Japan	Tallest tower	634 m (2,080 ft), for the Tokyo Sky Tree
3. Germany	Longest radio show broadcast by a team	73 hours, by Nora Neise and Tolga Aka for KISS FM Radio
4. UK	Most people in one pair of pants	57, by Pants to Poverty
5. UK	Tallest basketball player	231.8-cm (7-ft 7.25-in) Paul "Tiny" Sturgess
6. Netherlands	Most water rockets launched simultaneously	443, by students at Teylingen College in Noordwijkerhout
7. Japan	Largest rice cracker	1.6-m (5-ft 2-in) diameter, by Inzai City Tourism Association
8. UK	Fastest motorized shopping trolley	69 km/h (42.8 mi/h), by Tesco plc and The Big Kick
9. Germany	Most bottle caps removed with head (1 minute)	24, by Ahmed Tafzi
10. Germany	Longest full-body burn run (without oxygen)	120 m (393 ft 8.4 in), by Denni Düsterhöft
11. UK	Fastest time to wrap a person in newspaper	3 min 7 sec, by Francesca Librae for the *Daily Star Sunday*
12. UK	Fastest time to wrap a person in newspaper (by a team of eight)	1 min 31 sec, by *First News*
13. USA	Oldest yoga teacher	91-year-old Bernice Mary Bates (b. 30 June 1920)
14. UK	Largest cream tea party	334, by The English Cream Tea Company
15. Romania	Largest chocolate coin	265 kg (584 lb 3.5 oz), by the Sun Plaza shopping centre
16. China	Longest kissing chain	351, by Jiayuan.com
17. USA	Largest hula-hoop workout	221, by students from Longleaf Elementary School
18. UK	Most chin-ups (one hour)	993, by Stephen Hyland
19. Lebanon	Largest collection of model cars	27,777, by Nabil Karam
20. Germany	Most pine boards broken by a weight attached to the hair in one minute	10, by Janna Vernunft at the Joe Alexander Entertainment Group gym in Hamburg

GUINNESS WORLD RECORDS™

BE A RECORD-BREAKER

Have you got a record-breaking talent?

You don't need to be a super-athlete, a world-famous explorer or a multi-billionaire to have a Guinness World Record. We believe there's a world record in everyone – so why not attempt one yourself?

If you've got a world-beating skill, however off-beat you may think it is, get in touch with us! You could set or break a new world record online, at one of our live events, or even on television. To find out how, simply read on...

Records services

Aspiring record-holders can take advantage of various premium records services:

- Fast-track your claim
- Invite a GWR adjudicator to your event
- Launch a record-breaking product
- Promote your attempt using the official GWR logo

See **www.guinnessworldrecords.com** for more information.

HOW TO BE A RECORD-BREAKER

Follow Jonny on his mission to break the Guinness World Record for the most T-shirts worn at once. Everyone who wants to register a claim must follow this application process. Be sure to give us plenty of warning – at least a month.

START

1

I want to be a record-breaker.

Read the book, watch the TV shows or visit the website to see the kind of records we usually accept.

NO

Do you have a record in mind?

YES

2

Tell us as much as you can about your record idea at www. guinnessworldrecords.com. If it's an existing record, we'll send you the official guidelines that the previous claimant followed. If it's a new idea, and we like it, we'll write new guidelines for you.

If we don't think your idea is suitable for a record, we can help you adapt it so that it is record-worthy.

NO

Have we sent guidelines for your claim?

YES

FACT: Our most frequently broken record is that of **oldest living woman.**

FACT: GWR's most-applied-for record is the **longest film-watching marathon** – currently 120 hr 23 min!

Break your record on TV

When you make your record application through our website, let us know if you think your attempt would work well on television. We're always on the lookout for visually amazing records for our international TV shows. On the left, GWR adjudicator Kristian Teufel is pictured with Bollywood star Preity Zinta, host of *Guinness World Records – Ab India Todega*. Above right, GWR's Marco Frigatti and Lorenzo Veltri line up with two diminutive record holders on Italy's *Lo Show dei Record*. And on 10 January 2010, Brendan Mon Tanner (Australia, right, closely watched by GWR's Chris Sheedy), set a record for the **most fire torches extinguished with the mouth in one minute** (88) on the set of *Australia Smashes Guinness World Records*.

Break your record at a live event show

Guinness World Records hosts live events in supermarkets, shopping malls, holiday camps – wherever there's space for us! We stage record attempts every hour, on the hour. There are practice stations and GWR adjudicators are on hand to officiate. To find out when we'll be in your area, visit

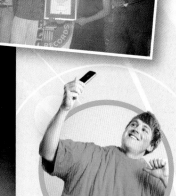

www.guinnessworldrecords. com/live-event. Above right, GWR's Talal Omar (far right) is in attendance as Chris Wones and Stuart Aitken (both USA) receive their certificate for the **most football passes in one minute by a pair** (101). On the left, GWR's Science Show visits Butlins in Bognor, UK.

FACT: The **most T-shirts worn at once** is 257, achieved by Sanath Bandara (Sri Lanka) in 2011.

Gather the evidence we ask for, such as photographs, video footage, press clippings and eyewitness signatures.

NO

Have you collated the evidence we've asked for?

YES

3

The guidelines explain how to attempt the record and how to collate the evidence. At the same time, we'll send you details of the current record – this is the figure you'll have to beat!

4

You're now ready to attempt the record. Be sure to follow every rule in the guidelines. If you're not sure about anything, let us know before you start.

If you think you've broken the record, send all your evidence to our adjudicators. The investigation can take a few weeks.

FINISH

5

If you've followed the rules and beaten the existing record (or set a new one), you will receive a letter of confirmation. You will also be sent your official Guinness World Records certificate welcoming you into the record-breaking family. Congratulations!

Evidence

Here's the kind of proof we need to show that you've followed our guidelines:

📷 Photographs

🎞 Full (unedited) video

📄 Witness statements

📔 Logbook

✂ Newspaper clippings

📑 Professional qualifications

⏱ GPS readings

 Birth certificates

Each record is different, so please read your guidelines carefully.

CHALLENGERS

Break your record online

If you want to start attempting world records *right now*, then be a GWR Challenger! Simply visit us at **www.guinnessworldrecords.com/challengers** and pick a world record you'd like to try – or suggest a new record you think you can set. Once we've given you the go-ahead, you're free to carry out your record attempt, but be sure to film yourself doing it. Next, upload your video and wait to hear from us – we adjudicate the best new videos every week. Who knows, you could be joining Silvio Sabba (Italy, left) – **most Ferrero Rocher chocolates stacked** (12) – and Stephen Kish (UK, above right) – **most coins stacked into a tower in 30 seconds** (44) – as Guinness World Record holders on Challengers!

PEACE ONE DAY

21 September...

"When you build a house, you start with one brick. If we want to build peace, we start with one day. That day has arrived."
Jeremy Gilley, founder, Peace One Day

Guinness World Records is proud to support Peace One Day – a global initiative to encourage an annual day of non-violence on Peace Day (21 September) to provide an opportunity for aid organizations to carry out essential life-saving work in war-torn communities. Already, the campaign has resulted in the vaccination of millions of children in Afghanistan. But there is much more to do... and you can be part of it.

By the time you read this, and if all goes to plan, the world will have experienced the largest reduction of violence ever recorded on a single day. The day in question – 21 September 2012 – is the focus of Peace One Day's Global Truce 2012 campaign, and is part of the ongoing initiative to establish an annual day of ceasefire and non-violence.

How it all began
Peace One Day was the brainchild of British actor-turned-film-maker Jeremy Gilley, who, in the late 1990s, "became preoccupied with questions about the fundamental nature of humanity and the issue of peace". His idea was a seemingly simple one: to achieve just one day of ceasefire around the world – an effort that would manifest in a documentary film following his attempts to secure this day of peace. From this audacious start, Gilley has spearheaded a successful global crusade to have an annual day of global ceasefire and

non-violence with a fixed date adopted by all United Nations member states. The resulting film, *The Day After Peace*, has inspired countless individuals, corporations, organizations and governments to recognize 21 September as an annual day of global unity.

Seeing results
Peace Days have already been a fantastic success. In Afghanistan, an initiative led by Peace One Day has achieved incredible results: on Peace Day 2008, the UN recorded a 70% reduction in violent incidents in that country. And on Peace Day 2010, over

50,000 children and women of child-bearing age across 23 high-risk locations in greater Kabul were vaccinated against deadly diseases including polio, meningitis, diphtheria and tetanus. In addition, a nationwide polio immunization campaign to

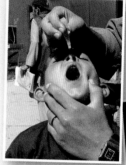

target 8 million children was launched. Already 4.5 million children have benefited from life-saving polio vaccinations as a result of Peace Day agreements since 2007.

Across the world
It's not just in Afghanistan that Peace Day activities have made an impact. In 2010, Peace One Day instigated a total of 88 life-saving and humanitarian activities by 28 organizations

in 31 countries. And the campaign's aim is not simply to stop violence in war-torn countries. Backed by Peace One Day ambassadors Jude Law and Thandie Newton (pictured above right), and Baroness

Scotland of Asthal (above), Peace One Day partnered the Eliminate Domestic Violence Global Foundation (EDV) for Peace Day 2012. Domestic violence affects people in all countries, and can have major consequences for children who see and hear it or even suffer from it at home.

OTHER RECORD-BREAKING PEACE INITIATIVES

Jeremy Gilley's Peace One Day campaign joins a host of other record-worthy initiatives to reduce poverty, encourage ceasefire, and redress the imbalance of power on our planet.

Indeed, the **largest Guinness World Records attempt ever staged** was a worldwide United Nations programme – "Stand Up Against Poverty" in October 2008 – in which a total of 116,993,629 participants in 7,777 events around the globe got to their feet to raise awareness of the "Global Call to Action Against Poverty" campaign.

Largest anti-war rally

On 15 February 2003, anti-war rallies took place across the globe – the largest occurring in Rome, Italy, where a crowd of 3 million gathered to protest the USA's threat to invade Iraq (pictured). Police figures report that millions more demonstrated in nearly 600 cities worldwide. On the same day, 1.3 million rallied in Barcelona, Spain, and 1 million people participated in a peace march through the streets of London, UK.

Largest book of signatures

Amnesty International gathered 10 million signatures from 125 countries in its one-year-long "Get Up, Sign Up" campaign pledging support for the Universal Declaration of Human Rights. The signatures were compiled into a book and presented to Kofi Annan, the UN Secretary General, in Paris, France, on the 50th anniversary of the Universal Declaration of Human Rights on 10 December 1998. Pictured below is the Dalai Lama adding his autograph to the book.

THE DAY AFTER PEACE

Against all odds an individual creates an annual global ceasefire/non-violence day. Will he silence the cynics and prove that the day can actually save lives?

Featuring:
Kofi Annan
The Dalai Lama
Angelina Jolie
Jude Law
Annie Lennox
Jonny Lee Miller

FACT:
Your own Peace One Day event could qualify as a world record. Find out how to apply on p.14.

Be a part of Peace Day

So how can you get involved? Every year on 21 September, Peace One Day invites you to celebrate peace in your community. It may be a soccer match – on Peace Day 2010, in a campaign entitled One Day One Goal, over 3,000 football matches took place in all 192 UN member states. You could also organize an event in any other sport, or put on a dance, theatrical or musical performance. According to the UN, 100 million people were active on Peace Day by 2007, and you can join them by simply contacting the organization through its website (www. peaceoneday.org).

You can also encourage teachers to download free education resources at the website. School teacher Betsy Sawyer from Groton, Massachusetts, USA, uses these resources in her after-school peace book club, called the Bookmakers and Dreamers. The teenagers in the club have Skyped fellow teenagers in rural Afghanistan and they found out exactly how important a sense of peace was in a country that has endured war for 30 years. For Afghani children, peace is not a grandiose ideal – like all children, they have the right to grow up without fearing for their safety.

JEREMY GILLEY IN HIS OWN WORDS

We all want answers to the big questions in the world: why is there so much starvation, destruction and killing of innocent people? But like most of us, I didn't think I could do anything about it. I had no qualifications (except a "D" in pottery!) and worked in acting. I began film-making, and wanted to make a film about peace, but there needed to be more than a series of soundbites and images. There had to be a mountain to climb. That's when I had the idea, a starting point for peace – could I create an annual day of global unity, a day when humanity comes together and realizes that we're all in this together?

I wanted the day to be 21 September because 21 was my grandfather's favourite number. He fought in World War II and died when I was 11. In one expedition, 700 men in his regiment left to fight, 23 came back and two died on the boat, leaving only 21 survivors.

The launch

So I launched Peace One Day in 1999, inviting hundreds of press organizations, but none turned up! A total of 114 people were there – but they were mostly my friends and family. It didn't matter – it was a start; it made a statement.

Gradually, after lots of letter-writing and telephoning, people started coming on board. Mary Robinson, UN Commissioner for Human Rights, said it was an idea whose time has come. UN Secretary General Kofi Annan told me the day would help his UN peacekeeping troops on the ground.

So on 7 September 2001, the UK and Costa Rican governments sponsored a resolution, with 54 co-sponsors, at the General Assembly of the United Nations, seeking to establish this annual day of non-violence on the UN International Day of Peace, fixed in the

calendar as 21 September. It was unanimously adopted by the member states of the United Nations – every single nation in the world! I was there at the top of the General Assembly, looking down, and I saw it happen. It really was a magnificent moment.

I was going to be present at a press conference with Kofi Annan on the morning of 11 September 2001 to announce the creation of the day. But obviously, after the planes crashed into the World Trade Center, Kofi Annan never arrived and the conference was cancelled. For me, though, the events of 9/11 simply confirmed exactly why we had to work harder. I left New York anxious but empowered – and inspired to stop events like 9/11 ever happening again.

Remarkable progress

By the end of the decade the progress was remarkable. Our efforts, and the efforts of all the parties in Afghanistan, resulted in Peace Day agreements leading to millions of children being vaccinated against polio and a 70% reduction in the violence on Peace Day 2008. I know if we can achieve that in Afghanistan, we can do it across the world – a global truce.

FACT:
A copy of the Hittite version of the treaty remains in the Karnak Temple in Luxor, Egypt.

First peace treaty

The earliest known surviving peace treaty was drawn up c. 1271 BC and signed by the Egyptian pharaoh Ramses II and Hattusilis III, King of the Hittites and ruler of Hatti (in present-day Turkey). Two copies of the treaty were made, one in hieroglyphics, the other in the Mesopotamian language of Akkadian (or Babylonian-Assyrian). Both parties agreed to end years of warring and form an alliance in the event of foreign aggression.

NOBEL PEACE PRIZES

The Nobel Peace Prize is one of the five categories of award bequeathed by Alfred Nobel (Sweden), the inventor of dynamite. It is awarded annually "to the person who shall have done the most or the best work for fraternity between nations, for the abolition or reduction of standing armies and for the holding and promotion of peace congresses". Notable laureates include:

Laureate	Year	Why?
Henry Dunant (Switzerland) & Frédéric Passy (France)	1901	**First Peace Laureates** (awarded jointly) – Dunant (pictured), for being a principal founder of the Red Cross and Passy for organizing the first Universal Peace Congress
Bertha von Suttner (Austria)	1905	**First female Peace Laureate**, for her novel *Lay Down Your Arms* (1889) and for assisting Alfred Nobel in founding the Peace Prize
Aung San Suu Kyi (Burma)	1991	For her non-violent struggle for democracy; endured the **longest house arrest** of the 20th century (lasting 5 years 355 days)
Rigoberta Menchú Tum (Guatemala)	1992	**Youngest Peace Laureate** (aged 33), for her work in asserting the rights of indigenous peoples
Barack Obama (USA)	2009	For his efforts to strengthen international diplomacy and cooperation; America has the **most Peace Prizes by nationality**, with 272 recipients

SPACE

CONTENTS

Largest concentration of observatories

The 13 telescopes on Hawaii's Mauna Kea include the world's largest infrared and submillimetre telescopes, along with some of the largest optical telescopes. Operated by 11 countries, the observatories are near the 4,205-m-high (13,796-ft) summit of the Mauna Kea volcano. As the atmosphere above the summit is dry, free of pollutants and rarely cloudy, astronomers see the faintest galaxies at the edge of the observable universe. This photograph was taken at the summit with a long exposure so that, as Earth rotates, the stars appear to leave trails.

HOW FAR WILL WE EXPLORE?

What are the limits to space travel?

The distances between the stars are vast and are measured using a unit called "light years". One light year is the distance travelled by light in one year. The speed of light is **299,792,458 m/s (671 million mi/h), so one light year is the same as 9,460,730,472,580.8 km (5,878,625,373,183.608 miles!).**

Our Sun is 8.3 "light minutes" away (i.e., it takes 8.3 minutes for sunlight to reach Earth), and the Moon – the farthest place humans have ever visited – just 1.3 "light seconds" away. So when we consider that our next nearest star is 4.2 light years away, what chances have we got of ever reaching it? Even if we consider light as our theoretical speed limit, how far *can* we expect to travel from Earth? Our journey starts at bottom left of the page...

Key

The history of exploring objects in space points to a trend of key stages:

 1. Study from Earth using telescopes

 2. Study briefly at close range using a flyby probe

 3. More in-depth close range study using an orbiting probe

 4. Land on the surface using a robotic probe

 5. Bring back samples using a robotic probe

 6. Send humans to explore

The distance stated at each stage is the average distance from Earth in astronomical units (AU). In which 1 AU is the distance between Earth and the Sun (roughly 149,597,870.7 km = 92,955,807 miles).

So rapid was humanity's progress in the development of flight that, for 18 years, Orville Wright (co-inventor of the **first powered aeroplane**) and Neil Armstrong **(first man on the Moon)** were alive at the same time!

Most remote man-made object

As of 12 February 2012, NASA's *Voyager 1*, launched in 1977 to help us study the outer solar system, was 17,960,000,000 km (120 AU) from the Sun. Should it ever be found by aliens, it contains a gold-plated disc carrying data on the human race, including photographs and music.

Proxima Centauri *(stage 1)*
At 4.24 light years away, this red dwarf is the **nearest star to the Sun.** Even travelling at the **fastest spacecraft speed** yet achieved (*Helios 2* at 252,792 km/h, 157,077 mi/h) it would take some 18,000 years to reach. To put this into perspective, 18,000 years ago our ancestors were creating cave art and using stone tools.

268,136 AU (4.24 light years)

Pluto *(stage 2)*
Despite its demotion from planet to dwarf planet, Pluto is the most distant Solar System object currently targeted by a robotic mission. NASA's *New Horizons* spacecraft is en route and will perform a flyby of Pluto and its four moons in July 2015.

39.5 AU (5.9 billion km)

Voyager 1
Currently nearly 18 billion km (120 AU) from Earth

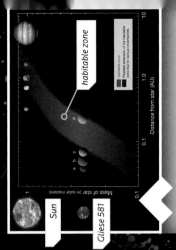

Mass of star (in solar masses)

habitable zone

Sun

Gliese 581

Distance from star (AU)

First confirmed exoplanet that could support Earth-like life

The "habitable zone" is the region around a star in which planets can sustain liquid surface water. Within this region of the star Gliese 581 is at least one planet ("d"); Gliese 581 is smaller than our Sun but "d" is correspondingly closer to its star.

Gliese 581 *(stage 1)*
This red dwarf star system is home to the planet Gliese 581 d, which lies in the "habitable zone" of its solar system and is therefore a contender for life (see panel below). A radio signal sent there in 2008 is due to arrive in 2029.

1.28 million AU (20.3 light years)

OGLE-2005-BLG-390L *(stage 1)*
Near the centre of the Milky Way, orb this red dwarf star, is OGLE-2005-BL 390Lb, the **most distant extrasolar** discovered to date. Even if we could t at 252,792 km/h (157,077 mi/h), it wo take 92 million years to get there!

1.3 x 10⁹ AU (21,500 light ye

Europa *(stage 3)*
The *Galileo* orbiter (1995–2003) suggested that, with its icy surface and the potential of liquid water oceans, this Jovian moon offers one of the best chances yet of finding extraterrestrial life. A robotic lander mission to Europa is under discussion as a concept but will launch no earlier than around 2030.

5.2 AU (778 million km)

Highest altitude achieved
The farthest distance ever travelled from Earth by humans is 400,171 km (248,655 miles), by the crew of Apollo 13 (Jack Swigert, Jim Lovell and Fred Haise, all USA) on 15 April 1970.

Apollo 13
Reached 400,171 km (248,655 miles) from Earth

International Space Station
Orbits at an altitude of 330–410 km (205–255 miles)

Longest high-fidelity spaceflight simulation
Mars-500 was a collaboration between the European Space Agency, Russia and China to simulate a 500-day manned mission to Mars. The crew of six men entered their sealed facility in Moscow, Russia, in June 2010 and emerged in November 2011. The project included a 20-minute time delay in communications between the crew and the outside world, just like a real Mars mission would.

Mars *(stage 4)*
The USSR *Mars 2* and *Mars 3* missions were the **first spacecraft to reach the surface of Mars**, in 1971. We have yet to see a successful sample return mission, but the first visit by humans should happen within the next few decades.

1.5 AU (225 million km)

Itokawa asteroid *(stage 5)*
On 13 June 2010, the unmanned spacecraft *Hayabusa* (Japan) landed on Earth with its cargo of tiny grains of material collected from the surface of the asteroid Itokawa. It was the **first spacecraft to lift off from an asteroid** and the **farthest land-and-return sample mission** launched.

0.706 AU (105.6 million km)

FACT:
To make the trip to Proxima Centauri – our nearest star neighbour – would take 100 times more energy than our civilization currently generates.

With current conventional rocket technology, a trip to the nearest star is out of the question. Even if we could develop an interstellar spacecraft (artist's impression below), Albert Einstein has taught us that as this theoretical spacecraft approached the speed of light, it would appear to gain mass, making it increasingly difficult to accelerate.

More advanced rocket technology, such as nuclear thermal or nuclear pulse, could theoretically send a manned mission to the nearest stars at a significant fraction of the speed of light – albeit at a great cost – within a century. If anyone manages to invent sci-fi technology such as a warp drive, it could happen much sooner!

Moon *(stage 6)*
Apollo 11, which landed on the Moon on 29 July 1969, was the first mission to reach stage 6; also counted as the first sample return mission (stage 5).

0.0027 AU (405,410 km)

Vostok 1
Reached apogee (farthest point from Earth) of 327 km (203 miles)

First manned spaceflight
Cosmonaut Flight Major (later Col.) Yuri Alekseyevich Gagarin (USSR) became the first human to travel into space, orbiting the Earth in *Vostok 1* on 12 April 1961.

VENUS

Hottest planet

Venus has an average surface temperature of 480°C (896°F). This scorching heat is hot enough to melt lead and, coupled with the atrocious atmosphere, makes exploration of the surface by landers very difficult. The circular forms and radiating concentric cracks seen in the main photograph above are known as arachnoids, as they resemble spiders' webs. They may have been caused by volcanic processes. The smaller picture is a colourized version of one of the images taken by the Soviet *Venera 13* and *14* landers, which touched down on Venus in 1982.

Largest planet with no magnetic field

Unlike Earth, Venus does not have a magnetic field. This allows particles from the solar wind to interact with the atmosphere, stripping away around 2×10^{24} hydrogen atoms into space every second. This image was pieced together from data from NASA's *Magellan* spacecraft, which used radar to map the surface.

Largest planet without a moon

Of the eight major planets of the Solar System only Mercury and Venus have no natural satellite. It is possible that Venus once had a moon, which crashed into the surface. With a 12,103.6-km (7,520.8-mile) diameter, Venus is similar in size to Earth.

Largest impact crater on Venus

Mead crater, north of a highland area called Aphrodite Terra, has a diameter of around 280 km (174 miles). Mead is quite shallow, suggesting it may have been filled by lava or impact melt after its formation.

Planet with the longest day

Venus has the longest rotation period (day) of all the major planets in the Solar System. While the Earth takes 23 hr 56 min 4 sec to complete one rotation, Venus takes 243.16 "Earth days" to spin once through 360 degrees. As it is closer to the Sun, the length of Venus's year is shorter than Earth's, lasting 224.7 days, so a day on Venus is actually longer than its year!

Brightest planet seen from Earth

Seen from Earth, the brightest of the five planets usually visible to the naked eye (Jupiter, Mars, Mercury, Saturn and Venus) is Venus, with a maximum magnitude of -4.4. Venus appears so bright because around 80% of the sunlight that reaches the planet is bounced back by its reflective cloud cover (see below). At maximum elongation, it is visible for quite some time before and after sunrise and sunset.

Thickest planetary atmosphere

Often referred to as the closest place to hell in the Solar System, Venus's atmosphere is the thickest of any planet, with a pressure nearly 100 times that of Earth's atmospheric pressure at sea level. The gases in the thick atmosphere cause a greenhouse effect which means the temperature on the surface reaches 480°C (896°F). Europe's *Venus Express* spacecraft is currently performing the most intensive study of Venus's atmosphere ever made (see p.23).

Most acidic rain in the Solar System

The highly reflective white clouds of Venus, which prevent direct viewing of the surface from space, are due to a layer of sulphuric acid 48–58 km (30–36 miles) above the surface. Rain of almost pure sulphuric acid falls from these clouds but never reaches the surface. At an altitude of around 30 km (18.5 miles), the rain evaporates, to be recycled into the Venusian clouds.

First successful interplanetary mission

Mariner 2 (USA) performed a fly-by of Venus on 14 December 1962, within 35,000 km (21,750 miles) of the planet's surface. Results from the fly-by revealed the extremely hot nature of the planet's surface. *Mariner 2*, now without power, is still in orbit around the Sun.

Largest highland region on Venus

Close to Venus's equator lies Aphrodite Terra, one of two major highland "continents" on the planet. First mapped in detail by the Soviet *Venera 15* and *16* orbiters in 1984, it covers an area of around 30 million km (11.6 million miles[2]), which is approximately the same size as Africa. The fractured appearance of Aphrodite suggests it has been subject to huge forces of compression in its geological history.

First European Venus orbiter

Venus Express, the European Space Agency's (ESA) first mission to Venus, is designed for long-term study of the Venusian atmosphere. The spacecraft is an orbiter with a complex array of instruments. It successfully entered orbit around Venus on 11 April 2006 after a main engine burn of just over 50 minutes, allowing the spacecraft to be captured by the planet's gravity. It has been operational ever since and is the only spacecraft currently studying the planet. Its discoveries to date include the first clear images of the planet's south pole and the discovery of an ozone layer in the upper atmosphere.

Tallest mountain on Venus

Maxwell Montes, on the Ishtar Terra plateau, is the highest point on Venus, reaching 11 km (6.8 miles) above the average surface level of the planet.

First detection of lightning on Venus

On 26 October 1975, the spectrometer onboard the Soviet *Venera 9* spacecraft detected optical flashes – consistent with lightning – in the Venusian atmosphere on the dark side of the planet. This represents the only time lightning has been witnessed optically by a spacecraft in the atmosphere of Venus.

On 25 December 1978, in its descent to Venus's surface, the USSR's *Venera 11* lander picked up a sound that scientists believe to be the first thunder heard on another planet.

Longest channel in the Solar System

Baltis Vallis on Venus is around 7,000 km (4,300 miles) in length and has an average width of around 1.6 km (1 mile). It was discovered by the *Magellan* radar mapper, which orbited Venus from August 1990 to October 1994. Experts believe that the channel was originally formed by molten lava.

FACT: Venus has an ozone layer, but it is between 100 and 1,000 times less dense than Earth's.

Venus at a glance

The vital statistics of this cloud-enshrouded planet

- **Mass:** 4.8×10^{21} tonnes (5.29×10^{21} tons)
- **Volume:** 9.38×10^{11} km^3 (22.2×10^{10} miles^3)
- **Equatorial (and polar) radius:** 6,051.8 km (3,760.4 miles)
- **Diameter:** 12,103.6 km (7,520.8 mile)
- **Surface gravity:** 8.9 m/s^2 (0.9 g)
- **Major atmospheric gases:** 96.5% carbon dioxide; 3.5% nitrogen
- **Mean surface temperature:** 480°C (896°F)
- **Closest distance to Earth:** 38.3 million km (23.7 million miles)
- **Rotation:** Retrograde. Venus and Uranus rotate in the opposite direction to all other planets in the Solar System. On both planets, the Sun rises in the west and sets in the east

Venusian geology

Crust
The crust of Venus was analyzed by Soviet landers and is basaltic in nature, with a thickness of around 50 km (30 miles). Underneath is the mantle, which is around 3,000 km (1,900 miles) thick.

Core
Probably a semi-molten, metallic mass, like the Earth's core.

Atmosphere
Mainly carbon dioxide (96.5%) and a small amount of nitrogen (3.5%). Smaller traces of sulphur dioxide, argon, water, carbon monoxide, helium and neon.

NB: The heavy cloud cover and extremely hostile conditions on Venus have made it very difficult for scientists to gather useful data about the internal composition of the planet. The mantle and core of the planet are still mysteries and require fuller investigation.

Largest Venusian atmospheric vortices

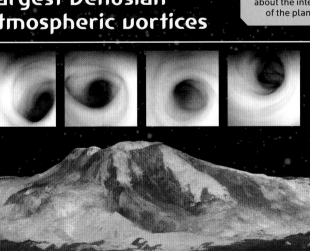

Huge double-eye vortices (whirlpool-like spirals in the atmosphere) up to 2,000 km (1,240 miles) across swirl around the north and south poles of Venus. The northern vortex was discovered by *Mariner 10* (USA) in 1974 and the southern vortex in 2006 by the ESA orbiter *Venus Express*. These swirling clouds are highly dynamic, shifting regularly between "S" shapes, "8" shapes and more chaotic patterns.

EARTH'S EVIL TWIN

If Venus is considered to be a twin planet to Earth, it's certainly an *evil* twin! Here are some of the hazards that make Venus the closest place to hell in the Solar System:

You'd be suffocated by the thick carbon dioxide (CO_2) atmosphere...

...fried by the 480°C surface temperature...

...and crushed by the pressure, which is 92 times greater than on Earth.

The beautiful white clouds of Venus are actually made of caustic sulphuric acid.

And if the atmosphere's not already nasty enough, there are trace elements of sulphur dioxide, carbon monoxide and hydrogen chloride.

Super-fast winds blow at speeds up to 300 km/h in the upper atmosphere.

There's a total absence of liquid water, all of which evaporated a long time ago... and to make matters worse, if you weren't instantaneously crushed, suffocated and fried, just a single day on this hellish planet would last the equivalent of 243 days on Earth!

THE SUN

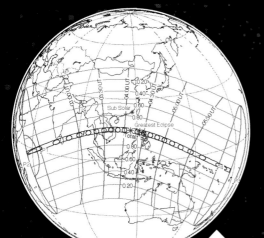

Longest total solar eclipse

A total solar eclipse occurs when the Moon completely obscures the Sun. The longest total solar eclipse since the year 1001 occurred on 20 June 1955, west of the Philippines, and lasted for 7 min 8 sec; the gridded area above shows the areas that fell into full or partial darkness. The longest possible solar eclipse is 7 min 31 sec; an eclipse of 7 min 29 sec will occur in the mid-Atlantic Ocean on 16 July 2186.

Coolest part of the Sun

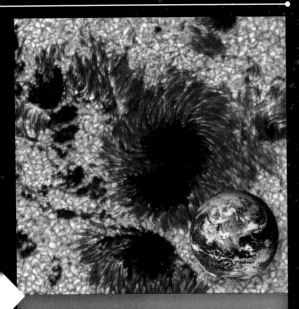

Sunspots form on the Sun's photosphere as a result of magnetic activity and have a temperature of c. 3,700 K, compared with c. 5,700 K for the surrounding photosphere. (The photosphere is the point at which the Sun becomes opaque and is regarded as its "surface".) These large spots would glow brightly if they could be seen against the background of space.

Highest number of sunspots in the current solar cycle

On 21 October 2011, observations of the Sun showed a total of 207 sunspots, the highest seen to date in the current solar cycle – number 24. Despite the sunspot number, flare activity was fairly light with only one X-class eruption event to date since then.

Fastest wind in the Solar System

The solar wind is a steady stream of (mostly) electrons and protons that is emitted from the Sun in all directions. The fastest component of the solar wind travels outward at around 750 km/sec (470 mi/sec) and is thought to originate from areas of open magnetic field lines around the Sun's poles.

FACT:
The strength of the Sun's magnetic field varies. When it peaks, dark "sunspots" appear.

Largest sunspot group

The most extensive group of sunspots ever recorded was in the Sun's southern hemisphere on 8 April 1947. Its area was about 18 billion km^2 (7 billion miles^2), with an extreme longitude of 300,000 km (187,000 miles) and an extreme latitude of 145,000 km (90,000 miles).

Largest solar prominence

"Prominences" are large, eruptive features of relatively cool plasma, or ionized gas, at around 80,000°C (144,000°F). Trapped within the Sun's magnetic field lines, they often form loops and can appear to twist and evolve above the Sun's photosphere for longer than a month. The largest to date have been around 500,000–700,000 km (310,000–435,000 miles) long.

FACT:
The four colour sections below show the Sun's surface as seen at different wavelengths.

Hottest place in the Solar System
Scientists estimate that the temperature at the Sun's core is around 15,600,000°C (28,000,000°F). The pressure there is around 250 billion times that of sea level on Earth.

Largest solar "tsunamis"

First captured using time-lapse imagery (left) in 1959, and subsequently confirmed by observations from spacecraft, Morton waves are the Sun's equivalent of tsunamis. Generated by eruptive solar flares, they travel across the solar surface like ripples from a stone dropped into water. They can reach speeds of 1,500 km/sec (930 mi/sec) in a radiating wave of hot plasma and magnetism that grows up to 100,000 km (62,130 miles) tall.

Largest object in the Solar System

The Sun dominates the Solar System. With a mass of 1.98×10^{30} kg, or 332,900 times that of Earth, and a diameter of 1,392,000 km (865,000 miles), it accounts for some 99.86% of the mass of the Solar System.

Largest explosions in the Solar System

Coronal mass ejections are often, though not always, associated with solar flares. They are huge bubbles of plasma threaded with magnetic field lines, which erupt from the Sun over a period of several hours. They can contain up to 100 billion kg (220.5 billion lb) of matter moving at 1,000 km/sec (620 mi/sec) with the equivalent energy of a billion hydrogen bombs. The next solar maximum, in 2013, could see several of these erupt from the Sun every day.

0.4 tesla, around 1,000 times that of their surrounding areas and around 13,000 times the strength of Earth's magnetic field at the equator.

Longest continuous observational science data

Astronomers have access to a continuous set of observational data of the number of sunspots on the Sun, dating back to 1750.

Longest solar minimum

The "solar minimum" is a period during the Sun's solar cycle when few sunspots are visible and solar activity is low. The Maunder Minimum lasted from 1647 to 1715, during which it appeared as if the solar cycle had broken down altogether. This period corresponded with a period of savage winters in Earth's northern hemisphere that became known as the "Little Ice Age".

Largest solar flare in the current solar cycle

On 8 January 2008, the Sun began its most recent solar cycle since records began in 1755. On 9 August 2011, a solar flare with an X-ray magnitude of X6.9 erupted from Sunspot 1263, near the western limb of the Sun. The associated coronal mass ejection caused some minor short-wave radio disruptions on Earth.

Largest magnetic structure in the Solar System

The magnetic field of the Sun is contorted into a vast spiral shape by the Sun's rotation and motion of the solar wind. Resembling the shape of a spinning ballerina's skirt, and known as the "Parker spiral", it extends all the way to the edge of the Solar System, into a region known as the "heliosheath". The magnetic structure of the Parker spiral is approximately 160–200 AU across, or 24–30 billion km (15–18 billion miles).

Strongest magnetic fields on the Sun's surface

Sunspots can have magnetic field strengths of up to

Largest solar granules

Convection currents within the Sun cause a phenomenon known as "granulation" on the photosphere. Each granule is formed as hot hydrogen rises in its centre and then falls again around its edge. A typical granule is around 1,000 km (620 miles) across and can last for less than 20 minutes. Discovered in the 1950s, supergranules measure around 30,000 km (18,640 miles) across and represent larger-scale currents in the Sun, which has several thousand of these features at any time.

FACT: The term "solar cycle" refers to a period of flux in the Sun's magnetic field. It lasts for around 11 years.

Largest recorded solar flare

Solar flares – huge bursts of energy on the Sun – are graded at three levels: C class (minor); M class (medium) and X class. M- and X-class events can have repercussions here on Earth, such as radio blackouts. On 4 November 2003, a flare erupted from the Sun's surface that was rated an X28 event by the Space Environment Center of the National Oceanic and Atmospheric Administration (NOAA) in Boulder, Colorado, USA.

FACT: Sunspots can be huge. The largest may reach 80,000 km (50,000 miles) in diameter.

SIZING UP THE SUN

The Sun dwarfs the planets in the Solar System. But when it comes to some of the other stars in the Milky Way, our Sun is pretty small fry (even if these stars weigh relatively little compared with their colossal size). Let GWR take you on an interstellar voyage:

Betelgeuse
Diameter: 1.3 billion km
(c. 15–20 x solar mass, the mass of our own sun)

Antares
Diameter: 970 million km
(15–18 x solar mass)

Rigel A
Diameter: 97 million km
(c. 17 x solar mass)

Aldebaran
Diameter: 59.77 million km
(c. 2 x solar mass)

Arcturus
Diameter: 36 million km
(c. 1.5 x solar mass)

Pollux
Diameter: 11.12 million km
(c. 2 x solar mass)

Sirius A
Diameter: 2.335 million km
(c. 2 x solar mass)

Sun
Diameter: 1.392 million km
Mass: 1.98×10^{30} kg

LIVING IN SPACE

FIRST...

Manned spaceflight

Soviet cosmonaut Yuri Gagarin was the first man in space when he orbited Earth in *Vostok 1* on 12 April 1961. Gagarin ejected 108 minutes into the flight as planned and landed back on Earth 10 minutes later by parachute. The maximum altitude on the 40,868.6-km (25,3948-mile) flight was 327 km (203 miles), with a top speed of 28,260 km/h (17,560 mi/h). Gagarin, invested a Hero of the Soviet Union and awarded the Order of Lenin and the Gold Star Medal, was killed in a jet plane crash in March 1968.

Flight between space stations

Mir EO-1 was the first expedition to the new Soviet *Mir* space station. Its crew, Leonid Kizim and Vladimir Solovyov, launched from Earth on 13 March 1986, docking with *Mir* two days later. They remained on *Mir* for six weeks, changing the station's orbit to match that of the *Salyut 7* space station. On 5 May 1986, the crew undocked their *Soyuz* spacecraft from *Mir* and flew to *Salyut 7*, the first flight between space stations. It took 29 hours. On 25 June, the crew undocked from *Salyut 7* and returned to *Mir*, bringing equipment from the old station to the new.

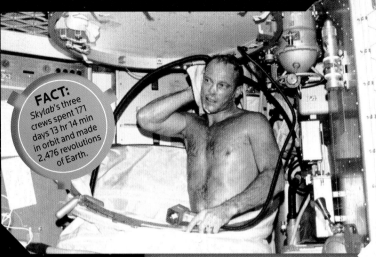

FACT: *Skylab*'s three crews spent 171 days 13 hr 14 min in orbit and made 2,476 revolutions of Earth.

Live music concert broadcast to space

Paul McCartney (UK) became the first artist to broadcast live to space when he sent a "wake-up call" to the *International Space Station* from his concert in Anaheim, California, USA, on 12 November 2005. In 2008, "Across the Universe", by McCartney's old band, The Beatles, became the **first song to be beamed into deep space**. NASA sent the song, at a speed of 300,000 km per second (186,000 miles per second), to celebrate the 50th anniversary of NASA's founding and the 40th anniversary of the song being recorded.

Untethered spacewalk

NASA astronaut Bruce McCandless II performed an untethered space walk from the space shuttle *Challenger* on 7 February 1984. His spacewalk was the first test of the Manned Maneuvering Unit backpack, which cost $15 million (£10 million) to develop.

Food smuggled into space

Gemini III was an orbital mission with a duration of 4 hr 52 min on 23 March 1965, crewed by US astronauts Gus Grissom and John Young. During the mission, Young was authorized to eat pre-approved space food, while Grissom was not scheduled to eat at all during the flight. However, Young, aware of Grissom's love of corned-beef sandwiches, smuggled one on board for his fellow astronaut. Young and Grissom were disciplined by NASA for this act.

First person to shower in space

The US space station *Skylab* orbited Earth from its launch on 14 May 1973 to its re-entry on 11 July 1979. During its life, it was home to three crews of three astronauts who all enjoyed the use of a shower. Users stood inside a ring on the floor and then lifted a circular curtain which attached to the ceiling. A hose would spray 2.8 litres (4.9 pints) of water, which was collected afterwards using a special vacuum cleaner.

Person to make an orbit of Earth on a bicycle

Skylab 3 was the second manned mission to the US *Skylab* space station, from 28 July to 25 September 1973. During the flight, Alan Bean, who walked on the Moon during Apollo 12, spent just over 90 minutes on a stationary bicycle, pedalling throughout a whole orbit of the Earth.

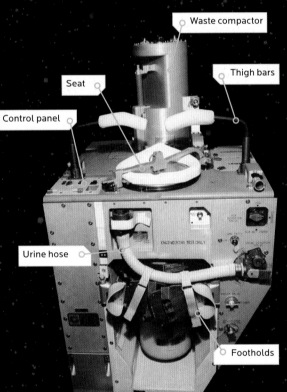

- Waste compactor
- Thigh bars
- Seat
- Control panel
- Urine hose
- Footholds

Most expensive toilet system

The space shuttle *Endeavour* launched on 13 January 1993 with a $23.4-million (£15.44-million) unisex toilet. The facility, described by NASA as a "complete sewage collection and treatment plant", works by suction rather than gravity. It contains 4,000 parts, including footholds and thigh bars to keep the user in place. In case of failure, the space shuttle carried faecal and urine collection bags.

FACT: Apollo 10 was intended as a "dry run" for Apollo 11, which saw the first Moon landing.

First crew to shave in space

Thomas Stafford, John Young and Gene Cernan, the crew of NASA's Apollo 10 mission, 18–26 May 1969, were the first men to shave in space. They found the mechanical shaver developed by NASA inadequate, and resorted to razors and shaving cream.

Most people together in space

When the space shuttle *Endeavour* docked on the *International Space Station* on 17 July 2009, it brought the number of people on the station to 13. The Russian space station commander, Gennady Padalka, rang a ceremonial bell to welcome the seven new *Endeavour* astronauts as they floated aboard.

Largest menu in space

The Russian crew of the *International Space Station* have access to more than 300 dishes, including borscht (beetroot soup), goulash (spicy stew), rice with meat and dried beef.

Person to vomit in space

Space sickness is similar to motion sickness and is caused by the changes in gravity. The first to suffer was Soviet cosmonaut Gherman Titov, who experienced nausea and vomiting on his *Vostok 2* flight on 6 August 1961. Some form of space sickness is felt by around half of all people who fly in space.

Fire on a space station

On 23 February 1997, a fire broke out on board the Russian space station *Mir*, caused by lithium perchlorate "candles" which supplied oxygen to the station. Although the fire was extinguished, the six-man crew came close to abandoning the station in their *Soyuz* "lifeboat", which was docked with *Mir*.

First person to sleep in space

Gherman Titov (USSR) slept on board his 25-hour flight on *Vostok 2* in August 1961. He awoke to find his arms floating in front of him, causing a hazard to the switches.

Commercial filmed in space

An advertising campaign for Tnuva Milk, showing cosmonaut Vasily Tsibliyev drinking milk on board the Russian *Mir* space station, was broadcast on 22 August 1997.

Dog in space

"Laika" became the first dog in space in November 1957 on board *Sputnik 2*, more than three years before the first human. She died early in the mission – her vehicle was not designed to return to Earth.

LONGEST...

Continuous human presence in space

Expedition 1's *Soyuz TM-31* was launched to the *International Space Station* on 31 October 2000 and its crew of three remained on board for 136 days. This marked the longest uninterrupted human presence in space to date, with more than 10 years of continuous occupation of the space station.

Mission by a spacesuit

On 3 February 2006, Russian cosmonaut Valery Tokarev and US astronaut Bill McArthur jettisoned an old Russian Orlan M spacesuit from the *International Space Station*. Equipped with a transmitter, "SuitSat-1" broadcast nearly 3,500 radio messages and data on the temperature inside the suit, which were picked up by amateur radio operators on Earth. The last transmission from SuitSat-1 was received on 18 February 2006, shortly before its battery died.

Running space grocery delivery programme

Russia's *Progress* vehicles are unmanned spacecraft designed to resupply cosmonauts in orbit with water, food and oxygen, as well as equipment for experiments and repairs. They have been in use since the first one was launched on 20 January 1978. Today's *Progress* vehicles can carry 1,700 kg (3,748 lb) of supplies in a 6-m³ (212-ft³) space. Upon docking to the *International Space Station*, it remains in place for months, during which time it is filled with rubbish from the station before undocking and burning up in a controlled deorbit.

First person to relieve himself on the Moon

After landing on the Moon on 20 July 1969, *Apollo 11* crew Neil Armstrong and Buzz Aldrin descended the ladder on to the lunar surface. While still on the ladder, Aldrin urinated into a special collection bag within his spacesuit.

FACT:
The *Apollo 13* crew were kept in quarantine for 21 days after they returned to Earth.

USING A TOILET IN SPACE

Here, quoting directly from the NASA Missions Operations handbook, are the instructions on using the Space Shuttle's Waste Collection System (WCS):

Foot/Toe Restraints – down, locked

Strap your feet into the WCS to ensure accurate positioning; body and thigh straps can also be used once seated.

VAC VLV – OP
Unstow urinal hose from Velcro strap, install hose in cradle

Open the vacuum pump; remove the urinal hose from its housing and mount it in its cradle.

✓CRADLE – AUTO
✓MODE – AUTO
FAN SEP SEL sw – "1"
Unstow hose from cradle (✓Airflow)

Check that the urinal hose is functioning (you can feel the suction using your hand); set the WCS to automatic and turn the "fan separator selector" switch to position "1" (this turns on an airflow that separates waste liquid off to a waste-water tank).

✓WCS ON lt – on

Check that the WCS light is on.

Unstow, install WCS Container, Bag & Hose, Mirror, Elbow Bag Dispenser Ventline mated in aux ✓Wet Trash

Solid waste goes down the commode; liquids down the urinal tube; non-human-waste (paper, wet wipes) is collected in a bag, so remove from container and attach to WCS; use mirror to check that you are aligned correctly; check that ventline is connected to Wet Trash hose; connect self to urinal hose; use.

SPACE WARFARE

First gun in space

Soviet cosmonaut Yuri Gagarin, the first man in space, allegedly carried a Makarov pistol on his historic *Vostok 1* flight on 12 April 1961. The weapon was to be used in self defence in case he landed back on Earth in hostile territory, or amidst dangerous wildlife.

FACT: Atlas V rockets have had a 100% success rate since their first launch in 2002.

First military space station

Salyut 2 was the first of the Soviet Union's Almaz military space stations. Measuring 14.55 m (47 ft 9 in) long with a diameter of 4.15 m (13 ft 7 in), it was launched on 3 April 1973. It was intended to be manned and conduct military activities including espionage from orbit. However, shortly after entering orbit it was struck by debris from the Proton rocket which had launched it. It remained in orbit for 55 days before re-entering the atmosphere and burning up and crashing into the Pacific Ocean, without having been visited by a crew.

First space-based submarine surveillance satellite

SEASAT was a US satellite designed to use synthetic aperture radar to monitor the oceans. Launched on 27 June 1978, it only operated for 105 days before malfunctioning. An unexpected feature of the radar system on board SEASAT was its ability to detect the movement of submerged submarines by seeing their "wake" on the ocean surface. This has led some people to conjecture that the satellite's malfunction is a cover story – they believe it was taken over by the US military upon discovery of its submarine-detecting ability.

First military space shuttle mission

STS-4, the fourth US space shuttle mission, was the first to handle a military payload. It launched on 27 June 1982 and landed back on Earth on 4 July 1982. Its military payload, known as P82-1, consisted of two sensors designed to detect missile launches from space.

Both sensors reportedly failed. Mission commander Ken Mattingly referred to the payload as "a rinky-dink collection of minor stuff they wanted to fly".

Largest spy satellite

On 21 November 2010, the USA launched the highly classified *NROL-32* satellite from Cape Canaveral, Florida, USA. Believed to be the latest in the series of Mentor-class satellites, *NROL-32* was claimed to be the largest ever put into space by the Director of the National Reconnaissance Office, the US body responsible for spy satellites. Although details of both the satellite and its mission are secret, some experts believe *NROL-32* has a main antenna larger than 100 m (328 ft) across.

First stealth satellite

When the space shuttle *Atlanti* launched on 28 February 1990, it carried into orbit a classified payload for the US Department of Defense. Two days later, *Atlantis* deployed what is believed to be the first of America's MISTY satellites. These spy satellites allegedly use an inflatable outer shell to reduce their visibility to radar.

Largest combat satellite

The Soviet *Polyus* satellite was an orbital weapons platform measuring 37 m (121 ft 4 in) long, 4.1 m (13 ft 5 in) in diameter and with a mass of 80 tonnes (176,370 lb). It could be equipped with an anti-satellite recoilless cannon, a sensor-blinding laser to confuse hostile satellites and nuclear space-mine launcher. Only one was ever launched, on 15 May 1987. It failed to reach orbit and crashed into the Pacific. It is unclear which weapon systems it had.

Smallest robotic space plane

The US's Boeing *X-37B* is an unmanned space plane which launches on an Atlas V rocket and returns to Earth as a glider, like the retired space shuttles, before touching down on wheels. Measuring 8.9 m (29 ft 2 in) long with a wingspan of 4.5 m (14 ft 9 in) and a loaded mass of around 4,990 kg (11,000 lb), it is only the second type of space vehicle to land unmanned on wheels, after the Soviet *Buran* shuttle. Two *X-37Bs* exist to date; the first was launched into orbit on 22 April 2010 and landed on 5 December 2010. The mission for a second vehicle began on 5 March 2011. The precise mission and payload of both flights are secret. The X-37 project was started by NASA in 2004 and taken over by the US Air Force in 2006 – its potential military applications include reconnaissance of enemy armed forces and the jamming of enemy satellites.

Largest handheld firearm in space

From 1986 to 2007, the Soviet Union began equipping their cosmonauts with a TP-82 firearm, a triple-barrelled combination pistol/carbine/shotgun and flare gun with a detachable stock which conceals a machete. Cosmonauts would use the weapon, which weighed 2.4 kg (5.3 lb), to protect themselves from wild animals if they landed in the Siberian wilderness.

Largest military satellite constellation

Initiated in 1973, the USA's Global Positioning System (GPS) is a coordinated constellation of at least 24 satellites in orbit around the Earth. They provide, via radio signals, precise 3D navigation data across the world, enabling users to quickly pinpoint their location using a receiver. The GPS constellation is operated by the US Air Force 50th Space Wing and was only available for military use until 1996.

Longest unexplained explosion detected from space

The *Vela* satellites were launched by the USA to monitor the Earth and detect illegal nuclear weapons tests which contravened the 1963 Partial Test Ban Treaty. On 22 September 1979, a double flash was detected by the *Vela 6911* satellite over the Indian Ocean between Crozet Islands and Prince Edward Islands. It was estimated that a 2–3-kiloton nuclear explosion would have been needed to create a double flash of such magnitude. However, no radioactive debris was ever unambiguously detected.

Highest-altitude nuclear explosion

A 1.7-kiloton nuclear weapon was detonated 749 km (466 miles) above Earth on 6 September 1958, as part of the USA's secret Operation Argus test series. The 98.9-kg (218-lb) W-25 warhead was launched by a modified three-stage Lockheed X-17A missile from the warship USS *Norton Sound*, located in the South Atlantic. There were two other Operation Argus nuclear explosions at lower altitudes. The aim was to create belts of trapped radiation that would destroy and disrupt enemy satellites and communication systems.

Most heavily armed space station

Of all the space stations to orbit Earth, only the Soviet *Salyut 3*, launched in 1974, was armed. For defence, it was fitted with a 23-mm Nudelman aircraft cannon.

First alleged shot at a manned spacecraft

According to some sources, the Soviet Union aimed a laser at the space shuttle *Challenger*, above, during the STS-41-G mission in 1984. As *Challenger* was orbiting over the Soviet Union, the crew allegedly felt unwell, as well as losing communications and experiencing other technical difficulties. The theory that the Terra-3 laser complex in Kazakhstan was used to fire at the shuttle is firmly denied by NASA.

Highest-altitude satellite destroyed from Earth

On 11 January 2007, the Chinese government launched a missile from the ground at its *Fegyun-1C* satellite, orbiting at an altitude of 865 km (537 miles). The missile, a type referred to as "kinetic kill", struck the satellite and destroyed it using its own kinetic energy, rather than with an explosive warhead. According to NASA, some 2,841 pieces of space debris were created in the collision. NASA are worried that the debris will endanger spacecraft in low orbit around Earth.

First weapon in space

During World War II, Germany developed military rocket technology, culminating in the V2, which was used to attack its enemies, mainly in London, UK, and Antwerp, Belgium. The rocket was 14 m (45 ft 11 in) long and weighed 12,500 kg (27,558 lb), with an operational range of 320 km (200 miles). The first successful firing of the V2 – on 3 October 1942 from Peenemünde on Germany's Baltic coast – was the first time any man-made object entered space. The V2's speed – about 5,760 km/h (3,580 mi/h) – and trajectory – it reached altitudes of about 100 km (62 miles) – made it invulnerable to anti-aircraft guns and fighters.

FACT:
The first V2 attack hit Paris on 2 September 1944; the last was aimed at Antwerp on 28 March 1945.

ARMING ORBITAL SPACE

The Cold War saw countless pieces of military hardware sent into space, from space stations in low orbit to top-secret satellites thousands of miles above us.

VELA SATELLITES
101,000 to 112,000 km

MILSTAR COMMUNICATIONS SATELLITES 35,786 km

GPS SATELLITE
20,200 km

GLONASS
19,100 km

LACROSSE 5
715 km

STS-4
365 km

X37B
318 km

KEYHOLE SPY SATELLITES 281–1,005 km

ALMAZ 2 STATION
257–278 km

COSMIC CURIOSITIES

Darkest extra-solar planet

On 10 August 2011, US astronomers announced their discovery of the planet TrES-2b, around 750 light years away in the constellation of Draco. Compared with Earth, which reflects about 37% of the light it receives, TrES-2b reflects less than 1%, making it darker than coal. The Jupiter-sized planet has an estimated temperature of 1,200°C (2,192°F), giving it a reddish glow.

FACT:
The darkness of TrES-2b may be due to materials such as gaseous sodium in its atmosphere.

Fastest matter in the universe

Blobs of superheated plasma are ejected from black holes in the cores of highly active galaxies known as blazars. These blobs, with as much mass as the planet Jupiter, move at 99.99% of the speed of light.

FACT:
Light moves most quickly in a vacuum, reaching 299,792,458 m/sec (983,571,056 ft/sec).

Fastest approaching galaxy

Despite the overall expansion of the universe, a small number of galaxies are approaching our own. M86, a lenticular galaxy around 52 million light years away, in the Virgo Cluster, is moving towards our Milky Way at 419 km/sec (260 miles/sec).

Fastest star in the galaxy

On 8 February 2005, a team of astronomers from the Harvard-Smithsonian Center for Astrophysics in Cambridge, Massachusetts, USA, announced their discovery of a star travelling at more than 2.4 million km/h (1.5 million mi/h). Named SDSS J090745.0+24507, the star was probably accelerated by an encounter with the supermassive black hole at the centre of our Milky Way galaxy nearly 80 million years ago.

Fastest spinning star

VFTS 102 is a star approximately 25 times more massive than the Sun and 100,000 times more luminous. It lies within the Tarantula Nebula in the Large Magellanic Cloud, around 160,000 light years away. Announced on 5 December 2011, VFTS 102 rotates at an estimated 300 times faster than our Sun, at around 2 million km/h (1.2 million mi/h). If it rotated any faster, it would be in danger of tearing itself apart with centrifugal forces.

Flattest star

The least spherical star studied to date in our galaxy is the southern star Achenar (Alpha Eridani). Observations made using the VLT Interferometer at the European Southern Observatory's Paranal Observatory in Atacama, Chile, have revealed that Achenar is spinning so rapidly that its equatorial diameter is more than 50% greater than its polar diameter. The observations were made between 11 September and 12 November 2002, and the results were released on 11 June 2003.

Most luminous star in the galaxy

The latest observations of LBV 1806-20, which is 45,000 light years from Earth, indicate that it is between 5 and 40 million times more luminous than the Sun. It has a mass of at least 150 times the mass of the Sun and is at least 200 times the Sun's diameter.

Shortest-lived stars

Less than 0.1% of the stars in our galaxy are blue supergiants. With masses of around 100 times that of the Sun, they burn through their fuel very quickly and can last as little as 10 million years. Their blue colour is a result of their high surface temperatures, around 20,000–50,000°C (36,000–90,000°F). One of the best known is Rigel in the constellation of Orion. It is the sixth brightest star in the sky despite being around 900 light years away.

Smallest stars

Neutron stars may have a mass around 1.5 times that of the Sun, but only have diameters of 10–30 km (6–19 miles).

Largest distant galaxy cluster

"El Gordo" is the nickname of a massive galaxy cluster some 7 billion light years away. It is actually two galaxy clusters that are colliding at a rate of several million kilometres per hour. Its combined mass is around 2×10^{15} times the mass of our Sun. Its discovery was announced on 10 January 2012.

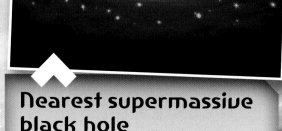

Nearest supermassive black hole

Sagittarius A* is the supermassive black hole that resides in the centre of our Milky Way galaxy, some 27,000 light years away. With a mass around 4 million times greater than our Sun, this black hole is orbited by several massive stars.

First proven collision of white dwarf stars

FACT: A white dwarf star is created when a star has burned all its nuclear "fuel". Only a superhot core is left.

SNR 0509-67.5 was a type 1a supernova in the Large Magellanic Cloud, a satellite galaxy of our own, which occurred around 400 years ago. The remnant of the explosion is a bubble of gas some 23 light years across, and expanding at more than 18 million km/h (11.2 million mi/h). In January 2012, astronomers studying the remnant proved that the supernova was caused by two white dwarf stars colliding. The remnant is around 160,000 light years away.

SUN AND STARS

Our galaxy, the Milky Way, is around 100,000 light years in diameter and has a spiral shape. The Sun is around 30,000 light years from its centre, located on one of the "arms" of the spiral:

KEY
1. Disk   2. Nucleus
3. Bulge   4. Sun

Side view

Top view

Spiral arm

0 5 10 15 20 25 30
Scale in kiloparsecs (1 kiloparsec = 3.26 light years)

20,000 astronomical units, or around 30 trillion km (18.6 trillion miles). This is around 100 times greater than our heliosphere (the distance from our sun to the point at which its gravitational force fades).

Most distant dwarf galaxy

On 18 January 2012, astronomers using the Keck II telescope on Mauna Kea, Hawaii, USA, announced that they had discovered a dwarf galaxy orbiting a large elliptical galaxy 10 billion light years away. It was found using a method called gravitational lensing, in which the mass of a foreground galaxy distorts and magnifies light from a much more distant galaxy behind it.

Most distant object in the universe

In January 2011, scientists announced that the Hubble Space Telescope had successfully imaged a galaxy so old that its light has taken 13.2 billion years to reach us. This means the galaxy as we see it today was formed less than 480 million years after the Big Bang, making it the earliest object to form in the universe.

Starstruck

How well do you know those twinkling lights in the night sky?

• Stars mostly consist of plasma (superhot matter) and gas.

• They form in dust-and-gas clouds called "nebulae".

• Scientists estimate there may be as many as 400 billion stars in our galaxy, the Milky Way. But there are more than 100 billion galaxies in our universe. And there may be more than 100 billion stars in each...

• Blue and white stars are hotter than orange or red stars. The temperature of a blue star may reach 25,000–40,000°C (45,000–75,000°F).

• Neutron stars are the core remnants of huge stars that have exploded. Although only around 20 km (12.5 miles) in diameter, their mass is approximately 1.5 times that of the Sun.

STAR SIZES

Stars range greatly in size, from the most massive supergiants (at 900 million km in diameter) down to the stellar remnants known as neutron stars (20–40 km wide).

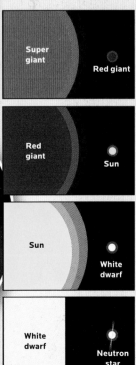

Super giant | Red giant

Red giant | Sun

Sun | White dwarf

White dwarf | Neutron star

Densest objects in the universe

Black holes are the remnants of stars that ended their lives as supernovae. They are characterized by a region of space in which gravity is so strong that not even light can escape. The boundary of this region is known as the event horizon, and at the centre of the black hole is the "singularity", where the mass of the dead star is compressed to a single point of zero size and infinite density. It is this singularity that generates the powerful gravitational field of a black hole.

Heaviest black hole
On 5 December 2011, astronomers using the Gemini North, Keck II and Hubble Space Telescope observatories reported their discovery of a supermassive black hole in the centre of the elliptical galaxy NGC 4889, some 336 million light years away. Its mass is estimated at around 21 billion times that of the Sun.

Largest structure in the universe
In October 2003, a team of astronomers from Princeton University in New Jersey, USA, announced that they had discovered a huge wall of galaxies which is some

1.37 billion light years long. The breakthrough had been made using data from the Sloan Digital Sky Survey, which mapped the locations of one million galaxies in the universe.

Largest circumstellar disk
M17-SO1 is a protostar (early stage of star formation) in the Omega Nebula, some 5,000–6,000 light years away. In 2005 it was discovered to have a disk of material orbiting it with a diameter of an estimated

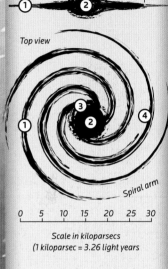

Farthest object ever visible to the eye
Gamma-ray bursts – the birth cries of black holes – are the largest explosions in the universe. At 2:12 EDT on 19 March 2008, a gamma-ray burst in a galaxy 7.5 billion light years away was visible for around 30 seconds and captured by a robotic telescope.

FACT: Later named GRB 080319B, the burst (artist's impression above) reached a brightness of magnitude 5.8.

VISIT THE CUTTING EDGE OF SCIENCE ON P.194

CONTENTS

GREEN EARTH

Largest cave

Hang Son Doong ("Mountain River Cave") is around 200 m (655 ft) high, 150 m (490 ft) wide and at least 6.5 km (4 miles) long. Located in Phong Nha-Ke Bang National Park, Bo Trach District, Quang Binh Province, Vietnam, this gigantic cave might be even larger than first thought, as it had not been completely surveyed as of February 2012. Hidden by forest, it was found in 1991 by a local farmer named Ho Khanh. In April 2009, he led a team of British cavers to the cave, and they made an initial survey of it.

FACT:
The figure nearest to us in this photograph is a full kilometre apart from the figure in the background.

HOW MUCH CLIMATE CHANGE CAN WE SURVIVE?

Do we have a future on Earth?

Earth's changing climate is one of the most complex systems ever studied. It is difficult to refute the data gathered by scientists, especially when very different methods show the same overall trend. The biggest questions are why is it changing, how much is human activity responsible, and can we survive as a race?

Earth's climate has changed before. The planet has undergone periods of severe glaciation (Ice Ages), which have occurred with no influence from humans. Around 14,600 years ago, as the ice sheets of the last Ice Age were retreating, a catastrophe happened: the partial collapse of the Antarctic ice sheet saw global sea levels rise by 20 m (66 ft) in less than 500 years.

Back then, though, there were no massive cities on the coastlines. In 2005, the US city of New Orleans was devastated by Hurricane Katrina, leaving more than 1,500 people dead. A sea-level rise of just 1 m (3 ft) could flood 17% of Bangladesh, creating tens of millions of refugees. Some island nations, such as the Maldives, would be completely submerged. Sea-level rise will destroy some of the world's largest cities, and contaminate fresh water for many of the others.

Illustrated here are three key influences on the climate, with a prognosis of how they might affect our future survival on Earth.

ICE CAPS

CAUSE

The Earth's average temperature has increased by around 0.5°C in the last 100 years. This has an effect on the size of the planet's ice caps. As ice is white, it reflects more solar radiation back into space. As the ice caps shrink, they reflect less and allow more solar radiation to be absorbed, meaning it can contribute to further warming. This is known as "positive feedback".

EFFECT

FACT: Pine Island glacier in Antarctica is shrinking by at least 16 m (52 ft) per year – and may be gone in 100 years.

Antarctica is a land mass covered by a vast ice cap, but the Arctic is an ocean on which the ice floats. The ice grows and shrinks with the seasons, and in the summer of 2007 the Arctic experienced the greatest shrinkage in the ice cap, reducing in size to an area of 4.11 million km². In the summer of 2011, it shrank to 4.33 million km², the second smallest Arctic ice cap recorded.

FUTURE

If the Arctic ice cap disappeared, it would not affect global sea levels. Why not? Because the ice is already floating on the ocean. But massive changes to Antarctica could change sea levels considerably. There is enough ice in Antarctica to raise the level of the oceans by around 61 m (200 ft), and the Greenland ice cap contains enough water to cause a 7-m (23-ft) rise. A recent report predicts a rise of 1.4 m (4 ft 7 in) by the end of the century. This could have devastating results for coastal cities.

Hockey stick graph

Published by the UN's Intergovernmental Panel on Climate Change in 2001, this graph is one of the most controversial in science. It is based on the one first published by US scientists Michael Mann, Raymond Bradley and Malcolm Hughes in 1998. It uses scientific data including tree-ring studies, ice cores, historical records, and coral and instrument data to show an overall rise in Earth's atmospheric temperature after 1900. The graph's name comes from the shape of the line.

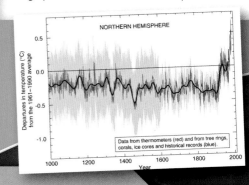

NORTHERN HEMISPHERE

Departures in temperature (°C) from the 1961–1990 average

Data from thermometers (red) and from tree rings, corals, ice cores and historical records (blue).

Year

MEET PIONEERING POLAR EXPLORERS ON P.118

ACID OCEANS

CO₂

FACT: In 1998, around 16% of the world's coral reefs were destroyed or seriously damaged in a once-in-a-millennium event. The 1998 El Niño phenomenon may have triggered the disaster.

The oceans are a natural "sink" for atmospheric carbon dioxide (CO_2) – they absorb around 22 million tonnes of CO_2 every day. CO_2 in the atmosphere comes from various natural sources, including volcanic activity and the respiration of animals, as well as human activity. The concentration of CO_2 in the atmosphere has increased since the beginning of the Industrial Revolution (c. 1750 onwards).

CO_2 is a natural component of the atmosphere. It only accounts for a small part of it but it has a significant effect on Earth's ability to trap in heat from the Sun. Most sources of CO_2 are natural but the study of air bubbles trapped in Antarctic ice cores shows a steady increase since 1832, corresponding to the increase in man-made emissions since the start of the Industrial Revolution. Exactly how much human activity has contributed to this remains unknown.

The absorption of CO_2 into the oceans is gradually changing their pH value, which is a measure of their acidity/alkalinity. (A pH value of 7 is neutral.) Between 1751 and 1994, the average pH of the oceans' surface water has decreased from around 8.25 to around 8.14. The current rate of change of ocean acidity is around 100 times greater than at any time in the last 20 million years.

From the 1950s to 2011, the atmospheric concentration of CO_2 has increased in volume from around 315 to 391.1 parts per million – the highest it has been in the last 800,000 years, and possibly a lot longer. After water vapour, CO_2 is the most abundant "greenhouse gas" in our atmosphere.

FACT: Earth would be significantly cooler without natural "greenhouse gases" such as CO_2.

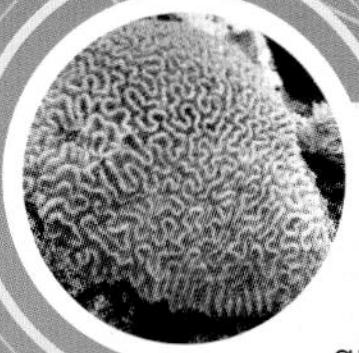

If the overall acidity of the oceans continues to rise, there will be various effects. Some species – for example sea grasses – flourish in water with elevated CO_2 in it. Other species, including some invertebrates, will find it tougher to form their shells, and some studies suggest up to 70% of corals (pictured) could be under threat by the end of the century.

If CO_2 levels in the atmosphere keep on rising, it will lead to an increase in Earth's natural greenhouse effect which, in turn, will make the planet warmer. A hotter atmosphere is expected to lead to not only sea-level rise but also a more energetic climate in general, with more tropical cyclones, droughts, flooding and heatwaves.

CAUSE

EFFECT

FUTURE

POLLUTION

Largest landfill reclamation project

The Fresh Kills Landfill at Staten Island, New York, USA, was opened in 1947. It was officially closed in early 2001 – although it temporarily reopened to receive debris from the 9/11 attack on the World Trade Center. At 890 ha (2,200 acres), it is three times bigger than Central Park – and, in places, it is 68 m (223 ft) high, taller than the Statue of Liberty. In October 2009, work began on a 30-year project to turn it into a public park.

Largest national producer of CO_2 emissions

According to the United Nations, as of 2008 China was responsible for 7,031.9 million tonnes (7,751 million tons) of carbon dioxide emissions. This represented 23.33% of the global total.
The rest of the top five:
2. USA: 18.11%
3. India: 5.78%
4. Russia: 5.67%
5. Japan: 4.01%

Worst SO_2 fire

A fire at a sulphur plant near Mosul, Iraq, which began on 24 June 2003, released an average of 21,000 metric tonnes (23,100 tons) of sulphur dioxide per day for nearly a month. In all, 600,000 metric tonnes (661,386 tons) escaped – representing the greatest man-made release of sulphur dioxide and exceeding the sulphur dioxide output from most volcanic eruptions.

Most lethal smog

Between 3,500 and 4,000 people, mainly the elderly and children, died in London, UK, from acute bronchitis caused by thick smog between 4 and 9 December 1952. It was caused by the burning of fossil fuels combined with a weather inversion that trapped smoke particles near the ground. Visibility in the streets was only 30 cm (12 in) and cinemas had to close because it was impossible to see the screens.

Largest red mud spill

On 4 October 2010, the collapse of a dam at the Ajkai Timföldgyár alumina plant in Ajka, Hungary, resulted in the release of about 1 million m³ (35 million ft³) of toxic red mud waste. The mud flooded nearby villages in a wave up to 2 m (6.6 ft) high. At least four people were killed and more than 100 injured as the mud covered around 40 km² (15.4 miles²). The flood also killed all life in the nearby Marcal river.

Most acidic acid rain

A pH reading of 2.83 was recorded over the Great Lakes, USA/Canada, in 1982 and a reading of 1.87 was recorded at Inverpolly Forest, Highland, Scotland, in 1983. These are the lowest pH levels ever recorded in acid precipitation, making it the most acidic acid rain.

Largest single oil spill

On 14 March 1910, an uncontrolled gusher began at the Midway-Sunset Oil Field in California, USA. The eruption of pressurized crude oil destroyed the mining derrick and produced a crater that prevented engineers from controlling the oil geyser. The leak, known as the Lakeview Gusher, lasted for 18 months and released around 9 million barrels (1.43 billion litres; 50.5 million ft³) of oil before the well sealed itself naturally.

Worst air pollution (country)

According to a 2011 World Health Organization report, Mongolia has the worst air pollution, with an annual average of 279 micrograms of "PM10" particles per cubic metre. In Mongolia, many factories burn coal and lots of people live in *gers*, felt-lined tents with central stoves in which coal or wood is burned. Ulan Bator, the Mongolian capital, which means "Red Hero", has been rechristened by the locals as Utan Bator, or "Smog Hero". It is the second most polluted city after Ahvaz (main image and record below).

Highest levels of CO_2

According to the National Oceanic and Atmospheric Administration (USA), the atmospheric carbon dioxide level for January 2011 was 391.19 parts per million (ppm). This is up on the average for 2010, which was 387.35 ppm.

City with the worst air pollution

According to a 2011 report by the World Health Organization (WHO), which measured air quality in 1,100 urban areas, Ahvaz, Iran, has the world's worst air pollution. (The main photo shows the oil fields of Ahvaz.) Air pollution is measured by the amount of particles less than 10 micrometres across per cubic metre. Ahvaz has an annual average of 372 micrograms of these "PM10" particles per cubic metre, nearly 20 times the WHO's recommended safe level.
The **city with the least air pollution** is Whitehorse in Yukon, Canada, which has an annual average of three micrograms of PM10 particles per cubic metre.

Welcome to WHITEHORSE
CAPITAL OF THE YUKON
CITY LIMIT

Largest DDT producer

The insecticide DDT has been banned for agricultural use but is still used to control malaria and the bubonic plague. India is the largest national producer – it made 6,344 metric tonnes (6,967 tons) in 2007.

FACT:
The creators of this map estimate that light pollution grows by 5–10% a year in both the USA and Europe.

Largest ocean landfill site

The North Pacific Central Gyre is a vast vortex of slow, clockwise-revolving, high-pressure ocean water that naturally concentrates floating litter in its centre. In 2002, environmental studies revealed that the centre of the Gyre contains around 6 kg (13 lb) of waste plastic for every 1 kg (2.2 lb) of natural plankton.

First global light pollution map

Light pollution in urban areas drowns out much of the natural night sky. In addition to representing energy waste, it can lead to confusion in nocturnal species. In 2001, Italian and American astronomers released the first global map highlighting the problem. According to the data, around 20% of the world's population can no longer see the Milky Way in the night sky from their homes. The Falkland Islands at the foot of South America have a surprising amount of light pollution because of light from fishing fleets and the gas flares on offshore oil and gas rigs.

Biggest contributor to the Atmospheric Brown Cloud

First observed in 1999 over parts of Asia, the Atmospheric Brown Cloud is a complicated mixture of air pollutants which can be 3 km (1.86 miles) thick. This type of pollution is caused by industrial activity, vehicle emissions and wood burning. The biggest single component of the cloud is black carbon "soot", the result of incomplete burning, which makes up around 55% of the cloud.

FACT:
The Brown Cloud problem is common in southern Africa, the Amazon Basin and the USA.

Largest e-waste site

Guiyu, a group of villages in Guangdong province, China, is the world capital of electronic waste. Around 1.5 million metric tonnes (1.65 tons) of discarded computers, phones and other electronics are processed here each year, within an area of 52 km² (20.1 miles²). As a result, the area has high levels of heavy metal and acid pollution.

Largest marine oil spill

During Iraq's retreat in the 1991 Gulf War, Saddam Hussein ordered troops to release oil from refineries and tankers in Kuwait. Some 2–4 million barrels (318–635 million litres; 11.2–22.4 million ft³) of oil was released into the sea.

Worst nuclear waste accident

In December 1957, an explosion at the nuclear plant at Kyshtym, Russia, released radiation that dispersed over 23,000 km² (8,900 miles²). More than 30 villages in a 1,200-km² (460-mile²) area were eliminated from maps of the USSR in the three years following the accident, and about 17,000 people were evacuated. A 1992 report indicated that 8,015 people died as a direct result of discharges.

Longest-lasting pollution

Nuclear waste, formed as a by-product of nuclear fission, gradually loses its radioactivity over time, until it can be considered "safe". "Half life" is the time it takes for half of a quantity of radioactive material to lose its radioactivity. Iodine-129, an unstable isotope of iodine, produced by the fission of uranium and plutonium in reactors, has a half life of 15.7 million years.

TOP 10 TOXIC POLLUTION PROBLEMS

The Blacksmith Institute's 2011 report on *The World's Worst Toxic Pollution Problems* reveals the most polluting industries, the key pollutants and the numbers of people directly at risk:

1. Artisanal gold mining
☠☠☠☠☠☠☠☠☠☠☠
Key issue: Mercury pollution
At risk: 3,506,600

2. Industrial estates
☠☠☠☠☠☠☠☠☠
Key issue: Lead pollution
At risk: 2,981,200

3. Agricultural production
☠☠☠☠☠☠☠
Key issue: Pesticide pollution (considering only local impact)
At risk: 2,245,000

4. Lead smelting
☠☠☠☠☠☠
Key issue: Lead pollution
At risk: 1,988,800

5. Tannery operations
☠☠☠☠☠☠
Key issue: Chromium pollution
At risk: 1,848,100

6. Mining/ore processing
☠☠☠☠☠
Key issue: Mercury pollution
At risk: 1,591,700

7. Mining/ore processing
☠☠☠
Key issue: Lead pollution
At risk: 1,239,500

8. Lead-acid battery recycling
☠☠
Key issue: Lead pollution
At risk: 967,800

9. Naturally occurring arsenic in ground water
☠☠
Key issue: Arsenic pollution
At risk: 750,700

10. Pesticide manufacturing and storage
☠☠
Key issue: Pesticide pollution
At risk: 735,400

Source: Blacksmith Institute/ Green Cross (Switzerland)

NUCLEAR ENERGY

First commercial nuclear power station

Calder Hall, in Cumbria, UK, was the first nuclear power station to provide electricity commercially. It was officially opened on 17 October 1956 by Queen Elizabeth II. Its four Magnox reactors were each capable of producing 60 MWe (megawatts). Its initial purpose was to produce weapons-grade plutonium; electricity generation was a by-product. It was decommissioned in 2003.

Country with the highest percentage of nuclear power use

France currently generates more than 75% of its electricity needs from nuclear power. There are 58 reactors in the country, with a total generating power of 63 GWe (gigawatts).

First floating nuclear power station

MH-1A, a pressurized-water reactor, was built inside a converted cargo ship for the US Army, and began operation in 1967. The ship, whose engines had been removed to make way for the reactor, was towed to the Panama Canal, where it provided electrical power to the Panama Canal Zone between 1968 and 1975. It was capable of providing 10 MWe of power.

Longest-operating nuclear power station

The nuclear reactor in Obninsk, Russia, ran from 27 June 1954 until it was decommissioned on 30 April 2002. It was the world's first operating civilian nuclear reactor. Obninsk is known as Russia's first science city, or *naukograd*.

Largest particle detector

The ATLAS Detector, part of the Large Hadron Collider (LHC) at the European Organization for Nuclear Research (CERN), measures 46 m (151 ft) long, 25 m (82 ft) wide and 25 m (82 ft) high. It weighs 7,000 metric tonnes (7,700 tons) and contains 100 million sensors that measure particles produced in proton-proton collisions in the LHC. ATLAS is being used to investigate the forces that have shaped the universe since the start of time, including the way particles gain mass, the differences between matter and antimatter, and the possibility of extra dimensions in space.

Largest mail irradiation programme

In October 2001, deadly anthrax spores were discovered in mail sent to congressional leaders and journalists in the USA, resulting in five deaths. In response, the US government initiated the irradiation of mail sent to key addresses. Between November 2001 and April 2008, around 1.2 million containers of federal mail were irradiated. All mail addressed to the White House is still reportedly irradiated.

First nuclear-powered pacemaker

In the late 1960s, two companies, Alcatel (France) and Medtronic (USA), created a nuclear pacemaker. It was first implanted into a patient in 1970. Before, patients would need surgery every few years to replace battery-powered pacemakers. Powered by a tiny piece of plutonium-238, the nuclear pacemaker resembled a hockey puck. In the 1980s, pacemakers powered by lithium batteries, which last around 10 years, superseded it.

ACTUAL SIZE

First commercial food irradiation

In 1957, a facility in Stuttgart, then West Germany, began irradiating spices with an electron beam to increase their storage life.

Highest nuclear fusion energy output

The highest energy output achieved using nuclear fusion is 16 MW, by the Joint European Torus (JET) tokamak nuclear fusion reactor, Culham, Oxfordshire, UK, in 1997.

Largest nuclear reactor building programme

China is currently building 27 new nuclear power stations, around 40% of the total under construction worldwide. The country's 13 operational nuclear power stations provide only around 2% of its electricity. The Chinese government suspended approval for further facilities after an earthquake and tsunami wrecked the nuclear plant at Fukushima, Japan, in March 2011.

First nuclear reactor in space

On 3 April 1965, the USA launched the System for Nuclear Power (SNAP) 10A into a polar orbit around the Earth. Designed to test remotely operated nuclear reactors, SNAP 10A began producing electricity at more than 600 W some 12 hours after launch. After 43 days of operation, the reactor shut down because of an electrical component failure. The spacecraft is still in orbit, about 1,200 km (746 miles) above Earth, and is not expected to re-enter the atmosphere for around 4,000 years.

Largest nuclear-powered lighthouse programme

During the Cold War, the USSR required navigational aids for shipping along its vast northern coast. Its solution was a chain of lighthouses powered by radioisotope thermal generators, which are more like "nuclear batteries" than reactors. These generators allowed isolated lighthouses to operate without supervision. The network of around 132 nuclear lighthouses began to fail after the fall of the USSR and some have been plundered by thieves for their metals.

Smallest nuclear-powered attack submarine

France currently operates six Rubis-class submarines, each of which has a length of 73.6 m (241 ft) and a displacement of 2,600 tonnes (2,860 tons) when submerged. Powered by a pressurized-water nuclear reactor, they have unlimited range and were designed to have an operational lifetime of around 25 years.

On 22 December 2006, the French government placed an order for six Barracuda submarines, which are expected to start replacing the Rubis subs by 2016. The Barracudas will be 99.4 m (326 ft) long.

Largest nuclear power station

Until going offline in March 2012, Kashiwazaki-Kariwa nuclear power station in Japan had a total output of 8,212 MWe. It supplied electricity to 16 million households and was the fourth largest electric-generating station in the world behind the hydroelectric plants at Itaipu on the Brazil-Paraguay border, Three Gorges Dam in China and Guri Dam in Venezuela.

NUCLEAR FISSION & FUSION

The nucleus of an atom is held together by strong forces, which means that the atom contains a huge amount of energy. Harnessing this energy means tapping into a source of power more than a million times more efficient than burning coal. There are two fundamental ways of releasing this energy: fission and fusion.

Fission

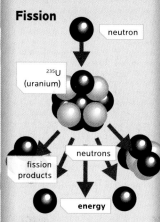

neutron

^{235}U (uranium)

neutrons

fission products

energy

Basics: Splitting of atomic nuclei into smaller fragments.
Occurrence: Very rare in nature.
Waste products: Many types of unwanted by-products requiring massive disposal efforts with short-, medium- and long-term environmental risks.
Energy released: Around a million times the energy released by chemical reactions.
Requirements: Critical mass of the fissile material plus high-speed neutrons.
Use history: Chicago Pile 1 was first tested in 1942. Commercial power supply from fission began in 1956.

Longest operation for a pressurized-water reactor

On 6 October 2009, the TMI-1 reactor at Three Mile Island, Pennsylvania, USA, was shut down for refuelling after 705 days of continuous operation. There are more than 200 pressurized-water reactors worldwide. Three Mile Island is famous for the partial meltdown of TMI-2 in March 1979.

Most powerful nuclear-powered cargo ship

Designed for Russia's northern sea route, the USSR-built *Sevmorput*, an ice-breaking container-cargo vessel, began active service in 1988. With a KLT-40 pressurized-water reactor, rated at 135 MWt, she is the most powerful of only four nuclear cargo ships ever built and the last in operation.

Strongest force

The four fundamental forces in the universe which account for all interactions between matter and energy are: the strong nuclear (which holds nuclei together), the weak nuclear (responsible for radioactive decay), electromagnetic and gravity. The strongest of these is the strong nuclear force, which is 100 times stronger than the electromagnetic force – the next strongest. Gravity, the weakest, is 10^{40} times weaker than the electromagnetic force.

Highest food irradiation dose

The irradiation of food is aimed at preventing the spread of disease. It can also increase the storage life of food. In 2003 the Codex Alimentarius, established in 1963 by the World Health Organization and the UN to maintain food standards, removed any upper limit on recommended radiation doses for food. Today the highest dose in general use is around 70 kGy (kilograys), to which some hospital food is subjected. About 0.0056–0.0075 kilograys would be a lethal dose to humans.

Largest radioactive exclusion zone

The accident at the Chernobyl nuclear power plant in Ukraine on 26 April 1986 resulted in a permanent exclusion zone roughly 30 km (19 miles) around the power plant. No one is officially allowed to live inside this zone, although some people are believed to have returned illegally.

FACT:
Nuclear fusion occurs all the time in stars – nuclei fuse together, releasing energy in the form of light and heat.

FOR SCIENCE STATS AND FACTS, TURN TO P.194

Fusion

^{3}H (hydrogen-3)

^{2}H (heavy hydrogen)

neutrino

helium

energy

Basics: The fusing together of two atoms to make a larger one.
Occurrence: Stars are powered by natural fusion reactions in their cores, where hydrogen is fused into helium and, later in a star's life, to heavier elements.
Waste products: None, apart from when a "fission trigger" is used.
Energy released: Between three and four times the energy released in fission.
Requirements: Very high temperatures and densities.
Use history: First lab demonstration in 1932. Longest sustained man-made fusion reaction stands at 210 seconds. No commercial use yet.

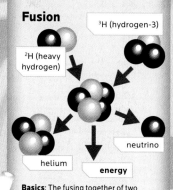

Longest sustained fusion reaction

In 2002, scientists at the experimental Tore Supra reactor in Cadarache, France, sustained a nuclear fusion reaction of 3 MW for 210 seconds. The picture shows a technician checking the heating system inside the reactor. Cadarache will be the site of the International Thermonuclear Experimental Reactor (ITER). When operational (planned for 2018), ITER is hoped to be the first large-scale fusion reactor to produce more energy than is used to initiate its fusion reactions.

BIOMES

Youngest biome

Arctic tundra, which encircles the North Pole along the northern coastlines of Russia and Canada, as well as parts of Greenland, was formed only 10,000 years ago. It is treeless, windy and receives only around 15–25 cm (6–10 in) of precipitation annually – mostly as snow. The 48 animal species found there include bears, polar bears, wolves, rodents, foxes and reindeer.

Geographical area with greatest biodiversity

The tropical Andes region covers 1,258,000 km^2 (485,716 miles^2) and runs through Venezuela, Colombia, Ecuador, Peru, Bolivia, Chile and a small area in north Argentina. So far, 45,000 species of vascular plants have been recorded (15–17% of the world's species) as well as 1,666 bird species, 414 mammal species and 1,309 reptile and amphibian species.

Fastest-declining biome

Tropical rainforests are being lost at a higher rate than any other biome. A 2002 study using satellite images revealed that around 58,000 km^2 (22,394 miles^2) a year were lost between 1990 and 1997. Between 2000 and 2005, Central America lost around 1.3% of its rainforests each year and about two-thirds of its rainforest has been turned into pasture since 1950.

Deepest hydrothermal vent

Hydrothermal vents, discovered in 1977, spew hot water laden with minerals from the ocean floor. The deepest ones found to date are in the Beebe Vent Field, south of the Cayman Islands, at a depth of 4,960 m (16,272 ft). Bacteria are able to convert minerals found in the vents' fluids into energy through chemosynthesis. They form the basis of the food chain – because, at these depths, there is no light for plants to photosynthesize.

FACT: The scaly-foot gastropod (or snail), right, lives near the vents and has a foot armoured with iron sulphides.

Smallest ecosystem

In October 2008, scientists discovered the first ecosystem on Earth with only one species. The bacteria *Desulforudis audaxviator* was found 2.8 km (1.7 miles) underground in the Mponeng gold mine, in South Africa. It exists in total isolation and total darkness in temperatures of around 60°C (140°F).

Highest concentration of heathers

The *fynbos* (Afrikaans for "fine bush") plant ecosystem, exclusive to South Africa's Cape floristic region, has more than 600 species of heather (*Erica*). Only 26 species of heather occur in the rest of the world.

LARGEST...

Temperate deciduous forest biome

Temperate deciduous forests are those with trees that lose their leaves each year and receive an average of 75–150 cm (30–60 in) of rainfall annually. They exist across the eastern USA, New Zealand and eastern China, but the largest example covers some 9.06 million km^2 (3.5 million miles^2) across Russia and Scandinavia.

Biome with the greatest biodiversity

The total number of animal and plant species in the world's tropical rainforests is unknown. However, current estimates of rainforest biodiversity suggest that perhaps 50–75% of all Earth's living species are concentrated in rainforests, although they cover only 6–7% of Earth's surface. The Wooroonooran National Park in Queensland, Australia, above, contains some of the oldest rainforests.

Largest biome

The open ocean, not close to the shore or sea bed, is known as the pelagic zone. Globally, its volume is around 1,330 million km^3 (319 million miles^3). This biome contains many of the largest animals on Earth, including *the* largest, the blue whale (below), as well as bluefin tuna and giant squid.

FACT: About 90% of marine life lives in the top 200 m (636 ft) of the ocean where the sunlight can reach.

Tropical rainforest

The Amazon rainforest covers an area of 5.5 million km^2 (2.12 million miles^2) across nine different South American countries: Brazil, Colombia, Peru, Venezuela, Ecuador, Bolivia, Guyana, Suriname and French Guiana. The second largest contiguous rainforest is in the Congo Basin, Africa.

Alpine biome

Alpine biomes occur in mountain regions across the world – the largest being the Tibetan alpine steppe in China which covers around 800,000 km² (309,000 miles²). They begin at an altitude of around 3,000 m (10,000 ft) and continue up to the snowline. The harsh conditions mean there are no cold-blooded animals, and plants tend to grow close to the ground because of the wind and cold. Alpine animals cope with the cold by hibernating, migrating or growing layers of insulating fat.

Marine reserve

The Papahānaumokuākea Marine National Monument covers 356,879 km² (137,791 miles²) of the Pacific Ocean surrounding the northwestern Hawaiian islands and atolls. The coral reefs here are home to more than 7,000 species, a quarter of which are unique to the region. It was designated a marine reserve on 15 June 2006 and was made a UNESCO World Heritage Site in 2010.

Tropical forest reserve

The largest tropical forest reserve is the Tumucumaque National Park in the northern Amazonian state of Amapá, Brazil. Measuring some 38,875 km² (15,010 miles²) in area, the reserve contains sloths, jaguars, freshwater turtles, eagles and agouti (a species of rodent). The creation of the park was announced on 22 August 2002 by Brazilian president Fernando Henrique Cardoso.

Forest biomes

Broadly speaking, there are three types of forest biome:

• **Boreal or taiga forest**, in the far north, is dominated by evergreen conifers, especially spruces and firs. In the long winters, many mammals hibernate and many birds migrate south.

• **Temperate deciduous forest** dominates in Europe and the USA and has trees that shed their leaves in autumn. Even in summer, lots of sun penetrates the canopy so forest-floor plants can photosynthesize and cold-blooded animals such as snakes and frogs can survive.

• **Tropical rainforest** near the equator has hundreds of species of trees, and the same species rarely grow next to each other. As vegetation is dense, little light reaches the forest floor. Many vines and epiphytes (plants which perch on other plants) cling to the branches.

Coastal mangrove forest

The Sundarbans (from the Bengali word for "beautiful forest") is a forested region stretching almost 15,540 km² (6,000 miles²) across India and Bangladesh. It acts as a natural barrier against tsunamis and cyclones that blow in from the Bay of Bengal. With saltwater-tolerant roots, this forest's mangrove trees sometimes exceed 21 m (70 ft) in height above islands of layered sand and grey clay, which have been deposited by rivers that flow 1,609 km (1,000 miles) from the Himalayas to the Bay of Bengal.

FACT: Rainforest trees are so dense that rain falling on the canopy can take 10 minutes to reach the floor.

Oldest terrestrial biome

Tropical rainforests, such as the Amazon rainforest (above), have been established for at least a million years. The last Ice Age, which ended around 10,000 years ago, covered much of the world's forests in ice, but left the equatorial forests uncovered.

Marine animal structure

The Great Barrier Reef, off Queensland, Australia, covers an area of 207,000 km² (80,000 miles²) and consists of billions of living and dead stony corals (order Madreporaria or Scleractinia). Over 350 species of coral are currently found there, and it is estimated to have formed over 600 million years ago. It was made a UNESCO World Heritage Site in 1981.

Unbroken intertidal mudflats

Stretching along some 500 km (311 miles) off the northern European coastline from the Netherlands to Denmark lies the Wadden Sea. Its total area of around 10,000 km² (3,861 miles²) contains many habitats, including tidal channels, sea-grass meadows, sandbars, mussel beds and salt marshes. Some 10–12 million migratory birds pass through each year, with up to 6.1 million present at any one time.

Deepest cold seep trench

First discovered in the Gulf of Mexico in 1983, cold seeps are an ocean floor biome sustained by methane and sulphide-rich fluids seeping from the seabed. The deepest yet discovered lies 7,326 m (24,035 ft) below sea level in the Japan Trench off the coast of Japan in the Pacific Ocean. Cold-seep ecosystems rely on the bacteria feeding on the escaping fluids, which in turn attract animals including mussels, clams and the *Lamellibrachia* tubeworm, right. *Lamellibrachia* tubeworms are believed to live for up to 250 years.

Japan

Pacific Ocean

Japan Trench

CATEGORIZING WORLD BIOMES

A biome is an ecosystem characterized by flora and fauna that have developed under specific conditions. There is no international agreement on how biomes should be organized, and there are many different lists; here is one such grouping by the University of California, Berkeley, USA.

TUNDRA	Arctic
	Alpine
FOREST	Boreal (taiga)
	Temperate
	Tropical
GRASSLAND	Temperate
	Tropical (Savannah)
DESERT	Cold
	Coastal
	Semi-arid
	Hot & dry
AQUATIC (FRESHWATER)	Wetlands
	Streams & rivers
	Ponds
	Estuaries
AQUATIC (MARINE)	Coral reefs
	Oceans

The climate has a major impact on biomes. Temperature and moisture play a key role in the terrestrial (land) biomes, while the aquatic biomes are determined by the availability of sunlight and nutrients.

TREES

The height scale on the right:
300 ft / 91.44 m
275 ft / 83.83 m
250 ft / 76.2 m
225 ft / 68.58 m
200 ft / 60.96 m
175 ft / 53.34 m
150 ft / 45.72 m

FACT:
"Centurion" was only found in 2008, although it is just 75 km (47 miles) from Tasmania's capital, Hobart.

Tallest hardwood tree: "Centurion", a specimen of Australian swamp gum tree (*Eucalyptus regnans*) located in Tasmania, Australia, stands 101 m (331.36 ft) tall.

Highest tree nest: Nests of the marbled murrelet (*Brachyramphus marmoratus*), a small north Pacific member of the auk family of seabirds, have been discovered as high as 45 m (147 ft), usually on moss-covered branches of old conifer trees.

Largest living tree by volume
"General Sherman", the giant sequoia (*Sequoiadendron giganteum*) in the Sequoia National Park, California, USA, has a volume of 1,487 m³ (52,508 ft³).

Most dangerous tree
The trunk of the manchineel (*Hippomane mancinella*), native to the Florida Everglades, USA, and Caribbean coast, exudes a sap so acidic that the merest contact with human skin causes a breakout of blisters, and blindness can occur if it touches a person's eyes. In addition, a single bite of its small, green, apple-like fruit causes blistering and severe pain, and can prove fatal. And if the tree catches fire, its smoke can cause blindness.

Most expensive tree
A single Starkspur Golden Delicious apple tree (*Malus domestica*) from near Yakima, Washington, USA, was sold to a nursery in 1959 for $51,000 (£18,000) – equivalent to $525,000 (£332,000) at today's prices.

Most trees destroyed by storms
Approximately 270 million trees were felled or split by storms that hit France on 26 and 27 December 1999.

Most parasitic tree
Unlike normal plants, the albino coastal redwoods (*Sequoia sempervirens*) lack chlorophyll and therefore are unable to feed themselves via photosynthesis. Instead, they permanently attach themselves to the roots of "parent" trees, from which they draw all of their sustenance. The trees are white with thin, limp, waxy needles, hence their nicknames "vampire redwoods" and "everwhites". Only between 25 and 60 exist, all in California, USA.

Remotest tree
The world's loneliest tree is believed to be a solitary Norwegian spruce (*Picea abies*) – over 100 years old – located on Campbell Island in Antarctica, whose nearest companion is over 222 km (119.8 nautical miles) away on the Auckland Islands.

Largest deforestation
Between 2005 and 2010, some 12,626,000 ha (31,199,525 acres) of forest were cleared in Brazil – an average rate of 2,525,000 ha (6,239,410 acres) per year. Data from the UN Food and Agriculture Organization shows that between 2000 and 2010, deforestation across 121 tropical countries averaged a total of 9,340,000 ha (23,079,642 acres) per year. At current rates, more than half of it will be lost by 2030.

First tree
The earliest surviving species of tree is the maidenhair (*Ginkgo biloba*) of Zhejiang, which first appeared in China about 160 million years ago during the Jurassic era. It was rediscovered by Engelbert Kaempfer (Germany) in 1690. It has been grown in Japan since c. 1100, where it is now known as *ichou*.

Longest-living forests
The forests of Patagonian cypresses (*Fitzroya cupressoides*) in the Andean mountains of southern Chile and Argentina have an average age of 2,500 years.

Largest tree transplanted
An oak tree (*Quercus lobata*) named "Old Glory", aged 180–220 years and weighing approximately 415.5 tonnes (916,000 lb), was moved 0.4 km (0.25 miles) by Senna Tree Company (USA) to a new park in Los Angeles, California, USA, on 20 January 2004. The tree was 17.67 m (58 ft) tall and had a branch span of 31.6 m (104 ft).

Longest pine cone
Steve Schwarz (USA) of Cuyahoga Falls, Ohio, USA, collected a pine cone measuring 58.2 cm (22.9 in) on 15 October 2002.

125 ft
38.1 m

100 ft
30.48 m

75 ft
22.86 m

50 ft
15.24 m

25 ft
7.62 m

0

FACT:
Redwoods use fog for more than 30% of their water needs – absorbing it directly into their leaves.

Tallest trees

Redwoods, a type of softwood tree, and eucalyptuses, often called gum trees, are the world's tallest tree species. This redwood from Prairie Creek Redwoods State Park in California, USA, was photographed with a camera suspended from the upper branches of the forest canopy so it could shoot the trunk all the way up from about 15.24 m (50 ft) away. A total of 84 photos were montaged together to create this image. This redwood is 91.44 m (300 ft) tall – but even this is dwarfed by **the tallest living tree**, "Hyperion", a coast redwood (*Sequoia sempervirens*) in the Redwood National Park, California, USA, which measured 115.54 m (379 ft) in September 2006.

Greatest girth of a living tree:
"El Arbol del Tule" (the Tree of Tule), a Montezuma cypress (*Taxodium mucronatum*), in Oaxaca state, Mexico, when measured in 1998 had a girth (circumference) of about 36 m (119 ft).

Slowest-growing tree

The white cedar (*Thuja occidentalis*) is the slowest-growing tree – one on a cliff in the Canadian Great Lakes area grew to less than 10.2 cm (4 in) tall after 155 years! It averaged a growth rate of 0.11 g (0.003 oz) of wood each year.

Fastest-growing tree by volume per year

"General Grant", a giant sequoia (*Sequoiadendron giganteum*) in Grant Grove, Kings Canyon National Park, California, USA, increased its trunk volume by a yearly average of 2.23 m³ (79 ft³) – from 1,218 m³ (43,038 ft³) in 1931 to 1,319 m³ (46,608 ft³) in 1976.

Most cold-tolerant trees

The trees most "tolerant" of cold weather are the larches (genus Larix). These include the tamarack larch (*L. laricina*), native to northern North America, mostly Canada, which can survive winter temperatures of at least −65°C (−85°F) and commonly occur at the Arctic tree line at the edge of the tundra.

Fastest-growing tree

The empress or foxglove tree (*Paulownia tomentosa*) can grow 6 m (20 ft) in its first year, and as much as 30 cm (1 ft) in three weeks. Native to central and western China, but naturalized now in the USA, this large species has purple foxglove-like flowers and produces 3–4 times more oxygen during photosynthesis than any other species of tree.

Highest tree

The highest altitude at which trees have been discovered is 4,600 m (15,000 ft). A silver fir (*Abies squamata*) was found in southwestern China at this height. Himalayan birch trees (*Betula utilis*) have also been discovered near this altitude.

Highest ring count

The highest ring count ever found on a tree is 4,867 and belonged to a bristlecone pine (*Pinus longaeva*) known as "Prometheus", which was cut down in 1963 on Mount Wheeler, Nevada, USA.

Oldest living tree

"Old Tjikko", a spruce tree at an altitude of 910 m (2,985 ft) in Dalarna Province, Sweden, has a root system that has been growing for 9,550 years, according to radiocarbon dating completed in April 2008. The roots are able to spawn new trees after each one dies. The **oldest continuously standing tree** is "Methuselah", a bristlecone pine (*Pinus longaeva*) in California's White Mountains, USA, dated in 1957 as being 4,600 years old.

Largest cork tree

The largest cork tree is the "Whistler Tree", named for the songbirds that sing in its branches, in the Alentejo region of Portugal. The tree is harvested every nine years by cutting the bark away with axes. The last harvest in 2009 produced 825 kg (1,818 lb) of raw cork – enough for 100,000 bottles of wine. The average tree produces enough cork for 40,000 bottles.

FOREST FACTS

The Forestry Department of the Food and Agriculture Organization (FAO) collects data from around the world in order to help nations manage their forests in a sustainable way.

AREA: In 2010, forests covered about 31% of the world's total land area – about 4,033 million ha. This is an area just over four times the size of the USA.

NATURAL v PLANTED: About 93% of the world's forest cover is natural forest and 7% is planted.

DEFORESTATION: Between 2000 and 2010, an estimated 13 million ha of forest was affected by deforestation per year – an area more than twice the size of France over 10 years.

NET LOSS: Afforestation projects and natural expansion help to replace lost trees at a rate of over 7 million ha a year (an area the size of Ireland). But the net loss is still 5.2 million ha of forest. The good news, at least, is that this figure is down from 8.3 million ha lost per year in the 1990s.

DON'T BE STUMPED, TURN TO P.244

CONTENTS

The Edge

EST. 1975

1300 W. 12

Longest living snake

Meet Medusa, a reticulated python (*Python reticulatus*) owned by Full Moon Productions Inc. of Kansas City, Missouri, USA. When measured on 12 October 2011, this outsize serpent was 7.67 m (25 ft 2 in) long – which also makes her the **longest captive snake ever**. She eats live animals, ranging from rats right up to deer. And though she doesn't bite, she can "butt" people and bring them down. Medusa is the star attraction at Kansas City's The Edge of Hell Haunted House – some of whose grisly denizens are lending a helping hand here.

7.67 M

HOW BIG CAN ANIMALS GET?

Is there a size limit to animal life?

Despite their epic size, dinosaurs were not the largest creatures to have ever lived. We don't need to look into prehistory to find this absolute record holder: we currently share our planet with the **largest animal that ever lived** – the blue whale (see below). But does the blue whale represent the absolute in animal size? What about terrestrial creatures, or birds? Here, GWR zoologist Dr Karl Shuker sizes up the planet's largest inhabitants.

Size comparison Here we see the relative sizes of the mightiest creatures on Earth. Nothing on land has ever exceeded c. 100 tonnes (220,000 lb); in the oceans, the upper limit is a 160-tonne (352,000-lb) whale.

Key
1: Blue whale
2: Argentinosaur
3: *Paraceratherium*
4: Giganotosaur
5: African elephant
6: *Quetzalcoatlus*

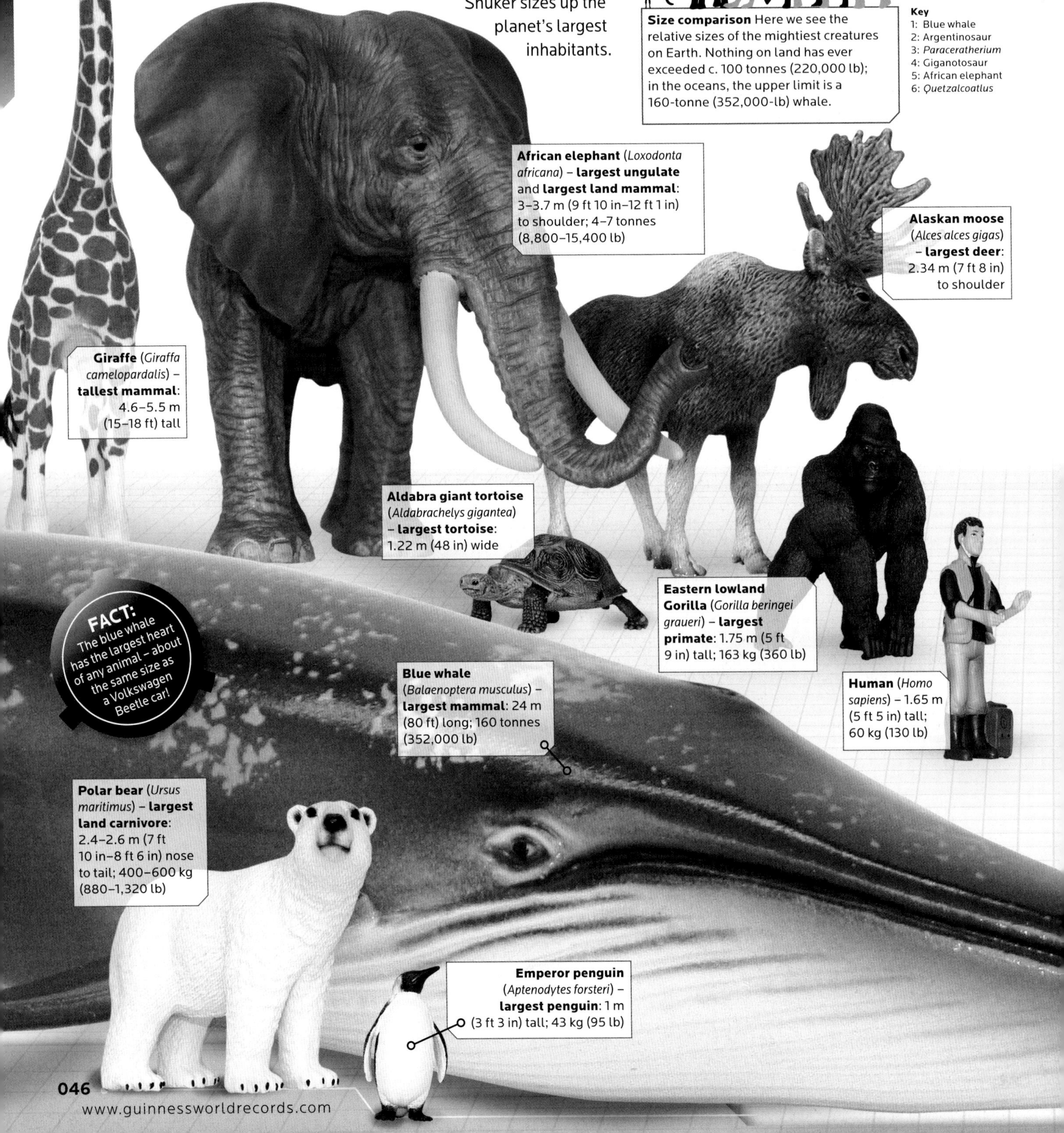

African elephant (*Loxodonta africana*) – **largest ungulate** and **largest land mammal**: 3–3.7 m (9 ft 10 in–12 ft 1 in) to shoulder; 4–7 tonnes (8,800–15,400 lb)

Alaskan moose (*Alces alces gigas*) – **largest deer**: 2.34 m (7 ft 8 in) to shoulder

Giraffe (*Giraffa camelopardalis*) – **tallest mammal**: 4.6–5.5 m (15–18 ft) tall

Aldabra giant tortoise (*Aldabrachelys gigantea*) – **largest tortoise**: 1.22 m (48 in) wide

Eastern lowland Gorilla (*Gorilla beringei graueri*) – **largest primate**: 1.75 m (5 ft 9 in) tall; 163 kg (360 lb)

Human (*Homo sapiens*) – 1.65 m (5 ft 5 in) tall; 60 kg (130 lb)

FACT: The blue whale has the largest heart of any animal – about the same size as a Volkswagen Beetle car!

Blue whale (*Balaenoptera musculus*) – **largest mammal**: 24 m (80 ft) long; 160 tonnes (352,000 lb)

Polar bear (*Ursus maritimus*) – **largest land carnivore**: 2.4–2.6 m (7 ft 10 in–8 ft 6 in) nose to tail; 400–600 kg (880–1,320 lb)

Emperor penguin (*Aptenodytes forsteri*) – **largest penguin**: 1 m (3 ft 3 in) tall; 43 kg (95 lb)

Quetzalcoatlus (*Quetzalcoatlus northropi*) – **largest flying creature**: 12 m (39 ft) wing-span; 113 kg (250 lb)

Guinness World Records is indebted to Schleich for supplying the models used in this feature.

A 160-tonne blue whale can exist because of the support it receives from the water. But on land, the upper weight limit – based on fossil evidence – is around 70–100 tonnes (154,000–220,000 lb), in the case of the herbivorous *Argentinosaurus*, which existed 95 million years ago.

A figure of about 100 tonnes is also the limit reached theoretically when examining the stress limits of bones – and the corresponding increase in muscle size – in terrestrial animals. Such a creature is feasible but would be limited by gravity, the availability of resources, the turnaround of offspring (larger animals produce fewer babies) and a lack of adaptability in times of crisis (such as a food shortage).

So if we were going to find an animal bigger than the blue whale, it would have to be in the oceans. Could the mysterious "Bloop" (see p.206) be a contender?

Theropods ("beast-footed" dinosaurs) – **largest ever land carnivores**: up to 13 m (43 ft) long; 6 tonnes (13,230 lb)

American bison (*Bison bison*) – **largest migrant on land**: 2 m (6 ft 5 in) to shoulder; c. 1 tonne (2,200 lb)

Red kangaroo (*Macropus rufus*) – **largest kangaroo**: 1.8 m (5 ft 11 in) tall; 90 kg (198 lb)

Hippopotamus (*Hippopotamus amphibius*) – **heaviest artiodactyl**: up to 3,630 kg (8,000 lb); 1.4 m (4 ft 7 in) to shoulder

Southern white rhinoceros (*Ceratotherium simum simum*) – **largest rhino**: 3.5–4.6 m (11 ft 6 in–15 ft) long; 3,500 kg (7,700 lb)

North African ostrich (*Struthio camelus camelus*) – **largest bird**: 2.75 m (9 ft) tall; 156.5 kg (345 lb)

Wolf (*Canis lupus*) – **largest canid**: 1–1.6 m (39.5–63 in) body length; 16–80 kg (35.25–176.5 lb)

Saltwater crocodile (*Crocodylus porosus*) – **largest crocodilian**: 7 m (23 ft) long; 520 kg (1,150 lb)

Siberian tiger (*Panthera tigris altaica*) – **largest felid**: 3.15 m (10 ft 4 in) nose to extended tail; 265 kg (580 lb)

Whale shark (*Rhincodon typus*) – **largest fish**: 12.65 m (41 ft 6 in) long; 15–21 tonnes (33,000–46,200 lb)

Great white shark (*Carcharodon carcharias*) – **largest predatory fish**: 4.3–4.6 m (14–15 ft) average length; 520–770 kg (1,150–1,700 lb)

SHARKS

First use of the term "shark"

Sailors originally described sharks as "sea dogs". The first use of the term "shark" occurred when sailors from the second expedition of 16th-century English seaman Sir John Hawkins exhibited a specimen in London in 1569 and referred to it as a "sharke". This soon became the accepted name for the creature.

Shark with the most gill slits

Most modern-day shark species have five pairs of gill slits. However, a few have six pairs, and two – the sharpnose sevengill shark (*Heptranchias perlo*) and the broadnose sevengill shark (*Notorhynchus cepedianus*) – have seven pairs. These sevengill species are related to some of the most ancient sharks; fossil sharks from the Jurassic Period, 200 to 145 million years ago, also had seven pairs.

Largest shark pups

The basking shark (*Cetorhinus maximus*) is the world's second largest shark species and it gives birth to the largest pups. A sexually mature female will give birth to one or two live pups at a time, each of which is about 1.7 m (5 ft 7 in) long.

Fastest shark

The shortfin mako (*Isurus oxyrinchus*), with recorded swimming speeds exceeding 56 km/h (34.8 mi/h), is the fastest shark. By comparison, the fastest human swims at only 7.5 km/h (4.7 mi/h). The shortfin mako is also the **highest leaping shark**. It can jump 6 m (19 ft 8 in) out of the water – that's longer than the average school bus. It has even leapt directly into fishermen's boats.

Largest fish

The rare plankton-feeding whale shark (*Rhincodon typus*) is found in the warmer areas of the Atlantic, Pacific and Indian oceans. The largest scientifically recorded example was 12.65 m (41 ft 6 in) long, and weighed an estimated 15–21 tonnes (33,000–46,200 lb). It was captured on 11 November 1949 off Baba Island, near Karachi, Pakistan. A whale shark has also produced the **largest egg** by any living creature. It was found on 29 June 1953 in the Gulf of Mexico and measured 30.5 x 14 x 8.9 cm (12 x 5.5 x 3.5 in).

Shark with the largest teeth (relative to body)

The largetooth cookiecutter (*Isistius plutodus*) measures only 0.4 m (1 ft 4 in) in length – however, its lower jaw's 19 triangular teeth with rectangular bases are huge in proportion. They are twice as large, relative to its total body length, as the great white shark's (*Carcharodon carcharias*) teeth are in relation to its own total body length. The shark uses the teeth to gouge flesh from larger fish.

ACTUAL SIZE

Most poisonous shark

The Greenland shark (*Somniosus microcephalus*) is the most poisonous species. Although its flesh is popularly eaten in Greenland and Iceland, it must be boiled in several changes of water first. This removes its poison – a neurotoxin known as trimethylamine oxide – which causes effects resembling extreme drunkenness.

Fish with greatest sense of smell

Sharks have a better sense of smell than any other fish. They can detect one part of mammalian blood in 100 million parts of water.

Most recently discovered shark family

The newest zoological family of sharks is Megachasmidae, which was created in 1981 for a large and dramatically different species of shark discovered as recently as November 1976.

In that year, an adult male specimen, measuring 4.5 m (14 ft 9 in) long, attempted to swallow the anchor of a US Navy research vessel near Oahu island, Hawaii. It was hauled out of the water to the astonishment of the scientific world. On account of its enormous mouth, the species became known as the megamouth shark (*Megachasma pelagios*). Up to August 2011, only 51 megamouths had been found.

Shark with the least varied diet

The crested bullhead shark (*Heterodontus galeatus*) is the fussiest eater of all the sharks. Despite measuring about 1.5 m (4 ft 11 in) in length, this species feeds almost exclusively on red sea urchins.

Shark with the most varied diet

Nicknamed the "garbage-can shark", the tiger shark (*Galeocerdo cuvier*) eats almost anything that moves. Confirmed prey of this 5-m-long (16-ft 5-in) predator includes seals; dolphins; seabirds such as cormorants and pelicans; reptiles including marine turtles and sea snakes; bony fishes; other sharks; invertebrates, such as lobsters, octopuses and crabs; and any land mammals that end up in the sea, including dogs, rats and even cattle.

Longest gestation

The common frilled shark (*Chlamydoselachus anguineus*), native to all oceans, has a gestation period (pregnancy) of 3.5 years, the longest known of any animal species.

FACT: Hammerheads swim so close to the surface, they can suffer from sunburn.

SEE IT 3D

Largest predatory fish

Adult great white sharks (*Carcharodon carcharias*) average 4.3–4.6 m (14–15 ft) long, and generally weigh 520–770 kg (1,150–1,700 lb). There are many claims of huge specimens up to 10 m (33 ft) long but few have been properly authenticated. However, there is plenty of circumstantial evidence to suggest that some great whites grow to more than 6 m (20 ft) long.

FACT: The hammerhead shark's "hammer" is known as a "cephalofoil".

SEE P.52 FOR OTHER CREATURES THAT ARE LONG IN THE TOOTH

Most bioluminescent shark

The cookiecutter shark (*Isistius brasiliensis*) from the central regions of the Atlantic and Pacific is the brightest shark. It is named after Isis, an Egyptian goddess associated with light. Up to 1.5 m (5 ft) long, it has a dull brown upper surface, but underneath it is often covered entirely with photophores, light-producing organs which emit a very bright, ghostly green glow. The purpose of this bioluminescence is unclear – it may serve to attract sharks of its own species, or to attract prey, or even as camouflage if viewed from below.

Largest hammerhead

Of the nine currently recognized species of hammerhead shark, by far the largest is the great hammerhead (*Sphyrna mokarran*). It attains a maximum length of 6.1 m (20 ft) – at least a third longer than any other hammerhead species. The great hammerhead inhabits tropical waters around the world's continents and, despite its size, can sometimes be encountered in reefs as shallow as 1 m (3 ft 3 in).

SHARK ATTA☠X

Galeophobia

is the fear of sharks, but you have very little to worry about. Movies such as *Jaws* (USA, 1975) – the **first blockbuster movie** – have unfairly portrayed sharks as ferocious man-eaters, but statistics show you're more likely to be killed by lightning or a falling coconut than by a shark. However, sharks *are* apex predators and will attack you if they mistake you for prey.

ALL SHARKS → **SHARKS THAT ATTACK HUMANS**

There are **>360** species of shark but only **35** have been reported to attack humans; of these, only a few are responsible for major incidents.

Top 5 attacking species

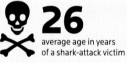

Great white: 10.6%
Tiger: 5.8%
Bull: 3.0%
Hammerhead: 0.9%
Lemon: 0.5%

☠ **26** average age in years of a shark-attack victim

Global shark attacks

YEAR	Total	Fatalities
2000	80	✝✝✝✝✝✝✝✝✝✝✝
2001	73	✝✝✝✝✝
2002	65	✝✝✝
2003	53	✝✝✝✝
2004	65	✝✝✝✝✝✝✝
2005	59	✝✝✝✝
2006	56	✝✝✝✝
2007	69	✝
2008	53	✝✝✝✝
2009	63	✝✝✝✝✝✝
2010	79	✝✝✝✝✝

Avoiding attack

- ☠ Do not wear shiny jewellery – to a shark this can look like fish scales
- ☠ Avoid the areas between sandbars and steep drop-offs
- ☠ Stay out of the water during hours of darkness or twilight
- ☠ Do not enter the water if you are bleeding or menstruating
- ☠ Remain in groups
- ☠ Stay near the shore

ANIMAL LIFE

MATING

Highest-pitch mating call

The male Colombian *Arachnoscelis* katydid (a type of bush-cricket) rubs its forewings together to create an intense burst of chirps peaking at a frequency of 130 kHz. This mating call is beyond the hearing threshold of humans.

Loudest penis

To attract a mate, *Micronecta scholtzi* – a small water boatman, just 2 mm (0.07 in) long – rubs its penis against its abdomen (a process known as "stridulation"). The chirping noise that this creates can be up to 99.2 decibels. This is equivalent to sitting in the front row listening to a loud orchestra playing.

Largest bowers

The bowerbirds of Australia and New Guinea construct and decorate elaborate "bowers" to attract females for mating purposes. The largest bowers are those of the Vogelkop gardener bowerbird (*Amblyornis inornata*) from New Guinea. These hut-like structures are some 160 cm (5 ft 3 in) across and 100 cm (3 ft 3 in) high, often with a front lawn-like area several square metres in area. The male clears this "lawn" of forest debris and then decorates it with bright, shiny objects such as colourful fruit, flowers and even shiny beetle wing-cases.

Most frequent mating

Native to the deserts of North Africa, a small gerbil-related rodent species known as Shaw's jird (*Meriones shawi*) has been observed mating 224 times in just two hours.

Smallest semelparous mammal

The male brown antechinus (*Antechinus stuartii*), a marsupial mouse from east Australia, is the world's smallest "semelparous" mammal, meaning that it has just one reproductive period during its entire lifetime. Every year the entire adult male population spends two weeks mating with as many females as possible before dying. Their deaths are believed to result from the stress of chasing females and fighting off rival males, causing their immune system to shut down, and leaving them vulnerable to ulcers, infection or, as they neglect to eat, starvation.

Most macaws born in a year

From 26 January to 30 October 2009, 105 macaws were born at the Xcaret Eco-Park on the Riviera Maya in Cancun, Mexico – a world record for one facility. Xcaret also holds the record for the **most dolphins born in a single facility in one year**, with 11 in 2008.

FACT:
Female pandas are ready to mate for just two to seven days a year, usually between March and May.

ORGANS

Longest animal penis relative to body size

A barnacle's body is just a few centimetres long, but its penis can be as much as 40 times longer. The long penis enables these immobile creatures to mate with other barnacles.

In absolute terms, the **longest penis** belongs to the blue whale at up to 2.4 m (8 ft).

Longest baculum

In many mammals, the penis has a bone called the baculum (although not in humans,

Smallest placental mammal baby relative to adult

The giant panda (*Ailuropoda melanoleuca*) produces the smallest baby of any placental mammal (that is, a mammal other than marsupials or those who lay eggs). A newborn panda is pink, hairless, blind, about 12 cm (5 in) long, and weighs about 100 g (3.5 oz). It is about 1/900th the size of its mother.

whales, marsupials, rabbits, hyenas and some hooved species). The walrus (*Odobenus rosmarus*) has the longest mammalian baculum; it can measure 75 cm (29.5 in) – the length of a human thigh bone.

Largest animal testes

The blue whale (*Balaenoptera musculus*), the **largest animal** on Earth, has testes that can measure in excess of 75 cm (2 ft 5.5 in) long, and weigh as much as 45 kg (99 lb), as heavy as a large male Alsatian dog. In whales, the testes are normally internal, and so only visible in dead specimens.

Most sires (bull)

Nordjydens Hubert, a Danish Holstein-Friesian bull, left 250,002 surviving offspring when he died at the age of 12 in January 1996.

Most eggs laid by a dinosaur

The largest clutch of eggs laid by a single dinosaur is 34, as discovered by palaeontologists alongside a fossilized skeleton of *Psittacosaurus*. This beaked dinosaur was around 1 m (3 ft 3 in) tall, walked on two feet, and lived in Mongolia 105–115 million years ago, during the Cretaceous Period.

Largest newborn marsupial

Newborn marsupials are born at a very early stage and continue to develop in their mothers' pouches. The red kangaroo (*Megaleia rufa*) produces the largest newborn marsupial, but even this only weighs 0.75 g (0.02 oz) – less than a paperclip. It would take at least 36,000 newborn babies to equal its mother's weight.

Largest bird egg relative to body size

The brown kiwi (*Apteryx australis*) of New Zealand lays the largest eggs relative to its body size. One female kiwi weighing 1.7 kg (3 lb 12 oz) laid an egg weighing 406 g (14 oz), which is almost a quarter of her total body mass. Weights of 510 g (1 lb) have been reliably reported for other kiwi eggs.

EGGS, ETC.

Most prolific chicken

The highest authenticated rate of egg-laying is 371 in 364 days, by a white leghorn in an official test that ended on 29 August 1979 at the University of Missouri in Columbia, Missouri, USA.

Biggest dinosaur nest

The biggest dinosaur nest on record measured 3 m (9 ft 10 in) in diameter and contained 28 long, cylindrical eggs, each roughly 30 cm (12 in) in length. The nest and eggs were from a *Macroelongatoolithus*, a dinosaur that lived in China about 70–90 million years ago.

Largest insect egg

The largest egg laid by an insect belongs to the 15-cm-long (6-in) Malaysian stick insect (*Heteropteryx dilitata*). At 1.3 cm (0.5 in) in length, each egg is larger than a shelled peanut. Some insects, notably mantids and cockroaches, lay egg *cases* which are much larger, but these contain as many as 200 eggs.

Fewest eggs produced by a fish in one spawning

The mouth-brooding fish *Tropheus moorii* of Lake Tanganyika in east Africa produces seven eggs or fewer during normal reproduction. As each egg is released, the female takes it into her mouth, where it is fertilized by the male.

Smallest bird egg

The smallest egg laid by any bird is that of the vervain hummingbird (*Mellisuga minima*) of Jamaica and two nearby islets. Two specimens measuring less than 10 mm (0.39 in) in length weighed 0.365 g (0.0128 oz) and 0.375 g (0.0132 oz) – you would need at least 136 of these to equal the weight of a medium-sized hen's egg.

Most protective female tortoise

The female Burmese brown tortoise (*Manouria emys*) remains close to her nesting site, guarding it from potential egg-snatchers, for several days after having laid her eggs. Other tortoises, conversely, either show no maternal interest in their eggs at all after laying them, or spend no more than an hour or so concealing their eggs and the nesting site.

Most fertile stick insect

The world's most fertile stick insect is *Acrophylla titan*, a species from north Australia that can grow to 30 cm (12 in). A single female can lay more than 2,000 eggs at a time.

Exceptional eggs

- The **heaviest hen egg** weighed 454 g (16 oz), with a double yolk and double shell, laid by a white leghorn on 25 February 1956.

- The **largest duck egg**, laid by a white Pekin duck in 1999, was 14 cm (5.5 in) high and weighed over 227 g (8 oz).

- The **largest fish egg** was produced by the whale shark (*Rhincodon typhus*). It measured 30.5 x 14 x 8.9 cm (12 x 5.5 x 3.5 in).

- The **heaviest goose egg** was 34 cm (13 in) around the long axis and weighed 680 g (24 oz). It was laid on 3 May 1977 by a white goose named Speckle.

ACTUAL SIZE

LARGEST LITTERS

A group of animals born at one birth is known as a litter, after the French word for "bed" – referring to the bed in which they are delivered. Listed here are a selection of litter world records.

● = died
○ = average litter size

Animal	Litter (dots)
Pigs	●●●●●●●●● / ●● ○○○○○○○○ / ○○○○○○○○○ / ○○○○○○
Mice	●●●●●●●●● / ○○○○○○○○ / ○○○○○○○○ / ○○○
Tenrecs*	○○○○○○○○ / ○○○○○○○○ / ○○○○○○○○ / ●
Hamsters	●●●●●●●●● / ○○○○○○○○ / ○○○○○
Dogs	●●●●●● / ○○○○
Rabbits	●●●●●● / ○○○○○○ / ○○○
Cats	○○○○○○○○ / ○○○○○
Ferrets	●●●●●●●● / ○○○○○○
Gerbils	●●●●● / ○○○○
Humans	● ○
Guinea pigs	●●●●
Tigers	●●●
Goats	● ○
Bears	●●
Koalas†	●

* This litter of 31 tail-less tenrecs (*Tenrec ecaudatus*) – a hedgehog-like insectivore native to Madagascar – represents the **largest litter for a wild animal**.

† A litter of two koalas is rare because the mother's pouch is usually only big enough to allow one baby to survive. In April 1999, the **first known koala twins** – Euca and Lyptus – were born in Queensland, Australia. DNA fingerprinting confirmed that the two babies were identical.

ANIMAL LONGEVITY

Longest-lived venomous lizard

The Mexican beaded lizard (*Heloderma horridum*) is a black-and-yellow forest-dwelling species that measures up to 90 cm (35.4 in) long. One specimen lived in captivity for 33 years 11 months.

Longest-lived armadillo

The La Plata three-banded armadillo (*Tolypeutes matacus*) is native to northern Argentina, south-western Brazil, Paraguay and Bolivia. A female specimen of this species was acquired by Lincoln Park Zoo in Chicago, Illinois, USA, in 1971, and died there in 2005 aged 36 years 9 months 18 days old.

FACT: If armadillos feel threatened, they curl up. Their hard, leathery shell gives them 360° protection.

LONG-LIVED SPECIES

Alligator

The greatest authenticated age for a crocodilian is 66 years, for a female American alligator (*Alligator mississippiensis*) that arrived at Adelaide Zoo, South Australia, on 5 June 1914 when she was two years old. She died on 26 September 1978.

Amphibian

The Artis Zoo in Amsterdam, Netherlands, owned two giant Japanese salamanders (*Andrias japonicus*), both of whom reached 52 years – the oldest confirmed age for an amphibian. The first giant Japanese salamander was given to the zoo in 1839, where it lived until 1881; the second arrived in 1903 and died in 1955.

Chelonian

The greatest authentic age recorded for a chelonian (tortoise, turtle or terrapin) is at least 188 years, for a Madagascar radiated tortoise (*Astrochelys radiata*) that was presented to the Tonga royal family by Captain Cook in either 1773 or 1777. The animal was called Tui Malila and remained in their care until its death in 1965.

Insect

On 27 May 1983, a splendour beetle (*Buprestis aurulenta*) appeared from the staircase timber in the home of Mr W Euston of Prittlewell, Southend-on-Sea, Essex, UK. It had spent at least 47 years as a larva. How do we know? The staircase had been in Mr Euston's house for the whole of this period, and as the beetle was a tropical species, not native to the UK, it must have already been present in the timber before the staircase was installed.

Lungfish

The longest-lived species of lungfish is the Australian lungfish (*Neoceratodus forsteri*). Popularly deemed to be more primitive in form than its South American and African relatives, it has lived to 19 years 8 months 12 days in captivity.

Marsupial

The oldest marsupial whose age has been reliably recorded was a common wombat (*Vombatus ursinus*) that was 26 years 22 days old when it died on 20 April 1906 at London Zoo. Although not verified, it is possible that the larger species of kangaroo can live up to 28 years in the wild.

Mollusc

A quahog clam (*Arctica islandica*) that had been living on the seabed off the north coast of Iceland was dredged by researchers from Bangor University's School of Ocean Sciences, UK, in 2006. On 28 October 2007, sclerochronologists (experts who examine growth patterns in algae and invertebrates) from Bangor University announced that they had studied the annual growth rings in the clam's shell and determined that it was 405–410 years old. It was nicknamed "Ming" after the Chinese dynasty that had been in power when the clam was born.

The **longest-lived species of freshwater bivalve mollusc** is the freshwater pearl mussel (*Margaritifera margaritifera*). In 2000, Russian malacologist Dr Valeriy Zyuganov determined the maximum

lifespan of this endangered Holarctic species to be 210–250 years, a remarkable discovery verified independently in 2008 by a team of malacological researchers in Finland.

Sponge

The longest-lived species of sponge is *Scolymastra joubini*, the Antarctic hexactinellid or glass sponge. It grows extremely slowly in this region's exceedingly cold waters, and an estimate of age for one 2-m-tall (6-ft 6-in) specimen in the Ross Sea gave a result of 23,000 years. Admittedly, this sea's fluctuating levels suggests that it could not survive there for more than around 15,000 years. Yet even if that latter, lower figure is itself an overestimate, this sponge is still one of the oldest – if not *the* oldest – specimens on the planet.

Wild bird

The oldest recorded age for a bird in the wild is 50 years for a Manx shearwater (*Puffinus puffinus*), a small seabird. It was first ringed in 1957 (when it was five years old) and then again in 1961, 1977 and finally in 2002. It was captured on Bardsey, an island off the Lleyn Peninsula, Wales, UK, on 3 April 2002.

FACT: Female murres lay eggs one at a time – on a ledge! The egg's conical shape helps stop it from rolling off.

Oldest carnivorous marsupial

One captive Tasmanian devil (*Sarcophilus harrisii*) was at least 13 years old when it died at Rotterdam Zoo, Netherlands, in 2005.

Longest-lived auk

The common European guillemot or murre (*Uria aalge*) is a puffin-related species of auk. Based on records obtained from ringed specimens, it can live to 38 years in the wild. The guillemot returns to land to breed, but otherwise passes most of its life at sea.

Longest-lived woodpecker

The longest-lived species of woodpecker is the red-bellied woodpecker (*Melanerpes carolinus*). Native to deciduous forests and with a breeding range spanning southern Canada and north-eastern USA, this species has been known to live more than 20 years 8 months in its wild state.

FACT: The lynx's super-sharp eyesight enables it to spot a mouse 75 m (250 ft) away.

Longest-lived lynx

The bobcat or red lynx (*Lynx rufus*) ranges from southern Canada through much of continental USA into northern Mexico. It is smaller than the Canada lynx (*L. canadensis*), with which it shares part of its range, but lives longer, with a maximum recorded longevity of 32 years 3 months 18 days, as opposed to 26 years 9 months 18 days for the Canada lynx.

Wild buffalo

The longest-lived species of wild buffalo is the anoa or dwarf buffalo (*Bubalus depressicornis*) of Celebes, Indonesia. The world's second smallest buffalo species, it has been recorded as living to 36 years 1 month 6 days in captivity.

SHORT-LIVED SPECIES

Fish

The shortest-lived fishes are various species of toothcarp, including several South American *Nothobranchius* species, which only live for about eight months in the wild. These small fishes thrive in temporary water sources, such as drainage ditches and even water-filled animal footprints. As soon as these sources dry up, however, the fishes die, but the eggs that they have laid in the meantime survive in the mud. When the rain returns and fills the pool, the eggs hatch, the fishes rapidly grow to their full size, then spawn, before their temporary homes dry out again.

Jackal

Based upon maximum recorded longevity, the shortest-lived species of jackal is the African side-striped jackal (*Canis adustus*). Its maximum recorded longevity is 13 years 8 months 12 days, in comparison with 18 years 9 months 18 days for the golden jackal (*C. aureus*) and 16 years 8 months 12 days for the African black-backed jackal (*C. mesomelas*).

Vertebrate

The animal with the shortest lifespan of all vertebrates is the coral-reef pygmy goby (*Eviota sigillata*), which has been recorded as surviving for an average of 59 days. In 2005, researchers at Australia's James Cook University were able to establish their age by studying the ear stones of 300 pygmy gobies, which collect daily growth rings.

Zebra

Based on maximum recorded longevity, the shortest-lived species of zebra is also the largest species – Grévy's zebra (*Equus grevyi*). The maximum recorded longevity for this species is 31 years, compared with 33 years 2 months 12 days for the mountain zebra (*E. zebra*) and 38 years for the plains zebra (*E. burchelli*).

Shortest-lived tapir

Also the smallest tapir, the mountain tapir *Tapirus pinchaque* – which lives in Colombia, Ecuador and Peru – has a maximum known longevity of 28 years 6 months.

Become a lizard wiz!

- Lizards smell with their tongues, as do snakes
- Some lizards can squirt blood 1.2 m (4 ft) from their eyes as a defence tactic
- Common lizards (*Zootoca vivipara*) can give birth both to live offspring and eggs
- The tails of some lizards detach if grabbed

Longest-lived lizard

In 1950, an adult male Grand Cayman blue iguana (*Cyclura lewisi*) nicknamed "Godzilla" (right) was captured alive on Grand Cayman by naturalist Ira Thompson, who estimated Godzilla's age to be 15 years at that time. In 1985, the iguana was purchased from Thompson and imported into the USA by an animal dealer, who donated him in 1990 to the Gladys Porter Zoo in Brownsville, Texas, USA. Here Godzilla remained until his death in 2004, giving a period of 54 years in captivity and an estimated total lifespan of 69 years.

FACT: The blue iguana is rated as Critically Endangered on the IUCN Red List of Threatened Species.

OLD-AGED PETS

You've read about the longest-lived species, but here are some OAPs (old-aged pets) and other individual animals who have also made it into Guinness World Records:

DOVE: Methuselah — 19 years

GOAT: McGinty — 22 years

KOALA: Sarah — 23 years

GIANT PANDA: Dudu — 37 years

SNAKE: Popeye — 40 years

RACEHORSE: Tango Duke — 42 years

PONY: Sugar Puff — 56 years

HORSE: Old Billy — 62 years

ELEPHANT: Lin Wang — 86 years

ANIMAL ODDITIES

ACTUAL SIZE

Largest unicorn

The largest ever mammal with a single central horn on its head was *Elasmotherium*, a prehistoric rhinoceros often referred to as the "giant unicorn". With a height exceeding 2.5 m (8 ft 2.5 in), a length sometimes exceeding 5 m (16 ft 5 in), and a weight of about 5 tonnes (11,000 lb), this rhino survived until at least as recently as 50,000 years ago, during the Late Pleistocene Epoch in the Black Sea region of Russia, extending north as far as Siberia. The horn, believed to be at least 2 m (6 ft 7 in) long, is thought to have been used for defence, attracting mates and digging for roots and water.

FACT:
Pictured is a 28-cm-long (11-in) "superprawn" amphipod caught off New Zealand in February 2012.

FACT:
Amphipods live at the bottom of oceans, where the pressure is 1,000 times greater than at sea level.

Largest amphipod crustacean

Amphipods are a large zoological order of superficially shrimp-like crustaceans with thin bodies. Most amphipods are very small, no more than a couple of centimetres long. However, the world's largest species of amphipod is *Alicella gigantea* – one specimen has been measured at 34 cm (1 ft 1 in) long.

Largest collection of two-headed animals

Former Grammy award-winning producer Todd Ray (USA) has 22 different specimens of two-headed animals, including an albino hog-nosed snake, a goat, a terrapin, a king snake and a bearded dragon (a species of lizard) named Pancho and Lefty. He also has the world's only living three-headed creature: a turtle named Myrtle, Squirtle and Thirdle (right). The smallest head is the middle one and only consists of eyes and a beak poking out from the carapace.

Fish with most eyes

The six-eyed spookfish (*Bathylychnops exilis*), which inhabits depths of 91–910 m (300–3,000 ft) in the northeastern Pacific, was only discovered by biologists in 1958. A slender 45-cm-long (17-in) pike-like species, it has a second, small pair of eyes – known as secondary globes – positioned, pointing downwards, within the lower half of its principal eyes. Each secondary globe possesses its own lens and retina, and may help to increase the spookfish's sensitivity to light in its shadowy surroundings. Moreover, located behind the secondary globes is a third pair of eyes, which lack retinas but divert incoming light into the fish's large principal eyes.

SEE IT 3D

ACTUAL SIZE

Only one previous purple cow is known – she was discovered in Florida in 1948.

ACTUAL SIZE

Smallest chameleon

The tiny leaf chameleons (*Brookesia minima*) of Madagascar are between 22 mm (0.87 in) and 48 mm (1.89 in) long, from head to tail.

Largest item of clothing woven from spider silk

In 2011, after eight years' work, 80 workers completed weaving a wide, full-length lady's cape with matching 4-m-long (13-ft 1-in) brocade scarf. Both cape and scarf were made from the golden-coloured silk of more than one million female Madagascan golden orb spiders (*Nephila madagascariensis*). Each day, the workers collected thousands of spiders from their webs in the wild and then used hand-powered machines to extract the silk from their spinnerets, after which the spiders were released unharmed. The cape alone contains 1.5 kg (3.3 lb) of silk. The project was masterminded by fashion designer Nicholas Godley (USA) and textiles expert Simon Peers (UK).

Most cannibalistic amphibian

Several amphibian species eat others of their own species, but the world's most cannibalistic amphibian is the alpine salamander (*Salamandra atra*), native to Europe's alpine regions. The female of this species carries up to 60 fertilized eggs in her body, but most of them are eaten by the first few salamander embryos that hatch inside her, so that only between one and four young are actually born.

Most colourful cattle

It was announced on 17 January 2012 that a male calf, lilac and white in colour, was born in Jezdina village near the city of Čačak in Serbia. Its owner is considering naming it Milkan, after the purple cow emblem of Milka chocolate.

Pictured here is Rosi, a Goliath bird-eating spider owned by Walter Baumgartner (Austria). This species has a record leg-span of 28 cm (11 in).

FACT:
Dr Beccaloni used his wife's former pet female Goliath spider – called Tracy – in the test!

Most clothing used in a bird's nest

In 1909, a 600-kg (1,323-lb) nest of a white stork (*Ciconia ciconia*) was removed from Colmar Cathedral, in Alsace in eastern France, to prevent the tower from toppling over. The nest's walls included 17 ladies' black stockings, five fur caps, three shoes, a sleeve from a white silk blouse, a large piece of leather and four buttons from the uniform of a railway porter!

Most bloodthirsty bird

The vampire finch (*Geospiza difficilis septentrionalis*) – which only inhabits Wolf Island and Darwin Island in the Galápagos Islands, Ecuador – lands on the tails of large seabirds (mainly the Nazca booby and blue-footed booby), pecks at the base of the wing feathers and then drinks the blood that seeps from the wound. It also eats seeds, eggs and invertebrates.

Strongest bird gizzard

The gizzard is the portion of a bird's stomach that grinds food into small pieces. The world's strongest recorded gizzard is that of the turkey *Meleagris gallopavo*. One specimen had crushed 24 walnuts in their shells within four hours, and had also ground surgical lancet blades into grit within 16 hours.

Most legs

Despite their names, centipedes do not have 100 legs and millipedes do not have 1,000. Normally, millipedes only have about 300 pairs of legs, although a millipede called *Illacme plenipes*, first discovered in California, USA, in 1926, had 375 pairs (750 legs).

Longest surviving Janus cat

A Janus cat is a domestic cat possessing two near-separate faces as a result of a very rare congenital condition known as diprosopia. In 2011, it was established that the world's longest-lived Janus cat was Frank and Louie, from Minnesota, USA, whose last-reported age, in June 2006, was six years old.

In autumn 2011, GWR was contacted by Marty Stevens – Frank and Louie's owner, now living in Massachusetts – who revealed that his now-famous two-faced cat was still alive and in good health, and in September 2011 celebrated his 12th birthday! Normally, Janus cats rarely survive more than a day or so following their birth. Since his first appearance in GWR last year, Frank and Louie has become an unlikely media star, appearing in countless newspaper reports and online news videos throughout the world.

Smallest frog

Paedophryne amauensis of Papua New Guinea is, on average, between 7 mm (0.27 in) and 7.7 mm (0.3 in) in length from snout to vent when fully grown.

ACTUAL SIZE

690% bigger

Largest spider

In July 2011, with the help of the Natural History Museum (NHM) in London, UK, GWR finally put to rest the notion that the Hercules baboon spider (*Hysterocrates hercules*) might be the world's largest spider species. According to GWR, the record holder is – and always has been – the Goliath bird-eating spider (*Theraphosa blondi*, left), a fact now confirmed by Dr George Beccaloni, Curator of Orthopteroid Insects. Using the NHM's own specimens, Dr Beccaloni used Archimedes' Principle to perform a volume test. This revealed that the Goliath is, in fact, more than twice the size of the Hercules. Case closed!

ODDEST ANIMAL?

One contender for the oddest animal of all is the platypus (*Ornithorhynchus anatinus*). When a specimen was first exhibited in London in the 19th century, many people thought it was a hoax owing to its seemingly random collection of features!

Bill (duck?)

+

Tail (beaver?)

+

Webbed feet (otter?)

+

Spurs (rooster?)

+

Eggs (turtle?)

+

Claws (reptile?)

+

Venom (snake?)

=

Platypus!

TEETH, TUSKS & HORNS

ACTUAL SIZE

Largest cat fangs

The 15-cm-long (6-in) dagger-like canine teeth of *Eusmilus*, a false sabre-tooth cat, were the largest feline fangs relative to body size – almost as long as its skull. It lived around 37–29 million years ago.

FACT: Horned lizards squirt jets of blood from the corners of their eyes if they feel threatened.

Longest whale tooth

The spiralled ivory tusk of the male narwhal (*Monodon monoceros*) was once thought to be the horn of the fabled unicorn, when it was found washed up with dead male narwhals. Narwhal tusks reach an average length of 2 m (6 ft 6 in), but occasionally exceed 3 m (9 ft 10 in) and weigh up to 10 kg (22 lb), with a maximum girth of approximately 23 cm (9 in). Narwhals live in the waters of the Arctic.

Dinosaur with the most teeth

Edmontosaurus, a hadrosaur (duck-billed dinosaur) that lived in the late Cretaceous Period, 65–61 million years ago, had more than a thousand teeth. They were diamond-shaped and set in columns known as "tooth batteries".

The **land mammal with the most teeth** is the giant armadillo (*Priodontes maximus*) of South America, which typically has up to 100 teeth.

The numbat or marsupial anteater (*Myrmecobius fasciatus*) of Western Australia is the **marsupial with the most teeth**

– up to 52, including a unique cheek tooth sited between the premolars and the molars.

Largest teeth used for eating

The largest teeth employed for eating (as opposed to tusks used for defence purposes) belonged to *Livyatan melvillei* – a prehistoric species of sperm whale that lived around 12 million years ago during the Miocene Epoch. Its teeth were up to 36 cm (1 ft 2 in) long.

FACT: An Asian water buffalo (*Bubalus arnee*) shot in 1955 had horns measuring 4.24 m (13 ft 10 in) from tip to tip.

Largest horned toad

The horned lizards of North America, popularly dubbed "horned toads", are named after the horns on their head – which are true horns, having a bony core. The largest species is the giant or long-spined horned lizard (*Phrynosoma asio*), which has a total length of up to 20 cm (7.9 in). It lives in desert regions along southern Mexico's Pacific coast.

Largest horn spread for domestic cattle (living)

"JR", a Texas Longhorn owned by Michael and Lynda Bethel (Australia), has a horn spread of 277 cm (9 ft 1 in). He was measured in Queensland, Australia, on 2 October 2011.

Largest antlers

An antler spread or "rack" of 1.99 m (6 ft 6.5 in) was recorded for a moose (*Alces alces*) killed near the Stewart River, Canada, in October 1897. It is now housed in the Field Museum in Chicago, Illinois, USA.

Longest elephant tusks (relative to body)

Anancus was a prehistoric gomphothere (an extinct family of elephantine mammals) that lived from the late Miocene Epoch to the early Pleistocene Epoch, 3–1.5 million years ago. Each of its two long, straight tusks measured up to 4 m (13 ft) – almost as long as its body!

Longest prehistoric tusks

The straight-tusked elephant (*Hesperoloxodon antiques germanicus*), which lived about 2 million years ago, had an average tusk length in adults of 5 m (16 ft 4.8 in).

The **longest tusks (non-prehistoric)** belong to an African elephant (*Loxodonta africana*) from the Democratic Republic of the Congo now housed at the New York Zoological Society in New York City, USA. The right tusk measures 3.49 m (11 ft 5 in) along the outside curve; the left is 3.35 m (10 ft 11 in).

Heaviest mammoth tusks

A pair of mammoth tusks found near Campbell, Nebraska, USA, in April 1915 weighs 226 kg (498 lb). One is 4.21 m (13 ft 9 in) long, the other 4.14 m (13 ft 7 in). They are in the University of Nebraska Museum, USA.

The **heaviest tusks (non-prehistoric)**, are a pair of African elephant tusks in the Natural History Museum, London, UK, from a bull shot in Kenya in 1897. They weigh 109 kg (240 lb) and 102 kg (225 lb) – giving a total weight of 211 kg (465 lb).

Longest horns on a sheep

The longest sheep horn measured 191 cm (6 ft 3 in) and belonged to a Marco Polo sheep (*Ovis ammon polii*). The species is indigenous only to the Pamir Mountains bordering Tajikistan, Afghanistan, Pakistan and China.

Most horns on a sheep

Ewes and rams of the Jacob sheep breed – a rare "polycerate" (multi-horned) sheep – typically grow two or four horns, but six is not uncommon. Of sheep that have four horns, one pair usually grows vertically, often to more than 60 cm (2 ft), while the other pair curls around the side of the head.

Most horns on a giraffe

A giraffe usually has three "ossicones" (horn-like projections under the skin): a pair on top of its head and a single one at the centre of its brow. A Rothschild's giraffe (*Giraffa camelopardalis rothschildi*) discovered in 1901 in Uganda, however, boasted five ossicones. It had an extra pair at the back of its head, behind its ears.

FACT:
The giant sawyer beetle is found in northern Venezuela, the Amazon Basin and eastern Brazil.

Longest beetle with enlarged jaws

Almost a third of the length of the male giant sawyer beetle (*Macrodontia cervicornis*) is accounted for by its huge jaws. The longest specimen on record was 17.7 cm (10 in), and was collected in Peru in 2007.

Heaviest horn for a hornbill

The hornbills, native to tropical Africa and Asia, are named after the horn-like structure, or "casque", on top of their bill's upper mandible. Usually, the casque is very light, being hollow, but uniquely in the helmeted hornbill (*Rhinoplax vigil*) of Malaysia and Indonesia it is solid. The skull of this species (including its casque) can account for up to 10% of the bird's weight of around 3 kg (6 lb 10 oz).

LONG IN THE TOOTH

When it comes to animal dentition, some creatures are way out ahead of the rest. GWR brushes up on the longest teeth in the animal world, from the prehistoric past to the present:

ALLIGATOR: 4 cm
LION: 9 cm
SPERM WHALE: 18 cm
WARTHOG: 23 cm
TYRANNOSAURUS REX: 30 cm
HIPPOPOTAMUS: 50 cm
WALRUS: 1 m
NARWHAL: 2 m
AFRICAN ELEPHANT: 3 m
WOOLLY MAMMOTH: 5 m

TO SCALE
= 50 cm

FACT:
Woolly mammoths may have used their curved tusks as shovels for clearing snow to reach food.

FACT:
It's not unusual for Texas Longhorn bulls to have a horn spread of 2 m (6 ft 6 in).

BIG CATS

Largest jaguar

FACT:
"Black panthers" – such as Boogie from Tbilisi Zoo in Georgia – are jaguars with an excess of dark melanin pigment.

The jaguar (*Panthera onca*) is the third largest species of cat (after the lion and tiger), and is therefore the largest cat in the New World. The largest subspecies of jaguar is the Pantanal jaguar (*P. o. palustris*), native to the Pantanal tropical wetlands in Brazil and Paraguay, as well as north-east Argentina. An adult of this subspecies weighs more than 135 kg (300 lb).

Largest cat not classed as a "true" big cat

There are five species of "true" big cats (all from the *Panthera* genus) – the lion, tiger, leopard, jaguar and snow leopard. However, four other large species – the clouded leopards, puma and cheetah – are often classified with them. The puma (*Puma concolor*) – also known as the cougar, mountain lion, catamount and painter – is the largest cat species apart from the true cats (only the lion, tiger and jaguar are bigger). It is up to 2.75 m (9 ft) long, stands 0.6–0.9 m (1 ft 11 in–2 ft 11 in) at the shoulder, and weighs 53–100 kg (116 lb 13 oz–220 lb 7 oz). The puma also has the **greatest north–south range for a big cat**. It lives in the New World from Alaska, USA, and Yukon, Canada, in the north down to Tierra del Fuego, an island group at the southern tip of South America – a distance of 14,400 km (8,950 miles).

First big cat in Europe

The earliest species of "true" big cat in Europe was the European jaguar (*P. gombaszoegensis*). Larger than present-day New World jaguars, this apex predator existed about 1.5 million years ago, during the early–mid Pleistocene epoch.

Highest-altitude big cat specimen

The famous frozen carcass of a leopard (*Panthera pardus*) discovered in 1926 at the rim of Mount Kilimanjaro's Kibo Crater in Tanzania, at a height of 5,700 m (18,700 ft), is the highest-found true big cat specimen. The highest-recorded cat of any species was a puma observed during the early 1990s at an altitude of 5,800 m (19,028 ft) in the South American Andes mountain range.

Largest population of white tigers

Nandankanan Zoo, in the state of Orissa, India, is home to the world's largest population of white tigers, with at least 34 specimens. This zoo has bred many white tigers, and has sent them to zoos all over the world.

Largest litter of tigers born in captivity

Eight tiger cubs were born to a Bengal tiger (*Panthera tigris tigris*) named Baghdad on 15 April 1979 at Marine World/Africa USA, Redwood City, California, USA (now called Six Flags Marine World and located at Vallejo, California).

Smallest big cat

The world's smallest species of "true" big cat is the snow leopard (*Panthera uncia*). Native to the mountain ranges of central and south Asia, this rare and highly elusive species has a head and body length of 0.75–1.3 m (2 ft 5 in–4 ft 3 in), a tail length of 0.8–1 m (2 ft 7 in–3 ft 3 in), and a shoulder height of 0.6 m (1 ft 11 in). It generally weighs around 27–55 kg (59–121 lb), although an extra-large male can weigh 75 kg (165 lb).

Least genetically diverse big cat

The big cat with least genetic diversity is the cheetah (*Acinonyx jubatus*). Studies conducted in the 1980s using two different populations of South African cheetah revealed that the cheetah not only exhibits less genetic diversity than any other species of cat but also less than almost any other species of large mammal.

Newest big cat

The newest species of big cat is the Bornean clouded leopard (*Neofelis diardi*). Traditionally classed merely as a subspecies of the mainland

Fastest mammal on land

FACT:
At top speed, the cheetah takes strides of about 7 m (23 ft) – the same stride length as a horse!

Over a short distance, the cheetah can maintain a steady maximum speed of approximately 100 km/h (62 mi/h) on level ground. In a timed run, Sarah, an eight-year-old cheetah, ran 100 m in 6.13 seconds on a specially designed course at Cincinnati Zoo, Ohio, USA, on 10 September 2009. If Usain Bolt had run against her, he would be just past halfway when she crossed the finish line. Here's why...

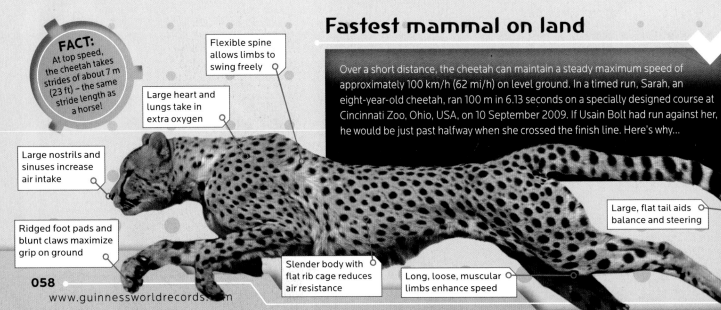

Flexible spine allows limbs to swing freely

Large heart and lungs take in extra oxygen

Large nostrils and sinuses increase air intake

Ridged foot pads and blunt claws maximize grip on ground

Slender body with flat rib cage reduces air resistance

Long, loose, muscular limbs enhance speed

Large, flat tail aids balance and steering

Most widely distributed big cat

Even today, after having become extinct in many parts of the world during the past century, the leopard (*Panthera pardus*) remains the world's most widely distributed true big cat. Inhabiting a range of habitats, it still exists throughout much of sub-Saharan Africa, north-west Africa, parts of the Middle East and west Asia, most of tropical Asia, and in isolated zones in eastern Russia, northern China, the Korean peninsula, Sri Lanka and Java.

clouded leopard (*Neofelis nebulosa*), it was reclassified in December 2006 after studies showed that its DNA and outward appearance were sufficiently distinct.

First record of a lion/tiger hybrid

Lion/tiger hybrids have frequently been bred in captivity, and are known as ligers if sired by a lion and tiglons or tigons if sired by a tiger. The earliest confirmed record of a lion/tiger hybrid is a colour plate of one that was prepared in 1798 by French naturalist Étienne Geoffroy Saint-Hilaire. The liger is the **largest hybrid of the cat family**, typically growing larger than both parents and reaching lengths of 3–3.6 m (10–12 ft).

Rarest tiger hybrids

In 1977, at Southam Zoo in Warwickshire, UK, a cub was born to a tigress that had mated with a black, or melanistic, leopard (commonly known as a black panther). The media dubbed the cub a "pantig", although strictly it is a "leoger". The only offspring ever to survive as a result of a tiger/leopard mating, it was sold to an American zoo as an adult.

Despite his father's all-black coat, the pantig closely resembled a normal leopard in coat colour, but its face was distinctly tiger-like. There has also been only one tiger/jaguar hybrid. Born at Altoplano Zoo in San Pablo Apetatlan, Mexico, in 2009, this "tiguar" was born to a Siberian, or Amur, tiger (*P. tigris altaica*) father and a jaguar mother from the Chiapas jungle, Mexico. It was named Mickey.

Smallest leopard

The smallest subspecies of leopard is the recently recognized, and critically endangered, Arabian leopard (*Panthera pardus nimr*). Males weigh about 30 kg (66 lb), and females 20 kg (44 lb) – notably smaller than any of the leopard's other eight subspecies. In the past, the Somali leopard was deemed the smallest leopard, but it is no longer recognized as a separate subspecies. The clouded leopard (*Neofelis nebulosa*) – native to Asia – is a different species from the leopard. An adult weighs about 15–23 kg (33–51 lb).

"FRANKENSTEIN" CATS

Several big cat species have been cross-bred – almost always in zoos rather than in the wild. Hercules, right, is a liger from South Carolina, USA, while the four tiglon cubs were born in Haikou city, China.

Breed	Hybrid name	Characteristics
Lion/tiger	Liger (from male lion) Tiglon/tigon (from male tiger)	Huge, sociable Smaller than parents
Lion/leopard	Lipard (from male lion) Leopon (from male leopard)	Large lion-like head Larger than leopards
Lion/jaguar	Liguar (from male lion) Jaglion (from male jaguar)	Anecdotal evidence Build of jaguar
Tiger/leopard	Tigard/tipard (from male tiger) Leoger (from male leopard)	Anecdotal evidence One recorded example
Tiger/jaguar	Tiguar (from male tiger) Jagger (from male jaguar)	One recorded example No evidence
Leopard/jaguar	Leguar/lepjag (from male leopard) Jagupard (from male jaguar)	Bigger than leopards Small, size of jaguar

Largest captive lion

The largest lion was a black-maned male named Simba, who had a shoulder height of 1.11 m (44 in) in July 1970. He lived in the UK until his death on 16 January 1973, aged 14.

Longest gestation period for a cat species

The gestation period of a lion (*Panthera leo*) varies between 100 and 114 days, with an average of 110 days. Close behind is the tiger (*P. tigris*), with a gestation period ranging from 93 to 112 days. The Asian elephant (*Elephas maximus*) has the **longest gestation period for a mammal**, taking an average of 650 days to give birth.

Mammal with most names
The puma (*Puma concolor*) has 40 common names – including deer tiger, ghost cat and mountain screamer – in the English language alone.

FACT:
The Asiatic lion (*Panthera leo persica*) is now only found in the wild in the Gir forest in Gujurat, India.

COMPARING CATS

A selection from the feline family in descending order of average weight:

Tiger
(*Panthera tigris*)
3 m (9 ft 10 in); 200 kg (441 lb)

Lion
(*Panthera leo*)
3 m (9 ft 10 in); 180 kg (400 lb)

Jaguar
(*Panthera onca*)
2.1 m (6 ft 10 in); 100 kg (220 lb)

Puma
(*Puma concolor*)
2.27 m (7 ft 5 in); 86 kg (190 lb)

Leopard
(*Panthera pardus*)
2 m (6 ft 6 in); 63 kg (140 lb)

Cheetah
(*Acinonyx jubatus*)
2 m (6 ft 6 in); 46 kg (100 lb)

Eurasian lynx
(*Lynx lynx*)
1.2 m (3 ft 11 in); 30 kg (66 lb)

Ocelot
(*Leopardus pardalis*)
1.1 m (3 ft 7 in); 13.5 kg (30 lb)

Serval
(*Leptailurus serval*)
0.8 m (2 ft 7 in); 13.5 kg (30 lb)

Domestic cat
(*Felis catus*)
0.75 m (2 ft 5 in); 4.5 kg (10 lb)

ON THE FARM

Most abundant farm mammal

The domestic cattle *Bos taurus* is the most abundant farm mammal. There are an estimated 1.3 billion individuals alive today around the world, which means that among large mammals of any kind, only our own species, *Homo sapiens*, is more abundant.

Largest dairy goat population

The greatest population of dairy goats in the world is found in China's Fuping County, which contains approximately 320,000 individuals. By comparison, there are around 310,000 dairy goats in the whole of the USA. Almost all of Fuping's dairy goats are Saanen goats, a large, all-white breed named after Switzerland's Saanen Valley.

Greatest milk-yielding goat breed

The breed of domestic goat (*Capra hircus*) that yields the greatest amount of milk is the Saanen goat, the largest of the dairy goat breeds. A Saanen nanny produces an average daily milk yield of 3.8 litres (1 gal).

Goat breed with the shortest ears

First bred in Oregon, USA, the breed of goat with the shortest ears is the LaMancha, of which there are two types in terms of ear size. The ear lobes of those with so-called "gopher" ears are either non-existent or measure no more than 2.54 cm (1 in) and contain little or no cartilage, whereas those with "elf" ears measure 5.08 cm (2 in) at most. As neither has normal outer ear lobes, on first sight LaMancha goats often appear earless.

Least dense goat coat

The breed of domestic goat with the least dense coat is the angora goat, from which mohair is derived. Other breeds of goat produce a double coat, consisting of coarse outer hair and softer under-down, but the angora goat's coat normally lacks any coarse outer hair, consisting only of a very fine, fleecy under-down.

Largest donkey sanctuary

The world's largest donkey sanctuary is the Sidmouth Donkey Sanctuary in Devon, UK. Founded in 1969 by the late Elisabeth Svendsen (UK), MBE, it currently owns eight farms in the UK, and has cared for more than 13,500 donkeys since it opened. It also oversees sanctuaries, foster homes and holding bays for donkeys in seven other European countries, as well as conducting international operations in Africa, Asia and Mexico.

Most widely used animal fibre

Wool from the domestic sheep (*Ovis aries*) is the most widely used natural fibre derived from animals. It is utilized throughout the inhabited world wherever sheep are farmed. There are just over a billion domestic sheep individuals currently in existence worldwide.

Shortest horse

Charly, a male five-year-old sorrel pony born in 2007, measures just 63.5 cm (25 in) to the withers (between the shoulders). He can be a bit bad-tempered, but is affectionate towards his owner, Bartolomeo Messina (Italy), who has trained Charly to take part in equine exhibition shows.

SNAP SHOT

• Big Jake's owner's son, Morgan, wanted to have a snap of his pet pony Nemo with Jake. Neither Morgan nor Nemo were afraid posing next to the lofty equine – Big Jake is a gentle giant with impeccable manners!

• Belgian draught horses are known for their athleticism rather than their bulk.

• Big Jake is now retired, after 11 years of hard work. It could be a long retirement: many Belgian draught horses live for 20 years or more.

Tallest living horse

Big Jake is a nine-year-old gelding Belgian draught horse who measured 20 hands 2.75 in (210.19 cm; 6 ft 10 in), without horse shoes, at Smokey Hollow Farms in Poynette, Wisconsin, USA, on 19 January 2010. Jerry Gilbert is the manager of Smokey Hollow Farms, and his daughter Caley is holding the reins here. The **tallest horse ever** was the shire gelding Sampson (renamed Mammoth), bred by Thomas Cleaver (UK). This horse, foaled in 1846, measured 21.2 ½ hands (2.19 m; 7 ft 2.5 in), in 1850.

FACT: Big Jake is 7 cm (2.75 in) taller than the previous tallest horse, a Clydesdale named Remington.

Shortest bull

Archie – a Dexter bull named and fully registered in the Northern Ireland livestock inventory in County Antrim, UK – measured 76.2 cm (30 in) from the hoof to the withers on 22 November 2011, when he was 16 months old. The **smallest breed of cattle** is the Vechur breed of Kerala, India. Its average height from the ground to a hump near its shoulders (a feature of certain cattle breeds) for the cow is 81–91 cm (31–35 in) and 83–105 cm (32–41 in) for the bull.

FACT: Archie's parents are both Dexter cows too, but their other calves are far larger than him.

Smallest breed of goat

According to the American Goat Society and Dairy Goat Association, adult males (bucks) of the Nigerian Dwarf breed should measure less than 60 cm (23.6 in) at the withers, and adult females (does) less than 57 cm (22.4 in).

Smallest breed of domestic pig

The Kunekune pig comes from New Zealand with a name that means "fat and round" in Maori. They grow up to 76 cm (30 in) and weigh up to 108 kg (240 lb).

Shortest donkey

KneeHi, a brown miniature Mediterranean jack who lives at Best Friends Farm in Gainesville, Florida, USA, measured 64.2 cm (25.29 in) to the top of the withers on 26 July 2011. KneeHi is owned by Jim and Frankie Lee (USA).

Donkey low-down

- Donkeys (*Equus asinus*) can live for more than 40 years in captivity. They became domesticated around 4,000 years ago.
- They are descendants of Africa's wild ass (*E. africanus*).
- Donkeys have to shelter in rain – unlike horses, their coats are not waterproof.
- Males are dubbed "jacks"; females are called "jennies".
- Mules are the offspring of a male donkey and a female horse. Female donkeys and male horses produce hinnies. Both these cross-breeds are usually sterile.

Hairiest domestic pig

The domestic pig (*Sus scrofa*) with the most hair is the Mangalitza. Uniquely among living breeds of pigs, the Mangalitza grows a remarkably long coat that resembles the fleece of sheep. The Mangalitza is divided into three breeds – the blonde Mangalitza (which is white), the swallow-bellied Mangalitza (which has a black body with white feet and belly) and the red Mangalitza (which is ginger). Mangalitzas originated in Hungary.

Largest sheep population

The country with the world's greatest domestic sheep population is China, which has more than 136 million sheep. Most of these belong to the fat-tailed breed, which is raised mainly for meat and dairy products, as the quality of its wool is generally low. Australia is in second place, with around 79 million sheep.

FACT: Some Mammoth Jackstocks grow as large as draught horses – so watch out, Big Jake!

Tallest living donkey

Oklahoma Sam, a four-year-old American Mammoth Jackstock, measured 15.3 hands (155.45 cm; 5 ft 1 in) tall on 10 December 2011. Jake's owner is Linda Davis of Watsonville, California, USA. Mammoth Jackstocks were bred by US president George Washington, who strongly advocated the use of large mules for farm work instead of horses.

THE PRODUCE WE PRODUCE...

We rely on farms for our basic food staples. In 2010 alone, the world's farmers produced the following jaw-dropping amounts of food and drink. It all adds up to more than 13 quadrillion calories!

MILK More than 760 million litres (or 304 Olympic-sized swimming pools – enough to fill a milk bottle more than twice the height of Nelson's Column, London, UK)

EGGS 68.9 million tonnes (enough to make an omelette the size of Northern Ireland)

POULTRY 97.9 million tonnes (around 16.4 times heavier than the Great Pyramid at Giza, Egypt)

PIG MEAT 109.2 million tonnes (some 4,430 times heavier than the **heaviest statue** – New York's Statue of Liberty)

BEEF AND BUFFALO MEAT 65.7 million tonnes (enough to create a burger with an area nearly 2.5 times greater than that of Mauritius)

SHEEP AND GOAT MEAT 13.6 million tonnes (more than 40 times heavier than the Empire State Building)

FISH (farmed – i.e., not caught fish) 56 million tonnes (around 560 times heavier than the world's **largest cruise ship**, the MS *Allure of the Seas*)

Source: Food and Agriculture Organization of the United Nations Statistical Yearbook 2012

FACT: Each year, a third of the food produced for us is lost or wasted – around 250 kg (551 lb) per person.

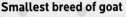

IF YOU HAVE A PENCHANT FOR PETS, SEE P.144

ANIMALYMPICS

Fish with the largest repertoire of tricks

Albert Einstein, a calico fantail goldfish, can perform a range of tricks, including eating from his owner's hand, swimming through a hoop, passing through a tunnel, fetching a ball from the bottom of his tank and swimming under a limbo bar. He even plays football by pushing a tiny ball along the floor of his tank and into a goal. He was trained by his owner, Dean Pomerleau (USA), at the Fish School in Gibsonia, USA.

MAD FOR SPORT? THEN RACE ON TO P.230!

FASTEST...

Guinea pig
A guinea pig appropriately named Flash took 8.81 seconds to run 10 m (32 ft 9 in) on 27 July 2009 in London, UK.

Skateboarding dog
Tillman, an English bulldog, covered a 100-m (328-ft) stretch of car park on a skateboard in 19.678 seconds at X Games XV in Los Angeles, California, USA, on 30 July 2009.

Canine rat catcher
During the early 1820s, an 11.8-kg (26-lb) "bull and terrier" dog named Billy dispatched 4,000 rats in 17 hours, a remarkable feat considering that he was blind in one eye. His most notable feat was the killing of 100 rats in 5 min 30 sec at the Cockpit in Tufton Street, Westminster, London, UK, on 23 April 1825.

Time for a dog to weave through 12 poles
Champion Mach Blazer, owned by Elaine Havens (USA), wove between 12 poles in a remarkable 1.87 seconds on the set of Animal Planet's *Guinness World Records: Amazing Animals* in Los Angeles, California, USA, on 24 September 2005.

The **fastest time for a dog to weave between 24 poles** is 5.88 seconds, by Alma, owned by Emilio Pedrazuela Cólliga (Spain), on the set of *Guinness World Records* in Madrid, Spain, on 16 January 2009.

Tortoise
A tortoise named Charlie covered a 5.48-m (18-ft) course in 43.7 seconds – a speed of 0.45 km/h (0.28 mi/h) – at Tickhill, UK, on 2 July 1977, during the National Tortoise Championship. The course had a gradient of 1:12.

FACT:
A greyhound named Bang set the doggy long-jump record with a leap of 9.14 m (29 ft 11 in).

Highest jump by a dog

Greyhound Cinderella May a Holly Grey, owned by Kate Long and Kathleen Conroy of Miami, Florida, USA, cleared 1.72 m (5 ft 8 in) at the Purina Incredible Dog Challenge National Finals at Gray Summit, Missouri, USA, on 7 October 2006. Her name derives partly from the rescue home that she came from – Hollydogs; the word "Grey" refers to her breed.

HIGHEST JUMP BY A...

Dolphin
Some bottlenose dolphins (*Tursiops truncatus*) have been trained to jump as high as 8 m (26 ft) above the surface of the water.

Dog (leap and scramble)
The canine high-jump record for a leap and scramble over a smooth wooden wall (without ribs or other aids) is 3.72 m (12 ft 2.5 in), achieved by an 18-month-old lurcher dog named Stag at the annual Cotswold Country Fair in Cirencester, Gloucester, UK, on 27 September 1993. The dog was owned by Mr and Mrs P R Matthews of Redruth, Cornwall.

Guinea pig
When it comes to high jumps, one guinea pig soars above the rest. Patch, owned by Philippa Sale (UK) and her family, cleared 22 cm (8.7 in) on 11 October 2011.

SNAP SHOT

• This photo shoot took place on Del Mar beach, which was full of dogs of all shapes and sizes. They were running around and chasing balls, but would often stop what they were doing and stare out in wonder at Abbie Girl surfing the waves!

• Abbie Girl's owner Michael adopted her as a shy rescue dog five years ago. To build her confidence, he would take her to a beach used by other dog owners. She would follow him into the water and enjoy jumping on his surf board. One day he allowed her to float with the wave and she didn't fall off. Since then, she's always loved to surf.

FACT:
Abbie Girl set her record at the Surf City Surf Dog event, beating more than 20 other paw-ticipants!

Longest wave surfed by a dog (open water)

A kelpie named Abbie Girl surfed a 107.2-m-long (351-ft 8-in) wave at Ocean Beach Dog Beach in San Diego, California, USA, on 18 October 2011. Kelpies are an Australian dog breed. They herd sheep, occasionally jumping on the backs of stubborn individuals to steer them while balancing on top – exactly the same balancing skills needed for surfing! Abbie has also happily gone skydiving with her owner, Michael Uy (USA).

Most races won by a sheep

When it comes to racing, a sheep named Lamborghini is way ahead of the pack. Born in January 2011, this woolly whirlwind has won 165 out of 179 races at Odds Farm Park in High Wycombe, UK. The track is approximately 250 m (820 ft) long and features hurdles and hairpin bends. Each competitor carries a jockey – although in the case of sheep racing, the jockeys are cuddly toys. Lamborghini – a Friesland/Dorset Down breed – races once a day from May to the end of October, when he has a well-earned rest.

FACT:
Lamborghini may be speedy, but he'd need to run 14 times faster to beat the car of the same name!

Horse

Unbroken now for more than 60 years, the Fédération Equestre Internationale record for a high jump by a horse outdoors is 2.47 m (8 ft 1.25 in), by Huaso ex-Faithful, ridden by Captain Alberto Larraguibel Morales (Chile). The record was set at Viña del Mar in Santiago, Chile, on 5 February 1949.

The **highest indoor jump by a horse** measured 2.4 m (7 ft 10.5 in) and was set by Optibeurs Leonardo, ridden by Franke Sloothaak (Germany), at Chaudefontaine, Switzerland, on 9 June 1991.

Miniature pygmy horse

A pygmy horse called Lovebug, owned by Krystal Cole (USA), performed a 61-cm (24-in) high jump on the set of Animal Planet's *Guinness World Records: Amazing Animals*. The jump took place on 24 September 2005 in Los Angeles, California, USA.

Pig

An 18-month-old pot-bellied pig named Kotetsu performed a 70-cm (27.5-in) high jump on 22 August 2004 at the Mokumoku Tedsukuri Farm in Mie, Japan. He was trained by Makoto Ieki (Japan).

Rabbit

The highest rabbit jump is 99.5 cm (39.2 in) and was achieved by Mimrelunds Tösen, owned by Tine Hygom (Denmark), in Herning, Denmark, on 28 June 1997.

LONGEST JUMP BY A...

Frog

The greatest confirmed distance ever leapt by a frog is 10.3 m (33 ft 9 in) – about half the length of a basketball court! The jump was made by a South African sharp-nosed frog (*Ptychadena oxyrhynchus*) named Santjie at a frog derby held at Lurula Natal Spa, Petersburg, KwaZulu-Natal, in eastern South Africa, on 21 May 1977.

Guinea pig

Truffles the guinea pig cleared a 48-cm (18-in) gap in Rosyth, Fife, UK, on 27 July 2009.

Kangaroo

The greatest confirmed long-jump by a kangaroo occurred during a chase in New South Wales, Australia, in January 1951, when a female red kangaroo made a series of bounds, including one measuring 12.8 m (42 ft).

Most slam dunks by a parrot in one minute

Who's a pretty smart boy, then? Zac the parrot, from the Happy Birds Performing Parrot Show in San Jose, California, USA, pulled off an impressive 22 slam dunks in 60 seconds on 11 November 2011 using his specially designed basketball net.

SEE IT 3D

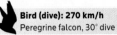

ANIMAL SPEED

The list below charts the speeds recorded by a selection of creatures. As you'll see, humans just can't compete when racing against the animal kingdom...

Bird (dive): 270 km/h
Peregrine falcon, 30° dive

Bird (level): 127 km/h
Albatross, timed over 8 hours

Fish: 109 km/h
Sailfish, over 91 m

Cat: 104.4 km/h
Cheetah, over 201.2 m

Bird (flightless): 72 km/h
Ostrich, burst speed

Horse: 70.76 km/h
Winning Brew, over 402 m

Greyhound: 67.3 km/h
Star Title, over 366 m

Insect: 58 km/h
Dragonfly, short bursts

Ungulate: 56 km/h
Pronghorn, over 6 km

Shark: 56 km/h
Shortfin mako, burst speed

Human: 37.58 km/h
Usain Bolt, over 100 m

Reptile: 34.9 km/h
Iguana, burst speed

Snake (on land): 19 km/h
Black mamba, burst speed

Animals not to scale

WEIGHTLIFTING WONDER

What about humans versus animals in the strength stakes? Again, puny *Homo sapiens* just can't compare...

x 850

The **strongest animals**, relative to body size, are the Scarabaeidae beetles. Larger members of this family support up to 850 times their own body weight – the human equivalent of the average man lifting 10 fully grown African elephants!

SEE IN 3D

ACTUAL SIZE

HUMANS

Shortest living man

The shortest man alive – and, indeed, the shortest living person on Earth – is Chandra Bahadur Dangi (Nepal), who measured 54.6 cm (21.5 in) tall at the CIWEC Clinic Travel Medicine Center in Lainchaur, Kathmandu, Nepal, on 26 February 2012. This measurement means that Chandra is also the shortest man in history whose height has been verified beyond doubt.

According to his identity card, Chandra is aged 72, which would also make him the oldest person to have achieved the shortest man record. He hails from the remote mountain village of Reemkholi, in the Dang district of Nepal, and made his first ever visit to the Nepali capital to have his height confirmed by Guinness World Records.

HOW LONG CAN WE LIVE?

What's the oldest age we can reach?

Guinness World Records' founding editor, Norris McWhirter, once stated: "No single subject is more obscured by vanity, deceit, falsehood and deliberate fraud than the extremes of human longevity." Extraordinary claims of old age continue to surface in the media but what, realistically, is the upper age limit for the human race? No authenticated account can be found of someone living beyond 122 years – and only one person ever reached this extreme age. But is this the absolute limit to life?

Here, GWR gerontologist Robert Young explains the limiting factors of longevity and makes his prediction for the oldest possible age...

How long will you live?

The table below reveals the odds of life. On the left, we look at the likelihood of *you*, the reader, reaching a given age. On the right is the likelihood that *anyone in history* ever lived to a given age.

Age	Odds of you surviving to this age	Likelihood of one person ever reaching this age
120	1 in 10 billion	48%
121	1 in 20 billion	24%
122	1 in 40 billion	12%
123	1 in 80 billion	6%
124	1 in 160 billion	3%
125	1 in 320 billion	1.50%
126	1 in 640 billion	0.75%
127	1 in 1.28 trillion	0.38%
128	1 in 2.56 trillion	0.19%
129	1 in 5.12 trillion	0.09%
130	1 in 10.24 trillion	0.05%

Calculations are based on current world life expectancy and assuming that annual mortality above 110 is .5

FACT: Telomeres give an indication of life expectancy. Can we lengthen our lives by using gene therapy to lengthen our telomeres?

Genetic limits Human cells tend to divide only 50 times, and the average human cell lives two years, so that's a limit of 100 years. Even for those who age 15% slower than normal, that's age 115. So, living beyond 115 is difficult at present, owing to the inevitable aging process. Some of the research into extending life is being directed on "telomeres" – the molecular strands attached to our chromosomes (pictured) that get shorter as we age.

Surviving old age

As we age, we all undergo inevitable physiological changes, some of which we can counteract or at least slow down. Those who live longer tend to "look young" as the effects of aging unfold at a slower rate than normal.

Youth

Skin: In our youth, the skin is full of moisture and very elastic; retain that youthful look by using moisturizers and avoiding the sun.

Hearing: With every passing year, the range of frequencies we can hear reduces, especially higher pitches.

Smell: We tend to lose our sense of smell as we age, and our taste buds become increasingly dulled.

Bones: Aging skeletons lose their density and become brittle as calcium levels drop. A diet rich in Vitamin D and calcium will slow this process.

Middle age

Respiratory system: The lungs can lose their elasticity as you age, leading to shortness of breath, fatigue and increased risk of infection. Avoid smoking, and take regular exercise.

Oldest man ever

Men fare relatively poorly in the survival stakes (there is only one man in the list of top ten oldest living people; see p.68). The greatest ever authenticated age for a male is 115 years 252 days by Denmark's Christian Mortensen (1882–1998).

23 — Dina Manfredini
Born: 4 Apr. 1897
Birthplace: **Italy**
Aged: **115**

24 — Marie Brémont
Born: 25 Apr. 1886
Died: 6 Jun. 2001
Birthplace: **France**
Aged: **115**

23 — Maud Farris-Luse
Born: 21 Jan. 1887
Died: 18 Mar. 2002
Birthplace: **USA**
Aged: **115**

22 — Hendrikje van Andel-Schipper
Born: Jun. 29, 1890
Died: Aug. 30, 2005
Birthplace: **Netherlands**
Age: **115**

21 — Augusta Holtz
Died: 3 Aug. 1871
Died: 24 Oct. 1986
Birthplace: **Germany**
Aged: **115**

20 — Susie Gibson
Born: 31 Oct. 1890
Died: 16 Feb. 2006
Birthplace: **USA**
Aged: **115**

19 — Maria de Jesus
Born: 10 Sep. 1893
Died: 2 Jan. 2009
Birthplace: **Portugal**
Aged: **115**

18 — Julie Winnefred Bertrand
Born: 16 Sep. 1891
Died: 18 Jan. 2007
Birthplace: **Canada**
Aged: **115**

17 — Bettie Wilson
Born: 13 Sep. 1890
Died: 13 Feb. 2006
Birthplace: **USA**
Aged: **115**

16 — Emiliano Mercado del Toro
Born: 21 Aug. 1891
Died: 24 Jan. 2007
Birthplace: **Puerto Rico**
Aged: **115**

15 — Gertrude Baines
Born: 6 Apr. 1894
Died: 11 Sep. 2009
Birthplace: **USA**
Aged: **115**

14 — Margaret Skeete
Born: 27 Oct. 1878
Died: 7 May 1994
Birthplace: **USA**
Aged: **115**

13 — Mary Ann Rhodes
Born: 12 Aug. 1882
Died: 3 Mar. 1998
Birthplace: **Canada**
Aged: **115**

TOP 25 VERIFIED SUPERCENTENARIANS OF ALL-TIME

Will you be joining the 110+ club?

The chart below details the chances of survival of supercentenarians (those over 110 years). It reveals that the longevity of Jeanne Calment, the **oldest person ever** (see below) is an anomaly, with the next oldest at 119 (one person only), two at 117 and three at 116.

SUPERCENTENARIAN SURVIVAL RATES

Age	Surviving	Deaths	Survival rate Yearly	Survival rate Cumulative	Mortality rate Yearly	Mortality rate Cumulative
123	0		0.00%			
122	1	-1	50.00%	0.00%	100.00%	100.00%
121	1	0	100.00%	0.07%	0.00%	99.92%
120	1	0	100.00%	0.07%	0.00%	99.92%
119	2	-1	50.00%	0.07%	50.00%	99.92%
118	2	0	100.00%	0.15%	0.00%	99.84%
117	4	-2	50.00%	0.15%	50.00%	99.84%
116	7	-3	57.14%	0.30%	42.86%	99.70%
115	23	-16	30.43%	0.52%	69.57%	99.48%
114	78	-55	29.49%	1.70%	70.51%	98.30%
113	167	-89	46.71%	5.77%	53.29%	94.23%
112	354	-187	47.18%	12.36%	52.82%	87.64%
111	683	-329	51.83%	26.20%	48.17%	73.80%
110	1,351	-668	50.56%	50.56%	49.44%	49.44%

Proof of age Living to a grand old age is one thing, but proving it is another. To qualify for a GWR certificate, claimants must provide sufficient proof of birth (preferably with an original certificate, issued at the time of birth; later-life certification does not count). Supporting documentation is then required to place a claimant at given key points in their life – so, national service papers, census reports, marriage certificates, medical reports and so on. Note: passports only really provide confirmation of nationality, not proof of age.

Hair: Greying occurs as pigment cells in the hair follicles die off. When the follicles themselves atrophy (waste away), the hair falls out. Hormonal differences between men and women result in differing patterns of baldness between the sexes.

Nervous system: Reaction times slow as signals take longer to pass from the nerves to the muscles.

Memory: Brain cells start to die from your early 20s, so by the time you reach your senior years, short-term memory will usually be affected.

Sight: The lenses in our eyes slowly lose their ability to "accommodate" – i.e., focus. As the focal length shortens, glasses are needed for reading. The pupils also shrink and it becomes difficult to see in lower light.

Later life

FACT: After the age of about 20 years, you lose around a gram of brain mass every year.

Oldest person ever

The greatest fully authenticated age to which any human has ever lived is 122 years 164 days by Jeanne Louise Calment (France, 1875–1997). She led an extremely active life, taking up fencing at 85 years old and still riding a bicycle at 100. Her keys to long life were olive oil, port and chocolate; she gave up smoking, aged 120.

To reach a record-breaking age, you will need to be a "longevity hybrid" – someone optimized for endurance, just as runners are optimized for strength. A diet low in fat and calories, and high in fresh fruit and vegetables, will help, as will regular, moderate exercise, a stimulated mind and a positive attitude to life. But you must also be capable of avoiding or managing disease and disability (and avoiding debilitating falls).

An increasing number of humans and the effects of better healthcare across a lifetime mean that we can and should expect humans to live longer in the future – and that a 130-year lifespan is possible.

12 Edna Parker
Born: 20 Apr. 1893
Birthplace: USA
Died: 26 Nov. 2008
Aged: 115

11 Charlotte Hughes
Born: 1 Aug. 1877
Birthplace: UK
Died: 17 Mar. 1993
Aged: 115

10 Christian Mortensen
Born: 16 Aug. 1882
Birthplace: Denmark
Died: 25 Apr. 1998
Aged: 115

09 Besse Cooper
Born: 26 Aug. 1896
Birthplace: USA
Age: 115

08 Maggie Barnes
Born: 6 Mar. 1882
Birthplace: USA
Died: 19 Jan. 1998
Aged: 115

07 Elizabeth Bolden
Born: 15 Aug. 1890
Birthplace: USA
Died: 11 Dec. 2006
Aged: 116

06 Tane Ikai
Born: 18 Jan. 1879
Birthplace: Japan
Died: 12 Jul. 1995
Aged: 116

05 Maria Esther de Capovilla
Born: 14 Sep. 1889
Birthplace: Ecuador
Died: 27 Aug. 2006
Aged: 116

04 Marie-Louise Meilleur
Born: 29 Aug. 1880
Birthplace: Canada
Died: 16 Apr. 1998
Aged: 117

03 Lucy Hannah
Born: 16 Jul. 1875
Birthplace: USA
Died: 21 Mar. 1993
Aged: 117

02 Sarah Knauss
Born: 24 Sep. 1880
Birthplace: USA
Died: 30 Dec. 1999
Aged: 119

01 Jeanne Calment
Born: 21 Feb. 1875
Birthplace: France
Died: 4 Aug. 1997
Aged: 122

OLDEST...

Oldest living man

Jiroemon Kimura (Japan) was born on 19 April 1897 and celebrated his 115th birthday in 2012. Seen here with GWR's Frank Foley, he is the only man verifiably born in the 19th century who is still alive today.

Living mixed twins
Pauline Shipp Love and Paul Gerald Shipp (both USA) were born on 22 April 1911. As of 23 March 2012 they were 100 years 11 months 1 day old.

As of 16 April 2012, the **highest aggregate age for two siblings** was 213 years 3 months 27 days for sisters Marjorie Phyllis Ruddle (b. 21 April 1907) and Dorothy Richards (b. 15 December 1903; both UK). Dorothy lives in Stamford, Lincolnshire, while Marjorie resides in Peterborough in Cambridgeshire (both UK).

Abseiler
Intrepid pensioner Doris Cicely Long, MBE (UK, b. 18 May 1914) completed a descent of 60 m (197 ft) from the top of Millgate House in Portsmouth, UK, on 21 May 2011 at the age of 97 years 3 days.

Acrobatic salsa dancer (female)
The UK's Sarah Paddy Jones (b. 1 July 1934) won first prize on Spain's TV talent show *Tú Sí Que Vales* (*You Are Worth It*) on 2 December 2009, aged 75 years 5 months 1 day.

Act to release a new album
Australian artist Smoky Dawson (1913–2008) released a new album of original songs, *Homestead of My Dreams*, at the age of 92 years 4 months 14 days. The album went on sale on 22 August 2005.

On 17 September 2011, aged 87 years 5 months 14 days, 1950s screen favourite Doris Day (USA, née Doris Kappelhoff; b. 3 April 1924) became the **oldest act to achieve a UK Top 10 album with a new recording** when *My Heart* peaked at No.9.

The star's 29th studio release featured eight new recordings, along with four songs that had appeared on earlier albums.

Author to have a first book published
Bertha Wood's (UK, b. 20 June 1905) *Fresh Air and Fun: The Story of a Blackpool Holiday Camp* was published on her 100th birthday.

BASE jumper
James Talbot Guyer (USA, b. 16 June 1928) parachuted off the 148-m-high (486-ft) Perrine Bridge near Twin Falls, Idaho, USA, on 2 August 2002, aged 74 years 1 month 17 days.

Bodybuilder (male)
Competitive bodybuilder Raymond "Ray" Moon (Australia, b. 1929) performed at the NABBA International Bodybuilding Figure and Fitness Championships in Melbourne, Australia, on 23 May 2010, aged 81.

Ballroom dancer
Frederick Salter (UK, b. 13 February 1911) passed his IDTA Gold Bar Level 3 exams in Latin and Ballroom with Honours, aged 100 years 8 months 2 days, in London, UK, on 15 October 2011.

Oldest living female twins
Evelyn Middleton (above far left) and Edith Ritchie (above left; both UK) were born on 15 November 1909. They are pictured celebrating their 102nd birthdays and (left) in their youth.

Oldest living person

Besse Cooper (USA, b. 26 August 1896) – seen here with GWR consultant Robert Young – became the world's oldest person on 21 June 2011, aged 114 years 10 months. As of 11 May 2012, she was 115 years 250 days old. Like Jiroemon Kimura, the **oldest living man** (see left), she puts her exceptional longevity down to a good diet and no junk food.

Darts player
As of 24 February 2012, Candy Miller (UK, b. 21 October 1920) was still playing in competitive darts matches in the Bournemouth and District Ladies Darts League, in Parkstone, Bournemouth, UK, aged 91 years 4 months 3 days.

Film director
Manoel de Oliveira (Portugal, b. 11 December 1908) began directing in 1931. His most recent movie was *O Estranho Caso de Angélica* (*The Strange Case of Angelica*, Portugal/Spain/France/Brazil, 2010).

Indoor bowls player
As of 1 March 2012, Jean Ella Cowles (UK, b. 10 September 1917) was a member of Spalding and District Indoor Bowls Club in Spalding, Lincolnshire, UK, aged 94 years 5 months 22 days.

Lifeguard (active)
Louis Demers (USA, b. 3 September 1923) of Quincy, Illinois, USA, was aged 88 years 6 months 4 days as of 7 March 2012. He has been a lifeguard since 1954.

MOBO winner
In 1998, B B King (USA, b. Riley B King, 16 September 1925) picked up the Music Of Black Origin (MOBO) Award for Lifetime Achievement aged 73. Over a recording career stretching back to 1949, King has won an impressive 16 Grammy Awards, including a Lifetime Achievement Award in 1987. His 1969 track "The Thrill is Gone" has also received a Grammy Hall of Fame Award.

Nobel laureate
Professor Francis Peyton Rous (USA, 1879–1970) shared the Physiology or Medicine prize in 1966 at the age of 87.

Patient
Jeanne Calment (France, 1875–1997) – the **oldest person ever** – was aged 114 years 11 months when she underwent a hip operation in January 1990.

Oldest living dwarf

Lowell DeForest Mason (USA) was born on 14 August 1937 and currently resides in Missouri, USA. He was aged 74 years 6 months 2 days as of 16 February 2012.

FACT: During his long career, Ted has delivered around 500,000 newspapers!

Oldest active flight attendant

As of 21 May 2012, at the age of 88 years 14 days, Robert Reardon (USA, b. 7 May 1924, above) was still a flight attendant with Delta Air Lines. He took up his first post as a flight attendant in 1951.

Ronald "Ron" Byrd Akana (USA, b. 8 September 1928, left) has enjoyed the **longest career as a flight attendant**. He joined United Airlines on 16 December 1949 and, as of 22 March 2012, had worked for 62 years 3 months 6 days.

TOP 10 OLDEST ALIVE

Below is a list of the 10 oldest people alive in the world, as of 11 May 2012. You'll notice that your chances of living to a very ripe old age are greatly increased if you happen to be a woman...

1. **Besse Cooper (USA)** born: 26 August 1896 age: 115 years 250 days
2. **Dina Manfredini (Italy/USA)** born: 4 April 1897 age: 115 years 28 days
3. **Jiroemon Kimura (Japan)** born: 19 April 1897 age: 115 years 13 days
4. **Misawo Okawa (Japan)** born: 5 March 1898 age: 114 years 58 days
5. **Kame Nakamura (Japan)** born: 8 March 1898 age: 114 years 55 days
6. **Marie-Thérèse Bardet (France)** born: 2 June 1898 age: 113 years 335 days
7. **Mamie Rearden (USA)** born: 7 September 1898 age: 113 years 238 days
8. **Hatsue Ono (Japan)** born: 31 October 1898 age: 113 years 184 days
9. **Ichi Ishida (Japan)** born: 15 January 1899 age: 113 years 108 days
10. **Maria Redaelli-Granoli (Italy)** born: 3 April 1899 age: 113 years 29 days

Oldest newspaper delivery person

Ted Ingram (UK, b. 18 March 1920) was still delivering the *Dorset Echo* in Weymouth, Dorset, UK, aged 91 years 11 months 4 days, as of 22 February 2012.

The **oldest female newspaper delivery person**, Joyce Pugh (UK, b. 10 September 1931), delivers the *Shropshire Star* in Shrewsbury, Shropshire, UK. She was 80 years 6 months 3 days old as of 13 March 2012.

Shopkeeper
Jack Yaffe (UK) ran his hardware store in Prestwich, Greater Manchester, UK, for 78 years. He retired in January 2012, on his 103rd birthday.

Person to complete a marathon
Dimitrion Yordanidis (Greece) completed a 42-km (26-mile) marathon in Athens, Greece, on 10 October 1976, aged 98.

Oldest gymnast

Johanna Quaas (Germany, b. 20 November 1925) is a regular competitor in the amateur competition Landesseniorenspiele, staged in Saxony, Germany.

She performed a floor-and-beam routine on the set of *Lo Show dei Record* in Rome, Italy, in April 2012 and can still perform cartwheels at the age of 86!

He finished in 7 hr 33 min.
On 12 December 2010, at the age of 92 years 19 days, Gladys Burrill (USA) completed the Honolulu Marathon in Hawaii, USA, making her the **oldest woman to complete a marathon**. Burrill completed the race in 9 hr 53 min 16 sec.

Person to swim the English Channel
Roger Allsopp (UK, b. 6 April 1941) swam the Channel from Shakespeare Beach, Dover, UK, to Calais, France, in 17 hr 51 min 19 sec, aged 70 years 4 months 24 days, on 30 August 2011.

The **oldest woman to swim the English Channel** is the UK's Linda Ashmore (b. 21 October 1946), who crossed from England to France in 15 hr 11 min, aged 60 years 9 months 29 days, on 19 August 2007.

Solo parachute jumper
Milburn Hart (USA) made a solo parachute jump near Bremerton National Airport, Washington, USA, on 18 February 2005, aged 96 years 2 months 1 day.

Sylvia Brett (UK) was 80 years 5 months 13 days old when she parachuted over Cranfield in Bedfordshire, UK, on 23 August 1986, making her the **oldest woman to make a solo parachute jump**.

Wing walker
At the age of 91 years 16 days, Thomas Lackey (UK, b. 22 May 1920) completed a wing walk across the English Channel from Lydd Airport, Kent, UK, to Calais Airport, France, on 7 June 2011.

Supercentenarians

As of 11 May 2012, there were 71 people over the age of 110. These "supercentenarians" are monitored by the Gerontology Research Group, which collects data such as age, gender, race and nationality:

Women/Men
5 Men
66 Women

Race
24 East Asian
38 White
7 Black
2 Hispanic

Nationality
1 Puerto Rico
1 Mexico
1 Germany
1 Barbados
1 Australia
2 Spain
2 Canada
2 Belgium
24 Japan
14 USA
6 UK
8 Italy
8 France

FACT: Johanna was a relatively late starter – she didn't take up gymnastics until she was in her 30s.

Oldest female bodybuilder
E Wilma Conner (USA, b. 9 May 1935) competed in the 2011 NPC Armbrust Pro Gym Warrior Classic bodybuilding championships in Loveland, Colorado, USA, on 20 August 2011, aged 77.

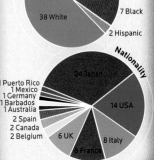

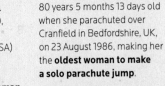

BIRTHS

HEAVIEST...

Birth

In February 2012, the birth of baby Chun Chun to mother Wang Yujuan in Henan Province, China, made headlines because of his impressive weight of 7.03 kg (15.5 lb) – twice the average birth weight. As remarkable as this new delivery was, it pales when compared with the heaviest birth of all time: on 19 January 1879, Anna Bates (Canada, pictured below right) – who measured 2.27 m (7 ft 5.5 in) tall – gave birth to a boy weighing 10.8 kg (23 lb 12 oz)!

Twins

The world's heaviest twins, with a combined weight of 12.58 kg (27 lb 12 oz), were born to Mary Ann Haskin of Fort Smith, Arkansas, USA, on 20 February 1924.

Triplets

The heaviest triplets ever weighed 10.9 kg (24 lb) and were born to Mary McDermott (UK) on 18 November 1914.

Quadruplets

Two girls and two boys, with a total weight of 10.42 kg (22 lb 15.75 oz), were born to Tina Saunders (UK) at St Peters Hospital in Chertsey, UK, on 7 February 1989.

Quintuplets

There have been two recorded cases of quintuplets with a combined birth weight of 11.35 kg (25 lb): on 7 June 1953 to Liu Saulian (China) and on 30 December 1956 to a Mrs Kamalammal (India).

LIGHTEST...

Birth

The lowest confirmed birth weight for a surviving infant is 260 g (9.17 oz), in the case of Rumaisa Rahman (USA), who was born at Loyola University Medical Center, Maywood, Illinois, USA, on 19 September 2004, after a gestation period of 25 weeks 6 days.

Twins

The lowest combined birth weight recorded for a surviving set of twins is 847 g (1 lb 13.57 oz) in the case of Hiba (580 g; 1 lb 4.4 oz) and Rumaisa (260 g; 9.17 oz) Rahman, who were born to Mahajabeen Shaik (India). The twins were born by Caesarean section (or C-section), a procedure whereby an incision is made in the mother's abdomen, through which the baby is delivered.

Triplets

With a combined weight of 1,385 g (3 lb 0.8 oz), Peyton (585 g; 1 lb 4.6 oz), Jackson (420g; 14.8 oz) and Blake (380g; 13.4 oz) Coffey (all USA) became the lightest triplets to survive when they were born by Caesarean section at the University of Virginia Hospital (USA) on 30 November 1998.

MOST...

Prolific mother

The wife of Russian peasant Feodor Vassilyev bore a total of 69 children. In 27 pregnancies from 1725 to 1765, she had 16 pairs of twins (the **most sets of twins born**), seven sets of triplets and four sets of quadruplets (the **most sets of quadruplets born**). *See far right for more information.*

The **most sets of triplets born** to one mother is 15, by Maddalena Granata (Italy, b. 1839).

Most siblings born on the same day

There are only five verified examples of a mother producing two sets of twins with the same birthdays in different years. The most recent case is that of Tracey Bageban (UK), who gave birth to Armani Jafar and Diego Mohamed on 27 February 2008 and Elisia Christina and Dolcie Falimeh three years later on 27 February 2011.

Most sets of mixed twins

Lightning struck twice for mixed-race parents Dean Durrant and Alison Spooner (both UK) when, in March 2009, Alison gave birth to a second set of twins with entirely different skin colourations: Leah and Miya. In 2001, she gave birth to the dark-skinned Hayleigh and fair-skinned Layren. Dr Sarah Jarvis, from the UK's Royal College of General Practitioners, has suggested that the odds of such an event happening twice in this way "must be one in millions".

FACT:
The odds of a mixed-race couple having just one set of twins of differing colour are around 500 to one.

Heaviest & longest birth
Giantess Anna Bates (Canada), who was 2.27 m (7 ft 5.5 in) tall, gave birth to a 10.8-kg (23-lb 12-oz), 76-cm-long (30-in) boy on 19 January 1879.

Heaviest triplets at birth (current)

Shown from left to right above are Gabriel James, Lilliana Mary and Nathan Andrew Kupresak (all Canada), who had a combined weight of 7.7 kg (17 lb 2.7 oz) when they were born on 6 November 2008, at Mount Sinai Hospital in Toronto, Canada. The triplets were born after a gestation period of 37 weeks, four weeks longer than the average period for triplets. Two years after their birth, there was still a significant size difference between the three children, with Gabriel and Lilliana weighing approximately 10.8 kg (24 lb) each and Nathan weighing around 15.4 kg (36 lb).

Triplet facts and figures

* More than 90% of triplets are born prematurely.

* Women who have children after the age of 30, especially those who use fertility treatment, have an increased chance of having triplets. Taller or heavier women are also more likely to give birth to triplets.

* Identical triplets have 100% of their DNA in common. They are of the same sex and the colour of their hair and eyes is the same, as is their blood type, although their fingerprints will be different.

Children delivered at a single birth

Nine children (nonuplets) were born to Geraldine Brodrick in Sydney, Australia, on 13 June 1971. Unfortunately, none of the children lived for longer than six days.

Children delivered at a single birth to survive

Nadya Suleman (USA) gave birth to six boys and two girls at the Kaiser Permanente Medical Center, Bellflower, California, USA, on 26 January 2009. The babies were conceived with the aid of *in vitro* fertilization (IVF) treatment and were nine weeks premature when they were delivered by Caesarean section.

Caesarean sections

Kristina House of California, USA, gave birth to 11 children (six girls and five boys), all by Caesarean section, between 15 May 1979 and 20 November 1998.

Premature

James Elgin Gill was born to Brenda and James Gill (both Canada) on 20 May 1987. He was 128 days premature and weighed 624 g (1 lb 6 oz).

CHECK OUT MORE YOUNG ACHIEVERS ON P.106

OLDEST...

Father

Les Colley (Australia, 1898–1998) had his ninth child to his third wife at the age of 92 years 10 months. Colley met Oswald's Fijian mother in 1991 through a dating agency.

Mother to give birth

Following IVF treatment, Maria del Carmen Bousada Lara (Spain, 1940–2009) gave birth by Caesarean section to twin boys, Christian and Pau, at the age of 66 years 358 days in Barcelona, Spain, on 29 December 2006. This achievement also gave Maria the record for the **oldest mother to give birth to twins**.

On 20 August 1997, a baby was born to Dawn Brooke (UK) who, at the age of 59 years, became the **oldest mother to conceive naturally** (i.e., without the aid of fertility treatments). She conceived him accidentally, having ovulated past her last period.

Woman to give birth to her grandchildren

Aged 56 years, Jacilyn Dalenberg of Wooster, Ohio, USA, acted as surrogate mother for her daughter, Kim Coseno (USA), and carried and delivered her own grandchildren: three girls. The triplets were delivered – two months premature – by Caesarean section.

Heaviest woman to give birth

Donna Simpson of New Jersey, USA, weighed 241 kg (532 lb; 38 st) when she gave birth to her daughter Jacqueline on 13 February 2007 at Akron City Hospital in Akron, Ohio, USA. Jacqueline was born after a gestation period of 37 weeks 4 days, and weighed 4 kg (8 lb 14 oz) at birth. Donna, who wears size XXXXXXXL clothing and was reportedly consuming around 15,000 calories a day at one point, has embarked on a diet since giving birth to Jacqueline. She had shed around 38.5 kg (85 lb) by December 2011.

FACT: The average woman only needs to consume around 2,000 calories per day.

MOST CHILDREN BORN TO ONE MOTHER

The peasant Feodor Vassilyev of Shuya, Russia, lived between c. 1707 and c. 1782 and fathered 69 children with his first wife (whose name is sadly not recorded). The births came in 27 confinements and consisted of four quadruplets, seven triplets and 16 twins*!

*The sexes of the children were not reported

The case was reported to the government in Moscow on 27 February 1782 by the Monastery of Nikolsk, where the births were recorded. The report revealed that Vassilyev married a second time and fathered a further 18 children in eight confinements of two triplets and six twins:

By the time of the 1782 report, Vassilyev was in "perfect health" at the age of 75 and boasted a total of 87 surviving children!

WEDDINGS

BRIDAL WEAR

Most expensive wedding dress

Jeweller Martin Katz and bridal couturier Renee Strauss (both USA) created a $12-million (£6.1-million) gown bedecked with 150 carats' worth of diamonds for the Luxury Brands Lifestyle Bridal Show held on 26 February 2006 at the Ritz-Carlton in Marina del Rey, California, USA.

Most crystals on a wedding dress

Özden Gelinlik Moda Tasarım Ltd (Turkey) created a wedding dress adorned with 45,024 crystals that was presented at the Forum Istanbul Shopping Mall, in Istanbul, Turkey, on 29 January 2011.

Longest wedding dress train

Measuring 2.48 km (1.54 miles) and created by Lichel van den Ende (Netherlands), the longest wedding train was presented and measured in Zoetermeer, Netherlands, on 22 December 2009.

Longest wedding veil

At the wedding of Sandra Mechleb to Chady Abi Younis (both Lebanon) in Arnaoon, Lebanon, on 18 October 2009, Sandra wore a veil 3.35 km (2 miles) long.

CAKES

Most expensive wedding cake slice

A piece of the Duke and Duchess of Windsor's 1937 wedding cake sold at Sotheby's, New York, USA, on 27 February 1998 for $29,900 (£18,163) to Benjamin and Amanda Yin of San Francisco, USA.

Oldest wedding cake

Two pieces of the wedding cake of Queen Victoria and Prince Albert, preserved since their wedding day on 10 February 1840, went on display at the Drawings Gallery, Windsor Castle, Windsor, UK, for the first time on 27 April 2007. On the opening day of the exhibition, which celebrated royal marriages, the cake was 167 years 2 months 17 days old.

Say it with flowers!

At the wedding ceremony for Arulanatham Suresh Joachim (Australia) and Christa Rasanayagam (Canada) on 6 September 2003, Christa held the largest wedding bouquet:

• 60.09 m (197 ft 1 in) long

• 92 kg (202 lb 12 oz) in weight

• 1,500 flowers, comprising: 500 roses, 400 carnations, 340 sprigs of baby's-breaths, 200 daisies and 60 lilies

The ceremony took place at King Catholic Church, Mississauga, Ontario, Canada.

OLDEST...

Bride

At the age of 102, Minnie Munro (Australia) married 83-year-old Dudley Reid (both Australia) at Point Clare, New South Wales, Australia, on 31 May 1991.

Bridegroom

Harry Stevens became the oldest bridegroom at the age of 103 when he married Thelma Lucas (both USA), then aged 84, at the Caravilla Retirement Home in Wisconsin, USA, on 3 December 1984.

Bridesmaid

On 31 March 2007, Edith Gulliford (UK, b. 12 October 1901; d. 29 April 2008) was bridesmaid at the wedding of Kyra Harwood and James Lucas (both UK) at Commissioner's House, Chatham, UK, at the age of 105 years 171 days.

Most expensive wedding

The wedding of Vanisha Mittal, daughter of billionaire Lakshmi Mittal, to investment banker Amit Bhatia (all India) was a wallet-busting affair. The six-day event, held in Versailles, France, in 2004, included a re-enactment of the couple's courtship and an engagement ceremony at the Palace of Versailles – the only private function ever to have been held there. The entertainers at the reception included Shah Rukh Khan and Kylie Minogue. The bride's father picked up a bill for $55 million (£28 million).

Best man

Gerald W Pike (USA, b. 12 October 1910) served as best man at the marriage of Nancy Lee Joustra and Clifford Claire Hill (both USA), aged 93 years 166 days on 26 March 2004 at Kent County in Michigan, USA.

Couple to marry (combined age)

On 1 February 2002, François Fernandez (France, b. 17 April 1906) and Berthe Andrée "Madeleine" Francineau (France, b. 15 July 1907) exchanged marriage vows at the rest home Le Foyer du Romarin, Clapiers, France, at the age of 96 years 290 days and 94 years 201 days, respectively. Their aggregate age at the time of the ceremony totalled 191 years 126 days.

YOU'RE NEVER TOO OLD! TURN TO P.68...

Largest underwater wedding

The marriage ceremony between Francesca Colombi and Giampiero Giannoccaro (both Italy) was attended by 261 divers at an event organized by the company Mares SpA (Italy) at the Morcone beach, Capoliveri, Elba, Italy, on 12 June 2010. The bride and groom were able to communicate by means of watches provided by Mares with a special "yes" and "no" function on their screens. The mayor of Capoliveri, who conducted the ceremony, was able to communicate with the couple using waterproof plastic boards on which pre-written text had been inscribed.

Heaviest wedding cake

6.8 tonnes

Weighing in at a belt-busting 6.818 tonnes (15,032 lb), the largest wedding cake was displayed during the New England bridal showcase at the Mohegan Sun Hotel and Casino, Uncasville, Connecticut, USA, on 8 February 2004. The seven-tiered cake could have fed 59,000 people and weighed more than a bull elephant. It was created by the Mohegan Sun's chef Lynn Mansel and a team of 57 chefs and "pastry artisans". Two fork-lift trucks were used to help raise each tier.

Most couples married underwater simultaneously

On Valentine's Day 2001 (14 February), 34 couples from 22 countries exchanged wedding vows at the same time, 10 m (32 ft 9 in) underwater near Kradan Island, Southern Thailand. The submarine service was organized by Trang Chamber of Commerce and Thai Airways International.

First robot wedding

A robot named I-Fairy conducted the wedding ceremony between robotics enthusiasts Tomohiro Shibata and Satoko Inoue (both Japan) in Tokyo, Japan, on 16 May 2010.

HIGHEST MARRIAGE RATES

Some nations are more in love with the idea of marriage than others. Below is a list of the countries with the highest marriage rates. (Number of marriages per 1,000 population; figures for 2009 or last available year.)

10 Barbados	10.1
9 Jordan	10.4
8 Bermuda	11.2
7 Iran	11.3
6 Mongolia	12.4
5 Guam	13.3
4 Tajikistan	13.7
3 British Virgin Islands	19.6
2 Antigua & Barbuda	21.7
1 Virgin Islands (US)	35.8

UNUSUAL WEDDINGS

Most wedding guests

On 7 September 1995, more than 150,000 people witnessed the wedding of V N Sudhakaran to N Sathyalakshmi (both India). The ceremony – shown on screens at the 20-ha (50-acre) grounds in Madras, India – was followed by the **largest wedding reception**!

First zero-gravity wedding

Erin Finnegan and Noah Fulmor (both USA) were sky high when they got married on 23 June 2009 – their weightless wedding took place aboard *G-Force One*, a modified Boeing 727-200.

Most weddings in a TV soap opera

A total of 79 wedding ceremonies have been celebrated on the British TV soap opera *Coronation Street*. The first took place on 8 March 1961.

Largest dog wedding

Some people even want their pets to get hitched! A group of 178 pooch pairs wed at the "Bow Wow Vows" event set up by the Aspen Grove Lifestyle Center (USA) on 19 May 2007.

FACT: The average age at which women in the UK now marry is 30. In 1981, it was just 23.

Largest mass wedding ceremony in a prison

On 14 June 2000, a group of 120 inmates of Carandiru prison, São Paulo, Brazil, married their fiancées in a mass ceremony organized by prison officers and volunteers from 19 local churches.

Although the brides wore traditional white dresses, the grooms were required to wear their prison trousers along with formal jackets and ties.

LOWEST MARRIAGE RATES

Marriage isn't for everyone, of course. Here's a list of those nations who don't care so much for the sound of wedding bells...

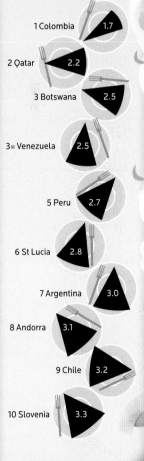

1 Colombia	1.7
2 Qatar	2.2
3 Botswana	2.5
3= Venezuela	2.5
5 Peru	2.7
6 St Lucia	2.8
7 Argentina	3.0
8 Andorra	3.1
9 Chile	3.2
10 Slovenia	3.3

Source: The Economist

BODY PARTS

Longest tongue

Stephen Taylor (UK) holds the record for the longest tongue, which stretches 9.8 cm (3.86 in) from the tip to the middle of his closed top lip. It was measured at Westwood Medical Centre in Coventry, UK, on 11 February 2009.

The **woman with the longest tongue** is Chanel Tapper (USA). Her lengthy licker was found to be 9.75 cm (3.8 in) from the tip to the middle of the lip when measured in California, USA, on 29 September 2010.

Most teeth

As of 17 October 2008, both Kanchan Rajawat (India) and Luca Meriano (Italy) could boast a more-than-full set of 35 adult teeth.

Oldest person to grow a new tooth

Spare a thought for Brian Titford (Australia, b. 14 January 1933): in March 2009, two of his upper wisdom teeth erupted when he was 76 years old. His dentist subsequently removed the teeth to restore the stability of Brian's denture.

Youngest person to have a wisdom tooth extracted

Matthew Adams (USA, b. 19 November 1992) had his lower two wisdom teeth removed at Midland Oral and Maxillofacial Surgery in Michigan, USA, on 24 October 2002. He was aged just 9 years 339 days.

Fewest toes

Some members of the Wadomo tribe of the Zambezi Valley, Zimbabwe, and the Kalanga tribe of the eastern Kalahari desert, Botswana, are born with only two toes. The three central toes are missing and the two outer toes are turned inwards. The condition is passed down via a single mutated gene.

Most fingers and toes on a living person

The greatest number of fingers and toes on a living person is 25, comprising 12 fingers and 13 toes. Two Indian citizens hold this record: Pranamya Menaria (b. 10 August 2005) and Devendra Harne (b. 9 January 1995). This digital abundance is the result of the congenital conditions polydactyly (a multiplicity of finger or toe) and syndactyly (in which fingers or toes have become fused together).

Largest feet ever

Robert Wadlow (USA, 1918–40), the **tallest man ever**, wore US size 37AA shoes (UK size 36 or approximately a European size 75), equivalent to 47 cm (18.5 in) in length.

Excluding cases of elephantiasis, the **largest feet on a living person** are those of Brahim Takioullah (Morocco), whose left foot measures 38.1 cm (1 ft 3 in) and right foot measures 37.5 cm (1 ft 2.76 in). The measurements were taken in Paris, France, on 24 May 2011.

Longest fingernails ever (male)

The fingernails of Melvin Boothe (USA, 1948–2009)

totalled 9.85 m (32 ft 3.8 in), when measured in Troy, Michigan, USA, in May 2009. When last measured in 2004, the fingernails on the left hand of Shridhar Chillal (India) totalled 7.05 m (23 ft 1.5 in) in length, the **longest fingernails on one hand**.

Largest "guns" (male)

Watch out, Popeye! Body-builder Mostafa Ismail (Egypt) has a right upper-arm circumference of 63.5 cm (25 in) flexed and 60.96 cm (24 in) non-flexed and a left upper-arm circumference of 64.77 cm (25.5 in) flexed and 62.23 cm (24.5 in) non-flexed. The measurement of his muscles – the biceps and triceps, or "guns" – were taken in Franklin, Massachusetts, USA, and verified on 24 November 2011.

Hairiest family

Victor "Larry" Gomez, Gabriel "Danny" Ramos Gomez, Luisa Lilia De Lira Aceves and Jesus Manuel Fajardo Aceves (all Mexico) are four members of a family of 19, spanning five generations, all of whom have a condition called congenital generalized hypertrichosis, characterized by excessive facial and torso hair. The women have a light-to-medium coat of hair, while the men have thick hair on around 98% of their bodies.

Longest hair (female)

Xie Qiuping's (China) hair measured 5.627 m (18 ft 5.54 in) on 8 May 2004.

The **longest nose on a living person** measures 8.8 cm (3.46 in) and belongs to Mehmet Ozyurek (Turkey).

Stretchiest skin

Garry Turner (UK) has a rare medical condition called Ehlers-Danlos Syndrome, a disorder of the connective tissues affecting the skin, ligaments and internal organs. He is able to stretch the skin of his stomach to a distended length of 15.8 cm (6.25 in). The condition makes the collagen that strengthens the skin, and determines its elasticity, defective. Its effects include a loosening of the skin and "hypermobility" of the joints.

More about Mostafa...

- Mostafa started body-building when he lived in Egypt, moving to the USA in early 2011 to participate in "naturally enhanced" body-building competitions
- He works as a manager of a petrol station, but his dream is to become a professional body-builder

FACT:
The term "guns" was used as early as 1929 to describe the throwing arm of baseball pitchers.

FACT:
In 2003, a peat farmer in Ireland discovered a 2,300-year-old corpse sporting a mohican.

FACT:
Moses is constantly being asked to show off his foot rotation at parties.

Tallest mohican

When it comes to mohican hairstyles, one man's achievements tower above the rest. Kazuhiro Watanabe (Japan) had a mammoth 113.5-cm (44.6-in) mohican as of 28 October 2011. Kazuhiro's lofty achievement easily broke his own world record: on 10 January 2011, his mohican had been measured at "just" 105 cm (41.3 in) in Sapporo, Hokkaido, Japan. And that was a hair-raising 25 cm (9.8 in) taller than the previous record holder...

1.1 m high

Longest beard ever

The beard of Hans N Langseth (Norway) measured 5.33 m (17 ft 6 in) at the time of his burial at Kensett, Iowa, in 1927, after 15 years' residence in the USA. His record-breaking beard was presented to the Smithsonian Institution, Washington, DC, USA, in 1967. The **longest beard on a living man** can be combed out to 2.495 m (8 ft 2.5 in). It belongs to Sarwan Singh (Canada), head priest of the Guru Nanak Sikh temple in Surrey, British Columbia, Canada.

Longest nose ever

There are historical accounts that Thomas Wedders, who lived in England during the 1770s and was a member of a travelling circus, had a nose measuring 19 cm (7.5 in).

Longest fingernails ever (female)

Lee Redmond (USA) began growing her fingernails in 1979 and nurtured them to a length of 8.65 m (28 ft 4.5 in), as verified in Madrid, Spain, on 23 February 2008. Sadly, in early 2009, Lee lost her nails in a car accident.

The current owner of the **longest fingernails (female)** is singer and recording artist Chris "The Dutchess" Walton (USA). Her left fingernails total 309.8 cm (10 ft 2 in) and her right total 292.1 cm (9 ft 7 in) – an overall length of 601.9 cm (19 ft 9 in) – as measured in Las Vegas, Nevada, USA, on 21 February 2011.

Longest eyeball pop

Keith Smith (USA) kept his eyes popped out of their sockets for 53.01 seconds. The eye-watering record attempt took place in Madrid, Spain, on 28 January 2009.

Greatest external foot rotation

Moses Lanham (USA) turns heads when he turns his feet around. He rotated them outwards, through an angle of 120°, on the set of *Lo Show dei Record* in Milan, Italy, on 10 March 2011. On the same day, Moses also achieved the record for the **fastest time to walk 20 m with the feet facing backwards.** He achieved the act of rapid reverse pedestrianism in a time of 19.59 seconds.

SNAP SHOT

- Aged 14, Moses fell off some gym bars at school and landed awkwardly, with his feet bent and apparently broken. Surprisingly, he didn't find it too painful...

- After lots of X-rays and tests, the doctors confirmed that Moses had a unique muscle and ligament make-up that he had probably endured since birth. It means he has the ability to turn his feet back to front

- Moses' son can also bend his feet to an unusual degree

LONGEST HUMAN HAIRS

Hairs are fine, thread-like strands of protein (largely keratin, which is also a part of the finger- and toenails) that grow on every part of the body apart from areas such as the soles, the palms and the lips.

ACTUAL SIZE

Eyelash	
Arm hair	
Nipple hair	
Leg hair	
Ear hair	
Eyebrow	
Chest hair	

0.00 cm · 6.99 cm · 14.61 cm · 15.16 cm · 16.51 cm · 18.1 cm · 22.8 cm

BIZARRE BEAUTY

Most facial piercings

Axel Rosales, from Villa Maria, Argentina, had a total of 280 piercings on his face as of 17 February 2012. On the day of the GWR adjudication itself, the count came in at 271 piercings. Axel wanted a round number for his record, however, and so invited his piercer friend to add nine more to reach a final total of 280.

Most extensive scarification

Women of the Tiv and Nuba peoples of Nigeria in west Africa endure extreme scarification rituals as part of a rite of passage (as in the case of the Nuba) or to accentuate their beauty. The scars are made using a knife or, more traditionally, stone or shards of glass or coconut shell. The deep wounds are rubbed with toxic plant juices to create swollen welts or "keloids".

Largest lip plates

For the Surma people of Ethiopia, lip plates serve a financial purpose. The process of inserting these plates (made by the women themselves from local clay) begins around a year before marriage and the final size indicates the number of cattle required by the girl's family from her future husband for her hand. The plates can reach 15 cm (6 in) in diameter, which would require a payment of 50 cattle.

Longest neck

The maximum known extension of a human neck is 40 cm (15.75 in). It was created by the successive fitting of copper coils – practised by the women of the Padaung or Kareni tribe of Myanmar as a sign of beauty.

TATTOOS

Most tattooed person

The acme of multi-layered tattooing is represented by the chainsaw-juggling, unicycling, sword-swallowing Lucky Diamond Rich (Australia, b. New Zealand), who has spent more than 1,000 hours having his body modified.

He began with a collection of colourful designs from around the world tattooed over his entire body. Lucky next opted for a 100% covering of black ink, including eyelids, the delicate skin between the toes, down into the ears and even his gums. He is now being tattooed with white designs on top of the black, and coloured designs on top of the white.

Most tattooed senior citizen

Tom Leppard (UK, b. c. 1934), has 99.9% of his body covered in tattoos. Tom opted for a leopard-skin design, with all the skin between the dark spots tattooed saffron yellow. Having lived alone in a cabin on the Isle of Skye, UK, for 20 years,

Ink-redible tattoos

• **Most bone tattoos:** As of 27 April 2011, Rick "Rico" Genest (Canada) had 139 bones tattooed on his body. By the same date, he also had the **most insect tattoos**: 176

• **Most flag tattoos:** Guinness Rishi (India) was tattooed with 366 tattoos of flags between July 2009 and July 2011

• **Most jigsaw-puzzle piece tattoos:** Artist The Enigma (USA, aka Paul Lawrence) had 2,123 tattoos in the shape of jigsaw-puzzle pieces as of 13 April 2011

Most tattooed woman ever

On 31 March 2011, licensed medical practitioners confirmed that Cynthia J Martell (USA, 1958–2011) had tattoos covering slightly more than 96% of her body. Cynthia – from Parker in Arizona, USA – was regularly tattooed for five years to attain her record-breaking skin coverage.

FACT:
Cynthia's palms and the soles of her feet were the only areas of her body that had no tattoos

he moved to one of the island's villages, Broadford, in 2008. The **most tattooed female senior citizen** is Isobel Varley (UK, b. 1938), who had covered 93% of her body with tattoos, as revealed on the set of *Lo Show dei Record*, in Milan, Italy, on 25 April 2009.

Longest tattoo session (multiple people)

Michael Cann (USA) tattooed multiple people in a marathon session lasting 35 hr 8 min at Skipass 2010 in Suffolk, Virginia, USA, from 18 to 19 November 2011. The **longest tattoo session by a team of two** lasted for 50 hours and was achieved

Most pierced tongue

FACT: The tongue has more than 2,000 taste buds on it. And we all have a unique "tongue print".

As of 17 February 2012, Francesco Vacca (USA) of Belleville, New Jersey, USA, had 16 piercings in his tongue. Francesco actually wants to take all of his piercings out... but only so that he can space them out more efficiently. Then he's aiming to fit in double the amount!

by tattooist Tyson Turk and tattooee Chris Elliott (both USA) at the Tyson Turk Body Mod Studio, Texas, USA, on 9–11 September 2011.

Most tattoos in 24 hours by a single artist

Hollis Cantrell (USA) performed 801 tattoos in 24 hours at Artistic Tattoo in Phoenix, Arizona, USA, on 16 November 2008.

The **most tattoos by a single artist in eight hours** is 331 and was achieved by John McManus (USA) at Joker's Tattoo Studio in Louisiana, USA, on 31 October 2008.

PIERCINGS

Most piercings in a lifetime (female)

Since first receiving a skin piercing in January 1997, Elaine Davidson (Brazil/UK) had been pierced a total of 4,225 times as of 8 June 2006. The former restaurant owner is constantly adding and replacing jewellery, mostly in her face; this number reflects her re-piercings.

FACT: Maria is sometimes referred to as "The Mexican Vampire Lady".

Elaine also holds the record for the **most piercings in a single count**. On examination on 4 May 2000, she was found to have a total of 462 piercings: 192 piercings on her facial area including ears, forehead, eyebrows, chin, nose and tongue (30), 56 piercings on her body including stomach, breasts and hands and 214 adorning her pubic area.

The **most pierced man** is Rolf Buchholz (Germany). Rolf had 453 piercings, including 158 around his lips, as of 22 February 2012.

Most 18-gauge surgical needle piercings

Jeremy Stroud (USA) had 1,197 18-gauge surgical needle body piercings inserted into his body at the Tyson Turk Tattoo Studio in Arlington, Texas, USA, on 2 May 2009. Jeremy broke the previous record with his back alone, which received 901 needles.

Subdermal (under the skin) forehead implants (and on the chest and forearms)

SNAP SHOT

• Francesco's piercer, who also came along to the photo shoot, knows another GWR body mod legend – Lucky Diamond Rich.

• Francesco is a licensed bounty hunter in his home state of New Jersey, USA.

Nine piercings in right eyebrow

Exposed titanium horn implants

Ten piercings in left eyebrow

Four upper-nose bars

Dental implants (fangs)

Both earlobes expanded with a "septum"

Most body modifications ◆

María José Cristerna (Mexico) has undergone a total of 49 body modifications, including a range of transdermal implants on her forehead, chest and arms, and multiple piercings in her eyebrows, lips, nose, tongue, earlobes, belly button and nipples. With 96% of her skin surface tattooed, María is also the **most tattooed woman (current)**.

One inner nose ring

Three lip piercings

Tattoos cover around 95% of her body

Five chest implants

COSMETIC SURGERY

Tattoos, piercings and body modifications aren't for everyone, of course. The quest for idealized beauty is seeing more and more people turn to cosmetic surgery. GWR takes a look at the world of nips and tucks.

TOP FIVE COSMETIC SURGICAL PROCEDURES

In 2011, there were more than 13 million cosmetic surgery operations in the USA:

1. Breast augmentation: 307,180 (up 4% from 2010)

2. Nose re-shaping: 243,772 (down 3% from 2010)

3. Liposuction: 204,702 (up 1% from 2010)

4. Eyelid surgery: 196,286 (down 6% from 2010)

5. Facelift: 119,026 (up 5% from 2010)

Kristina Ray (Russia) has had more than 100 silicone injections to boost the size of her lips.

TOP FIVE COSMETIC "MINIMALLY INVASIVE" PROCEDURES

When it comes to less dramatic surgery, botox implants are way out in front:

1. Botox: 5,670,788 (up 5% from 2010)

2. "Soft-tissue" implants (e.g. collagen): 1,891,158 (up 7% from 2010)

3. Chemical peel: 1,110,464 (down 3% from 2010)

4. Laser hair removal: 1,078,612 (up 15% from 2010)

5. Microdermabrasion: 900,439 (up 9% from 2010)

Source: American Society of Plastic Surgeons. Figures for 2011

LARGEST...

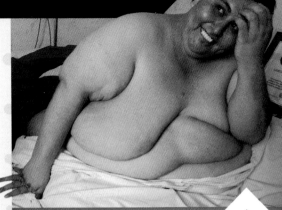

Heaviest person to finish a marathon
Kelly Gneiting (USA) completed the 2011 Los Angeles Marathon weighing 181.44 kg (400 lb; 28 st 8 lb) in California, USA, on 20 March 2011. He finished in 9 hr 48 min 52 sec.

HEAVIEST...

Man
The heaviest person in medical history was Jon Brower Minnoch (USA, 1941–83), who had suffered from obesity since childhood. He was 185 cm (6 ft 1 in) tall and weighed 178 kg (392 lb; 28 st) in 1963, 317 kg (700 lb; 50 st) in 1966 and 442 kg (975 lb; 69 st 9 lb) in September 1976.

In March 1978, Minnoch was admitted to University Hospital in Seattle, Washington, USA, where consultant endocrinologist Dr Robert Schwartz calculated that he must have weighed more than 635 kg (1,400 lb; 100 st), a great deal of which was water accumulation due to his congestive heart failure.

Woman
Rosalie Bradford (USA, 1943–2006) was claimed to have registered a peak weight of 544 kg (1,200 lb; 85 st 9 lb) in January 1987.

The **heaviest woman living** is Pauline Potter (USA) of Sacramento, California, USA, who weighed 291.6 kg (643 lb; 46 st) on 13 May 2010.

Twins
Billy Leon (1946–79) and Benny Loyd (1946–2001) McCrary, alias McGuire (both USA), were average in size until the age of six. In November 1978, Billy and Benny weighed 337 kg (743 lb; 53 st) and 328 kg

(723 lb; 51 st 9 lb) respectively. Each brother had waists measuring 213 cm (84 in) in circumference.

TALLEST...

Actor
Matthew McGrory (USA, 1973–2005) stood 229 cm (7 ft 6 in) tall. His film career began in 1999 with *The Dead Hate the Living!* (USA, 2000). He also featured in Tim Burton's *Big Fish* (USA, 2003), playing the role of Karl the Giant alongside Ewan McGregor.

Two actors hold the title for the **tallest actor in a leading role**, with a height of 194 cm (6 ft 5 in). Christopher Lee (UK) has played most of the major horror characters in films since 1958. Vince Vaughn (USA) had his first leading role in *Return to Paradise* (USA, 1998).

Four women share the record for the **tallest actress in a leading role**. Margaux Hemingway (USA, 1955–96), Sigourney Weaver (USA), Geena Davis (USA) and Brigitte Nielsen (Denmark) all stand 182 cm (6 ft) tall.

Basketball player
Suleiman Ali Nashnush (1943–91) was 245 cm (8 ft 0.25 in) tall when he played for the Libyan national team in 1962.

Heaviest man living
The heaviest living man is Manuel Uribe (Mexico), who weighed 444.6 kg (980 lb; 70 st) as of March 2012. At his absolute heaviest, in January 2006, Manuel peaked at 560 kg (1,235 lb; 88 st 3 lb). Since then – and with medical assistance – he has gradually been able to lose weight. Although he has been bed-bound since 2002, Manuel married his second wife, Claudia Solis, in 2008.

Tallest tribe
The Tutsi (also known as the Watutsi) are the tallest major tribe in the world. Young adult males of the tribe average 180 cm (6 ft) in height. The Tutsi are native to Rwanda and Burundi in Central Africa.

Know sumo
• Japan's favourite sport, sumo is a form of wrestling. It originated centuries ago.

• Sumo bouts take place on a raised ring called a *doyhō*.

• The wrestler (or *rikishi*, meaning "strong man") who leaves the ring first – or touches the floor with anything other than the soles of the feet – loses.

• A sumo champion is called a *yokozuna*. Champions never lose titles, but are expected to step down when their performances worsen.

Heaviest sportswoman
The heaviest competing sportswoman is Sharran Alexander of London, UK, who weighed 203.21 kg (448 lb; 32 st) on 15 December 2011. Sharran actively competes around the world as an amateur sumo wrestler and is recognized by the British Sumo Federation in the UK. The 180-cm (6-ft) sumo star is looking to retire from competition level in 2013, when she will turn 48 years old.

FACT: Sharran dines on pasta, pasties, Corn Flakes, chicken and plenty of rice – 5,000 calories a day!

FACT: To date, Sharran has won four gold medals in sumo competitions around the world.

Tallest living twins

Michael and James Lanier (USA) stand 223 cm (7 ft 3 in) tall. Ann and Claire Recht (USA) are the **tallest female twins**, at 201 cm (6 ft 7 in). Both sets of twins are identical.

Boxer

The tallest professional boxer was Gogea Mitu (Romania, 1914–36). In 1935, he was 223 cm (7 ft 4 in) tall and weighed 148 kg (327 lb; 23 st 5 lb). John Rankin, who won a fight in New Orleans, Louisiana, USA, in November 1967, measured 223 cm tall too. Jim Cully (Ireland), "The Tipperary Giant" who fought as a boxer and wrestled in the 1940s, was reputedly also this height.

Crown prince

The current heir apparent to the Spanish throne, Príncipe de Asturias, Don Felipe de Borbón y Grecia (Spain), stands at 197 cm (6 ft 5.5 in).

Tallest teenager ever

Aged 17, Robert Wadlow (USA, 1918–40) was 245 cm (8 ft 0.38 in) tall. He grew up to become the **tallest man ever** – an incredible 272 cm (8 ft 11.1 in) when measured on 27 June 1940. He's pictured above, aged 18, with his family, and on the right, aged 10, with an 11-year-old boy.

Tallest man

Sultan Kösen (Turkey) is the tallest person alive today. He was last measured in Ankara, Turkey, on 8 February 2011, at the age of 26 years, when he stood at an incredible 251 cm (8 ft 3 in).

This photo shoot took place on a basketball court in Manhattan, New York, USA. Sultan is a big basketball fan – as a teenager, he was signed to the Galatasaray team but proved *too* big to play!

Ice hockey player (NHL)

At 205 cm (6 ft 9 in) tall, Zdeno Chára (Slovakia), of the Boston Bruins (USA), is the tallest player in National Hockey League history.

Tallest female teenager

Anna Haining Bates, born Anna Haining Swan (Canada, 1846–88), had grown to 241 cm (7 ft 11 in) by the time she was 15 years old. And as an adult, she set another world record – see p.70.

Professional model

Amazon Eve (USA) topped out at 201 cm (6 ft 7.4 in) when measured on 25 February 2011.

Grand Slam tennis player

Ivo Karlović (Croatia) stands at 208 cm (6 ft 10 in), taller than any other Grand Slam player in history.

Juan Martín Del Potro (Argentina) measured 198 cm (6 ft 6 in) when he triumphed in the 2009 US Open in New York, USA, on 14 September 2009, making him the **tallest tennis player ever to win a Grand Slam**.

Tallest living woman

Yao Defen (China, right) was 231 cm (7 ft 7 in) tall when last documented. Zeng Jinlian (China) (1964–82) measured 248 cm (8 ft 1.6 in) when she died, making her the **tallest woman ever**.

SHOOT TO P.250 FOR BASKETBALL WORLD-BEATERS

NATIONS BY HEIGHT

According to Statistics Netherlands, the Dutch are, on average, the world's **tallest citizens**, reaching 181 cm (5 ft 11.2 in); the **shortest citizens** are the Cambodians at 160.3 cm (5 ft 3.1 in).

Cambodians: 160.3 cm
Average: 168.1 cm
Dutch: 181 cm

NATIONS BY WEIGHT

Body Mass Index (BMI) is a calculation made by dividing your body weight by the square of your height. It was devised by Adolphe Quetelet (Belgium) in the 19th century to track the problem of obesity in the population. According to the Global Burden of Metabolic Risk Factors of Chronic Diseases Collaborating Group, Nauru in the South Pacific has the heaviest citizens, with an average BMI of 34.4; Bangladesh has the lightest citizens, averaging 20.4.

Bangladeshis: 20.4
Average: 25.5
Nauruans: 34.4

Sources: Interbasket; Global Burden of Metabolic Risk Factors of Chronic Diseases Collaborating Group

SHORTEST...

Shortest siblings

Bridgette and Brad Jordan (both USA) are 69 cm (2 ft 3 in) and 98 cm (3 ft 2.5 in) tall respectively, giving them a combined height of 167 cm (5 ft 5.5 in). Their reduced height is caused by the condition Majewski osteodysplastic primordial dwarfism type II. They both enjoy full and active lives; Bridgette wants to become a model.

Shortest man

In February 2012, Guinness World Records travelled to the Nepalese capital of Kathmandu to investigate the case of a 72-year-old man supposedly standing 5 cm (2 in) shorter than the current shortest living man, Junrey Balawing (Philippines) at 59.9 cm (1 ft 11.5 in, or 23.5 in). Following a series of measurements (see below) at the CIWEC Travel Clinic Medicine Center in the Lainchaur district, Chandra Bahadur Dangi from Reemkholi, Nepal, did indeed prove to be shorter, averaging 54.6 cm (1 ft 9.5 in, or 21.5 in). This also makes him the **shortest man ever measured**.

Shortest woman

On 16 December 2011, former **shortest living teenager** Jyoti Amge (India) reached the age of 18 and so took the title of **shortest living woman**. Dr Manoj Pahukar, an orthopaedic consultant, performed the official measurements at the Wockhardt Hospital in Nagpur, India, in the presence of GWR's Rob Molloy. Jyoti's average height was 62.8 cm (2 ft 0.7 in) – 6.2 cm (2.3 in) shorter than the previous record holder.

Measuring stature

When assessing absolute "shortest" and "tallest" claims, Guinness World Records insists on making a series of measurements over the duration of a day. The principal assessment is standing height, or stature, which is the length of the claimant standing as straight as possible, measured using a stadiometer (a ruler with a vertical sliding head-piece). Three measurements are taken then averaged.

Shortest twins

Matyus and Béla Matina (1903–c. 1935) of Budapest, Hungary, who later became naturalized American citizens, both measured 76 cm (30 in). Primordial dwarfs, they appeared in *The Wizard of Oz* (USA, 1939), billed as Mike and Ike Rogers.

The **shortest identical twin sisters** are 124.4-cm (4-ft 1-in) Dorene Williams and Darlene McGregor (both USA, b. 1949).

Shortest married couple

Brazilian couple Douglas Maistre Breger da Silva and Claudia Pereira Rocha measured 90 cm (2 ft 11 in) and 93 cm (3 ft 0.6 in) respectively when married on 27 October 1998, in Curitiba, Brazil.

Shortest newborn baby

Nisa Juarez (USA) was born on 20 July 2002, measuring just 24 cm (9.4 in) long, at the Children's Hospital and Clinic in Minneapolis, Minnesota, USA. (The average newborn length in the USA is 43 cm, or 17 in.) Born 108 days premature, Nisa weighed 320 g (11.3 oz) – more than 10 times the average weight of 3.5 kg (7 lb). She was discharged from hospital on 6 December 2002.

Recent "shortest" record holders

He Pingping
74.6 cm (2 ft 5.3 in)

Edward "Niño" Hernández
70.2 cm (2 ft 3.6 in)

Khagendra
Thapa Magar
67 cm (2 ft 2.4 in)

Junrey Balawing
59.9 cm (1 ft 11.5 in)

Chandra Bahadur Dangi
54.6 cm (1 ft 9.5 in)

FACT:
Musters, aka "Princess Pauline", was 30 cm (12 in) at birth; by the age of 19, she had only doubled in size.

SHORT AND SHORTER

The difference in height between He Pingping and Chandra Bahadur Dangi is illustrated here actual size, with their fellow record-breakers included for comparison.

CERTIFICATE

The shortest living man is Junrey Balawing (Philippines, b. 12 June 1993) as verified in Sindangan, Zamboanga del Norte, Philippines on 12 June 2011

GUINNESS WORLD RECORDS LTD

Lightest person

Lucia Zarate (Mexico, 1863–89) of San Carlos, Mexico, an emaciated ateleiotic dwarf who stood 67 cm (2 ft 2 in) tall, weighed 1.1 kg (2 lb 6 oz) at birth and only 2.1 kg (4 lb 11 oz) at the age of 17. She had fattened up to 5.9 kg (13 lb) by the time of her 20th birthday.

Most variable stature

Adam Rainer (Austria, 1899–1950) measured 118 cm (3 ft 10.5 in) at the age of 21. He then suddenly started growing at a rapid rate and by 1931, he had reached the height of 218 cm (7 ft 1.8 in). Sadly, he became so weak as a result of his dramatic growth spurt that he was bedridden for the rest of his life.

Shortest actor in a leading adult role

The Indian actor Ajay Kumar, who performed in the lead role of his debut

Junrey Balawing

In June 2011, shortly after we went to press with *Guinness World Records 2012*, our adjudicators visited the home of Junrey Balawing in the Philippines to confirm him as the **shortest living man**. Measured three times on the advent of his 18th birthday, Balawing reached 59.9 cm (1 ft 11.5 in) and claimed the title from Khagendra Thapa Magar from Nepal. Yet he held the record for less than a year, ceding the title to another Nepali, Chandra Bahadur Dangi, as this year's book goes to print.

feature film, *Albhutha Dweep* (India, 2005), measures 76 cm (2 ft 6 in) in height.

Tamara de Treaux (USA, 1959–90) was, at 77 cm (2 ft 6.3 in) tall, the **shortest actress ever to appear in a leading adult role**. Her most celebrated (shared) role was as E.T. in Steven Spielberg's *E.T. The Extra-Terrestrial* (USA, 1982).

Shortest stuntman

Kiran Shah (UK, b. Kenya) is the shortest professional stuntman now working in the movie industry, standing 126 cm (4 ft 1.7 in) when measured on 20 October 2003. He has appeared in 52 movies since 1976 and performed stunts in 31 of them. He doubled as Elijah Wood in the *Lord of the Rings* trilogy.

Dwarfism

An adult is regarded as a dwarf if he or she is less than 147 cm (4 ft 10 in) in height.

• Body growth is stimulated by the activation of different hormones. If this process is disrupted, the individual can experience delayed or extremely slow body growth – resulting in dwarfism.

• There are around 200 forms of the condition.

• Pygmies – native to various regions worldwide, including central Africa, the Philippines and Brazil – also have a reduced height, but not because of dwarfism. Their smaller size is hereditary.

Shortest facts

Pictured here are the eight shortest record holders from the past five years.

• Over this period, the male record has fallen an incredible 20 cm (7.8 in).

• In the female category, height has dropped nearly 10 cm (4 in).

• At the (unconfirmed) age of 72, Chandra Bahadur Dangi, the current **shortest living man**, is by far the oldest person to take this record.

• Extreme short stature is usually the result of a medical condition. Each person in our line-up has a form of dwarfism.

Heights to one decimal place

75 cm
60 cm
40 cm
20 cm
0 cm

Elif Kocaman
72.6 cm (2 ft 4.5 in)

Bridgette Jordan
69 cm (2 ft 3 in)

Jyoti Amge
62.8 cm (2 ft 0.7 in)

GUINNESS WORLD RECORDS 2012
BURSTING WITH AMAZING NEW RECORDS

He Pingping
74.6 cm (2 ft 5.3 in)

Elif Kocaman
72.6 cm (2 ft 4.5 in)

Edward "Niño" Hernández
70.2 cm (2 ft 3.6 in)

Bridgette Jordan
69 cm (2 ft 3 in)

Khagendra Thapa Magar
67 cm (2 ft 2.4 in)

Jyoti Amge
62.8 cm (2 ft 0.7 in)

Junrey Balawing
59.9 cm (1 ft 11.5 in)

Increases in 1-cm increments

Chandra Bahadur Dangi
54.6 cm (1 ft 9.5 in)

CONTENTS

Fastest time to fit into a box

Contortionist extraordinaire Skye Broberg (New Zealand) crammed herself into a 52 x 45 x 45-cm (20.4 x 17.7 x 17.7-in) box in just 4.78 seconds at the Melia Whitehouse Hotel in London, UK, on 15 September 2011. Once Skye's body was entirely inside the box, the lid was closed from the outside and the clock was stopped.

Along with fellow New Zealanders Nele Siezen and Jola Siezen, Skye also set the record for the **longest time spent in a box by three contortionists**. The elastic trio remained inside a 66 x 68.5 x 55.8-cm (26 x 27 x 22-in) box for 6 min 13.52 sec on the set of *NZ Smashes Guinness World Records* at the Sylvia Park shopping mall in Auckland, New Zealand, on 20 September 2009.

HOW HEAVY CAN WE LIFT?

NEW WORLD RECORD HOLDERS OF SUPER HEAVYWEIGHT CATEGORY

472.5 kg
HOSSEIN REZAZADEH (Iran)
Sydney, Australia (2000)

465 kg
RONNY WELLER (Germany)
Reisa, Germany (1998)

462.5 kg
ANDREI CHEMERKIN (Russia)
Chiang Mai, Thailand (1996)

457.5 kg
ALEXANDER KURLOVICH (Belarus)
Istanbul, Turkey (1994)

450 kg
ANDREI CHEMERKIN
Sokolov, Czech Rep. (1994)

442.5 kg
RONNY WELLER
Melbourne, Australia (1993)

In 1993 and 1998, the weight categories were reclassified – therefore Leonid Taranenko's 1988 record of 475 kg is no longer recognized.

1. The clean and jerk is the heaviest lift over the head. Grab the bar, palms down, with a shoulder-wide grip.

2. The clean – pulling the barbell to shoulder height – must be done in one continuous movement. So, without stopping...

3... extend the body, pulling the bar upwards. At the same time, bend at the knees to descend under the bar, flip the wrists and bring the bar to the clavicle.

4. From the squat position, stand up straight with the bar, completing the "clean" part of the two-part lift.

5. Bend at the knee to begin the "jerk." (There are various jerk options – pictured is a "split jerk" with the feet apart.)

6. Finish the lift by standing upright, raising the bar and holding it above the head with locked arms.

What is the heaviest weight a human can lift?

The super heavyweight category of Olympic weightlifting can, arguably, be considered the ultimate test of a human's lifting ability. Powerlifters may well disagree, but whoever holds the total world record in the over-105-kg category – the combined weight of a snatch lift plus the clean and jerk – can rightly consider themselves the strongest in the world. But it's not just about brute strength – technique is equally as important. So what's the lifting limit in competition?

Height: The average height of recent record-breaking lifters (see right) is 1.84 m (6 ft). The taller the lifter, the more difficult it is to stand up from the squat position (see steps 3–4, right).

Heart: Weightlifting is anaerobic – meaning that it does not need oxygen. This means the cardiopulmonary aspect of the training is less important than the musculoskeletal.

Bodyweight: In the over-105-kg category, there is no upper weight limit for the athlete, so any increase in bodyweight is justified as long as it results in even a small increase in performance, especially in the clean and jerk – it could make the difference between gold and silver. Ideally, of course, it will be as muscle, not fat.

Body shape: Thick and solid barrel-shape; muscle needs to be developed only in those areas that need it.

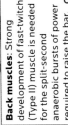

Back muscles: Strong development of fast-twitch (Type II) muscle is needed for the split-second anaerobic bursts of power required to raise the bar.

472.5 kg

Hossein Rezazadeh

Double Olympic champion and the athlete dubbed the "strongest man in the world" by his peers, Iran's Hossein Rezazadeh holds the total lifting record in the over-105-kg category (athletes compete in different classes depending on their body mass). He achieved this twice in the Olympics (2000 and 2004) with snatches of 212.5 and 210 kg, and clean and jerks of 260 and 263.5 kg.

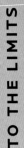

GUINNESS WORLD RECORDS™

Limbs: Short arms and legs make better levers (but too short and the corresponding reduction in bodyweight means the risk of dropping down a category in competition).

Support belts

Weightlifting rules allow competitors to wear a belt – no wider than 12 cm (4.72 in) – outside their clothing, to provide support and protection. The belt stiffens the torso and increases intra-abdominal pressure, allowing the muscles to work more efficiently; it also gives the torso more of an elastic "bounce" during lifts.

Leg muscles: The quadriceps and hamstrings work with the back muscles (spinal erectors) and the glutes to provide most of the lifting power.

Stance: Bad positioning and technique can effectively add weight to a lift: moving the bar just 1 cm (0.4 in) away from the vertical (as opposed to lifting straight up) adds a load of up to 4.8 kg to the total.

Mobility: Getting the body *under* the bar during the "clean" is just as important as getting the bar *over* the head. Lifters must be flexible and nimble enough to react quickly.

Feet: Flexibility is needed to move the feet through a range of movements. Approved "lifting shoes" provide stability, keep the foot at the optimal angle and help balance the lifter during holds.

475 kg
LEONID TARANENKO (USSR)
Canberra, Australia (1988)

472.5 kg
ALEXANDER KURLOVICH
Ostrava, Czech Rep. (1987)

467.5 kg
ANTONIO KRASTEV (Bulgaria)
Reims, France (1987)

465 kg
ALEXANDER GUNYASHEV (USSR)
Reims, France (1984)

Rezazadeh's total record of 472.5 kg has stood for more than a decade (although his eight-year reign as snatch world record holder ended in November 2011 when fellow Iranian, Behdad Salimikordasiabi, lifted 214 kg).

Combining the heaviest-ever results of both types of lift – a 216-kg snatch by Antonio Krastev (Bulgaria) in 1987 and a 266-kg clean and jerk by Leonid Taranenko (USSR) in 1988, both of which are now considered "historical" following the recategorizing of classes – gives a theoretical total of 482 kg. As simplistic as this calculation is, it certainly gives current contenders something to aspire to.

Zhou Lulu

Lifting is not just for the boys – women have been competing at Olympic level since 2000. Pictured is Zhou Lulu (China), the current world record holder for the "total" in the over-75-kg category – the heaviest female class. She achieved a snatch of 146 kg and a clean and jerk of 182 kg to give a world-beating total of 328 kg at the World Weightlifting Championships in Paris, France, on 13 November 2011.

328 kg

FOR MORE SPORTING GREATS, SEE PP.230–277

STRENGTH

HEAVIEST...

Vehicle lifted with the breath

On 23 July 2011 at the Arrowhead Mall in Muskogee, Oklahoma, USA, Brian Jackson (USA) lifted a 2011 Ford Festiva weighing 1,143 kg (2,520 lb) by blowing into a bag that, when inflated, raised the vehicle off the ground.

Weight lifted by both eye sockets

Yang Guang He (China) lifted two buckets of water weighing 23.5 kg (51 lb 12.96 oz) with both eye sockets on the set of Lo Show dei Record in Milan, Italy, on 28 April 2011. Yang rested hooks on the bones under his eyes and connected them to the buckets.

Combined weight of aircraft pulled simultaneously

More than 200 Hong Kong citizens pulled four aircraft weighing 474.72 metric tonnes (1,046,578 lb) for 50 m (164 ft) at Hong Kong International Airport in Hong Kong, China, on 17 March 2011. The aircraft were a Boeing 747-400, an Airbus 330-343, an Airbus 300-200 and a Zlin Z-242 L, and the feat took 2 min 53 sec.

Weight lifted by nipples

Sage Werbock (USA), aka "The Great Nippulini", lifted a 31.9-kg (70.5-lb) weight from his pierced nipples in Hulmeville, Pennsylvania, USA, on 26 September 2009.

Vehicle pulled by a woman with her hair

Rani Raikwar (India) pulled an 8,835.5-kg (19,479-lb) truck on the set of Guinness World Records – Ab India Todega in Lalitpur, Bhopal, India, on 3 March 2011. Ajit Kumar Singh (India) holds the record for **heaviest vehicle pulled by a man with his hair**. He pulled a 9,385-kg (20,690-lb) truck in Nawada, Bihar, India, on 21 September 2010.

Weight lifted by tongue

Thomas Blackthorne (UK) lifted a 12.5-kg (27-lb 8.96-oz) weight hooked through his tongue on the set of El Show Olímpico, in Mexico City, Mexico, on 1 August 2008.

Fastest 100 m light aircraft pull

Montystar Agarawal (India) pulled a light aircraft 100 m (328 ft) in 29.84 seconds on the set of Guinness World Records – Ab India Todega in Baramati, Maharashtra, India, on 23 February 2011.

Most World's Strongest Man wins

Nicknamed "The Dominator", "Super Mariusz" and "Pudzian", Mariusz Pudzianowski (Poland) has won the World's Strongest Man competition five times: in 2002, 2003, 2005, 2007 and 2008. Magnús Ver Magnússon and Jón Páll Sigmarsson (both Iceland) have each won the title four times.

5 wins

FACT:
Events in the World's Strongest Man include the farmer's walk, shown here.

Deadlift in one hour (male)

Nick Molloy (UK) deadlifted 45,702 kg (100,755 lb) in an hour at the White Swan pub in London, UK, on 25 May 2011. For his total, Molloy completed 164 repetitions of a 75.5-kg (166-lb) barbell and 490 repetitions of a 68-kg (150-lb) barbell to reach his total.

Deadlift in one minute (male)

Markus Rücker (Germany) deadlifted 4,680 kg (10,317 lb) at the Marktplatz in Eilenburg, Germany, on 13 June 2011. Rücker lifted a bar and weighted plates, with a combined weight of 120 kg (264 lb), for 39 repetitions.

MOST...

Vehicles to run over the stomach

Tom Owen (USA) had nine pick-up trucks, each weighing between 3,000 kg (6,614 lb) and 4,000 kg (8,818 lb), run over his stomach on the set of Lo Show dei Record, in Milan, Italy, on 26 April 2009.

Consecutive bench presses underwater

Marcello Paredi (Italy) achieved 20 bench presses while holding his breath underwater, on the set of Lo Show dei Record in Rome, Italy, on 25 February 2010. His barbell weighed 50 kg (110 lb).

Mariusz's wins and near misses...

• 2000: Finishes fourth, after first place in the car lift and second in the power stairs.

• 2001: Misses the event while in jail for assault.

• 2002: Wins first title after coming second in his qualifying heat.

• 2003: Wins with record points score of 66.

• 2006: Leads for two days, but is edged out in the Atlas stones, the last event on the final day, by Phil Pfister (USA).

• 2008: Clinches title by beating Derek Poundstone (USA) in the Atlas stones to disappoint the American crowd in Charleston, Virginia.

• 2009: Finishes second and retires to start career in mixed martial arts.

Fastest time to push a car one mile

On 28 February 2011, Konda Sahadev (India) pushed a Tata Winger van one mile (1.61 km) down Shamshabad Airport Road in Hyderabad, India, in 11 min 39 sec. The van weighed 2,700 kg (5,952 lb).

Heaviest aircraft pulled over 100 m by a wheelchair team

A team of Belgian wheelchair users from Blijf Actief (Stay Active) pulled an aircraft weighing 67.19 metric tonnes (148,128.59 lb) at Melsbroek Air Base in Brussels, Belgium, on 29 May 2011. The team consisted of 84 connected individuals who pulled a C-130 Hercules without stopping, for nearly four minutes.

FASTEST...

Farmer's walk over 20 m
On the set of *CCTV Guinness World Records* in Beijing, China, on 5 December 2011, Laurence Shahlaei (UK) completed a 20-m (66-ft) farmer's walk (see p.84) in 6.73 seconds, carrying a 150-kg (330-lb) weight in each hand. Laurence won England's Strongest Man competition in 2009.

20 m carrying 300 kg on shoulders
Derek Boyer (Australia) carried a 300-kg (661-lb) weight between his shoulders for 20 m (66 ft) in 6.88 seconds on the Gold Coast in Queensland, Australia, on 2 September 2011.

20 m carrying a car on the shoulders
Žydrunas Savickas (Lithuania) carried a car 20 m (66 ft) strapped to his shoulders in 14.44 seconds on the set of *Lo Show dei Record*, in Milan, Italy, on 10 March 2011.

Bus-pull over 50 m by an individual
Jarno Hams (Netherlands) pulled a bus weighing 17.2 tonnes (37,920 lb) over 50 m (164 ft) in 1 min 13.12 sec on the set of *CCTV Guinness World Records Special* in Beijing, China, on 16 August 2011. Jarno has won Holland's Strongest Man competition on six occasions, most recently in 2010.

LONGEST...

Time holding a 500-kg weight with shoulders
Kevin Fast (Canada) held a 500-kg (1,102.31-lb) weight on his shoulders for 1 min 1.4 sec on the set of *CCTV Guinness World Records Special* in Beijing, China, on 19 August 2011.

Time restraining two aircraft
Using ropes, Chad Netherland (USA) prevented two Cessna planes from taking off by pulling in opposite directions for 1 min 0.6 sec at Richard I. Bong Airport in Wisconsin, USA, on 7 July 2007.

Stacked benches held between the teeth
For 10 seconds, Huang Changzhun (China) held 17 benches between his teeth on the set of *CCTV Guinness World Records Special* in Beijing, China, on 19 August 2011.

Weight lifted by arm curls in one hour
In Castlebar, County Mayo, Ireland, on 12 November 2011, Keith Cresham (Ireland) used arm curls to lift 29,570.5 kg (65,191.8 lb) in one hour. Keith completed 1,253 repetitions of 23.6 kg (52.02 lb) during the record attempt.

Chin-ups in 24 hours
Lucas Garel (Canada) completed 5,045 chin ups in 24 hours at Fitness Force gym in Keswick, Ontario, Canada, on 17–18 July 2011.

Consecutive 90° push-ups
Starting from a headstand, Jesus Villa (USA) completed 13 consecutive push-ups, attaining a 90° angle at the elbow on each, in Las Vegas, Nevada, USA, on 18 September 2011.

World's Strongest Woman wins
Aneta Florczyk (Poland) has won the World's Strongest Woman competition on four occasions, in 2003, 2005, 2006 and 2008. The annual event is staged by the International Federation of Strength Athletes.

PLEASE DON'T TRY THIS WITH A FRIEND – YOU NEED SPECIALIST TRAINING

Heaviest barbell lifted by a pair
Matthias Steiner and Almir Velagić (both Germany) lifted a barbell weighing 333.3 kg (734.8 lb) in Wiesbaden, Germany, on 5 February 2011.

FACT: The duo had to each lift the bar simultaneously above their heads and lock their arms.

FOR WEIGHTY HUMANS, TURN TO P.78

HEAVIEST DEADLIFT

TWO-ARM
455 kg (1,003 lb)
Andy Bolton (UK)
4 November 2006

ONE-ARM
301 kg (663 lb 8 oz)
Hermann Goerner (Germany)
29 October 1920

ONE-FINGER
116.90 kg (354.72 lb)
Benik Israelyan (Armenia)
11 June 2011

LITTLE-FINGER
104.43 kg (230 lb 3 oz)
Kristian Holm (Norway)
3 November 2008

MOST PUSH-UPS IN ONE MINUTE CARRYING...

40 lb pack Paddy Doyle (UK)	60 lb pack Neil Bryant (Australia)	80 lb pack Paddy Doyle (UK)	100 lb pack Paddy Doyle (UK)
61	50	38	34

MOST WEIGHT LIFTED IN ONE HOUR...

BENCH PRESS:	138,480 kg
BARBELL ROWS:	36,384 kg
DUMBBELL ROWS:	32,730 kg
LATERAL RAISES:	19,600 kg

All held by multiple record holder Eamonn Keane (Ireland).

MOST PULL-UPS

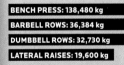

1 hr	= 993	16 Nov 2011
6 hr	= 3,288	23 Jul 2011
12 hr	= 4,020	23 Jul 2011

All set by Stephen Hyland (UK) in Stoneleigh, Surrey, UK.

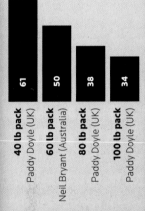

TEAMWORK

LARGEST ENSEMBLES

- **Air guitar:** On 22 September 2011, a group of 2,377 air-guitar aficionados performed at an event organized by San Manuel Indian Bingo & Casino (USA) in Highland, California, USA.
- **Carol singers:** 15,111 singers performed eight Christmas carols at the Hong Myung-bo Charity Soccer Game in Seoul, South Korea, on 25 December 2010, in an event organized by the Hong Myung-bo Foundation (South Korea).
- **Choir:** The Art of Living (India) assembled a 121,440-strong choir who sang in unison in Perungalathur, Chennai, India, on 30 January 2011.
- **Gospel choir:** 1,138 gospel singers performed 17 songs in an event organized by Mano Ezoh (Germany) at the Olympiahalle, Munich, Germany, on 15 October 2011.
- **Human beatboxers:** A group of 2,081 human beatboxers

– including artists Shlomo and Testament (both UK), and staff at Google (Ireland) – performed at the Convention Centre in Dublin, Ireland, on 14 November 2011.
- **Ukulele players:** On 20 August 2011, a group of 1,547 ukulele players strummed "Leende Guldbruna Ögon", by Vikingarna, in Helsingborg, Sweden, in an event organized by ABF, Folkuniversitetet and Studieförbundet Vuxenskolan (all Sweden).
- **Violinists:** 4,645 violinists played at Changhua Stadium, Chinese Taipei, China, on 17 September 2011, in a performance set up by the Changhua County Government.
- **Whistlers (one venue):** 672 members of the Make-A-Wish Club at the Nazareth Area Middle School whistled "God Bless America" and "America the Beautiful" in the Andrew S Leh Stadium at the Nazareth Area High School in Nazareth, Philadelphia, USA.

Most people on one motorcycle

The greatest number of people mounted on one moving motorcycle is 54 and was achieved by the Army Service Corps Motorcycle Display Team "Tornadoes" (all India) at Air Force Station Yelahanka in Bangalore, India, on 28 November 2010. The men rode a single 500 cc Royal Enfield motorcycle a distance of 1,100 m (3,609 ft) and were supervised by Major M K Jha. The overladen motorcycle was driven by Havi Idar Ram Pal Yadav and was modified, as permitted in the GWR guidelines, with a platform around the edge to carry all the riders. None of the participants touched the ground during the attempt.

Most people crammed into a Mini Cooper

The maximum number of people to have squeezed into a Mini Cooper (old model) is 21 and was last achieved by female members of the Caless Dance School (Japan) on the set of *100 Beautiful Women Who Have Guinness World Records*, at the Shiodome Nihon TV Studios in Tokyo, Japan, on 5 May 2011. How do you fit 21 dancers into a Mini Cooper? Twelve in the back of the car, eight in the front and one person in the boot! This superlative feat of tight-fitting equalled an existing record, achieved by 21 students from INTI College Subang Jaya at INTI College Subang Jaya Campus in Selangor, Malaysia, on 17 June 2006.

MOST PEOPLE...

On a theme-park ride (costumed)
A total of 330 riders took to the Steel Force ride in costume at Dorney Park & Wildwater Kingdom in Pennsylvania, USA, on 18 August 2011.

Head shaving at once
On 19 September 2010 in Port Colborne, Ontario, Canada, 57 people shaved their heads at once in an event set up by Nancy Salvage (Canada).

Inside a soap bubble
Fan Yang, Deni Yang and Melody Yang (all Canada) popped 118 people into a soap bubble at the Discovery Science Center in Santa Ana, California, USA, on 4 April 2011.

Wearing underwear
Clad only in their underwear, 2,270 people (all USA) met up at the Utah Undie Run in Salt Lake City, USA, on 24 September 2011.

21 PEOPLE

FACT: You can fit even more people in the new-style Mini – the record is 27, achieved in Eastbourne, UK, on 18 November 2011.

MOST PEOPLE DRESSED AS...

Category	People	Organizer/event	Location	Event date
Pirates	8,734	Angie Butler and the town of Penzance (both UK)	Penzance, Cornwall, UK	26 Jun 2011
Zombies	4,093	New Jersey Zombie Walk (USA)	Asbury Park, New Jersey, USA	30 Oct 2010
Wally/Waldo	3,872	Street Performance World Championship (Ireland)	Dublin, Ireland	19 Jun 2011
Bees	2,176	Yateley and Westfield schools campus (UK)	Hampshire, UK	6 Apr 2011
Skeletons	2,018	Jokers' Masquerade (UK)	Swansea, UK	8 Oct 2011
Comic-book characters	1,530	Opening ceremony of International Animation CCJOY LAND (China)	Changzhou City, Jiangsu Province, China	29 Apr 2011
Star Trek characters	1,040	Official Star Trek Convention	Las Vegas, Nevada, USA	13 Aug 2011
Vampires	1,039	Kings Dominion (USA)	Doswell, Virginia, USA	30 Sep 2011
Turkeys	661	44th Annual Capital One Bank Dallas YMCA Turkey Trot (USA)	Dallas, Texas, USA	24 Nov 2011
Superman	437	Nexen Inc. (Canada)	Calgary, Alberta, Canada	28 Sep 2011
Videogame characters	425	BUYSEASONS, Inc. (USA)	New Berlin, Wisconsin, USA	5 Oct 2011
Garden gnomes	331	Bayview Glen Day Camp (Canada)	Don Mills, Ontario, Canada	19 Jul 2011
Cows	250	Bel Nederland BV, Maud Peters and John Smit (all Netherlands)	Wassenaar, Netherlands	10 Sep 2011
Sunflowers	229	Thorndown Community Infant School and Junior School (both UK)	St Ives, Cornwall, UK	27 May 2011

MASSIVE PARTICIPATION

Records for mass participations can involve literally hundreds of thousands or even millions of attendees, as these great gatherings – the largest in the GWR archive – attest.

The areas of the circles are in direct proportion to the amount of participants.

116.9 million
Largest "stand-up" for charity in one week
"Stand Up Against Poverty"
17–19 October 2008

20 million
Largest religious crowd
Hindu festival of Kumbh Mela, Allahabad (Prayag), Uttar Pradesh, India, 30 January 2001

>8 million
Largest gathering of Sikhs
300th anniversary of the founding of the Sikh Khalsa order, Anandpur Sahib *gurdwara* (Sikh temple), Punjab, India, 13–17 April 1999

2.5 million
Largest annual gathering of women
Attukal Pongala festival, Kerala, India, 10 March 2009

2 million
Largest Muslim pilgrimage
Hajj to Mecca, annually

559,493
Most people jumping (multiple venues)
Science Year launch (UK), 7 September 2001

Most people dressed as Gandhi

On 29 January 2012, a group of 485 children dressed up as Mohandas "Mahatma" Gandhi in Kolkata, India, in an event organized by the charity Training Resource and Care for Kids (TRACKS). The children, all of whom were from disadvantaged backgrounds, were aged 10 to 16 and had been taught about Gandhi's philosophy prior to the attempt. TRACKS has been rehabilitating underprivileged young women and their children since 1991.

FACT:
GWR's Andrea and Lucia checked that all the children remained garbed as Gandhi for a full 10 minutes.

ESCAPOLOGISTS • FUNAMBULISTS • PYROMANIACS

CIRCUS ARTS

Fastest escape from a straitjacket

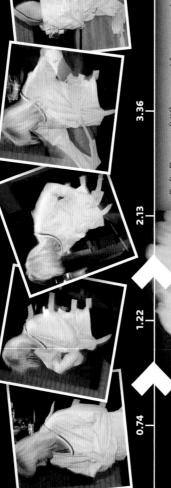

0.74	1.22	2.13	3.36	4.69 SEC

Sofia Romero (UK) escaped from a regulated Posey straitjacket in 4.69 seconds at the Aylestone Leisure Centre in Leicester, UK, on 9 June 2011.

Highest flame by fire-breather

Antonio Restivo (USA) blew himself into the record books with a 8.05-m-high (26-ft 5-in) flame at a warehouse in Las Vegas, Nevada, USA, on 11 January 2011. In fact, Antonio succeeded in hitting the warehouse ceiling with the fire!

FACT: Antonio used liquid paraffin as fuel for his fire-breathing. Definitely don't try this at home!

ACROBATS

Longest neck hang
Rebecca Peache (UK) and Donovan Jones (USA) carried out a neck hang lasting 1 min 12.29 sec for CCTV – *Guinness World Records Special* in Beijing, China, on 14 August 2011.

Farthest indoor aerial trapeze flight
The leader of Russian aerial flying team "The Tur", Sergei Tur, flew 19 m (62 ft 4 in) through the air between two swinging cradles, to be caught by a fellow acrobat. The feat was performed at the Anaheim Pond in Anaheim, California, USA, on 29 July 1998.

First...
• flying return trapeze act
Jules Léotard (France) demonstrated the first flying return trapeze act at Cirque Napoleon in Paris, France, on 12 November 1859.

• triple somersault on the trapeze This feat was first performed in public at the Chicago Coliseum in Illinois, USA, in 1920.

• double-back somersault on the flying return trapeze
Eddie Silbon (UK) performed this feat for the first time at the Paris Hippodrome in Paris, France, in 1879.

• triple-back somersault on the flying return trapeze
The debut performance of a triple-back somersault on the flying trapeze was by Lena Jordan (Latvia) to Lewis Jordan (USA) in Sydney, Australia, in April 1897.

FIRE-BREATHERS

Most flames blown in one breath
The most consecutive flames blown without re-fuelling was 129, by Ambika Niraula (Nepal) in Kathmandu, Nepal, on 27 February 2012.

Most torches put out in 30 seconds
On 21 February 2011, Hubertus Wawra (Germany) extinguished 39 torches in 30 seconds using only his mouth on the set of *Guinness World Records – Ab India Todega* in Mumbai, India.

Greatest flame distance blown by a fire breather
Reg Morris (UK) blew a flame from his mouth to a distance of 9.4 m (31 ft) at The Miner's Rest, Chasetown, Staffordshire, UK, on 29 October 1986.

Farthest tightrope walk (unsupported)

The greatest distance for an unsupported tightrope walk is 130 m (429 ft) and was achieved by funambulist Bello Nock (USA) across a wire attached to poles on board Royal Caribbean International's *Majesty of the Seas* cruise ship, in Coco Bay, The Bahamas, on 10 November 2010.

FACT: The walk lasted – not an easy feat when the sea is moving the ship all the time!

TIGHTROPE WALKERS

Longest tightrope crossing (supported)
The longest walk by any funambulist was 3,465 m (11,368 ft), achieved by Henri Rochetain (France) along a wire slung across a gorge at Clermont-Ferrand in France on 13 July 1969.

Longest tightrope crossing by bicycle
Nik Wallenda (USA) cycled across a 71.63-m (235-ft) tightrope in Newark, USA, on 15 October 2008.

Steepest tightrope
Aisikaier Wubulikasimu (China) and Maurizio Zavatta (Australia) walked a tightrope set at an angle of 36° in Changzhou City, China, on 28 November 2011.

Fastest motorcycle wheelie on a tightrope
On 13 August 2005, Johann Traber (Germany) performed a 53-km/h (33-mi/h) motorcycle wheelie on a tightrope in Flensburg, Germany.

Oldest tightrope walke
In 1948, William Ivy Baldwin (USA) crossed the Eldorado Canyon in Colorado, USA, on a tightrope on his 82nd birthday.

Most knives thrown around a human target in one minute

Dr David R Adamovich (USA) hurled 102 throwing knives around his partner, "Target Girl" Tina Nagy (USA), in one minute in Freeport, New York, USA, on 26 December 2007.

FACT:
Dr Adamovich (aka "The Great Throwdini") practised for five years before aiming his knives at a human.

JUGGLERS AND JOGGLERS

Fastest 100 m joggling three objects (women)

In July 1990, Sandy Brown (USA) ran 100 m while joggling three objects in 17.2 seconds at the International Juggling Association's Joggling Championships in Los Angeles, California, USA.

Longest duration juggling three objects blindfolded

On 11 August 2011, Niels Duinker (Netherlands) juggled three objects for 6 min 29 sec while blindfolded in Rotterdam, Netherlands.

Farthest distance on a unicycle juggling three objects

On 25 April 2011, Chayne Hultgren (Australia) unicycled 1,005 m (3,297 ft) while juggling three objects at the Royal Easter Show in Sydney, Australia.

Most juggling catches in one minute (three firestaffs)

Johan Eklund (Sweden) caught three lit firestaffs 48 times in one minute in Skyttorp, Sweden, on 5 January 2011.

Longest duration juggling four objects

Zdeněk Bradáč (Czech Republic) juggled four objects, without dropping any of them, for 2 hr 46 min 48 sec in Jablonec nad Nisou, Czech Republic, on 30 November 2010. The prolific Zdeněk also holds a further 15 GWR records!

2 hours plus!

ESCAPOLOGY

Fastest escape from a straitjacket (suspended)

Peng Deming (China) escaped from a suspended straitjacket in 25.37 seconds on the set of *CCTV – Guinness World Records Special* in Beijing, China, on 17 August 2011.

The **fastest escape while suspended and chained** is 19.2 seconds, by Lucas Wilson (Canada) in Simcoe, Ontario, Canada, on 8 October 2011.

Fastest handcuff escape blindfolded

Zdeněk Bradáč (Czech Republic) escaped from a pair of handcuffs while blindfolded in 4.06 seconds in Jablonec nad Nisou, Czech Republic, on 29 November 2010.

HUNGRY FOR MORE RISKY THRILLS? TRY P.110

HISTORY OF THE SHALLOW DIVE

Centimetre by centimetre, the record for the highest shallow dive edges ever more skywards. As per GWR rules, daredevil divers are allowed just 30 cm (12 in) of water in which to land, cushioned by a mattress a mere 25 cm (10 in) thick...

Current GWR – 11.2 m
Darren Taylor, USA (2011)
Changzhou City, Jiangsu, China

10.99 m
Darren Taylor (2010)
Louisville, Kentucky, USA

10.9 m
Darren Taylor (2009)
Atlanta, Georgia, USA

10.83 m
Darren Taylor (2008)
Tokyo, Japan

10.75 m
Darren Taylor (2007)
Cologne, Germany

10.65 m
Darren Taylor (2006)
Madrid, Spain

10.3 m
Darren Taylor (2005)
Denver, Colorado, USA

Largest-ever increase in record (1.35 m)

8.95 m
Danny Higginbottom, USA (2004)
Twickenham, Middlesex, UK

8.86 m
Danny Higginbottom (2000)
Therme Erding Spa, Germany

8.83 m
Danny Higginbottom (1999)
Metairie, Louisiana, USA

The current Guinness World Record holder, Darren Taylor, aka Professor Splash, hits the water at an estimated speed of 53 km/h (33 mi/h)!

Regulation-sized paddling pool: 30 cm (12 in) deep, 1.82 m (6 ft) wide, 3.65 m (12 ft) long.

30 cm (12 in)

FUN WITH FOOD

AGAINST THE CLOCK

Lasagne (30 sec): Rafael Bujotzek ate 358 g (12.6 oz) of lasagne in 30 seconds at an event organized by Twentieth Century Fox (Germany) at the Theatre Cinedom in Cologne, Germany, on 3 August 2006.

Mashed potato (30 sec): On 23 November 2011, Hasib Zafar (UK) consumed 266 g (9.38 oz) of mashed potato at the British Potato Conference in Harrogate, North Yorkshire, UK.

Brussels sprouts (1 min): Linus Urbanec (Sweden) downed a record 31 Brussels sprouts in one minute in Rottne, Sweden, on 26 November 2008.

Jaffa Cakes (1 min): Gustav Schulz (Germany) scoffed eight Jaffa Cakes in a minute in Essex, UK, on 9 October 2009. His feat was matched by Connor Whiteford (UK) in Hull, UK, on 6 October 2011.

Marshmallows (1 min): Prolific record-setter Ashrita Furman (USA) consumed 12 marshmallows in a minute at the Panorama Café in New York City, USA, on 13 January 2011.

Mince pies (1 min): Catherine Jones, Michael Xuereb and Luke Chilton (all UK) each ate two mince pies in one minute at the offices of *Real People* magazine in London, UK, on 22 November 2010.

Oranges peeled and eaten (3 min): Ashrita Furman (USA) ate six oranges, which he had also peeled, at the Panorama Café in New York City, USA, on 14 July 2010.

Sausages (1 min): On 22 July 2001, Stefan Paladin (New Zealand) chomped his way through eight whole sausages at the Ericsson Stadium in Auckland, New Zealand.

Dumplings (2 min): Seth Grudberg (USA) ate a stomach-bulging 18 dumplings in just two minutes at the Third Annual Tang's Natural NYC Dumpling Festival in New York City, USA, on 17 September 2011.

Baked beans (3 min): Nick Thompson (UK) consumed 136 baked beans from a plate with a cocktail stick in three minutes at an event organized by the advertising agency Claydon Heeley Jones Mason (UK) at Harrow School, Harrow-on-the-Hill, Middlesex, UK, on 18 August 2005.

Grapes (3 min): Ashrita Furman (USA) downed 186 grapes in three minutes at the Sri Chinmoy Center in New York City, USA, on 31 May 2011.

Jam doughnuts (3 min): Lup Fun Yau downed six sugared jam doughnuts, without licking his lips, in three minutes at the offices of *The Sun* in London, UK, on 2 May 2007. This equalled the record set in 2002 by Steve McHugh (UK).

Oysters (3 min): Colin Shirlow (UK) ate a belt-busting 233 oysters in three minutes at the annual World Oyster Eating Championship held in Hillsborough, County Down, UK, on 3 September 2005.

Shrimps (3 min): On 26 February 2003, William E Silver (USA) worked his way through 272.1 g (9.6 oz) of shrimps in three minutes at the Calabash West Restaurant in Asheville, North Carolina, USA.

Baked beans (5 min): Gary Eccles (UK) consumed a total of 258 baked beans with a cocktail stick in five minutes on 18 March 2011.

Most mashed potato eaten in one minute

Amy Varney (USA) ate 365 g (12.875 oz) of mashed potato in one minute at Sierra Studios, in East Dundee, Illinois, USA, on 14 January 2012.

SNAP SHOT

• Patrick broke an amazing 11 records – and equalled another – in just one day!

• He competes in food competitions all around the world. His passion has recently taken him to Thailand, Australia and the UK.

• Of all the records that Patrick has broken, by far the most nausea-inducing for him was the one involving garlic cloves!

An appetite for record-breaking

Patrick Bertoletti (USA) has stacked up a mouth-watering array of food-related records. They include the **most chicken nuggets eaten in one minute** (12) – at Sierra Studios in East Dundee, Illinois, USA, on 14 January 2012. And on the set of ABC's *Live with Regis & Kelly* in New York City, USA, he set the record for the **most ice-cream eaten in 30 seconds** (382 g; 13.5 oz). But that's just for starters. Check out his other records – all set in one minute!

Grapes: 40

Jam doughnuts: three

Yoghurt: 1.272 kg (2 lb 12.875 oz)

Olives: 30

Bananas peeled and eaten: eight

Mini gherkins: 16

Peanut-butter-and-jelly sandwiches: six

Cream-filled biscuits: seven

Shrimps: 167 g (5.89 oz)

Chocolate bars: three. Record shared with Joey Chestnut (USA)

Garlic cloves: 36

Ferrero Rocher chocolates: nine. Record shared with Peter Czerwinski (Canada)

Most hot dogs eaten in three minutes

Takeru Kobayashi (Japan) worked his way through six hot dogs in three minutes for *Bikkuri Chojin 100 Special #2* (Fuji TV) at Kashiwanohakoen Sogokyogijo, Kashiwa, Japan, on 25 August 2009. Takeru's healthy appetite has earned him a few GWR records and seen him become a big cheese in the world of competitive eating (see right)...

Takeru won Nathan's Annual Hot Dog Eating Contest a record six times in a row! Other feasting feats include:

Most hamburgers eaten in three minutes: 10

Most meatballs eaten in one minute: 29

Most Twinkies (cake snacks) eaten in one minute: 14

Fastest time to eat 100 g of pasta: 45 sec

Fastest time to eat a 12-inch pizza: 1 min 9.36 sec

FASTEST TIME TO EAT...

A raw onion
Peter Czerwinski (Canada) consumed a raw onion in 43.53 seconds in Mississauga, Ontario, Canada, on 2 November 2011.

A lemon
Ashrita Furman (USA) peeled then ate a lemon in 8.25 seconds at the Songs of the Soul offices in New York City, USA, on 3 May 2010.

Three eclairs
Jonathan Coull (UK) scoffed three pastry eclairs in 1 min 11 sec at the offices of *Zoo* magazine, London, UK, on 17 November 2011 in celebration of GWR Day.

Three chillies (Bhut Jolokias)
Birgit Tack (Germany) ate three Bhut Jolokia chillies in 1 min 11 sec on *Guinness World Records: Wir holen den Rekord nach Deutschland* in Berlin, Germany, on 2 April 2011.

Most jelly eaten with chopsticks in one minute

Ashrita Furman (USA) tucked away 610 g (1 lb 5 oz) of jelly in one minute – using a pair of chopsticks – at the Panorama Café in New York City, USA, on 7 December 2010.

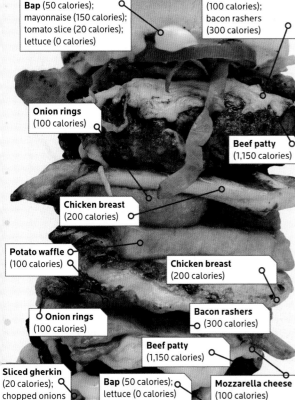

Bap (50 calories); mayonnaise (150 calories); tomato slice (20 calories); lettuce (0 calories)

Mozzarella cheese (100 calories); bacon rashers (300 calories)

Onion rings (100 calories)

Beef patty (1,150 calories)

Chicken breast (200 calories)

Potato waffle (100 calories)

Chicken breast (200 calories)

Onion rings (100 calories)

Bacon rashers (300 calories)

Beef patty (1,150 calories)

Sliced gherkin (20 calories); chopped onions (10 calories)

Bap (50 calories); lettuce (0 calories)

Mozzarella cheese (100 calories)

Most calorific burger

As of February 2012, Oscar's Diner in Telford, Shropshire, UK, is serving up a 1.1-kg (2-lb 8-oz) burger packing 4,200 calories for £15 ($24). Finish it off, along with complementary milkshake, chips and coleslaw, within 45 minutes and you'll win a free meal, T-shirt and photo to mark the event. One customer did it in seven minutes!

MOST...

Competitors in a hot-dog eating contest
A total of 3,189 participants took part in a hot-dog eating contest at an event organized by Oscar Mayer (Spain) in Puente de las Flores, Valencia, Spain, on 12 March 2011.

Watermelons crushed with the head (1 min)
Tafzi Ahmed (Germany) smashed 43 watermelons with his head in a minute at the Rose Festival, Saxony-Anhalt, Germany, on 27 May 2011.

Apples snapped (1 min)
The greatest number of apples snapped in one minute is 40, a feat achieved by Ashrita Furman (USA) in New York City, USA, on 31 December 2011.

Ashrita, who has recently turned to food in order to satisfy his hunger for record-breaking, also holds records for the **most bananas snapped with both hands (1 min)** – he broke 99 of them at the Sri Chinmoy Center in New York City, USA, on 4 May 2010 – and the **most cucumbers snapped (1 min)** – 118 at the Smile of the Beyond Luncheonette in New York City, USA, on 24 March 2011.

Mentos and soda fountains
A total of 2,865 mint and soda fountains were unleashed in an event organized by Perfetti Van Melle (Philippines) at the SM Mall of Asia Complex in Manila, Philippines, on 17 October 2010 (pictured below).

YOU'LL FIND MORE TASTY RECORDS ON P.94

THE FIZZ-ICS OF CANDY-SODA FOUNTAINS

Physicists at Appalachian State University in Boone, North Carolina, USA, have applied their scientific minds to explaining – and perfecting – the ever-popular candy-soda fountain:

1 For optimum results, use mint Mentos. They're not as smooth as they seem: they're covered in layers of liquid sugar, creating a surface of microscopically tiny pits.

2 Sodas are fizzy because carbon dioxide (CO_2) is dissolved in the liquid. Bubbles of CO_2 get released when the molecules come into contact with tiny bumps – such as minute scratches on a drinking glass or flecks of dust – known as "nucleation points".

3 Bubbles of CO_2 quickly form on all the millions of nucleation points on the Mentos, creating a raging foam as the mints sink to the bottom. This release of pressure forces the foaming liquid upwards and outwards!

DIET

4 The best soda to use is Diet Coke – it contains the sweetener aspartame, which lowers the surface tension of the liquid, allowing the CO_2 to escape more easily. (Caffeine-free Diet Coke works just as well!)

BIG FOOD

LARGEST...

- **Cheese slice:** Long Clawson Dairy (UK) created a 110.5-kg (243-lb 9.7-oz) piece of Stilton cheese. It was presented and weighed in Long Clawson, Leicestershire, UK, on 20 September 2011.

- **Chocolate Easter egg:** Tosca (Italy) made an Easter egg that measured 10.39 m (34 ft 1.05 in) tall on 16 April 2011.
- **Doner:** On 26 August 2011, Doner Restaurant (UAE) created a 468-kg (1,031-lb 12-oz) doner on Jumeirah Beach Road, in Dubai, UAE.

Heaviest pineapple

Tipping the scales at 8.28 kg (18 lb 4 oz), and measuring 32 cm (12.5 in) long, is the pineapple (far right) picked in November 2011 by amateur gardener Christine McCallum (Australia). The prodigious pineapple has a girth of 66 cm (25.9 in) and took two-and-a-half years to grow in Christine's garden in Bakewell, Northern Territory, Australia.

Largest hot dog commercially available

Made by Gorilla Tango Novelty Meats (USA), the Big Hot Dog weighs 3.18 kg (7 lb) and is available for $89.95 (£57) as of December 2011. Pictured here is the CEO of Gorilla Tango Novelty Meats, Dan Abbate (USA), with his hands full of one of the record-breaking snacks. The hot dog – which is made from veal, beef and pork – is 40.64 cm (16 in) long and has a diameter of 10.16 cm (4 in). Just one of these humongous hunger-quashers can provide 40 regular-sized servings!

FACT:
US baseball fans gobble up around 26 million hot dogs every season.

SNAP SHOT

- Dan's original plan was to create a rectangular hot dog that wouldn't spin out of the bun when pressed. That idea didn't take off, so he decided to go much, much bigger and aim for a Guinness World Record.

- During the photo shoot a small dog named Dorian went by, licking his lips. He ended up eating quite a lot of one end of the super-sized snack. Dorian is a dachshund – also known as a "sausage dog"...

- **Cocktail:** A margarita with a volume of 32,176 litres (7,077.73 UK gallons) was made by Margaritaville Casino in Las Vegas, Nevada, USA, on 14 October 2011.
- **Falafel:** The Santa Clarita Valley Jewish Food and Cultural Festival (USA) prepared a 23.9-kg (52-lb 12-oz) falafel ball at the College of the Canyons in Valencia, California, USA, on 15 May 2010.
- **Lasagne:** Weighing a titanic 3.71 tonnes (8,179 lb 2 oz), and measuring 21.33 x 2.13 m (70 x 7 ft), the largest lasagne was created by the Food Bank for Monterey County at Salinas, California, USA, on 14 October 1993.
- **Pasty:** On 19 August 2010, the Proper Cornish Food Company produced a pasty that weighed 728 kg (1,604 lb) in Fowey, Cornwall, UK.
- **Ploughman's lunch:** Sylwia Ciszewski, from Seriously Strong Cheddar (UK), made a ploughman's lunch weighing 1,853.9 kg (4,086 lb), which was shown at the Foodies Festival in London, UK, on 29 July 2011.

Long lunch

• Peckish? Try the longest cooked salami, at 16.09 m (52 ft 9.46 in), made by Fratelli Daturi snc (Italy).

• Some greens, perhaps? The longest cucumber is 107 cm (42.1 in) and was grown by Ian Neale (UK).

• For after, how about the longest ice-cream dessert, a 45.72-m (150-ft) sundae made by the parents of the Parent and School Association of St Anne School, Bethlehem, Pennsylvania (USA)?

LARGEST SERVING OF...

• **Baked potatoes:** Shopping centre El Mirador (Spain) baked 1,116 kg (2,460 lb 5.7 oz) of potatoes at Las Palmas de Gran Canaria, Spain, on 28 May 2011. The dish – *papas arrugadas* ("wrinkly potatoes") – is popular in the Canary Islands.

• **Chilli con carne:** On 19 July 2003, the Keystone Aquatic Club (USA) cooked up a pot of chilli con carne that weighed 652.4 kg (1,438 lb 5.1 oz) at the Broad Street Market, Harrisburg, Pennsylvania, USA.

• **Fish and chips:** Weighing in at 45.83 kg (101 lb 7 oz), the heftiest helping of fish and chips was created by the Wensleydale Heifer hotel (UK) in West Witton, Yorkshire, UK, on 2 July 2011.

• **Fried chicken:** Weighing 1,076 kg (2,372 lb 2.7 oz), the largest serving of fried chicken

was produced by NOAS FM (Japan) at the Fourth Karaage Festival at AEON Mall Sanko in Nakatsu City, Oita, Japan, on 23 September 2011.

• **Potato salad:** Spilva Ltd (Latvia) exhibited a 3.27-tonne (7,209-lb 1-oz) potato salad at the International Exhibition Centre of the Riga Technical University in Latvia, on 1 September 2002.

• **Risotto:** On 26 November 2004, the Ricegrowers' Association of Australia served up a 7.51-tonne (16,556-lb 11-oz) helping of risotto at First

Fleet Park, Sydney, Australia.

• **Salsa:** A team led by Bob Blumer (Canada) created a super-sized salsa weighing 1,212 kg (2,672 lb) at the 26th Annual Tomato Festival in Jacksonville, Texas, USA, on 12 June 2010.

• **Snails:** The Câmara Municipal de Loures (Portugal) created a 1,111-kg (2,449-lb) serving of snails in Loures, Portugal, on 11 July 2009.

• **Stir-fry:** On 5 September 2011, the University of

Massachusetts Dining Services (USA) created a 1,818.91-kg (4,010-lb) stir-fry in Amherst, Massachusetts, USA.

• **Vegetable stew:** The city council of Tudela (Spain) created a 2,040-kg (4,497-lb 6.8-oz) vegetable stew in Tudela, northern Spain, on 30 April 2011. The recipe included locally grown artichokes, peas, broad beans, green beans, asparagus, onions and garlic.

Largest meatball

This mountain of meat weighs 503.71 kg (1,110 lb 7.84 oz) – making it around 5,926 times larger than a more conventional 85-g (3-oz) meatball – and has a diameter of 1.38 m (4 ft 6.5 in). It was prepared by the Columbus Italian Club (USA) at the St John's Italian Festival, in Columbus, Ohio, USA, between 5 and 8 October 2011. The meat and spices were mixed in batches of 22.5 kg (50 lb), then refrigerated, moved to another location, packed into a pod-like vessel and cooked in a specially made oven.

HEAVIEST FRUIT & VEG

The largest produce grown in our gardens is the pumpkin, the mightiest of which is the 821.23-kg (1,810-lb 8-oz) monster grown by Chris Stevens (USA) of Wisconsin, USA. The pumpkin is 10 times heavier than its nearest rival, the cabbage, as this list of garden giants reveals...

Cabbage	57.61 kg (127 lb)
Sweet potato	37 kg (81 lb 9 oz)
Radish	31.1 kg (68 lb 9 oz)
Cantaloupe	29.4 kg (64 lb 13 oz)
Courgette	29.25 kg (64 lb 8 oz)
Celery	28.7 kg (63 lb 4.8 oz)
Cauliflower	24.6 kg (54 lb 3 oz)
Beetroot	23.4 kg (51 lb 9.4 oz)
Turnip	17.7 kg (39 lb 3 oz)
Broccoli	15.87 kg (35 lb)
Cucumber	12.4 kg (27 lb 5 oz)
Leek	9.2 kg (20 lb 5 oz)
Carrot	8.61 kg (18 lb 13 oz)
Brussels sprout	8.3 kg (18 lb 4 oz)
Pineapple	8.3 kg (18 lb 4 oz)
Onion	8.15 kg (17 lb 15 oz)
Parsnip	7.8 kg (17 lb 4 oz)
Lemon	5.26 kg (11 lb 9 oz)
Potato	4.98 kg (10 lb 14 oz)
Tomato	3.51 kg (7 lb 12 oz)
Mango	3.43 kg (7 lb 8 oz)
Grapefruit	3.21 kg (7 lb 1.2 oz)
Pear	2.94 kg (6 lb 8 oz)
Avocado	2.19 kg (4 lb 13 oz)
Apple	1.84 kg (4 lb 1 oz)
Garlic	1.19 kg (2 lb 10 oz)
Peach	725 g (1 lb 9 oz)
Pepper	290 g (10.08 oz)
Strawberry	231 g (8.14 oz)
Cherry	21.69 g (0.76 oz)
Blueberry	11.28 g (0.4 oz)

Pictured is record vegetable grower Peter Glazebrook (UK) with his prize-winning onion, weighed at the Harrogate Flower Show in Yorkshire, UK, on 16 September 2011.

Largest box of popcorn

Cineplexx International (Austria/Serbia/Croatia) made a 52.59-m³ (1,857-ft³) popcorn box. It was filled in 1 hr 57 min at an event near Avenue Mall in Osijek, Croatia, on 16 April 2011 to mark the opening of two new malls, along with two new Cineplexx cinemas, in Croatia.

52,73m³
51,51m³
50,03m³
47,91m³
45,57m³

FACT: Native Americans were popping corn in North America 5,000 years ago!

SWEET TREATS

Fastest time to sort 30 jelly babies

Alfie Binnie (UK) sorted 30 jelly babies by colour using chopsticks in a record time of 40 seconds in London, UK, on 17 February 2012.

FACT:
Michael Patrick Buonocore (USA) survived a blood-sugar level of 147.6 mmol/L in 2008 – 25 times the normal figure!

FACT:
The world's **first chocolate bar** was manufactured by Joseph Fry & Son of Bristol, UK, in 1847.

Pez In May 1998, David Welch (USA) sold three Pez dispensers for $6,000 (£3,660) each – a total of $18,000 (£10,980) – making them the **most expensive sweet dispensers**. Around 50 years old at the time, they had three separate designs: a one-piece shiny gold elephant, a Mickey Mouse softhead and a headless dispenser embossed with the words "PEZ-HAAS". All three were bought by an anonymous dealer.

Oreo cookies
The world's **best-selling cookie** is the Oreo, with total sales in excess of 500 billion since its introduction in the USA in 1912. If every Oreo ever made were to be stacked on top of each other, the pile would reach to the Moon and back more than six times.

FACT:
You could circle the Earth more than five times with all the jelly beans eaten last year!

Chocolate coins
The world's **largest chocolate coin** was unveiled at the Sun Plaza shopping centre in Bucharest, Romania, on 17 November 2011. The enormous 1,325,000-calorie coin measured 14 cm (5.5 in) thick with a diameter of 1.35 m (4 ft 5 in) and weighed in at 265 kg (584 lb 3.5 oz). If it had been made from gold, it would have cost £9.5 million ($15 million)!

KitKat
The KitKat is the **chocolate bar with the greatest number of flavour variants**. To date, the standard four-finger KitKat has been available in more than 120 flavours, including cucumber, wasabi, watermelon and salt – and, of course, milk chocolate.

Candy floss
The **longest candy floss (cotton candy)** measures 1,400 m (4,593 ft 2 in) and was spun by Kocaeli Fuar Müdürlüğü (Turkey) in Izmit, Kocaeli, Turkey, on 10 July 2009.

Cadbury's Dairy Milk
The **best-selling chocolate bar** is Cadbury's Dairy Milk, generating annual sales worth $852 million (£551 million) globally. It is especially popular in the UK – the British get through an average of 8.6 kg (19 lb) of chocolate per person every year.

Coconut ice
A 140.14-m-long (459-ft 9-in) coconut candy was made to celebrate the Coconut Festival at Tecolutla, Mexico, on 28 February 1998.

Ferrero Rocher
Silvio Sabba (Italy) stacked a record 12 Ferrero Rocher chocolates on top of each other in Pioltello, Milan, Italy, on 30 January 2012.

After Eights
Anthony Falzon (Malta) downed a record-breaking 10 After Eight thin mints in one minute, without using his hands, in Sliema, Malta, on 14 December 2011.

FACT:
The earliest samples of chocolate – found in Honduras, Central America – date back to 1150 BC.

M&M's
With annual sales worth $1.8 billion (£900 million) in the USA alone as of 2007, the world's **most popular sweet** is the M&M. The candy-coated chocolate drops were introduced in 1941 by Americans Forrest Mars, Sr and R Bruce Murrie, who named the product after themselves.

Largest chocolate bar

Made by Thorntons plc (UK) in Alfreton, Derbyshire, UK, on 7 October 2011, the largest chocolate bar weighed 5,792.50 kg (12,770 lb 4.48 oz) and measured 4 x 4 x 0.35 m (13 ft 1.48 in x 13 ft 1.48 in x 1 ft 1.78 in). The bumper-sized bar was made as part of the celebrations for Thorntons' centenary.

Hershey's Kiss
The **largest individual chocolate** was a Hershey's Kiss weighing 13,852.71 kg (30,540 lb). It was made to celebrate the iconic chocolate's 100th anniversary and was displayed at Chocolate World, Hershey, Pennsylvania, USA, on 7 July 2007.

FACT: The world's largest chocolate bar (see above) is heavier than a bull elephant!

Pick 'n' Mix
An 800-g (1-lb 12-oz) bag of "pick 'n' mix" sweets, including fizzy cola bottles, white mice and jelly worms, sold for £14,500 ($23,653) at a charity auction for Retail Trust (UK) on 21 February 2009. It was the last pick 'n' mix to be sold by the now-defunct Woolworths chain. Proceeds went towards a helpline for retail workers and their families affected by redundancy.

FACT: The Chinese have used liquorice plants as a medicine for thousands of years.

Smarties
Using chopsticks, Kathryn Ratcliffe (UK) ate a record 170 Smarties in three minutes at the Guinness World Records 2005 Roadshow at the Trafford Centre, Manchester, UK, on 27 November 2004.

FACT: More than 10 billion Maltesers are produced each year by the Mars company's UK factory!

Highest chocolate consumption
Switzerland has the **highest per capita chocolate consumption**. On average, its citizens manage to consume 10.55 kg (23 lb 4 oz) of chocolate each per year – hardly surprising, given the legendary quality of Swiss chocolate.

Fudge
The **largest slab of fudge** weighed 2.61 tonnes (5,754 lb) and was made by Northwest Fudge Factory (Canada) in Levack, Ontario, Canada, on 23 October 2010.

FACT: It took a week to make this bumper block of vanilla-, chocolate- and maple-flavoured fudge.

Maltesers
The **farthest distance to blow a Malteser with a straw** is 14.07 m (46 ft 1 in), achieved by Ashrita Furman (USA) in the gymnasium of the Jamaica YMCA, New York City, USA, on 29 November 2010.

Bubble-gum
The **largest bubble-gum bubble blown through the nose** had a diameter of 27.94 cm (11 in). It was created by Joyce Samuels (USA) on the set of *Guinness World Records: Primetime* in Los Angeles, USA, on 10 November 2000.

TITANIC TREATS

Jelly beans
3 m tall

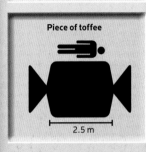
Piece of toffee
2.5 m

String of liquorice
244 m long

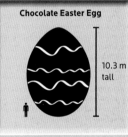
Chocolate Easter Egg
10.3 m tall

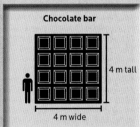
Chocolate bar
4 m tall
4 m wide

Gummy bear candy
81 cm tall

HE COLLECTS...

Airline boarding passes
Miguel Fernández Díaz (Spain) had a collection of 1,020 airline boarding passes from 54 airlines as of May 2009.

Armoured vehicles
As of 3 February 2007, Jacques Littlefield (USA) had 229 de-activated armoured fighting vehicles, including a German Panzer IV tank, displayed at his ranch in California, USA.

Autographed baseballs
Dennis M Schrader (USA) had collected 4,020 baseballs, all autographed by different professional baseball players, as of August 2011.

Autographed books
As of 11 March 2011, Richard Warren of Lake Forest, California, USA, had collected 2,381 books, all signed by their original authors.

Harry Potter memorabilia

The largest collection of Harry Potter memorabilia belongs to Steve Petrick of Pittsburgh, USA, and consisted of 608 individual items as of 30 October 2011. Steve's huge hoard includes lifesize cardboard cut-outs of all the main characters, adult and children's versions of the books, Quidditch trophies, goggles and snitches, and a large assortment of toy owls and wands. He also has numerous soft toys, including one of Hagrid's three-headed dog, Fluffy.

Back scratchers
Manfred Rothstein (USA) has amassed 675 back scratchers from 71 countries, housed in his dermatology clinic in Fayetteville, North Carolina, USA.

Beatles memorabilia
Rodolfo Renato Vazquez (Argentina) had 7,700 different Beatles-related items, as of August 2011.

SNAP SHOT

• Steve is 1.66 m (5 ft 5.5 in) tall – the same height as Harry Potter actor Daniel Radcliffe. He's 23 years old and studies Fine Art at university.

• Steve actually auditioned for the role of Harry in the first film – and his English accent is pretty good.

• He has been collecting Harry memorabilia since the first book came out in 1997.

• When J K Rowling signed his arm, Steve had a tattoo inked on top so that it would last forever.

Superman memorabilia

As of 22 February 2012, Herbert Chavez (Philippines) had a collection of 1,253 Superman-related items. They include life-size statues, figurines, clothing, cushion and duvet covers, and comics and posters. Herbert has taken his obsession with the Man of Steel to even greater extremes – he has admitted to having a nose job, chin augmentation, silicone lip injections and thigh implants to make himself look like his (super)hero.

Candles
Lam Chung Foon (Hong Kong) owned 6,360 different candles, as of 23 December 2011. He keeps them in four temperature-regulated showrooms.

Charlie's Angels memorabilia
Jack Condon (USA) has 5,569 items of *Charlie's Angels* memorabilia, which he has been collecting since 1976.

Dioramas
Nabil Karam (Lebanon) has 333 unique dioramas (three-dimensional models of a scene). Nabil also has the **largest collection of model cars**, with 27,777 unique items (see p.13). Both collections were counted on 17 November 2011.

"Do Not Disturb" signs
Jean-François Vernetti (Switzerland) has collected 11,111 different "Do Not Disturb" signs from hotels in 189 countries since 1985.

Film cameras
Richard LaRiviere (USA) owns 894 different film cameras that he has collected since 1960.

Film projectors
Christos Psathas (Greece) had 1,919 film projectors, as of 29 July 2011.

Fireman's patches
Bob Brooks (USA) has 8,158 fireman's patches, all of which he displayed at the Albany Fire Department in Albany, Oregon, USA, on 22 June 2011. Bob was a fireman for 35 years.

Hats
Roger Buckey Legried (USA) has collected hats since 1970 and, as of 2 March 2010, he had 100,336 of them.

Horse-related items
Edgar Rugeles (Colombia) had 2,149 horse-related items, as of 26 August 2011.

Miniature champagne bottles
Christoph Bermpohl (Germany) had 1,030 different miniature champagne bottles, as of July 2011.

Moutai bottles
Zhang Jinzhong (China) had 432 different bottles of Moutai liquor, as of May 2011. He's been collecting since 2003.

Number plates
Brothers Péter and Tamás Kenyeres (both Hungary) had 11,345 different number plates from 133 countries, as of April 2011. They have been collecting since 1990.

Pizza-related items
Brian Dwyer (USA) had 561 different pizza-related items, as of 31 July 2011. He has only been collecting since 2010. His collection includes games, puzzles and matchboxes.

ACTUAL SIZE

Miniature books

Jozsef Tari (Hungary) owns 4,500 miniature books, including one that measures only 2.75 mm high and 1.75 mm wide – that's almost the same size as the "H" in "Hungary" in this sentence. Jozsef, a printer by trade, has been collecting miniature books since 1972 and he has even made some of his own miniature books. He has a special bookcase for his collection – each shelf is about half the height of a matchbox.

FACT: The German airline Hapag-Lloyd Express had bags that stated: "Thank you for your criticism!"

Sick bags

Niek Vermeulen (Netherlands) had 6,016 airline sickness bags from 1,142 different airlines from more than 160 countries, as of 29 January 2010, which he has accumulated since the 1970s. All the sick bags have an airline company name or company logo printed on them. His favourite bag, however, is not from an airline – it's from the NASA space shuttle *Columbia*.

SHE COLLECTS...

Hello Kitty memorabilia

Asako Kanda (Japan) had amassed 4,519 different Hello Kitty items as of 14 August 2011. Her house is filled with a huge range of products relating to the white bobtail cat whose full name is Kitty White, including a frying pan, an electric fan and even a Hello Kitty toilet seat!

Angels

Since 1976, Joyce and Lowell Berg (both USA) have collected 13,165 angelic objects, including angel and cherub figurines, music boxes and even an angel smoke alarm.

Bells

Myrtle B Eldridge (USA) has built up a collection of 9,638 bells since the 1980s.

Butterflies

As of September 2011, Nina Merinova (Russia) owned a total of 735 different butterfly ornaments. She started her collection in 1996 and makes many of the ornaments herself.

Cats

Carmen de Aldana (Guatemala) had 21,321 different cat-related items as of 14 March 2011. She began her collection in 1954 with three ceramic kittens, one of which she still owns.

Coca-Cola memorabilia

Rebecca Flores (USA) began collecting Coca-Cola items in 2005. As of 15 December 2008, she had 945 unique objects.

Donald Duck memorabilia

Mary Brooks (USA) had 1,411 objects related to Donald Duck as of March 2011. Her collection began more than 35 years ago and it now occupies a spare room in her house.

Flamingos

Sherry Knight (USA) owned 619 flamingo-related items as of 19 February 2011. Her collection is displayed at the Path Shelter Store in Lecanto, Florida, USA.

Fridge magnets

Louise J Greenfarb (USA) has amassed a total of 35,000 non-duplicated fridge magnets. Her collection dates back to the 1970s.

Gnomes and pixies

Ann Atkin (UK) had 2,042 unique garden gnomes and pixies as of March 2011.

Handmade dolls

Isabel Romero Jorques (Spain) has made 500 felt dolls by hand, each 10 cm (3.9 in) high. Although she made dolls as a child, it was only aged 69, prompted by her grandchilden, that she began creating her record-breaking collection.

Shoes

Darlene Flynn (USA) had 15,665 unique shoe-related items as of 20 March 2012, in a collection that dates back to 2000. It's still growing, too – Darlene receives shoes from well-wishers the world over. Her favourite films are *Cinderella* and *The Wizard of Oz* and, as you might expect, she owns replicas of both Cinderella's glass slippers and Dorothy's red shoes. Darlene lives very close to Denise Tubangui – the owner of the **largest collection of cows** (2,429, as of March 2011) – and they speak to each other regularly about their joint passion for collecting.

FACT: The oldest known leather shoe dates back 5,500 years. It was found in Armenia in 2008.

Mickey Mouse memorabilia

Janet Esteves (USA) owned 2,760 different Mickey Mouse items as of 11 December 2008.

Pandas

Miranda Kessler (USA) had put together a collection of 1,225 unique panda items by March 2011.

Pigs

Anne Langton (UK) has a collection of 16,779 pig items which she has been collecting for more than 40 years.

Barbie dolls

Bettina Dorfmann shares her home in Düsseldorf, Germany, with 15,000 unique Barbie dolls. She received her first doll back in 1966, but has only been collecting seriously since 1993. Barbie was first released by US toy giants Mattel in 1959. Her full name is Barbara Millicent Roberts, the name of the daughter of Mattel founders Elliot and Ruth Handler (USA).

Pokémon memorabilia

Lisa Courtney (UK) was the proud owner of 14,410 different items of Pokémon memorabilia as of 14 October 2010, after more than 14 years of collecting.

Rubber ducks

Charlotte Lee (USA) owned 5,631 unique rubber ducks by 10 April 2011.

Spice Girls memorabilia

As of April 2011, Elizabeth West (UK) owned 2,066 different Spice Girls items.

FACT: According to Mattel, there are in excess of 100,000 collectors of Barbie dolls worldwide.

SNAP SHOT

- Bettina posed for this photo in October 2011, when her collection surpassed 15,000 dolls.

- She received her first doll when she was five years old – but it wasn't Barbie, it was Midge, Barbie's best friend.

- She's now the proud owner of an original (and rare) 1959 Barbie.

- Got a broken Barbie? Bettina runs a doll hospital, where she fixes broken legs, untangles matted hair and replaces missing limbs!

COLLECTORMANIA
13,788,795

total number of unique items collected by Guinness World Records collectors*

current holders only; not including public collections amassed by libraries or universities

Top 10 largest collections

Matchbook covers	3,159,119
Human teeth	2,000,744
Books (privately owned)	1,500,000
Matchbox labels	1,054,221
Cigarette cards	1,000,000
Buttons	439,900
Beer labels	424,868
Scratchcards	319,011
Ballpoint pens	285,150
Cigar bands	211,104

10

items in the **smallest record-breaking collection**: playable musical instruments made of matchsticks. A total of 106,000 matches were used to make, among other instruments, a violin, a mandolin, a recorder and a ukulele! The collection is owned by Tony Hall (UK).

TOP 10 COLLECTING NATIONS

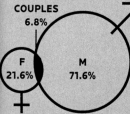

- USA: 34.0%
- UK: 13.9%
- GERMANY: 9.3%
- INDIA: 4.6%
- CHINA: 3.9%
- ITALY: 3.9%
- CANADA: 3.1%
- THE NETHERLANDS: 3.1%
- SPAIN: 3.1%
- SWEDEN: 2.3%

Male vs female collectors

COUPLES 6.8%

F 21.6% M 71.6%

Most hotly contested collections

Certain items are more appealing to collectors. Here are the most popular objects to collect – each record has been broken five times in the last 10 years:

Beer bottles · Book-marks · Model cars · Pencils

BIGGEST...

Artificial climbing wall
Scared of heights? The tallest artificial climbing wall measured 41.89 m (137.42 ft) and was constructed at Historic Banning Mills in Whitesburg, Georgia, USA. It was scaled in 12 minutes by experienced climber Kalib Robertson on 9 December 2011.

Bar chimes
Consisting of 1,221 parts, the largest playable bar chimes reach 19.58 m (64 ft 2 in) in length. They were built by Universal Percussion Inc., TreeWorks Chimes, Tom Shelley and Mitch McMichen (all USA) and presented and played at the Drum Festival in Columbiana, Ohio, USA, on 28 August 2011.

Bed
On 28 May 2011, the biggest bed was created by Commissie Zomerfeesten St Gregorius Hertme (Netherlands) in Hertme, Netherlands. It is 26.5 m (86 ft 11 in) long and 16.44 m (53 ft 11 in) wide.

Cup of coffee
At 12,847.69 litres (2,826.09 UK gal; 3,394 US gal), the largest cup of coffee contained around 54,304 regular servings. It was made by PuertoRicoIsCoffee.com and served at the Puerto Rico Coffee Expo 2011 held in San Juan, Puerto Rico, on 9 October 2011.

Drum
A drum measuring 5.54 m (18 ft 2 in) in diameter, 5.96 m (19 ft 6 in) tall and weighing 7 tonnes (15,432 lb 5.76 oz) was built by the Yeong Dong-Gun local government and Seuk Je Lee (all South Korea) in Simcheon-Meon, South Korea, on 6 July 2011.

Flag (flown)
The city of Piedras Negras in Coahuila, Mexico, raised a flag measuring 34.3 m x 60 m (112 ft 6.39 in x 196 ft 10.2 in) on 2 December 2011.

The **largest draped flag**, unveiled in Rayak, Lebanon, on 10 October 2010 in honour of the Lebanese Army, was 325 m x 203 m (1,066 ft x 666 ft).

Garden gnome
A giant garden gnome built by Ron Hale (Canada) in 1998 reached a record height of 7.91 m (25 ft 11 in). It was measured officially on 19 August 2009.

Biggest glove
Taking a whopping 128 hours to manufacture, the biggest glove measures 2.82 m (9 ft 3 in) tall and 93 cm (3 ft) wide and was created by Held GmbH (Germany). It was presented in Burgberg im Allgäu, Germany, on 20 April 2011.

Jacket
A jacket measuring 12.95 m (42 ft 6 in) from collar to base and 15.32 m (50 ft 3 in) across from sleeve to sleeve was made at St George's Church (UK) in Stockport, UK, on 29 June 2011.

Jigsaw puzzle
When measured by number of pieces, the largest jigsaw is a 551,232-piece puzzle completed on 24 September 2011 by 1,600 students of the University of Economics of Ho Chi Minh City (Vietnam), at a local stadium. It had an overall size of 14.85 x 23.20 m (48 ft 8.64 in x 76 ft 1.38 in).

The **largest jigsaw by area** comprised 21,600 pieces and measured 5,428.8 m² (58,435 ft²). Devised by Great East Asia Surveyors & Consultants Co. Ltd, it was assembled by 777 people at the former Kai Tak Airport in Hong Kong on 3 November 2002.

FACT: Mark is a pastor and has been described by some of his flock as "God's drummer"!

Biggest drum kit
The largest drum kit comprises 340 pieces, is owned by Dr Mark Temperato (USA) and was counted in Lakeville, New York, USA, on 31 October 2011. A huge converted truck is used to transport the drum kit around the USA when Dr Temperato is on tour.

FACT: Mark has a compartment under his tour truck for the drum set's gigantic gong.

FOR BIG THINGS WITH WHISKERS, TURN TO P.58

Biggest telephone

The world's largest operational telephone was exhibited on 16 September 1988 to celebrate the 80th birthday of Centraal Beheer, an insurance in Apeldoorn, Netherlands. It was 2.47 m (8 ft 1 in) high and 6.06 m (19 ft 11 in) long, and weighed 3.5 tonnes. The handset, being 7.14 m (23 ft 5 in) long, had to be lifted by crane for a call to be made.

Magazine
An edition of *Veronica Magazine* was the largest magazine ever, at 190 cm x 270 cm (6 ft 2 in x 8 ft 10 in). It was measured in Hilversum, Netherlands, on 31 October 2011.

Pocket knife
When opened, the world's largest pocket knife measures 6.02 m (17 ft 33 in) and has a steel blade 2.46 m (8 ft 1 in) long. It was designed and manufactured by Garima Foundation and Pankaj Ojha (all India) and was presented at the Pink Square Mall, Jaipur, India, on 21 December 2010.

Screwdriver
A giant screwdriver was created by Biswaroop Roy Chowdhury (India) and was unveiled in New Delhi, India, on 20 April 2011. It is 2.27 m (89.2 in) long and has an acrylic handle which measures 24.13 cm (9.5 in) at its widest point and is 71.12 cm (28 in) long. The steel shaft is 8.89 cm (3.5 in) thick and can be extended a further 1.55 m (61.2 in).

Biggest skateboard

At 11.14 m (36 ft 7 in) long, 2.63 m (8 ft 8 in) wide and 1.10 m (3 ft 7.5 in) high, the largest skateboard was created by *MTV* presenter Rob Dyrdek with Joe Ciaglia and team from California Skateparks (all USA) in Los Angeles, USA. It made its grand entrance on 25 February 2009 on the *MTV* series *Rob Dyrdek's Fantasy Factory*.

Largest spade
At 3.90 m (12 ft 9 in) tall, with a blade 64 cm (1 ft 11 in) wide, the biggest spade was produced by Yeoman Quality Garden Products (UK) on 4 October 2011 in Droitwich, UK.

Sock
A sock measuring 9.93 m (32 ft 7 in) x 6.86 m (22 ft 6 in) x 2.49 m (8 ft 2 in) was displayed on 2 December 2011 at the Rhode Island Convention Center in Providence, Rhode Island, USA. Made by Project Undercover, Inc. (USA), it was designed to resemble a "sock monkey" puppet.

Tea bag
Capable of producing over 50,000 cups of tea, the biggest tea bag weighs 120 kg (264 lb 8.8 oz) and was achieved by All About Tea (UK) aboard HMS *Warrior* in Portsmouth, Hampshire, UK, on 16 November 2011. The tea bag measures 2.48 m (8 ft 1.64 in) in length and width.

White cane
On 27 August 2011, the largest white cane measured 23.55 m (77 ft 3.16 in) and was achieved by the Swiss Federation of the Blind and Visually Impaired Fribourg Section (Switzerland) in Fribourg, Switzerland.

Wine glass
At 3.37 m (11 ft) tall and 1.73 m (5 ft 8 in) at its widest, the biggest wine glass was completed by the Limassol Municipality in Cyprus on 8 September 2011. It was revealed at the 50th anniversary of the Limassol wine festival, where it was filled with five bottles of wine.

SNAP SHOT

• Joe Ciaglia and team (USA) took less than three months to build this skateboard, which is exactly 12.5 times the size of a standard board.

• They regularly design and help construct skateparks around the world, including a new one in Arad, Israel.

• Fans are welcome to go and see the board, which has also been ridden through Times Square in New York, USA.

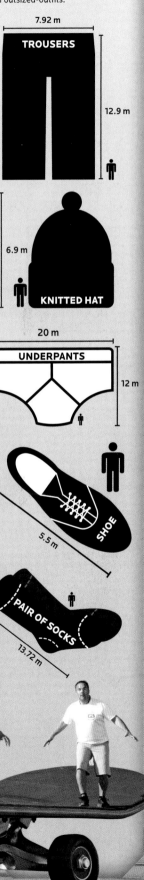

FANTASTIC FASHION
For the gentleman or lady with the fuller figure, we present the Guinness World Records wardrobe of outsized-outfits.

TROUSERS — 7.92 m / 12.9 m

KNITTED HAT — 6.9 m

UNDERPANTS — 20 m / 12 m

SHOE — 5.5 m

PAIR OF SOCKS — 13.72 m

BUT IS IT ART?

LARGEST...

Drawing (one artist)
A pencil drawing by Ashok Nagpure (India) measuring 98.75 x 2.43 m (324 x 8 ft), depicting the life of Indian film-maker Dadasaheb Phalke, was shown in Nashik, Maharashtra, India, on 24 May 2010.

Finger painting
On 26 November 2009, a total of 3,242 students created a finger painting measuring 2,101.43 m² (22,619.51 ft²). The event was organized by the Organizing Committee of the Anti Youth Drug Abuse Campaign at Victoria Park in Hong Kong, China.

Largest panoramic painting

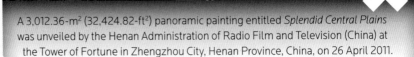

A 3,012.36-m² (32,424.82-ft²) panoramic painting entitled *Splendid Central Plains* was unveiled by the Henan Administration of Radio Film and Television (China) at the Tower of Fortune in Zhengzhou City, Henan Province, China, on 26 April 2011.

Largest sand painting
More than 2,500 participants created a sand painting measuring 9,028 m² (97,176.19 ft²), based on the theme of "peace", on 26 November 2010. The event was organized by the Brahma Kumaris (India) at Firodia School in Ahmednagar, Maharashtra, India.

Handprint painting
A handprint painting covering 5,893 m² (63,431 ft²) – larger than an American football field – was created by 5,000 children in an event organized by the UN Relief and Works Agency. It was made at the Khan Younis Stadium in Southern Gaza, Palestinian Entity (West Bank-Gaza) on 21 July 2011 and depicted the United Nations logo as the sun rising over the Gaza Strip.

Painting-by-numbers
In celebration of GWR Day 2010, a painting-by-numbers artwork measuring 3,130.55 m² (33,696.95 ft²) was unveiled by the Ecole de Dessin in Lagos State, Nigeria.

Footprint painting
On 29 May 2011, in an event organized by Creative Campus in Ealing, London, UK, 200 participants created a 1,489.45-m² (16,000-ft²) painting using their feet.

Painting by mouth
R Rajendran (India) painted a 9.14 x 6.10-m (30 x 20-ft) artwork, as a tribute to Mother Teresa, with his mouth. It was measured on 30 October 2007.

Spray-painted picture
Made for Coca-Cola İçecek by 580 Turkish students, the largest spray-painted image measured 760.28 m² (8,183.58 ft²). It was completed at Hezarfen Airport, Istanbul, Turkey, on 16 August 2004.

FACT: Only around 10% of the human lung is solid tissue. The remaining 90% is filled with air.

Largest model of a human organ
Pfizer Japan Inc. created a 5.02 x 5.78-m (16-ft 5-in x 18-ft 11-in) model of a human lung at Ario Sapporo, Sapporo, Hokkaido, Japan, on 2 October 2010. One side displayed a healthy lung; the other showed a smoker's lung.

Underwater painting
Alexander Belozor (Ukraine) created a 0.8-m² (8.61-ft²) submarine painting at diving site El Mina in the Red Sea, off the coast of Hurghada, Egypt, on 18 December 2010.

Largest art contest
A total of 4,850,271 children from 6,601 schools across India entered the All India Camel Colour Contest, which was judged on 8 December 2011.

2,975 balloons

Largest modelling balloon sculpture

Adam Lee (USA, below) created a balloon sculpture in the shape of a gigantic spider measuring 6.76 m (22 ft 2 in) long and 13.77 m (45 ft 2 in) wide. Consisting of 2,975 balloons, it was measured at the Grand Mound Great Wolf Lodge in Washington, DC, USA, on 6 October 2011.

LONGEST...

Cartoon strip (team)
The longest cartoon strip made by a team measured 1,012 m (3,320 ft). It was created by students of Ecole Emile Cohl, ECAM and Centrale Lyon (all France) in an event staged by Lyon BD Organisation in Lyon, France, on 28 May 2011.

Graffiti scroll
Almeersegraffiti (Netherlands) organized 300 participants in the creation of a gigantic graffiti scroll measuring 1,576.3 m (5,171 ft 6 in) – longer than 22 747 jumbo jets – in Almere, Netherlands, on 2 July 2011.

Painting
A 6-km-long (19,690-ft) artwork on the theme of government transparency was painted by 3,000 students from local schools (all Mexico) at an event held at Parque Tangamanga in San Luis Potosí, Mexico, on 28 May 2010.

The **longest painting by an individual** measured 2,008 m (6,587 ft) and was created by Thommes Nentwig (Germany). It was completed, presented and measured in Vechta, Germany, on 10 July 2008.

The **longest anamorphic painting** – that is, a distorted artwork that when viewed from the correct angle looks three-dimensional – measures 128.7 m (422 ft 3 in) and was created by Qi Xinghua (China). Entitled *Macao's One Impression*, it was unveiled at the One Central Macao shopping centre in China on 6 December 2011. (*See below for an example of anamorphic pavement art.*)

Painting by numbers
Entitled *Birds and Wetlands*, the longest painting by numbers measures 959.35 m (3,147 ft 5 in). It was created by 2,041 participants in an event organized by the Hong Kong Wetland Park at their premises in Hong Kong, China, on 17 October 2009.

Scaled-up sculpture
Who needs clay or marble? GWR presents the largest sculptures made out of:

- **Ice lolly (popsicle) sticks**
840,000 sticks, in the form of a map of Thailand; made by Wall's (Thailand)

- **Plastic bottles**
3,528 bottles, in the shape of a tree; made by Wing Lee (China)

- **Blu-Tack**
4,000 packs of Blu-Tack, weighing 200 kg (440 lb), in the shape of a spider; made by Elizabeth Thompson (UK)

Most plastic bags used in an artwork
Miha Artnak (Slovenia) created *Plastic Bag Monster* in November 2010, using 40,000 plastic bags (and 7,500 plastic cups).

Largest anamorphic pavement art

Joe Hill of 3D Joe and Max (both UK) created an anamorphic pavement artwork measuring 1,160.45 m² (12,490.93 ft²). The sensational street art was unveiled at West India Quay, London, UK, to celebrate Guinness World Records Day, on 17 November 2011.

FACT:
The skull-pture was designed to highlight the huge levels of waste that humanity produces.

FACT:
Anamorphic (from the Greek for "transformation") means that it only displays properly if viewed from one specific spot.

Woodblock print
A group of 80 students from De Eindhovense School (Netherlands) made a woodblock print 151.5 m (497 ft) long that was exhibited at their school in Eindhoven, Netherlands, on 30 January 2009. Entitled *Holland and Nicaragua*, it was created to raise awareness of Chinandega – Eindhoven's twin city in Nicaragua.

MOST EXPENSIVE ART
Art is big business. And business is getting bigger all the time...

 The **most expensive book illustration sold at auction** is a Beatrix Potter (UK) watercolour titled *The Rabbits' Christmas Party*. Created in the 1890s, it was bought on 17 July 2008 by a British collector for £289,250 ($579,232).

 The **most expensive photograph** is an image of the Rhine taken by the German artist Andreas Gursky (b. 1955). It fetched $4,338,500 (£2,706,490), including buyer's premium, at Christie's in New York City, USA, on 8 November 2011. (*See p.149*)

 Danseuse au repos (c. 1879), a pastel of a ballet dancer by French artist Edgar Degas, sold for £17,601,500 ($27,854,400) at Sotheby's, London, UK, on 28 June 1999, making it the **most expensive work of art on paper**.

The **most expensive drawing by an Old Master** is the *Head of a Muse* by Raphael (Italy), which sold for £29,200,000 ($47,788,400) on 9 December 2009 at Christie's, London, UK.

 The **most expensive sculpture** sold at auction is Alberto Giacometti's (Switzerland) bronze sculpture entitled *L'Homme qui marche I* (*The Walking Man I*, 1960), which sold to an anonymous bidder at Sotheby's, London, UK, for a record £65,000,000 ($103,676,000) on 3 February 2010.

 Damien Hirst (UK) made £111 million ($200.8 million) during an auction on 15 and 16 September 2008, the **most money made at auction by an artist**. Of the 167 works that went on sale at Sotheby's in London, UK, only three were not sold.

The **most expensive painting in private sale** is French artist Paul Cézanne's *The Card Players*. One of a series of five, it was sold to the royal family of Qatar for more than $250 million (£158.3 million) in 2011. *Vanity Fair* magazine broke news of the sale in February 2012.

All currency conversions have been calculated as of the date of sale when known.

YOUNGEST...

You might be surprised at just how young some GWR record holders are! Here's a selection of remarkably young achievers, listed by ascending age.

No.1 box-office star

Film star Shirley Temple (USA, b. 23 April 1928) was seven years old when she became No.1 at the box office in 1935, retaining the title until 1938.

Temple's great popularity saw her become the **youngest millionairess (non-inherited)**.

She had earned more than $1 million (£204,498) before she reached the age of 10.

The **youngest millionaire (non-inherited)** was the American child film actor Jackie Coogan (1914–84), who was born in Los Angeles, California, USA. In 1923–24, he was earning $22,000 (£11,936) per week and retained approximately 60% of his films' profits. By the age of 13, Coogan had become a millionaire in his own right.

Club DJ

Jack Hill (UK, b. 20 May 2000) played at CK's Bar and Club in Weston-super-Mare, Somerset, UK, on 26 August 2007 aged 7 years 98 days.

Film director

The youngest director of a professionally made feature-length film is Kishan Shrikanth (India, b. 6 January 1996), who directed *C/o Footpath* (India, 2006) – about an orphaned boy who wants to go to school – when he was nine years old.

Graduate

Michael Kearney (USA) obtained his BA in anthropology from the University of South Alabama, USA, in June 1994, at the age of 10 years 4 months. He went on to gain his Master of Science degree in biochemistry on 9 August 1998, aged just 14 years 8 months.

Author of a best-selling book series

Born on 17 November 1983, Christopher Paolini (USA) is the author of the *Inheritance Cycle* series. It had sold in excess of 20 million copies as of May 2011 and remains a firm favourite of fantasy fans the world over.

Drummer

The youngest professional drummer is Julian Pavone (USA, b. 14 May 2004). As of 24 January 2012, he was 7 years 8 months 10 days old. Julian started off by playing while seated on his father's lap, at the age of just three months, and released his first CD, *Go Baby!*, at the age of just 23 months. He plays a 22-piece kit, including 17 cymbals.

Chess grandmaster

Child prodigy Sergey Karjakin (Ukraine, b. 12 January 1990) qualified as an international chess grandmaster on 12 August 2002, at the age of 12 years 212 days. The title has been in existence since 1950.

Doctorate

On 13 April 1814, Carl Witte of Lochau, Austria, was made a Doctor of Philosophy (PhD) at the University of Giessen, Germany, at the age of 12.

Olympic gold medallist

The youngest female Olympic champion was Kim Yun-mi (South Korea, b. 1 December 1980), aged 13 years 85 days, in the 1994 women's 3,000 m short-track speedskating relay event.

Composer of a musical

Adám Lörincz (Hungary, b. 1 June 1988) was aged 14 years 76 days when his 92-minute musical *Star of the King* was performed on 16 August 2002 in Székesfehérvár, Hungary.

SNAP SHOT

• Julian's father used to play music to his mother's pregnant belly and Julian would kick back with some amazingly tuneful rhythms.

• Rock musician Tom Petty has been in touch with Julian and already regards him as a major talent in the making.

• When Julian first took the record title, he was four years younger than the previous youngest drummer, Tiger Onitsuka (Japan).

FACT: The first drum kits date way back to the 19th century, when pedals for bass drums were invented.

Professional poker player

Joe Cada (USA, b. 18 November 1987) became the youngest winner of the World Series of Poker main event at the age of 21 years 357 days on 10 November 2009. Joe earned $8,547,044 (£5,250,449).

FIFA World Cup finals goalscorer
Pelé (b. Edson Arantes do Nascimento) was 17 years 239 days old when he scored for Brazil against Wales at Gothenburg, Sweden, on 19 June 1958.

NBA player
Jermaine O'Neal (USA, b. 13 October 1978) made his debut for the Portland Trail Blazers against the Denver Nuggets on 5 December 1996 at the age of 18 years 53 days.

Hollywood producer
Steven Paul (USA) was 20 when he produced and directed *Falling in Love Again* (USA, 1980), starring Elliott Gould and Susannah York, which saw the film debut of actress Michelle Pfeiffer. He has produced a further 28 films and directed the 1993 *NYPD Blue* TV series.

Super Bowl player
At 21 years 155 days, Jamal Lewis (USA, b. 26 August 1979) of the Baltimore Ravens is the youngest player to ever appear in the Super Bowl. Lewis ran for 102 yards and a touchdown in a 34–7 romp over the New York Giants at Super Bowl XXXV on 28 January 2001.

Oscar winner (Best Actress)
On 30 March 1987, aged 21 years 218 days, Marlee Matlin (USA, b. 24 August 1965) won the Best Actress award for playing Sarah Norman in *Children of a Lesser God* (USA, 1986).

The **youngest winner of an Oscar for Best Actor** is Adrien Brody (USA, b. 14 April 1974). He picked up the award on 23 March 2003 for his performance as Wladyslaw Szpilman in *The Pianist*

(France/Germany/UK/Poland, 2002), aged 29 years 343 days.

Formula One World Champion
Sebastian Vettel (Germany, b. 3 July 1987) won his first Formula One World Championship aged 23 years 134 days. He took the title on 14 November 2010, at the Abu Dhabi Grand Prix in the United Arab Emirates.

Vettel is also the **youngest driver to win a Formula One World Championship race**. He was 21 years 72 days old when he won the Italian Grand Prix on 14 September 2008, driving for Toro Rosso.

Prime minister
William Pitt (1759–1806) was 24 years 205 days old when he assumed office on 19 December 1783. He had previously declined the premiership at the age of 23 years 275 days. (In fact, the term "prime minister" wasn't officially used to describe the role until 1905.)

Astronaut
Major (later Lieutenant-General) Gherman Stepanovich Titov (USSR, b. 11 September 1935) was aged 25 years 329 days when he launched in *Vostok 2* on 6 August 1961.

The **youngest female astronaut** was Valentina Tereshkova (USSR, b. 6 March 1937), who was 26 years 102 days old when she became the **first woman in space** on 16 June 1963 in *Vostok 6*.

Antarctic solo trekker
On 20 December 1998, 26-year-old Swede Ola Skinnarmo arrived on his own, unaided, at the Scott Base in Antarctica after a 47-day, 1,200-km (750-mile) trek on skis across the frozen continent. Ola was pulling a sled that weighed approximately 120 kg (260 lb) when fully laden, yet still managed to finish 10 days earlier than he had expected.

Chief Scout
The youngest Chief Scout is Edward "Bear" Grylls (UK). He was 34 years old when he received the appointment from The Council of the Scout Movement in London, in 2009.

X Games gold medallist

Lyn-z Adams Hawkins (USA, b. 21 September 1989) became the youngest female to win a gold medal at the X Games in any discipline when she won the Skateboard Vert competition aged 14 years 321 days at X Games 10, Los Angeles, California, USA, on 7 August 2004.

GUINNESS WORLD RECORDS

BIRTH RATES
Average number of children per woman (estimated, 2010–15)

Highest		
1	Niger	7.2
2	Afghanistan	6.6
3	Mali	6.5
	Timor-Leste	6.5
5	Somalia	6.4
	Uganda	6.4
7	Chad	6.2
	Zambia	6.2
9	Congo-Kinshasa	6.1
10	Malawi	6.0

Lowest		
1	Hong Kong	1.0
	Macau	1.0
3	Bosnia	1.2
4	Hungary	1.3
	Japan	1.3
	Malta	1.3
	Poland	1.3
	Romania	1.3
	Singapore	1.3
	Slovakia	1.3
	South Korea	1.3

FACT: As of 2010, an estimated 52% of the world's population was under the age of 30.

YOUNG PLANET
Figures from the US Census Bureau for 2010 revealed that there were more than 2.4 billion people under 19 years old on Earth:

	0–4	5–9	10–14	15–19
♂	320,032,992	306,710,315	306,644,307	309,742,265
♀	299,175,551	288,524,929	285,899,964	288,768,476

CURIOUS CONTESTS

Most World Gravy Wrestling Championships

The most prolific winner of the World Gravy Wrestling Championships, held annually at the Rose 'n' Bowl pub in Stacksteads, Lancashire, UK, is Joel Hicks (UK). Out of the four competitive tournaments held to date, he has won the title twice, in 2009 and 2011.

MOST WINS

World Conker Championships (men)

The most World Conker Championships won in the men's category is three, by P Midlane (UK), who took the title in 1969, 1973 and 1985, and J Marsh (UK), who won in 1974, 1975 and 1994. The annual contest started in Ashton, Northamptonshire, UK, in 1965.

Gurning World Championships (women)

Between 1977 and 2010, Anne Woods (UK) won 27 Women's Gurning World Championships at the Egremont Crab Fair in Cumbria, UK.

Tommy Mattinson (UK) has recorded the **most wins of the Men's Gurning World Championships**, with 12. His flexible face took top prize at the annual Gurning World Championships at Egremont Crab Fair, UK, in 1986–87 and 10 times between 1999 and 2010.

Horseshoe Pitching World Championships (women)

Vicki Chappelle Winston (USA) won 10 Women's Horseshoe Pitching World Championships. She took the first of her titles in 1956, and the last in 1981.

Log Rolling World Championships (men)

Between 1956 and 1969, Jubiel Wickheim (Canada) triumphed in 10 Log Rolling World Championships.

World Pea Shooting Championships (men)

Mike Fordham (UK) won an unprecedented seven Championships, in 1977–78, 1981, 1983–85 and 1992.

Sandra Ashley (UK) has picked up the **most Women's World Pea Shooting Championships**, producing three wins consecutively in 2005–07.

Sauna World Championships

Timo Kaukonen (Finland) has won the Sauna World Championships in Heinola five times, in 2003, 2005–07 and 2009.

Tiddlywinks World Championships (pairs)

Larry Kahn (USA) has won the greatest number of pairs titles at the Tiddlywinks World Championships. He secured 16 victories between 1978 and 2011.

Contestants must push an opponent's foot to the other side of a ring called a "toerack" using only their toes.

Karen Davies (UK) won four times consecutively in the women's category, between 1999 and 2002 – the **most Women's Toe Wrestling World Championships**.

Most Wife Carrying World Championships (male)

Margo Uusorg (Estonia) won the World Championships five times, in 2000–01, 2003 and 2005–06.

The **most Wife Carrying World Championships won by a female** is two. The record is shared by four Estonians: Annela Ojaste (1998–99), Birgit Ullrich (2000–01), Egle Soll (2003 and 2005) and Inga Klauso (2004 and 2007).

Most underwater draughts players

The most people to play draughts (checkers) underwater at once is 88, at an event organized by Normunds Pakulis (Latvia) in Riga, Latvia, on 21 May 2011.

FACT:
Usually, around 60 divers enter these championships in Latvia. The games last up to six minutes.

Most Tiddlywinks World Championships

"Winker" extraordinaire Larry Kahn (USA) won 21 World Championships singles titles from 1983 to 2011. He discovered the game in 1971 as a student at Massachusetts Institute of Technology (MIT), USA.

Toe Wrestling World Championships (men)

Alan Nash (UK) has won six World Championships, in 1994, 1996–97, 2000, 2002 and 2009. Nash, nicknamed "Nasty", has also had the honour of being knighted by His Majesty King Leo 1st of Redonda in the West Indies.

The contest is held annually at Ye Olde Royal Oak in Wetton, Staffordshire, UK.

Wok Racing World Championships (team)

Two teams have won the Wok Racing World Championships twice each: ProSieben (Germany) in 2004–05 and TV Total (Germany) in 2009–10.

FIND MORE CONVENTIONAL SPORTS ON P.230

World Conker Championships (women)

Two women have won the World Conker Championships twice: Sheila Doubleday (UK) won the inaugural women's event in 1988 and took the title again in 1993, in a competition organized by Ashton Conker Club. Tina Stone (UK) won the event in 1994 and 2007.

World Unicycle Hockey titles

UNICON, the world championships of unicycling, has been held every two years since 1984. Unicycle hockey was added to the programme of events in 1994, since when nine tournaments have been contested. The Swiss Power Team (Switzerland) has won the title a record three times, in 2004, 2006 and 2010.

Most Men's Horseshoe Pitching World Championships

Alan Francis (USA) won the men's championships a record 15 times between 1989 and 2009.

The art of log rolling

- Both competitors ("birlers") step off a dock and on to a floating log. Assistants offer them poles so that they can steady themselves.

- The two birlers push away from the dock. When both are balanced, they dispense with the poles and set the log spinning quickly.

- Each opponent tries to slow or stop the log to dislodge their rival and send them into the water ("wetting"). If neither falls within a set time limit, they continue on a smaller log.

FASTEST TIME IN THE...

Men's World Bog Snorkelling Championships

Andrew Holmes (UK) completed the course in 1 min 24.22 sec at Llanwrtyd Wells, Powys, UK, on 28 August 2011.

Men's World Mountain Bike Bog Snorkelling Championships

Graham Robinson (UK) won the men's World Mountain Bike Bog Snorkelling Championships in 51 min 37 sec at the 2010 games in Llanwrtyd Wells, Powys, UK.

World Roof Bolting Championships

This vocational "sport" tests competitors' accuracy and skill with a roof-bolting drill machine. Brian McArdle and Les Bentlin (both Australia) secured the 1998 World

FACT: Held in Wisconsin, USA, the Lumberjack World Championships began way back in 1960.

Most Women's Log Rolling Championships

Tina Bosworth (USA, née Salzman) has taken 10 International Championships for log rolling. She won the contest – part of the Lumberjack World Championships – in 1990, 1992 and 1996–2003.

Championships by finishing the required tasks in 1 min 50.85 sec at Fingal Valley, Tasmania.

Wife Carrying Championships

On 1 July 2006, Margo Uusorg and Sandra Kullas (both Estonia) completed the 253.5-m (831-ft 8-in) obstacle course at the World Wife Carrying Championships in 56.9 seconds. This is the fastest time since a minimum "wife weight" was introduced in 2002.

Woolsack race (male)

Pete Roberts (UK) achieved the fastest men's individual time of 45.94 seconds in the 2007 World Woolsack Championships. The event is held annually at Tetbury in Gloucestershire, UK, and involves competitors racing up and down the 1-in-4 Gumstool Hill while carrying a 27.21-kg (60-lb) bag of wool on their shoulders.

The **fastest woolsack race by a woman** in the event is 1 min 6.3 sec in 2009, by Zoe Dixon (UK). Women competitors carry a 13.6-kg (30-lb) bag of wool on their shoulders.

Most Wok Racing World Championships

In wok racing, competitors make timed runs down Olympic bobsled tracks on modified Chinese woks. Georg Hackl (Germany) won six Wok Racing World Championships, in 2004–05 and 2007–10. Georg is pretty good at more conventional sports too. He has picked up five medals at consecutive Olympic Games in the luge contest, the **most consecutive individual event Olympic medals won**.

THE COTSWOLD OLIMPICKS

The modern Olympic Games was the brainchild of France's Baron de Coubertin at the end of the 19th century. But 284 years prior to the Games' revival, the Cotswold Olimpicks in Gloucestershire, UK, were first staged. Once described as a "unique blend of history, eccentricity, amateurism and enthusiasm bordering on the obsessive", this competition involves a range of rather curious disciplines:

DANCING
The medieval Morris-dancing equivalent of *Strictly Come Dancing*

CHESS
It's not all physical – this is a mental match of minds

COCKFIGHTING
Pitting one angry, aggressive rooster against another to the death

JUMPING IN SACKS
Jumping. In sacks

PIKE DRILL
Wielding a long spear with grace and aplomb

SHIN KICKING
Kicking your opponent to the ground by stamping on their shins

SPURNING THE BARRE
Middle England's version of Scotland's Highland Games caber toss

HAY BALE RACING
Shifting a bundle of hay using a wheelbarrow at high speed

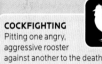

RISKY BUSINESS

FASTEST TIME TO...

Change a wheel on a spinning car
Terry Grant (UK) changed a wheel on a spinning car in 3 min 10 sec on the set of *Lo Show dei Record* in Rome, Italy, on 4 March 2010.

Drink a pint of stout upside down
Peter Dowdeswell (UK) imbibed a pint of stout while being held upside down in 5.24 seconds on the set of *Lo Show dei Record* in Milan, Italy, on 21 April 2011.

Eat a drinking glass
The fastest time to eat a drinking glass is 1 min 27 sec and was achieved by Patesh Talukdar (India) on the set of *Guinness World Records – Ab India Todega* in Mumbai, India, on 10 March 2011.

Most arrows caught blindfolded (two minutes)

Joe Alexander (Germany) caught four arrows blindfolded in two minutes at the gym of Joe Alexander Entertainment Group in Hamburg, Germany, on 16 November 2011. He was 8 m (26 ft 3 in) from the archer, Peter Dubberstein (Germany). Joe also holds the record for the **most arrows caught (two minutes)** – 43 in all – set on 17 November 2010.

Pierce four coconuts with one finger
Ho Eng Hui, aka "Master Ho" (Malaysia), took just 12.15 seconds to pierce four coconuts with a finger on the set of *Lo Show dei Record* in Milan, Italy, on 21 April 2011.

Climb the Burj Khalifa
The fastest time to climb the world's **tallest building** (see p.170) is 6 hr 13 min 55 sec by Alain Robert (France). "Spider-man", as he is known, climbed it barehanded (and with the aid of only rubber-soled shoes) between 6:03 p.m. and 12:17 a.m. on 29–30 March 2011.

HEAVIEST WEIGHT LIFTED BY...

Eye socket
Manjit Singh (UK) lifted a 14-kg (30-lb 13.7-oz) weight with his eye socket in Punjab, India, on 7 July 2011.

Beard
On 18 December 2010, Antanas Kontrimas (Lithuania) raised a female model weighing 63.4 kg (139 lb 12 oz) a distance of 10 cm (3.9 in) off the ground using only his beard on the set of *Zheng Da Zong Yi – Guinness World Records Special* in Beijing, China.

Little fingers
The heaviest deadlift using the little fingers is 67.5 kg (148 lb 12 oz), achieved by Kristian Holm (Norway) in Herefoss, Norway, on 13 November 2008.

Neck
Frank Ciavattone (USA) lifted a weight of 366.5 kg (808 lb) supported by the neck at the New England Weightlifting Club in Walpole, Massachusetts, USA, on 15 November 2005.

94 catches

Most chainsaw-juggling catches
Ian Stewart (Canada) showed he was a cut above the rest by making 94 chainsaw-juggling catches at the Hants County Exhibition in Windsor, Nova Scotia, Canada, on 25 September 2011.

Most kicks to the head in one minute (self)
The greatest number of self-administered kicks to the head in one minute is 115, by Joshua William Reed (USA) on the set of *Guinness World Records Gone Wild* at the Staples Center in Los Angeles, California, USA, on 28 September 2011.

⚠ **PLEASE DON'T** try any of these records at home! They have been set by trained professionals and are not safe enough to be attempted by members of the public.

Longest duration full-body burn (without oxygen)

Jayson Dumenigo (USA) endured a full-body burn without oxygen for 5 min 25 sec in Santa Clarita, California, USA, on 27 March 2011. Having set a new world record, Jayson stopped the attempt earlier than planned, to allow assistants to free him from his protective layers and allow him to breathe freely again. He has worked on a number of big-budget blockbusters, including *Fantastic Four*, *Ocean's Eleven*, *Ocean's Twelve* and the first three instalments of *Pirates of the Caribbean*.

MOST...

Champagne bottles sabred simultaneously
A group of 196 participants sabred champagne bottles at once in an event organized by Centro Empresarial e Cultural de Garibaldi (Brazil) at the Fenachamp 2011 champagne festival in Garibaldi, Rio Grande, Brazil, on 8 October 2011.

Concrete blocks broken in a stack with the head
Wasantha De Zoysa (Sri Lanka) broke a stack of 12 concrete blocks using only his head in Anuradhapura, Sri Lanka, on 23 August 2009.

Most concrete blocks broken on the head with a bowling ball
John Ferraro (USA) stacked 45 concrete blocks on his head and had his assistant smash them by dropping a 7.3-kg (16-lb) bowling ball on to them on the set of *Lo Show dei Record* in Milan, Italy, on 14 April 2011.

Cups kicked off a head (one minute)
David Synave (France) kicked 89 plastic cups off the head of an assistant in one minute in Nord-Pas-de-Calais, France, on 17 September 2011.

Born to burn

When it comes to fiery daredevils, Jayson has some company...

• The **greatest number of simultaneous full-body burns** is 17 and was achieved during an event set up by Ted Batchelor and the "Ohio Burn Unit" (all USA) in South Russell, Ohio, USA, on 19 September 2009.

• Ted also holds the record for the **longest distance run while on fire** – 150.23 m (492 ft 10 in), set at King's Home in Chelsea, Alabama, USA, on 4 December 2011.

• The **longest distance pulled by a horse while on full-body burn** was 472.8 m (1,551 ft 2 in) by Halapi Roland (Hungary) in Kisoroszi, Hungary, on 12 November 2008.

JAYSON BEAT THE PREVIOUS RECORD BY 40 SECONDS

Fastest time to jump over three moving cars

The fastest time to leap over three moving cars head-on is 1 min 11.79 sec and was achieved by Aaron Evans (USA) on the set of *Guinness World Records Gone Wild* at the Staples Center in Los Angeles, USA, on 28 September 2011. Each of the cars was driven head-on towards Aaron at a speed of 40 km/h (25 mi/h). He took a run-up towards each vehicle before jumping off the ground and performing a front flip over it, clearing its length completely without touching any part of the vehicle itself.

FACT: Aaron's feat was inspired by a video in which NBA star Kobe Bryant seems to jump a moving Aston Martin.

UNDER RISK UNDERWATER

If a record doesn't feel quite demanding enough, why not try it underwater? These people did...

Greatest depth cycled underwater
• 66.5 m (218 ft 2 in)
• Vittorio Innocente (Italy)
• Santa Margherita Ligure, Liguria, Italy
• 21 July 2008

Farthest distance cycled underwater
• 3.04 km (1.87 miles)
• Ashrita Furman (USA)
• Complexo Olímpico de Piscinasde Coimbra, Coimbra, Portugal
• 22 September 2011

Farthest distance on a pogo stick underwater
• 512.06 m (1,680 ft)
• Ashrita Furman (USA)
• Nassau County Aquatic Center, East Meadow, New York, USA
• 1 August 2007

Fastest escape from a straitjacket underwater
• 15.41 seconds
• Matthew Cassiere aka "Matt the Knife" (USA)
• *Zheng Da Zong Yi – Guinness World Records Special*, CCTV Studios, Beijing, China
• 13 September 2007

Fastest escape from handcuffs underwater
• 4 seconds
• Zdeněk Bradáč (Czech Republic)
• Jablonec nad Nisou swimming pool, Jablonec nad Nisou, Czech Republic
• 15 February 2011

Longest submergence underwater in a controlled environment
• 4 days 4 hours (100 hours total)
• Ronny Frimann (Norway)
• Central Station, Oslo, Norway
• 14–18 June 2007

Longest time breath held underwater voluntarily
• 21 min 33 sec
• Peter Colat (Switzerland)
• Ebikon, Switzerland
• 17 September 2011

Deepest underwater escape using equipment
• 183 m (601 ft)
• Norman Cooke and Hamish Jones (both UK)
• From submarine HMS *Otus* in Bjørnefjorden, off Bergen, Norway
• 22 July 1987

CONTENTS

Longest journey by quad bike

Quad Squad Expedition team members Valerio De Simoni, Kristopher Davant and James Kenyon (all Australia) started out from Istanbul, Turkey, on 10 August 2010, and went on to set a new record for the longest journey on a quad bike (ATV) by covering 56,239 km (34,945 miles). The trip ended in Sydney, Australia, with a 500-strong motorcycle escort, on 22 October 2011 after 437 days 19 hr 9 min. The team had traversed 37 countries.

HOW DEEP CAN WE GO?

What's the greatest depth we can reach?

With his Virgin Oceanic project, Richard Branson (UK) hopes to achieve a solo trip to the deepest points in every ocean. But just how far will he be able to descend in his *Deep Flight Challenger* submersible? What's the absolute limit when it comes to plumbing the depths of our planet?

FACT: The depth of water was traditionally measured in "fathoms" – the length of a man's outstretched arms (1.8 m; 6 ft).

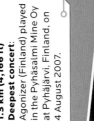

1.3 km (4,166 ft)
Deepest concert: Agonizer (Finland) played in the Pyhäsalmi Mine Oy at Pyhäjärvi, Finland, on 4 August 2007.

212 m (695 ft)
Deepest half marathon: A competition between 11 racers in the Bochnia salt mine in Poland on 4 March 2004.

2.191 km (1.3 miles)
Deepest cave: In September 2007, Ukranian cavers (speleologists) reached a new record depth at the Krubera Cave in the Arabika Massif of Georgia.

3.9 km (2.4 miles)
Deepest mine: The TauTona gold mine near Carletonville, South Africa, began operation in 1962 and, by 2008, had reached 3.9 km (2.4 miles) deep. The lift journey can take one hour.

1.3–3.6 km (0.8–2.2 miles)
Deepest land-dwelling creature
The 0.5-mm-long (0.02-in) nematode worm *Halicephalobus mephisto* – aka the "worm from hell" – was found in a South African goldmine in 2011.

FACT: Water pressure is the weight of the sea above you, where 1 bar = 1.19 kg/cm² (14.5 lb/in²).

318.2 m (1,044 ft) Deepest scuba dive: Nuno Gomes (South Africa) descended a fifth of a mile in the Red Sea off Dahab, Egypt, on 10 June 2005.

1 km (3,345 ft)
Deepest operational combat submarine: No military sub has gone deeper than the Russian K-278.

2 km (1.2 miles) Deepest dive by a mammal: A bull sperm whale (*Physeter macrocephalus*) was studied off the coast of Dominica in the Caribbean in 1991.

2.4 km (1.5 miles)
Deepest live TV broadcast by a presenter: Alastair Fothergill (UK) relayed *Abyss Live* for the BBC on 29 September 2002 from inside a Mir submersible, along the Mid-Atlantic Ridge off the eastern coast of the USA.

4 km (2.5 miles) Wreck of RMS Titanic
The pride of the White Star Line (UK) was sunk on 15 April 1912 off Newfoundland, Canada, with the loss of 1,517 lives. The **youngest person to dive to the Titanic** is Sebastian Harris (UK), who was 13 years old when he visited the site in the *Mir 2* submersible on 2 August 2005.

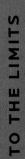

-1,000 m
-2,000 m
-3,000 m
-4,000 m
-5,000 m

(1 bar)
-1,000 m (101 bar)
-2,000 m (202 bar)
-3,000 m (302 bar)
-4,000 m (403 bar)
-5,000 m (503 bar)

1 bar = 100,000 Pascals (a unit of pressure); rounded off to nearest whole number

On land: Even at 12.2 km (7.6 miles), the deepest bore hole (see below) is barely a scratch on the Earth's surface. The planet's outer crust comprises 35 km (21.5 miles) of solid rock. Assuming we could stop water seeping into our hole – a constant problem in mines – we'd also have to contend with temperatures that rise the deeper we go; at the bottom of the 3,900-m-deep (2.4-mile) TauTona mineshaft (above), our current depth limit on land, the heat rises to 55°C (131°F).

On breaking through the crust, we'd then face the challenge of the mantle: 3,000 km (1,864 miles) of super-heated rock at 400–900°C (752–1,652°F) – depending on depth. Temperatures here are far beyond the operational limits of any known heatproof suit. Still want to keep digging?

In the ocean: Human beings evolved to live on land. Under the water, we soon discover the limits this places on us. We can't breathe, our senses become dulled, and the pressure exerted by the water as we travel deeper becomes increasingly dangerous. Here, we are little more than well-equipped cavemen, using technology to plunge our Stone Age bodies into the abyss.

However, by shielding our fragile bodies from the effects of pressure, nitrogen narcosis and oxygen toxicity, we can voyage to the deepest, darkest crevices of our oceans. As humans have already travelled to the deepest known point in the ocean, this is one record that has already reached its absolute limit. The Virgin team now faces the added challenge of making the first solo dives to the deepest points in the oceans. Good luck!

5.8 km (3.6 miles)
Deepest shipwreck: World War II German blockade runner SS *Rio Grande*, discovered in 1996 at the bottom of the South Atlantic Ocean, on 30 November 1996.

6.5 km (4 miles)
Deepest submersible in service
Built in 1990, the Shinkai 6500 is a Japanese three-man research submarine with a 7.35-cm-thick (2.9-in) hull. It made its 1,000th dive in 2007.

Deepest points in each ocean
Arctic: 5.60 km
Southern: 7.23 km
Indian: 8.04 km
Atlantic: 8.38 km
Pacific: 11.03 km

FACT:
At these depths, the oceans rarely get above 4°C (39°F) – even in the warmest tropical regions.

8.4 km (5.2 miles)
Deepest fish: A 20-cm-long (8-in) species of cusk eel (*Abyssobrotula galatheae*) found in the Puerto Rico Trench of the Atlantic Ocean.

Depth to which Mt Everest would descend

10.9 km (6.7 miles)
Deepest descent by a manned vessel
Jacques Piccard (Switzerland) and Donald Walsh (USA) piloted the bathyscaphe *Trieste* to the "Challenger Deep" section of the Mariana Trench (see below) on 23 January 1960. On 25 March 2012, James Cameron (USA) made the same journey alone – the **deepest solo descent** – in the *DEEPSEA CHALLENGER* (pictured), a "vertical torpedo" that allowed him to make the first ever exploration of the trench.

10.1 km (6.2 miles)
Deepest oil well:
The *Deepwater Horizon* semi-submersible drilling rig operated to this depth in the Tiber oil field in the Gulf of Mexico.

FACT:
To reach the centre of the Earth, you'd have to dig through about 6,370 km of solid rock and molten magma!

11 km (6.8 miles)
Deepest part of the ocean:
The Mariana Trench in the Pacific Ocean is the deepest natural point on the surface of the Earth.

12.3 km (7.6 miles)
Deepest penetration into Earth's crust:
A geological exploratory borehole near Zapolyarny on the Kola peninsula of Arctic Russia. It was begun on 24 May 1970 and had reached this record depth by 1983, when work stopped because of a lack of funds.

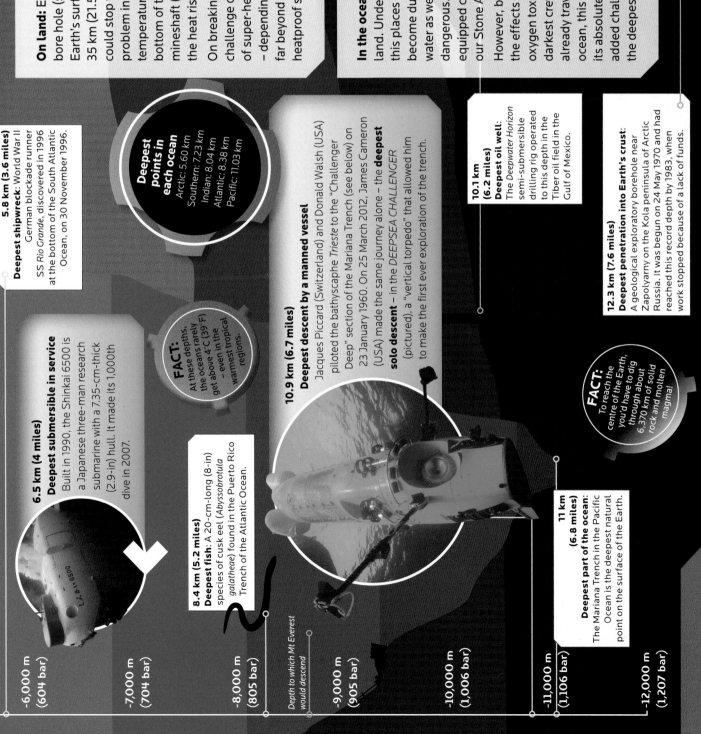

-6,000 m (604 bar)
-7,000 m (704 bar)
-8,000 m (805 bar)
-9,000 m (905 bar)
-10,000 m (1,006 bar)
-11,000 m (1,106 bar)
-12,000 m (1,207 bar)

CIRCUMNAVIGATION

Fastest circumnavigation by bicycle

The speediest circumnavigation by bicycle took 106 days 10 hr 33 min and was achieved by Alan Bate (UK), who cycled a distance of 29,467.91 km (18,310.47 miles) and travelled 42,608.76 km (26,475.8 miles), including transfers. The journey lasted from 31 March to 4 August 2010, starting and finishing at the Grand Palace in Bangkok, Thailand.

Fastest circumnavigation by yacht

On their arrival at Ushant, France, on 6 January 2012, Loïck Peyron (France) and the 13-man crew of *Banque Populaire V* became record holders. They had sailed their yacht around the world in a time of 45 days 13 hr 42 min 53 sec – more than two days faster than the previous record, set by Franck Cammas (France). The feat saw the team take the Jules Verne Trophy – a competition for the fastest circumnavigation by yacht – which Peyron's brother Bruno has won three times.

FIRST...

Ever circumnavigation
History's first circumnavigation of the world was accomplished on 8 September 1522, when the Spanish vessel *Vittoria*, under the command of the Spanish navigator Juan Sebastián de Elcano, reached Seville in Spain. The ship had set out from Sanlúcar de Barrameda, Andalucía, Spain, on 20 September 1519, along with four others as part of an expedition led by the Portuguese explorer Ferdinand Magellan. They rounded Cape Horn, crossed the Pacific via the Philippines, and returned to Europe after sailing around the Cape of Good Hope. *Vittoria* was the only ship to survive the voyage.

By walking
The first person reputed to have walked round the world is George Matthew Schilling (USA), from 1897 to 1904. The first verified achievement was by David Kunst (USA), who walked 23,250 km (14,450 miles) through four continents from 20 June 1970 to 5 October 1974.

By aircraft without refuelling
Richard G "Dick" Rutan and Jeana Yeager (both USA) circumnavigated the world westwards from Edwards Air Force Base, California, USA, in nine days from 14 to 23 December 1986 without refuelling.

Via both Poles by aircraft
Captain Elgen M Long (USA) achieved the first circumpolar flight in a twin-engined Piper PA-31 Navajo from 5 November to 3 December 1971. He covered 62,597 km (38,896 miles) during the course of 215 flying hours.

Via both Poles by helicopter
Jennifer Murray and Colin Bodill (both UK) flew around the world, taking in both Poles, from 5 December 2006 to 23 May 2007, in a Bell 407 helicopter. The journey started and finished in Fort Worth, Texas, USA.

FACT: *Banque Populaire V* sailed 21,600 nautical miles (40,030 km; 24,870 miles).

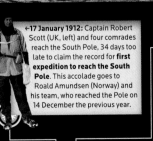

- Circumnavigation
- Polar
- Mountaineering
- Land & Air
- Sea

←17 January 1912: Captain Robert Scott (UK, left) and four comrades reach the South Pole, 34 days too late to claim the record for **first expedition to reach the South Pole**. This accolade goes to Roald Amundsen (Norway) and his team, who reached the Pole on 14 December the previous year.

→7 March 1912: Roald Amundsen arrives at Hobart in Tasmania, Australia, with confirmation of his successful polar trip.

29 March 1912: Scott and his crew perish on their return journey from the South Pole.

→1914–15: Ernest Shackleton (UK) attempts to cross Antarctica via the South Pole but his ship, *Endurance*, freezes in pack ice and eventually sinks.

↑14 June 1919: John Alcock and Arthur Brown (UK) fly from Newfoundland in Canada to Connemara in Ireland, the **first non-stop transatlantic flight**. They touch down the following day and win themselves a £10,000 prize (equivalent today of £360,000; $570,000).

1912   1913   1914   1915   1916   1917   1918   1919   1920   1921

FACT: TÚRANOR PlanetSolar is 31 m (101 ft) long and has a displacement of 85 tonnes, making it the **largest solar-powered boat**.

First circumnavigation by solar-powered boat

MS *TÛRANOR PlanetSolar* (Switzerland) circumnavigated the world in a westward direction from Monaco in 1 year 7 months 7 days from 27 September 2010 to 4 May 2012. The catamaran's upper surface is covered in 537 m² (5,780 ft²) of solar panels, allowing it to be powered by solar energy alone.

FASTEST...

Sailing solo
Francis Joyon (France) sailed the world non-stop in 57 days 13 hr 34 min 6 sec, from 23 November 2007 to 20 January 2008, in the 29.5-m (97-ft) maxi-trimaran *IDEC II*. The 21,600-nautical-mile (38,900-km; 24,170-mile) trip began and ended in Brest, France.

The **fastest solo sailed circumnavigation by a woman** was achieved by Ellen MacArthur (UK). She sailed non-stop around the world in 71 days 14 hr 18 min 33 sec from 28 November 2004 to 7 February 2005 in the trimaran *B&Q*.

By passenger aircraft
The fastest flown circumnavigation under the Fédération Aéronautique Internationale (FAI) rules, which permit flights that exceed the length of the Tropic of Cancer or Capricorn (36,787.6 km; 22,858.8 miles), was one of 31 hr 27 min 49 sec. The aircraft was an Air France Concorde, piloted by captains Michel Dupont and Claude Hetru (both France). The flight lasted from 15 to 16 August 1995; a total of 80 passengers and 18 crew were also on board.

By balloon solo
Steve Fossett (USA) flew around the world alone in 13 days 8 hr 33 min in *Bud Light Spirit of Freedom* from 19 June to 2 July 2002. He took off from Northam, Western Australia, and landed at Eromanga in Queensland, Australia.

By helicopter
Edward Kasprowicz (USA) and his crewman Stephen Sheik flew around the world in an easterly direction in an AgustaWestland Grand helicopter in 11 days 7 hr 5 min, completing their epic trip on 18 August 2008. The journey started and finished in New York, USA, travelling via Greenland, UK, Italy, Russia, USA and Canada.

By car
The record for the first and fastest man and woman to have circumnavigated the Earth by car covering six continents under the rules applicable in 1989 and 1991 embracing more than an equator's length of driving (24,901 road miles; 40,075 km), is held by Saloo Choudhury and his wife Neena Choudhury (both India). The journey took 69 days 19 hours 5 minutes from 9 September to 17 November 1989. The couple drove a 1989 Hindustan "Contessa Classic" starting and finishing in Delhi, India.

Going global

These are the current rules for a "true" circumnavigation, as defined in the official GWR guidelines:

- A circumnavigation must pass through two antipodes (opposite points of the Earth's surface)

- The traveller must start and finish at the same point – and travel in only one direction

- All lines of longitude must be crossed

- A minimum distance of 40,000 km (24,855 miles), or 21,600 nautical miles (40,030 km; 24,870 miles), should be covered

- Claimants must be aged 16 or older.

First circumnavigation in a hydrogen-powered car

Mercedes-Benz (Germany) was the first manufacturer to circumnavigate the world with a hydrogen-powered "fuel cell" vehicle. A fleet of three identical cars (based on the company's B-Class hatchback) carried out the 125-day journey to mark the car-maker's 125th anniversary. The trip started and finished in Stuttgart, Germany.

1924: First Olympic medal for alpinism (mountain climbing) is awarded at the Chamonix Winter Games to the team led by Brigadier Charles Bruce (UK) for the (failed) 1922 Mount Everest expedition.

↓**4 June 1924:** A British duo set off on an attempt to be the first climbers to summit Mount Everest – but disappear. George Mallory (pictured) and Andrew Irvine are last seen a few hundred metres from the summit, but we will never know if they reached the peak. Mallory's body is eventually found in 1999.

28 September 1924: Two US Army Douglas DWC seaplanes complete the **first circumnavigation by aircraft**; they do so in a series of 57 "hops" starting and finishing in Seattle, Washington, USA.

↗**20 May 1927:** Charles Lindbergh (USA) sets off on the **first solo flight across the Atlantic Ocean** in his monoplane *Spirit of St Louis*.

31 May 1928: Charles Kingford Smith (Australia) captains the **first transpacific flight**, from the USA to Australia.

→**29 November 1929:** Richard Byrd (USA) captains the **first flight over the South Pole** in the *Floyd Bennett* Ford trimotor.

26 July 1930: Charles Creighton and James Hargis (both USA) set off from New York on the **fastest drive across the USA in reverse**; they arrive at Los Angeles, California, without once stopping the engine.

1922 1923 1924 1925 1926 1927 1928 1929 1930 1931

POLAR JOURNEYS

FASTEST...

Solo journey to the South Pole (unsupported and unassisted)

On 13 January 2011, Christian Eide (Norway) completed a solo and unsupported trek to the South Pole in 24 days 1 hr 13 min. He set off on the 1,150-km (715-mile) adventure on 20 December 2010 and covered an average of 47 km (29 miles) per day. Eide smashed the previous record – Todd Carmichael's (USA) 39 days 7 hr 49 min – and has set a benchmark that many polar explorers consider near-impossible to beat.

Ray Zahab, Kevin Vallely and Richard Weber (all Canada) reached the South Pole from the Hercules Inlet, Antarctica, on 7 January 2009 after 33 days 23 hr 30 min, the **fastest journey to the South Pole by a team (unsupported and unassisted)**.

Trek to the North Pole

David J P Pierce Jones (UK), Richard Weber, Tessum Weber (both Canada) and Howard Fairbanks (South Africa) trekked to the North Pole in 41 days 18 hr 52 min, from 3 March to 14 April 2010. The team set out on 3 March from 82°58'02"N, 77°23'3"W and were picked up after reaching the North Pole, 90°N, on 14 April 2010.

Trek to the North Pole by a female (unsupported)

Cecilie Skog (Norway) made an unsupported trek to the North Pole in 48 days 22 hr. She left Ward-Hunt Island with teammates, Rolf Bae and Per Henry Borch (both Norway), on 6 March 2006 and reached the North Pole on 24 April 2006.

Owing to this trek, Skog is also the **fastest female to complete the Three Poles Challenge** (conquering both poles and Mount Everest), taking just 1 year 336 days.

FIRST...

Person to reach the North Pole

The question of who first reached the North Pole has long been a matter of debate. Robert Peary, travelling with Matt Henson (both USA), indicated he had reached the North Pole on 6 April 1909. Frederick Cook (USA) claimed he had done so a year earlier, on 21 April 1908. Neither claim has been convincingly proven.

Person to reach the South Pole

A Norwegian party of five men led by Captain Roald Amundsen reached the South Pole at 11 a.m. on 14 December 1911 after a 53-day march with dog sledges from the Bay of Whales, Antarctica.

Youngest person to ski to the South Pole

Amelia Hempleman-Adams (UK, b. 1 June 1995) was aged just 16 years 190 days when she reached the South Pole on 9 December 2011, after skiing 156 km (97 miles). She and her father David spent 17 nights in Antarctica, enduring white-outs and temperatures as low as -50°C (-58°F).

Surface crossing of Antarctica

A party of 12 led by Sir Vivian Ernest Fuchs (UK) completed a crossing of Antarctica on 2 March 1958, after a trek of 3,473 km (2,158 miles) lasting 99 days from 24 November 1957. They crossed from Shackleton Base to Scott Base via the Pole.

Person to visit both Poles

Dr Albert Paddock Crary (USA) reached the North Pole in a Dakota aircraft on 3 May 1952. On 12 February 1961, he arrived at the South Pole by Sno-Cat on a scientific traverse party from the McMurdo Station.

Person to walk to both Poles

Robert Swan (UK) led the three-man "In the Footsteps of Scott" expedition, which arrived at the South Pole on 11 January 1986. Three years later, he headed the eight-man "Icewalk" expedition, reaching the North Pole on 14 May 1989.

Person to walk to both Poles solo and unsupported

Marek Kamiński (Poland) reached the North Pole from Ward Hunt Island on 23 May 1995, an 880-km (546-mile) trip, in 72 days. He trekked 1,400 km (870 miles) to the South Pole from Berkner Island, Antarctica, in 53 days, arriving on 27 December 1995.

First female to ski solo across Antarctica

Felicity Aston (UK) became the first woman to ski solo across Antarctica when she arrived at the Hercules Inlet on the Ronne Ice Shelf on 23 January 2012 after a 1,744.5-km (1,084-mile) journey lasting 59 days. She made the trip while pulling two sledges and without the assistance of kites or any other propulsion aids.

Most South Pole treks in a year

There were 19 Antarctic expeditions in 2011, mostly to mark the centenary of the race to the South Pole between Roald Amundsen and Captain R Scott.

○ **Circumnavigation**

✳ **Polar**

⛰ **Mountaineering**

◦ **Land & Air**

⊙ **Sea**

→21 May 1932: Female aviator Amelia Earhart (USA) becomes the **first woman to fly solo across the Atlantic.**

↓22 July 1933: Wiley Post (USA) is the **first person to fly around the world solo** in the Lockheed Vega *Winnie Mae*, starting and finishing in New York, USA.

15 August 1934: William Beebe and Otis Barton (both USA) descend to a then-record 923 m (3,028 ft) in a tethered bathysphere, the **first deep-ocean dive**.

20 February 1935: Caroline Mikkelsen (Denmark), the wife of a Norwegian whaling captain, makes history by becoming the **first woman to set foot on Antarctica**.

2 July 1937: Amelia Earhart vanishes over the Pacific Ocean during an attempt at flying around the world.

24 July 1938: A German-Austrian team solve the "last great problem of the Alps" by completing the first ascent of the north face of the Eiger in Switzerland.

| 1932 | 1933 | 1934 | 1935 | 1936 | 1937 | 1938 | 1939 | 1940 | 1941 |

Aircraft flight over the North Pole

The first verified flight over the North Pole was achieved on 12 May 1926 by the crew of a 106-m (348-ft) airship led by Norwegian explorer Roald Amundsen and Umberto Nobile (Italy), the airship's designer and pilot.

Ivan André Trifonov (Austria) flew a one-man Thunder and Colt Cloudhopper balloon 1 km (0.6 miles) over the geographic North Pole at 18:30 GMT on 20 April 1996, the **first hot-air balloon flight over the North Pole**.

Hot-air balloon flight over the South Pole

Ivan André Trifonov floated over the geographic South Pole at an altitude of 4,570 m (15,000 ft) with two Spanish crew members on 8 January 2000.

Winter expedition to the North Pole

Matvey Shparo and Boris Smolin (both Russia) began the earliest winter expedition to the North Pole on 22 December 2007, the day of winter solstice, from the Arktichesky Cape, the northern point of the Zevernaya Zemlya Archipelago. They reached the North Pole on 14 March 2008, eight days before the vernal equinox, the official beginning of the polar "day".

Unsupported journey to the North Pole

Along with husband Thomas, Tina Sjögren (both Sweden) made the journey in 68 days from 22 March to 29 May 2002. The couple received no external support on their trek.

Tina is also the **first woman to complete an unsupported journey to the South Pole**. With her husband, she made the journey from the Hercules Inlet in 63 days, from 30 November 2001 to 1 February 2002.

Fastest overland journey to the South Pole

To mark the 100th anniversary of Amundsen's epic polar trip (see p.118), Jason De Carteret and Kieron Bradley (both UK) travelled to the South Pole in a record time of 1 day 15 hr 54 min. They set off on 18 December 2011 in the Thomson Reuters Polar Vehicle, driving from Patriot Hills at an average speed of 27.9 km/h (17.34 mi/h) – also beating the record for the **fastest average speed for a South Pole journey**.

FACT:
Aleksander travelled without the aid of food drops, snowmobiles, kites or any form of assistance.

FACT:
There is no sun at the South Pole for 182 days of the year. At the North Pole, the figure is 176 days.

Farthest unsupported solo ski journey

Aleksander Gamme (Norway) skied 2,270 km (1,410 miles) across Antarctica from Hercules Inlet to the South Pole and returning to a point 1 km (0.6 miles) from his start. There, he waited almost five days to cross the finish line, on 24 January 2012, with skiers James Castrission and Justin Jones (both Australia), who had travelled a similar route.

Prior to her polar treks, Tina had summitted Mount Everest on 26 May 1999; the mountain is often regarded as a "pole" owing to its inaccessibility. Tina's success at reaching all three landmarks constitutes the **first completion by a female of the Three Poles Challenge**.

Married couple to reach both Poles

Mike and Fiona Thornewill (UK) skied to the South Pole on 4 January 2000, and the North Pole on 6 May 2001. Both trips were air-supported and on both the duo were accompanied by teammate Catharine Hartley (UK). She and Fiona became the first British women to walk to the North and South Poles.

Person to complete the Three Poles Challenge

Erling Kagge (Norway) became the first person to complete the trio of the North Pole (reached on 8 May 1990), the South Pole (on 7 January 1993) and the peak of Mount Everest (on 8 May 1994).

Person to complete the Explorers' Grand Slam

Park Young-Seok (South Korea) reached the North Pole on foot on 30 April 2005, becoming the first person to achieve the Explorers' Grand Slam. This involves climbing the highest peaks on all seven continents (the "Seven Summits") and the 14 peaks over 8,000 m (26,246 ft), and reaching the North and South Poles on foot.

Polar opposites

• As well as the geographic Poles (the most northerly and southerly points of the Earth) there are Magnetic North and South Poles. These are the most northerly and southerly points of the Earth's magnetic field.

• Antarctica is far colder than the Arctic. In 1983, it saw the **lowest-ever temperature**: -89.2°C (-128.6°F).

• Unlike the geographic South Pole, the North Pole is covered by a floating ice cap. There is no land beneath it.

↓**1943:** Jacques Cousteau (pictured) and Émile Gagnan (both France) develop the Aqua-Lung, giving divers an unprecedented degree of freedom to explore.

1946: Alpinism is dropped as an Olympic sport.

1946–47: Operation Highjump sees the **largest expedition to Antarctica** as a 4,700-strong US Navy force establishes a presence on the continent.

↑**14 October 1947:** US test pilot Chuck Yeager takes his Bell X-1 through the sound barrier, the **first supersonic flight**.

↓**1949:** Otis Barton (USA) breaks his own deep-dive record with a 1,372-m (4,500-ft) descent in his benthoscope submersible. This remains the deepest solo **descent by a cable-suspended submersible**.

19 July 1950: Ben and Elinore Carlin (both Australia) begin the **first** – and to date only – **successful circumnavigation by amphibious car**. Wife Elinore abandons their jeep *Half-Safe* – and their marriage – during a rest break during the trip.

1942 1943 1944 1945 1946 1947 1948 1949 1950 1951

MOUNTAINEERS

Deadliest mountain

According to the Himalayan Database, between 1950 and 2009 the death toll at Annapurna I was 62 from 1,524 attempts (in 169 expeditions), giving the peak a 4.07% mortality rate. (The mean death rate in the Himalayas is 1.55%.) The latest fatalities came in October 2011, when Young-Seok Park, Dong-Min Shin and Gi-Seok Gin (all South Korea) perished during their descent.

First person to climb all 8,000-m peaks

Reinhold Messner (Italy) became the first person to climb the world's 14 peaks over 8,000 m (26,246 ft) when he summitted Lhotse (8,501 m; 27,890 ft), on the border between Nepal and Tibet, on 16 October 1986. His quest started in June 1970. The difficulty of Messner's feat is illustrated by the fact that, by the first half of 2012, only 27 people had achieved it.

Messner, who was the first person to summit the world's three highest mountains, is considered the greatest climber of all time. He achieved all of the 14 ascents without supplementary bottled oxygen, making him the **first person to climb all 8,000-m peaks without oxygen** – a feat that, to date, has been achieved by only 12 climbers.

Fastest time to climb all 8,000-m peaks

Jerzy Kukuczka (Poland) conquered all of the 14 main peaks over 8,000 m in a time of 7 years 11 months 14 days.

First person to climb the "Seven Summits"

The Seven Summits – the highest peaks on all seven continents – are categorized in two alternative ways. The Messner list has the highest point in Oceania as Puncak Jaya in Indonesia. The Bass list recognizes Mount Kosciuszko in New South Wales, Australia, instead. Patrick Morrow (Canada) was the first person to complete the Messner list, summitting Puncak Jaya on 5 August 1986.

Oldest female to climb the Seven Summits

Caroline (Kay) LeClaire (USA, b. 8 March 1949) completed her last Seven Summits climb with her ascent of Mount Everest on 23 May 2009, at the age of 60 years 77 days.

First person to climb Annapurna I solo

On 28 October 2007, Tomaž Humar (Slovenia) completed his solo climb of Annapurna I. He chose a new route along the right side of the south face in pure "alpine" style – he carried his equipment and food with him. In "expedition" style, the climber benefits from porters and fixed lines.

Fastest time to climb El Capitan

The fastest ascent of the "Nose" of El Capitan in California, USA, was made

Oldest man to climb Mount Kilimanjaro

Richard Byerley (USA, b. 26 March 1927) reached the summit of Mount Kilimanjaro, Tanzania, aged 84 years 71 days, on 6 October 2011. The farmer from Washington, USA, began scaling the mountain on 2 October 2011 at noon, through the Machame route, accompanied by his grandchildren – Annie, aged 29 (above left), and Bren, aged 24 (above right).

by Hans Florine (USA) and Yuji Hirayama (Japan) in 2 hr 48 min 50 sec in September 2002.

The **fastest solo ascent of the "Nose" of El Capitan** was achieved by Hans Florine in 11 hr 41 min on 30 July 2005.

First ascent of K2 by a woman

Wanda Rutkiewicz (Poland) reached the summit of K2 – the world's second highest mountain, at 8,611 m (28,251 ft) – on 23 June 1986.

First ascent of K2 (west face)

Russia's Andrew Mariev and Vadim Popovich completed the first successful ascent of the notoriously vicious west face of K2. The expedition – led by Viktor Kozlov (Russia) – reached the 8,500-m-high

(28,251-ft) peak on 21 August 2007, after a gruelling 10-week climb. Incredibly, none of the team used oxygen for the climb.

Fastest time to climb Mount Everest and K2

Karl Unterkircher (Italy) summitted the Himalayan peaks of Mount Everest (8,848 m; 29,029 ft) on 24 May 2004 and K2 on 26 July 2004. In both cases he achieved this without extra oxygen. There was a 63-day gap between his ascents.

First solo summit of Mount Everest

Reinhold Messner (Italy) topped Mount Everest, solo, on 20 August 1980. It took Reinhold three days to make the ascent from his base camp at 6,500 m (21,325 ft).

First woman to climb all 8,000-m peaks

On 17 May 2010, Edurne Pasaban Lizarribar (Spain) became the first woman to climb all 14 of the peaks over 8,000 m. She began her conquest of the "8,000-ers" by reaching the top of Mount Everest on 23 May 2001 and completed it by summitting Shishapangma in Tibet, the lowest of the 14 peaks.

FACT:
Mount Everest is known to locals as Qomolangma, meaning "holy mother".

Circumnavigation

Polar

Mountaineering

Land & Air

Sea

→**29 May 1953:** Edmund Hillary (New Zealand) and Sherpa Tenzing Norgay (Nepal) succeed in the **first ascent of Mount Everest**, the world's **highest peak**.

31 July 1954: The **first ascent of K2** (the second highest mountain) is made by Achille Compagnoni and Lino Lacedelli (both Italy).

↘**November 1956:** A US Navy crew begin building the Amundsen-Scott South Pole Scientific Station, which goes on to become the **longest-serving polar research station**, continuously occupied to the present day.

23 January 1960: Jacques Piccard (Switzerland) and Don Walsh (USA) achieve the **deepest manned submarine dive** when they descend 10,911 m (35,810 ft) down the Marianas Trench in the Pacific Ocean.

1952   1953   1954   1955   1956   1957   1958   1959   1960   1961

Fastest time to climb the Seven Summits by a married couple

Rob and Joanne Gambi (UK) achieved the fastest (and **first**) Seven Summits ascent by a married couple, climbing the highest peak on each continent in 404 days for the Kosciuszko list (which takes Mount Kosciuszko as the highest point in Australasia). The couple later climbed the Carstensz Pyramid, or Puncak Jaya (Australasia's highest point, if Indonesia is included), in 799 days.

His climb was made all the more difficult by the fact that he did not use bottled oxygen.

Oldest person to climb Mount Everest (male)

According to the Senior Citizen Mount Everest Expedition, Min Bahadur Sherchan (Nepal, b. 20 June 1931) reached the Everest summit on 25 May 2008 at the age of 76 years 340 days.

Tamae Watanabe (Japan, b. 21 November 1938) became the **oldest woman to summit Everest** when she reached the peak at 9:55 a.m. on 16 May 2002 aged 63 years 177 days.

First ascent of Mount Everest (female)

Junko Tabei (Japan, b. 22 September 1939) reached the summit of Mount Everest on 16 May 1975.

Most ascents of Mount Everest by a woman

Lakpa Sherpa (Nepal) topped Mount Everest for the fifth time on 2 June 2005. She made the climb with her husband, George Dijmarescu (USA), who was himself completing his seventh ascent of Everest.

First married couple to reach the summit of Mount Everest

Phil and Susan Ershler (USA) were the first married couple to successfully climb Everest. They made it to the summit on 16 May 2002, the same day that a record 54 people also reached the top.

Most conquests of Mount Everest

Apa Sherpa (Nepal), Climbing Leader of the Eco Everest Expedition 2011, reached the summit of Mount Everest for a record-breaking 21st time on 11 May 2011. Apa made his first ascent of Everest back in May 1990 (see right). He is pictured here receiving his official GWR certificate in Gyalthum, Sindhupalchowk, Nepal, in February 2012, while trekking on the 1,700-km-long (1,056-mile) Great Himalayan Trail.

Apa's 21 ascents

Date	Expedition name
10 May 1990	International
8 May 1991	Sherpa Support
12 May 1992	New Zealand
7 Oct 1992	International
10 May 1993	USA
10 Oct 1994	International
15 May 1995	American on Sagarmatha
26 Apr 1997	Indonesian
20 May 1998	EEE
26 May 1999	Asian-Trekking
24 May 2000	Everest Environmental
16 May 2002	Swiss 50th anniversary
26 May 2003	Commemorative US expedition
17 May 2004	Dream Everest
31 May 2005	Climbing for a Cure
19 May 2006	Team No Limit
16 May 2007	SuperSherpas
22 May 2008	Eco Everest
21 May 2009	Eco Everest
21 May 2010	Eco Everest
11 May 2011	Eco Everest

3 September 1966: John Ridgway and Chay Blyth (both UK) row from Cape Cod, USA, to the Aran Isles, Ireland, in *English Rose III*, the first ocean row of the 20th century. The row takes place 70 years after the **first ocean row** by Norwegians George Harbo and Gabriel Samuelsen in June–August 1896.

↓22 April 1969: Robin Knox-Johnston (UK) arrives at Falmouth as the only competitor left in the Sunday Times Golden Globe Race, making him the **first person to sail around the world solo and non-stop**.

↓19 July 1969: John Fairfax (UK) returns home triumphant after the **first solo row across any ocean**, crossing the Atlantic east to west in *Britannia*.

21 July 1969: Neil Armstrong and Edwin "Buzz" Aldrin (both USA) become the **first humans to walk on the Moon**.

↘30 July–1 August 1971: Alfred M Worden (USA) of *Apollo 15* becomes the **most isolated human** in history. While his fellow astronauts explore the lunar surface, Worden is alone in the command module 2,596.4 km (2,234 miles) from the nearest person.

6 August 1971: Chay Blyth (UK) becomes the **first person to sail non-stop westward around the world** on *British Steel*.

| 1962 | 1963 | 1964 | 1965 | 1966 | 1967 | 1968 | 1969 | 1970 | 1971 |

EPIC JOURNEYS

FARTHEST FLIGHT BY...

Airship

The longest non-stop flight by an airship, both in terms of distance and duration, was one of 6,384.5 km (3,967 miles) by Hugo Eckener (Germany), piloting the *Graf Zeppelin* in November 1928. The 71-hour flight took place between Lakehurst, New Jersey, USA, and Friedrichshafen, Germany.

Autogyro

Wing Commander Kenneth H Wallis (UK) holds the straight-line distance record of 874.32 km (543.27 miles) in a WA-116/F gyrocopter. His non-stop flight from Lydd, Kent, UK, to Wick, Highland, UK, took place on 28 September 1975.

Commercial aircraft

From 9 to 10 November 2005, a Boeing 777-200LR Worldliner was flown 11,664 nautical miles (21,601.7 km; 13,422.7 miles) non-stop and without refuelling from Hong Kong to London, UK. At 22 hr 42 min, it was the longest flight ever by an unmodified commercial aircraft. The 777-200LR is powered by two General Electric GE90-115Bs, the world's **most powerful jet engines**. The first aircraft were delivered to customer airlines early in 2006.

Paraglider (male)

The farthest straight distance achieved by a male paraglider is 502.9 km (312.5 miles) by Nevil Hulett (South Africa) at Copperton, South Africa, on 14 December 2008.

Kamira Pereira (Brazil) carried out the **farthest paraglider flight by a woman**, travelling 324.5 km (201.63 miles) in a straight line west from Quixada, Brazil, on 14 November 2009. In doing so, she beat her own record of 323 km (200 miles), which she had set six days earlier.

FASTEST TIME TO...

Cycle across Canada

Arvid Loewen (Canada) cycled across Canada in 13 days 6 hr 13 min between 1 July and 14 July 2011.

Cycle across Europe (North Cape to Tarifa)

From 20 June to 29 July 2011, Glen Burmeister (UK) cycled solo across Europe, north to south, in 39 days 11 hr 24 min 24.71 sec.

Cycle across the Sahara desert

Reza Pakravan (Iran) crossed the Sahara desert by bicycle in 13 days 5 hr 50 min 14 sec. He set out on 4 March at 30°00'5"N, 2°57'2"E in Algeria and completed his journey at 17°59'2"N, 30°59'4"E, in Sudan, on 17 March 2011.

Fly across the Atlantic Ocean

The transatlantic flight record stands at 1 hr 54 min 56.4 sec. USAF Major James V Sullivan and Major Noel F Widdifield (both USA) flew a Lockheed SR-71A Blackbird eastwards on 1 September 1974. The average speed for the New York–London stage of 5,570.80 km (3,461.53 miles) was 2,908.02 km/h (1,806.96 mi/h). The pilots slowed their speed only once, to allow for refuelling from a specially modified tanker aircraft.

Longest journey on a 50cc scooter

The greatest distance covered on a 50cc scooter was 12,441.29 km (7,730.66 miles) by Claudio Torresan (Italy). He travelled from Shumen, Bulgaria, to Almaty, Kazakhstan, between 25 May and 25 November 2010.

Longest journey on crutches

Guy Amalfitano (France) travelled 4,004.12 km (2,488.04 miles) through France, on crutches, ending in Orthez on 27 July 2011.

Fastest time to cycle from Cairo to Cape Town

Robert Knol (Netherlands) cycled from Cairo, Egypt, to Cape Town, South Africa, in 70 days 3 hr 50 min from 24 January to 4 April 2011. The trip was unsupported and unaided. Robert's bicycle had to be repaired only once, in Zambia. In Sudan, with temperatures approaching 45°C (113°F), he drank around 15 litres (3.08 gal) of water every day.

🌐 **Circumnavigation**	**22 April 1972:** Sylvia Cook (UK) becomes the **first woman to row across any ocean**, as she and John Fairfax (UK) row the Pacific east to west – in absolute terms, the **first row across the Pacific**.	**7–19 December 1972:** The *Apollo 17* crew take part in the **longest lunar mission**, remaining on the Moon's surface for 74 hr 59 min 40 sec. Commander Eugene Cernan (USA) becomes the **last man on the Moon**.	←**16 May 1975:** Junko Tabei (Japan) is the **first woman to reach the summit of Mount Everest**.	↓**8 May 1978:** Reinhold Messner (Italy, below) and Peter Habeler (Austria) are the **first people to summit Mount Everest without oxygen**.	↓**29 August 1982:** Sir Ranulph Fiennes and Charles Burton (both UK) return from the **first circumnavigation via both poles**, a 56,000-km (35,000-mile) round trip from Greenwich, London, UK.
✳ **Polar**					
⛰ **Mountaineering**					
◈ **Land & Air**					
◉ **Sea**					

1972	1973	1974	1975	1976	1977	1978	1979	1980	1981

A CENTURY OF

FACT: Human beings cannot survive extended periods at altitudes beyond around 6,000 m (20,000 ft).

Highest altitude on a tandem paraglider

Lifting off from the summit of Everest on 21 May 2011, Babu Sunuwar and Lakpa Sherpa (both Nepal) reached a height of approximately 8,878 m (29,127 ft), the greatest altitude achieved on a tandem paraglider. The two men then travelled 31 km (19.3 miles) around Mount Nuptse before landing safely at the airport in Namche Bazaar, Nepal.

Run from John o'Groats to Land's End

The fastest run between John o'Groats and Land's End lasted 9 days 2 hr 26 min and was achieved by Andrew Rivett (UK) from 4 to 13 May 2002.

The **fastest confirmed journey from Land's End to John o'Groats by a woman** is 12 days 15 hr 46 min 35 sec, by Marina Anderson (UK), from 16 to 28 July 2008.

LONGEST JOURNEY...

By car

Emil and Liliana Schmid (Switzerland) have covered 665,712 km (413,653 miles) in their Toyota Land Cruiser since 16 October 1984. In the course of their travels, they have crossed 172 countries and territories. Although the Schmids have returned to Switzerland for short periods several times during their adventure, they have no permanent home there.

By helicopter

Robert Ferry (USA) piloted his Hughes YOH-6A helicopter from Culver City, California, USA, to Ormond Beach, Florida, USA, without refuelling, a distance of 3,561.6 km (2,213.1 miles). The flight ended on 6 April 1966.

By motorcycle

Emilio Scotto of Buenos Aires, Argentina, completed the longest ever journey by a motorcycle, covering more than 735,000 km (457,000 miles) and 214 countries and territories, from 17 January 1985 to 2 April 1995.

The **longest continuous journey by motorcycle within one country** is 18,301 km (11,371.69 miles)

by Mohsin Haq (India), who toured all 28 states of India between 2 October and 26 November 2011.

By mouth-controlled motorized wheelchair

The longest continuous journey by mouth-controlled motorized wheelchair is 28,000 km (17,398 miles) and was achieved by Chang-Hyun Choi (South Korea) between 10 May 2006 and 6 December 2007. Choi, who is affected by cerebral palsy and paralysed from the neck down, travelled at a maximum speed of 13 km/h (8 mi/h) across 35 countries in Europe and the Middle East.

FACT: Dixie and Sam exploited wind power during their trek by kite-skiing part of the way.

Walking backwards

The greatest ever exponent of reverse pedestrianism was Plennie L Wingo (USA), who completed a 12,875-km (8,000-mile) transcontinental walk from Santa Monica, California, USA, to Istanbul, Turkey, from 15 April 1931 to 24 October 1932.

Most travelled toy mascot

Toy bear Raymondo, owned by ISPY (UK), flew 636,714.8 km (395,605 miles) from 27 September 2009 to 3 September 2010, via 35 countries.

Expedition by numbers

- 74 days on the ice
- 68 km (42 miles) per day travel, on average
- 24 days on which they covered more than 100 km (62 miles)
- 11 days of enforced rest owing to inclement weather
- 3,147 m (10,324 ft) average altitude
- -30.4°C (-22.72°F) average temperature
- 10.77 km/h (6.69 mi/h) average speed (on active days)

Longest unassisted snow-kiting trek in Antarctica

On 3 February 2012, Dixie Dansercoer and Sam Deltour (both Belgium) completed their Antarctic ICE Expedition across unexplored regions of eastern Antarctica. They carried out their 5,013-km (3,114.93-mile) trip without any external assistance or the use of motorized vehicles.

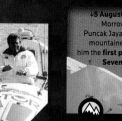

→**14 June 1983:** Peter Bird (UK) becomes the **first person to row the Pacific solo**, travelling east to west in *Hele-on-Britannia*.

↓**5 August 1986:** Patrick Morrow (Canada) adds Puncak Jaya in Indonesia to his mountaineering tally, making him the **first person to climb the Seven Summits** (highest peaks on each continent).

5 June 1988: Kay Cottee (Australia) spends 189 days at sea to become the **first woman to sail non-stop around the world solo**.

↙**14 May 1989:** Robert Swan (UK) completes the Icewalk Expedition to the North Pole, becoming the **first person to walk to both poles**. Swan had trekked to the South Pole on 11 January 1986.

↘**4 May 1990:** Børge Ousland (pictured) and Erling Kagge (both Norway) become the **first to reach the North Pole unsupported**; a third team member – Geir Randby – is airlifted after a fall and does not complete the trip.

| 1982 | 1983 | 1984 | 1985 | 1986 | 1987 | 1988 | 1989 | 1990 | 1991 |

SEA JOURNEYS

Fastest English Channel crossing by canoe (kayak)

Paul Wycherley (UK) took just 2 hr 28 min to row a kayak across the English Channel between Dover Harbour, UK, and Cap Gris Nez, France, on 2 October 2011. There are busy shipping lanes in the Channel, and Paul found himself rowing around ferries and tankers en route. But he didn't mind – in fact, he found that the waves that the ships created broke up the monotony of rowing constantly!

Most solo ocean crossings

In 2000, Emmanuel Coindre (France) became the first person to cross the Atlantic Ocean east to west in a pedal-boat. He then rowed the Atlantic east to west in 2001, west to east in 2002, and east to west in 2004 before setting a speed record, also in 2004, by rowing the Atlantic again, west to east, in 62 days 19 hr 48 min. To cap it off, he rowed the Pacific west to east, from Chōshi in Japan, to Coos Bay in Oregon, USA, in 2005, taking 129 days 17 hr 22 min.

Most ocean rows

Simon Chalk (UK) has rowed oceans six times, including one solo crossing of the Indian Ocean in 2003. The remaining crossings were completed as a member of various teams of different sizes. As one half of a duo, he rowed the Atlantic east to west in 1997; as part of a five-strong team, he rowed the Atlantic east to west again in 2007–08; in an octet, he rowed the Indian Ocean east to west in 2009; in a team of 14, he rowed the Atlantic east to west in 2011; and finally, in another octet, he rowed the Atlantic east to west in 2012.

First row across an ocean solo (male)

John Fairfax (UK, 1937–2012) rowed the Atlantic Ocean east to west in *Britannia* between 20 January and 19 July 1969.

In addition, his crossing of the Pacific with Sylvia Cook (UK, see above) made John the **first person to row two oceans**.

Youngest person to row an ocean solo

On 14 March 2010, Katie Spotz (USA, b. 18 April 1987) completed a 70-day row across the Atlantic Ocean east to west from Dakar in Senegal to Georgetown in Guyana. She set off on 3 January 2010, aged just 22 years 260 days.

The **youngest male to row across an ocean solo** is Tommy Tippetts (UK, b. 26 March 1989), who was 22 years 301 days old at the start of his row across the Atlantic east to west from San Sebastián in La Gomera, Canary Islands, to Barbados, West Indies, from 21 January to 12 April 2012 in *Ked Endeavour*. In all, Tippetts spent 82 days 8 hr 40 min at sea, raising money for Mind, the mental health charity.

Oldest person to row an ocean solo

Tony Short (UK, b. 28 March 1944) was 67 years 252 days old when he began rowing the Atlantic east to west from La Gomera to Barbados in *Spirit of Corinth*. The row lasted from 5 December 2011 to 22 January 2012, a total of 48 days 8 hr 3 min.

First row across the Pacific Ocean

The first people to row across the Pacific Ocean were John Fairfax and Sylvia Cook (both UK) in *Britannia II* between 26 April 1971 and 22 April 1972.

FACT: Gábor's canoe capsized twice, leaving him without communication from 6 February 2012 to the end of his row.

First canoeist to paddle across an ocean

Gábor Rakonczay (Hungary) crossed the Atlantic Ocean east to west in his 7.5-m-long (24-ft 7-in) canoe after 76 days at sea. He set off from Lagos in Portugal on 21 December 2011. After stopping off at Las Palmas in the Canary Islands to rest and gather supplies, he continued on 25 January 2012, arriving at the Caribbean island of Antigua in the Leeward Islands, West Indies, on 25 March 2012.

- Circumnavigation
- Polar
- Mountaineering
- Land & Air
- Sea

May 1996: Freak weather conditions result in the **most deaths on Everest in a day**, as eight climbers succumb to blizzards and 112-km/h (70-mi/h) winds; 1996 becomes the **deadliest year** in Everest's history.

←**15 October 1997:** Andy Green (UK) drives the **first car to break the sound barrier**, averaging a speed of 1,236 km/h (763 mi/h) behind the wheel of *Thrust SSC*.

20 March 1999: Bertrand Piccard (Switzerland) and Brian Jones (UK) complete the **first non-stop circumnavigation by balloon** in the *Breitling Orbiter 3*.

→**2 July 2002:** Steve Fossett (USA) becomes the **first person to circumnavigate the globe by balloon solo** in the 42.6-m-tall (140-ft) *Bud Light Spirit of Freedom*.

| 1992 | 1993 | 1994 | 1995 | 1996 | 1997 | 1998 | 1999 | 2000 | 2001 |

Fastest circumnavigation of Australia by catamaran

Bruce Arms (New Zealand) sailed his 14-m (45-ft 11-in) catamaran around Australia in 38 days 21 hr 40 min 42 sec, setting the record for the swiftest circumnavigation of Australia. He completed his round trip at Mooloolaba, Queensland, on 18 August 2011 at 9:41:06 a.m. AEST.

FACT:
The coastline of the Australian mainland is around 35,000 km (21,750 miles) long.

Longest solo row across an ocean

From 10 July 2007 to 17 May 2008, Erden Eruç (Turkey) rowed the Pacific Ocean solo, east to west, from California, USA, to Papua New Guinea on board *Around-n-Over* in a time of 312 days 2 hr.

Fastest solo row across the Atlantic

The fastest solo east to west Atlantic crossing in a classic ocean-rowing boat was by Fyodor Konyukhov (Russia), who made the 4,678-km (2,907-mile) journey between San Sebastián in La Gomera, Canary Islands, and Port St Charles in Barbados in 46 days 4 hr from 16 October to 1 December 2002.

Andrew Brown (UK) achieved a faster solo row along the same route, in a one-of-a-kind ocean-rowing boat with a modified hull – the **fastest crossing of the Atlantic east to west in an open-class ocean-rowing boat**. Andrew set off from San Sebastián on 5 December 2011 and arrived in Port St Charles on 14 January 2012, having spent 40 days 9 hr 41 min at sea.

The **fastest solo row across the Atlantic east to west on the "Trade Winds II" route** was by Charles Hedrich (France), who rowed 4,035 km (2,507 miles) between Dakar in Senegal, and Guara Point in Brazil, in 36 days 6 hr 37 min, from 18 December 2006 to 23 January 2007.

First person to sail and row the Indian Ocean

James Kayll (UK) sailed from Thailand to Djibouti, on board *Ocean Song*, from 8 January to 13 February 2005; he then rowed from Geraldton, Western Australia, to Mauritius, on board *Indian Runner 4*, from 21 April to 6 July 2011.

The trimaran *Groupama 3*, skippered by Franck Cammas (France), sailed the Indian Ocean in 8 days 17 hr 40 min from 15 to 23 February 2010, the **fastest sailed crossing of the Indian Ocean**.

The **first** and **youngest person to row the Indian Ocean solo** is Sarah Outen (UK, b. 26 May 1985), between 1 April and 3 August 2009, starting off at the age of 23 years 310 days.

Fastest time to swim the Persian Gulf

Open-water swimming takes place in open oceans, seas, rivers, canals and so on. The first, and therefore fastest, swim along the length of the Persian Gulf is by 34-year-old Mohammad Kobadi (Iran). In 84 days between 19 December 2011 and 12 March 2012, Kobadi swam 1,051 km (653 miles), in stages, from the Strait of Hormuz to Arvandkenar along the coast of southeastern Iran, averaging 11.7 km (7.2 miles) per day. The achievement was ratified by Open Water Source.

Fastest time to swim around Manhattan

On 28 September 2011, Oliver Wilkinson (Australia) swam around the island of Manhattan in New York, USA, in a time of 5 hr 44 min 2 sec, beating the record of 5 hr 44 min 47 sec set earlier that day by Rondi Davies (USA/Australia). The achievement was ratified by NYC Swim, the governing body of the Manhattan Island Marathon Swim.

FACT:
By the end of her third crossing, Roz had spent 510 days at sea, the **most days at sea by a female ocean rower**.

rozsavage.com

First female to row three different oceans

British rower Roz Savage conquered the Atlantic Ocean east to west from the Canary Islands, Spain, to Antigua in the West Indies in 2005–06, the Pacific Ocean east to west from San Francisco, USA, to Madang, Papua New Guinea (via Hawaii, USA, and Tarawa, Kiribati) in 2008–10 and the Indian Ocean east to west from Perth, Australia, to Mauritius in 2011.

↓30 April 2005: Park Young-Seok (South Korea) reaches the North Pole on foot, becoming the **first person to complete the Explorers' Grand Slam**: climbing the Seven Summits and the 14 peaks over 8,000 m (26,246 ft), reaching both poles on foot and climbing Everest.

→November 2005: Olivier de Kersauson (France) sets the record for the **fastest sail across the Pacific**, taking 4 days 19 hr 13 min 37 sec on board *Geronimo*.

←May 2006: Dee Caffari (UK) sails *Aviva* on the **fastest solo non-stop circumnavigation westbound** in 178 days 3 hr 5 min 34 sec.

7 January 2009: A Canadian team reaches the South Pole after 33 days 23 hr 30 min – the **fastest unsupported and unassisted journey to the South Pole**.

↘13 January 2011: Christian Eide (Norway) completes the **fastest unsupported solo journey to the South Pole** after a trek lasting 24 days 1 hr.

2002   2003   2004   2005   2006   2007   2008   2009   2010   2011   2012

World Tour

GWR goes global

Packed your suitcase? Got your passport? Then fasten your seatbelt, settle back and relax. It's time to take a trip around the world with Guinness World Records!

Over the next 12 pages, we present a tour of some of the most amazing record-breaking places on our planet. Every record you'll see is a destination you can visit as a tourist, and taken together they comprise a route around the globe, continent by continent. Well, we haven't sent you to Antarctica – we've limited it to places you could realistically be expected to spend a holiday. For polar adventures, meanwhile, see p.118.

Bon voyage!

Europe

Largest trilithons

1

"Trilithon" is a Greek word that means "three stones", and describes structures comprising two upright stones with a third laid across the top. The largest trilithons are at Stonehenge, to the south of Salisbury Plain (UK), with single sarsen blocks weighing more than 45 tonnes (49.5 tons). The tallest upright stone stands 6.7 m (22 ft) above ground, with a further 2.4 m (8 ft) below ground. The earliest stage of the construction of the ditch has been dated to 2950 BC.

FACT:
Around 44 million tourists visit Paris annually. Disneyland Paris attracts 15 million people alone, while around 8.8 million art lovers head for the Louvre.

Most popular city for tourism

2

The city that has the greatest number of international visitors is Paris, France: 31 out of every 150 foreign tourists to the country arrive in the city. Housed in Paris's Louvre art gallery, Leonardo da Vinci's *Mona Lisa* (c. 1503–19, above) is considered to be the **most valuable object ever stolen**. It was stolen from the Louvre on 21 August 1911 but was recovered in Italy in 1913. Vincenzo Perugia (Italy) was charged with its theft.

Most expensive hotel room

3

The Royal Penthouse Suite at the Hotel President Wilson in Geneva, Switzerland, costs $65,000 (£41,676) per day. For this sum, clients have access to 1,680 m² (18,083 ft²) of space plus views of Mont Blanc – through 6-cm-thick (2-in) bullet-proof windows – along with a private cocktail lounge, a jacuzzi, a fitness centre and a conference room.

FACT:
The Royal Penthouse Suite, which can be accessed via a private lift, also features a grand piano, a library and a billiards table.

9256300

9256300

Largest annual food fight

4

On the last Wednesday in August the town of Buñol, near Valencia, Spain, holds its annual tomato festival, La Tomatina. In 2004, 38,000 people spent one hour at this giant food fight, throwing about 125 tonnes (137.7 tons) of tomatoes at each other. Attendants dump the red fruit from the backs of lorries on to the streets for people to throw.

Largest amphitheatre

5

The Flavian amphitheatre or Colosseum of Rome, Italy, completed in AD 80, covers 2 ha (5 acres) and has a capacity of 87,000. It has a maximum length of 187 m (612 ft) and a maximum width of 157 m (515 ft).

9

Largest ice structure

The Ice Hotel in Jukkasjärvi, Sweden, which is rebuilt each winter, has a total floor area of 4,000–5,000 m² (43,000–54,000 ft²) and in the winter of 2004–05 featured 85 rooms. The hotel also features the Ice Globe theatre – based on the design of William Shakespeare's famous playhouse – an ice bar and an ice church. Lying 200 km (124 miles) north of the Arctic Circle, the hotel has been recreated every December since 1990.

FACT:
Empress Elizabeth Petrovna, one of Peter the Great's daughters, commanded the Winter Palace to be built as a royal residence in 1754.

FACT:
3738562   3738562
Many large cities in medieval Europe had pleasure gardens, featuring fireworks, games and basic amusement rides. Most of them closed down in the 18th century.

8

Most art gallery space

You would have to walk 24 km (15 miles) to visit each of the 322 galleries of the Winter Palace within the State Hermitage Museum in St Petersburg, Russia. The galleries are home to nearly 3 million works of art and objects of archaeological interest.

7

Oldest amusement park in operation

Bakken, located in Klampenborg, north of Copenhagen, Denmark, opened in 1583 and is the world's oldest operating amusement park. It is home to five roller coasters, including the wooden "Rutschebanen", built in 1932.

6

Largest beer festival

In terms of the quantity of beer consumed, Munich's Oktoberfest 2011 (17 September–3 October 2011) was history's largest beer festival. Some 6.9 million visitors consumed 7.5 million litres (1.65 million gal) of beer in 35 beer tents.

Asia

Most Muslim pilgrims

1

The Hajj annual pilgrimage to Mecca, Saudi Arabia, attracts an average of 2 million people a year, more than any other Islamic pilgrimage. Pilgrims enter a spiritual state called *ihram*, which for men includes wearing a white seamless garment (intended to show the equality of all Muslims in the eyes of Allah).

Most visited Sikh shrine

2

The Golden Temple in Amritsar, India, the world's most important Sikh shrine, has up to 20,000 visitors a day. This figure rises to 200,000 on special festivals such as Guru Purab (the birthday of one of the 10 Sikh gurus) and Baisakhi (the day Sikhism was established). The temple's second storey is covered in precious stones and about 400 kg (881 lb) of gold leaf.

Highest mountain

3

Mount Everest epitomizes humanity's sense of adventure. Located in the Himalayas, at 8,848 m (29,029 ft) high, it was named in 1865 after Sir George Everest (1790–1866), a Surveyor-General of India. But it was only in 1953 that New Zealander Edmund Hillary and Tenzing Norgay, a Nepali from India, managed to climb it. In the snow at the top, Norgay left sweets as an offering to Buddhist gods and Hillary left a small cross.

FACT:
By the end of 2010's climbing season, there had been 5,104 ascents to the top of Everest – 80% of these since 2000. In total, 219 Everest climbers have lost their lives there.

5527488   5527488

Largest religious structure

5

Angkor Wat (City Temple) in Cambodia covers an area of 1.62 million m² (17.5 million ft²) and has an external wall measuring 1,280 m (4,200 ft). It was built for the Hindu god Vishnu by the Khmer King Suryavarman II in the period 1113–50, and housed a population of 80,000 before it was abandoned in 1432.

Most expensive elephant painting

4

Tourists visiting the Maesa Elephant Camp in Chiang Mai, Thailand, can marvel at the paintings produced by the pachyderms. The most expensive – entitled *Cold Wind, Swirling Mist, Charming Lanna I* – sold for 1.5 million baht (£20,660, $32,970) to Panit Warin (Thailand) on 19 February 2005.

FACT:
The Angkor settlement, which included Angkor Wat, covered more than 1,000 km² (386 miles²) – the world's largest preindustrial metropolis.

Largest observation wheel

6

The Singapore Flyer, in Marina Bay, Singapore, consists of a 150-m-wide (492-ft) wheel, built over a three-storey terminal building, giving a total height of 165 m (541 ft). It was opened to the public on 1 March 2008.

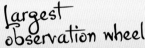

Largest palace

The Imperial Palace in the centre of Beijing, China, covers a rectangle measuring 960 x 750 m (3,150 x 2,460 ft) over an area of 72 ha (178 acres). The outline survives from the construction of the third Ming Emperor, Yongle (1402–24), but most of the buildings are from the 18th century.

11

10

Longest wall

The main part of the Great Wall of China is 3,460 km (2,150 miles) long – nearly three times the length of Britain. It also has 3,530 km (2,195 miles) of branches and spurs. Built to protect the northern border of the Chinese empire, it runs from Shanhaiguan on the Gulf of Bohai to Yumenguan and Yangguan.

9

Steepest roller coaster

The Takabisha ride at the Fuji-Q Highland park in Fujiyoshida City, Japan, has a 121° "beyond vertical" drop for 3.4 m (11 ft 2 in). The carriages descend from a 43-m (141-ft 1-in) tower, enter the steepest stretch at 29 m (95 ft 1 in) and, for a stomach-churning 0.38 seconds, the riders are travelling down and inwards at the same time.

FACT:
Before the Ming Dynasty started in 1368, the wall was built from rammed earth, stones and wood. During Ming rule, bricks were used, quickening the wall-building.

0084033 0084033

Tallest stone Buddha

The Leshan Giant Buddha in the Sichuan Province of China was carved out of a hillside in the 8th century. It measures 71 m (233 ft) in height, making it the tallest statue of Buddha to be carved entirely out of stone. The statue and surrounding area have been designated a UNESCO World Heritage Site.

8

FACT:
Buddha was a spiritual teacher who lived about 500 years before Christ. He was born in Nepal or India and his teachings are the basis of Buddhism.

7

Largest orangutan sanctuary

Since 1964, the Sepilok Orangutan Rehabilitation Centre, in the Malaysian state of Sabah, in northern Borneo, has rehabilitated more than 100 orphaned orangutans back into the wild. Baby orangutans usually stay with their mothers for six years but often have to be rescued during logging and forest clearances or from poachers. At Sepilok, a buddy system is used to replace a mother's teaching.

Africa

FACT: The far side of the Great Hassan II mosque sits above the sea. This was inspired by a Qur'an verse that states: "The throne of Allah was built on water".

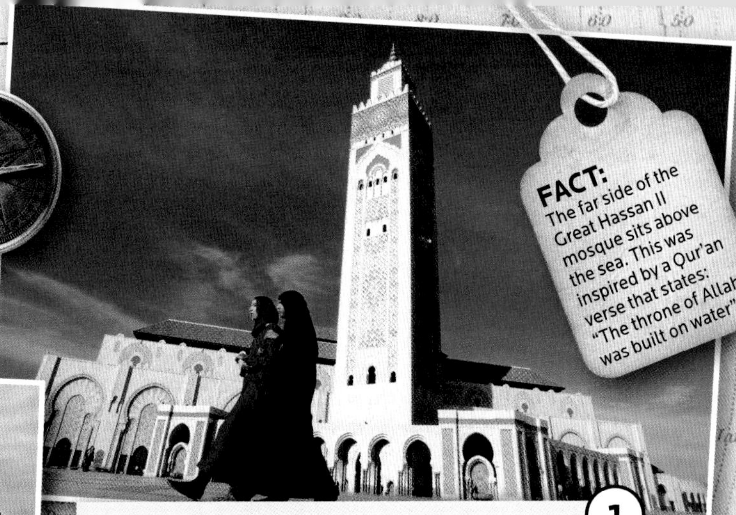

1 Tallest minaret

The minaret of the Great Hassan II mosque in Casablanca, Morocco, measures 200 m (656 ft). The mosque, built from 1986 to 1993, cost 5 billion dirhams (£360 million, $574 million) and can accommodate 25,000 worshippers in its prayer hall, which has a retractable roof, and a further 80,000 within its environs.

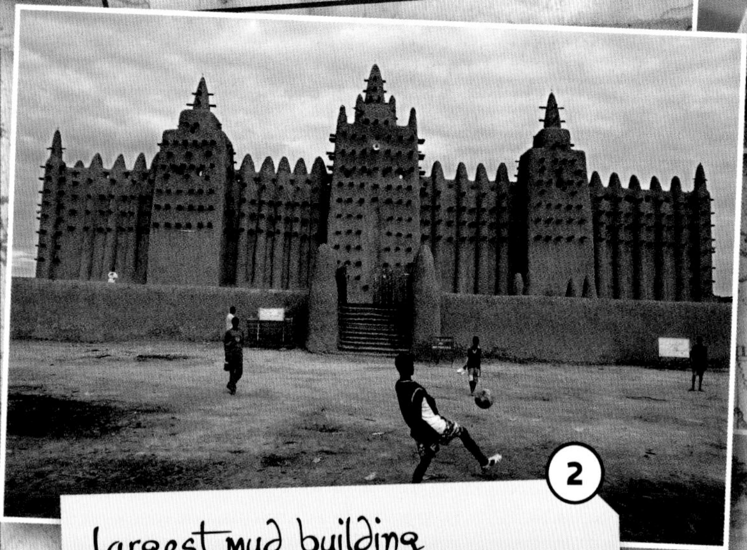

2 Largest mud building

The Great Mosque in Djenné, Mali, measures 100 m (328 ft) long and 40 m (131 ft) wide. The present structure was built in 1905 and is made from sun-baked mud bricks, fixed with a mud-based mortar and coated with a mud plaster to give a smooth, sculpted look. It is replastered every year.

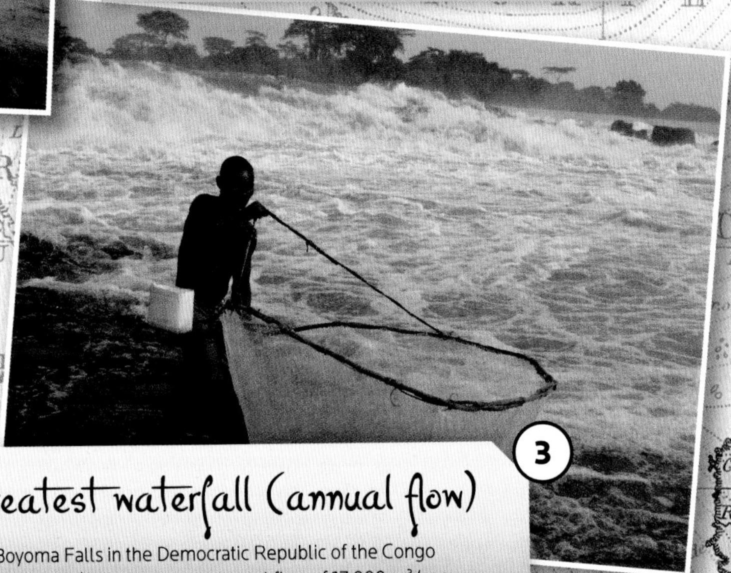

3 Greatest waterfall (annual flow)

The Boyoma Falls in the Democratic Republic of the Congo (formerly Zaire) has an average annual flow of 17,000 m^3/sec (600,000 ft^3/sec). Formerly known as Stanley Falls, it has seven cataracts and extends for 100 km (60 miles) along a curve of the Lualaba River between Ubundu and Kisangani.

FACT David Livingstone (UK, 1813–73) named the Victoria Falls in honour of his Queen, but locals called it *Mosi-oa-Tunya* (Smoke that Thunders).

4 Largest waterfall (vertical area)

The Victoria Falls, on the Zambezi River between Zimbabwe and Zambia, is neither the tallest nor the widest waterfall in the world, but it is the largest by vertical area. At 1,708 m (5,604 ft) wide and 108 m (354 ft) high, it creates a sheet of falling water with an area of around 184,400 m^2 (2,017,400 ft^2).

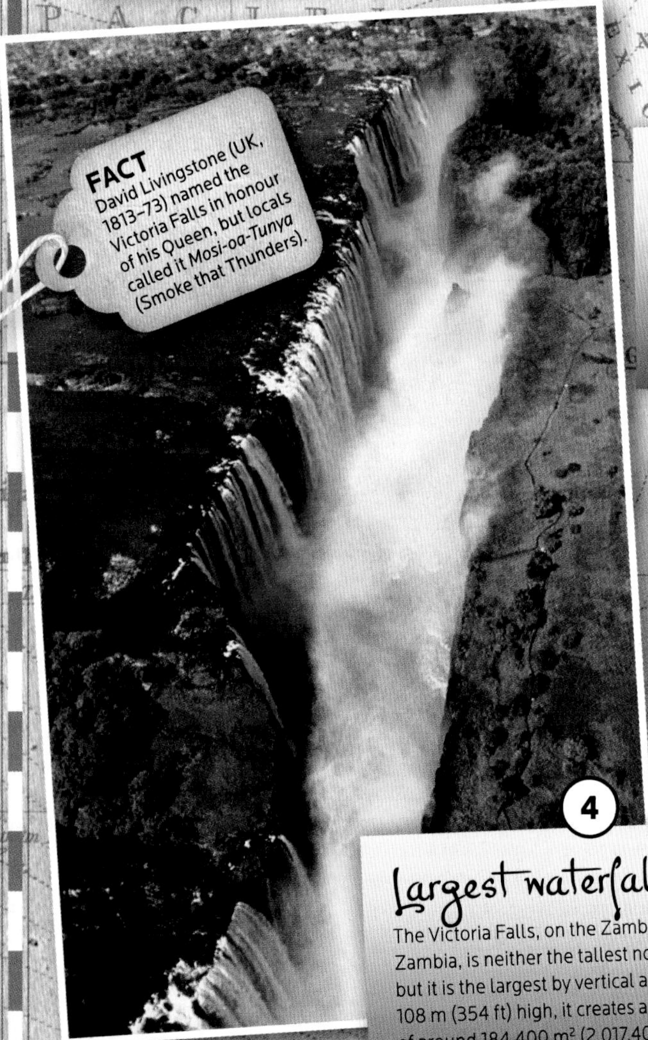

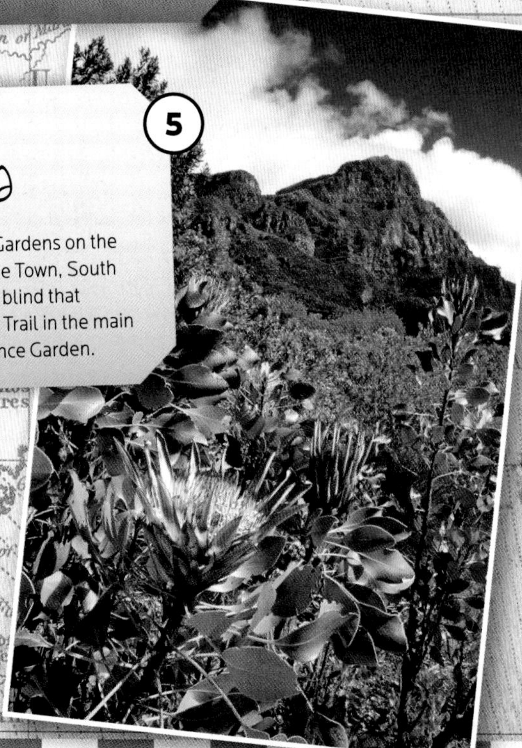

5 Largest scented garden for the blind

The Kirstenbosch National Botanical Gardens on the eastern slopes of Table Mountain, Cape Town, South Africa, has a Fragrance Garden for the blind that measures 36 ha (88.9 acres). A Braille Trail in the main gardens starts and ends at the Fragrance Garden.

10

Tallest pyramid

Khufu's pyramid at Giza, Egypt, also known as the Great Pyramid, was 146.7 m (481.4 ft) high when completed about 4,500 years ago, but erosion and vandalism have reduced its height to 137.5 m (451.4 ft) today. In this photo, it is the far pyramid – as it is in the distance, it looks smaller than Khafre's pyramid in the middle.

FACT:
In 2004, an expedition led by Hendrik Coetzee (South Africa) kayaked the Nile, from Lake Victoria to the Mediterranean. The trip took 126 days.

9

Longest river

The Nile's main source is Lake Victoria in east central Africa. From its farthest stream in Burundi, it extends 6,695 km (4,160 miles) in length.

8

Longest rift system

The Great Rift Valley is about 6,400 km (4,000 miles) long with an average width of 50–65 km (30–40 miles). It begins in Jordan and extends along the Red Sea into east Africa. The African section, from Ethiopia to Mozambique, is about 3,500 km (2,175 miles) long and includes the Ol Doinyo Lengai volcano in Tanzania, right. The valley has been forming for about 30 million years.

FACT:
The reserve was named after hunter Frederick Selous (UK). He died in the reserve in 1917, aged 66, fighting in the British Army against the Germans in Africa.

7725226

Largest game reserve

Larger than Switzerland, the Selous Game Reserve extends over 55,000 km² (21,236 miles²) of woodland, grassland swamp and forest in southern Tanzania. It was designated a UNESCO World Heritage Site in 1982. This was as a result of its diverse wildlife, which includes one of the world's largest populations of wild dogs, and its undisturbed nature – there is no permanent human habitation in the reserve, only tourist facilities.

7

6

Oldest island

Madagascar, in the Indian Ocean, became an island around 80–100 million years ago, when it split off from the Indian subcontinent. It is now only 400 km (248.5 miles) off the coast of Africa (at the shortest point) and is considered part of the African continent. Lemurs, such as the diademed sifaka (*Propithecus diadema*) above, are indigenous to Madagascar.

Oceania

1 Oldest operating open-air cinema

Sun Picture Theatre, in Broome, Western Australia, first opened on 9 December 1916. The cinema played only silent films until 1933, when it showed its first "talkie" – *Monte Carlo* (USA, 1930), a musical starring Jeanette MacDonald and Jack Buchanan (both USA).

Largest sandstone monolith

Uluru, also known as Ayers Rock, rises 348 m (1,143 ft) above the surrounding desert plain in Northern Territory, Australia. It is 2.5 km (1.5 miles) long and 1.6 km (1 mile) wide. Uluru's distinctive reddish colour is caused by the oxidation of iron-bearing minerals in the rock.

2

FACT:
Uluru was originally part of an ancient mountain range. The surrounding peaks have been eroded away over hundreds of millions of years.

5647250

3

Widest bridge

The widest long-span bridge is the 503-m-long (1,650-ft) Sydney Harbour Bridge, Australia, which is 48.8 m (160 ft) wide. It carries two electric overhead railway tracks, eight lanes of roadway and a cycle track and footway. The bridge was officially opened on 19 March 1932.

4

Most southerly capital city

Wellington, North Island, New Zealand, which had a population of around 393,000 as of June 2011, is the southernmost capital city of an independent country (41°17'S). The world's southernmost capital of a dependent territory is Port Stanley, Falkland Islands (51°43'S).

5

Oldest koala sanctuary

Established in 1927 by Claude Reid (Australia), the Lone Pine Koala Sanctuary in Brisbane, Queensland, Australia, is the world's oldest koala sanctuary. The sanctuary currently houses more than 130 animals – the greatest number of koalas in captivity.

Carstensz Pyramid, Indonesia

At 4,884 m (16,023 ft), the Carstensz Pyramid (also known as Puncak Jaya), in Papua Province, Indonesia, is Oceania's tallest peak. It features on one of the two Seven Summits lists (see below). Henrik Kristiansen (Denmark) set the **fastest time to climb the highest peak on each continent (Carstensz list)**, in 136 days from 21 January 2008 to 5 June 2008.

FACT:
There are two "Seven Summits" lists. One has Mount Kosciuszko (2,228 m; 7,310 ft), the highest peak on the Australian continent, instead of Carstensz.

9856460

FACT:
There are more than 400 types of coral in the Great Barrier Reef. It is home to around 1,500 species of fish and 4,000 types of mollusc.

Longest reef

The Great Barrier Reef off Queensland, north-eastern Australia, is 2,027 km (1,260 miles) in length. It is not actually a single structure, but consists of thousands of separate reefs. On three occasions (between 1962 and 1971, 1979 and 1991, and 1995 and the present), corals on large areas of the central section of the reef were eaten away by the crown-of-thorns starfish (*Acanthaster planci*).

Largest sand island

Fraser Island, located off the south coast of Queensland, Australia, covers approximately 163,000 ha (402,750 acres). It is home to a sand dune 120 km (75 miles) long and more than 100 freshwater lakes. In 1992, the island was recognized by the United Nations Educational, Scientific and Cultural Organization (UNESCO) as a World Heritage Site.

North America

Largest jazz festival

The Festival International de Jazz de Montréal in Québec, Canada, is the world's largest jazz festival. The event attracted 1,913,868 people in July 2004, its 25th anniversary year.

FESTIVAL INTERNATIONAL DE JAZZ DE MONTRÉAL
RioTintoAlcan
25 JUIN AU 4 JUILLET 2011
JUNE 25 TO JULY 4, 2011
32E É

Most visited waterfall

Located on the border between Canada and the USA, Niagara Falls receives 22.5 million visitors a year. It is also the fifth most popular tourist attraction in the world, beating the Disney theme parks, the Notre Dame Cathedral in Paris, France, and the Great Wall of China.

FACT:
Las Vegas (Spanish for "the meadows") became a city in 1905. Its parent state, Nevada, was part of Mexico until 1864, when it became the 36th state of the USA.

6026523

FACT:
The term "light pollution" refers to an excess of artifical light. Up to two-thirds of humanity lives with this condition, according to the latest research.

Highest concentration of theme hotels

There are 14 theme hotels on the Strip in Las Vegas, Nevada, USA, all of which boast extravagant designs. The Luxor has a sphinx, a black pyramid and an obelisk; New York New York recreates a scaled-down version of the New York skyline; and Paris features a half-scale Eiffel Tower.

First dark sky park

The International Dark Sky Association has named Utah's Natural Bridges National Monument as the first dark sky park. This is an area where the night sky can be seen clearly, without any light pollution.

Oldest national park

Yellowstone National Park, USA, was the first area in the world to be designated a national park. It was given its status in 1872 by US president Ulysses S Grant, who declared that it would always be "dedicated and set apart as a public park or pleasuring ground for the benefit and enjoyment of the people". The park covers 8,980 km² (3,470 miles²), mainly in the state of Wyoming.

⑨

Heaviest statue

Unveiled on 28 October 1886, the Statue of Liberty weighs 24,635.5 tonnes (27,156 tons), of which 28.1 tonnes (31 tons) is copper, 113.4 tonnes (125 tons) is steel and 24,494 tonnes (27,000 tons) makes up the concrete foundation. It was presented to the USA as a gift from France to commemorate friendship between the two countries.

FACT:
The tablet that the Statue of Liberty holds in her hand bears the date "July 4, 1776" – the day on which the USA declared its independence from Great Britain.

FACT:
Walt Disney's first theme park, Disneyland, opened in July 1955. It had just 20 attractions and five "lands", each of which had an individual theme.

Most visited theme park

⑧

As of 2010, the Magic Kingdom at Walt Disney World in Florida, USA had been visited by more than 16.9 million visitors, according to a report compiled by Themed Entertainment Association (TEA) and Economics Research Associates (ERA). It was followed by Disneyland in Anaheim, California, USA, which had 15.9 million guests, and Tokyo Disneyland in Japan, which had 14.4 million visitors.

Largest monument

The volume of the Quetzalcóatl Pyramid at Cholula de Rivadavia in Central Mexico has been estimated at 3.3 million m³ (151 million ft³). The pyramid stands 54 m (177 ft) tall and its base covers an area of nearly 18.2 ha (45 acres). The structure is now mostly overgrown (and a Spanish church was built on top in the 1590s) but recent excavations and renovations have revealed some of the original structure (inset).

⑦

⑥

Largest land gorge

The Grand Canyon was created over the course of millions of years by the Colorado river in north-central Arizona, USA. It runs from Marble Gorge to the Grand Wash Cliffs, covering a distance of 446 km (277 miles). The gorge extends to a depth of 1.6 km (1 mile) and its width ranges from 0.5 km to 29 km (0.3–18 miles).

FACT:
The Grand Canyon stretches over an area of more than 404,685 ha (1 million acres). Each year it attracts at least 5 million visitors.

South America

Largest Inca discovery

The two Yale University Peruvian Expeditions of 1911–12 and 1914–15, both led by historian Hiram Bingham (USA), uncovered the lost Inca cities of Machu Picchu (left) – which is the largest Inca site yet discovered – and Vitcos. These sites are regarded as two of the most important archaeological finds in the Americas. It is believed that the Spanish conquistadors, who conquered the Incas, failed to find Machu Picchu.

FACT: Completed c. 1450, Machu Picchu was only inhabited for around 100 years. It is located 2,340 m (7,677 ft) above sea level in the Andes mountains.

Highest waterfall

The Salto Angel in Venezuela, on a branch of the Carrao River, an upper tributary of the Caroni River, has a total drop of 979 m (3,212 ft), with the longest single drop being 807 m (2,648 ft). The "Angel Falls" were named after the American pilot James "Jimmie" Angel, who recorded them in his log book on 16 November 1933.

Largest geoglyphs

The so-called "Nazca lines" are a group of huge figures engraved on the desert ground of Nazca (Peru) representing plants, animals, insects and various geometric shapes. Most can only be appreciated from the air. The designs occupy a 500-km² (193-mile²) area and average 180 m (600 ft) in length.

FACT: Titicaca is home to the **largest man-made reed islands**. Because the reeds rot away, the Uros people who live there need to constantly rebuild their islands.

Tallest moai

"Moai" are monolithic human figures that were carved from rock on Easter Island (Rapa Nui) between 1250 and 1500. In all, 887 of these statues have been discovered so far. The tallest standing moai, which has been named "Paro", measures 9.8 m (32 ft 1 in) in height and is located at Ahu Te Pito Kura, Easter Island. It weighs 74.39 tonnes (82 tons).

FACT:
The Amazon is c. 6,400 km (4,000 miles) long, though the figure varies according to the way it is measured. The Nile is the **longest river**, at 6,695 km (4,160 miles).

4953588

4953588

Greatest river flow

On average, the Amazon discharges water at 200,000 m³/sec (7,100,000 ft³/sec) into the Atlantic Ocean, increasing to more than 340,000 m³/sec (12,000,000 ft³/sec) in full flood. The lower 1,450 km (900 miles) of the river average 17 m (55 ft) in depth, but the river has a maximum depth of 124 m (407 ft).

Largest carnival

Rio de Janeiro's annual carnival is usually held for four days in February or March and attracts about 2 million people each day. In 2004, the carnival drew in a record 400,000 foreign visitors, of which 2,600 were thought to have been from the *Queen Mary II* ocean liner. Samba schools spend many months creating the fabulous, colourful costumes that they wear when they dance through the city's streets.

Highest navigable lake

The highest commercially navigable lake is Lake Titicaca, which lies in the Altiplano at a height of 3,810 m (12,500 ft) above sea level on the Andean border between Peru and Bolivia. Its surface area covers approximately 8,300 km² (3,200 miles²) and it has an average depth of 140–180 m (460–590 ft), i.e. deep enough for the safe passage of commercial vessels.

Tallest water slide

The world's loftiest water slide is Kilimanjaro at Águas Quentes Country Club in Barra do Piraí, Rio de Janeiro, Brazil. Constructed in 2002, it reaches a vertiginous 49.9 m (163 ft 9 in) – that's taller than the Statue of Liberty – and descends at an angle of 60°. If you're brave enough to tackle this skyscraping slide, you'll find yourself racing downwards at speeds approaching 96 km/h (60 mi/h)!

FACT:
During the rainy season, (December–May), 80% of the Pantanal is flooded, and it contains the greatest diversity of water plants in the world.

6038533

6038533

Largest swamp

Located principally in south-western Brazil but with small areas within neighbouring Bolivia and Paraguay too, the Pantanal (which is Spanish for "marshland") covers a surface area of 150,000 km² (57,915 miles²) – greater than the total surface area of England!

Largest swimming pool

The San Alfonso del Mar seawater pool in Algarrobo, Chile, is 1,013 m (3,324 ft) long and has an area of 8 ha (19.77 acres). It was completed in December 2006, after 10 years' work. The pool employs advanced technology to draw seawater into one end of the pool from the Pacific Ocean, filter, treat it and pump it out at the other end.

139

CMS AUDITORIUM

CONTENTS

39,437

Largest school

The largest school in terms of pupils is the City Montessori School in Lucknow, India, which had a record enrolment of 39,437 children on 9 August 2010 for the 2010–11 academic year. The school admits boys and girls between ages two and five, who can then continue their education to degree level. In 2002, it won the UNESCO Prize for Peace Education. The City Montessori has come a long way since Jagdish Gandhi and his wife Bharti first opened it in 1959 with a loan of just 300 rupees ($63, £22). Then it had a grand total of five pupils!

HOW RICH CAN YOU GET?

Endless pursuit of wealth

There was a time when real wealth was largely inherited. It was tied up in land and the right to farm that land. Over time, the ability to exploit the oil, gas, minerals and precious metals that lay beneath the surface of the land changed the face of wealth. It also served to feed the demands of emerging industries such as steel and shipping – and the powerful men who went on to make fortunes from them.

Fortunes are still made and maintained in the old industries, but a new source of wealth has emerged based on technologies that barely existed 50 years ago. Telecoms and computing – convergent technologies that seem to change almost daily – are the new engines of wealth creation, but will today's technology billionaires ever reach, or exceed, the heady heights of the Rockefellers and the Vanderbilts? Is there a limit to just how much money one person can actually accrue?

$1 billion = £647 million

TOP TEN RICHEST LIVING PEOPLE, 2012

The world's wealthiest according to Forbes (and how their wealth compares to the GDP of various countries – yes, these people are personally richer than some countries!)

	Name	Business	Worth
	1. Carlos Slim Helú (Mexico) *Richer than: Puerto Rico*	Telmex and América Móvil (telecoms)	$69 billion £44.5 billion
	2. Bill Gates (USA) *Richer than: Slovenia*	Microsoft (computing)	$61 billion £39.5 billion
	3. Warren Buffett (USA) *Richer than: Luxembourg*	Berkshire Hathaway (holdings: retail, rail, media, utilities)	$44 billion £28.5 billion
	4. Bernard Arnault (France) *Richer than: North Korea*	LVMH (apparels/accessories)	$41 billion £26.5 billion
	5. Amancio Ortega Gaona (Spain) *Richer than: Jordan*	Inditex/Zara (fashion)	$37.5 billion £24 billion
	6. Larry Ellison (USA) *Richer than: Honduras*	Oracle (computing)	$36 billion £23 billion
	7. Eike Batista (Brazil) *Richer than: Afghanistan*	EBX Group (mining, oil)	$30 billion £19.5 billion
	8. Stefan Persson (Sweden) *Richer than: Senegal*	H&M (fashion)	$26 billion £17 billion
	9. Li Ka-shing (China) *Richer than: Senegal*	Hutchison Whampoa & Cheung Kong Holdings (diverse)	$25.5 billion £16.5 billion
	9=. Karl Albrecht (Germany) *Richer than: Senegal*	Aldi (discount supermarkets)	$25.5 billion £16.5 billion

WHO: Cornelius Vanderbilt (USA)
WEALTH: $170 billion
WHY: New York and Harlem Railroad
DETAILS: At the time of his death at 82 in 1877, the engineering entrepreneur was worth $105 million – roughly 1/87th of the GDP of the entire USA!

WHO: Basil II (Byzantine Empire)
WEALTH: $172 billion
WHY: Byzantine Emperor (976–1025)
DETAILS: Basil, aka the "Bulgarslayer", ruthlessly expanded his empire, taxing the nobility as he went; died aged 67, leaving behind a full treasury.

WHO: Marcus Licinius Crassus (Italy)
WEALTH: $172.5 billion
WHY: Consul of the Roman Republic (115–53 BC)
DETAILS: Historian Pliny estimated Crassus' wealth at 200 million sestertii from slavery, mining and real estate.

WHO: Henry Ford (USA)
WEALTH: $191 billion
WHY: Founder of the Ford Motor Company
DETAILS: Didn't invent the car but the Model-T entrepreneur was practically responsible for the assembly line.

WHO: Andrew W Mellon (USA)
WEALTH: $192 billion
WHY: Oil, steel and shipping magnate
DETAILS: Banker, politician, statesman, philanthropist, art collector; wealth peaked at $400 million in 1930.

Top ten richest people of all time

Richest people in history

This filthy-rich line-up of billionaires represents our best estimation of the wealthiest people of all time. It includes rulers, business magnates and entrepreneurs from across history, with their estimated wealth adjusted for inflation to allow comparison. How do these people – all men – compare? And how do they compare with today's money-makers?

FACT: Even if you spent £1,000 a day, it would still take you around 2,739 years to spend £1 billion!

Who's not on the list? Excluded are historical figures deemed to "own" entire nations or empires, such as the Pharaohs of ancient Egypt, Alexander the Great, Mongol leader Genghis Khan, and the monarchs of Europe.

THE COAT OF ARMS

CONCORDIA INTEGRITAS INDUSTRIA

Richest family?

The House of Rothschild – a German/Jewish dynasty that founded banks and financial institutions in 18th-century Europe – could be considered the richest family in history. Renowned for their secrecy, as well as their philanthropy, the many generations of Rothschilds are believed to have a wealth valued in excess of $1 trillion in today's money. Their businesses continue to thrive, still driven by family members. The price of gold, for example, is fixed daily at the Rothschild & Sons offices in London.

The World Bank puts the GDP of the world at $63.04 trillion. Yet John D Rockefeller, the richest person in history, managed to acquire just a fraction of that – and at the peak of his wealth he owned 85% of the crude oil known to exist at the time and 95% of the world's oil refineries! So what might have stopped him going any further and grabbing the lot?

Economic systems require stability if they are to function properly. Any imbalance will inevitably require that the system be rebalanced. This means that while an individual might in theory be able to acquire all the money in the world, the tipping point for a chaotic imbalance in the system will have been reached long before they do so, causing the kind of economic crash that would result in their money not being worth the paper it was printed on.

WHO: John D Rockefeller (USA)
WEALTH: $322 billion
WHY: Standard Oil (Esso)
DETAILS: Founded his oil company in 1870 and became America's first billionaire as the demand for petroleum and gasoline exploded; like Carnegie, gave much of it away – he spent 40 years of his retirement as a philanthropist.

WHO: Andrew Carnegie (UK/USA)
WEALTH: $302 billion
WHY: Steel magnate
DETAILS: Born in Dunfermline, Scotland, Carnegie emigrated to the USA in 1848, where he founded a steel company that he would eventually sell in 1901 for $480 million; gave most of it away in philanthropic ventures.

WHO: Nicholas II (Russia)
WEALTH: $257 billion
WHY: Last (and worst?) Emperor of Russia
DETAILS: Wealthiest monarch in history, reported to be worth $881 million at the age of 48 in 1916; abdicated the following year, then murdered in 1918 by the Bolsheviks.

WHO: William Henry Vanderbilt (USA)
WEALTH: $235 billion
WHY: Son of Cornelius (see no.10, left)
DETAILS: Inherited c. $100 million from daddy but managed to nearly double it in just nine years by expanding the family railway business. Famously unhappy with his wealth.

WHO: Osman Ali Khan, Asaf Jah VII (Hyderabad)
WEALTH: $213 billion
WHY: Ruler of Hyderabad (now India)
DETAILS: His Exalted Highness The Nizam of Hyderabad (ruled 1911–48) enjoyed the royalties from Hyderabad's diamond mining – until the country was forcibly annexed by India.

1 = 10 billion US $

PETS

Oldest living rabbit
Do is a Jersey Wooley owned by Jenna Antol of New Jersey, USA. He was born on 1 January 1996 and was 16 years 1 month 14 days old on 15 February 2012.

Largest living pet snail
A pet snail named Homer measured 26.1 cm (10.27 in) from shell tip to nose when fully extended, with a shell length of 18 cm (7.08 in), on 15 December 2011. The African land snail is owned by Joseph Billington (UK) of Whitstable, Kent, UK.

Farthest distance tracked by a lost dog
In 1979, Jimpa, a labrador/boxer cross, arrived at his old home in Pimpinio, Victoria, Australia, after walking 3,220 km (2,000 miles) across Australia. His owner, Warren Dumesney (Australia), had taken Jimpa with him 14 months earlier when he went to work on a farm at Nyabing, Western Australia. During his trek, the dog negotiated the almost waterless Nullarbor Plain.

Largest pet gathering
A group of 4,616 pets went for a walk with their owners at La Feria de las Flores ("Flower Fair") in Medellín, Colombia, on 7 August 2007.

Longest cat whiskers
At 19 cm (7.5 in), the longest whiskers on a cat belong to Missi, a Maine coon who lives with her owner, Kaija Kyllönen. The whiskers were measured in Iisvesi, Finland, on 22 December 2005.

Pet photographed with the most celebrities
A white Maltese dog called Lucky Diamond has been photographed with 363 different celebrities, including Kim Kardashian, Richard Branson, Snoop Dogg and Kristin Stewart (all above, left to right). Lucky's owner is Wendy Diamond (USA).

FACT: Savannah cats are a cross between the domestic cat and the African serval (*Leptailurus serval*).

Longest dog tail
As of 12 April 2012, the longest dog tail measured 66.04 cm (26 in) and belonged to Bentley, a great dane from Colorado, USA. He is owned by Patrick Malcom (USA) and his family.

Most expensive pet wedding
In September 1996, two rare "diamond-eyed" cats, Phet and Ploy, were married at a lavish ceremony at Phoebus House, Thailand's biggest discotheque. The wedding cost Phet's owner, Wichan Jaratarcha, $16,241 (£10,444) on top of an additional dowry of $23,202 (£14,920).

Most prolific cat
A tabby named Dusty from Texas, USA, produced 420 kittens during her life. She gave birth to her last litter (a single kitten) on 12 June 1952.

Shortest living domestic cat
The shortest cat alive is Fizz Girl, a two-year-old female munchkin cat, who measured 15.24 cm (6 in) from the floor to the shoulders on 23 July 2010. The pint-size pet is owned by Tiffani Kjeldergaard of San Diego, USA.

Wealthiest cat
When Ben Rea (UK) died in May 1988, he bequeathed his £7-million ($12.5-million) fortune to Blackie, the last surviving of the 15 cats with whom he shared his mansion. The millionaire antiques dealer and recluse refused to recognize his family in his will.

Similarly, the **wealthiest dog** was a standard poodle named Toby, who was left $15 million (£10.5 million) in the will of Ella Wendel of New York, USA, in 1931.

Tallest domestic cat
Savannah Islands Trouble is 48.3 cm (1 ft 7 in) tall. He is owned by Debby Maraspini (USA) and was measured at the Silver Cats Cat Show at the Grand Sierra Resort in Reno, Nevada, USA, on 30 October 2011.
The **longest domestic cat** is Mymains Stewart Gilligan at 123 cm (48.5 in) long. He is owned by Robin Hendrickson and Erik Brandsness (both USA) and was measured on 28 August 2010.

FACT: Savannah Islands Trouble is 2.4 cm (0.93 in) taller than the previous record holder.

FACT: Great danes usually reach a height of around 76–86 cm (30–34 in).

TOP DOGS

Humanity's fondness for a canine companion shows no sign of abating. GWR presents a list of the most popular dog breeds, based on registrations made at the UK's Kennel Club for 2011.

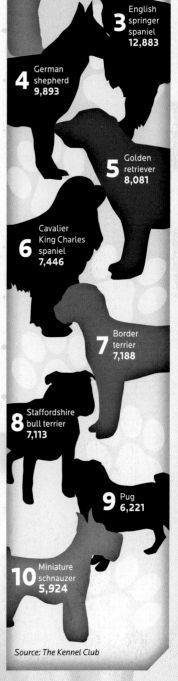

1 Labrador retriever **39,964**

2 Cocker spaniel **23,258**

3 English springer spaniel **12,883**

4 German shepherd **9,893**

5 Golden retriever **8,081**

6 Cavalier King Charles spaniel **7,446**

7 Border terrier **7,188**

8 Staffordshire bull terrier **7,113**

9 Pug **6,221**

10 Miniature schnauzer **5,924**

Source: The Kennel Club

Tallest dog

A great dane named Zeus measured 111.8 cm (3 ft 8 in) tall on 4 October 2011 – making him both the **tallest living dog** and the **tallest dog ever**. The Olympian canine is owned by Denise Doorlag (pictured) and her family of Otsego in Michigan, USA.

Cat: A cat named Creme Puff, born on 3 August 1967, lived until 6 August 2005 – an amazing 38 years 3 days! She lived with her owner, Jake Perry, in Austin, Texas, USA.

The **oldest living cat** is Pinky, who was born on 31 October 1989 and lives with her owner, Linda Anno (USA), in Hoyt, Kansas, USA.

Chinchilla: A chinchilla named Bouncer, born on 1 July 1977 and owned by Jenny Ann Bowen (UK) of Great Barr in Birmingham, UK, died on 3 October 2005, at the incredible age of 28 years 94 days.

Goldfish: A goldfish named Tish, owned by Hilda and Gordon Hand (UK), lived for 43 years after Hilda's son Peter won the fish at a fairground stall in 1956.

Guinea pig: Snowball the guinea pig, who lived in Nottinghamshire, UK, died on 14 February 1979, aged 14 years 10 months 2 weeks. Guinea pigs have an average life span of 4–8 years.

Mouse: A house mouse called Fritzy (b. 11 September 1977), who belonged to Bridget Beard of Edgbaston, West Midlands, UK, died at the age of 7 years 7 months on 24 April 1985. Mice usually live for 1.5–2 years.

Rat: A common rat called Rodney (b. January 1983), belonging to Rodney Mitchell of Tulsa in Oklahoma, USA, died aged 7 years 4 months on 25 May 1990.

OLDEST...

Bearded dragon: Guinness, a lizard owned by Nik Vernon (UK), was born on 26 July 1997 and was 14 years 268 days old as of 20 April 2012.

Budgerigar: Charlie, born in April 1948 and owned by J Dinsey (UK), died on 20 June 1977, aged 29 years 2 months.

Dog: The greatest reliable age recorded for a dog is 29 years 5 months for an Australian cattle-dog named Bluey (d. 1939), who was obtained as a puppy in 1910 by Les Hall of Rochester, Victoria, Australia.

Shortest dogs

In terms of length, the shortest dogs are Cupcake (left) – a five-year-old female long-haired teacup chihuahua owned by Angela Bain of Moorestown, New Jersey, USA – and Heaven Sent Brandy (below), a chihuahua who lives with owner Paulette Keller in Largo, Florida, USA. Both dogs are just 15.2 cm (6 in) long!

SEE IT 3D

SCHOOLS

Complete class

Here are the largest lessons in some of your favourite subjects...

Lesson/date	Students	Location
Business 18 November 2011	1,864	DAV Centenary College in Faridabad, Haryana, India
Chemistry 22 September 2011	4,207	Multiple venues across Israel
History 8 November 2011	14,257	Third-grade children from Orange County, California, USA, at Angel Stadium, California
Hockey 11 February 2009	459	Streatham & Clapham High School in London, UK
Maths 3 December 2010	4,076	Multiple venues – 30 schools across the UK
Meteorology 7 May 2009	16,110	"School Day at the K" at Kauffman Stadium, Kansas City, Kansas, USA
Painting 16 September 2011	879	Warren Road Primary School in Orpington, Kent, UK
Physics 7 May 2009	5,401	Coors Field in Denver, Colorado, USA

First country to impose compulsory education
Prussia made education compulsory in 1819.

Lowest pupil-to-teacher ratio
San Marino has six pupils to every teacher in primary schools. At secondary level, Monaco has the lowest ratio, with 5.8 pupils per teacher.

Country with most higher education students
The USA has 14,261,800 students in higher education (attending universities, colleges and comparable institutions).

Most primary schools
India had 664,000 primary schools, as of September 2011. China, previously the holder of the record, now has 456,900 primary schools (down from 849,123 in 1997) as a result of its one-child-per-family policy.

Most schools attended
Wilma Williams, now Mrs RJ Horton, attended 265 schools, from 1933 to 1943, when her parents were in showbusiness in the USA.

Most multiple birth sets in one year at one school
Maine South High School in Park Ridge, Illinois, USA, has 17 birth sets – 14 sets of twins and 3 sets of triplets. All 37 students are due to graduate in 2014.

Most twins in one year at one school
A total of 16 pairs of twins are enrolled in the 9th grade at Valley Southwoods Freshman High School in West Des Moines, USA, for the academic year 2011–12.

Most triplets in one school
In the school year 1998–99, Kirkby Centre School, Ashfield, Nottinghamshire, UK, had five sets of triplets on its student register.

Oldest person to begin primary school

Kimani Ng'ang'a Maruge (Kenya) was 84 when he enrolled at Kapkenduiyo Primary School, Eldoret, Kenya, in 2004. Two of his 30 grandchildren were in the school above him! He wore the school uniform and, after straight "A"s in his first end-of-term exams, he was made a senior headboy. Sadly, Mr Maruge passed away on 15 August 2009, aged 90.

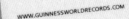

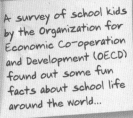

Largest school reunion
A total of 3,299 former pupils of Stadium High School, Tacoma, Washington, USA, attended a reunion on 16 September 2006.

Longest lesson
Kathiravan M Pethi and 36 students (all India) took part in a lesson entitled "Ghandhi's Vision and Mission in Life" that lasted 78 hr 3 min. The lesson took place at the Association of Physicians of India, Bangalore, India, from 31 October to 3 November 2008.

Largest class with perfect attendance
In the year 1984–85, Ms Melanie Murray's class of 23 at David Barkley Elementary School, San Antonio, Texas, USA, had a perfect attendance with no absences.

Longest-running annual class reunion
The class of 1929 at the Cherokee County Community High School held its 77th class reunion in Columbus, Kansas, USA, on 27 June 2006.

Longest-serving headteacher
John Aitkenhead (UK) founded the Kilquhanity House School in Dumfries and Galloway, Scotland, in 1940, and worked there for 57 years until it closed in 1997. Although he was headteacher, the school was libertarian and governed by its pupils and staff.

Longest wait for a class reunion
The 1929 class of Miss Blanche Miller's Kindergarten and Continuation School, Bluefield, West Virginia, USA, had its first reunion after 70 years. Ten members of the class had died but, of those remaining, 55% were in attendance.

Longest-serving music teacher
Charles Wright (USA) taught piano for 76 years from 1931 until he passed away on 19 July 2007, aged 95.

Longest career as a teacher
Medarda de Jesus Leon de Uzcategui (b. 8 June 1899), alias La Maestra Chucha, started teaching at the Modelo de Aplicacion, Caracas, Venezuela, in 1911. In 1942, she started her own school, the Escuela Uzcategui, from her home in Caracas, where she was still teaching in 1998, so her career spanned 87 years. She is reported to have died in 2002.

Highest pupil-to-teacher ratio
In the Central African Republic, there are 95 pupils for every primary school teacher and 92 pupils for every secondary school teacher.

A survey of school kids by the Organization for Economic Co-operation and Development (OECD) found out some fun facts about school life around the world...

Mexican kids have the coolest teachers...
71%
say their teachers really listen to them.

Australian kids are the most popular...
93%
say they are liked by fellow students.

Latvian kids respect school the most...
81%
believe that it is preparing them well for later life.

Uruguayan kids are the worst timekeepers...
57%
say they are late for lessons at least once every two weeks.

Indonesian kids are most likely to be maths swots...
70%
say they enjoy the subject.

AUCTIONS

MOST EXPENSIVE...

The following selection of records reflects the highest prices paid for items at auction, presented in ascending order of sale price.

Most expensive popstar costume

Elvis Presley's (USA) white peacock jumpsuit – designed by Bill Belew (USA) – sold for $300,000 (£153,560) in an online auction on 7 August 2008.

Calendar

A wall calendar featuring sketches of costume designs for characters from *Alice in Wonderland* was sold to an anonymous bidder for £36,000 ($57,848). The sale took place as part of a fund-raising auction in aid of the Muir Maxwell Trust and the Fettes Foundation (both UK). It was held at The Mad Hatter's Tea Party on The Queen's Lawn at Fettes College, Edinburgh, UK, on 3 July 2011.

Signed baseball

At an auction in Dallas, Texas, USA, on 5 May 2006, a baseball signed in 1961 by legendary baseball player Joe DiMaggio and film star Marilyn Monroe (both USA) – DiMaggio's former wife – was sold for $191,200 (£103,766) by Heritage Auction Galleries.

Doll

A rare French doll dating from c. 1914, by sculptor Albert Marque, realized $263,000 (£162,181) at a Theriault's auction in Atlanta, Georgia, USA, on 12 July 2009. The doll, dressed in its period clothing to honour the Ballets Russes of Paris and first introduced to international acclaim in 1909, was won by a prominent collector from Boston, USA.

Batman memorabilia

A Batmobile used in Joel Schumacher's movie *Batman Forever* (USA, 1995) sold at the Kruse International collector car auction in Las Vegas, Nevada, USA, in September 2006 for $335,000 (£175,770) to John O'Quinn (USA).

Football memorabilia

The most valuable piece of football history is an original FA Cup – one of four produced for the first competition held in 1871 and given to the winning team between 1896 and 1910. An anonymous telephone bidder bought the cup for £420,000 ($773,136) from Christie's, UK, on 19 May 2005.

James Bond memorabilia

On 20 January 2006, a Swiss businessman paid $1.9 million (£1.1 million) for a silver 1965 Aston Martin DB5 coupé that was used to promote the 007 films *Goldfinger* (UK, 1964) and *Thunderball* (UK, 1965).

Guitar

A Fender Stratocaster guitar signed by a host of music legends including Mick Jagger, Eric Clapton, Paul McCartney, Jimmy Page and Brian May (all UK) fetched $2.7 million (£1.6 million) at a charity auction for Reach Out to Asia at the Ritz-Carlton Hotel, Doha, Qatar, on 17 November 2005. The Reach Out to Asia campaign seeks to support worthy causes around the world, with particular emphasis on the Asian continent.

Clock

The world record for a clock sold at auction is £1,926,500 ($3,001,294) for a Louis XVI Ormulu-Mounted Ebony Grande Sonnerie Astronomical Perpetual Calendar Regulateur de Parquet. The auction took place at Christie's, London, UK, on 8 July 1999.

Jacket

Price: $1.8 million (£1.1 million)
Date: 26 June 2011
Auction: Julien's Auction, Beverly Hills, USA
Details: Black-and-red calf-leather jacket with winged shoulders worn by singer Michael Jackson (USA) in his 1983 *Thriller* video

Truffle

Price: $330,000 (£160,000)
Date: 1 December 2007
Place: The Grand Lisboa Hotel, Macau, China
Details: White truffle (*Tuber magnatum pico*) unearthed in Pisa, Italy, on 23 November 2007

Handbag

Price: $203,150 (£129,477)
Date: 9 December 2011
Auction: Heritage Auctions, Dallas, Texas, USA
Details: Hermès Diamond Birkin handbag, featuring diamond-and-white-gold hardware

Toy soldier

Price: $200,000 (£124,309)
Date: 7 August 2003
Auction: Heritage Comics Auctions, Dallas, Texas, USA
Details: First handcrafted 1963 GI Joe prototype

False teeth

Price: £15,200 ($23,700)
Date: 29 July 2010
Auction: Keys auctioneers, Aylsham, Norfolk, UK
Details: Set of dentures that once belonged to wartime British prime minister Winston Churchill

Barbie doll

Price: $27,450 (£14,600)
Date: May 2006
Auction: Held by Sandi Holder's Doll Attic (USA)
Details: Original 1959 Barbie in mint condition

Most expensive photograph

Rhein II, a photograph of the River Rhine under grey skies taken by Andreas Gursky (Germany, b. 1955), fetched $4,338,500 (£2,706,490), including buyer's premium, at a Christie's auction in New York, USA, on 8 November 2011. The glass-mounted 363.5 x 185.4-cm (143 x 73-in) image, created in 1999, is one of an edition of six works. The buyer is unknown.

Letter (signed)

A letter written in 1787 by George Washington to his nephew Bushrod – in which he urges adoption of the country's new constitution – sold for $3,200,000 (£1,932,600) on 5 December 2009 at Christie's, New York City, USA.

Musical instrument

A violin known as the "Hammer", made in 1707 by Antonio Stradivari in Cremona, Italy, sold for $3.5 million (£1.8 million) to an anonymous buyer, at Christie's, New York City, USA, on 15 May 2006. It is one of 620 instruments made by Stradivari thought to exist.

Dress

The ivory rayon-acetate dress worn by Marilyn Monroe in *The Seven Year Itch* (USA, 1955) raised $4.6 million (£2.8 million) in an auction at The Paley Center for Media in Los Angeles, USA, on 18 June 2011.

Coin

The most expensive coin is a 1933 Double Eagle: a $20 gold coin that was minted but never officially circulated (most of the coins were melted down shortly after being produced). The rare coin was auctioned at Sotheby's in New York City, USA, on 30 July 2002, where it fetched $7,590,020 (£4,856,370) with premium.

Diamond

A "D" colour internally flawless pear-shaped diamond weighing 100.10 carats sold for CHF 19,858,500 ($16,561,171; £10,548,444) at Sotheby's in Geneva, Switzerland, on 17 May 1995. It also holds the record for the **most expensive jewel sold at auction**.

Chair

An armchair made *c.* 1917–19 by Irish-born designer Eileen Gray which had belonged to designer Yves Saint Laurent (France) sold at auction for €21.9 million ($28 million; £19.4 million). The buyer, Cheska Vallois (France), was the same dealer who originally sold the chair to the French designer in the 1970s. The auction took place at Christie's in Paris, France, on 24–26 February 2009.

Whisky
Price: £46,850 ($72,975)
Date: 14 December 2011
Auction: Bonhams, Edinburgh, UK
Details: Bottle of rare 55-year-old Glenfiddich single-malt whisky. Proceeds of the sale were donated to the charity WaterAid

Teddy bear
Price: €213,720 ($182,400; £125,617)
Date: 14 October 2000
Auction: Christie's, Monaco
Details: Steiff "Louis Vuitton" teddy bear made in 2000 and measuring 45 cm (17 in) tall

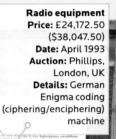

Radio equipment
Price: £24,172.50 ($38,047.50)
Date: April 1993
Auction: Phillips, London, UK
Details: German Enigma coding (ciphering/enciphering) machine

Pearl necklace
Price: $11,842,500 (£7,601,630)
Date: 14 December 2011
Auction: Christie's, New York City, USA
Details: 50.6-carat necklace known as "La Peregrina", dating from the 16th century. It was a present to actress Elizabeth Taylor from her then husband Richard Burton, who bought it in an auction in 1969 for $37,000 (£15,400)

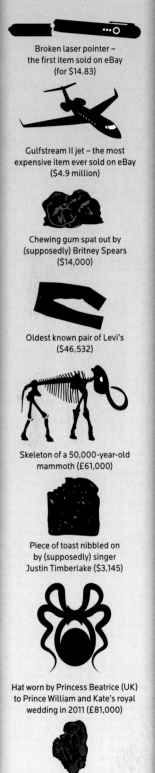

ODDEST THINGS SOLD ON EBAY

eBay is the world's **largest online auction house**, with 98.7 million active users as of December 2011. In 2010, a total of 24.4 million packages – worth £40 billion ($62 billion) – were shipped via the site. Here is a selection of the stranger items listed over the years, with sale or final bid prices:

Broken laser pointer – the first item sold on eBay (for $14.83)

Gulfstream II jet – the most expensive item ever sold on eBay ($4.9 million)

Chewing gum spat out by (supposedly) Britney Spears ($14,000)

Oldest known pair of Levi's ($46,532)

Skeleton of a 50,000-year-old mammoth (£61,000)

Piece of toast nibbled on by (supposedly) singer Justin Timberlake ($3,145)

Hat worn by Princess Beatrice (UK) to Prince William and Kate's royal wedding in 2011 (£81,000)

Cornflake in the shape of the state of Illinois, USA ($1,350)

THE ECONOMY

Largest bank collapse
According to the International Monetary Fund (IMF), the worst banking crisis suffered by any country, relative to its economy, occurred in 2008–11 with the collapse of the three largest banks in Iceland.

FACT:
Iceland's banks had made loans equivalent to nine times its gross domestic product (GDP).

Largest stock-market flotation (IPO)
The stock-market launch – or "Initial Public Offering" (IPO) – of the Agricultural Bank of China (aka AgBank) raised a record $22.1 billion (£13.8 billion) on 13 August 2010. Shares were listed on both the Shanghai and the Hong Kong Stock Exchanges. The bank has over 30 million customers and over 440,000 employees.

Largest trading volume in a day
The largest volume of shares traded at one stock exchange in one day was 5,799,792,281. This incredible figure was achieved on the New York Stock Exchange on 16 August 2007.

Highest share value
On 27 March 2000, the share price for one share of Yahoo! Japan stood at 120.4 million yen ($1.12 million; £706,573). Yahoo! Japan is the nation's dominant information portal, and the scarcity of the stock contributed to the dramatic rise in price. As of 2004, Japanese company

FACT:
John is 122 days younger than the previous title holder, Jason A Earle (USA).

Softbank owned 41.93% of the company, with US-based Yahoo! owning 33.49%. Yahoo! Japan's share price had increased 4,700% since December 1998.

Highest closing price on the FTSE 100
The FTSE 100 index lists the share prices of the 100 UK companies with the highest market value. It reached an overall closing high of 6,930.2 on 30 December 1999.

The **lowest closing price on the FTSE 100** was on 12 July 1984, when it fell to 978.7.

Greatest annual net loss by a company
AOL Time Warner (USA) reported an annual net loss of $98.7 billion (£60 billion) on 30 January 2003.

Most billionaires (city)
According to Forbes, the Russian capital Moscow currently boasts an unprecedented 79 billionaires. Between them, the Moscow billionaires share a total of $375.3 billion (£231.6 billion). The richest Muscovite – and Russia's richest man – is the steel magnate Vladimir Lisin. The photograph above shows a millionaire's shopping fair in Moscow.

The USA is the **country with the most billionaires**: 412 out of a global total of 1,210, as of 2011.

Largest takeover
German conglomerate Mannesmann merged with Vodafone AirTouch (UK) in February 2002. Under the terms of the £112-billion ($159-billion) deal, Mannesmann shareholders received 49.5% of the merged company, with Vodafone providing 58.96 of its shares for each Mannesmann share.

Largest public company
According to Forbes, banking firm JP Morgan Chase (USA) was the world's largest public company as of 2010/11 – a record for the second year running. Forbes' calculations are based on four categories: sales, profits, assets and overall market value. For 2010/11, JP Morgan Chase registered

Youngest investment banker
John Wang Clow (USA, b. 23 May 1994) passed the Investment Banking Examination (Series 79), administered by the Financial Industry Regulatory Authority (FINRA), on 5 August 2011. He became a licensed investment banker on 8 August 2011, at the age of 17 years 77 days.

WHY NOT INVEST YOUR TIME IN AUCTIONS, ON P.148?

Youngest billionaire
Facebook co-founder Dustin Moskovitz (USA) left the social networking website in 2008 to form his own company. Now aged 27, he is worth $3.5 billion (£2.2 billion) according to Forbes.

Most profitable restaurant chain

When it comes to restaurants, McDonald's (USA) is first in line. For the 2010/11 financial year, the ubiquitous burger chain served up profits of $4.9 billion (£2.9 billion), while the company itself was valued at a mouth-watering $80.1 billion (£48 billion). The first McDonald's fast-food restaurant opened in 1948 in San Bernardino, California, USA.

figures of $115.5 billion (£69.3 billion) in sales, $17.4 billion (£10.4 billion) in profits, $2,117.6 billion (£1,270.5 billion) in assets and $182.2 billion (£109.3 billion) in market value.

Largest company
• **By assets**: Mortgage association Fannie Mae (USA) had assets totalling $3,222 billion (£1,933 billion), according to Forbes' Global 2000 list for 2010/11.

Largest financial rescue plan

Between 2008 and 2012, the central banks of the USA, UK, Japan and the 17 countries that use the euro issued loans to the value of $8.8 trillion (£5.5 trillion) to ease the effects of the Global Financial Crisis (GFC). This figure includes $2.95 trillion (£1.86 trillion) from the US Federal Reserve and $3.58 trillion (£2.26 trillion) from the European Central Bank.

• **By market value**: According to the Forbes Global 2000 list for 2010/11, the oil and gas giant Exxon Mobil had a market value of $407.2 billion (£244.3 billion) as of April 2011.
• **By profits**: Swiss food company Nestlé made $36.7 billion (£22 billion) profit in 2010/11.
With revenues totalling $112 billion (£69.3 billion) for the 12 months up to 11 March 2011, Nestlé is also the **largest food company** in terms of annual sales. The company owns business units including Food and Beverage, Nestlé Waters and Nestlé Nutrition.
• **By sales**: Forbes places Wal-Mart Stores, Inc., as the company with the highest sales, with world-beating figures of $421.8 billion (£253 billion).

Largest corporate bankruptcy
US investment bank Lehman Brothers Holdings Inc. filed for bankruptcy to the tune of $613 billion (£341.5 billion) on 15 September 2008. The bank succumbed to the sub-prime mortgage crisis, which started the worldwide recession in 2008.

Largest advertising agency (revenues)
Omnicom Group Inc., whose headquarters are on Madison Avenue in New York, USA, had revenues of $12.5 billion (£8 billion) for the fiscal year ending 31 December 2010.

Richest investor
Warren Edward Buffett (USA), chairman of Berkshire Hathaway, is the world's richest investor, estimated to be worth $45 billion (£29 billion) as of September 2011.

Richest media tycoon
Michael Bloomberg's (USA) media empire Bloomberg L.P., which includes the Bloomberg financial news firm, was worth an estimated $22.5 billion (£14 billion) as of March 2011.

FACT: Economists regard a "recession" as a period of two or more fiscal quarters in which GDP shrinks.

FACT: The GFC is widely regarded as the worst financial crisis since the Great Depression of the 1930s.

WORLD WEALTH
The colour bars here represent the world share of Gross Domestic Product as of 2010, according to a yearly average for 1990 to 2010 calculated by the World Bank. In all, 190 countries are listed, with the top 10 richest nations named. These 10 countries own 66.5% of the world's wealth.

10. CANADA $1,577,040 million
9. INDIA $1,721,111 million
8. ITALY $2,051,412 million
7. BRAZIL $2,087,890 million
6. UK $2,248,831 million
5. FRANCE $2,560,002 million
4. GERMANY $3,280,530 million
3. JAPAN $5,458,837 million
2. CHINA $5,926,612 million
1. USA $14,586,736 million

*includes overseas departments
†excludes Chinese Taipei, Hong Kong and Macau

151

CITIES

Oldest skyscraper city

The population of Shibam in Yemen – amounting to about 7,000 people – live in densely clustered mud-brick high-rise buildings, some of which are above 30 m (98 ft 5 in) tall and have up to 12 storeys. The high-rise construction began after Shibam was flooded in 1532–33, with most of the approximately 500 towers built in the 16th century.

First city

Dating back to around 3200 BC, the world's first city was Uruk, located in southern Mesopotamia (modern Iraq). Home to some 50,000 inhabitants, it was the largest settlement of its time, covering 450 ha (1,112 acres) and encircled by a 9.5-km (5.9-mile) city wall. Thriving as a result of trade and agriculture, Uruk also became a great artistic centre, featuring many elaborate mosaics and monuments.

First use of postal codes

In 1857, Sir Rowland Hill (UK) divided London into postal districts based on compass points – "N" for North, "S" for South, etc. The UK's present form of the postcode – a mixture of letters and numbers decoded by machine to allow faster sorting – was first used in Norwich, Norfolk, UK, in October 1959. The similar ZIP (Zone Improvement Plan) code came into use in the USA in July 1963.

Largest arcology project

An arcology is a city designed to provide an alternative to modern urban sprawl. First proposed by Italian-American architect Paolo Soleri in the 1960s, an arcology's aim is to be self-sufficient and prevent wasteful consumption of land, energy and time. The largest arcology underway is Masdar City in Abu Dhabi, UAE. Initiated in 2006, it occupies 6 km² (2.3 miles²) and is planned to host around 50,000 people and 1,500 businesses.

Largest city with no major road connection

Iquitos, founded in the Peruvian rainforest in the 1750s, has a population of around 430,000 and is a major port on the Amazon River. The only road from Iquitos stops at the small town of Nauta, about 100 km (62 miles) to the south. This makes the city accessible only by air and river.

Largest slum

Neza-Chalco-Itza is one of Mexico City's *barrios* (slums). Most of its approximately four million inhabitants live there illegally. Mexico City's slums have been growing for more than 100 years, after the railways allowed new industry to begin in the city.

Most expensive city to park in

According to a 2011 report by Colliers International, the two most expensive urban zones in which to park a car are both in London, UK. Median monthly parking rates are £657 ($1,083) in the City of London, the financial district, and £615 ($1,014) in London's West End, the entertainment district.

Largest shopping centre

The Dubai Mall, located in Downtown Dubai, UAE, consists of four levels with a floor area of 548,127 m² (5.9 million ft²) and has 1,200 retail outlets and over 160 food and beverage outlets. Construction began in 2004, with the mall opening its doors on 4 November 2008.

Busiest metro network

The Moscow Metro in Russia carries 8–9 million passengers each day. By comparison, the New York City Subway, USA, carries 4.5 million people each day and the London Underground, UK, carries just over 3 million.

Oldest metro system

The London Underground, UK, opened its first section – from Paddington station to Farringdon – in 1863.

Metro with most stations

New York City Subway has 468 stations (277 of which are underground) in a network covering 370 km (230 miles).

Longest driverless metro network

The Dubai Metro (UAE) consists of two driverless lines (Red and Green) that totalled 74.694 km (46.41 miles) when the Green line was officially opened on 9 September 2011.

City with most skyscrapers

According to the Council on Tall Buildings and Urban Habitat, in 2010 there were 2,354 buildings in Hong Kong that were at least 100 m (328 ft) tall. They have an estimated combined height of around 330 km (205 miles), which is only 25 km (15.5 miles) shy of the altitude at which the Chinese *Tiangong 1* space station orbits the Earth.

City with the densest population

Manila, capital of the Philippines, had 1,660,714 inhabitants according to its 2007 census. Crammed into just 38.55 km² (14.88 miles²), its population density is 43,079 people per square kilometre.

First parking meters

Parking meters were invented by Carl C Magee (USA) and first installed in Oklahoma City, Oklahoma, USA, in July 1935. They reached New York in 1951 and London in 1958.

Largest urban tram network

From 1897 to the 1960s, Buenos Aires in Argentina boasted a huge tram network. At its maximum, it had an estimated 857 km (532.5 miles) of lines, including those underground. The trams were replaced by modern buses.

Oldest bus rapid-transit network

Curitiba, the capital of the Brazilian state of Paraná, is home to around 1.75 million people. In 1974, it became the first city in the world to implement a bus rapid-transit network. Superior to normal bus routes, it uses dedicated lanes for buses, articulated long buses and more frequent vehicles, allowing its 2.3 million daily users to commute at speeds similar to light rail networks.

Longest metro escalator

The St Petersburg metro in Russia has an escalator with a vertical rise of 50.5 m (195 ft).

Most escalators in a metro system

The metro in Washington, DC, USA, has 557 escalators which are maintained by approximately 90 technicians.

Busiest station

Shinjuku Station in Tokyo, Japan, has an average of 3.64 million passengers pass through it each day. It has more than 200 exits.

Longest continuous subway

The Moscow metro Kaluzhskaya underground railway line from Medvedkovo to Bittsevsky Park, completed in early 1990, is 37.9 km (23.8 miles) long.

City with most bridges

Hamburg, Germany, is located on the River Elbe at the point where it meets the Bille and Alster rivers. The canals, rivers and streams within the city are crossed by a total of 2,302 bridges – more than the cities of Venice and Amsterdam combined.

Largest car park

The world's largest car park can hold 20,000 vehicles and is situated at the West Edmonton Mall in Edmonton, Alberta, Canada. There are overflow facilities on an adjoining car park for 10,000 more vehicles.

FACT: "A Symphony of Lights", a light show with music, illuminates 44 Hong Kong skyscrapers every night.

FOR MORE HIGH-RISE RECORDS, TURN TO P.270

LARGEST CITIES

The top 15 largest urban areas ("urban agglomerations"), as defined by the most recent United Nations World Urbanization Prospects report.

TOKYO, JAPAN 36,669,000

DELHI, INDIA 22,157,000

SÃO PAULO, BRAZIL 20,262,000

MUMBAI, INDIA 20,041,000

MEXICO CITY, MEXICO 19,460,000

NEW YORK, USA 19,425,000

SHANGHAI, CHINA 16,575,000

KOLKATA, INDIA 15,552,000

DHAKA, BANGLADESH 14,648,000

KARACHI, PAKISTAN 13,125,000

BUENOS AIRES, ARGENTINA 13,074,000

LOS ANGELES, USA 12,762,000

BEIJING, CHINA 12,385,000

RIO DE JANEIRO, BRAZIL 11,950,000

MANILA, PHILIPPINES 11,628,000

Circles to scale = 10 million people

MYSTERIOUS WORLD

Largest collection of "haunted" dolls

Located south of Mexico City within a network of canals, Mexico's tiny La Isla de las Muñecas ("Island of the Dolls") houses thousands of broken, mutilated and decaying dolls. Locals claim that at night the dolls come to life, animated by the spirits of the dead. The grotesque collection began in the 1950s, when a hermit named Don Julian Santana Barrera settled here. Claiming that he was being haunted by the ghost of a young girl who had drowned in one of the canals in the 1920s, he began placing dolls around the island as a sort of shrine to appease her restless spirit.

FACT:
In 2001, Don Barrera died in the same canal that the young girl had drowned in...

First scientific treatise on spontaneous human combustion

Spontaneous human combustion (SHC) is defined as the burning of a living human body without any clear external source of ignition. Approximately 200 cases have been reported worldwide during the past three centuries alone. Author Charles Dickens even incorporated an SHC event into the plot of his novel *Bleak House* (1852). The first scientific, non-sensationalized investigation into spontaneous human combustion appeared in 1673. Entitled *De Incendiis Corporis Humani Spontaneis*, it was written by Jonas Dupont (France) and comprised SHC-related cases and studies.

First "haunted" battle scene

The famous Battle of Marathon between the citizens of Athens and Persian armies took place on the Plain of Marathon in 490 BC, and was won by the Greeks. However, shortly afterwards, observers claimed to have seen a ghostly "action replay" of this battle, and comparable spectral re-enactments have reputedly been witnessed at the site on several occasions since then, up to modern times.

Oldest ghost

Ghost Ranch, in Rio Arriba County, New Mexico, has earned its name from the many sightings of a huge ghostly reptile that have been made there over the years. Measuring 6–9 m (19 ft 6 in–29 ft 6 in) long, it has been dubbed "Vivaron, the snake-demon" by local inhabitants.

In 1947, paleontologist Edwin H Colbert (USA) unearthed a huge cache of fossil skeletons in this same area, derived from various prehistoric reptiles. These not only included more than a thousand dinosaur specimens but also a 9-m-long (29.5-ft) crocodile-like creature known as a phytosaur. Its discovery led to speculation that the paranormal "snake-demon" that had been reported by the locals was the ghost of this phytosaur. If this were true – and bearing in mind that its fossil skeleton is 220 million years old, dating from the Triassic Period – the phytosaur's spectre would be the world's oldest ghost!

Longest continuous house construction

Winchester House in San Jose, California, USA, was under construction for 38 years. Once an eight-room farmhouse on a 65-ha (161-acre) estate, its transformation into a mansion was begun in 1886 by the widowed Sarah Winchester, heiress to the Winchester rifle fortune. It is known as the "Winchester Mystery House" because of its many oddities, such as closets opening into blank walls, a window in the floor, and staircases leading nowhere. Some believe that after the death of her husband (son of the inventor of the famous rifle) the widow was told by a medium that endless remodelling would confuse and calm the ghosts of all the people killed by the "gun that won the West". The house has 13 bathrooms, 52 skylights, 47 fireplaces, 10,000 windows, 40 staircases, 2,000 doorways and trapdoors and three elevators.

FATE

HAS ATLANTIS BEEN FOUND?

Longest-running paranormal magazine

US magazine *Fate* began in 1948 and for many years was published monthly. Since July 2009, it has appeared bi-monthly online only.

Most participants in a scientific study of a haunted house

Between 26 May and 4 June 2000, psychologist Richard Wiseman from the University of Hertfordshire, UK, led an experiment in which 1,027 volunteers walked around parts of Hampton Court Palace, reputedly one of the most haunted locations

Tallest bigfoot

According to researchers who investigate reports of the bigfoot (sasquatch), visibly different types of this hairy bipedal mystery primate occur in North America. The tallest is the so-called true giant, which, witnesses say, is 3–6 m (9 ft 10 in–19 ft 6 in) tall. The most common sightings are in the high mountains of the west and in the northern spruce forests. Pictured is GWR consultant Karl Shuker with a cast of the "Grays Harbor Footprint", taken from tracks discovered in 1982 in Washington state, USA.

SASQUATCH XING

Largest crop glyph

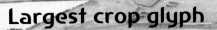

Members of the XL D-Sign team (all Netherlands) created a 530 x 450-m (1,739 x 1,476-ft) cropfield image of a "mothman" in Zeeland, Netherlands, over the course of one night in August 2009. It covered around 24 ha (59 acres) and was dubbed "Project Atlas". XL D-Sign has been producing huge, elaborate cropfield-sited images for more than 10 years.

FACT: The image is around 60 times larger than the pitch at Rotterdam's De Kuip stadium (left).

STRANGEST FALLS

ELECTRIC RAIN
1 November 1844 – Paris, France
Witnessed by Dr Morel-Deville, rain sparked and crackled as it hit the ground and buildings, and gave off a phosphorus smell.

BIRD BLOOD
15 May 1890 – Messignadi, Calabria, Italy
Rain of blood formally identified as birds' blood fell, but no bird carcasses were found.

GREEN RAIN
June 2002 – India
Fell for two days; shown to be pollen-containing droppings of a huge swarm of honeybees.

NAILS
12 October 1888 – Texas, USA
Cascade of nails rained from the sky on to the wife of Point Isabel's lighthouse keeper.

BLUE RAIN
8 April 1954 – USA
Blue rain fell over several USA towns; when examined, found to be radioactive.

HAILSTONE-ENCASED TORTOISE
11 May 1894 – Vicksburg, Mississippi, USA
During a hailstorm, a gopher tortoise entirely encased in a giant hailstone and measuring 15.2 x 20.3 cm (6 x 8 in) fell from the sky.

FROGS
28 Aug 1977 – Canet-Plage, France
Thousands of tiny frogs the size of peas seen falling to the ground from the sky just before a heavy rain shower began.

PWDRE SER (STAR ROT)
21 January 1803 – Silesia, Germany
The day after a meteor fell to Earth, an unexplained jelly-like mass (*pwdre ser*) was found on the ground.

SILVER COINS
30 September 1956 – Meshehera, Russia
Shower of silver coins fell all over the district during a storm.

ANGEL HAIR
20 September 1892 – Florida, USA
Great white sheets of spiderweb-like gossamer (known as angel hair) floated down with rain, some measuring 45 m (150 ft) or more in length. Seen and collected by Gainesville's postmaster.

---

in the UK. The volunteers documented any unusual experiences or sensations and the results were collected for psychological analysis.

Largest flock of birds to invade a house

On the evening of 4 May 1998, the Fire Department in Pasadena, California, USA, was called to investigate a strange happening in an empty house. Firefighters discovered that more than 1,000 swifts (family Apidae) had flown down the chimney, spreading soot everywhere. Some of the swifts were dead, having apparently flown headlong into the walls in panic. It took at least two hours for the firefighters, led by Fire Dept Battalion Chief Joe Nestor (USA), to shoo the rest of the huge flock out of the house, through windows and doors. It is unclear why the swifts flew down the chimney en masse.

Deadliest lake

The lake responsible for the most deaths not brought about by drowning is Lake Nyos in Cameroon, west Africa, where toxic gases have claimed nearly 2,000 lives in recent decades. On one night in August 1986, about 1,700 people and countless animals were killed by a large natural release of carbon dioxide gas.

Largest area of glowing sea

In 1995, scientists at the US Naval Research Laboratory discovered an area of luminous sea in the Indian Ocean off the coast of Somalia using satellite images. The patch of water measured more than 250 km (155 miles) long and had an area of around 14,000 km² (5,400 miles²). Bioluminescent bacteria are believed to have been responsible for the water's striking appearance.

Largest pink lake

Retba Lake, better known as Lac Rose ("Pink Lake"), is the world's largest pink body of water, measuring around 1.5 x 5 km (0.9 x 3 miles) at low water. A shallow lagoon, located 30 km (18 miles) north of Dakar, Senegal (famous as the last leg in the Paris–Dakar Rally), the lake's intense colour is the result of micro-organisms and a strong concentration of minerals.

First stigmatic

The term "stigmatic" refers to a person who seems to have wounds mirroring those suffered by Jesus Christ during his crucifixion. Depicted here is Francis of Assisi (1181/2–1226, canonized 1228), who was reportedly visited by an angel in 1224 while praying. Francis later found that he bore a series of wounds corresponding to those of Jesus. Stigmatics continue to make claims to the present day (inset photo).

Longest Loch Ness monster vigil

FACT: This 1934 photo is the most famous image of "Nessie". Its authenticity remains a matter for debate.

Steve Feltham (UK, right) arrived at Loch Ness, Scotland, in 1991 in search of the legendary monster, and remains there full-time. Feltham lives on the shore in a converted mobile library and spends every day scanning the loch in search of the monster.
The **most prolific Nessie eyewitness** is Alex Campbell, a water bailiff who worked at the loch for more than 40 years – he claimed to have made 17 observations of Nessie, starting in May 1934.

NATIONS

FACT:
The USA spent $7,421 (£4,684) per person on healthcare in 2009 – a total bill of $2.2 trillion (£1.38 trillion).

01 Highest budget for health care The USA spent 16.2% of its Gross Domestic Product (GDP) on healthcare in 2009.

02 Fewest smokers According to the latest available figures from Nationmaster.com, only 17% of Canadians smoke at least one cigarette daily.

03 Lowest population density Greenland has a population density of around 0.02 people per km² (0.06 people per mile²).

04 Fastest-growing body mass index The average US citizen grew 1 kg (2 lb 3 oz) heavier per decade from 1980 to 2008.

Most computers per capita Canadians had 108.6 computers per 100 citizens as of 2009.

05 Largest emigrant population According to the latest World Bank report, 11.9 million Mexican citizens were living abroad as of 2010.

Most internet users per capita Iceland had 93.5 internet users per 100 population as of 2009, according to *The Economist*.

06 Fewest divorces Guatemala registers just one divorce per 10,000 people, according to *The Economist*.

Lowest marriage rate Colombia has an average of just 1.7 marriages per 1,000 population, according to *The Economist*.

Largest producer of coffee Brazil produced more than 2.36 million tonnes (2.6 million tons) of coffee in 2009–10.

At a glance...

GWR's one-stop guide to the world's populations:

• **Global population:** reached 7 billion on 31 October 2011

• **Population growth rate:** the annual birth rate is currently 1.915% – meaning 252 babies are born every minute; but the mortality rate is 0.812%, which means 107 deaths every minute and therefore a net growth of 1.092% (based on estimates for 2011)

• **Countries:** 195

• **Land boundaries:** 322

• **Total labour force:** 3.228 billion (2010 estimate)

• **Registered refugees:** at least 8.8 million (2010 estimate)

Source: CIA Factbook

07 Highest murder rate The United Nations recorded 60.87 murders per 100,000 citizens in Honduras in 2008.

08 Happiest country As of 2009, Costa Rica ranked first on the Happy Planet Index, with a 76.1% rating.

JUST HOW LONG CAN WE LIVE FOR? FIND OUT ON P.66

Leaving a big footprint

With a population of some 500,000, Luxembourg is one of the tiniest nations. As of 2009, however, it had the **largest ecological footprint** of any nation. The equivalent of 20.2 ha (25.2 acres) of land would be needed to meet each Luxembourger's needs and absorb their carbon emissions.

Most popular tourism destination According to the United Nations, France attracted 76.8 million tourists in 2010.

Highest alcohol consumption Moldovans drank the equivalent of 19.2 litres (4.1 gal) of pure alcohol per person in 2005, according to the World Health Organization (WHO).

Highest ratio of foreign aid Sweden gives 1.03% of its GDP to official development aid.

Greatest gender difference in life expectancy Russian males have a life expectancy of 59.33 years, compared with 73.14 years for females – a difference of 13.81 years.

Most democratic country The 2011 Economist Intelligence Unit report rates Norway as the most democratic country, with a score of 9.8 out of 10.

FACT: A total of 46 nations and other territories are completely land-locked.

Most blind people There are more than 15 million blind people in India.

Most official languages The Republic of South Africa has 11 official languages. They are: English, Afrikaans, isiZulu, isiXhosa, Sesotho, Setswana, Sepedi, Xitsonga, siSwati, isiNdebele and Tshivenda.

Newest independent country On 9 July 2011, South Sudan peacefully seceded from Sudan. One day earlier, Sudan had become the first country to recognize South Sudan as a country in its own right.

Highest population According to figures from 2010, China's population now exceeds 1.33 billion.

Highest birth rate Based on figures for 2005–10, there are 49.5 births per 1,000 population in Niger.

Least corrupt country New Zealand scores 95% on the Corruptions Perception Index.

FACT: As of 2011, there are roughly two cows and seven sheep to every person in New Zealand.

LIFE EXPECTANCY

The average life expectancy in the world is 66.57 years: 64.52 for males and 68.76 for females.

Average age in years

89.73 Monaco	
	Iceland 81.79
81.81 Australia	Italy 81.77
81.38 Canada	France 81.19
81.17 Spain	Sweden 81.07
	New Zealand 80.59
80.20 Norway	Ireland 80.19
80.07 Germany	UK 80.05
79.92 Greece	Netherlands 79.68
79.27 Finland	
78.63 Denmark	Portugal 78.54
78.37 USA	Chile 77.70
77.19 Czech Rep	Argentina 76.95
	Mexico 76.47
75.77 Paraguay	Poland 76.28
75.40 Slovakia	Croatia 75.35
74.70 Hungary	
	Estonia 72.82
72.81 Colombia	Egypt 72.66
71.99 Brazil	Turkey 71.69
70.74 Peru	Iraq 69.96
69.89 India	
68.20 Belize	Ukraine 68.25
	Mongolia 67.65
66.89 Bolivia	**WORLD 66.57**
66.03 Russia	
	The Bahamas 65.78
	Kiribati 63.22
	Haiti 60.78

Key

Africa	Asia	Europe
N. America	S. America	Oceania

Source: CIA Factbook

WORLD LEADERS

Youngest current head of state

Kim Jong-un of North Korea ascended to the leadership position on 17 December 2011, following the death of his father, Kim Jong-il. Kim Jong-un's exact age has never been confirmed: it has been speculated that he was 27 upon succeeding his father, though his date of birth has also been listed as 8 January 1982, or the same date in 1983 or 1984. The younger Kim also holds the title of Supreme Commander of the Korean People's Army and carries the rank of Daejang, the equivalent of a general.

Simultaneous head of state of most countries

Her Majesty, Queen Elizabeth II (UK) is head of state of 16 countries, as of March 2012. The Queen's role is nominal and ceremonial (she has no political power), yet more than 128 million people in 15 Commonwealth states (plus the UK and its 14 Overseas Territories) recognize her as their monarch.

She is also the oldest British monarch ever. Her coronation was on 2 June 1953 and, in 2012, she remains on the throne at the age of 85.

First female president

Maria Estela Martínez de Perón (known as Isabel, or Isabelita), the widow of General Juan Perón (both Argentina), was the first female president. She was sworn in as interim leader of Argentina on 29 June 1974, as delegated by her husband, the president, who died on 1 July. She was deposed in a military coup on 24 March 1976.

Richest monarch

According to Forbes, as of July 2011 the wealthiest monarch is Thailand's King Bhumibol Adulyadej, King Rama IX of the Chakri dynasty. Although his wealth declined by some $5 billion (£3 billion) in the year following the global financial crisis of 2008, he is still managing to get by, with an estimated fortune exceeding $30 billion (£18.2 billion), much of which stems from investment in Thai businesses.

Oldest president

Joaquín Balaguer (1907–2002) was president of the Dominican Republic in 1960–62, 1966–78 and 1986–96. He left office at the age of 89, having held the presidency for over 23 years.

The **oldest currently reigning monarch** is Abdullah bin Abdulaziz Al Saud, the King of Saudi Arabia. He took the record on 11 May 2007, at the age of 82 years 253 days. King Abdullah took to the throne on 1 August 2005.

Morarji Ranchhodji Desai (India, 1896–1995) was 81 when he began leading India in March 1977, the **oldest age at which a prime minister has first been appointed**.

Youngest current monarch

King Oyo – aka Rukirabasaija Oyo Nyimba Kabamba Iguru Rukidi IV – is the 20-year-old ruler of Toro, a kingdom in Uganda, East Africa. Born on 16 April 1992, he came to power at the age of three and now reigns over 3% of Uganda's 33-million-strong population.

Largest parliament (legislative body)

China's National People's Congress, or NPC, has 2,987 members and meets annually in Beijing's Great Hall of the People. Its formal leader is Wu Bangguo, who holds the title of Chairman and Party Secretary of the Standing Committee of the National People's Congress.

中国人民政治协商会议第十一届全国委员会第五次会议

Longest-serving head of state (non-royal)

Fidel Castro (Cuba) held the top political position in his country, first as prime minister (1959–76) and then president (1976–2008), for a span of 49 years 10 months 3 days.

Longest imprisonment for a deposed leader

Former Panamanian general and "Maximum Leader" Manuel Noriega (effective ruler of Panama from 1983 to 1989) was taken prisoner by US military forces on 4 January 1990. He was first imprisoned in the USA, then France and currently in Panama and, as of 4 March 2012, he had been detained for 22 years 2 months.

The **youngest monarchs ever** were a king of France and a king of Spain, who were sovereigns from the moment of their birth. Jean (John) I of France was the posthumous son of Louis X and succeeded at birth on 14 November 1316, but died five days later. Alfonso XIII of Spain was the posthumous son of Alfonso XII and succeeded at birth on 17 May 1886.

Tallest world leader

Canadian prime minister Stephen Harper is the tallest current world leader, at 188 cm (6 ft 2 in). Harper edges out US president Barack Obama, whose height is 185 cm (6 ft 1 in), and British prime minister David Cameron, who stands at 184 cm (6 ft 0.5 in).

The world's **shortest national leader** was Benito Juarez (1806–72), five-term president of Mexico, who served from 1858 until 1872. He stood a mere 137 cm (4 ft 6 in) tall. Juarez led Mexico during the period known as La Reforma. He fought the French occupation of Mexico and made early efforts to liberalize and modernize the country.

Shortest presidency

The shortest presidency was that of Pedro Lascuráin, who governed Mexico on 18 February 1913 for one hour. Lascuráin was the legal successor to President Madero, who was murdered on 13 February 1913. The vice-president of Mexico was disqualified as he was under arrest at the time and thus Lascuráin was sworn in, immediately appointed General Victoriano Huerta as his successor and then resigned.

First fascist dictator

Benito Mussolini became Italy's youngest prime minister on 31 October 1922, having led the country's right-wing, fascist political movement since 1919. He made it clear that he would govern authoritatively and soon obtained full dictatorial powers, securing his position in a fraudulent election in 1924. He became the first of the fascist dictators, siding with Adolf Hitler's Germany in World War II. He was caught by Italian partisans and killed on 28 April 1945 while trying to flee to Switzerland.

Longest time for an embalmed leader to be on public display

The body of Vladimir Ilyich Lenin (1870–1924), the first leader of the Soviet Union, has been on public display in the Mavzoléy Lénina (Lenin's Tomb) in Red Square, Moscow, Russia, since six days after his death on 21 January 1924. Lenin's features are moisturized every day and preservatives injected beneath his clothes. The body was removed for safety during World War II.

Most failed assassinations

In 2006, an ex-bodyguard claimed that there had been 638 plots to take Castro's life. The schemes included:

• Cigars packed with explosive, and others laced with poison
• Poisoned pills
• A fountain pen containing a syringe full of poison
• Infecting Castro's diving suit with a lethal fungus
• Rigging sea shells, in one of Castro's favourite diving areas, with explosives

Longest imprisonment of a future head of state

Nelson Mandela, who was president of South Africa from 1994 to 1999, was a political prisoner interned in three different prisons (most notably Robben Island) from 5 August 1962 to 11 February 1990 – a total of 27 years 6 months 6 days.

First female prime minister

Sirimavo Ratwatte Dias Bandaranaike (Sri Lanka, 1916–2000) was the first and **longest-serving female prime minister** in modern times. She held the post three times: 21 July 1960–27 March 1965, 29 May 1970–23 July 1977 (Ceylon re-named itself as Sri Lanka in 1972) and 14 November 1994–10 August 2000.

LONGEST-SERVING CURRENT HEADS OF STATE

Some heads of state hold onto their position rather longer than others. GWR presents a selection of world leaders who, as of 4 May 2012, are still occupying the top spot. This list excludes disputed countries.

65 years — King Bhumibol Adulyadej: Thailand

60 years — Queen Elizabeth II: UK and Commonwealth

44 years — Sultan Hassanal Bolkiah: Brunei

41 years — Sultan Qaboos bin Said al Said: Oman

40 years — Queen Margrethe II: Denmark

38 years — King Carl XVI Gustaf: Sweden

36 years — King Juan Carlos: Spain

33 years — President Teodoro Obiang Nguema Mbasogo: Equatorial New Guinea

32 years — President José Eduardo dos Santos: Angola

32 years — Queen Beatrix: Netherlands

Sources: *Daily Telegraph*; *CIA World Factbook*

PEOPLE AT WAR

Deadliest conflict since World War II

The conflict that began in Zaire – now the Democratic Republic of the Congo – in August 1998, and officially ended in July 2003, is known as the Second Congo War or the Great African War. It involved Zaire, Rwanda, Uganda, Angola, Zimbabwe, Chad, Namibia and Sudan. About 5.4 million people died – most owing to disease and starvation – and many millions were displaced.

World War II remains the **deadliest conflict ever**, with around 56 million fatalities.

Largest armed force (relative to population)

The Democratic People's Republic of Korea (DPRK, aka North Korea) boasts 1.19 million active personnel in its regular armed forces. This is the largest active armed force relative to population – almost 49 military personnel for every 1,000 head of population. It is also the world's fourth largest army *(see "Armed forces" feature far right)*. When combined with the reserve and paramilitary services, and the Peasant Red Guard, the number of military personnel rises to 7.68 million.

Leading country of origin for refugees

According to the Global Trends 2010 Report from the United Nations' Refugee Agency, more than three million Afghan refugees are distributed throughout 75 countries; 96 per cent of them are in Pakistan and Iran.

Country least at peace

According to the Global Peace Index 2011, the country least at peace is Somalia. The index, published by the Institute for Economics and Peace, ranks 153 nations and takes into account issues such as domestic and international conflict, safety and security in society, and militarization. The **country most at peace** in the index is Iceland.

Country with most hostage-taking

The Centre for Strategic and International Studies reports that Pakistan had 5,333 incidents of hostage-taking in the period 2007–10.

Leading host country for refugees

According to the UNHCR's Global Trends 2010 report, Pakistan has 1.9 million

refugees. Developing countries host around 80% of the world's refugee population – more than half of whom are children. The report puts the global total at 43.7 million, consisting of refugees, people displaced within their country by conflict and natural disasters, and asylum seekers.

Youngest state leader to control nuclear weapons

The leader of the Democratic People's Republic of Korea (North Korea), Kim Jong-un, who succeeded his father Kim Jong-il as leader of the country on 24 December 2011, is, according to official reports, only 29 years old (although other sources put his age at 26 or 27).

Most highly decorated servicewoman of World War II

Born in New Zealand and raised in Australia, Nancy Grace Augusta Wake worked with the French Resistance during World War II as a British agent with the Special Operations Executive (SOE). The German Gestapo called her the "White Mouse" owing to her ability to evade capture. Her awards include: the British George Medal; the French Croix de Guerre (with two palms), Médaille de la Resistance and Chevalier de la Légion d'Honneur; and the US Medal of Freedom. She died on 7 August 2011, aged 98.

Most military personnel rescued at sea

On 8 May 1942, 2,735 people from the US aircraft carrier USS *Lexington* (CV-2) were rescued after it had been sunk by the Japanese between Australia and New Caledonia in the Battle of the Coral Sea.

Shortest war

On 27 August 1896, Britain and Zanzibar (now part of Tanzania) officially went to war at 9 a.m. The conflict ended at 9:45 a.m., with Zanzibar suffering about 500 casualties and its leader, Sultan Khalid, seeking refuge in the German consulate.

First woman to command a fighting warship

Commander Sarah West (UK), right, of the British Royal Navy, became the first woman to take charge of a major warship when she assumed command of the British frigate HMS *Portland*, main picture, in May 2012. On 10 June 1998, Commander Maureen A Farren (USA) became the first woman to command a combatant ship, when she took charge of USS *Mount Vernon*, a dock landing ship.

FACT:
At the end of World War II, the US Navy had 6,798 active ships; in 2011, the figure was just 285.

F79

LARGEST...

Tank battle
On 12 July 1943 during World War II, the Battle of Kursk – part of Germany's Operation Zitadelle – saw a total of 1,500 German and Russian tanks amass for close-range fighting in the Prokhorovka region of Russia. Both sides lost over 300 tanks each in one day.

Air and sea battle
During World War II's Battle of Leyte Gulf in the Philippines, 218 Allied warships battled 64 Japanese warships from 22 to 27 October 1944. In the skies above, 1,280 US and 716 Japanese aircraft were engaged in combat. In the end, 26 Japanese and six US vessels were sunk and the Allies secured a base on the island of Leyte.

Most wanted man

According to the US Federal Bureau of Investigation, the world's most wanted man is al-Qaeda leader Ayman al-Zawahiri (Egypt). A sum of $25 million (£15.88 million) has been offered by the Rewards for Justice Program for his capture or conviction. Although the FBI does not provide a ranking of its most wanted, no one else has a larger bounty attached to their name.

Largest NATO operation

NATO, the North Atlantic Treaty Organization, is an intergovernmental mutual-defence alliance based on the North Atlantic Treaty signed on 4 April 1949. As of 6 June 2011, NATO's International Security Assistance Force (ISAF) in Afghanistan totalled 132,457 personnel from 49 countries. ISAF was set up by the UN in 2001 and came under NATO control in 2003 – its aims are to defeat the Taliban insurgency, provide economic aid, and train the police and army.

Evacuation of military personnel
From 26 May to 4 June 1940, as France fell to Nazi Germany, 1,200 Allied naval and civil craft – including fishing boats, pleasure cruisers and Royal National Lifeboat Institution lifeboats – evacuated 338,226 British and French troops from the beachhead at Dunkerque (Dunkirk), France.

Landlocked navy
The landlocked country with the largest naval force is Bolivia. As of 2007, it had 4,800 personnel, of which marines comprised 1,700 (including 1,000 Naval Military Police). These forces patrol Lake Titicaca as well as the country's river systems, preventing smuggling and drug trafficking.

Naval battle
The greatest sea battle involving only ships and submarines was the Battle of Jutland on 31 May 1916, in which 151 British Royal Navy warships squared up against 101 German warships. The Royal Navy lost 14 ships and 6,097 men, and the German fleet 11 ships and 2,545 men.

Combined military operation
On 6 June 1944, the Allied Forces launched Operation Overlord, the invasion of German-occupied mainland Europe. Three million men were assembled in the UK under General Eisenhower's command. In the first wave of landings on five beaches in Normandy, France, some 5,300 ships carried 155,000 men, supported by 1,500 tanks and 12,000 aircraft.

Most sniper kills
Simo Häyhä, a Finn, killed over 500 Soviet soldiers in World War II. On 6 March 1940, Soviet soldiers finally shot the man they called "White Death" in the jaw. He survived and died in 2002.

Most sniper kills of 21st century
Ex-US Navy SEAL, Chris Kyle, is the deadliest sniper so far in the 21st century. Nicknamed "the Devil of Ramadi" by Iraqis, he has 160 kills confirmed by the US defence authorities.

MILITARY MIGHT AT A GLANCE

Armed forces
The chart below identifies the top 10 largest armed forces based on the number of personnel as of 2010.

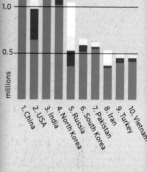

Legend:
- Other
- Air Force
- Navy
- Army

millions

1. China
2. USA
3. India
4. North Korea
5. Russia
6. South Korea
7. Pakistan
8. Iran
9. Turkey
10. Vietnam

Military spending

The global expenditure on the military in 2011 was $1.73 trillion (represented by this square block). This equates to 2.6% of world Gross Domestic Product. But which countries spend the most? Here is the top 10, based on the total annual spend in $ for the year 2011.

Rank	Country	Spending
1.	USA	$711 bn
2.	China	$143 bn*
3.	Russia	$71.9 bn*
4.	UK	$62.7 bn
5.	France	$62.5 bn
6.	Japan	$54.5 bn
7.	Saudi Arabia	$48.2 bn
8.	India	$46.8 bn
9.	Germany	$46.7 bn*
10.	Italy	$37 bn*

* estimates

Sources: *The Economist*, International Institute for Strategic Studies, Stockholm International Peace Research Institute.

SURVIVORS

Longest time adrift at sea

Captain Oguri Jukichi and one of his sailors, named Otokichi (both Japan), survived approximately 484 days after their ship was damaged in a storm off the Japanese coast in October 1813. They drifted in the Pacific before being rescued by a US ship off the Californian coast on 24 March 1815.

Greatest rescue without loss of life

The US vessel *Susan B Anthony* was sunk off Normandy, France, on 7 June 1944. All 2,689 passengers on board survived.

Longest time adrift at sea alone

Poon Lim (b. Hong Kong) lived for 133 days on a raft after his ship, the SS *Ben Lomond*, was sunk on 23 November 1942. He was picked up off the north coast of Brazil on 5 April 1943.

Most lightning strikes survived

The only man in the world to be struck by lightning seven times was ex-park ranger Roy C Sullivan, the "human lightning conductor" of Virginia, USA. A single lightning strike is made up of several 100-million volts (with peak current in the order of 20,000 amps).

Longest time trapped in a lift

Kively Papajohn of Limassol, Cyprus, was trapped in her apartment block lift for six days from 28 December 1987 to 2 January 1988. She was 76 years old at the time. Kively survived the cold and beat dehydration by rationing the fruit, vegetables and bread that she had in her shopping bag.

Farthest vertical ski fall survived

In April 1997, while she was competing in the 1997 World Extreme Skiing Championships in Valdez, Alaska, Bridget Mead (New Zealand) fell a vertical distance of nearly 400 m (1,312 ft). Remarkably, she suffered no broken bones, just bruises and severe concussion. Doctors credit her survival to her excellent physical condition and to the fact that she was wearing a helmet.

Farthest car accident flight survived

Paramedic Matt McKnight (USA) was helping at an accident scene on 26 October 2001 when he was struck by a car travelling at 112 km/h (70 mi/h). He was thrown a distance of 35.9 m (118 ft) along Route 376, Monroeville, Pennsylvania, USA. Matt dislocated both his shoulders (fracturing one), suffered a collapsed lung, had a thigh ripped open to the bone, and fractured his pelvis and legs. He made a full recovery and returned to work a year later.

Farthest distance survived in a tornado

Matt Suter (USA) was caught in a tornado and carried 398 m (1,307 ft) in Missouri, USA, on 12 March 2006.

First person to survive two nuclear attacks

Tsutomu Yamaguchi (Japan, 1916–2010) was in Hiroshima on 6 August 1945, when the US Army Air Forces dropped the "Little Boy" atomic bomb on the city. Suffering burns to his upper body, Tsutomu returned to his home town of Nagasaki on 8 August. The next day, US forces dropped "Fat Man", a 20–22-kiloton bomb, on the city. Miraculously Tsutomu again survived with only minor injuries – although his left eardrum was irreperably damaged and in later life he was to suffer from illness related to his exposure to radiation. In both cities he was within 3 km (1.8 miles) of ground zero.

Longest fall survived in a lift

Betty Lou Oliver (USA) survived a plunge of 75 storeys – more than 300 m (1,000 ft) – in a lift in the Empire State Building in New York City, USA, on 28 July 1945, after an American B-25 bomber crashed into the building in thick fog.

Youngest person to survive a car crash

On 25 February 1999, Virginia Rivero from Misiones, Argentina, went into labour at her home and walked to a nearby road in order to hitchhike to hospital. Offered a lift by two men, she then gave birth to a baby girl in the back seat of their car. When she told them she was about to have a second baby, the driver overtook a car in front, only to collide with a third vehicle. Virginia and her newborn daughter were ejected through the back door of the car, suffering minor injuries, but Virginia was able to flag down another car, which took them to the hospital. Once there, she gave birth to a baby boy.

Longest time survived with no pulse

For one week, starting on 14 August 1998, surgeons used a blood pump to support Julie Mills (UK), who had had severe heart failure. For three of those days, she had no pulse.

Highest speed survived in a motorcycle crash

Ron Cook (USA) crashed a 1,325 cc Kawasaki motorcycle while travelling at an estimated 322 km/h (200 mi/h) during the SCTA time trials at El Mirage Dry Lake, California, USA, on 12 July 1998. He broke his right arm, wrist and leg in the crash.

Highest percentage of burns to the body survived

Two people have survived burns to 90% of their bodies. David Chapman (UK) was burned after a petrol canister exploded and drenched him with burning fuel on 2 July 1996. Following the accident, surgeons spent 36 hours removing his dead skin.

Tony Yarijanian (USA) underwent 25 surgeries, including multiple skin grafts, after suffering similar injuries from an explosion at his wife's beauty spa in California, USA, on 15 February 2004.

Longest time to survive without food

Doctors have estimated that a well-nourished individual can survive without medical consequences on a diet of sugar and water for 30 days or more. The longest period for which anyone has lasted without solid food is 382 days in the case of Angus Barbieri (UK) of Tayport, Fife, who lived on tea, coffee, water, soda water and vitamins in Maryfield Hospital, Dundee, UK, from June 1965 to July 1966. During that period, his weight declined from 214 kg (33 st 10 lb) to 80.74 kg (12 st 10 lb).

FACT:
It took around 15 minutes to winch each of the miners up to the surface in the rescue capsule.

FACT:
Luis Urzua (left), seen here with Chilean president Sebastián Piñera, was the last man rescued.

World coverage

• "When the last miner exited the depths of the mine, I was moved as every Chilean was." – President Piñera

• "We have done what the entire world was waiting for. The 70 days that we fought so hard were not in vain. We had strength, we had spirit, we wanted to fight, we wanted to fight for our families." – Luis Urzua, miner

• "We are really religious, both my husband and I, so God was always present. It is a miracle, this rescue was so difficult, it's a grand miracle." – Monica Ávalos, miner's wife

Longest time to survive trapped underground

"The 33 of San José" (32 Chileans and one Bolivian) were trapped 688 m (2,257 ft) underground for 69 days after the collapse of the San José copper-gold mine, near Copiapó, Chile, on 5 August 2010. All the miners made it back to the surface in a rescue capsule. The last man was lifted to safety from the capsule at 21:55 CLDT on 13 October 2010.

MEDICAL MARVELS

GWR pays tribute to those individuals who have undergone major surgery and survived...

LONGEST SURVIVING ARTIFICIAL HEART TRANSPLANT PATIENT
Peter Houghton (UK, 1938–2007)
Date of operation: 20 June 2000
Survived: 7 years 5 months 5 days

LONGEST SURVIVING SINGLE LUNG TRANSPLANT PATIENT
Wolfgang Muller (Canada, 1934–2008)
Date of operation: 15 September 1987
Survived: 20 years 11 months 21 days

LONGEST SURVIVING HEART TRANSPLANT PATIENT
Tony Huesman (USA, 1957–2009)
Date of operation: 30 August 1978
Survived: 30 years 11 months 10 days

LONGEST SURVIVAL WITH HEART OUTSIDE BODY
Christopher Wall (USA, b. 19 August 1975)
Survived: 36 years 5 months 29 days, as of 17 February 2012

LONGEST SURVIVING DOUBLE-KIDNEY TRANSPLANT PATIENT
Brian K Bourgraf (USA)
Date of operation: 23 March 1968
Survived: 43 years 10 months 25 days, as of 17 February 2012

LONGEST SURVIVING KIDNEY TRANSPLANT PATIENT
Johanna Leanora Rempel (née Nightingale, Canada, b. 24 March 1948)
Date of operation: 28 December 1960
Survived: 51 years 1 month 20 days, as of 17 February 2012

SOCIAL MEDIA

Most viewed video online

FACT:
Bieber had 21,927,059 Twitter followers as of 18 May 2012 – not far off Lady Gaga's record (see p.165).

Justin Bieber's (Canada) video for "Baby", directed by Ray Kay (Norway), is not only the top music video on YouTube but the most viewed video online of any kind. As of 18 May 2012, it had 738,166,041 views on the video-sharing website. However, it is also the **most "disliked" video online** – as of 18 May 2012, it had 2,563,872 "dislikes". "Friday", a 2011 single by US pop star Rebecca Black, was previously the most disliked video, but it was removed temporarily from YouTube for copyright reasons.

Highest price paid for a social network developer

The games developer Playdom, which initially made its reputation creating games for Myspace, was sold to the Walt Disney Company for a record $563 million (£350 million) in July 2010.

Fastest to 1 million followers on Twitter

Actor Charlie Sheen (USA) racked up 1 million followers on Twitter in just 25 hours 17 minutes on 1 and 2 March 2011. Sheen was big news at the time, having had his contract terminated on his CBS hit sitcom *Two and a Half Men*.

Largest online music playlist

The social entertainment site Myspace.com (launched January 2004) has a published playlist of more than 200 million tracks, with 500 new artists being added each week.

Largest video sharing website

YouTube dominates video on the internet. As of April 2012, it had more than 4 billion views a day, and more than 60 hours of video were being added every minute – the equivalent of more than 250,000 full-length movies per week. In 2010, over 13 million hours of video were uploaded and, in 2011, it attracted 490 million unique users a month.

Most tweets per second

During a television screening of Hayao Miyazaki's *Castle in the Sky* (Japan, 2009) in Japan on 9 December 2011, Twitter went crazy, reaching 25,088 tweets per second. In the anime film, a spell of destruction is cast with the word "balse" to bring down the city of Laputa. The moment this happened, the film's fans hopped on Twitter to tweet the word "balse" too.

First satirical social network game

Cow Clicker involves clicking on a picture of a cow every six hours and is designed to satirize other social network games, such as *FarmVille*. Its designer, Ian Bogost (USA), describes it as "a Facebook game about Facebook games". It drew an all-time monthly high of 54,245 users, and has spawned a puzzle game, an iPhone game and an alternate reality game, making it the most successful satirical social game to date. It also sells new cow pictures to click on – the most expensive, the "Roboclicker", had an asking price of 5,000 "mooney" or $340 (£208).

First to 1 million followers on Twitter

In April 2009, actor Ashton Kutcher (USA) became the first person to amass over 1 million Twitter followers. Kutcher is now no longer king of the celebrity tweeters, being only the 17th most-followed, with 10,668,643 followers as of 18 May 2012. That's well behind first-placed Lady Gaga (see p.165).

Biggest social games company

Despite having only existed since July 2007, US firm Zynga is the most popular social games developer. It attracted 252,274,991 monthly active users on Facebook as of 18 May 2012. Its most popular game, *CityVille*, in which players create their own city, claimed a staggering 26 million players within 12 days of its launch in 2010, making it the **fastest-growing social network game**. As of 18 May 2012, *CityVille* had 36,900,000 active monthly users.

Largest online social network

As of March 2012, Facebook boasted over 901 million monthly active users, with more than 125 billion friend connections. Each day, 3.2 billion "likes" and comments are generated by its users, who upload over 300 million photos to the service. Facebook's largest shareholder is Mark Zuckerburg (right), who was recently overtaken by fellow Facebook founder Dustin Moskovitz (both USA) as the world's **youngest billionaire** (see p.151).

Most "liked" video online

With 908,668 thumbs up on YouTube as of 18 May 2012, "Charlie bit my finger – again!" is the favourite online video. It shows Harry Davies-Carr having his finger bitten by his baby brother Charlie (both UK) – with a little more force than he was expecting.

First arcade game to integrate Twitter

Sega's *Virtua Fighter 5: Final Showdown* is the first arcade game to allow players to link together their Virtua Fighter and Twitter accounts. This means players can follow each other's fortunes while they punch and kick their way through bouts. Cool combat moves are posted automatically on Twitter.

Most social networking

- **Most comments on a Facebook item in 24 hours:** 80,030, achieved by Greenpeace on 14 April 2011. Greenpeace were trying to get Facebook itself to use green energy rather than electricity from burning coal.
- **Most comments on a single Facebook item in total:** 1,001,552, in response to a post made on 30 October 2011 by Tracey Hodgson (UK) on the Facebook page FFG Pioneers. Tracey's post was on the Zynga game *Frontierville*, now called *The Pioneer Trail*.
- **Most "likes" on a Facebook page:** 88,051,895, on Facebook for Every Phone, as of 18 May 2012.
- **Most "likes" on a Facebook item in 24 hours:** 588,243, in response to a post on 15 February 2011 by rapper Lil Wayne (USA, b. Dwayne Carter, Jr). He was competing with cookie company Oreo for the record.

Tweets on Twitter...

all in 140 characters or less:

- Twitter has donated access to all its tweets to the Library of Congress for research.
- The name Twitter was used as its definitions – "chirps from birds" and "a short burst of inconsequential information" – fitted perfectly.
- Traffic usually peaks at 9 p.m. GMT (4 p.m. on the East Coast of the USA and 1 p.m. on the West Coast of the USA).

Most followers on Twitter

Lady Gaga (USA, b. Stefani Germanotta) had more than 24,285,376 Twitter followers of her @ladygaga Twitter feed as of 18 May 2012. She was also the **first tweep to attain 10 million followers**, on 15 May 2011.

Most content uploaded to an online video service

An average of 70.49 hours per minute is uploaded to Ustream.tv, a website that broadcasts live events. This figure, based on the 37.05 million hours of content uploaded to the site from June 2010 to May 2011, beats YouTube's 60 hours of content per minute.

Most talked-about topics on Facebook

Since 2009, Facebook has been tracking the phrases most used in status updates. In 2009, "Facebook applications" was the favourite topic. In 2010, it was "HMU" (hit me up), with "World Cup" (soccer) coming in second. In 2011, it was "Death of Osama bin Laden".

Most pictures downloaded from a website in 24 hours

Erik Kessels (Netherlands) downloaded 950,000 pictures from the Flickr website for his *What's Next?* exhibition held in Amsterdam, Netherlands, in 2011. He printed 350,000 of the images to create "a sea of images you can drown in" and left them heaped on the floor. Kessels said he wanted to show "how public private photos have become" and to unnerve visitors by making them "walk over personal memories".

IN JUST ONE DAY...

375 Mb of data are consumed per average household

294 billion e-mails are sent

22 billion text messages are sent

8 years of footage is added to YouTube: the equivalent of 60 hours of video every minute!

3 billion YouTube clips are viewed; in 2010, 700 billion playbacks were logged

400 million people log into Facebook

300 million photos are added to Facebook

50 million people log into Twitter

230 million tweets are sent – equal to 2,662 messages tweeted every second!

460,000 new Twitter accounts are opened

4.3 million new images are uploaded to Flickr, enough to fill 540,000 pages of a photo album!

ENGINEERING

CONTENTS

Largest truck body

The WESTECH Flow Control Body, designed and manufactured in Wyoming, USA, is the largest mining truck body by volume. Specially made for the Liebherr T 282 C truck, it was measured on 14 June 2011 at North Antelope Rochelle Mine in Wyoming carrying 470.4 m³ (16,612 ft³) of coal. That's about the same capacity as 5,875 bathtubs, or 600 pickup truckloads. To move such a great weight, the T 282 C has a 20-cylinder engine and 5,350-litre (1,171-gal) fuel tank. It costs about 5 million (£3.2 million).

The driver needs to climb 21 steps to get to his cab...

and sits 6 m (19 ft 8 in) off the ground.

The total height of the truck is 9.3 m (30 ft 6 in)...

and the wheels are 3.6 m (11 ft 10 in) high.

The engine weighs 10,480 kg (23,104 lb)...

and generates a top speed of 64 km/h (39.7 mi/h).

470.4 m³

HOW TALL CAN WE BUILD?

How high can we go?

In the Old Testament tale of the Tower of Babel (below left), mankind tries to reach God by building a super-tall structure to heaven. But is there any upper limit to our towering ambitions today?

The 20th century saw skyscrapers dominate city skylines. By 1980, more than 80% of the world's buildings over 150 m (500 ft) were in North America. Today, however, Asia and the Middle East are the pre-eminent builders of super-tall structures. Every building now sits in the shadow of the 828-m-tall (2,717-ft) Burj Khalifa, the glittering glass-and-steel trophy that opened in Dubai, UAE, in 2010. But for how long?

Concrete: A super-high-pressure pump was used to raise the concrete upwards during construction of the Burj Khalifa.

FACT: This illustration shows a design for Saudi Arabia's Kingdom Tower, planned to top out at around 1 km (3,280 ft)!

TOP 100 TALLEST BUILDINGS

Born in the USA, the skyscraper has latterly been taken to spectacular new heights in the Middle East and Asia. Our timeline (right) shows the history of the 100 tallest buildings constructed – and their distribution across the world – since 1930.

Source: skyscrapercenter.com

Middle East — Europe
The Americas — Oceania
Asia

Wind: The top of a skyscraper can sway 1 m (3 ft) in high winds. Typically, a tall building is designed to sway by no more than 1/500th of its height. Large objects called "mass dampers" help to shift a building's weight, to balance the pressure of the wind. Pictured left is the 660-tonne (728-ton) mass damper, housed – in full public view – near the top of the 508-m-tall (1,667-ft) skyscraper Taipei 101 in Chinese Taipei.

THE RISING CHALLENGE OF WASTE DISPOSAL

Sewage: Tall buildings must be located where there is sufficient municipal sewage systems – otherwise there is the risk of congestion. Until recently, Dubai had an insufficient sewage system, so a constant stream of trucks had to ferry the contents of septic tanks between its tall buildings and the city's only sewage-treatment plant.

Office rental: The cost of office space is inexorably on the rise, with rates in the **most expensive office location** – Hong Kong, China – at an eye-watering $2,299.41 (£1,435.27) per m² ($213.70, or £133.39, per ft²) per annum as of June 2011. One way to combat these hefty costs is to build upwards, rather than taking up more space on the ground.

Logistics: The higher you build, the greater the mechanical infrastructure needed to support the building.

SKY-HIGH RENTS AND SKYSCRAPERS

OFFICE SPACE
FOR LEASE

SHOP SPACE
FOR LEASE

CALL

£133 per ft²

FACT: In Hong Kong, skyscraper heights are limited by law to that of the area's surrounding mountains.

Timeline years: 1930 1930 1931 1953 1974 1975 1975 1977 1982 1982 1983 1984 1985 1986 1987 1989 1989 1990 1990 1990 1990 1991 1992 1992 1993 1993 1996 1996 1996 1997 1997 1997 1998 1998 1998 1999 1999 1999 1999 1999 1999 2000 2000 2000 2000 2001 2001 2003 2003 2004

Height scale (m): 0 100 200 300 400 500 600 700 800 900

LINE KEY

▬	Hotel
▬	Hotel/Office
▬	Hotel/Residential
▧	Hotel/Office/Retail
⋯	Office
⋮	Residential
▮	Residential/Office
≡	Residential/Office/Hotel

Economics: Super-tall buildings are often begun at the end of a boom era, when money is available and confidence is high. But the long construction times involved may dissuade financiers.

FACT: Out of the 100 tallest buildings listed here, 61 have been built in the 21st century.

FIRE SAFETY FIRST

Evacuation: Fire and smoke can be lethal in a tall building, as was the case in the aftermath of the terrorist attacks on the World Trade Center towers on 11 September 2001 (above).

Maintenance: The size of super-tall buildings makes them highly vulnerable to the elements. The building's façade will deteriorate over time and will require re-cladding. Adequate surface drainage is also vital. To avoid corrosion in a building's metal structures and components, an electrical current is sometimes passed through them, a treatment known as "cathodic protection".

In theory, a building's height is limited only by an architect's imagination. But a skyscraper is a complex creation, involving engineering, architecture, economics and even politics, with each having its own set of limitations. Location matters, too: tall buildings may topple in earthquake-prone regions and existing building materials can only withstand a certain amount of structural pressure and movement.

All these factors may explain why the Kingdom Tower is the only building with a projected height of around 1,000 m (3,280 ft) to have been given the go-ahead.

Lifts: Moving large numbers of people to a great height – and promptly – is a challenge. The higher you build, the more lifts you need, but every extra bank of lifts reduces the available floor space to rent. Express lifts also have a speed limit, beyond which passengers begin to feel queasy – the upper limit is around 64 km/h (40 mi/h).

FACT: At 64 km/h (40 mi/h), the **fastest lifts** are those of the Burj Khalifa's observation deck.

Height: The Burj Khalifa was an impressive 60% taller than the previous highest building, Taipei 101. But the Kingdom Tower would be another 20% taller than the Burj Khalifa!

Financial climate: When recessions kick in, the construction of showcase tall buildings is often put on hold. The Burj Dubai was finished (and renamed the Khalifa) only when the bankrupt emirate of Dubai was bailed out by the president of neighbouring Abu Dhabi. Ultimately, the revenue generated per square metre must be greater than the building costs per square metre.

Foundations: The **deepest foundations** are those of the Petronas Towers, Kuala Lumpur, Malaysia, which extend 120 m (394 ft) into the bedrock.

SKYSCRAPERS

Tallest structure

The top of the drilling rig of the Ursa tension leg platform, a floating oil production facility operated by Shell in the Gulf of Mexico, is 1,306 m (4,285 ft) above the ocean floor. The platform is connected to the sea-floor by oil pipelines and four massive steel tethers at each corner, with a total weight of approximately 16,000 tonnes (35 million lb).

Tallest chimney

The coal power-plant No. 2 stack at Ekibastuz, Kazakhstan, completed in 1987, is 420 m (1,378 ft) tall. The diameter tapers from 44 m (144 ft) at the base up to 14.2 m (46 ft 7 in) at the top, and it weighs 60,000 tonnes (132 million lb).

Tallest monument

The stainless-steel Gateway Arch in St Louis, Missouri, USA, was completed on 28 October 1965 to commemorate the westward expansion after the Louisiana Purchase of 1803. It is a sweeping arch rising to 192 m (630 ft).

Tallest obelisk

An obelisk is a tapered four-sided column, usually with a pointed top. The Washington Monument in Washington, DC, USA, is an obelisk that stands 169 m (555 ft) tall. Completed in 1884, it was built – without any steel enforcement – to honour George Washington, the first president of the USA, making it the world's tallest unreinforced masonry structure.

1. Red Pyramid, Egypt
2. Great Pyramid, Egypt
3. Lincoln Cathedral, UK
4. St Mary's Church, Germany
5. St Nikolai, Germany
6. Cologne Cathedral, Germany
7. Washington Monument, USA
8. Chrysler Building, USA
9. Eiffel Tower, France
10. Empire State Building, USA
11. Ostankino Tower, Russia
12. CN Tower, Canada
13. Burj Khalifa, UAE

Tallest self-supporting structures

Here are the world's tallest buildings since the 104-m-high (341-ft) Red Pyramid was built for the pharaoh Sneferu in c. 2600 BC. The Great Pyramid, built for the pharaoh Khufu to a height of 146 m (481 ft) in c. 2560 BC, soon superseded it. However, it took another 3,771 years for the record to be broken again, when Lincoln Cathedral with its central spire (now collapsed) reached 160 m (525 ft). Today's tallest building – the Burj Khalifa at 828 m (2,716 ft 6 in) high – is almost eight times as high as the Red Pyramid.

STATUE OF LIBERTY

You can compare the height of all the buildings on these pages against the Statue of Liberty, which, from the bottom of the pedestal to the tip of the torch, is 92.99 m (305 ft 1 in) tall.

TALLEST HOSPITAL

The Li Shu Pui block of the Hong Kong Sanatorium and Hospital in Wan Chai, Hong Kong, is 148.5 m (487 ft) tall. The 38-floor hospital was designed by Wong & Ouyang (HK) Ltd and completed in 2008.

TALLEST PYRAMID

The Great Pyramid of Giza, Egypt (also known as the pyramid of Khufu), was 146 m (481 ft) high when completed around 4,500 years ago, but erosion and vandalism have reduced it to 137.5 m (451.4 ft) today.

TALLEST OBSERVATION WHEEL

The Singapore Flyer comprises a 150-m (492-ft) diameter wheel built over a three-storey terminal building, giving it a total height of 165 m (541 ft). It is located in Marina Bay, Singapore, and was opened to the public on 1 March 2008.

TALLEST UNSUPPORTED FLAGPOLE

The Dushanbe Flagpole, unveiled on 24 May 2011 in the Tajikistan capital of Dushanbe, measures 165 m (541 ft 4 in). It flies a 60 m (196 ft 10 in) x 30 m (98 ft 5 in) Tajikistan flag.

TALLEST UNIVERSITY

The MV Lomonosov Moscow State University on the Lenin Hills, south of Moscow, Russia, stands 240 m (787.5 ft) tall and has 32 storeys and 40,000 rooms. It was constructed between 1949 and 1953.

TALLEST ATRIUM

The atrium of the Burj Al Arab hotel in Dubai, UAE, is 180 m (590 ft) high. It forms a vast central cavity, around which the hotel is built.

TALLEST TOWER

The Tokyo Sky Tree in Sumida, Tokyo, Japan, rises 634 m (2,080 ft) to the top of its mast, making it the world's tallest tower. The Sky Tree serves as a broadcasting tower.

TALLEST BUILDING

At 828 m (2,716 ft 6 in) tall, the Burj Khalifa (Khalifa Tower) in Dubai, UAE, became the tallest building in the world when it was officially opened on 4 January 2010. Part of a 2-km² (490-acre) development called Downtown Dubai, the Burj has residential, office and hotel use.

TALLEST HOTEL

The 120-storey Makkah Royal Clock Tower Hotel – aka the Abraj Al-Bait Hotel Tower – in Mecca, Saudi Arabia, stands 601 m (1,972 ft) high. The hotel is part of a seven-building complex that has a record floor space of 1,500,000 m² (16.15 million ft²). The **tallest all-hotel building** (as opposed to a mixed-use building) is the 333-m (1,093-ft) Rose Rayhaan by Rotana in Dubai.

TALLEST RESIDENTIAL BUILDING

Completed in 2012, Princess Tower in Dubai, United Arab Emirates, is 413.4 m (1,356 ft) high and has 101 storeys, dedicated to residential use.

TALLEST TWIN TOWERS

The 451.9-m-tall (1,482-ft 7-in) Petronas Towers in Kuala Lumpur, Malaysia, are the tallest matching pair of buildings. The 88-storey office buildings opened in March 1996. The towers are joined at level 41 and level 42 by a double-decker "Skybridge".

FACT:
Close to 26,000 glass panels, each hand-cut, were used in the exterior cladding of the Burj Khalifa.

TALL BUILDINGS

Guinness World Records uses the definition of tall and supertall buildings as specified by the Council on Tall Buildings and Urban Habitat (CTBUH).

Tall v Supertall

The CTBUH defines "supertall" as taller than 300 m (984 ft). By the end of 2011 there were only 59 completed structures worldwide.

300 m

Tall   Supertall

How do you measure a tall building?

GWR only recognizes buildings measured to their "architectural top", which is defined by the CTBUH as the height "including spires, but not including antennae, signage, flag poles or other functional-technical equipment".

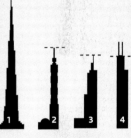

1. Burj Khalifa, UAE: 828 m
2. Taipei 101, Chinese Taipei: 508 m
3. Zifeng Tower, China: 450 m*
4. Willis Tower, USA: 442 m†

*381 m to roof but spire considered part of structure

†527 m to top of antennae (not considered part of the structural height of the building)

Buildings v Towers

GWR defines a "tower" as a building in which usable floor space occupies less than 50% of its height (usable floor space shown in blue).

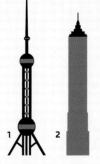

1. Oriental Pearl Tower, China
2. Jin Mao Tower, China

AIRPORTS

Longest ice runway

The two ice runways at Antarctica's McMurdo Station are the longest of their type in the world, each measuring 3,048 m (10,000 ft) long and 67 m (220 ft) wide. The runways are carved out of sea ice each year, before the ice breaks in December. They can take large aircraft such as the Lockheed C-5 Galaxy (above).

Largest airport

King Fahd International Airport (DMM), near Dammam in eastern Saudi Arabia, is the largest airport by area. It occupies 780 km² (301 miles²) – bigger than the entire country of Bahrain (which has three airports of its own).

Largest airport park

A park at Amsterdam Schiphol Airport (AMS) in the Netherlands opened on 11 May 2011 by the Dutch Princess Irene, is the world's largest (and currently only) park within an airport. The park has indoor and outdoor sections, measures 2,000 m² (21,528 ft²) and features projected butterflies and the sounds of bicycle bells and children. People can recharge their mobile phones in the park by pedalling static bicycles.

Largest airport library

Schiphol is also home to the largest airport library in terms of area, covering 90 m² (967 ft²). It opened in July 2010.

Largest airport golf course

Don Mueang International Airport (DMK) in Bangkok, Thailand, is home to an 18-hole golf course. It fills much of the gap between the two runways, which are 3,700 m (12,139 ft) and 3,500 m (11,482 ft) long.

Busiest beach airport

Despite being submerged daily by the incoming tide, the Barra beach airport (BRR) in the Scottish Western Isles handles over 1,000 flights per year. It is the only beach airport to handle scheduled airline services.

Highest airport

At 4,334 m (14,219 ft) above sea level, Qamdo Bangda Airport (BPX) in Tibet is the highest airport operating a scheduled service. Because planes have extended stopping distances at high altitude (due to reduced atmospheric resistance), the airport requires an extra-long runway at 4,204 m (13,794 ft).

Largest model airport

Knuffingen Airport, located at Miniatur Wunderland in Hamburg, Germany, is a 45.9-m² (494-ft²) model of Hamburg's Fuhlsbüttel Airport. Built to a scale of 1:87, it took seven years to make at a cost of about $4.8 million (£3 million). A computer can move the planes and cars and, because of wires, the planes can even fly.

TOP 10 MOST EXTREME AIRPORTS

In 2010, the History Channel ranked the most challenging airports for pilots. Tenzing-Hillary tops the list – the Yeti Airlines crash there (right) in 2008 left 18 people dead.

Airport	Dangers
1. Tenzing-Hillary (LUA), Lukla, Nepal	Mountainous location with high winds and changing visibility
2. Toncontín (TGU), Tegucigalpa, Honduras	Difficult approach through hills, short runway
3. Gustaf III (SBH), St Barthélemy, Caribbean	Steep approach and short airstrip – planes often end up on beach
4. Princess Juliana (SXM), St Maarten, Caribbean	Short runway – planes fly in just metres above beach (pictured right)
5. Gibraltar (GIB)	Road runs across runway, high winds, restricted air corridors
6. Kai Tak, Hong Kong (HGK, now closed)	Nearby multi-storey buildings means tricky low-altitude approach
7. Courchevel (CVF), France	Mountain-top runway is short, sloping and ends with a cliff drop
8. Eagle County (EGE), Gypsum, Colorado, USA	Difficult mountainous approach and changeable weather
9. Madeira (FNC), Funchal, Madeira, Portugal	High winds, mountainous terrain, runway built over ocean
10. San Diego (SAN), California, USA	Busy airspace, multi-storey car park close to end of runway

The three-letter airport codes are identifiers assigned by the International Air Transport Association.

F-GETA

FACT: Planes at Princess Juliana Airport fly just metres above the beach. A two-lane road separates beach and runway.

FACT:
At peak hours, a plane lands every minute at Hong Kong International.

Aviation at a glance

• Global air passenger traffic rose by 6.6% in 2010, topping the 5 billion passenger mark for the first time.

• According to the US National Air Traffic Controllers Association (NATCA), there are roughly 5,000 (non-military) planes in the sky above the USA at any one time.

• It's impossible to give an accurate figure for the actual number of people flying at any one time globally, but estimates range from 100,000 to 2 million passengers.

• NATCA claim that your chances of dying on a flight out of the USA to be 1 in 14 million; boffins at the Massachusetts Institute of Technology have deemed flying to be 22 times safer than driving.

Busiest cargo airport

Hong Kong International Airport (HKG), also known as Chek Lap Kok Airport, is the world's **busiest airport in terms of cargo handling**. According to the Airports Council International, the airport overtook Memphis International Airport (MEM) in 2010, when it handled 4,168,852 tonnes (4,102,984 tons) of cargo. With a floor area of 280,500 m² (3.2 million sq ft), the airport's SuperTerminal 1 is the world's **largest cargo terminal** under one roof.

Most northerly airport

Svalbard Airport (LYR), which serves a cluster of Norwegian islands in the Arctic Ocean, is the most northerly public airport, located at 78.2° latitude and 15.4° longitude. Completed in 1975, the 2,319-m (7,608-ft) runway is built on a layer of permafrost.

Closest airports

The distance between the airports of Papa Westray (PPW) and Westray (WRY), neighbouring destinations in the Scottish Orkney Islands, is a mere 2.83 km (1.76 miles). Flights between the two airports take an average of just 96 seconds (two minutes including taxiing time).

Steepest runway at an international airport

Courchevel Airport (CVF) in the French Alps possesses the world's steepest runway. At just 525 m (1,722 ft) long and angled at 18.5°, it is definitely not for the faint-hearted.

Longest airstrip on a purpose-built island

Kansai International Airport (KIX), constructed on an artificial island 4.8 km (3 miles) offshore in Osaka Bay, Japan, is home to a 4,000-m-long (13,123-ft) airstrip. The island is connected to the mainland by a road and rail bridge.

Airport with the longest bridge-supported runway extension

Extended into the sea to accommodate large aircraft such as Boeing 747s, the runway at Madeira Airport (FNC), Portugal, is 2,781 m (9,124 ft) long with the bridge-supported section measuring 1,020 m (3,346 ft) long and 180 m (591 ft) wide.

Shortest commercially serviceable runway

Juancho E Yrausquin Airport (SAB), on the Caribbean island of Saba, Netherlands Antilles, has the shortest commercially serviceable runway. At just 396 m (1,300 ft) in length, it is only slightly longer than the runways on most aircraft carriers. At either end of the runway, cliffs drop into the sea.

Largest air terminal
Measuring 1,185,000 m² (12.76 million ft²), Dubai International Airport's (DXB) Terminal 3 is the world's largest airport building in terms of floor space.

BUSIEST AIRPORTS

The Airports International Council produces annual figures on the world's busiest airports based on three criteria:

ATL (89.33 million)
PEK (73.94 million)
ORD (66.77 million)
LHR (65.88 million)
HND (64.21 million)

= 10 million passengers arriving, departing or transferring

HKG (4.16 million tonnes)
MEM (3.91 million tonnes)
PVG (3.22 million tonnes)
ICN (2.68 million tonnes)
ANC (2.57 million tonnes)

= 1 million tonnes of cargo loaded and unloaded

ATL (950,119)
ORD (882,617)
LAX (666,938)
DFW (652,261)
DEN (630,063)

= 100,000 take-offs and landings

KEY TO AIRPORT CODES

Code	Airport
ANC	Ted Stephens Anchorage (USA)
ATL	Hartsfield Jackson Atlanta (USA)
DEN	Denver (USA)
DFW	Dallas/Fort Worth (USA)
HND	Tokyo (Japan)
LAX	Los Angeles (USA)
LHR	London Heathrow (UK)
ICN	Incheon (South Korea)
MEM	Memphis (USA)
ORD	Chicago O'Hare (USA)
PEK	Beijing Capital (China)
PVG	Shanghai Pudong (China)

AIR FRANCE

TRAINS & RAILWAYS

FACT:
The line has cut journey times between Beijing and Tianjin from 70 minutes to 30 minutes.

Longest continually operating tramway

The St Charles Avenue Line in New Orleans, Louisiana, USA, began operation in September 1835 and still runs today. It was one of the USA's first passenger railways. Initially, carriages were moved by a number of different means, including mules and steam engines, until overhead electric cables were adopted in 1895.

Fastest train speed

• **Average speed:** A French SNCF TGV train recorded an average speed of 306.37 km/h (190.37 mi/h) between Calais and Marseille on 26 May 2001. The train, which was unmodified and identical to Eurostar trains, covered the 1,067 km (663 miles) between the cities in 3 hr 29 min, reaching a top speed of 366 km/h (227 mi/h).

• **Maglev:** The highest speed by a manned superconducting magnetically levitated (maglev) train is 581 km/h (361 mi/h) by the MLX01, operated by the Central Japan Railway Company and Railway Technical Research Institute, on the Yamanashi Maglev Test Line, Yamanashi Prefecture, Japan, on 2 December 2003.

• **Jet-powered:** The M-497 Black Beetle was a prototype experimental train powered by two General Electric J47-19 jet engines. It was developed and tested in 1966 in the USA and reached speeds of up to 296 km/h (183 mi/h).

• **Diesel:** The former British Rail inaugurated its high-speed train (HST) daily service between London, Bristol and south Wales, UK, on 4 October 1976, using InterCity 125 trains. One of these reached a speed of 238 km/h (148 mi/h) on a test run between Darlington and York, UK, on 1 November 1987.

• **Steam:** The fastest steam locomotive is the London North Eastern Railway "Class A4" No. 4468 *Mallard*. It achieved a speed of 202.8 km/h (126 mi/h), hauling seven coaches weighing 243 tonnes (535,722 lb), down Stoke Bank, near Essendine, between Grantham and Peterborough, UK, on 3 July 1938.

Fastest scheduled speed between two rail stops

Between Lorraine and Champagne-Ardenne in France, trains reach an average speed of 279.4 km/h (173.6 mi/h), according to the *Railway Gazette International* World Speed Survey study.

Fastest train on a national rail system

The highest speed recorded by a train on a national rail network (rather than a dedicated test track) is 574.8 km/h (357.2 mi/h), by a French SNCF modified version of the TGV on 3 April 2007. The peak speed was achieved between the Meuse and Champagne-Ardenne stations on the LGV Est high-speed rail line in eastern France.

Largest railway system

The country with the most extensive railway network is the USA, with 224,792 km (139,679 miles) of railway lines.

The country with the **shortest railway track** is Vatican City, with an 862-m (2,828-ft) spur entering the Holy See from Italy. It is used only for goods and supplies.

Oldest railway station

Liverpool Road station in Manchester, UK, was first used on 15 September 1830 and was finally closed on 30 September 1975. Today, part of the station serves as a museum.

The **oldest independent railway company** is the Ffestiniog Railway (UK), which was founded by an act of Parliament on 23 May 1832. It is still operating today, running tourist trains along the 597-cm (23.5-in) narrow-gauge tracks between Porthmadog and Blaenau Ffestiniog in Gwynedd, Wales – a distance of 21.6 km (13.5 miles).

The **oldest locomotive roundhouse** is the Derby Roundhouse, which was built in 1839 by the North Midland Railway (UK). The restored structure now forms part of the Derby College campus.

First public electric railway

The earliest public electric railway was opened on 12 May 1881 at Lichterfelde near Berlin, Germany. It was 2.5 km (1.5 miles) long, ran on 100 V current and carried 26 passengers at a speed of 48 km/h (30 mi/h).

Longest train journey without changing trains

The longest run without a change of train stretches 10,214 km (6,346 miles), from Moscow in Russia to Pyongyang in North Korea. One train a week makes the journey, which incorporates sections of the famous Trans-Siberian line. The journey is scheduled to take 7 days 20 hr 25 min in total.

Fastest train – maximum speed

On the 114-km-long (70.84-mile) Beijing–Tianjin Intercity Rail line in China, trains run at a maximum operating speed (MOS) of 350 km/h (217.48 mi/h). Tests have demonstrated that the trains have an unmodified capability of 394 km/h (244.82 mi/h), but their speed has been limited for safety reasons.

Fastest train journey (average speed)

The West Japan Railway Company operates its 500-Series *Nozomi* bullet trains ("Shinkansen") at an average speed of 261.8 km/h (162.7 mi/h) on the 192-km (119-mile) line between Hiroshima and Kokura on the island of Honshu.

Japan has the **busiest railway network**, with around 23 billion passengers recorded for the year 2010, across all rail companies. Japan Railway, the country's main rail company, recorded approximately 8.9 billion passengers alone in that year.

Japanese trains get very full indeed – particularly at rush hour – so white-gloved "pushers" are used to encourage passengers to fill all available space (left).

Oldest model train set

Made at an unknown location before 1868, the oldest model train set can be found in the Bowes Museum in Barnard Castle, County Durham, UK.

Smallest commercially available working model railway

"T" Gauge, developed by K K Eishindo of Japan, has a track with a gauge of just 3 mm (0.1 in). The models are 450 times smaller than the real thing.

ACTUAL SIZE

Longest train

A 7.35-km-long (4.57-mile) train consisting of 682 ore cars pushed by eight diesel-electric locomotives was assembled by BHP Iron Ore (Australia). The train travelled 275 km (171 miles) from the company's Newman and Yandi mines to Port Hedland in Western Australia on 21 June 2001.

Longest passenger train

Comprising 70 coaches and one electric locomotive, a train created by the National Belgian Railway Company – in aid of a cancer charity – measured 1,732.9 m (5,685 ft 4 in) on 27 April 1991. It travelled 62.5 km (38.9 miles) from Ghent to Ostend (both Belgium).

First preserved railway

The 11.6-km (7.25-mile) Talyllyn Railway in Gwynedd, UK, dates from 1865 and was built to carry slate from local quarries. Over the years, the railway fell into a state of disrepair until it was eventually taken over by enthusiasts and volunteers, who formed the Talyllyn Railway Preservation Society and re-opened the line as a tourist attraction. The first trips on the revived railway took place on 14 May 1951.

Longest runaway train

On 26 March 1884, a wind of great force set eight coal cars on the move at Akron in Colorado, USA. The chance event resulted in the longest journey by a runaway train: a distance of 160 km (100 miles) down the Chicago, Burlington and Quincy Railroad east of Denver, Colorado.

Longest railway platform

The platform at Kharagpur station in West Bengal, India, is 1,072 m (3,517 ft) long.

India is also home to the **longest 2-ft-gauge passenger railway line**, which runs for 199.8 km (124.14 miles) between Gwalior and Sheopur Kalan.

Longest pleasure-pier railway

The pleasure-pier railway at Southend-on-Sea, Essex, UK, measures 1,889.8 m (6,200 ft 1 in) in length.

Most northerly tramway terminus

The northernmost tramway terminus is St Olav's Gate station in Trondheim on the Gråkallbanen, or Trondheim Tramway line, in Norway. The city is located at 63° 36'N latitude, 10° 23'E longitude.

Longest continuous publication of a model railway magazine

An issue of *Model Railroader* has been produced every month since issue No. 1 appeared in January 1934. As of April 2012 the magazine, which is published by Kalmbach Publishing (USA), had produced 940 monthly issues specifically related to model railroading in a variety of scales and gauges.

FACT: The first Japanese bullet train line began operation in October 1964.

Highest railway line

The Qinghai-Tibet railway in China is a 1,956-km-long (1,215-mile) line, most of which lies 4,000 m (13,120 ft) above sea level. Its highest point reaches an altitude of 5,072 m (16,640 ft). Carriages are pressurized, like aircraft cabins, and oxygen masks are available.

At an altitude of 5,068 m (16,627 ft) above sea level, the Tanggula railway station in Tibet is the **highest railway station** in the world. The unstaffed station opened on 1 July 2006 and is located at the highest point on the Qinghai-Tibet railway.

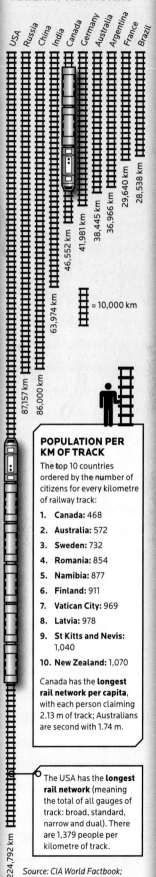

TOP 10 LONGEST RAILWAY NETWORKS

Country	Length
USA	224,792 km
Russia	87,157 km
China	86,000 km
India	63,974 km
Canada	46,552 km
Germany	41,981 km
Australia	38,445 km
Argentina	36,966 km
France	29,640 km
Brazil	28,538 km

= 10,000 km

POPULATION PER KM OF TRACK

The top 10 countries ordered by the number of citizens for every kilometre of railway track:

1. **Canada:** 468
2. **Australia:** 572
3. **Sweden:** 732
4. **Romania:** 854
5. **Namibia:** 877
6. **Finland:** 911
7. **Vatican City:** 969
8. **Latvia:** 978
9. **St Kitts and Nevis:** 1,040
10. **New Zealand:** 1,070

Canada has the **longest rail network per capita**, with each person claiming 2.13 m of track; Australians are second with 1.74 m.

The USA has the **longest rail network** (meaning the total of all gauges of track: broad, standard, narrow and dual). There are 1,379 people per kilometre of track.

Source: CIA World Factbook; International Union of Railways

MANUFACTURING

FACT:
The Grupo Modelo plant can produce 6,000 cans and 144,000 bottles per hour.

Largest manufacturer of silicon chips

In 2011, the revenue of US firm Intel topped $54 billion (£34.5 billion). It has been the largest silicon-chip firm by revenue since 1991.

First factory to use standardized parts

Originally built around 1104, but extended in about 1320, the Venetian Arsenal was a group of shipyards in Venice, Italy. It was the first manufacturing factory in the modern world to use standardized and interchangeable parts to build products. At its height, it employed around 16,000 people and could make almost one ship each day. The new techniques allowed lighter, faster and more cost-effective ships to be built.

First production car factory

René Panhard and Émile Levassor started as woodworkers, moved into coach building, and, in 1889, built the first factory to make petrol-powered cars. Their first car – using a Daimler engine – rolled out of their workshop in 1890. Panhard-Levassor produced cars in the 1890s with pedal-operated clutches, chain transmission and, crucially, a front-mounted engine driving rear wheels. This became standard in the motor industry, and is known as "System Panhard".

Strongest commerically available manufacturing robot

Kuka Robotics' KR 1000 Titan robot – designed for heavy lifting and placement tasks in the automotive, building and foundry industries – has a load capacity of 1,000 kg (2,200 lb). It can move in six independent directions at once and uses nine motors to attain better than +/- 0.1-millimetre precision handling. The robot weighs 4,950 kg (10,912 lb) and has a reach of 3.2 m (10 ft 6 in).

Best-selling car

The Toyota Corolla is the world's best-selling car, with more than 35 million sold (to February 2011) over 10 generations since 1966. It was also the first car in the world to eclipse 30 million sales. However, the Volkswagen Beetle is the best-selling car of a single design (the core structure and shape of the Beetle remained largely unchanged from 1938 to 2003). The Beetle's tally when production ended was 21,529,464.

Highest production of aircraft (company)

The Cessna Aircraft Company of Wichita, Kansas, USA, has been the most productive aerospace company, with total production of 192,991 aircraft through to the end of 2009. Company founder Clyde Cessna built and flew his first aeroplane in 1911.

Largest automated factory

The brewers Grupo Modelo have built a bottling factory at Piedras Negras in Coahuila state, northern Mexico, that has 37 robots that give a total bottling capacity of up to 10 million hectolitres (220 million gal) a year. Alongside the bottling robots, there are laser-guided automated transport trolleys. The plant cost $520 million (£338 million) and reached full production capacity in 2011.

Highest production of military jet aircraft

It is estimated that over 11,000 Russian MIG-21 "Fishbed" jet fighters have been produced since the first prototype flew in 1955, making it the most common jet-powered military aircraft ever, and the military aircraft produced in the greatest numbers in the post-World War II era. The aircraft has been produced in over 30 different variants and has seen service with around 50 air forces around the world.

LARGEST...

Bell foundry

Since 1839, John Taylor & Co. has been casting bells in Loughborough, Leicestershire, UK. It has the largest bell foundry by area, occupying half of a 10,000-m² (107,600-ft²) site, the rest of which is devoted to the Taylor Museum of bell casting and tuning. John Taylor & Co. is responsible for casting many famous bells, including "Great Paul" in St Paul's Cathedral, London, UK, the largest bell in the UK, weighing 17,002 kg (37,483 lb). The business has been in the hands of the Taylor family since 1784.

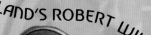

SCOTLAND'S ROBERT WILLIAM THOMSON INVENTED THE PNEUMATIC TYRE IN 1846

Largest tyre manufacturer

In 2010, Lego made 381 million tyres, easily beating all other tyre manufacturers. Lego tyres may not fit an everyday car, but they are remarkably life-like. Even the rubber compound used for the Lego products would be suitable for a domestic car.

FACT:
Lego's minifigures were all yellow until 2003, when the firm introduced realistic skin tones.

Highest national manufacturing output

Manufacturer of artificial limbs
The Artificial Limbs Manufacturing Corporation of India (ALIMCO), based in Kanpur, Uttar Pradesh, is a non-profit organization that makes 355 different types of artificial limbs and prosthetic aids. In the 2008–09 financial reporting period, the firm made 1,644,232 limbs.

Manufacturer of ball bearings
Svenska Kullagerfabriken (SKF), a Swedish company founded in 1907 with headquarters in Gothenburg, is the biggest ball-bearing firm by turnover. In 2011, SKF, which employs around 40,000 people, had a turnover of 49,285 million Swedish krona (£4,633 million).

Manufacturer of musical instruments
The Yamaha Corporation, although renowned for its motorbikes and engines, is the world's largest manufacturer of musical instruments by revenue. In 2011, the income from musical instruments was 271.1 billion yen (£2.26 billion), which accounted for 72.5% of the Yamaha group turnover. The company was founded in 1887 by Torakusu Yamaha as the Japan Musical Instrument Manufacturing Corporation.

Manufacturer of snowboards
With an average annual turnover of about $230 million (£149.5 million) from 2006 to 2010, Burton Snowboards is the largest money-earner of all snowboard manufacturers. The firm, whose flagship store is located in Burlington, Vermont, USA, was started in 1977 by Jake Burton Carpenter. He built the world's first snowboard factory in Burlington, although since March 2010 the boards have been produced in Austria.

In 2010, China was estimated to have produced 19.8% of the world's manufactured goods, fractionally ahead of the USA at 19.4%. This broke the USA's 110-year history as the world's leading manufacturer. China has around 100 million manufacturing workers – significantly more than any other country.

Long-lived manufacture
• The UK's Royal Mint has been manufacturing coins since the reign of Alfred the Great (871–899). From about 1279 to 1812, the mint was based at the Tower of London. Now it is in Llantrisant, Wales, UK.

• The Marinelli family set up their bell foundry in Agnone, Italy in 1339. In 2009, about 90% of their orders came from the Catholic church.

• Italy's Beretta firm have been making guns since 1526 when Bartolomeo Beretta received 296 ducats from the Arsenal of Venice as payment for 185 gun barrels.

Manufacturer of toilets
Toto Ltd, a Japanese company founded in 1917, sells a range of toilets called Washlets. With an annual sales revenue in 2006 in excess of $4.2 billion (£2.6 billion), the firm is the largest manufacturer of toilets.

Abandoned factory
The old Packard car factory in Detroit, USA, at 325,160 m² (3.5 million ft²), is the largest abandoned factory by size. The factory, which once produced 75% of the world's cars, was closed in 1956 and has stood empty ever since.

FACT:
Boeing offer tours of their factory – on 14 November 2007, they received their 3-millionth visitor.

Largest factory (volume)
The Boeing Everett factory in Washington state, USA, has a total volume of 13,385,378 m³ (472,370,319 ft³), and covers a floor area of 399,483 m² (4.3 million sq ft²). The facility is used to build the Boeing 747, 767, 777 and the new 787 Dreamliner aircraft.

UNITS PRODUCED IN ONE YEAR...

Lego bricks
36,000,000,000

Mobile phones
1,600,000,000

Tyres
1,400,000,000

Computers
364,000,000

Bicycles
105,000,000

Cars
51,971,000

Washing machines
50,100,000

iPads
19,500,000

Book titles published
1,004,725

WEAPONS

Most advanced sniper rifle

The L115A3, made by Accuracy International (UK) and used by the British Army since 2008, is the most advanced sniper (or long-range) rifle. Weighing 6.8 kg (15 lb), this 8.59-mm calibre weapon is fitted with a telescopic day sight, which offers up to 25 times magnification, as well as a night sight and a laser-range finder. It can achieve a first-round hit at 600 m (1,969 ft) and harassing fire out to more than 1,100 m (3,609 ft).

FIRST...

Boomerang
The boomerang is usually associated with the Australian Aborigines, but they were also used in ancient Egypt and Europe. The oldest boomerang discovered is about 23,000 years old. It was made from a mammoth tusk and found in a cave in the Oblazowa Rock in south Poland.

Gun
It is believed that the earliest guns were constructed both in China and in Northern Africa c. 1250. The invention of the gun certainly dates from before 1326. Gunpowder may have been invented in China, India, Arabia or Europe in the 13th century; the earliest known example of a gun was found in the ruins of the castle of Monte Varino in Italy, which was destroyed in 1341.

True flintlock mechanism
Marin le Bourgeoys (France), a gun-maker at the court of Louis XIII of France, invented the first true flintlock in the early 17th century. The flintlock is the firing mechanism used

on muskets and rifles, which includes a striking device that operates a firing pin to hit and ignite the primer in the gun cartridge. Le Bourgeoys combined and adapted earlier firing mechanisms so that the cock and trigger acted vertically instead of horizontally. His guns also incorporated a half-cocked position, which allowed it to be loaded without firing – providing greater safety for the user.

Machine gun
In 1862, Richard Gatling (USA) produced the first workable, hand-cranked, multiple-barrel machine gun. Loose cartridges were fed under gravity into the open breach from a top-mounted hopper. It was this feature, rather than the multiple rotating barrels, that permitted unskilled operators to achieve high rates of fire. It was first used in warfare during the American Civil War of 1861–65. Although capable of continuous fire, it was not a true automatic weapon as it required human power to turn it.

Automatic weapon
Sir Hiram Maxim built his first self-powered, single-barrelled machine gun in 1883 in the UK and demonstrated it in 1884. It used the recoil force

Newest sea-launched ballistic missile

Following successful testing in December 2011, the Bulava Intercontinental Ballistic Missile (ICBM) is set to be used by the Russian Navy. The missile can carry several individually targeted warheads and has a range of 8,000 km (5,000 miles). It will be deployed aboard the newest class of Russian sub, the Burei.

Final B53 weapon to be dismantled

Brought into service in 1962 and decommissioned in 1997, the US B53 nuclear bomb had 9,000 kilotons of explosive power. It was a major weapon in the Cold War, often deployed on the B-52 Stratofortress aircraft. On 25 October 2011, it was announced that the last B53 had been dismantled. High-explosive material weighing 136 kg (300 lb) was removed from the enriched uranium heart of the bomb.

Most advanced pilot helmet
BAE Systems' (UK) newest fighter-pilot helmet projects the image of enemy aircraft on to the visor; it also tracks the pilot's eye movements, allowing the weapons systems to quickly lock on to the target the pilot is looking at.

of the fired round to extract the fired case and place another in the chamber, cocking the action in the process. By holding the trigger down, the gun fired continuously or until it overheated or jammed. Various designs of the Maxim gun were used in World War I and it also continued in service in various guises throughout World War II.

Large-scale use of poison gas in war
While the earliest documented use of a biological agent in war was in the 6th century BC, the first large-scale use of poison gas was during World War I. The German Army used a form of tear gas unsuccessfully against the Russians at the Battle of Bolimov in Poland on 31 January 1915. They then used chlorine gas during the

Second Battle of Ypres in France between 22 April and 25 May 1915, when 171 tonnes (188 tons) of the poisonous gas were released over a 6.4-km (4-mile) front. The British first used poison gas at the Battle of Loos in France on 25 September 1915.

Battlefield ray-gun deployment

A battlefield ray gun, or direct-energy weapon, was deployed for the first time in Iraq by the Americans in 2008. "Zeus" – named after the Greek god of thunder – is designed to allow operators to neutralize targets such as roadside bombs and other unexploded ordnance at a safe distance of 300 m (984 ft). The conventional way to neutralize bombs is by using explosives, for instance with a rocket-propelled grenade. However, compared with direct-energy weapons, this method can be inaccurate and often more expensive.

MOST ADVANCED...

Weapon for drones

In 2011, the US defence company Raytheon successfully tested the Small Tactical Munition bomb specifically designed to be fired from a drone, or unmanned aerial vehicle (UAV). Using a laser seeker together with GPS, the 60-cm-long (2-ft) weapon is capable of hitting fixed and moving targets regardless of weather conditions.

Warhead casing material

A new material that replaces steel in warhead casings was demonstrated at the US Naval Surface Warfare Center (NSWC) in Dahlgren, Virginia, USA, on 2 December 2011. Called High-Density Reactive Material (HDRM), it consists of metals and polymers that combine and explode only on impact with the target. The kinetic force of impact and the disintegration of the casing inside the target – with an additional release of chemical energy – creates an explosion up to five times greater than conventional casings. It can be used for new warheads or incorporated into current ones.

First combat use of a stealth aircraft

Stealth aircraft cannot be detected by enemy radar. The first one used on military operations was the US F-117 Nighthawk, made by Lockheed Martin. It first flew in 1981 and remained classified until November 1988; in all, 64 Nighthawks were built. The first combat use of the aircraft was in the US invasion of Panama in December 1989, when it bombed the Rio Hato airfield, near Panama's south coast.

FACT: In the 1991 Gulf War, the F-117 flew for a total of 6,905 hours in nearly 1,300 combat sorties.

Most adaptable electronic camouflage

BAE Systems' (UK) electronic camouflage system, Adaptiv, consists of an exterior cover of hexagonal tiles that can be used on tanks, aircraft or ships. It can disguise one type of vehicle as another type, as shown right, where a tank appears to be an ordinary car, and can also "merge" a vehicle with its background so it becomes invisible to thermal-imaging sensors. It works by altering the temperature of the tiles, effectively turning the vehicle's exterior into a large thermal infra-red "television screen", with each tile representing a pixel.

System OFF

System ON

FACT: The Adaptiv system can also send signals that enable it to be identified by friendly forces.

TOP 10 COUNTRIES BY GUN OWNERSHIP

The annual Small Arms Survey estimates the number of firearms and small weapons in circulation around the world. Here are the top 10 countries for civilian gun ownership (main figures in millions).

USA 270.0
83–97 firearms per 100 people

INDIA 46.0
3–5.6 per 100

CHINA 40.0
24–36 per 100

FRANCE 19.0
30–34 per 100

PAKISTAN 18.0
2.3–3.9 per 100

GERMANY 25.0
15 per 100

MEXICO 15.5
12 per 100

BRAZIL 15.3
8.8 per 100

RUSSIA 12.7
5–13 per 100

YEMEN 11.5
32–96 per 100

*Largest civilian firearm holdings in millions (**bold**), with average number of firearms per 100 people (italics)*
source: Small Arms Survey 2007

FIGHTING VEHICLES

First tank
The British No. 1 Lincoln, modified to become "Little Willie", first ran on 6 September 1915 and first saw action on 15 September 1916 in World War I.

Highest rate of tank production
Designed to be easily produced and maintained, the M-4 Sherman Main Battle Tank was first made in the USA in 1942 during World War II. More than 48,000 of them were turned out over three years.

Deadliest unmanned aerial vehicle
The Predator C Avenger Unmanned Aerial Vehicle is capable of 740 km/h (460 mi/h) at 18,288 m (60,000 ft) for up to 20 hours. The ability to carry 1,360 kg (3,000 lb) of weapons and its stealthy design – there are no sharp angles, reducing its radar signature – make it the world's deadliest drone to date. Its first flight was on 4 April 2009.

Most Spitfires flown
Alex Henshaw (UK) flew and tested more than 3,000 Spitfires between April 1932 and October 1995, when he flew his last one in a Battle of Britain memorial flight at Coningsby, Lincolnshire, UK.

Longest development of a Main Battle Tank
Work on the development of the Arjun Main Battle Tank for the Indian Army started in 1972. In 1996, the Indian government decided to mass-produce the tank but tests by the Indian Army highlighted its poor performance and reliability so the first deliveries were not made until 2004 – 32 years after its conception. By 2011, 124 Arjuns were in service with the Indian Army.

Most expensive single weapon system
The USS *Ronald Reagan*, the CVN 76 class, nuclear-powered aircraft carrier launched in 2001, cost about $4.5 billion (£3.1 billion) including crew, armament, 85 aircraft, and defence and communication systems.

Heaviest route-clearance vehicle
The US Army's Buffalo weighs 24,267 kg (53,500 lb) empty and has a load capacity of 10,205 kg (22,500 lb), giving a total weight of nearly 34.47 tonnes (38 tons). Part of the Mine Resistant Ambush Protected (MRAP) family of vehicles, it was developed to counter the threat from landmines, improvised explosive devices (IEDs) and ambushes in Iraq and Afghanistan. Made by Force Protection Inc., the Buffalo has a V-shaped hull to deflect explosions. It can carry up to 13 personnel in addition to driver and co-driver.

FIRST...

Armoured car squadron
On 3 December 1914, three armoured cars were delivered to British Royal Naval Air Service. Each comprised a Rolls-Royce Silver Ghost chassis with a Vickers machine gun mounted on a single turret. They were used in World War I for reconnaissance and to rescue downed pilots. In the 1920s, the Royal Air Force used Rolls-Royce armoured cars to protect oil supplies in Mesopotamia (modern-day Iraq).

Combat wing for an unmanned aerial vehicle
On 1 May 2007, the US Air Force (USAF) created the first combat wing of unmanned aerial vehicle – the 432nd Wing of Air Force Special Operations Command. The combat wing

Landmine casualties
In 2006, the Department of Social and Spatial Inequalities at the University of Sheffield, UK, estimated the nations most affected by landmines. They calculated deaths and injuries per year, per million people living in each nation.

1. Cambodia 69
2. Iraq. 50
3. Burundi. 42
3=. Afghanistan. 42
5. Laos. 33
6. Colombia 19
7. Guinea-Bissau. 14
7=. Angola. 14
9. Bosnia and Herzegovina 12
9=. Eritrea. 12

Heaviest armoured vehicle

Weighs 62,500 kg (137,789 lb)

The Titan, a British bridge-laying vehicle that enables ground troops to cross rivers, weighs 62,500 kg (137,789 lb) and can carry a 26-m-long (85-ft) bridge or two 12-m-long (39-ft) bridges. It is the **fastest bridge-laying system** in the world, able to lay the 26-m bridge within two minutes. Equipped with the chassis of the Challenger 2 Main Battle Tank, the Titan has remote-controlled CCTVs to help position the bridges and a bulldozer blade to clear obstacles. The British Army has 33 Titans, the final one being delivered in 2008.

fly Predator and Reaper drones from Creech Air Force Base in Nevada, USA. They can be armed with missiles and are capable of flying remotely anywhere in the world.

Laser gunship

On 4 December 2007 at Kirkland Air Force Base, New Mexico, USA, Boeing completed the installation of a high-energy chemical laser on a Hercules C-130H aircraft. It was part of the development of the US military's Advanced Tactical Laser, which will be able to destroy ground targets more accurately and with less collateral damage than conventional guns or missiles.

Aerial battle involving an unmanned aerial vehicle

In December 2002, a US Air Force RQ-1 Predator drone conducting surveillance in Iraqi airspace was engaged by an Iraqi MiG-25 fighter jet. The two planes fired air-to-air missiles at each other, with the MiG eventually downing the Predator.

FASTEST ...

Armoured four-wheel drive carrier

The Kombat T-98, an armoured VIP car built by Kombat Armouring in St Petersburg, Russia, since 2003, can reach 180 km/h (111 mi/h). It has an 8.1-litre V8 engine and can be equipped with gun ports and a machine gun.

Largest unmanned logistic vehicle

Developed by Lockheed Martin, the US Army's unmanned Squad Mission Support System (SMSS) is designed to carry military supplies by remote control. It is 3.68 m (12 ft) long, 1.8 m (6 ft) wide and 2.15 m (7 ft) tall, and can carry 540 kg (1,200 lb) of equipment for up to 13 men. The SMSS was first used in Afghanistan in 2011 to counter deaths in manned vehicles caused by improvised explosive devices (IEDs). It uses Global Positioning System (GPS) technology to navigate automatically.

Combat jet

The Russian Mikoyan MiG-25 fighter (NATO code-name "Foxbat") entered service in 1970 and had a reconnaissance version, "Foxbat-B", which was tracked by radar at about Mach 3.2 (3,395 km/h; 2,110 mi/h).

Flying-boat

The Martin XP6M-1 SeaMaster, the US Navy four-jet-engined minelayer flown in 1955–59, had a top speed of 1,040 km/h (646 mi/h).

Military submarine

The Russian Alpha-class nuclear-powered submarines, produced from 1974 to 1981, had a reported maximum speed of more than 40 knots (74 km/h; 46 mi/h). In all, seven Alpha-class submarines were made.

Tank

A production-standard S 2000 Scorpion Peacekeeper tank, developed by Repaircraft PLC (UK), attained a speed of 82.23 km/h (51.1 mi/h) at the QinetiQ test track in Chertsey, UK, on 26 March 2002.

Warship

The US Navy test surface-effect ship the SES-100B reached 91.9 knots (170 km/h; 105 mi/h) on 25 January 1980 at Chesapeake Bay, Maryland, USA. Similar to hovercraft, surface-effect ships travel on a cushion of air, but also have two sharp, rigid hulls that remain in the water. Large fans under the ship create air pressure that is trapped between the hulls and raises the ship.

Largest family of personnel carriers

The US-made BAE M113 is the most used tracked armoured personnel carrier still in service worldwide. There are more than 80,000 M113s currently deployed, in over 40 variants, and they are used in more than 50 countries. The vehicle is due to retire from service from the US military in 2018.

Most produced Main Battle Tank

First produced in 1945, the Soviet T54/55 Main Battle Tanks entered production in 1947 and eventually became the most produced tank in the world, as they were supplied not only to the Soviet Union but also to its allies in eastern Europe and elsewhere. Production numbers are estimated at over 80,000 and they have been deployed in nearly 80 countries.

FACT: T55 tanks were used by both sides in the Libyan Civil War that ended Gaddafi's rule in 2011.

GLOBAL FIREPOWER

TANK NUMBERS

The Chinese People's Republic has the army with the greatest number of Main Battle Tanks. The most recent estimates give it 7,050 tanks, while the US Army possesses 5,795 (excluding the 447 in the US Marine Corps) and the Russian Army 2,800 (rises to 3,319 when Naval Infantry (Marines), Coastal Defence Forces and Interior Troops are included), if the 18,000 in store are disregarded.

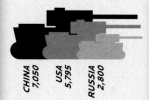

CHINA 7,050   USA 5,795   RUSSIA 2,800

AIRCRAFT-CARRIER NUMBERS

Source: Haze Gray & Underway World Aircraft Carrier List

USA – 11, Spain – 2, Italy – 2, Brazil – 1, India – 1, UK – 1, France – 1, Russia – 1, Thailand – 1

COMBAT AIRCRAFT

Source: Haze Gray & Underway

Country	Fighters	Bombers	Attack
Egypt	644	25	–
India	1,130	118	370
Israel	233	10	264
N. Korea	899	60	211
Pakistan	325	30	250
PLAAF	901	91	110
Russia	1,264	166	1,267
S. Korea	648	60	352
UK	345	50	209
USA	3,043	171	1,185

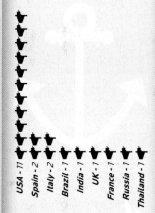

HELICOPTERS

FIRST...

"Helicopter" design

Leonardo da Vinci (Italy, 1452–1519) proposed the idea of a helicopter-type craft for a human passenger in 1493. The so-called "air screw" consisted of a platform with a helical screw designed to allow it to take off and land vertically. Da Vinci's sketch was discovered in the 19th century.

Helicopter flight

On 13 November 1907, Paul Cornu (France) flew an experimental helicopter in untethered flight for the first time in Lisieux, Calvados, France. This event is widely credited as the first free flight of a rotary-wing aircraft, though in reality it was probably no more than a hop or series of airborne hops. Another two machines were built, but the control system proved to be ineffective and no further progress was made.

Design for a production helicopter

Igor Sikorsky (Russia, now Ukraine) designed the world's first true production helicopter. Sikorsky's US Patent 1,994,488, filed on 27 June 1931, marked the crucial breakthrough in helicopter technology and led to the Sikorsky R-4. It proved itself in active service for US forces during World War II and became the world's first mass-produced helicopter.

Turbine-powered helicopter

The Kaman K-225 helicopter was built in 1949, principally for use as a crop duster. In 1951, the reciprocating engine was replaced with a Boeing 502-2 gas turbine (jet) engine to demonstrate the reduced weight, higher power-to-weight ratio – thus allowing greater payloads – and the greater reliability and easier maintenance offered by such engines. On 11 December 1951, the modified K-225 became the first helicopter to fly with turbine-powered transmission.

Following development of his K-225, aeronautical engineer Charles Kaman (USA) introduced the world's **first twin-turbine- (jet-) powered helicopter** in March 1954.

Largest helicopter ever

The Russian Mil Mi-12 was 37 m (121 ft 4.7 in) long, with a maximum take-off weight of 103.3 tonnes (227,737 lb). Powered by four 4,847-kW (6,500-hp) turboshaft engines, it had a rotor diameter of 67 m (219 ft 10 in). The Mil Mi-12 first flew in 1968, but never went into production.

Largest helicopter in active use

The five-man Russian Mil Mi-26 first flew in 1977. It has a maximum take-off weight of 56,000 kg (123,460 lb) and is 40.025 m (131 ft) long.

Helicopter at the South Pole

The first helicopters to land at the South Pole were three Bell UH-1B turbo-powered Iroquois from Mount Weaver, Antarctica. They arrived on 4 February 1963 after a 2-hr 24-min flight, the aim being to fly back to McMurdo Station via the Pole. Despite arriving successfully, the helicopters were eventually dismantled and flown back to McMurdo in Lockheed Martin LC-130s.

FACT: The A/MH-6X can be piloted or programmed to fly autonomously.

Fully autonomous flight by unmanned helicopter

In June 2010, the Piasecki Aircraft Corporation, together with the Carnegie Mellon University (both USA), demonstrated a navigation and sensor system that enables a full-sized helicopter to fly, unmanned, at low altitude. It can also avoid obstacles and evaluate and select suitable landing sites in unmapped terrain.

The sensors – which are mounted in an unmanned Little Bird helicopter testbed – build three-dimensional maps of the ground and identify obstacles in the path of the helicopter. In time, the system will be used to allow unmanned helicopters to evacuate wounded soldiers from the battlefield and other dangerous situations.

Remotely piloted helicopter

On 30 July 1957, a modified Kaman helicopter, the HTK-1K, became the first rotorcraft to fly while being remotely controlled. It was developed as part of a US Army/Navy programme and designed for use in difficult and dangerous situations. Earlier that year, on 23 May, it had been flown from the USS *Mitscher*, while being operated from the ship, with a safety pilot on board.

Unmanned cargo resupply helicopter

On 17 December 2011, the US 2nd Marine Air Wing used a Kaman K-Max to make the first unmanned helicopter cargo delivery to troops on a battlefield. Having successfully demonstrated a remotely controlled, unmanned resupply helicopter to the US Marine Corps in January 2010, some 1,590 kg (3,500 lb) of freight was moved from Camp Dwyer to Combat Outpost Payne in the Helmand Province, Afghanistan, in around 1.5 hours.

Electric helicopter

On 4 August 2011, the first authenticated, manned flight of a helicopter powered by an electric motor took place at Venelles, France. The aircraft was flown by Pascal Chretien

First true hybrid manned/ unmanned helicopter

On 20 September 2006, the A/MH-6X, a light-turbine helicopter constructed at the Boeing Rotorcraft Facility in Mesa, Arizona, USA, flew for the first time. It combines features from Boeing's A/MH-6M Mission Enhanced Little Bird (MELB) and the Unmanned Little Bird (ULB) Demonstrator, a modified MD 530F civil helicopter. The A/MH-6X has been designed both for military and civil use.

Most common military helicopter

More than 16,000 Bell Helicopter Textron (USA) UH-1 Iroquois ("Huey") helicopters have been produced since 1959.

Largest helicopter manufacturer

As of 2011, Eurocopter held a 43% share of the global civil and private helicopter market, with over 11,300 helicopters in service in a total of 149 countries.

Smallest helicopter

In terms of rotor length, the smallest helicopter is the GEN H-4 made by Gen Corporation (Japan) with a rotor length of only 4 m (13 ft), a weight of 70 kg (154 lb 5 oz) and consisting of one seat, one landing gear and one power unit. It has two sets of coaxial contra-rotating rotors, removing the need for a traditional tail rotor to act as a balance.

FACT: The GEN H-4 can reach an altitude of 1,000 m (3,280 ft) and a top speed of 90 km/h (56 mi/h).

HOW WE LEARNED TO HOVER

In the 4th century BC, children in China tied feathers to small sticks, spun them and watched them rise into the air. But it took nearly 2,000 years before the first plans for a practical 'copter were drawn up. GWR presents highlights from the history of the helicopter:

1493
Leonardo da Vinci (Italy) sketches his idea for a human-powered "air screw".

1784
Launoy and Bienvenu (both France) demonstrate a small model helicopter, propelled by a tightly wound cord, for the French Academy of Sciences.

(France) and hovered about 50 cm (19 in) above the ground for 2 min 10 sec. The first flight was tethered, but the machine later made its first free flight on 12 August 2011. In July and August 2011, the aircraft flew for a total of 99.5 minutes in 29 flights, some of which extended for 6 minutes.

SEE IT 3D

1907
Gyroplane No.1 – created by Louis and Jacques Breguet, under the direction of Charles Richet (all France) – becomes the first rotary-wing craft to be manned; is unsteerable and reaches up just 60 cm (2 ft).

First manned electric multicopter

On 21 October 2011, the first manned flight of the "e-volo" – an electric multicopter – took place in south-west Germany. It lasted 1 min 30 sec and the pilot was Thomas Senkel (Germany). Powered by 16 lithium ion batteries running electric motors, each driving its own propeller to provide lift, the multicopter is capable of flying for 20 minutes. It weighs 80 kg (176 lb 6 oz).

Swarming mini choppers

A team from General Robotics, Automation, Sensing and Perception (GRASP) Laboratory at the University of Pennsylvania, USA, has developed a fleet of mini four-bladed helicopters, properly named "quadrotors". About the size of a human hand, they are designed to carry out autonomous, synchronous flying. Working together as a swarm, they are capable of carrying items through small openings, and it is envisaged that they will operate in environments dangerous to humans such as on oil rigs or in war or disaster zones. At the beginning of 2012, the helicopters were demonstrated operating in "swarms" (multiple formations) of up to 20 aircraft.

1907
Bicycle manufacturer Paul Cornu (France) makes the first true "free" manned helicopter flight.

1931
Igor Sikorsky (Russia) secures a patent for first production helicopter, the Sikorsky R-4.

Largest helicopter carrier

Few classes of ship cater for helicopters in force. The largest ships in this role currently in service, by tonnage and helicopter capacity, are those of the US Wasp Class, such as the USS *Boxer* (below), of which eight are in use. If not carrying fixed-wing aircraft they can carry 42 CH-46 Sea Knight helicopters or 22 MV-22 Osprey aircraft.

1959
Bell UH-1 Iroquois "Huey" military helicopters enter production.

SPEC:
Length: 253.2 m
Beam: 31.8 m
Draft: 8.1 m
Displacement: 41,150 tonnes

IN SEARCH OF AN AIRPORT? LAND ON P.172

WACKY VEHICLES

First flying car

The ultimate off-roader, the Terrafugia Transition is the first "roadable" aircraft – or flying car. Previous "flying cars" have needed extra equipment or wings to be added but this two-seater plane can, at the touch of a button, fold its wings and turn into a car. The Transition took flight for the first time in March 2009 at Plattsburgh International Airport in New York state, USA. It can reach a top speed of 100 knots (185 km/h; 115 mi/h) in the air – although Terrafugia have not said how fast it can go on land. The company is now developing a production version, which they are marketing with the line: "Simply land at the airport, fold your wings up and drive home."

Smallest van

The smallest roadworthy van is *Wind Up*, which measures 104.14 cm (41 in) high, 66.04 cm (26 in) wide and 132.08 cm (52 in) long. Perry Watkins (UK) made the car from a Postman Pat coin-in-the-slot children's ride in seven months up to May 2011. The van has insurance, road tax and all the usual features including lights, indicators, brake lights and windscreen wipers.

Fastest scooter

Colin Furze (UK) has supercharged a mobility scooter so that it can reach a top speed of 115.21 km/h (71.59 mi/h). It took Colin three months to convert the scooter, which features five gears, a 125-cc motorbike engine and twin exhausts.

First submarine car

The Swiss company Rinspeed created the world's first true submersible car, called the "sQuba". First shown at the Geneva Motor Show in March 2008, the carsub is powered electrically by three rechargeable lithium-ion batteries. It can drive straight into the sea and then float until a hatch is opened to allow water to flood the body and gradually sink the car. Underwater, it effectively flies at a depth of 10 m (33 ft).

Longest bicycle

The longest true bicycle (with two wheels and no stabilizers) measures 35.79 m (117 ft 5 in). It was built by the Mijl van Mares Werkploeg (gang of workers) in Maarheeze, Netherlands, and ridden on 5 August 2011. Two people ride the bike: one steers at the front and one pedals at the back.

Tallest unicycle ride

Sem Abrahams (USA) rode a 35-m-tall (114-ft 9-in) unicycle for a distance of 8.5 m (28 ft) at the Silverdome in Pontiac, Michigan, on 29 January 2004.

Largest tricycle

Made by Kanyaboyina Sudhakar (India) and ridden in Hyderabad, India, on 1 July 2005, the largest pedal tricycle is 11.37 m (37 ft 4 in) long and has an overall height of 12.67 m (41 ft 7 in).

Most transformations of a vehicle

An Ellert – a three-wheeled car – was successfully transformed in Denmark into a hotrod, a rocket-powered hydrofoil and, finally, on 8 September 2006, an aircraft. Each of these transformations took two weeks to complete.

Lowest roadworthy car

The *Mirai* – the word means "future" in Japanese – measures 45.2 cm (1 ft 5.79 in) from the ground to the highest part of the car. It was created on 15 November 2010 by Hideki Mori (pictured) and his students on the automobile engineering course at Okayama Sanyo High School in Asakuchi, Japan. Previous projects on the course have included building an amphibious car and a huge glider plane.

FACT:
The **lightest car** was built by Louis Borsi (UK) – it weighed 9.5 kg (21 lb) and had a 2.5-cc engine.

Fastest bathroom

The *Bog Standard*, created by Edd China (UK), consists of a motorcycle and sidecar hidden under a bathroom suite – including a bathtub, basin and laundry bin. Using controls hidden under the basin, Edd has driven the vehicle at a top speed of 68 km/h (42.25 mi/h).

68 km/h

FACT: Edd China also holds the record for **fastest garden shed, fastest bed** and **fastest office.**

for *The Gadget Show*'s 200th episode in Bentwaters Parks, Suffolk, UK, on 9 August 2011. Jason's luge, essentially a liquid-fuel-powered skateboard, had no brakes – so Jason superglued pieces of car tyre to his boots to help him stop.

TITANIC TYRES
Looking for a tyre for your giant mining truck? You need a Titan 63, the new **largest production tyre**:

4.26 m — **5,670 kg**

But that's nothing. The **tallest tyre** of all – the 24-m Uniroyal Giant in Michigan, USA – is nearly six times as big!

24 m

FASTEST...

Car powered by compressed air
Toyota's three-wheeled KU:RIN car reached a top speed of 129.2 km/h (80.3 mi/h) at the Japan Automobile Research Institute's Ibaraki test track on 9 September 2011. The car has a compressed-air "fuel tank" – as air is released, it generates thrust.

Vehicle powered by powertool
Jon Bentley (UK) reached 117 km/h (72.74 mi/h) on a dragster powered by a chainsaw for the 200th episode of *The Gadget Show* at Santa Pod Raceway, Northamptonshire, UK, on 22 August 2011.

Bicycle powered by electric-ducted fans
Ortis Deley (UK) recorded a top speed of 115.87 km/h (72 mi/h) on a bicycle fitted with electric-ducted fans – propellers used for model aircraft. The fans, along with about 10 kg

(22 lb) of batteries, were fixed to the back rack of the bike. Ortis completed his feat for the 200th episode of *The Gadget Show* at Santa Pod Raceway in Northamptonshire, UK, on 24 August 2011.

Powered street luge
Lying down on his jet-powered street luge, Jason Bradbury (UK) attained a speed of 186.41 km/h (115.83 mi/h)

Water-jet-powered car
Jason Bradbury (UK) achieved a top speed of 26.8 km/h (16.65 mi/h) in a water-jet-powered car for *The Gadget Show* at Wattisham Airfield, Ipswich, UK, in March 2010.

Heaviest rideable pedal bike

Built by Wouter van den Bosch (Netherlands), the *Monsterbike* weighs 750 kg (1,650 lb) and was ridden for the first time in Arnhem, Netherlands, in May 2010. It is made from steel tubes, bicycle parts, four small tyres at the back and one mammoth Michelin tractor tyre, measuring 1.95 m (6 ft 4.7 in) high, at the front. Wouter made the bike for his fine art degree – but he is not sure whether or not it is art.

WOUTER'S "MONSTERBIKE" VIDEO ON YOUTUBE HAS MORE THAN 3,300,000 VIEWS

SNAP SHOT

• The photographer Ranald Mackechnie almost ended up in one of Arnhem's canals trying to get far enough back to capture the whole bike in the shot!

• During the shoot, a police van stopped and all the policemen inside had their photos taken with the bike.

• When taking his bike for a spin, Wouter finds that most people stop, stare and smile – however, a few fellow cyclists get annoyed as the bike tends to block cycle lanes.

ROADS

Shortest street

The length of Ebenezer Place in Wick, Caithness, Scotland, was found to be a mere 2.05 m (6 ft 9 in) when measured on 28 October 2006. The stunted street has a postal address (No.1), a doorway and even a street sign above the door.

Longest continuous road

Australia's Highway One circumnavigates the whole country via a network of fully interconnected roads. Its total length is 14,523 km (9,024 miles), making it more than 3,500 km (2,200 miles) longer than its nearest rival, the Trans-Siberian Highway.

Longest straight road

Built originally as a private road for Saudi Arabia's King Fahd, the road that connects the Harad area with Badha in Saudi Arabia is 240 km (149.13 miles) long. It cuts straight through the desert with no bends to the left or right, and no significant rise or fall.

Longest one-way road

The M2 Southern Expressway in Adelaide, South Australia, is 21 km (13 miles) long and allows only one direction of traffic flow at a time. The road runs towards Adelaide in the morning, swapping to a southbound flow in the afternoon.

Longest ring-road

The M25 London Orbital Motorway is 195.5 km (121.8 miles) long. Work on the ring-road began in 1972 and was completed in 1986 at an estimated cost of $1.33 billion (£909 million).

Most lanes on a road

The Toll Plaza of the San Francisco–Oakland Bay Bridge has 23 lanes running east-bound through the tolls.

Oldest road surface still in use

Stretches of the Via Appia (the Appian Way) in Italy date from its original construction in 312 BC. The route formed the main connection between Rome and Brindisi, south-east Italy. On the best-preserved parts, close to Rome itself, people may walk or cycle on the old stone-paved road. In the area of Velletri, it is still possible to drive on the original Roman-paved surface.

First motorway

In 1924, the world's first dual-carriage highway built for higher-speed traffic was opened between the Italian towns of Milan and Varese, with a single lane in each direction separated by a crash barrier. Today, it is part of the A8 and A9 motorway network.

First solar-powered road

The A18 Catania–Siracuse motorway in Sicily incorporates three tunnels covered with more than 80,000 individual solar panels, which provide power for lighting, tunnel fans, emergency phones and signage. The road is estimated to produce 12 million kWh of power per year across the 2.8-km (1.7-mile) length covered by the tunnels.

Coldest road

The Kolyma Highway (M56) in Russia passes through some of the coldest inhabited places on Earth. The road is 2,031 km (1,262 miles) long and goes from Nizhny Bestyakh in the west to Magadan in the east. Temperatures as low as -67.7°C (-89.86°F) have been recorded along this route.

Most southerly road

The McMurdo–South Pole Highway is a 1,450-km (900-mile) road constructed in Antarctica from the McMurdo Station to Amundsen-Scott base at the South Pole. The road is made from flattened and graded ice and snow.

Oldest functional traffic light

The oldest working traffic signal was first installed on a junction in Ashville, Ohio, USA, in 1932 and operated until 1982. The signal has four faces, and a rotating red/green lamp inside alternately illuminates each face. Designed by Ashville resident Teddy Boor, it still works today and was only retired from service because colour-blind individuals found it more difficult to read than modern lights.

Steepest road

Located in Dunedin, New Zealand, Baldwin Street is the world's steepest paved road over a continuous distance of more than 10 m (33 ft). At just over 350 m (1,150 ft) in length, with 34 houses located along it, the road rises a total of 69.2 m (227 ft) at a rate of 1 m (3 ft 4 in) vertically for every 2.86 m (9 ft 4 in) horizontally travelled. The road is surfaced with specially grooved concrete to ensure cars can grip the surface.

FACT: The "Baldwin Street Gutbuster" is an annual race up and down the steepest street.

Most crooked road

Comprising eight tight hairpin turns as it meanders down a hill in San Francisco, USA, Lombard Street is the world's most crooked road. Many roads twist and turn, but only a 400-m-long (0.25-mile) section of Lombard Street, which descends a 27% incline, can claim so many hairpin turns in such a short distance – a total of 1,440 degrees twisted and turned.

4,700-m (15,420-ft) drop

Most complex junction

The Judge Harry Pregerson Interchange in Los Angeles, USA, is a multiple-stack motorway interchange that connects Interstate Highway 105 and Interstate Highway 110 with the Harbor Gateway North area of Los Angeles. A four-level interchange, it offers the possibility of driving from any direction on to any other direction of travel on the intersecting roads as well as possessing restricted access lanes for high-occupancy vehicles. The topmost lane stands at a height of 36.5 m (120 ft).

First road-traffic death
On 31 August 1869, Mary Ward (Ireland) fell out of her cousin's experimental steam car and was run over, breaking her neck. The speed of the vehicle was estimated to be 5.6–6.4 km/h (3.5–4 mi/h).

Most complex roundabout
The "Magic Roundabout" in Swindon, UK, comprises five smaller roundabouts around the circumference of a larger roundabout. It is possible to travel in both directions around the larger roundabout to exit via the driver's chosen road. Each of the smaller roundabouts has three entry and three exit lanes.

Deepest road tunnel
The Eiksund road tunnel in Norway connects the Norwegian mainland with Hareidlandet island and lies 287 m (942 ft) below sea level. It is 7,765 m (25,476 ft) long and was opened in 2008.

THERE IS A FIVE-STAR HOTEL ON THE ROUNDABOUT!

Largest roundabout
One roundabout in Putrajaya, Malaysia, has a 3.4-km (2.1-mile) circumference. Circled by the Persiaran Sultan Salahuddin Abdul Aziz Shah road, it has 15 entry/exit points.

FACT:
The North Yungas Road is known in Spanish as El Camino de la Muerte – "Road of Death".

Most dangerous road

The road considered by many to be the most lethal in the world is the North Yungas Road that runs for 69 km (43 miles) from La Paz to Coroico in Bolivia, and sees up to 300 deaths annually – 4.3 per km (6.9 per mile). For most of the stretch, the single-lane mud road (with two-way traffic) has an unbarricaded vertical drop, measuring 4,700 m (15,420 ft) at its highest point. It's most deadly in the rainy season.

GUINNESS WORLD RECORDS

= 300,000 km

TOP 10 LONGEST ROAD NETWORKS

384,000 km: Distance from Earth to the Moon.

10. Spain 681,298 km
9. Australia 818,356 km
8. France 951,200 km
7. Russia 982,000 km
6. Canada 1,042,300 km
5. Japan 1,203,777 km

1,390,000 km: Diameter of the Sun.

4. Brazil 1,751,868 km

FACT:
Peruvians drive more than any other nationality – the average Peruvian drives 38,553 km each year!

c. 3,000,000 km: Distance travelled by light in 10 seconds.

3. India 3,320,410 km

2. China 3,860,800 km

*4,667,097 km: Distance clocked up as of December 2010 by a 1966 P-1800S Volvo owned by Irvin Gordon (USA), equivalent to 2.9 million miles, the **highest vehicle mileage** for a single car.*

*4,830,086 km: Distance driven by professional truck driver William Coe, Jr (USA) between 1986 and 2009, the **greatest distance driven without accident in a commercial vehicle**.*

*5,565,600 km: Total distance covered annually by drivers for every kilometre of road in Hong Kong, the nation with the **most used road network** in the world. The **most crowded roads**, however, are in Kuwait, where there are nearly 271 vehicles per kilometre of road!*

1. USA 6,506,204 km

Source: The Economist

EPIC ENGINEERING

Largest concrete dam

The Three Gorges Dam on the Yangtze River in China, was begun on 14 December 1994, and was operational from 2005. It has a concrete volume of 14.86 million m³ (525 million ft³) and is 2,335 m (7,661 ft) long, with the top 185 m (607 ft) above sea level. The dam is still in progress, but it is reported to be the most expensive single construction project on Earth, with unofficial estimates over US $75 billion (£43.5 billion).

Highest dam
The Nurek Dam, on the Vakhsh River in Tajikistan is 300 m (984 ft) high and was completed in 1980.

Longest dam
Completed in 1964, the Kiev Reservoir across the Dnieper River in Ukraine has a crest length of 41.2 km (25.6 miles).

Longest rubber dam
The Xiaobudong Rubber Dam, on the Yihe river in Shandong Province, China, measures 1,135 m (3,723 ft) long and consists of 16 sections, each 70 m (229 ft) long. It was completed on 1 July 1997.

Strongest dam
The Sayano-Shushenskaya Dam on the Yenisey River in Russia, is designed to bear a record load of 18 million tonnes (19,841,600 tons) from a fully filled reservoir of 31,300 million m³ (1,100,000 million ft³) capacity. The dam, which was completed in 1987, is 803 ft. (245 m) high.

AT SEA

Longest bridge spanning open sea
The 36-km-long (22.4-mile) Hangzhou Bay Bridge, linking the cities of Cixi and Zhapu in the Zhejiang Province of China, is the bridge spanning the greatest width of open ocean. Construction on the £860 million ($1.4 billion) bridge began in June 2003 and ended in 2007. It was officially opened in 2008.

Longest suspension bridges

1. Akashi-Kaikyō Bridge
Length: 1,990.8 m (6,532 ft)
Links: mainland Japan (Honshu) to Shikoku Island
Built: 1998

2. Xihoumen Bridge
Length: 1,650 m (5,414 ft)
Links: mainland China to Zhoushan Archipelago
Built: 2009

3. Great Belt Bridge
Length: 1,624 m (5,328 ft)
Links: Danish islands of Zealand and Funen
Built: 1998

ON LAND

Longest bridge
The Danyang-Kunshan Grand Bridge on the Jiangsu high-speed railway (from Beijing to Shanghai) is 164 km (102 miles) long. This line, opened in June 2011, also crosses the 114-km (70.8-mile) Langfang–Qingxian viaduct, the second longest bridge in the world.

Longest bridge over continuous water
The Second Lake Pontchartrain Causeway, completed in 1969, joins Mandeville and Metairie, Louisiana, USA and is 38.42 km (23.87 miles) long.

Longest footbridge
The 2.06-km (1.28-mile) Poughkeepsie Bridge (also known as the "Walkway Over the Hudson State Historic Park") in New York, USA, was re-opened to the public on 3 October 2009 as the world's longest pedestrian bridge.

Longest road bridge
The six-lane elevated Bang Na Expressway (also known as the Burapha Withi Expressway) runs for 54 km (33.5 miles) through Bangkok, Thailand, and was constructed using 1.8 million m³ (63.5 million ft³) of concrete. It was opened on 7 February 2000 at a cost of $1 billion (then £770 million).

Longest canal
The Belomorsko-Baltiysky Kanal, or the White Sea-Baltic Canal, from Belomorsk to Povenets in Russia, is 227 km (141 miles) long and has 19 locks. It was built using forced labour between 1930 and 1933.

Longest big-ship canal
The Suez Canal in Egypt, linking the Red and Mediterranean Seas, is 162.2 km (100.8 miles) long from Port Said lighthouse to the town of Suez. Opened on 17 November 1869, it took 10 years to build, with a workforce of 1.5 million, of whom 120,000 died during the construction. It has a maximum width of 365 m (1,198 ft).

Highest cable-stayed bridge

A cable-stayed bridge has cables supporting the bridge deck from one or more columns (often called towers or pylons). The deck of the 1,124-m-long (3,688-ft) cable-stayed Baluarte Bicentennial Bridge in Mexico is, at its highest point, 402.57 m (1,321 ft) above the average water level of the Baluarte River. The bridge is supported by 12 concrete towers, the tallest of which measures 153 m (502 ft) from its underground foundations to the road level.

Highest suspension bridge

FACT: To build this bridge, the first cable to be secured was fired across the valley with a rocket.

The deck of the Si Du River Bridge in Badong County, Hubei, China, is 472 m (1,549 ft) above the bottom of the valley – more than high enough to accommodate the Empire State Building beneath it.

Ship with greatest lifting capacity

The MV *Fairplayer* and MV *Javelin*, operated by Jumbo Shipping of Rotterdam, Netherlands, are J-class mega-ships with two Huisman mast cranes each capable of carrying a load of 900 tonnes (992 tons), giving a lifting capacity of 1,800 tonnes (1,984 tons). Each cargo ship has a transport capacity (deadweight tonnage or DWT) of 12,673 tonnes (13,969 tons). Particularly heavy loads are welded to the deck.

Heaviest object lifted at sea

The crane vessel *Saipem 7000*, the second largest in the world, broke the offshore weightlifting record when it transported a 12,150-tonne (13,393-ton) single integrated deck (SID) from a heavy-transport carrier to the Sabratha platform in Libya's Bahr Essalam gas field in October 2004. The lift took just four hours to complete. The lifting capacity, from two 140-m-long (459-ft) 15,600-hp (11,630-kW) fully revolving Amhoist cranes, is 14,000 tonnes (15,432 tons).

Largest cruise ship

At 362 m (1,187 ft) long, 66 m (216 ft) wide and weighing 225,282 gross tonnage, MS *Allure of the Seas* (USA) is the largest passenger ship. It has 16 passenger decks and can take 6,318 passengers.

Largest container ship

With a length of 397 m (1,300 ft), a beam of 56 m (183 ft) and a depth from deck to keel of 30 m (98 ft), the MV *Emma Maersk* (Denmark) is the largest container vessel. It could fill a freight train over 70 km (43.5 miles) long.

Largest land vehicle

The largest machine capable of moving under its own power is the 14,196-tonne (31.3-million-lb) RB293 bucket wheel excavator, manufactured by MAN TAKRAF of Leipzig, Germany. Used to move earth in an open-cast coal mine in the German state of North Rhine-Westphalia, it is 220 m (722 ft) long, 94.5 m (310 ft) tall, and capable of shifting 240,000 m³ (8.475 million ft³) of earth per day.

Largest tunnel boring machine

FACT: The Mixshield can tunnel distances of up to 26 m (85 ft) per day.

The Mixshield tunnel boring machine built by Herrenknecht AG (Germany) measures 15.43 m (50 ft 7.48 in) in diameter and weighs 2,300 tonnes (5.07 million lb). Two Mixshields were used to create two tunnels under the Yangtze River in China from Shanghai to Changxing Island. The tunnels, built from 2006 to 2008, are 7.47 km (4.64 miles) long and 65 m (213 ft) deep.

隧道股份

BRIDGE TYPES

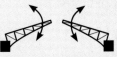

Drawbridge (bascule)

Has two "leaves" that can be raised to enable ships to pass underneath; the **longest drawbridge** is the Charles Berry Bridge across the Black River in Lorain, Ohio, USA, at 101.5 m (333 ft).

Span suspension bridge

Deck is suspended by cables attached to vertical supports; the **longest suspension bridge for both road and rail traffic** – with a main span of 1,377 m (4,517 ft), a width of 40 m (131.2 ft) and a length of 2.2 km (1.3 miles) – is the Tsing Ma Bridge in Hong Kong (China).

Steel arch bridge

Deck passes beneath a steel arch and through (often) concrete supports; the **longest steel arch bridge** is the Chongqing-Chaotianmen Bridge over the Yangtze River in China with a main span of 552 m (1,811 ft).

Swing bridge

Movable bridge that pivots horizontally (as opposed to upwards like a drawbridge). The El Ferdan Railway Bridge across the Suez Canal near Ismailia, Egypt, has a central span of 340 m (1,115 ft) that rotates 90° in order to allow ships to pass and is the world's **longest swing bridge**.

Tibetan bridge

A narrow walkway between two banks and supported loosely by cables or ropes; the world's **longest Tibetan bridge** has a span of 374 m (1,227 ft) over the river Po in Turin, Italy.

CONTENTS

Largest particle accelerator

The Large Hadron Collider – a 27-km-long (17-mile) circular tunnel underground on the Franco-Swiss border near Geneva, Switzerland – is history's largest and most complex machine. Its purpose is to smash together two opposing beams of protons at very high energies, to study the results. In use, the collider's 9,300 magnets are frozen at -271.3°C (-456.3°F), colder than deep space, making the collider the world's **largest fridge**!

WHAT'S THE SPEED LIMIT?

Can anything travel faster than light?

The biggest news in physics in 2011 was the revelation that the **fastest speed possible** may have been broken. One of the backbones of science is that nothing can travel faster than the speed of light in a vacuum. This speed limit affects everything – heat, gravity, radio waves. But an experiment that fired tiny particles called neutrinos through the Earth towards a detector seemed to show these subatomic particles travelled very slightly faster than the speed of light. Was our understanding of the universe wrong?

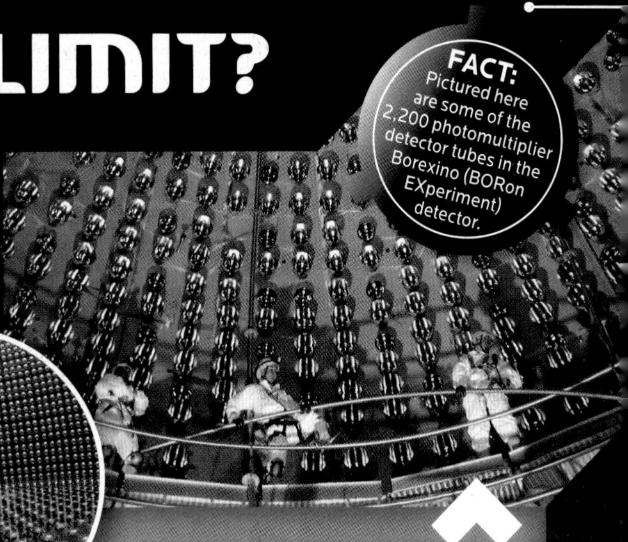

CERN
The European Organization for Nuclear Research, CERN, is an international laboratory in the suburbs of Geneva. It was founded in 1954 and currently consists of 21 member countries. Its biggest project is the Large Hadron Collider.

1. Pions and kaons
To create the neutrinos, a beam of protons is first generated by the Super Proton Synchrotron (SPS) at CERN. The beam of protons hits a graphite target that creates subatomic particles known as pions and kaons.

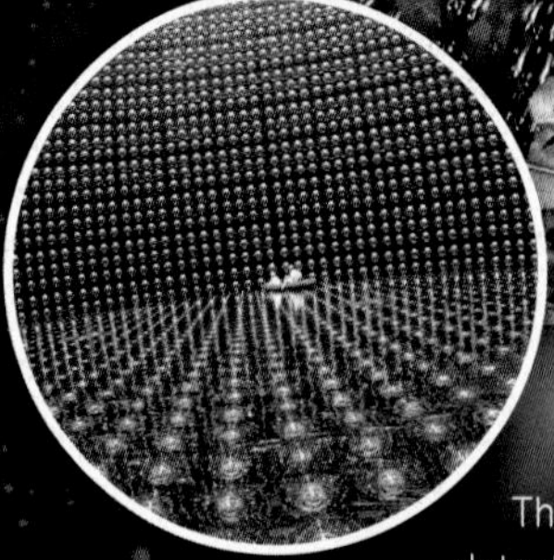

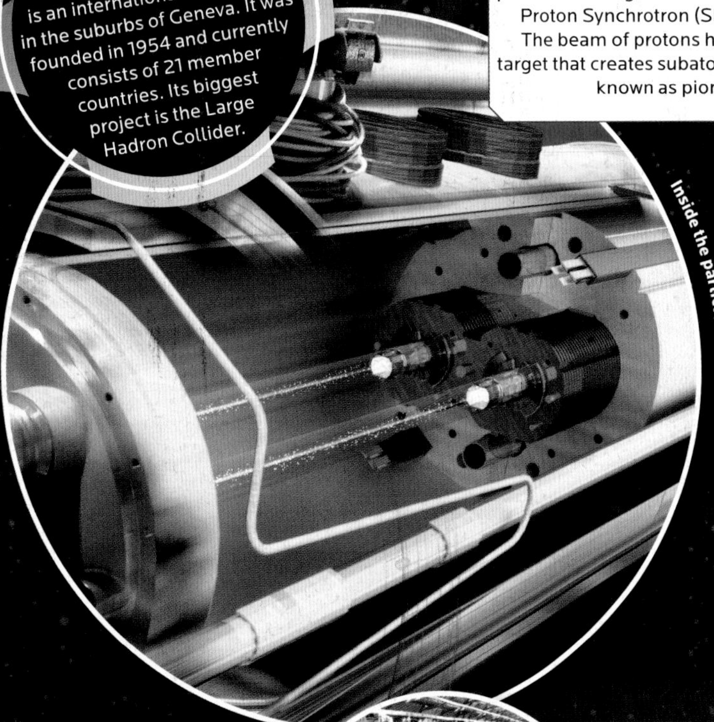

Borexino
The Borexino Experiment is designed to detect low-energy neutrinos emanating from the Sun. Situated underground at Gran Sasso, Italy, it is shielded from cosmic rays but not from neutrinos, which pass through the rock around it. Photomultiplier tubes detect individual photons produced whenever a neutrino from the Sun interacts with an atom in the detector's internal fluid (inset, showing liquid filling the detector).

Neutrinos, unlike protons and electrons, have no electric charge. They can easily pass through matter. Every second, the Sun produces over two hundred trillion trillion trillion of them, and every second, billions of them pass through your body.

The sensational results of 2011 came from a beam of artificial neutrinos fired from CERN in Switzerland, home to the Large Hadron Collider. The beam was aimed through the Earth to the OPERA detector at Gran Sasso in Italy, 732 km (454 miles) away. The mystery was that the CERN neutrinos appeared to arrive 60.7 billionths of a second earlier than they should have, if travelling at the speed of light.

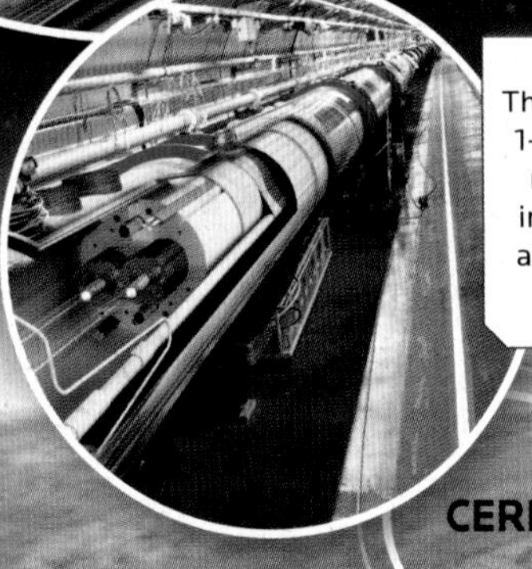

Inside the particle accelerator

2. Neutrinos
The subatomic particles produced by the SPS enter a 1-km-long (0.62-mile) tunnel, where they decay into muons and muon neutrinos. They are then focused into a beam and fired in the direction of the detector at Gran Sasso. When these particles encounter solid rock, only the muon neutrinos pass through.

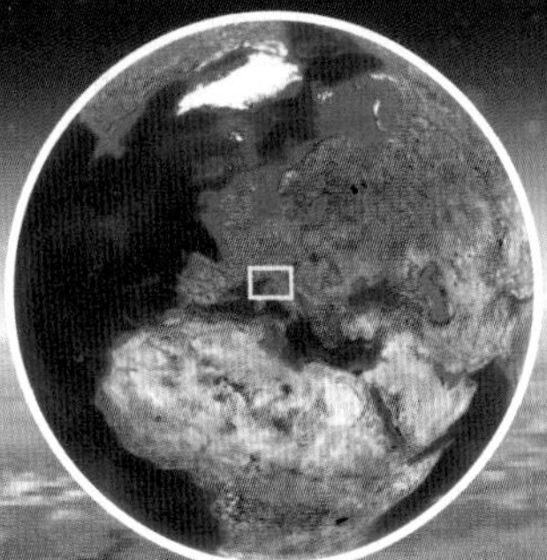

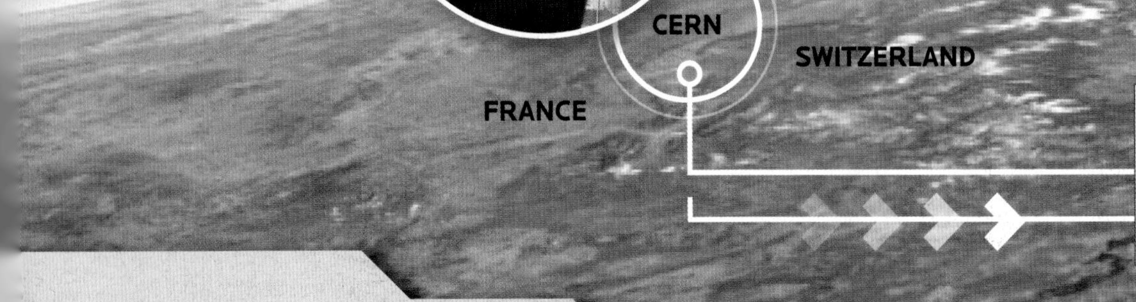

CERN
SWITZERLAND
FRANCE

3. Through the Earth
The neutrinos travel straight through the Earth – 11.4 km (7 miles) from the surface at the deepest point – and make the 732-km (454-mile) journey to Italy. GPS is used to monitor even the most subtle shifting of the Earth.

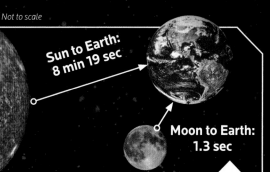

Not to scale

Sun to Earth: 8 min 19 sec

Moon to Earth: 1.3 sec

Speed of light

Albert Einstein's Theory of Special Relativity proposes that the speed of light is the maximum speed at which all energy and matter can travel. The idea that light has a "speed" was first demonstrated by Denmark's Ole Christensen Rømer (1644–1710), whose studies of the moons of Jupiter led to a better understanding of how light travels. Today, the speed is ratified as a constant by the Conférence Générale des Poids et Mesures – the body that manages the International System of Units.

FACT: $E = mc^2$ is Einstein's most famous equation. It is a direct result of his Theory of Special Relativity.

Measuring the speed of light
The figures below track the increasing accuracy with which scientists throughout history have determined the speed of light.

Date:	Scientist:	Speed of light (km/s):
1675	Ole Rømer (Denmark) and Christiaan Huygens (Netherlands)	220,000
1729	James Bradley (UK)	301,000
1849	Hippolyte Fizeau (France)	315,000
1862	Léon Foucault (France)	298,000±500
1907	Edward Rosa and Noah Dorsey (both USA)	299,710±30
1926	Albert Michelson (USA)	299,796±4
1950	Louis Essen and A C Gordon-Smith (both UK)	299,792.5 ±30
1958	Keith Davy Froome (UK)	299,792.5 ±0.10
1972	K M Evenson (USA) et al	299,792.4562 ±0.0011
1983	17th Conférence Générale des Poids et Mesures	299,792.458 (exact)

The OPERA team measured the speed of the CERN neutrinos 16,000 times, and each result showed the particles arriving faster than they should have. The race was on to independently measure neutrino velocities. If a different lab could confirm the results, then the speed of light barrier could indeed have been broken.

The ICARUS experiment, also at Gran Sasso, used liquid argon to detect neutrinos arriving in the beam from CERN and found no sign of the faster-than-light anomaly. In the meantime, the team at OPERA discovered a faulty connection between a fibre optic cable and a GPS receiver used to synchronize timing measurements between CERN and Gran Sasso. It seems that scientists including Albert Einstein and James Clerk Maxwell were right all along and that the speed of light *is* the **fastest possible speed in the universe**, even for neutrinos!

5. OPERA detector
The OPERA detector consists of 150,000 "bricks" of photographic film separated by lead sheets. It is located underground at Gran Sasso, insulating it from other particles and radiation which cannot pass through matter as easily as neutrinos. When a neutrino does interact with the matter making up the bricks, the photographic film records the event, which can then be analysed by developing the film in each brick separately.

Gran Sasso National Laboratory

4. Gran Sasso
At Gran Sasso, the neutrinos arrive and are detected by OPERA after travelling 732 km through Earth's crust in just 0.0024 seconds. They appeared to be arriving 0.000000067 seconds earlier than they should have if they were obeying the speed of light.

ITALY

GRAN SASSO

732 km

SCIENCE FRONTIERS

Most detailed map of Antarctic bedrock

BEDMAP2, by the British Antarctic Survey (BAS), is a view of Antarctica beneath its ice. It is a digital map created from some 27 million data points collected by radar, which can "see" through the ice. The data has been compiled from measurements taken from aircraft, satellites and dog-sled teams. BEDMAP2 was first shown in December 2011, and updated the first BEDMAP, made in 2000.

Fastest camera

In December 2011, the Massachusetts Institute of Technology, USA, revealed a camera that acquires visual data from repetitive events at a rate of half a trillion frames per second. The camera, which builds up the data from many repetitions of the event, therefore has an effective shutter speed of two-trillionths of a second. It can show a pulse of light moving through a bottle.

Deepest multicellular life

In June 2011, scientists announced the discovery of a new species of nematode worm which lives at depths of 1.3–3.6 km (0.8–2.2 miles) below the Earth's surface. The nematodes (*Halicephalobus mephisto*) survive in rock fractures filled with fluid, where they eat bacteria. *Find out more on p.114.*

First living laser

In June 2011, Malte Gather and Seok Hyun Yun at the Wellman Center for Photomedicine at Massachusetts General Hospital, USA, announced they used a cell derived from the human kidney to create laser light. The scientists injected the kidney cell with DNA from glowing jellyfish, which made the kidney cell glow green when bombarded with blue light. By using mirrors, they eventually made the cell emit green laser light. The cell survived the process even after several minutes of emitting laser light.

Highest frequency microelectronic device

In January 2012, researchers at Technische Universität Darmstadt, Germany, announced they had created an experimental resonance tunnel diode less than 1 mm² (0.04 in²) which can transmit at 1.111 THz, or 1,111 billion cycles per second. The tiny transmitter, which works at room temperature, could lead to new methods in medical diagnostics.

Longest trapped antimatter

On 5 June 2011, scientists working on the ALPHA experiment at CERN, Geneva, Switzerland, reported they had successfully trapped 112 antihydrogen atoms for 16 minutes. The ALPHA experiment mixed antiprotons with positrons in a vacuum chamber, where they combined to form antihydrogen. This was then trapped within a magnetic bottle. The antihydrogen atoms were detected by turning off the magnetic field within the magnetic bottle and observing flashes of light as each antihydrogen atom met normal matter. Both the normal and antimatter atoms were annihilated.

Most accurate clock

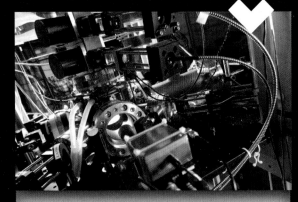

The caesium-fountain atomic clock, CsF2, at the UK's National Physical Laboratory, Teddington, London, is part of a global network of highly accurate atomic clocks providing consistent time measurements for the world. As of 26 August 2011, the CsF2 clock was accurate to one part in 4,300 trillion, meaning it would take 138 million years for it to lose or gain less than one second.

Largest Cherenkov telescope

The Major Atmospheric Gamma-ray Imaging Cherenkov (MAGIC) Telescope consists of a pair of almost identical telescopes on La Palma in the Canary Islands, Spain. Each telescope has a diameter of 17 m (55 ft 9 in) and a surface area of 236 m² (2,540 ft²). They detect faint blue Cherenkov radiation produced in the Earth's atmosphere by high-energy gamma rays from distant cosmic events. The two telescopes began operation in 2004 and 2009.

FACT:
The active mirror surfaces comprise 974 diamond-milled, quartz-coated aluminium pieces.

FACT:
The laser's energy could propel a 0.9-tonne (1-ton) vehicle at 161 km/h (100mi/h).

Highest laser energy (on a single target)

The laser at the National Ignition Facility at Lawrence Livermore National Laboratory, San Francisco, USA, consists of 192 laser beams. In October 2010, it fired a one-megajoule shot on a peppercorn-sized pellet of nuclear fuel. The energy crushed the pellet instantly, releasing about 10 trillion neutrons and signalling the successful fusion of some tritium and deuterium atoms. Ultimately, the objective is to create a fusion reaction that offers unlimited, pollution-free energy.

First image of charge distribution in a single molecule

On 27 February 2012, scientists at IBM Research in Zurich, Switzerland, announced that they had used "Kelvin probe force microscopy" to image and measure the positive and negative charge distribution in a molecule of naphthalocyanine. This breakthrough should make it possible to investigate charges at a molecular level when chemical bonds are formed.

Darkest man-made substance

A low-density carbon-nanotube array created by researchers from Rensselaer Polytechnic Institute and Rice University (both USA) demonstrated reflectance of 0.045% when tested at Rensselaer Polytechnic Institute on 24 August 2007.

Smallest magnetic memory bit

In January 2012, IBM and the German Center for

Free-Electron Laser Science announced they had managed to store one bit of data on a storage device consisting of just 12 atoms of iron, measuring 4 x 16 nanometres. By comparison, a modern PC requires around one million atoms to do the same. The device was created atom by atom using a scanning tunnelling microscope at IBM's Almaden Research Center in San Jose, California, USA.

Fastest computer
The K computer at the RIKEN Advanced Institute for Computational Science in Kobe, Japan, is the world's fastest supercomputer, achieving 10.51 quadrillion calculations per second using LINPACK benchmarking. Built in conjunction with Fujitsu, it took its second consecutive top place in the TOP500 list – which ranks the most powerful supercomputers – in 2011.

Fastest-running humanoid robot

FACT:
The new ASIMO has improved hand dexterity – it can now open bottles and pour drinks into cups.

ASIMO (short for Advanced Step in Innovative Mobility) is the latest in a series of prototype humanoid robots developed by Honda (Japan) since 2000. On 8 November 2011, Honda revealed the latest ASIMO, which can run at 9 km/h (5.6 mi/h) with both feet momentarily leaving the ground.
For more robots, just turn the page.

Largest planetary rover

On 26 November 2011, NASA launched its Mars Science Laboratory mission towards the planet Mars. On board was the *Curiosity* rover, which is 3 m (9 ft 10 in) long and weighs 900 kg (1,984 lb), including 80 kg (176 lb) of scientific instruments. It is designed to travel at up to 0.09 km/h (0.056 mi/h) while it explores the geology of Gale crater on Mars.

Laser and camera to analyse rocks and soil

Meteorological sensor

Spectrometer and camera on robotic arm for close-up rock studies

Suspension built for driving over Mars rocks

Wheels double up as landing gear

EVOLUTION OF THE SUPERCOMPUTER

The human brain can perform no more than about five calculations per second, while the fastest computers (see left) can now perform more than 10 quadrillion calculations in the same time. Here we look at the number of calculations (operations) per second by computers over time:

OPS *Operations per second*	1943	5,000 OPS
	1944	100,000 OPS
	1955	400,000 OPS
MFLOPS *Millions of floating point operations per second (FLOPS)*	1960	1.2 MFLOPS
	1964	3 MFLOPS
	1969	36 MFLOPS
	1974	100 MFLOPS
	1976	250 MFLOPS
	1981	400 MFLOPS
	1983	941 MFLOPS
GFLOPS *Gigaflops: 10^9 – 1,000,000,000 (one billion) – FLOPS*	1984	2.4 GFLOPS
	1985	3.9 GFLOPS
	1989	10 GFLOPS
	1990	23.2 GFLOPS
	1993	43 GFLOPS
	1994	170 GFLOPS
	1996	368 GFLOPS
TFLOPS *Teraflops: 10^{12} – 1,000,000, 000,000 (one trillion) – FLOPS*	1997	1.34 TFLOPS
	1999	2.38 TFLOPS
	2000	7.23 TFLOPS
	2002	35.8 TFLOPS
	2004	70.7 TFLOPS
	2005	280 TFLOPS
	2007	478 TFLOPS
PFLOPS *Petaflops: 10^{15}– 1,000, 000, 000, 000,000 (one quadrillion) – FLOPS*	2008	1.1 PFLOPS
	2009	1.76 PFLOPS
	2010	2.5 PFLOPS
	2011	10.51 PFLOPS

Sources: Peer1 Hosting; TOP500

AI & ROBOTICS

Most advanced synthetic human brain

Researchers at the Blue Brain Project, part of the Swiss Federal Institute of Technology in Lausanne, are building an artificial human brain by simulating the operation of individual brain cells, or "neurons", inside a supercomputer. In 2008, scientists on the project perfected the software needed to describe the behaviour of a human "neocortical column" – a sub-unit in the brain, consisting of some 10,000 neurons. In 2011, 100 of these virtual neocortical columns were joined together to form a network of a million artificial neurons. This marks the most sophisticated software emulation of a human brain to date.

Deadliest anti-personnel robot

In 2010, South Korea recruited some serious robotic firepower in the form of the Super aEgis 2 – a robot sentry gun packing a heavy-duty 12-mm machine gun, 40-mm grenade launcher and even surface-to-air missiles. The weapon uses infrared sensors and a camera to lock on to human targets up to 3 km (1.8 miles) away in daylight and 2.2 km (1.3 miles) at night. Targets are recognized and tracked in the images using sophisticated artificial intelligence algorithms. A laser range-finder enables the computer to adjust its aim, while a gyroscope helps it correct for recoil.

First AI robot toy

The Furby – built by Tiger Electronics (Japan) – was the first truly robotic cyber pet with artificial intelligence (AI). It went on sale in 1998 and took the form of a cuddly toy, resembling Gizmo from the *Gremlins* movies, which had to be fed (by placing objects in its mouth to activate a button), could "learn" to speak English and would take naps (snoring as it did so). It sold in excess of 40 million units in three years.

Most life-like android

In March 2011, a team of scientists from Osaka University and robotics company Kokoro (both Japan) unveiled an android – a robot with features modelled closely on those of a human – the most life-like yet. Named Geminoid DK, the android has been made in the likeness of technology professor Henrik Scharfe, of Aalborg University in Denmark. It cost $200,000 (£123,674) to develop.

First computer film critic

British company Epagogix has developed an artificial intelligence computer program that can accurately predict the box-office returns of movies. First, human readers score a prospective script, assigning numerical values to hundreds of variables describing its content. The software then compares these numbers to those of previously released movies – together with their box-office receipts – which yields a forecast of what a full production of the new script is likely to make. The company claims its software can estimate a movie's box office takings to within +/- $10 million (£6.3 million).

FACT: Geminoid DK has rubber "skin". Pneumatic devices enable it to show expressions and move.

Biggest stock-market crash caused by automated trading

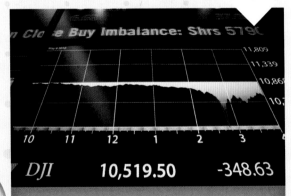

On 6 May 2010, the Dow Jones, an index of value on the US stock market, plunged more than 600 points (about 6%). It recovered 20 minutes later. Dubbed the "flash crash", it was thought to have been caused by "algorithmic trading" – a term that describes AI computers trading automatically in accordance with pre-programmed rules.

FACT: An algorithm is a set of instructions that a computer can follow to carry out a calculation.

Highest score on a quiz show by a computer

In 2011, IBM fielded a computer named "Watson" in the US TV game show *Jeopardy!* against two highly successful contestants; it comprehensively defeated them both, winning $77,147 (£48,734). On many questions, its opponents simply couldn't press their buzzers fast enough to beat the machine. Prior to the game, engineers fed Watson with a huge volume of data. This not only taught it how humans communicate, but also turned it into a general-knowledge genius.

First computer to beat a world chess champion (regular time controls)

On 11 May 1997, world chess champion Garry Kasparov (Russia) was beaten by the IBM chess computer Deep Blue – a super-powerful parallel processor capable of evaluating 200 million board positions every second, and holding in its memory details of 700,000 past games played by grandmasters.

First poker bot to beat human professionals in a live tournament

In 2008, a program called "Polaris", written by computer scientists from the University of Alberta, Canada, beat a six-strong team of human professionals in a tournament held in Las Vegas, USA. Against each of the pros, it played a 500-hand game of Limit Texas Holdem ("limit" means the bet sizes are fixed). Whoever finished each game with the most chips was the winner. Polaris won three games, lost two and tied one.

Fastest time to solve a Rubik's Cube by a robot

A robot can now solve a Rubik's Cube faster than a human. On 11 November 2011, CubeStormer II finished a scrambled 3 x 3 cube in 5.27 seconds at *Wired* magazine's offices in London, UK. It was commissioned by ARM Holdings and built by Mike Dobson and David Gilday (all UK) from four LEGO Mindstorms NXT kits and a Samsung Galaxy S2 mobile phone. The human record, held by Feliks Zemdegs (Australia), stood at 5.66 seconds as of 18 February 2012.

First AI scientist

In 2009, researchers at the Creative Machines Lab, part of Cornell University in New York, USA, unveiled a software program called Eureqa. Feed the program some data on pretty much anything and it will try to come up with a mathematical law explaining how the data is related. As a proof of concept, the team fed the program data on the motion of a pendulum – to which it responded by "discovering" Newton's second law of motion and the conservation of energy.

> **Brain that learns from errors**

> **FACT:** Unlike androids, humanoid robots are not necessarily designed with human-like faces.

> **Single eye powerful enough to match human stereoscopic vision**

> **Tendons, muscles and bones made from a special plastic**

> **FACT:** Ecci's name derives from the Latin word "ecce", meaning "behold".

Most advanced humanoid robot

In June 2011, scientists at the University of Zurich, Switzerland, unveiled a remarkable humanoid robot called Ecci. The robot has the electromechanical equivalent of muscles, tendons and nerves to move the bones in its skeleton. These are controlled by a highly advanced synthetic brain – a computer that learns from its experiences. This enables Ecci to develop coordination skills and ensure that it doesn't repeat its mistakes. Ecci's development involved 25 scientists, working for a period of three years.

> **Electric motors move joints**

> **Rotatable forearms**

TURN TO P.204, WHERE SCIENCE MEETS SCI-FI

RISE OF THE ROBOTS

The idea of a machine capable of independent movement dates back to ancient times. Mechanisms for entertainment, such as toy figures, clockwork toys and music boxes, have existed for centuries. But genuinely functional robots, or machines capable of processing calculations, are a far more recent development...

MECHANICAL CALCULATOR

Definition: any automated counting device

First example: Antikythera Mechanism, considered the **oldest analogue computer** (early 1st century BC)

INDUSTRIAL ROBOT

Definition: non-human-like machine used to perform tasks in industrial manufacturing

First example: Unimate robot, introduced by General Motors (1961)

HUMANOID

Definition: more autonomous robot; anthropomorphic structure: head, arms, trunk, sometimes legs

First example: WABOT-1 (1973)

ANDROID
(female equivalent: "gynoid")

Definition: robot with features that convincingly mimic those of humans, and which can process information and respond to it

First examples: early 2000s, including the Actroid and EveR-1 (both 2003)

CYBORG

Definition: partly mechanical, partly organic being, fitted with integral, advanced technology*

First example: British scientist Kevin Warwick, who implanted an electronic chip into his nervous system (2002)

* not including humans with artificial aids, such as hearing aids, prosthetic limbs or false eyes

NUMBERS

Most irrational number

Numbers are considered "irrational" if they cannot be written down precisely as a fraction or in decimal form, – you would need an infinite number of digits. The geometric constant pi is one example (see below).

The most irrational number is 1 plus the square root of 5 all divided by 2 – a figure roughly equal to 1.618. This number is known as the "Golden Ratio". Shapes with side lengths in this proportion tend to be especially pleasing to the eye – a fact that was known to artists and architects dating back to the 5th century BC. The painting above, which uses the "Golden Ratio", is *Bathers at Asnières* (1884) by Georges Pierre Seurat.

Most precise value of pi

Pi (π) is a number that is frequently used in geometry, where it denotes the ratio of a circle's circumference to its diameter. It has the value 3.141592, but that is only the value to six decimal places – in fact, as it is an "irrational" number, it is impossible to write down its full value. The most digits of pi ever calculated were worked out in 2011 by Shigeru Kondo (Japan) and student Alexander J Yee (USA). Kondo used computer software written by Yee to calculate pi to 10,000,000,000,000 (10 trillion) decimal places – a computation that took 371 days!

Oldest irrational number

The first irrational number discovered was the square root of 2, by Hippasus of Metapontum (then part of Magna Graecia in southern Italy), in around 500 BC.

Largest named number

The largest lexicographically accepted named number in the system of successive powers of 10 is the "centillion", first recorded in 1852. It is the hundredth power of a million, or 1 followed by 600 noughts (although only in the UK and Germany).

The words googol (10^{100}) and googolplex (10^{googol}) have entered the language to describe large numbers but are mostly used informally.

Largest prime number

A "prime" number is any positive number divisible only by 1 and itself. The largest prime number found to date was discovered by the Great Internet Mersenne Prime Search project on 23 August 2008. It is a Mersenne prime, which means it can be written as $2^n - 1$, where "n" is a power; $2^{43112609} - 1$ contains around 12,978,189 digits. The **lowest prime number** is 2.

Lowest composite number

A "composite" number is a number higher than 1 that can be divided exactly by numbers other than 1 or itself. Examples are 22 (2 x 11) and 20 (2 x 10, 4 x 5). The lowest of the composite numbers is 4.

Largest hyperbolic crochet

The ancient Greek philosopher Euclid argued that parallel lines remain parallel forever. Later, however, mathematicians realized that his laws only apply in flat space. On the Earth's curved surface, for example, lines of longitude are parallel at the equator but cross at the poles. Mathematicians have also envisaged theoretical curved spaces in which lines start as parallel but then diverge; such "hyperbolic" spaces have a kind of saddle shape. Daina Taimina, a Latvian mathematician, has crocheted models of hyperbolic shapes, the largest of which measures 70 x 70 x 50 cm (27.5 x 27.5 x 19.6 in) and weighs 6.3 kg (13 lb 14 oz). It is woven from 7.8 km (4.8 miles) of yarn.

Lowest perfect number

A number is said to be "perfect" if it is equal to the sum of all its divisors (i.e., all the other numbers that go into that number exactly) other than itself. For example, 28 is perfect: 1 + 2 + 4 + 7 + 14 = 28. The next two perfect numbers are 496 and 8,128. The lowest perfect number is therefore 6, as 1 + 2 + 3 = 6.

Oldest unsolved number problem

All the perfect numbers discovered so far are even – but could a perfect number ever be odd? This puzzle perplexed the ancient Greeks, back to the time of Nicomachus of Gerasa in the 1st century

FACT: Coral grows "hyperbolically", expanding its surface area to take in more nutrients.

and maybe even back as far as Euclid, who lived 500 years earlier. In the centuries since, other mathematicians, including Pierre de Fermat and René Descartes, have attempted a solution but none has so far succeeded.

Newer number

Most numbers are not invented or discovered; they just "are". But one number had to be invented: zero. It was

Fastest time to complete an Easy Sudoku puzzle

Thomas Snyder (USA) completed an Easy Sudoku puzzle in 2 min 8.53 sec at BookExpo America, Washington, DC, USA, on 20 May 2006. Sudoku is one of the world's most popular number puzzles – pictured inset are some of the 1,714 students from Fairfield Methodist Primary School in Singapore who set the record for **most people playing Sudoku simultaneously**, on 1 August 2008.

introduced by the Babylonians in the 4th century BC to indicate nothing – the absence of any other number. Originally, the Babylonians used a space (and later a placeholder symbol) between numerals to indicate the lack of a digit or value; the actual symbol "0" did not arise until the 8th century in India.

Longest proof

Originally proposed in 1971 by Daniel Gorenstein, the "Enormous Theorem" relates to the symmetry of geometric shapes. It took 100 mathematicians and some 15,000 pages of workings to prove it, a task that was finally completed in 2004.

Culture with the fewest numbers

The Pirahã tribe, who live in the Amazon region of Brazil, South America, have a very special vocabulary: it has no numbers. As a result, the Pirahã are unable to count (though they do have expressions for "more than" and "less than"). Other linguistically innumerate societies (such as Australia's aborigines) borrow number systems from other languages, but the Pirahã seem to show no interest in learning to count.

Most popular number

Of the numbers 1–9, the most commonly occurring is the number 1. You might expect all numbers to occur with equal likelihood. But studies of data in many forms, from train times to fundamental constants of nature, show that 1 crops up with a probability of 30%, and that higher numbers occur with steadily diminishing frequency.

Longest binary number memorized in five minutes

The everyday numbers we use are termed "base-10", meaning there are 10 basic numbers (0, 1, 2, 3, 4, 5, 6, 7, 8, 9) from which all others are constructed. For example, 625 stands for six hundreds, two tens and five units. The term "binary" is another name for base-2 numbering. In binary, there are just two basic numbers: 0 and 1. The number 6 would be written 110 – one 4, one 2 and zero units. In 2008, Ben Pridmore (UK) set the world record for memorizing the most binary digits in five minutes – accurately reciting every digit from a randomly generated sequence 930 digits long. Ben set his impressive record at the 2008 UK Memory Championships in London, UK, and he was also the overall winner of the event. *See right for a binary record attempt that you can try yourself.*

Largest Menger sponge

A Menger sponge (named after its originator, Austrian mathematician Karl Menger) is a kind of fractal made by taking a cube, dividing each face into nine squares (like a Rubik's cube) and from each face removing the middle square and all the material beneath it. The process is then repeated on every remaining square on the cube. The largest model of a Menger sponge measures 1.4 m (4 ft 6 in) along each side and weighs 70 kg (154 lb 5 oz). It was built from 66,048 business cards by computer scientist Dr Jeannine Mosely (USA). She spent 10 years on the task, finishing in 2005.

FACT:
A fractal is a geometric shape. Small regions resemble copies of the original fractal.

Fastest time to type from 1 to 1,000,000

Les Stewart (Australia, right), has typed from 1 to 1,000,000, in words, on 19,990 sheets of quarto-sized paper. Starting in 1982, he became a "millionaire" on 7 December 1998.

In a related record attempt in 2007, Jeremy Harper (USA, inset) verbally counted up to one million in a series of live internet broadcasts. Starting on 18 June 2007, he reached 1,000,000 on 14 September 2007, after 89 days, averaging just over 11,200 numbers per day – the **highest sequence of numbers counted out loud**.

FACT:
As of March 2012, the last stages of Jeremy's feat are still viewable at: http://bit.ly/cOT1IC

PUT YOUR BRAIN TO THE TEST – AND BREAK A RECORD

Jayasimha Ravirala (India) committed to memory a binary number sequence consisting of a record 264 numbers, in just one minute, at the Holy Mary Institute of Technology in Hyderabad, India, on 8 March 2011. (It took him 9 minutes to accurately recall every number!) Can you beat his record? Below is a string of 265 numbers, and if you can memorize them all in just one minute, you'll be a record-breaker. Give it a go!

```
1111011001011001111110111
0011011111001001010010
0000111001001000000101
0010011001001111000110
0100001101000010000110
1111100010110001100000
1011101011011110010010 0
0000001101111101000110
0111010010000011101110 1
1001001101001000001000
0000101010101110000101
00100011100100010000
```

Mathletics

If mind-blowing maths is more your thing, could you beat the feat of France's Alex Lemaire (below)? On 10 December 2007, in an event organized by the Science Museum, in London, UK, this "mathlete" was able to mentally evaluate the 13th root of a randomly generated 200-digit number (i.e., he found a number which when multiplied by itself 13 times gave the original 200-digit answer).

Lemaire completed this feat in just 70.2 seconds, calculating a value for the 13th root of:

83,689,466,882,369,569, 398,373,286,622,256,452, 247,267,804,664,938,366, 774,973,575,581,573,035, 075,704,089,625,288,023, 857,831,568,376,802,934, 938,201,056,343,363,855, 595,931,514,150,415,149, 490,709,419,097,704,449, 305,660,268,402,771,869, 624,155,688,082,648, 640,933

And here's the answer, just in case you were having trouble!

2,407,899,883,032,220

LIGHT FANTASTIC

Longest burning light bulb

The Livermore Centennial Light Bulb, at Firestation 6 in Livermore, California, USA, has been burning since it was installed in 1901. The hand-blown bulb has operated at about 4 watts, and has been left on 24 hours a day to provide illumination of the fire engines. In 2011, the city of Livermore threw a street party to celebrate the bulb's 110th birthday.

Longest underwater fibre-optic cable

Fibre-optic cables transmit light and form the basis of modern communication. There are many thousands of kilometres of fibre-optic cables at the bottom of the oceans. The longest of these "light pipes" is the Sea-Me-We-3 (South-East Asia–Middle East–Western Europe), which is 39,000 km (24,000 miles) long. Operated by India's Tata Communications and fully commissioned in late 2000, the cable provides a high-speed connection from Germany to Australia and Japan. From Germany, the cable runs around Europe via the North Sea, Atlantic and Mediterranean, then into the Red Sea and Indian Ocean. It splits in two just below Thailand; one branch goes north to Japan and one goes south to Australia.

Fastest single-core fibre-optic cable

In April 2011, NEC Laboratories, in Princeton, New Jersey, USA, demonstrated a data-sending rate of 101.7 terabits a second through 165 km (103 miles) of fibre-optic cable. This is the equivalent of sending 250 Blu-ray discs a second and was achieved by sending light from 370 separate lasers of different wavelength outputs into the fibre. Each laser emitted its own waveband of infrared light, containing several polarities, phases and amplitudes to code information.

Oldest light

The oldest light in the universe is the Cosmic Microwave Background (CMB), created in the Big Bang. The radiation has been cooled and stretched out by the expansion. It is present everywhere and almost uniformly distributed. It was discovered in 1964 by astronomers Arno Penzias and Robert Wilson (both USA), who noticed a faint glow in space not related to any star, galaxy, or other object. The current estimated age of the CMB light, and hence the universe itself, is 13.75 ± 0.13 billion years (4.336×10^{17} seconds in SI units, or 13.75 gigayears).

First calculation using an optical computer

In 2009, scientists at the University of Bristol, UK, used four photons of light to interact with silicon chips to implement an algorithm to calculate the factors of 15 (3 and 5). The calculation was a simple process, but the work should pave the way for super-fast optical computers that will ultimately calculate at the speed of light.

First hologram

In 1962, Emmett Leigh and Juris Upatnieks of the University of Michigan, USA, made the first hologram – a three-dimensional image captured on a two-dimensional surface. It showed a toy train and a bird and was captured on photographic silver halide film emulsion on glass. The image is viewed by shining a laser from behind the image. Later in 1962, Soviet physicist Yuri Denisyuk (1927–2006) invented what became known as a reflection hologram that could be viewed using a simple light bulb in front of the image. Capturing a three-dimensional image on a photographic plate was first conceived by Hungarian-British physicist Dennis Gabor (1900–79) in 1947. However, holography only became possible in the early 1960s with the development of the laser, which creates coherent light that generates an interference pattern.

First infrared photograph

Infrared light is electro-magnetic radiation with a wavelength longer than that of visible light – it sits beyond the "red" end of the spectrum. The first photographic emulsions capable of capturing infrared light were developed by Professor Robert Williams Wood (USA, 1868–1955). He published the first infrared photographs in the October

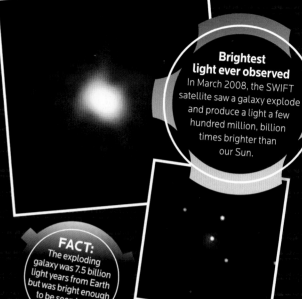

Brightest light ever observed
In March 2008, the SWIFT satellite saw a galaxy explode and produce a light a few hundred million, billion times brighter than our Sun.

FACT: The exploding galaxy was 7.5 billion light years from Earth but was bright enough to be seen by the naked eye.

Greatest colour vision

Stomatopod crustaceans, which include the mantis shrimps, contain eight different types of colour photoreceptor. This compares to four in most birds and reptiles, three in humans and other primates, and two in most other mammals. The stomatopods can distinguish numerous shades within the electromagnetic spectrum's ultraviolet waveband – which is entirely invisible to humans. The eyesight may be used to identify prey (which are often semi-transparent), or avoid predators.

Brightest bioluminescence
The fire beetle (Pyrophorus noctilucus), from the tropical regions of the Americas, has a brightness of 45 millilamberts (as bright as a modern single-LED torch).

ACTUAL SIZE

1910 Photographic Journal of the Royal Photographic Society (RPS). Today, infrared photography has many practical as well as artistic uses. Infrared cameras are used to detect changing blood flow, overheating in electrical apparatus and heat loss in buildings. Military night-vision devices also use infrared illumination – as do many household appliances including heaters, TV remote controls and the solid state lasers that play CDs.

Longest optical tape measure

Optical tape measures use lasers rather than a physical piece of tape and are used in the construction industry. The longest optical tape measure, however, works all the way to the Moon. Light from lasers based in the USA, France and Russia can be bounced off reflectors left on the Moon's surface from 1969 to 1971 by the astronauts of the USA's *Apollo* 11, 14 and 15 missions. From these lasers, it is possible to measure the distance of the Moon from the Earth. The distance averages 384,400 km (238,855 miles) now – but because the Moon moves away from the Earth by 38 mm (1.5 in) each year, this record will continually be broken. The light takes a 2.5-second round trip.

First living "neon" sign

Scientists at the University of California, San Diego, USA, have created bioluminescent bacteria that have been biologically programmed to synchronize their blue flashes like a neon sign. The scientists are hoping to use the bacteria as low-cost biosensors – in the presence of pollutants or disease-causing organisms, for instance, they would change the rate at which they flash.

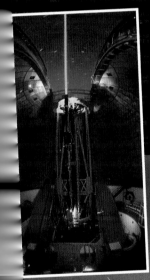

Largest light bulb

Appropriately, the world's largest light bulb is fixed at the top of the Thomas Alva Edison Memorial Tower, a monument dedicated to the inventor of the electric light bulb. It is 3.96 m (13 ft) tall, weighs 7,257 kg (8 tons) and is illuminated at night. The 40-m (131-ft) tower was built in 1937, on the site of Edison's laboratory in Menlo Park, New Jersey, USA.

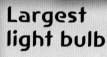

First artificial guide star

On 1 June, 1992, scientists at Lick Observatory and Lawrence Livermore National Labs (both in California, USA) shot a laser beam into the sky to create an artificial "star" of glowing atmospheric sodium ions. Astronomers used this star to observe how much "distortion" the Earth's atmosphere introduced into a telescope's image. They could then compensate for this distortion when viewing other objects in space, creating much more accurate images. The laser technology was developed from the USA's "Star Wars" missile defence system of the 1980s and 1990s.

COLOUR SPECTRUM

White light is comprised of many individual colours, or wavelengths, of light. The visible spectrum is one continuous band of electromagnetic radiation with decreasing wavelength (and increasing frequency).

620–740 nm RED

Red – *derives its name from the Sanskrit word for "blood"*

590–620 nm ORANGE

Orange – *named after the fruit (before which the colour was known as simply yellow-red)*

570–590 nm YELLOW

Yellow – *an ancient name with its origins in proto-European language. The first written record is believed to be in the ancient epic Beowulf, in which the unknown author uses the Old English word "geolwe" to describe a shield carved from a Yew tree (with yellowish wood)*

520–570 nm GREEN

Green – *name derived from the word for "grow"; exists in nature largely because of chlorophyll, the pigment in plants that allows the absorption of energy from sunlight*

450–470 nm BLUE

Blue – *the colour of the daytime sky. Why? Because particles in the atmosphere scatter light from the Sun; the portions of the spectrum with a shorter wavelength (i.e., blues) are scattered more than those with longer wavelengths (reds) so we see the sky as blue*

Indigo – *a subtle colour that's more difficult for the human eye to detect. The name is derived from the Greek word "Indic", describing a purplish-blue dye obtained from India*

Violet – *the last colour the human eye can perceive at the UV end of the spectrum; the effects of UV are visible whenever we acquire a suntan*

380–420 nm VIOLET

MAD SCIENCE

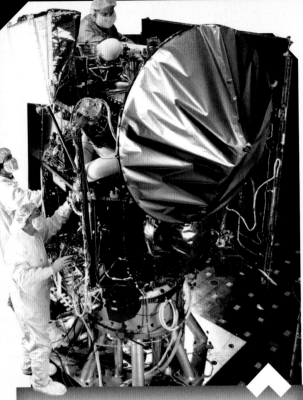

Most expensive conversion error

On 23 September 1999, NASA's *Mars Climate Orbiter* probe passed behind the planet Mars – and disintegrated in the Martian atmosphere. The cause? Human error. The on-board software had been written using metric units of thrust, but imperial units had been used to enter course correction commands from the ground. The mission had cost $327.6 million (£200.5 million).

Fastest cell

On 3 December 2011, the American Society for Cell Biology announced the results of their first World Cell Race: some 50 laboratories across the world chose different types of cell to compete in a race along a 0.4-mm (0.01-in) race track. The winner was a line of fetal mesenchymal bone marrow cells from Singapore, which were clocked at 5.2 microns per minute, or 0.000000312 km/h (0.000000194 mi/h).

Highest prize offered for a scientific proof of paranormal ability

The James Randi Educational Foundation Million Dollar Paranormal Challenge was first offered in 1968 by American magician and sceptic James Randi, initially as a prize of $100. The money has increased to $1 million (£631,305, as of 5 March 2012), which will be awarded to the first group to scientifically prove the existence of paranormal or supernatural abilities. Between 1997 and 2005, some 360 applications were made. No one has yet been awarded the prize.

Lowest Bacon number

In 1994, a trivia game emerged based on the "small world phenomenon", linking people in the movie industry to US actor Kevin Bacon (below right). A person's Bacon number marks the fewest steps from them to Bacon, based on movie appearances. For example, UK actor Sir Patrick Stewart was in *Star Trek Generations* (USA, 1994) with Glenn Morshower (USA), who was in *X-Men: First Class* (USA, 2011) with Bacon. This gives Stewart a Bacon number of 2. Kevin Bacon has the lowest Bacon number: zero.

Lowest Erdös–Bacon number

An Erdös–Bacon number is the sum of an "Erdös" number (the fewest steps to link academics to the prolific Hungarian mathematician Paul Erdös) and a "Bacon" number. Two people share the record for the lowest Erdös–Bacon number. Professor Daniel Kleitman (USA, right) has co-authored multiple research papers with Erdös, giving him an Erdös number of 1. Kleitman was also a consultant and extra in the movie *Good Will Hunting* (USA, 1997) – starring Minnie Driver (UK), who starred with Bacon in *Sleepers* (USA, 1997). This gives him a Bacon number of 2 and a resulting Erdös–Bacon number of 3.

Bruce Reznick (USA) was an extra in *Pretty Maids All in a Row* (USA, 1972) with Roddy McDowall (UK) – who starred with Bacon in *The Big Picture* (USA, 1989) – giving him a Bacon number of 2. Reznick also has an Erdös number of 1. This gives him an Erdös–Bacon number of 3.

First ESP experiment in space

On the Apollo 14 mission from 31 January to 9 February 1971, Lunar Module Pilot Edgar Mitchell tried a private, prearranged extra-sensory perception (ESP) experiment. He looked at, and thought about, five shapes on Zener cards, in random order, hoping that his thoughts would be received by four friends on Earth. Out of 200 attempts, his friends got 51 right.

FACT:
Daniel Kleitman (above) teaches applied mathematics at Massachusetts Institute of Technology.

First remote-controlled bull

In 1963, Spanish physiology professor José Manuel Rodriguez Delgado implanted a device he had created, called a "stimoceiver", into the brains of bulls at a breeding ranch in Córdoba, Spain. He was later able to use a hand-held transmitter to halt a charging bull by using the stimoceiver to stimulate the animal's caudate nucleus.

First complete robotic digestive system

Ecobot III was created in 2010 by scientists at the Bristol Robotics Laboratory (University of the West of England and University of Bristol), UK. It is a robot powered by organic matter, which, along with water, it can collect itself from its environment. The organic matter, which can include human waste, is digested by an array of 48 on-board microbial fuel cells in order to generate electricity. The organic waste products from this process are then excreted by the robot.

First graphene distillery

Discovered by scientists at the University of Manchester, UK, and the Institute for Microelectronics Technology, Russia, in 2004, graphene is the **thinnest material** known to science. It forms a sheet made from a single layer of carbon atoms and its discoverers earned the Nobel Prize in Physics in 2010. In January 2012, researchers at the University of Manchester announced they had used a membrane of graphene oxide to seal a bottle of vodka "just for a laugh", and discovered that the spirit became stronger over time as water molecules escaped through the membrane.

Largest Rube Goldberg
In 2012, the Purdue Society of Professional Engineers (PSPE) Rube Goldberg Team (all USA) made a machine with 300 "steps". Its goal? To blow up and pop a balloon.

First sensory deprivation tank

In 1954, US scientist John Lilly built a soundproofed and darkened tank filled with warm salty water, at body temperature, designed to isolate the human brain from external stimuli. Lilly – who, with a colleague, was the first person to try the tank – reported that he entered dream-like, euphoric states within its environment. Sensory deprivation tanks are now commonly used for meditation and in alternative therapies.

Longest man-made lightning

Nikola Tesla (Croatia) created the longest man-made bolt of lightning – 40 m (130 ft) – in 1899, at his laboratory in Colorado, USA. The accompanying thunderclap was reported to have been heard 35 km (22 miles) away.

Largest single dose of LSD administered

On 3 August 1963, Tusko, a 14-year-old Indian elephant residing at Oklahoma City Zoo, USA, was injected with 297 milligrams of the hallucinogenic drug LSD (lysergic acid diethylamide). The experiment was carried out by Louis Jolyon West, Chester M Pierce (both of University of Oklahoma School of Medicine) and Warren Thomas (Director of the zoo) to test if the drug could trigger a mental state known as "musth", a mad, often violent, hormonal surge during which bull elephants produce temporin (a sticky fluid) from glands between the ears and eyes. Tusko trumpeted once, ran around his enclosure, suffered a crippling seizure and died after 80 minutes.

ACTUAL SIZE

First electronic dialogue between nervous systems

In March 2002, UK scientist Kevin Warwick had a tiny 100-electrode array (seen above, on a UK 5p coin) set into the median nerve fibres of his left arm. A second implant was surgically added to Kevin's wife, Irena. The implants communicated over the internet, allowing Kevin to feel signals from Irena's implant. Via a radio transmitter/receiver connected to the implant, Kevin also interacted with objects without touching them. His arm movements are making his wife's necklace glow in the photograph above.

First heat-ray gun

The Active Denial System projects an invisible heat-energy microwave beam within a range of 500 m (1,640 ft). Typically, the gun is mounted on a Humvee vehicle, and while a human target would feel a burning sensation, the weapon is non-lethal. It was first publically demonstrated at Moody Air Force Base in Georgia, USA, on 24 January 2007.

First scientific probe into "tin-foil hats"

Many conspiracy theorists believe that a hat made from aluminium foil can protect the brain from telepathic interference. In 2005, a group of graduate students at the Massachusetts Institute of Technology (MIT), USA, concluded that foil hats can actually amplify radio signals at some frequencies that are controlled by the US government.

IG NOBEL PRIZE

A satirical version of the Nobel Prizes, the Ig Nobels have been awarded annually by the Annals of Improbable Research since 1991. Ten are awarded each year for research that "first makes people laugh and then makes them think". Recent awards include:

BIOLOGY, 2011
For discovering that a certain kind of beetle mates with a certain kind of Australian beer bottle.

PEACE, 2011
Awarded to the Mayor of Vilnius, Lithuania, for demonstrating that the problem of illegally parked luxury cars can be solved by running them over with an armoured tank.

MEDICINE, 2011
For demonstrating that people make better decisions about some kinds of things – but worse decisions about other kinds of things – when they have a strong urge to urinate.

ENGINEERING, 2011
For perfecting a method to collect whale snot using a remote-controlled helicopter.

2010, PHYSICS
For demonstrating that, on icy footpaths in wintertime, people slip and fall less often if they wear socks on the outside of their shoes.

MANAGEMENT, 2010
For demonstrating mathematically that organizations would become more efficient if they promoted people at random.

SCI-FI SCIENCE

its Sun-like star in around 290 days. The luminosity of its star, coupled with the orbital distance, means Kepler-22b is believed to reside within its star's habitable zone. If the planet has an Earth-like greenhouse effect then its surface temperature could be a comfortable 22°C (71.6°F).

EVOLUTION BECOMES REVOLUTION

RISE OF THE PLANET OF THE APES

IN CINEMAS AUGUST 4

First prehistoric extinct cloning project

Sci-fi: In *Jurassic Park*, extinct dinosaurs are brought back to life using DNA manipulation.

Science: Some intact specimens of woolly mammoths have been found in Siberian permafrost. In January 2011, Japanese researchers announced plans to insert woolly mammoth DNA into African elephant cells to create an elephant-mammoth hybrid. It will take around two years before an embryo is ready to be implanted into an elephant.

First planet found to orbit two stars

Sci-fi: Luke Skywalker's home planet of Tatooine from *Star Wars* is in a binary (two-sun) system.

Science: Kepler-16b was discovered by NASA's Kepler mission and unveiled on 15 September 2011. The planet is similar in mass to Saturn and it orbits the binary star Kepler-16 every 229 days in a stable, roughly circular orbit.

Largest tractor-beam study

Sci-fi: A technology familiar to fans of *Star Trek* and *Star Wars*, tractor beams can pull large objects from a distance.

Science: In October 2011, NASA awarded a $100,000 (£62,000) grant to scientists at its Goddard Space Flight Center in Greenbelt, Maryland,

First inter-species web chat

Sci-fi: *Rise of the Planet of the Apes* features great apes with artificially boosted intelligence.

Science: Koko the gorilla has been taught more than 1,000 American Sign Language signs and more than 1,000 spoken words. On 28 April 1998, she took part in a web chat in which around 8,000 AOL subscribers asked her questions. Her teacher, Dr Penny Patterson, put the questions to Koko, interpreted her signs and replied to the questioners via AOL.

First Earth-like extrasolar planet

Sci-fi: The forested planet of Pandora in *Avatar* is located in the Alpha Centauri system.

Science: To date, more than 700 planets have been found that orbit other stars, but the first potentially Earth-like example is Kepler-22b – so its discovery, announced on 5 December 2011, caused excitement among astronomers. The planet is about 2.4 times the size of Earth and orbits

First robot policeman

Sci-fi: The *Robocop* TV shows and movies feature a robot-human hybrid law-enforcement agent.

Science: In 2007, the Russian city of Perm gained a fully robotic real-life version. R Bot 001 is a 1.7-m-tall (5-ft 6-in) robot crime fighter that moves on four wheels and scans its environment with five cameras to look for crimes being committed. It can issue simple orders and serve as a point of contact for its human counterparts.

FACT: R Bot 001's first test patrol ended in failure: rain caused the non-waterproof robot to short-circuit!

РОБОПАТРУЛЬНАЯ СЛУЖБА

Р•БОТ 001 59 RUS

FACT: Krikalev's achievement is consistent with Albert Einstein's Theory of Special Relativity.

Greatest time dilation

Sci-fi: In the *Back to the Future* movies, Marty McFly travels through time in a modified Delorean DMC-12 sports car.

Science: The greatest "time travel" experienced by an individual is around 1/48th of a second, for cosmonaut Sergei Krikalev (USSR) – a consequence of the 803 days 9 hr 39 min he has spent in orbit, travelling at around 27,000 km/h (17,000 mi/h). Relative to everyone else, he has essentially "time travelled" a fraction of a second into the future.

USA, to study three potential methods for manipulating and transporting particles using laser light. NASA hopes to use future tractor-beam technology for tasks including extraterrestrial sampling and the cleaning up of space debris.

Largest tricorder competition

Sci-fi: The medical tricorder in *Star Trek* is a hand-held device used by doctors for on-the-spot medical diagnosis.

Science: On 10 January 2012, the X-Prize Foundation and the Qualcomm Foundation announced a $10-million (£6.4-million) incentive for the first working version of a medical tricorder. The prize will be awarded to the research group that develops a mobile platform able to best diagnose a set of 15 diseases in 30 people in three days.

Oldest automated nuclear weapons control system

Sci-fi: In the *Terminator* movies, Skynet is a computer-controlled "Global Digital Defense Network" that maliciously launches the US nuclear arsenal towards Russia, resulting in a global nuclear war that kills half of humanity.

FACT: Confirmation of the moray eel's pharyngeal jaws (shown here in blue) was made in 2007.

Pharyngeal jaws

First documented use of pharyngeal jaws to catch prey

Sci-fi: The Xenomorphs in the *Alien* movies have a second – and very vicious – set of protruding jaws.

Science: Known as pharyngeal jaws, these exist within the throats of around 30,000 species of fish. While most species with these extra jaws use them to help swallow food, moray eels project theirs forward into their mouths to help capture prey.

Science: When US President Ronald Reagan announced his Strategic Defense Initiative in 1983, the Soviet Union saw it as a sign that the USA may be preparing for a nuclear "first strike" against them. In response, they developed "Perimeter", a doomsday weapon that would automatically retaliate. Perimeter became active in 1985 and was designed to seismically detect nuclear strikes in the USSR.

Most powerful radio signal deliberately beamed into space

Sci-fi: In *Close Encounters of the Third Kind* and countless other sci-fi fables, humans make contact with an alien race.

Science: In 1974, scientists at the Arecibo Radio Telescope in Puerto Rico transmitted basic data on humanity, in the form of a 2,380-MHz binary radio signal, to the M13 globular cluster in the constellation of Hercules. The 169-second message will arrive in around 25,000 years – though it will take another 25,000 years for us to receive any answer...

FACT v FICTION

The *International Space Station* (ISS) is the **largest space station** ever built, while the Space Shuttle is, to date, the **largest reusable space craft**. But how do these real-world examples compare with their sci-fi counterparts? Below are some classic fictional craft – how many can you identify? *(Answers on p.283.)*

Shuttle: 37.2 m long

ISS: 105.8 m wide

First dextrous robotic astronaut in space

Sci-fi: Science fiction is populated with intelligent, robot droids such as *Star Wars'* C-3PO and R2-D2.

Science: In February 2011, the space shuttle *Discovery* set off for the *International Space Station*. Part of its cargo was Robonaut 2, a humanoid robot designed to test how robots can assist astronauts in space. On 15 February 2012, in its latest test, it performed a firm handshake with *ISS* commander Daniel Burbank.

FACT: Robonaut 2 has highly dextrous hands and arms which enable it to handle tools as a human can.

Four cameras behind visor

Infra-red camera for depth perception

Backpack contains batteries or a system for power conversion

Each arm can hold 9 kg (19 lb 13 oz)

Stomach houses 38 PowerPC processors

Fingers controlled by tendons

Thumb has four joints

SOUND

Loudest burp

Paul Hunn (UK, above right, with GWR's Craig Glenday), blasted out a burp at 109.9 decibels (dB). Decibels measure sound intensity, with silence equal to 0 dB, a normal conversation registering at 60 dB and a large orchestra at 98 dB. Hunn claimed his record for the loudest male burp at Butlins in Bognor Regis, UK, on 23 August 2009.

suggested it originated far off the west coast of southern South America, giving a range of around 5,000 km (3,100 miles). Nicknamed "The Bloop", this sound was picked up several times that summer and has never been detected since. Its origin remains unknown, although some scientists have speculated it was caused by ice calving in Antarctica or even an unknown giant marine species.

Loudest possible sustained sound in air

Sound takes the form of a wave, and the loudness of any sound relates to how high and low the peaks and troughs of the wave are. The peaks and troughs of a sound wave oscillate at an average of 1 atmospheric pressure. The lowest possible troughs of a wave are at 0 atmospheres, or a pressure of zero. The highest troughs of such a wave would be at 2 atmospheres. A sound wave with an amplitude range of 2 atmospheres corresponds to 194 dB. Any event louder than 194 dB is considered a shock wave.

Deepest note in the universe

The lowest note in the universe is caused by acoustic waves generated by a supermassive black hole in the centre of the Perseus cluster of galaxies, 250 million light years away. The sound, which propagates through the extremely thin gas surrounding the black hole, is that of a B-flat note, 57 octaves below middle C. The sound waves are estimated to have been consistently produced by the black hole for around 2.5 billion years.

Loudest sound

The island-volcano Krakatoa, in the Sunda Strait between Sumatra and Java, Indonesia, exploded in an eruption on 27 August 1883. The sound was heard 5,000 km (3,100 miles) away. The noise is estimated to have been heard across 8% of the Earth's surface and to have had 26 times the power of the largest ever H-bomb test.

Loudest unexplained underwater sound

In the 1960s, the US Navy began installing arrays of underwater microphones in the South Pacific and North Atlantic regions to track the movements of Soviet submarines. In the summer of 1997, a sound was heard that rose in frequency for one minute and was powerful enough to be detected by multiple sensors in the Equatorial Pacific Ocean autonomous hydrophone array. Analysis of the signal

Strongest measured sonic boom created by an aircraft

In 1967, the US Government performed a series of tests to discover whether or not an aircraft's sonic boom could be used as a weapon. An F-4 Phantom was used to perform extremely low and fast fly-bys over Nevada, one of which resulted in a sonic boom measuring 703 kg-force/m^2 (144 lb per ft^2). No injury was reported by the researchers who were present, despite them being exposed to a sonic boom produced by a jet fighter travelling at Mach 1.26 and at an altitude of just 29 m (95 ft) above ground level.

Loudest animal sound

Blue whales (*Balaenoptera musculus*) and fin whales (*B. physalus*) emit a low-frequency pulse when communicating. These calls reach an amazing 188 dB on the decibel scale, the loudest sounds by any living source.

First voice recording

The oldest recorded human voice is a 10-second fragment of the French folk song "Au Clair de la Lune". It was recorded on 9 April 1860 by inventor Édouard-Léon Scott de Martinville (France, 1817–79). Discovered in 2008 by researchers in Paris, the clip was created on paper using a phonautograph, a device for recording sounds visually, without being able to play them back. The paper recording was analysed by scientists at Lawrence Berkeley National Laboratory (USA), who used optical imaging as a "virtual stylus", allowing the clip to be played back for the very first time.

Rarest speech sounds

The least common speech sound is "ř" in Czech – technically speaking a "rolled post-alveolar fricative". It occurs in very few languages and is the last sound mastered by Czech children.

In the southern Bushman language "!xo", there is a click articulated with both lips which is written "Ⓧ". This character is usually referred to as a "bull's-eye" and the sound – essentially a kiss – is termed a "velaric ingressive bilabial stop".

Loudest siren

The Chrysler air raid sirens are the loudest sirens ever constructed, capable of producing 138 dB at a distance of 30 m (100 ft). The sirens are so loud that a normal person would be deafened within 60 m (200 ft) of one during operation.

Most common language sound

No language lacks the vowel "a" (as in the English word "father").

CHRYSLER

Largest acoustic mirror

Acoustic mirrors were developed by the British as an experimental early warning system to detect enemy aircraft. The two largest examples were built in the 1920s and early 1930s near Dungeness, UK (above), and Maghtab in Malta. Both had the same design: a curved concrete wall 61 m (200 ft) long by 8.2 m (27 ft) high, which focused sound into a "listening trench" in which microphones were installed. The invention of radar made them obsolete.

First acoustic hyperlens

In October 2009, scientists at the US Department of Energy's Lawrence Berkeley National Laboratory announced that they had created an acoustic hyperlens – a device to magnify details obtained by sound imaging, including submarine sonar and ultrasound foetal scans. Their hyperlens consists of 36 brass fins arranged in a fan shape. This arrangement allows physical manipulation of imaging sound waves in order to resolve details one-sixth the size of the sound waves themselves.

Loudest land animal

Male howler monkeys (*Alouatta*) of Central and South America have an enlarged bony structure at the top of the windpipe, allowing sound to reverberate. In full voice, they are audible 4.8 km (3 miles) away.

Loudest pipe organ

The Vox Maris organ produced a reading of 138.4 dBA when tested in Urspringen, Germany, on 21 October 2011.

Least appealing sound

A year-long survey by Trevor Cox, Professor of Acoustic Engineering at Salford University, UK, found the most repellent sound to the human ear is someone vomiting. It beat such sounds as a baby wailing and a dentist's drill.

Loudest insect

The African cicada (*Brevisana brevis*) makes a calling song with an average sound pressure level of 106.7 dB at a distance of 50 cm (1 ft 7.5 in). Its songs play a vital role in communication and reproduction.

Quietest place on Earth

The world's quietest place is the Anechoic Test Chamber at Orfield Laboratories in Minneapolis, Minnesota, USA. Ultra-sensitive tests in this specially constructed room on 21 January 2004 gave a background noise level of just -9.4 dBA (decibels, A-weighted).

First man-made object to break the sound barrier

Bullwhips have been used by humanity for millennia. The sharp "crack" that a whip makes when it is cast occurs because the tip of the whip has broken the speed of sound.

FACT: In the photo above, Adam Winrich (USA) is casting the **longest whip ever cracked**: 65.83 m (216 ft).

Largest anechoic test chamber

The Benefield Anechoic Facility at Edwards Air Force Base in California, USA, is a vast echo-free chamber with a volume of 130,823 m³ (4.62 million ft³). The chamber is insulated from outside noise and its interior surfaces do not reflect sound or electromagnetic waves. Built in 1988–89, it is used to test aerospace and defence projects including tanks, aircraft and air-defence systems.

FACT: The speed of sound is 342.3 m/sec (1,123 ft/sec) in dry air at 20°C (68°F).

FACT: The term "dBA" covers sound levels audible to the human ear – i.e., excluding extreme highs and lows.

IF YOU PREFER THE SOUND OF MUSIC, SEE P.218

SOUND SPECTRUM

GWR explores the extremes of sound, from the faintest rustling of leaves to the eardrum-popping noises of guns and fireworks.

Decibel scale

Category	dB	Example
Painful and dangerous		
Avoid or use hearing protection	140	Fireworks
		Gunshots
		Custom car stereos at full volume
	130	Jackhammers
		Ambulances
Uncomfortable		
Dangerous over 30 seconds	120	Jet planes during take-off
Very loud		
Dangerous over 30 minutes	110	Concerts
		Car horns
		Sporting events
	100	Snowmobiles
		MP3 players at full volume
	90	Lawnmowers
		Power tools
		Blenders
		Hair-driers

Over 85 dB for extended periods can cause permanent hearing loss

Category	dB	Example
Loud		
	80	Alarm clocks
	70	Traffic
		Vacuum cleaners
Moderate		
	60	Normal conversation
		Dishwashers
	50	Moderate rainfall
Soft		
	40	Quiet library
	30	Whisper
Faint		
	20	Leaves rustling

Source: American Academy of Audiology; South Carolina Department of Health and Environmental Control

CONTENTS

Highest revenue generated by an entertainment product in 24 hours

Within 24 hours of its launch on 8 November 2011, military shooter *Call of Duty: Modern Warfare 3* had sold more than 6.5 million copies in the USA and UK. The record sales generated around $400 million (£250 million) according to the game's publisher, Activision Blizzard.

HOW FAMOUS CAN YOU GET?

Who is the most famous person on Earth?

Fame, renown, repute, glory: there are many words for the state of being known or talked about by lots of people. But what is fame, how can we quantify it and what, if any, are the limits on fame?

We live in an age where the line between fame and celebrity is blurred. Where once someone became famous for their extraordinary deeds, many people are now celebrated merely for being famous.

The great Julius Caesar (100–44 BC) was known throughout the Roman Empire and beyond, having extended Rome's power to the west across the English Channel and to the north into the Rhinelands. Even then, his fame (or infamy) cannot compare with that of Justin Bieber, who has conquered the internet with three entries in the top ten most popular YouTube videos of all time (see p.219), reaching well over a billion people in the process. Admittedly, Bieber also attracted a record number of "dislikes", but he fared rather better than Caesar, who received multiple stab wounds from *his* "dislikers"!

Top 10 most influential people in history

1	Mohammed	Prophet of God, founder of Islam
2	Isaac Newton	English scientist, devised laws of motion
3	Jesus Christ	Son of God, central figure of Christianity
4	Buddha	Indian teacher, philosopher, founder of Buddhism
5	Confucius	Chinese teacher, philosopher, founder of Confucianism
6	St Paul	Christian apostle, missionary, Bible contributor
7	Cài Lún	Chinese inventor of paper-making process
8	Johannes Gutenberg	German inventor of printing press and movable type
9	Christopher Columbus	Italian navigator, explorer, led to European colonization of the New World
10	Albert Einstein	German physicist, devised theory of relativity

Source: The 100: A Ranking of the Most Influential Persons in History, Michael H Hart

In essence, there would appear to be two ages of fame: pre- and post-internet. *The 100*, a book that ranks those people who have played a pivotal role in the course of human history, features not a single person in its top ten who was born after the beginning of the 20th century.

The five leading figures are Mohammed, Isaac Newton, Jesus Christ, Buddha and Confucius – clearly significant figures. Yet who among us could quote more lines of Confucius than we could the lyrics of a song by Michael Jackson – the man once referred to (in 2006) as the most famous living person on Earth by Guinness World Records? How many of us know the limits of Newtonian mechanics better than we know the chorus of "Poker Face" by Lady Gaga, the most famous of the faces in our 2011–12 snapshot of celebrity fame (right)?

CELEBRITY SNAPSHOT 2011–12

Plotted here are the top 25 celebrities currently making the news (to the year ending 14 March 2012), in terms of hits on Google, news sites and picture sites, as well as Forbes' power rating, imdb star rating and first-name rank (chance of a Google hit from the first name only).

The ratings given – and the corresponding celebrities' head sizes – have been calculated by assigning a score out of 100 to each of the criteria mentioned above. The larger the head, the more "famous" the face...

Interestingly, if you take the average age, occupation and nationality from a list of the top 50 celebs, we end up with a 34-year-old male musician from the USA. The top 25 celebrity who fits this profile most closely is rapper/songwriter/producer Kanye West (who actually appears at No.12 on the list)!

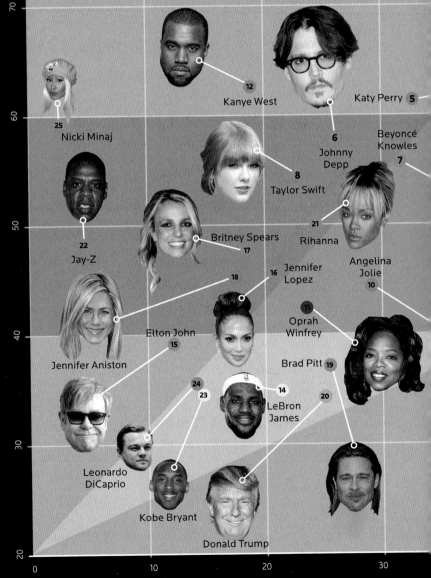

GUINNESS WORLD RECO

FACT:
The fastest-rising query on Google in 2011 was "Rebecca Black" – the American 13-year-old whose pop single "Friday" went viral on YouTube.

3 Madonna

Most famous celebrity
According to our rinse of celebrity statistics, Lady Gaga is currently the most famous celeb on the planet. The First World bias of the list reflects the ubiquity of the internet in the West. How will a shift in this balance change the face of celebrity in the future?

9 Adele

George Clooney

1 Lady Gaga

4 Justin Bieber

FACT:
George Clooney made headlines in March 2012 after being arrested outside Sudan's Embassy in Washington, DC – he was protesting about the country's human rights issues.

FACT:
Musicians account for more than half of the names in the celebrity top 50.

Roger Federer **13**

FACT:
Global population at the time of Julius Caesar (c. 50 BC): 100 million; weekly viewing figures for Baywatch in 1996: 1.1 billion.

Facebook currently has 845 million active users, and between them the faithful helped to generate revenues in excess of $3.7 billion (£2.4 million) in 2011. This networking site drives much of the internet's traffic, with users tipping each other off about new uploads, be they from musicians, actors or simply ordinary people. For a fleeting moment, these celebrities attract the fame that eluded Julius Caesar – merely by walking into a door, falling off a skateboard or getting bitten by a baby.

As access to the net grows, which it inevitably will, so too will the limits of fame – in June 2011 the United Nations declared that free access to the internet was a fundamental human right, on a par with access to clean water. Only when everyone is online will these limits be reached, and by then perhaps we will *all* be afforded our allotted 15 minutes – or at least 15 megabytes – of fame.

40 50 60 70 80 90 10

● Music ● Movies ● TV ● Sports ● Business

WHO'S HAD THE MOST FACEBOOK "LIKES" THIS YEAR? FIND OUT ON P.165

COMICS

Most expensive page of comic art

An unknown collector paid €312,500 (£279,875; $461,503) for one hand-drawn page from the 1963 Tintin book *The Castafiore Emerald* on 10 May 2009. The selling price was three times that of its catalogue estimate.

First comic

Most experts agree that Swiss cartoonist Rodolphe Töpffer's *Histoire de M. Vieux Bois* ("The Adventures of Mister Wooden Head"), created in 1827 and first published a decade later, was the earliest comic. The story, published in North America in 1842 as *The Adventures of Obadiah Oldbuck*, consisted of around 30 pages of comic strip. Each page was cut into six panels, with a narrative caption below each drawing.

First sequential newspaper strip

Hogan's Alley, by Richard Felton Outcault (USA), is credited as the first regular newspaper strip. It featured Mickey Dugan, better known as the "Yellow Kid" because of his distinctive long, yellow nightshirt. The sequential strip version of *Hogan's Alley* appeared in Randolph Hearst's *New York Journal* from 25 October 1896 and continued for three series.

First graphic novel

Graphic novels are book-length comics. The term "graphic novel" first appeared in 1976 on the dust jacket of *Bloodstar* by illustrator Richard Corben and author Robert E Howard (both USA). In the same year, George Metzger's (USA) comic book *Beyond Time and Again* was subtitled "A Graphic Novel", and *Red Tide* by Jim Steranko (USA) was labelled both a "visual novel" and a "graphic novel".

Best-selling comic (single edition)

Created by Chris Claremont (UK) and Jim Lee (USA), *X-Men 1*, published by Marvel Comics, sold a total of 8.1 million copies. Lee also drew four variant covers for the issue, all of them published simultaneously and which integrated to form one image, bearing the cover date October 1991.

Most translated comic

The Adventures of Asterix, created by René Goscinny and Albert Uderzo (both France) in 1959, has been translated into 111 languages and dialects, including Welsh, Latin, Swiss German and Esperanto. It sold 320 million copies worldwide and has been adapted nine times as a cartoon for TV and three times for the cinema.

FACT:
Asterix debuted in the first issue of *Pilote* magazine, on 29 October 1959.

Most expensive comic

A copy of *Action Comics* #1, first published in 1938, was bought by an anonymous bidder via the US auction website ComicConnect.com for $2.161 million (£1,388,850) on 30 November 2011. The comic, which features the first appearance of Superman, was graded at Very Fine/Near Mint: 9.0 by the Certified Guaranty Company (CGC).

Most expensive Silver Age comic

The years 1956 to 1970 mark the "Silver Age" of comics. A copy of *Amazing Fantasy* #15, first published in 1962, was purchased by an anonymous buyer via the US auction website ComicConnect.com for $1.1 million (£686,000), in March 2011. The comic marked the debut of Spider-Man.

FACT:
The "Golden Age" of comics began in the 1930s and lasted until the mid/late 1950s.

Largest comic festival

Japan's Comiket, a three-day comics festival held in Tokyo in the summer and winter each year, attracted 560,000 visitors during summer 2009. The last day – Sunday, 16 August – was the busiest, with around 200,000 visitors attending. This record was equalled at the summer 2010 Comiket. The event is especially known for its *dojinshi* – self-published manga comics.

Longest-running weekly comic

British humour comic *The Beano* was launched on 30 July 1938, and has been published weekly ever since – except for a period during World War II, when its frequency was reduced due to paper shortages. As of 11 February 2012, *The Beano* has been published for 3,622 issues, making it the longest-running weekly comic to have retained its name and numbering system throughout its history. It is published by DC Thompson & Co. (UK).

Most editions of any comic

The Mexican comic *Pepin* printed its first edition on 4 March 1936 as a weekly comics anthology. It eventually became a daily, running until 23 October 1956. In all, 7,561 issues were published.

Largest publisher of comics

Marvel Comics is the biggest publisher of comics, boasting the greatest market share of any comic publisher, claiming an amazing 45.63% of the total market at the end of 2009. The second largest is DC Comics with 35.22%.

THE EISNER AWARDS – MOST WINS

Category	Winner	Details
Best writer	Alan Moore (UK)	Nine-times winner, 1988–2006
Best artist/ penciller	P Craig Russell and Steve Rude (both USA)	Four wins each
Best painter/ multimedia artist (interior art)	Alex Ross and Jill Thompson (both USA)	Five wins each
Best letterer	Todd Klein (USA)	Has won 16 times since category opened in 1993
Best cover artist	James Jean (USA)	Won six times consecutively between 2004 and 2009

Most professional contributors to a graphic novel

In one working day in September 1991, a group of 133 cartoonists gathered at the Guinness World of Records museum at the Trocadero in London, UK, to create a 76-m-long (250-ft) comic strip entitled *The Worm*. The strip's story – concerning a cartoonist who journeys through time – was conceived by legendary writer Alan Moore (UK). The finished comic was published in 1999 by Slab-O-Concrete Press to help raise money for the Cartoon Art Trust.

Largest collection of comics in a museum

The Serial and Government Publications Division of the Library of Congress in Washington, DC, USA, houses more than 5,000 titles and over 100,000 individual issues. The oldest comic book in the collection is *Popular Comics*, first published in February 1936.

Most movies from the work of a comic-book creator

As of March 2012, the comic-book creations of Stan Lee (USA) have been adapted into Hollywood films 15 times.

Smallest comic

Agent 327, drawn and written by Martin Lodewijk (Netherlands), was published by Comicshop "Sjors" in June 1999. It measured just 2.58 x 3.7 cm (1 x 1.4 in). Printed in full colour with 100 lines per centimetre, 2,000 copies of the 16-page comic were made, each sold with a free magnifying glass.

First superhero

Contrary to popular belief, Superman was not the first comic-strip superhero. That honour falls instead to The Phantom, created in 1936 by the American cartoonist Lee Falk, two years before Superman. The *Phantom* newspaper strip featured the adventures of Kit Walker, who sported a mask and a figure-hugging purple outfit as "the ghost who walks".

Fastest time to produce a comic book

Kapow! Comic Con produced a comic book in 11 hr 19 min 38 sec in London, UK, on 9 April 2011.

FACT: Inspired by the blank eyes of classical statues, Falk drew The Phantom without pupils.

Largest auction of comic books

On 5 and 6 May 2011, an auction of comic books, art and comic-related memorabilia took place in New York City, USA. Conducted by Heritage Auction Galleries, the auction raised $6,077,355 (£3,712,000).

PREFER BATSMEN TO BATMAN? THEN FLY TO P.244

Most film adaptations of a comic character
Batman has starred in eight full-length live-action movies, from *Batman* (USA, 1996) to *The Dark Knight Rises* (USA, 2012).

SPRING ISSUE
No. 1
BATMAN
10¢
ALL BRAND NEW ADVENTURES OF THE BATMAN AND ROBIN, THE BOY WONDER!

SUPERHERO TIMELINE

The Phantom (1936)
Superman (1938)
Batman (1939)
Green Lantern (1940)
Robin, the Boy Wonder (1940)
Captain America (1941)
Catwoman (1941)
Wonder Woman (1941)
Supergirl (1959)
Fantastic Four (1961)
The Hulk (1962)
Spider-Man (1962)
Thor (1962)
Iron Man (1963)
Nick Fury (1963)
X-Men (1963)
The Avengers (1963)
Daredevil (1964)
Silver Surfer (1966)
Ghost Rider (1972)
Punisher (1974)
Wolverine (1974)
Watchmen (1986)
Hellboy (1993)
Kick-Ass (2008)

Human | God | Mutant | Alien | Hero | Anti-hero | Side-kick | Heavy hitter | Superpowers | Gadgets

AT THE MOVIES

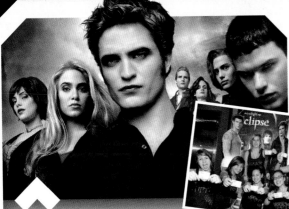

MOST...

Money lost by a film

Costing about $98 million (£63 million) to produce, and with a US domestic gross of just $10,017,322 (£6,411,086), *Cutthroat Island* (USA, 1995) made a net loss of $104,982,678 (£67,188,914).

"Original Screenplay" Oscar wins

At the 84th Oscars ceremony in February 2012, Woody Allen (USA) won the best "Original Screenplay" award for *Midnight in Paris* (Spain/USA, 2011), his third award in the category, following previous wins for his films *Hannah and Her Sisters* (USA, 1986) and *Annie Hall* (USA, 1977). He also holds the record for the **most "Original Screenplay" nominations**, with 15.

Highest-grossing midnight screening

Directed by David Slade (UK), *The Twilight Saga: Eclipse* (USA, 2010), the third film in the *Twilight* series, opened with midnight screenings (including one in Los Angeles, USA, right) on 30 June 2010 in over 4,000 US cinemas, grossing an estimated $30 million (£20 million).

Highest-grossing film series

As of 19 July 2011, the eight films of the Harry Potter series had grossed $6,853,594,569 (£4,251,047,730) at the international box office. The first film, *Harry Potter and the Philosopher's Stone* (USA/UK), came out in 2001.

Oldest actor to receive an Oscar

At the 84th Academy Awards on 26 February 2012, Christopher Plummer (Canada) won the Best Supporting Actor category for his role in *Beginners* (USA, 2010). At the age of 82 years 65 days, this makes him the oldest ever winner of an acting Oscar.

Longest red carpet at a première

At the world première of *Harry Potter and the Deathly Hallows – Part 2* (USA/UK, 2011) in London, UK, on 7 July 2011, Warner Bros. created a red carpet that stretched 455 m (1,492 ft 9 in) from Trafalgar Square to Leicester Square.

Highest-grossing opening weekend

During the weekend of its US release on 4–6 May 2012, *The Avengers* (USA, 2012) took $207,438,708 (£128,806,936), beating the record set by *Harry Potter and the Deathly Hallows: Part II* in 2011. The Marvel-inspired movie hit the $150-million mark within 48 hours of its US release, grossing $150,371,975 (£93,377,990) by the end of Saturday 5 May.

"Razzie" nominations in a year

Adam Sandler (USA) holds the dubious honour of having earned 11 separate nominations for the 2012 "Razzie" Awards (also known as the Golden Raspberries), reflecting his work as actor, producer or screenwriter for such critically reviled 2011 films as *Bucky Larson*, *Just Go with It* and his cross-dressing comedy *Jack and Jill* (all USA).

Most successful feature-film spin-off

The Hasbro Transformers toy line first appeared on screen as a cartoon series in the 1980s. It has had three live-action feature-film spin-offs, the most successful being *Transformers: Dark of the Moon* (USA, 2011), which had accumulated over $1 billion (£644 million) by the start of 2012. The movie also holds the record for the **most vehicles destroyed in the making of a film** – 532 cars were "totalled", easily surpassing the record of 150 held by *The Junkman* (USA, 1982). According to director Michael Bay (USA), the cars were flood-damaged vehicles donated by the film's insurance company: "By law, the cars have to be crushed. So I am a perfect guy to do that."

FACT: Technically, "dark of the moon" is the last few days of the lunar cycle, when the night sky is devoid of moonlight.

ZOMBIES, MUMMIES AND BORGS

Portrayed character in film

The Devil has been featured in 544 different films as of March 2012. The second most common character is Santa Claus, with 303 portrayals; third is the Grim Reaper, with 290; fourth is Jesus Christ, with 239; and fifth is God, with 231. Count Dracula is the **most portrayed literary character on screen**, with 155 portrayals, followed by Sherlock Holmes, with 147.

Successful box-office month

The release of *Harry Potter and the Deathly Hallows – Part 2* (USA/UK), *Captain America*, *Transformers: Dark of the Moon* and *Cars 2* (all USA, 2011) helped to make July 2011 the highest-earning month at the worldwide box office, with ticket sales totalling $1,395,075,783 (£883,833,103).

Sequels released in one year

During 2011, Hollywood broke its record for most sequels released in a calendar year. According to Box Office Mojo, 27 films released in 2011 were sequels, beating the 24 released in 2003. That averages about one every other week and roughly one-fifth of total releases.

Product placements in a film

POM Wonderful Presents: The Greatest Movie Ever Sold, directed by Morgan Spurlock (USA) and released on 22 April 2011, had 3,463 product placements. The film is a documentary about advertising and product placement, and, ironically, its finance came from advertising and product placement. The **greatest product placement return for a film** is held by the James Bond film *Die Another Day* (UK/USA, 2002) – it earned MGM £45 million ($71 million). In all, 20 companies had their product featured in the film, including Ford, British Airways, Sony and Finlandia Vodka.

Most Oscar nominations for an actress

Meryl Streep (USA) has been Oscar nominated 17 times. She's won three of them, including the 2012 Best Actress for playing former UK prime minister, Margaret Thatcher, in *The Iron Lady* (UK/France, 2011).

THE ACTING A-LIST

According to research published in 2011 by the US media company Forbes, the highest-earning Hollywood actors and actresses are...

	Actor/actress	Yearly earnings
01	Leonardo DiCaprio	$77 million (£48.5 million)
02	Johnny Depp	$50 million (£31.5 million)
03	Adam Sandler	$40 million (£25.1 million)
04	Will Smith	$36 million (£22.6 million)
05	Tom Hanks	$35 million (£22 million)
06	Ben Stiller	$34 million (£21.4 million)
07	Robert Downey, Jr.	$31 million (£19.5 million)
08 =	Angelina Jolie	$30 million (£18.8 million)
08 =	Sarah Jessica Parker	$30 million (£18.8 million)
10 =	Jennifer Aniston	$28 million (£17.6 million)
10 =	Mark Wahlberg	$28 million (£17.6 million)
10 =	Reese Witherspoon	$28 million (£17.6 million)

SFX characters portrayed

As of 6 May 2011, Bill Blair (USA) has played 202 special-effects (SFX) characters in US feature films and TV shows. These include a caveman in *Dinosaur Valley Girls* (1996), a captured human pet in *Masked and Anonymous* (2003), a mummy in *Monster Night* (2006), zombies in *Voodoo Moon* (2006) and *Resident Evil: Afterlife* (2010), and assorted Klingons, Bajorans, Asoths, Cardassians, Vulcans and Borgs in the TV series *Star Trek: Deep Space Nine* (1993–99).

Highest-grossing limited opening

In its 425-cinema US opening weekend on 16–18 December 2011, *Mission: Impossible – Ghost Protocol* (USA/UAE) grossed $13 million (£8.24 million), the highest amount for an opening in fewer than 600 cinemas. The record was previously held by *Bridget Jones: The Edge of Reason* (UK/France/Germany/Ireland/USA, 2004).

OSCAR WINNERS

Most wins by a film: 11
Ben-Hur (1959), *Titanic* (1997), *The Lord of the Rings: The Return of the King* (2003)

Films that have won the "Big Five" (Best Picture/Director/Actor/Actress/Screenplay): 3

- *It Happened One Night* (1934) Frank Capra/Clark Gable/Claudette Colbert/Robert Riskin
- *One Flew Over the Cuckoo's Nest* (1975) Miloš Forman/Jack Nicholson/Louise Fletcher/Lawrence Hauben and Bo Goldman
- *The Silence of the Lambs* (1991) Jonathan Demme/Anthony Hopkins/Jodie Foster/Ted Tally

Most Best Director: 4
John Ford for *The Informer* (1935), *The Grapes of Wrath* (1940), *How Green Was My Valley* (1941), *The Quiet Man* (1952)

Most Best Leading Actor: 2
Spencer Tracy, Fredric March, Gary Cooper, Marlon Brando, Dustin Hoffman, Tom Hanks, Jack Nicholson, Daniel Day-Lewis, Sean Penn

Most Best Leading Actress: 4
Katharine Hepburn for *Morning Glory* (1934), *Guess Who's Coming to Dinner* (1967), *The Lion in Winter* (1968), *On Golden Pond* (1981)

Most Best Cinematography: 4
- Leon Shamroy for *The Black Swan* (1942), *Wilson* (1944), *Leave Her to Heaven* (1945), *Cleopatra* (1963)
- Joseph Ruttenberg for *The Great Waltz* (1938), *Mrs. Miniver* (1942), *Somebody Up There Likes Me* (1956), *Gigi* (1958)

Winner of both Best Actor/Actress and Best Screenplay: 1
Emma Thompson for *Howards End* (1992) and *Sense and Sensibility* (1995)

BOX-OFFICE HITS

Fantasy
The Lord of the Rings: The Return of the King (USA/New Zealand, 2003)
$1.1 billion
(£796.7 million)

Anime
Spirited Away
(Japan, 2001)
$275 million
(£188 million)

Animation series
Shrek (USA, 2001–07)
$2.2 billion
(£1.1 billion)
total gross

Gangster
The Departed
(USA/Hong Kong, 2006)
$290 million
(£154 million)

Crime
Ocean's Eleven
(USA, 2001)
$451 million
(£320 million)

Zombie
Resident Evil: Afterlife
(Germany/France/USA, 2010)
$296 million
(£203 million)

Disaster
2012
(USA, 2009)
$770 million
(£477 million)

Bond
Casino Royale
(UK/Czech Republic/USA/Germany/The Bahamas, 2006)
$587.6 million
(£304.6 million)

Horror
The Twilight Saga: New Moon
(USA, 2009)
$710 million
(£440 million)

Animation
Toy Story 3
(USA, 2010)
$1.063 billion
(£732 million)

Videogame spin-off
Prince of Persia: The Sands of Time
(USA, 2010)
$326.8 million
(£211.8 million)

Sci-fi
(and highest-
grossing movie
of all time)
Avatar
(USA/UK, 2009)
$2.71 billion
(£1.7 billion)

Post-
apocalyptic
I Am Legend
(USA, 2007)
$585 million
(£297 million)

High-school
comedy
Superbad
(USA, 2007)
$170 million
(£86 million)

Musical
Mamma Mia!
(USA/UK/
Germany, 2008)
$610 million
(£311 million)

Spy
*The Bourne
Ultimatum*
(USA/Germany,
2007)
$443 million
(£222 million)

Superhero
The Dark Knight
(USA/UK, 2008)
$1.002 billion
(£508 million)

Silent
The Artist
(France/
Belgium, 2011)
$105.5 million
(£67.4 million)

Martial arts
The Karate Kid
(USA/China, 2010)
$359 million
(£247 million)

Swashbuckler
*Pirates of the
Caribbean:
Dead Man's Chest*
(USA, 2006)
$1.066 billion
(£572 million)

Comedy
*The Hangover:
Part II*
(USA, 2011)
$581 million
(£354 million)

Foreign
language
*The Passion of the
Christ* (USA, 2004)
$604.3 million
(£309.7 million)

THE ULTIMATE BLOCKBUSTER

The films on these pages grossed more than any other movie in their genre. But what elements should the ideal blockbuster include? GWR has created a composite movie that *should* be box-office gold. The calculations are based on the *average* box-office grosses for the most successful movies and film-makers since 1995.*

GENRE: Superhero
Gross: $131.7 million

DIRECTOR:
Steven Spielberg (USA)
Gross: $150.9 million

PRODUCER:
David Heyman (UK)
Gross: $192.7 million

LEAD ACTOR:
Daniel Radcliffe (UK)
Gross: $244.4 million

LEAD ACTRESS:
Emma Watson (UK)
Gross: $245.6 million

SCREENPLAY:
George Lucas (USA)
Gross: $224.9 million

COMPOSER:
John Williams (USA)
Gross: $139 million

PRODUCTION METHOD:
Animation/live action
Gross: $138.4 million

DISTRIBUTED BY:
DreamWorks SKG
Gross: $77.7 million

RATED: PG-13
Gross: $42.3 million

SOURCE: Comic/
graphic novel
Gross: $86.5 million

RELEASE TIME:
summer

** Sources: the-numbers.com;
boxofficemojo.com. The
box-office figure for each
category is based on
a minimum of 10 movies*

217

PICK OF THE POPS

Youngest chart entrant (US)

The "breathing, cries and coos" of Blue Ivy Carter, the daughter of Beyoncé and Jay-Z (both USA), appeared on Jay-Z's track "Glory". It charted just days after her birth on 7 January 2012.

Adele-uge of records

Adele has been sweeping up records since *21* was released in January 2011. Here are some of them:

Biggest-selling UK album by a solo female By 7 April 2012, *21* had sold 4,181,000 copies in the UK.

Biggest-selling UK album artist in one year In 2011, *21* sold 3,772,346 units and *19* sold 1,207,600 units – 4,979,946 units in total.

Biggest-selling US digital track in one year "Rolling in the Deep", the lead single from *21*, was downloaded 5.81 million times in 2011.

Fastest album to reach US digital sales of one million *21* registered 1 million US digital sales on 16 July 2011, just 19 weeks after its No.1 debut on 12 March 2011.

FACT: Katy Perry became the first artist to achieve five four-million-selling digital tracks in the USA.

Biggest-selling digital album in US and UK

Adele (UK, b. Adele Adkins) raised the bar for digital album sales in both the USA and the UK in 2011. Within five months of its February 2011 release, *21* had eclipsed Eminem's *Recovery* as the biggest-selling digital album in US chart history, with sales of 1.1 million units. By the end of the year, sales were 1.8 million. In the UK, *21*'s digital sales rose to more than 700,000 in 2011, replacing Lady Gaga's *The Fame* as the biggest-selling UK digital album.

First solo artist to have three No.1 US albums before the age of 18

Justin Bieber (Canada, b. 1 March 1994) claimed three chart-topping US albums before reaching his 18th birthday: the singer's *My World 2.0* made its debut at No.1 on 10 April 2010 with first-week sales of 283,000, *Never Say Never: The Remixes* made its chart-topping entrance on 5 March 2011 with sales of 165,000 and *Under the Mistletoe* was the first Christmas album by a male artist to debut at No.1 on the US albums chart. *Under the Mistletoe* topped the countdown on 19 November 2011 after first-week sales of 210,000.

First artist to win two Mercury Music Prizes

Let England Shake, the eighth studio album by UK alternative rock singer PJ Harvey, claimed the prestigious Mercury Music Prize on 6 September 2011, making her the only artist to win the award twice in its 20-year history. In 2001, Harvey became the first female to take home the prize with her fifth studio effort, *Stories from the City, Stories from the Sea*.

Longest gap between top 10 albums (UK)

When Leonard Cohen (Canada) debuted at No.2 on 11 February 2012 with his 12th studio album, *Old Ideas*, it was his first showing in the top 10 since *Songs of Love and Hate* in 1971.

Most simultaneous hits on UK singles chart (solo female)

On 25 February 2012, Whitney Houston (USA) had 12 new entries in the top 75, including three tracks in the top 40: "I Will Always Love You" (No.14), "I Wanna Dance with Somebody (Who Loves Me)" (No.20) and "One Moment in Time" (No.40). The record-breaking artist was found dead at the Beverly Hilton Hotel in Beverly Hills, California, USA, on 11 February 2012.

First female with five No.1 US singles from one album

When "Last Friday Night (T.G.I.F.)" followed "California Gurls", "Teenage Dream", "Firework" and "E.T." to the singles chart summit in August 2011, it gave singer Katy Perry (USA, b. Katheryn Hudson) a fifth US chart-topper from her No.1 album *Teenage Dream*. The only other artist to achieve five US No.1 singles from one album is Michael Jackson (USA), who notched up five No.1s from his 1987 album *Bad*.

Youngest male to enter US albums chart at No.1

Scotty McCreery (USA), winner of the 10th season of *American Idol*, was 18 years 13 days old when he made his albums chart bow with *Clear as Day* on 22 October 2011. McCreery, the sixth *American Idol* contestant to crown the *Billboard* 200, was also the first country artist to enter at No.1 with a debut studio album.

First UK group to debut at No.1 in USA with debut album

UK boy band One Direction (Niall Horan, Zayn Malik, Liam Payne, Harry Styles and Louis Tomlinson) became the first UK group to make a chart-topping bow on the *Billboard* 200 albums chart, with *Up All Night*'s first-week sales of 176,000 on 31 March 2012. The band finished third in the 2010 series of talent show *The X Factor* (UK, 2004–present).

Most simultaneous tracks on US singles chart by a solo artist

Grammy-winning American rapper Lil Wayne (b. Dwayne Carter, Jr, aka Weezy) placed an unprecedented 12 tracks on the *Billboard* Hot 100 on 17 September 2011. Weezy scored eight new entries to add to his four existing Hot 100 entries in the same week his *Tha Carter IV* album debuted at No.1 on the *Billboard* 200.

Fastest-selling US digital album

Lady Gaga's (USA, b. Stefani Germanotta) *Born this Way* is the fastest-selling digital album in Nielsen SoundScan history (i.e., since March 1991, when accurate sales figures were introduced in the USA), generating 662,000 first-week sales to debut at No.1 on 11 June 2011. *Born this Way* – the **first album to debut in a social network game** (*GagaVille*) – sold 1.1 million copies in its first week (retailing on Amazon for just 99 cents).

Biggest TV audience for a Super Bowl act

A record 114 million people watched Madonna's (USA, b. Madonna Ciccone) half-time show at Super Bowl XLVI, at Lucas Oil Stadium, Indianapolis, Indiana, USA, on 5 February 2012. The performance also featured UK rapper M.I.A. (b. Mathangi Arulpragasam) and US hip-hop star Nicki Minaj (b. Onika Minaj) on Madonna's new single, "Give Me All Your Luvin'".

Biggest-selling US digital artist

By the end of 2011, Rihanna (Barbados, b. Robyn Rihanna Fenty) had sold an incredible 47.57 million digital tracks in the USA, according to sales tracked by Nielsen SoundScan. The 24-year-old singer, who made her debut in 2005, held off The Black Eyed Peas (42.4 million career digital sales), Eminem (42.29 million), Lady Gaga (42.08 million) and Taylor Swift (41.82 million).

Fastest-selling rock concerts in UK history

On 21 October 2011, The Stone Roses (UK) sold 220,000 tickets in 68 minutes for their three comeback gigs at Heaton Park in Manchester, UK, on 29 June–1 July 2012. A total of 150,000 tickets for the first two concerts were bought in just 14 minutes from 9:30 a.m.; 70,000 tickets for the third date were made available at 10 a.m. and sold out in 38 minutes. The event grossed over £12 million ($19.04 million) in ticket sales.

YOUTUBE SENSATIONS

Here are the top 10 most viewed music videos on YouTube. The total number of views (y axis) are charted over time (x axis) to show how rapidly the songs reached their total viewing figures (accurate to 24 March 2012). The numbers of "likes" and "dislikes" are also listed.

Views

Date

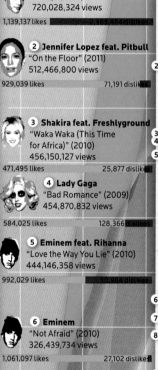

1 Justin Bieber feat. Ludacris
"Baby" (2010)
720,028,324 views
1,139,137 likes · 2,383,464 dislikes

2 Jennifer Lopez feat. Pitbull
"On the Floor" (2011)
512,466,800 views
929,039 likes · 71,191 dislikes

3 Shakira feat. Freshlyground
"Waka Waka (This Time for Africa)" (2010)
456,150,127 views
471,495 likes · 25,877 dislikes

4 Lady Gaga
"Bad Romance" (2009)
454,870,832 views
584,025 likes · 128,366 dislikes

5 Eminem feat. Rihanna
"Love the Way You Lie" (2010)
444,146,358 views
992,029 likes · 30,984 dislikes

6 Eminem
"Not Afraid" (2010)
326,439,734 views
1,061,097 likes · 27,102 dislikes

7 Don Omar feat. Lucenzo –
"Danza Kuduro" (2010/11)
325,290,637 views
405,014 likes · 29,529 dislikes

8 Justin Bieber feat. Jaden Smith
"Never Say Never" (2010/11)
307,746,944 views
549,818 likes · 241,697 dislikes

9 Justin Bieber
"One Time" (2009/10)
288,637,158 views
400,707 likes · 391,452 dislikes

10 Miley Cyrus
"Party in the U.S.A." (2009)
277,926,168 views
443,677 likes · 99,653 dislikes

2011   2012

ROCK OF AGES

Most consecutive US No.1 singles

Whitney Houston (USA, 1963–2012) achieved seven consecutive No.1 singles on the *Billboard* Hot 100 between 1985 and 1988: "Saving All My Love for You" (1985), "How Will I Know" (1986), "Greatest Love of All" (1986), "I Wanna Dance with Somebody (Who Loves Me)" (1987), "Didn't We Almost Have it All" (1987), "So Emotional" (1987) and "Where Do Broken Hearts Go" (1988).

The Grammy-winning soundtrack to the blockbuster movie *The Bodyguard* (1992), in which Houston starred, remains the **best-selling soundtrack**, with more than 44 million copies sold worldwide. The album, which has been certified for shipments of 17 million copies in the USA alone, spent 20 non-consecutive weeks at No.1 between 12 December 1992 and 29 May 1993.

First video on MTV

The first music video aired on the Music Television network (based in New York City, USA, and launched on 1 August 1981) was the appropriately titled "Video Killed the Radio Star", a UK No.1 single for The Buggles (UK) in 1979.

The first video seen on MTV Europe, launched on 1 August 1987, was "Money for Nothing" by Dire Straits (UK), which topped the *Billboard* Hot 100 in 1985. The track starts and ends with the lyric: "I want my MTV".

Largest rock concert TV audience

On 13 July 1985, an estimated global audience of 1.9 billion people in 150 countries watched the dual-venue Live Aid charity concerts to raise money for famine-hit Ethiopia. Organized by musicians Bob Geldof (Ireland) and Midge Ure (UK), the event was broadcast simultaneously from Wembley Stadium in London, UK, and John F Kennedy Stadium in Philadelphia, Pennsylvania, USA, and featured many of the biggest names in rock including The Beach Boys, David Bowie, Bob Dylan, Elton John, Led Zeppelin, Paul McCartney, Queen and U2. The concerts raised about £40 million (then $50 million).

Best-selling single
Bing Crosby's (USA) "White Christmas" has sold an estimated 50 million copies worldwide. Written by Irving Berlin (USA) in 1940, it reached No.1 in the USA in October 1942, where it remained for 11 consecutive weeks.

The **first album to debut at No.1 in the USA** was *Captain Fantastic and the Brown Dirt Cowboy* by Elton John (UK, b. Reginald Dwight), which hit the top spot on 7 June 1975. The second album to go straight to No.1 was Elton's next album, *Rock of the Westies*.

The Beatles (UK) hold the record for the **most consecutive weeks at No.1 on the UK albums chart (group, one album)**, with their chart debut *Please Please Me* (1963). It topped the charts for 30 weeks from 11 May to 30 November 1963.

ABBA (Sweden), along with Led Zeppelin (UK), see right, hold the record for the **most successive UK No.1 albums**, with eight. ABBA first ascended to No.1 with their *Greatest Hits* collection, above, in May 1976 and scored their eighth consecutive chart-topper with *The Singles – The First Ten Years* in November 1982.

Released in November 1982, *Thriller* by Michael Jackson (USA, 1958–2009) is the world's **biggest-selling album**. Sales figures vary, but *Thriller* has definitely exceeded the 65-million mark.

The record for the **most cumulative weeks on the US chart (one album)** is held by Pink Floyd's (UK) 1973 album *The Dark Side of the Moon*. On 28 April 2012, it recorded its 802nd week – more than 15 years – on the *Billboard* 200.

FACT: Claims on the internet that *Dark Side* was written as a soundtrack for *The Wizard of Oz* are denied by the band!

ROCK around the clock
BILL HALEY and COMETS

UK No.1 versions [same song]

[...d]ifferent versions of ["Unch]ained Melody" have [topped] the UK chart. Jimmy [... (UK, 1955), The [Righte]ous Brothers (USA, [...), Robson Green and [Jerom]e Flynn (UK, 1995) and [Gareth] Gates (UK, 2002) have [score]d No.1s with this 1955 [song] written by Alex North [and Hy] Zaret (both USA).

[Most] simultaneous [...] UK singles [...] (group)

[...m]onths after The Jam [a]nnounced their split [in Nov]ember 1982, the New [...rio's] entire singles [c]atalogue was re-issued. [Sev]en tracks reached the [chart] on 5 February 1983, [most n]otably the double A-side ["Going] Underground"/"Dreams [of Chil]dren" at No.21.

[Most] charts topped [by] one album

[...Rele]ased on 14 November [...,]*Confessions on a Dance*

Floor by Madonna (USA), topped charts in 40 countries around the world. The lead single, "Hung Up", reached No.1 in the singles charts of 41 countries.

Most No.1 singles

In little more than six years, between 1964 and 1970, The Beatles (UK) crowned the *Billboard* Hot 100 a record 20 times, including six times in 1964 and four in 1965. Their first No.1 was "I Want to Hold Your Hand" in January 1964 and their last "The Long and Winding Road" in June 1970.

First group inducted into the Songwriters Hall of Fame

Queen (Freddie Mercury (b. Zanzibar), Brian May, Roger Taylor and John Deacon, all UK) were the first complete group inducted into the Songwriters Hall of Fame, in 2003. The first induction ceremony was staged in 1969, and 389 individuals have been inducted since then.

First single to sell one million copies

In 1955, "Rock Around the Clock" by Bill Haley and the Comets (USA) became the UK's first million-selling single. It is also the only single to return to the top 20 on five separate occasions.

Oasis (UK) claimed the record for the **fastest-selling album in UK chart history** when their third studio album, *Be Here Now*, sold 663,389 copies in just three days on 21–23 August 1997, including 350,000 copies on the first day. The album sold its millionth copy 17 days after its release.

Released on 21 March 2000, *No Strings Attached* by *NSync (USA), the group that introduced Justin Timberlake to the world, is the **fastest-selling album in the USA**. It shifted a staggering 2.42 million copies in its first week, more than doubling the 1.13 million copies sold by Backstreet Boys' *Millennium* in 1999.

Fleetwood Mac's *Rumours* has spent the **most weeks on the UK albums chart**. Between 26 February 1977 and 28 April 2012 the album racked up 490 weeks in the top 75 (the chart was a top 100 from 1981 to 1989).

Led Zeppelin (UK) share with ABBA (Sweden), see left, the record for the **most successive UK No.1 albums**, with eight. Led Zeppelin's chart-topping run began with *Led Zeppelin II*, above, in February 1970 and concluded with *In Through the Out Door* – recorded at ABBA's Polar Studios in Stockholm, Sweden – in September 1979.

FACT:
As a youngster, future *NSync member Justin Timberlake performed at beauty pageants.

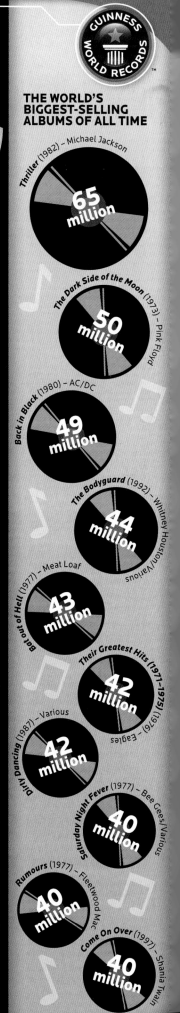

GUINNESS WORLD RECORDS™

THE WORLD'S BIGGEST-SELLING ALBUMS OF ALL TIME

Thriller (1982) – Michael Jackson — **65 million**

The Dark Side of the Moon (1973) – Pink Floyd — **50 million**

Back in Black (1980) – AC/DC — **49 million**

The Bodyguard (1992) – Whitney Houston/Various — **44 million**

Bat out of Hell (1977) – Meat Loaf — **43 million**

Their Greatest Hits (1971–1975) (1976) – Eagles — **42 million**

Dirty Dancing (1987) – Various — **42 million**

Saturday Night Fever (1977) – Bee Gees/Various — **40 million**

Rumours (1977) – Fleetwood Mac — **40 million**

Come On Over (1997) – Shania Twain — **40 million**

All sales figures are estimated.

THEATRE

Française is the oldest national theatre in the world. During the French Revolution of 1789, the theatre's company split: the conservatives went to the Théatre de la Nation, while the more revolutionary actors became the Théatre de la République at the Palais Royal. In 1803, the Comédie Française was reformed and has remained in existence ever since.

Longest solo theatrical performance

Adrian Hilton (UK) recited the complete works of Shakespeare in 110 hr 46 min in a "Bardathon" at the Shakespeare Festival in London and Gold Hill Baptist Church in Chalfont St Peter (both UK) on 16–21 July 1987.

Best-selling playwright

English playwright William Shakespeare (1564–1616) is the world's best-selling playwright, with sales of his plays and poetry thought to have exceeded 4 billion copies since his death. He is also the third most translated author in history behind Agatha Christie (UK) and Jules Verne (France).

The **most valuable edition of a Shakespeare work** is one of only five copies of the First Folio, dated 1623, which was sold at Christie's in New York City, USA, on 8 October 2001 for $6,166,000 (£4,156,947). It is also the highest price ever paid for a 17th-century book.

Longest theatrical run

As of 23 April 2012, there have been 24,757 continuous performances of *The Mousetrap* by Dame Agatha Christie (UK). The show opened at the Ambassadors Theatre in London's West End on 25 November 1952, transferring to St Martin's Theatre in 1974. The legendary whodunnit will mark its diamond anniversary (60 years) on 25 November 2012.

First permanent theatre

The Theatre of Dionysius was the world's oldest theatre, built in ancient Athens in approximately 500 BC. With an estimated capacity of up to 17,000 people, the outdoor theatre was "in the round", with tone rows built up a slope overlooking the stage.

Both tragedies and comedies were performed here and it was used for "competitions", in which the audience served as judges to vote for a prize for best play.

Oldest indoor theatre

The Teatro Olimpico in Vicenza, Italy, was designed in the Roman style by Andrea di Pietro, alias Palladio (1508–80). Work on the theatre began three months before his death and was finished by his pupil Vicenzo Scamozzi in 1583. It is preserved today in its original form.

Largest theatre

The Great Auditorium is part of the Great Hall of the People (Renmin Dahuitang) in Tiananmen Square, Beijing, China, which was completed in 1959. The Auditorium is 76 m (249 ft) long, 60 m (196 ft)

wide and 33 m (108 ft) high. When used as a theatre, it seats 10,000.

The **smallest regularly operated professional theatre** is the Kremlhof theater in Villach, Austria, which has a maximum capacity of eight seats. It is jointly run by the organizations VADA and kärnöl (both Austria) and has hosted regular performances since 12 January 2010.

Largest theatre stage

The Hilton Theater at the Reno Hilton in Reno, Nevada, USA, measures 53.3 x 73.4 m (175 x 241 ft). The stage has three main lifts, each of which

can raise 1,200 performers (up to a total weight of 65.3 tonnes, or 143,961 lb), as well as two turntables, each with a circumference of 19.1 m (62 ft 6 in).

Largest theatre cast

A total of 2,100 children appeared in the finale of the *Rolf Harris Schools Variety Spectacular* held at Sydney Entertainment Centre, Sydney, Australia, in November 1985.

Oldest national theatre

Founded in 1680 by Louis XIV of France, the Comédie

> **FACT:**
> Spider-Man was created by writer Stan Lee and artist Steve Ditko (both USA) back in 1962.

Most expensive theatre production

By the time *Spider-Man: Turn Off the Dark*, the musical based on the legendary comic superhero, opened on 14 June 2011 at the Foxwoods Theatre on Broadway, its cost had climbed to $75 million (£46 million). It is the largest investment for a theatrical production anywhere in the world. With 182 previews (performances before an official opening) from 28 November 2010 until its official opening on 14 June 2011, it has also registered the **most previews for a Broadway show**.

Longest continually operating theatrical management organization

The Theatrical Management Association (TMA) was founded in London, UK, 108 years ago, on 24 January 1894, though initially under a variant of this name. The great English actor-managers Sir Henry Irving and Sir Herbert Beerbohm Tree were among its creators, with Irving becoming the organization's first president.

Oldest opera

The Chinese form of opera, *Kunqu*, appeared in the 14th century during the Yuan Dynasty (1271–1368). It combined opera with ballet, drama and the recitation of poetry and music, drawing on earlier Chinese theatrical forms such as mime and acrobatics. "Kun" refers to Kunshan (the district where the opera originated, near Suzhou, in modern Jiangsu Province, China) and "qu" means music.

Most prolific contemporary playwright

Sir Alan Ayckbourn (UK) has written 76 full-length plays since 1959. His first full work, *The Square Cat*, debuted at the Library Theatre in Scarborough, North Yorkshire, UK, when Ayckbourn was just 20. His latest play, *Surprises*, is due to debut in 2012. He has had a new full-length play produced nearly every year over 53 years. Only six of those years have not seen the premiere of a new Ayckbourn play.

Agile Ayckbourn

Sir Alan's writing output has also encompassed two short, one-act plays, 11 revues, seven plays for children, five adaptations (also full length plays), one screenplay and one book, *The Crafty Art of Playmaking*.

FACT:
Hugh Jackman made his New York theatrical debut way back in 2002, in the musical *Carousel*.

Highest weekly gross for a one-man show on Broadway

Hugh Jackman (Australia) grossed $2,057,354 (£1,323,380) during the holiday week 27 December 2011–1 January 2012, performing *Hugh Jackman, Back on Broadway* at the Broadhurst Theater in New York City, USA.
Jackman also took the record for the **most money raised for a charity by a Broadway show**: $1,789,580 (£1,151,140) for Broadway Cares/Equity Fights AIDS.

Most performances in one Broadway show

George Lee Andrews (USA) gave 9,382 performances in the Broadway staging of *The Phantom of the Opera*. The show opened on 26 January 1988 at the Majestic Theater with Andrews in the cast and he played several roles in the show until 3 September 2011.

Most performances of a one-man show

Hal Holbrook (USA) had performed *Mark Twain Tonight!* 2,237 times as of 26 February 2012. Holbrook began performing the show in 1954, so 2012 marks his record 58th consecutive year as the American writer!

Your ticket to Broadway

• New York's world-renowned Broadway Theater District includes Times Square and stretches from West 41st Street to West 54th Street, between 6th Avenue (Avenue of the Americas) and 8th Avenue. It includes 39 professional theatres.

• Its nickname, the "Great White Way", alludes to the district's adoption of electric advertising signs and lighting in the late 19th century.

• "Off Broadway" theatres usually have between 100 and 499 seats. Even smaller professional productions can be seen in "Off Off Broadway" venues seating under 100. The smallest Broadway theatre has 650 seats.

Longest-running show on Broadway

The Andrew Lloyd Webber (UK) musical *The Phantom of the Opera* is the longest-running show in the history of Broadway – musical or play – having reached the milestone 10,000 performances at the Majestic Theater in New York, USA, on 11 February 2012.

The **longest-running musical in London's West End** is *Les Misérables* by Claude-Michel Schönberg (France), which opened on 4 December 1985 and is currently in its 27th year. It celebrated its 10,000th performance on 5 January 2010.

Highest-grossing Broadway show

By April 2012, Disney's *The Lion King* had grossed $853.8 million (£537.7 million) since opening on Broadway in October 1997. It overtook *The Phantom of the Opera*, which had grossed $853.1 million (£537.3 million) in its Broadway run since January 1988.

AND THE WINNER IS...

The UK's Laurence Olivier Awards and the USA's Tony Awards are benchmarks of theatrical excellence. GWR raises the curtain on the most lauded performers and productions.

Most Tony Awards for a play
The Coast of Utopia, by Tom Stoppard (UK) – 7

Performer with the most Tony Award nominations
Julie Harris (USA) – 10

Most Tony Awards for an actor
Boyd Gaines (USA) – 4

Most Tony Awards for an actor/actress in performance
Julie Harris (USA) and Angela Lansbury (USA, b. UK) – 5 (Julie Harris also has a Lifetime Achievement Tony)

Most Tony Awards (individual)
Harold Prince (USA) – 21

Most Tony Awards for a composer
Stephen Sondheim (USA) – 8

Most Olivier Awards for a show
Matilda the Musical, from the book by Roald Dahl (UK) – 7

Most Olivier Awards for an actor
Sir Ian McKellen (UK) – 6

Most Olivier Awards for an actress
Dame Judi Dench (UK) – 7 (including the Special Award for Outstanding Contributions to the British Theatre)

Most Olivier Awards (individual)
Dame Judi Dench and designer William Dudley (both UK) – 7

Usually, GWR considers only world records. London's West End and New York's Broadway are such cornerstones of the theatre, however, that we have also included records specific to those districts.

TV

Highest-paid comedy actor

As of 2011, Ashton Kutcher (USA, centre above) earned $700,000 (£453,000) per episode for sitcom *Two and a Half Men* (CBS), making him TV's highest-paid comedy actor. He replaced previous record holder Charlie Sheen (USA).

FACT: Sheen had earned as much as $1.2 million (£750,000) per episode on the same show.

Most widely viewed factual programme

Airing in 212 different territories worldwide, the UK's *Top Gear* (BBC) is the most widely viewed factual programme on TV. The motoring show began in 1977 and relaunched in 2002. It is currently hosted by Jeremy Clarkson, Richard Hammond and James May (all UK).

First regular TV broadcasts

At 3 p.m. on 2 November 1936 in London, UK, the BBC launched the world's first regular public television broadcasts. That said, experimental services had operated across the world from the 1920s.

First TV broadcaster to show a live sporting event in 3D

BSkyB was the first TV broadcaster to relay a sporting event live in 3D. On 31 January 2010, it screened a football match between Arsenal and Manchester United in 3D via its Sky Sports platform to a public audience in selected pubs in the UK.

First TV sitcom

Character actor James Hayter (UK) starred as J Pinwright, owner of the smallest multiple store in the world, in the first television sitcom *Pinwright's Progress* (BBC, 1946–47).

Longest-running sitcom (episode count)

The current (and, in fact, all-time) longest-running sitcom on US television is *The Simpsons* (Fox), which completed its 23rd series in spring 2012. The show debuted on 17 December 1989 and its 500th episode was broadcast on 19 February 2012. Doh!

Most expensive TV series

Screened in late 2011, Steven Spielberg's 13-part series *Terra Nova* (Fox, 2011) carried a $70-million (£45.3-million) price tag, or around $200,000 (£130,000) for each minute of action. Not far behind were the HBO giants *Game of Thrones* – $60 million (£36 million) for its first series – and *Boardwalk Empire* – $50 million (£32 million) per series.

FACT: The pilot episode of *Boardwalk Empire* cost $18 million (£11.6 million) alone!

Longest-running TV variety show

Sábado Gigante (Univision Television Network) is a Spanish-language US TV variety show that has been broadcast every Saturday evening since 8 August 1962. It was created – and has been continually hosted – by Mario Kreutzberger (Chile), more popularly known as "Don Francisco". Each three-hour episode is filmed in front of a live audience.

Longest marathon TV talk show

Lasting 52 hours, the longest marathon TV talk show took place on Channel 5 (Ukraine) from 23 to 25 August 2011. The hosts were Pavlo Kuzheyev and Tetiana Danylenko (both Ukraine) at the Channel 5 Studio in Kiev, Ukraine.

Most durable TV presenter

Sir Patrick Moore (UK) has hosted the monthly UK series *The Sky at Night* (BBC) since the first edition aired in 1957. The series is also the **longest-running TV show presented by the same host**.

Most watched man on TV

Actor David Hasselhoff (USA) is the most watched man in television history. Having debuted as the eponymous hero of the popular US series *Knight Rider* (NBC), he went on to star as LA County lifeguard Mitch Buchannon in the series *Baywatch* (NBC), which, at its peak in 1996, had an estimated weekly audience of 1.1 billion viewers.

TV star and daredevil...

• David Hasselhoff has achieved another world record – for the **highest reverse bungee**: the greatest height a human has been catapulted using a reverse bungee system.

• "The Hoff" was catapulted a height of 70 m (229 ft 7 in).

• The height was verified by a UK Bungee Club official, who supervised the attempt on behalf of UK TV show *Red or Black*. (See the record for this show on the next page.)

• This record took place on 30 June 2011 at Battersea Power Station, London, UK.

Highest-rated TV series (current)

The Metacritic website assembles ratings for movies, TV shows, music and games releases from several sources and provides an average value for each. As of 9 March 2012, the fourth season of *Southland* (TNT) – starring Michael Cudlitz and Lucy Liu, pictured – registered the highest ratings for a current show, with a score of 90/100. The **highest-rated TV series of all time** was season four of Baltimore-based crime show *The Wire* (HBO), which scored 98/100.

TV'S TOP GENRES

In 2009, we all broke records by watching more TV than ever before, a global average of 3 hr 12 min per day! But what were we watching?

Longest TV career by an entertainer (male)

Sir Bruce Forsyth (UK) made his TV debut in 1939 as an 11-year-old on the BBC (UK) show *Come and Be Televised* and hosted his first show, *Sunday Night at the London Palladium* (ATV/ITV, UK), in 1958. His most recent TV appearance was on 25 December 2011 when he co-hosted the BBC's *Strictly Come Dancing Christmas Special*, giving him a TV career of 72 years.

Most expensive TV commercial)

A four-minute feature film made by director Baz Luhrmann (Australia) advertising Chanel No.5 perfume is the world's most expensive TV advert, costing £18 million ($33 million) to produce. It premiered on US TV on 11 November 2004 and starred Nicole Kidman (Australia) as a Marilyn Monroe-style actress who is hounded by paparazzi. Kidman, who wore couture outfits by designer Karl Lagerfeld in the advert, was paid £2 million ($3.7 million) for her appearance (the **highest fee for a TV commercial**).

Highest advertising rates for a TV show

Excluding specials and one-off sporting events, the costliest television series for advertising slots is currently *American Idol* (Fox), during which a 30-second advert will cost $623,000 (£413,000), earning the show $7 million (£4.6 million) every 30 minutes. However, the hour-long final episode of *Friends* (NBC) holds the all-time record for a TV series, costing advertisers $2 million (£1.1 million) per 30 seconds on 6 May 2004.

Highest annual earnings for a TV talent show judge

His appearances as a judge on television shows *Pop Idol* (UK), *American Idol* (USA) and *The X Factor* (UK) have made Simon Cowell (UK) the highest-paid TV talent show judge. He earned £56.7 million ($90 million) in 2010–11 according to Forbes.

Highest-paid TV cast

The cast of *The Sopranos* (HBO), a New Jersey-based Mob drama, earned a combined salary of $52 million (£26 million) for their work on the show's seventh series. According to Forbes' Celebrity 100, James Gandolfini (USA), who played Mob boss Tony Soprano, secured himself a fee of $1-million (£505,000) for each of the last eight episodes.

Highest annual earnings ever for a television actor

Seinfeld star Jerry Seinfeld (USA) made an estimated $267 million (£159.5 million) in 1998 according to the 1999 Forbes Celebrity 100 list.

Highest-paid TV actress

Eva Longoria (above left) of *Desperate Housewives* (ABC), which finished in 2012, and Tina Fey (above) of *30 Rock* (NBC) each earned a record $13 million (£8.4 million) a season. Fey's salary also includes her writing fees.

Most expensive game show

The most expensive TV game show ever was the UK's *Red or Black* (ITV), devised by Simon Cowell (UK, *see above*) and hosted by Ant & Dec (aka Anthony McPartlin and Declan Donnelly, both UK, pictured). The programme was stripped – i.e., shown on consecutive nights – across seven nights in September 2011, and four contestants each walked away with £1 million ($1.5 million). The budget for the show was £15 million ($23 million).

Greatest prize winnings on a TV game show

The largest cash prize won on a TV game show is €3,000,000 (£2,559,122; $4,183,594) by Nino Stefan. He beat host Stefan Raab (both Germany) on the popular German Pro 7 show *Schlag den Raab* (*Beat the Raab*), on 23 May 2009.

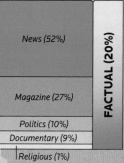

FICTION (42%)
- Series (?%)
- Movies (12%)
- Soap operas (12%)
- Telenovelas (9%)
- Cartoons (2%)
- TV movies (2%)
- Sitcoms (1%)

ENTERTAINMENT (38%)
- Event (30%)
- Reality show (28%)
- Variety show (18%)
- Game show (12%)
- Talk show (7%)
- Comedy (5%)

FACTUAL (20%)
- News (52%)
- Magazine (27%)
- Politics (10%)
- Documentary (9%)
- Religious (1%)

Source: International Television Expert Group (2009 figures)

STAR WARS

Largest fortune made from a film franchise

Rather than taking a director's fee for *Star Wars* (USA, 1977), George Lucas (USA) acquired the rights to all sequels and future merchandise. In 2011, Forbes assigned him a net worth of $3.2 billion (£2 billion).

Highest average box-office gross for a director

The six feature films directed by George Lucas, from *THX 1138* (USA, 1971) to *Star Wars: Episode III – Revenge of the Sith* (USA, 2005), have grossed a total of $1.74 billion (£1.08 billion) at the box office, at an average of $290.6 million (£145.4 million) per movie.

(Of those film directors who have made 10 movies or more, US director Steven Spielberg has the highest average box-office gross; see p.216.)

The 15 movies *written* by George Lucas have grossed $3.33 billion (£2.16 billion) in global box-office receipts, the **highest box-office gross for a screenwriter**.

Highest-grossing space-opera movie

Star Wars Episode I – The Phantom Menace (USA, 1999) had grossed $924 million (£577 million) worldwide by 3 February 2000.

Largest simultaneous premiere – territories

Star Wars: Episode III – Revenge of the Sith (USA, 2005) was released simultaneously in 115 territories by 20th Century Fox on 19 May 2005. It went on to secure an international gross of $303 million (£165.9 million).

Largest entertainment voice-over project

More than 200,000 lines of dialogue were recorded by several hundred voice actors for the LucasArts videogame *Star Wars: The Old Republic* (Electronic Arts, BioWare and LucasArts, 2011). The MMORPG (massively multiplayer online role-playing game) was first released on 20 December 2011. Pictured above are some of the game's creative team.

Biggest opening weekend ever for a re-released film

Shown in cinemas in 1997 as the first of Lucasfilm's 20th anniversary Special Editions of the original *Star Wars* trilogy, *Episode IV: A New Hope* (USA) grossed $35,906,661 (£21,903,063) in US cinemas on the weekend of 31 January–2 February 1997.

A New Hope took $579,646,015 (£353,584,069) worldwide to June 1997 – the **highest theatrical gross for a film re-release**.

First *Star Wars* videogame

The inaugural *Star Wars* videogame, *The Empire Strikes Back* (Parker Brothers, 1982) was based on the second film in the series and made for the Atari 2600 and Intellivision.

Most Oscars won for visual effects

Dennis Muren (USA) won the Academy Award for Visual Effects a total of six times between 1983 and 1994. He has also received two Special Achievement Awards, in 1981 for *Star Wars: Episode V – The Empire Strikes Back* (USA, 1980) and in 1984 for *Star Wars: Episode VI – Return of the Jedi* (USA, 1983). He also received the Technical Achievement Award in 1982 "For the development of a Motion Picture Figure Mover for animation photography". In addition, Muren holds the record for the most Oscar nominations for visual effects. He has been nominated on 13 occasions, the first being in 1982 for *Dragonslayer* (USA, 1981) and the most recent being in 2006 for *War of the Worlds* (USA, 2005).

Best-selling single of instrumental music

A 1977 disco arrangement of John Williams's (USA) music to *Star Wars* – entitled "Star Wars Theme/Cantina Band" – by record producer Meco, aka Domenico Monardo (USA), remains the only instrumental single to have reached platinum status, according to the Recording Industry Association of America (RIAA), having sold more than 2 million units. The track featured on the album *Star Wars and Other Galactic Funk* (1977), which outsold the original movie soundtrack and was also certified platinum.

FACT:
"Star Wars Theme/Cantina Band" was a US No.1 hit in 1977.

THE EMPIRE STRIKES GOLD

Taking into account the original movies, re-releases and special editions, the six Star Wars movies represent the **highest-grossing sci-fi series ever**. Take a look at the worldwide box-office figures...

Star Wars: Episode VI – Return of the Jedi
$475.1 M

Star Wars: Episode V – The Empire Strikes Back
$538.4 M

Star Wars: Episode II – Attack of the Clones
$649.4 M

Star Wars: Episode IV – A New Hope
$775.4 M

Star Wars: Episode III – Revenge of the Sith
$848 M

Star Wars: Episode I – The Phantom Menace
$1.026 B

Most spoofed film series

There have been direct references to the Star Wars series in more than 170 feature films, and in countless TV shows, comics, adverts and online videos. One episode of the cartoon comedy Family Guy, "Blue Harvest" (Fox, 2007, left), was an hour-long parody of the film.

A number of full-length Star Wars spoofs have been made, of which the best known is Spaceballs (USA, 1987, below left). Individual Star Wars spoof scenes have been a staple of comedy movies for more than 30 years, from Airplane II: The Sequel (USA, 1982) and Get Crazy (USA, 1983) to Austin Powers: The Spy Who Shagged Me (USA, 1999) and The Simpsons Movie (USA, 2007).

Most successful book series based on a film series

Lucas Licensing has recorded more than 100 million sales of Star Wars-related books, with over 850 novelizations, original novels, reference books, children's books and role-playing supplements, including 80 New York Times best-sellers. The first original novel based on Star Wars characters was Splinter of the Mind's Eye (1978), written by Alan Dean Foster (USA).

Largest film merchandising campaign

In May 1996, PepsiCo (owners of Pepsi, Pizza Hut, KFC, Taco Bell and Frito Lay) signed a deal with Lucasfilm for the right to link their products with Star Wars during the Special Edition re-releases of the original trilogy, leading up to the 1999 release of Episode I: The Phantom Menace. At a reported $2 billion (£1.34 billion), it is the most extensive single cross-promotion deal in history.

Most prolific videogame series based on a licensed property

As of April 2012, a total of 279 Star Wars videogames had been released across 41 different platforms.

Most successful action-figure range

As of 2007, the Star Wars toy lines from Kenner/Hasbro had generated more than $9 billion (£4.5 billion) in sales. In 1978 alone, Kenner's first range of Star Wars figures sold more than 40 million units, earning in excess of $100 million (£52 million).

Most successful film merchandising franchise

As of 2012, the value of the Star Wars franchise is estimated at $30.57 billion (£19.51 billion), of which the box-office returns for the six films in the series account for only $4.27 billion (£2.72 billion). Lucas Licensing on behalf of Lucasfilm has noted more than $20 billion (£12.76 billion) in sales of tie-in merchandise globally, along with more than $3 billion (£1.9 billion) profit from Star Wars videogames and $2.5 billion (£1.6 billion) in DVD sales.

Sources for box-office figures: boxofficemojo.com; imdb.com

VIDEOGAMERS

Most prolific dancing game high scorer

Elizabeth "Kitty McScratch" Bolinger (USA) holds more Twin Galaxies high-score records for *Dance Central*, *Just Dance* and *Just Dance 2* than any other player. She is first on the leaderboard for more than 85 different songs. Her highest score is for *Dance Central* track "C'mon Ride It (The Train)" by Quad City DJs, for which she scored 432,793 points on 5 December 2010.

FACT:
The International Video Game Hall of Fame is based in Kitty's hometown, Ottumwa, Iowa, USA.

Best-selling computer game console

The PlayStation 2 (PS2), made by Sony and released in 2000, had sold over 153.6 million units as of 21 November 2011. The second best-selling console is the Nintendo DS, released in 2004. The DS overtook the PS2 in January 2011, when it registered 147 million sales, but has since lost ground.

Best-selling music game

As of May 2011, more than 7.32 million copies of Ubisoft's Wii game *Just Dance 2* (2010) had been sold around the globe, making it more successful than the single-platform versions of all other music games. The second best-selling title in the genre is the original *Just Dance* (Ubisoft, 2009) with sales of 5.78 million.

Biggest MMO hack

In April 2011, Sony revealed that due to a huge online hack user details from 24.6 million accounts in its massively multiplayer online (MMO) gaming arm, Sony Online Entertainment (SOE), may have been stolen. The games affected were *EverQuest I & II*, *Free Realms*, *Vanguard*, *Clone Wars Adventures* and *DC Universe Online*. About 12,700 credit or debit card numbers and expiration dates, plus 10,700 direct-debit records, could have been compromised as part of the hack, leading to SOE taking all of its MMOs offline for 12 days.

First fitness game

In 1979, a full 25 years before Nintendo popularized fitness gaming, Mattel's Intellivision blazed a trail for health-conscious software with Jack LaLanne's *Physical Conditioning*. The game featured the recorded voice of veteran US fitness fanatic LaLanne (then already aged 65), encouraging gamers to try various exercises, while basic animations showed the movements on screen.

Largest collection of videogames

Richard Lecce (USA) had a total of 8,068 different videogames when counted in Delray Beach, Florida, USA, on 22 December 2011.

Largest fee paid for an appearance in a videogame advert

Helen Mirren (UK) was paid a reported £500,000 ($800,000) to appear in a series of television adverts for *Wii Fit* (Nintendo, 2007) from October 2010.

Largest game of *Angry Birds*

The 3 March 2011 edition of *Conan*, the American talkshow hosted by Conan O'Brien, featured a man-sized real-life version of *Angry Birds* (Rovio, 2009) in his studio set. The game was recreated by the show's production staff and featured obstacles made from furniture, while inflatable balls were used to represent the game's birds and pigs.

Largest mobile phone gaming party

On 13 April 2011, a total of 316 participants joined a mobile phone gaming party organized by Kick Energy (UK) at the *Gadget Show Live*, in the NEC, Birmingham, UK.

FACT:
To use this controller like a standard hand-held pad, you would need to be 51 m (167 ft) tall.

Largest videogame controller

Officially verified in August 2011 as the largest console game controller, this fully functional Nintendo Entertainment System (NES) pad measures an enormous 366 cm x 159 cm x 51 cm (12 ft x 5 ft 3 in x 1 ft 8 in). Its main creator is engineering student Ben Allen (bottom right), who was helped by Stephen van't Hof and Michel Verhulst, all of whom study at the Delft University of Technology in the Netherlands. The fantastic facsimile is 30 times the size of a standard NES controller, and requires two gamers to navigate its enormous buttons.

First videogame theme to win a Grammy award

On 13 February 2011, *Civilization IV* became the first game to feature a Grammy-winning theme song. Composer Christopher Tin (USA) won in the Best Instrumental Arrangement Accompanying Vocalist(s) category with "Baba Yetu".

Most expensive PlayStation 3 game sold at auction

On 2 August 2011, Damian Fraimorice (Israel) sold a factory-sealed copy of *NBA Elite 11* (EA, 2011) to a buyer in the USA for $1,500 (£915). Damian also holds the record for the **most expensive Xbox 360 game sold at auction**. On 2 February 2011, he sold a copy of *Dead Space Ultra Limited Edition* to a buyer in New York, USA, for $2,999 (£1,865).

Most gamers voting in a gaming award

In a poll conducted by the entertainment news service IGN at the 2011 Gamescom exhibition in Cologne, Germany, a total of 258,367 people voted for their favourite game. The winner, *DOTA 2* (2012) from Valve Software, collected 68,041 votes.

Most guns in a videogame

Borderlands (Gearbox Software, 2009) has a tagline boasting "87 bazillion" guns in the game. In reality, the figure is 17,750,000 – still by far the most guns in any videogame. Weapons are generated randomly, with different ammo, components and elemental effects.

Most prolific videogames magazine

Enterbrain, Inc. (Japan) had published 1,120 issues of *Famitsu* as of 1 December 2011. The first issue appeared on 20 June 1986.

Most valuable Xbox sold at auction

Excluding one-off competition prizes, and consoles not on general sale, the rarest Xbox is the white Panzer Dragoon-themed original, released to promote *Panzer Dragoon Orta* (Sega, 2002). Only 999 were produced. On 10 June 2011, one was sold on eBay for $1,250 (£760).

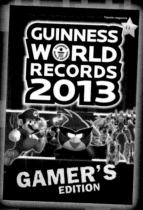

GUINNESS WORLD RECORDS 2013
GAMER'S EDITION

For even more gaming world records, check out GWR Gamer's Edition 2013!

FACT: Ryan dressed as the character Ryu for a special Guinness World Records shoot in London's Chinatown.

Most international *Street Fighter* wins

Ryan Hart (UK) won more than 450 *Street Fighter* events in 13 different countries from 1998 to 2011. He also holds the record for the **longest winning streak on *Street Fighter IV*** (Capcom/Dimps, 2009). Ryan remained unbeaten for 169 matches at the GAME event in the Prospect Centre, Hull, UK, on 27 March 2010.

Fastest completion of *Mario Kart* Circuit 1

Speedy Sami Çetin (UK) has been a fixture of the competitive *Mario Kart* scene for over 10 years, but 2010 was his golden season. He took the chequered flag for the fastest completion of the iconic Circuit 1 on the very first game in the series, *Super Mario Kart* (Nintendo, 1992). He holds the record on both the PAL and NTSC versions of the game, with times of 58.34 seconds and 56.45 seconds respectively, as of August 2011.

GAMING MARATHONS

Some videogamers just can't stop playing their favourite games, as these endurance marathons demonstrate...

Motion-sensor game: (*Dance Central 2*) Christopher Lawrence Trasmaño (Philippines) — **16 hr 21 min 44 sec**

Dance game: (*Dance Dance Revolution*) Chris McGivern (UK) — **20 hr 24 min 43 sec**

Mobile game: (Various) Martin Fornleitner, Hans Peter Glock and Stefan Reichspfarrer (all Austria) and Paul Dahlhoff (Germany) — **24 hr 10 min**

Survival horror game: (*Resident Evil* series) Tim Turi (USA) — **27 hr 8 min**

Racing game: (*Need for Speed Shift*) Sebastian Giessler and Marcus Wiessala (both Germany) — **30 hr**

Fighting game: (*Mortal Kombat*) Melissa Estuesta, Cristopher Bryant, Paul Chillino and Jameson Moose (all USA) — **32 hr 5 min 47 sec**

Japanese RPG: (*Final Fantasy* series) Philip Kollar (USA) — **34 hr**

Football game: (*Pro Evolution Soccer 2012*) Marco Ramos and Efraim Ie (both Portugal) — **38 hr 49 min 13 sec**

RPG: (*Elder Scrolls: Oblivion*) Bryan Vore (USA) — **43 hr 21 min**

Stealth game: (*Metal Gear Solid* series) Ben Reeves (USA) — **48 hr**

Platform game: (*LittleBigPlanet*) David Dino, Lauren Giuliano and Sean Crowley (all USA) — **50 hr 1 min**

Action-adventure game: (*Assassin's Creed: Brotherhood*) Tony Desmet, Jesse Rebmann and Jeffrey Gamon (all Belgium) — **109 hr**

SPORTS

CONTENTS

www.guinnessworldrecords.com

Most prize money in an ATP season

Novak Djokovic (Serbia) served up a stunningly successful 2011 season on the Association of Tennis Professionals (ATP) circuit, which saw him net a hefty $12.6 million (£8 million) in prize money. By winning 10 titles in all – including the Australian Open, Wimbledon and the US Open – the world No.1 took his career earnings to $32.9 million (£21.2 million), making him the fourth highest-earning tennis player of all time.

HOW FAST CAN WE RUN?

How quickly can a human run 100 metres?

When Usain Bolt (Jamaica) ran the 100 m in 9.58 seconds, he smashed not only the world record but also the mathematical theories about athletic ability.

Scientists did not expect anyone to go that fast until 2060. Can he go faster? If so, what's the fastest speed that it is physically possible to reach?

Sports scientist John Brenkus has written about this very subject in his book *The Perfection Point*. The perfect athlete would benefit from the ultimate in genetics, nutrition and training. But how much faster than Usain Bolt could this perfect athlete travel at if he were to make a flawless run in ideal conditions?

As Brenkus explains, the 100 m is a simple concept – you run from A to B as quickly as possible – but this involves four key stages:

1. Reacting to the gun: Starting pistols are a thing of the past. Why? The sound takes 0.025 seconds to travel the 11 m (36 ft) from lane 1 to lane 9, giving the first athlete an advantage. Today, the race starts with a beep from a speaker placed behind each runner. The key is to react quickly, but not too quickly. The perfect start is one-tenth of a second (100 milliseconds) after the beep. Moving off the blocks sooner than this will trigger a false start. If Usain Bolt had managed to get away in one-tenth of a second for his record-breaking run in 2009, he would have finished in 9.51 seconds.

2. Getting out of the blocks: While it's good to have strong calf and thigh muscles to get that explosive start, if they're too powerful, they'll be too heavy for a record-worthy sprint.

WORLD RECORD 100-M RUNS UNDER 10 SECONDS

9.95
JIM HINES
Mexico City, Mexico
14 October 1968

9.93
CALVIN SMITH
Colorado Springs, USA
3 July 1983

9.83
BEN JOHNSON*
Rome, Italy
30 August 1987

9.93
CARL LEWIS
Rome, Italy
30 August 1987

Zürich, Switzerland
17 August 1988

9.92
CARL LEWIS
Seoul, South Korea
24 September 1988

9.90
LEROY BURRELL
New York, USA
14 June 1991

9.86
CARL LEWIS
Tokyo, Japan
25 August 1991

9.85
LEROY BURRELL
Lausanne, Switzerland
6 July 1994

THE PERFECT 100 M ATHLETE

Height: 1.87 m (6 ft 2 in)

Reaction time: 100 milliseconds

Head: shaved, with aerodynamic sunglasses

Altitude: 1,000 m (3,280 ft)

Tailwind: 2 m/sec (4.4 mi/h)

9.84
DONOVAN BAILEY
Atlanta, USA
27 July 1996

9.79
MAURICE GREENE
Athens, Greece
16 June 1999

9.78
TIM MONTGOMERY
Paris, France
14 September 2002

9.77
ASAFA POWELL
Athens, Greece
14 June 2005

JUSTIN GATLIN*
Doha, Qatar
12 May 2006

ASAFA POWELL
Gateshead, England
11 June 2006
Zürich, Switzerland
18 August 2006

9.74
ASAFA POWELL
Rieti, Italy
9 September 2007

9.72
USAIN BOLT
New York, USA
31 May 2008

9.69
USAIN BOLT
Beijing, China
16 August 2008

9.58
USAIN BOLT
Berlin, Germany
16 August 2009

233

Leg inseam:
1 m (40 in)

Muscles: ideal balance of muscle fibres: 55–65% fast-twitch; 35–45% slow-twitch; 30.4-cm-wide (12-in) thighs

Climate: barometric pressure of 986.78 millibars (29.14 in), 11% humidity, 27.7°C (82°F)

Running suit: skin-tight material to make air flow smoothly around body

Top speed: 47.3 km/h (29.4 mi/h)

Weight: 87 kg (192 lb) – only 4% fat

Shoes: lightweight 87-g (3-oz) spiked shoe (see left)

USAIN BOLT

*These records were later rescinded

ASAFA POWELL

CARL LEWIS

So, taking Usain Bolt's record time of 9.58 seconds

and adjusting for what we've learned from the four stages, the result is a potential time of 9.01 seconds.

But just think. It took humanity 190,000 years of development to run a mile in under 4 minutes. Once this barrier was breached – a barrier more psychological than physical – it took just 46 days for someone else to do it; 10 years later, 336 people had achieved it!

So if 9.01 seconds seems an absolute scientific limit, then breaking the 9-second barrier will become the new holy grail of athletics. And as humans seem to have an inbuilt desire to overcome apparently insurmountable obstacles, it is surely conceivable that the barrier will be broken. Therefore, the real limit is 8.99 seconds.

3. Accelerating to your top speed:

Air resistance increases as the square of the speed, which means that if you double your speed, the drag increases fourfold. At speeds of 40 km/h (25 mi/h), this is four times the resistance a marathon runner will face. Luckily, tailwinds up to 2 m/sec (4.4 mi/h) are allowed by the Olympic committee. (Bolt broke his record with no tailwind; imagine how much quicker he would have been with one!) If the track is at an altitude of 1,000 m (3,280 ft), the air will be thinner and provide less resistance. Any higher, and records don't count.

4. Slowing down as little as possible:

The final challenge is not decelerating too quickly. Air resistance continues to act on runners, but by now their muscles will start to tire too and they won't be able to speed up the rate at which they are taking individual steps. Instead, they should increase their stride length – so that they can cover as great a distance as possible with each pace.

AMERICAN FOOTBALL

Most first downs by a team in a season

Darren Sproles (USA, pictured above right) helped the New Orleans Saints set a National Football League (NFL) record for most first downs in a season, with 416 in 2011.

Most field goals converted (50 yards or more)

Jason Hanson (USA) shares the NFL record for most successful field goals of 50 yards or greater in a regular season, with eight. He achieved this in 2008, place-kicking for the Detroit Lions. Jason equalled the 1995 record set by Morten Andersen (Denmark) with the Atlanta Falcons.

NFL SEASONS

Longest NFL field goal

The NFL record for longest field goal is 63 yards, by Sebastian Janikowski (Poland) of the Oakland Raiders against the Denver Broncos on 12 September 2011. He equalled the record set by Jason Elam (USA) of the Denver Broncos, against the Jacksonville Jaguars, on 25 October 1998, and Tom Dempsey (USA) of the New Orleans Saints, against the Detroit Lions, on 8 November 1970.

Most passes thrown without an interception

Quarterback Tom Brady (USA) achieved an NFL regular-season record by throwing 358 consecutive passes in a row without one being intercepted while playing for the New England Patriots from 17 October 2010 to 12 September 2011. Brady, who joined the team in 2000, broke the record of 319 attempts without an interception set by Bernie Kosar (USA) while playing for the Cleveland Browns in 1990 and 1991.

Most passes completed in a Super Bowl game

The NFL record for most completions in a Super Bowl game is 32, by Tom Brady for the New England Patriots in 2004's Super Bowl XXXVIII. His record was equalled by Drew Brees (USA) for the New Orleans Saints in Super Bowl XLIV in 2009. Both players' teams went on to victory, as the Patriots defeated the Carolina Panthers 32–29 and the Saints won against the Indianapolis Colts 31–17.

Most receptions by a tight end

Tony Gonzalez (USA) made 102 catches for the Kansas City Chiefs in 2004, the most by a tight end in a season. He also set the record for **most catches made by an NFL tight end during a career**, with 1,149, playing for the Kansas City Chiefs and Atlanta Falcons.

Most penalty yards by a team

The Oakland Raiders set an NFL record for most penalty yards in a season with 1,358 in 2011. In the same year, they also set the NFL record for **most penalties incurred by a team in a season**, with 163.

Most receiving yards by a tight end

Rob Gronkowski (USA) racked up 1,327 receiving yards while playing for the New England Patriots in the 2011 season. Gronkowski also claimed the NFL record for **most touchdown catches in a season by a tight end**, making 17 for the Patriots in the same year.

Most offensive yards by a team

The New Orleans Saints achieved the most offensive yards in a season, with 7,474 in 2011. The Saints also set an NFL record for the **most yards passing by a team in a season**, with 5,347 in 2011.

The **most passing yards by both teams in a single game** is 971, set when the

Most pass completions in a play-off

Drew Brees (USA) set the NFL record for most pass completions in a play-off game with 39. He was playing for the New Orleans Saints against the Seattle Seahawks on 8 January 2011. He also holds the NFL record for **highest completion percentage by a quarterback in a season** with 71.2%, playing for the New Orleans Saints in 2011. Brees completed 468 of 657 attempts to break his own mark of 70.6% in 2009.

Championship wins, touchdowns and stadiums

Most Super Bowls won	6	Pittsburgh Steelers	Most NFL touchdowns	208	Jerry Rice (San Francisco 49ers, Oakland Raiders)
	5	Dallas Cowboys San Francisco 49ers		175	Emmitt Smith (Dallas Cowboys, Arizona Cardinals)
	4	Green Bay Packers New York Giants		162	LaDainian Tomlinson (San Diego Chargers, New York Jets)
Most AFC Championships won	8	Pittsburgh Steelers	Largest stadiums (by capacity)	109,901	Michigan Stadium Home of Michigan Wolverines Ann Arbor, Michigan
	7	New England Patriots			
	6	Denver Broncos			
Most NFL Championships won	8	Dallas Cowboys		107,282	Beaver Stadium Home of Penn State Nittany Lions University Park, Pennsylvania
	5	Washington Redskins New York Giants San Francisco 49ers		102,455	Neyland Stadium Home of Tennessee Volunteers Knoxville, Tennessee

Statistics correct as of 19 March 2012

Longest touchdown reception

A 99-yard touchdown reception has been made 13 times, most recently by New York Giants teammates Victor Cruz from Eli Manning. The record was claimed when the Giants played the New York Jets (all USA) on 24 December 2011.

Green Bay Packers (469) beat the Detroit Lions (502) 45–41 on 1 January 2012.

Most seasons at the same NFL team

The most seasons played with one team is 20, shared by three players:
• Offensive tackle Jackie Slater (USA) played for the Los Angeles Rams from 1976 to 1995
• Cornerback Darrell Green (USA) played for the Washington Redskins between 1983 and 2002
• Place-kicker Jason Hanson (USA), currently active, has played for the Detroit Lions since 1992.

NFL CAREERS

Most points scored

Morten Andersen (Denmark) scored 2,544 points in his career as a place-kicker from 1982 to 2007. Andersen played for the New Orleans Saints, Atlanta Falcons, New York Giants, Kansas City Chiefs and Minnesota Vikings.

Andersen also holds the NFL record for **most field goals in career**, with 565.

Most kick returns for a touchdown

Devin Hester (USA) set the NFL record for the most combined kick-return touchdowns, with 17. Hester had 12 punt return touchdowns and five kick-off return touchdowns. He also holds the NFL record for **most kick-off return touchdowns by an individual in a regular season game**, with two against the St Louis Rams on 11 December 2006.

Most punt return touchdowns in a career

The NFL record for most punt return touchdowns is 12, by Devin Hester (USA). He has played for the Chicago Bears since 2006. Devin also has the record for the **most punt return touchdowns in an NFL season**, with four in 2007. Patrick Peterson (USA) equalled it for the Arizona Cardinals in 2011.

Most passing yards in a first season

The NFL record for most passing yards by a quarterback playing in his first season is 3,893, set by Cam Newton (USA) playing for the Carolina Panthers in 2011.

Newton also set the NFL record for **most passing yards in an NFL debut**, with 432 against the Green Bay Packers on 18 September 2011. That same year, he set the NFL record for **most rushing touchdowns by a quarterback in a season**, with 14.

Most fumble return touchdowns

Jason Taylor (USA) achieved six fumble return touchdowns as a defensive end and linebacker, playing for the Miami Dolphins, Washington Redskins and New York Jets between 1997 and 2011.

Most receiving yards by a tight end

Tony Gonzalez (USA) racked up 13,338 yards playing for the Kansas City Chiefs and Atlanta Falcons from 1997 through to the 2011 season.

Most punts

The NFL record for most career punts is 1,713, by Jeff Feagles (USA) during his 22-year career with the New England Patriots, Philadelphia Eagles, Arizona Cardinals, Seattle Seahawks and New York Giants from 1988 to 2009. Feagles also holds the record for **most career punting yards**, with 71,211.

Highest field-goal percentage

Nate Kaeding's (USA) career field-goal percentage is 86.5%, playing for the San Diego Chargers since 2004.

Most field goals in a season

David Akers (USA) set the NFL record for most field goals in a season with 44, for the San Francisco 49ers in 2011. Akers secured his 44 successful goals out of a record 52 attempts – the **most field goals attempted in a single season by an individual**. Akers joined the 49ers in July 2011, after an 11-year career with the Philadelphia Eagles.

BALL SPORTS

GAELIC FOOTBALL

Most All-Ireland Ladies Championship wins

Kerry won the All-Ireland Ladies Gaelic Football Championship a record 11 times between 1976 and 1993. The first Championships were held in 1974, the year in which the Ladies Gaelic Football Association itself was formed.

Most players in an exhibition match

Whitehall Colmcille GAA Club (Ireland) organized a Gaelic football exhibition match with 399 players in Dublin, Ireland, on 22 May 2011. The participants ranged in age from the club's under-8 members to its senior players.

Most pass completions in a CFL career

Anthony Calvillo (USA) has completed 5,444 passes in the Canadian Football League (CFL) with the Las Vegas Posse (USA), the Hamilton Tiger-Cats and the Montreal Alouettes (both Canada). He set the record from 1994 to 2011, when he also recorded the **most touchdown passes in a CFL career**, with 418, and the **most passing yards in a CFL career**, with 713,412.

Most pass receptions in Grey Cup history

The Grey Cup is awarded to the winners of the Canadian Football League (CFL). Ben Cahoon (USA) is the all-time leading receiver in Grey Cup history, making 46 catches in the championships. Playing with the Montreal Alouettes (Canada) from 1998 to 2010, he also set the CFL record for **most pass receptions in a career**, with 1,017. The **single season CFL record for most pass receptions** was set by Derrell Mitchell (USA), with 130 for the Toronto Argonauts (Canada) in 1998.

FACT:
The Ladies Gaelic Football Players' Player of the Year Award was awarded for the first time in 2011. The winner was Juliet Murphy (Ireland), who plays for Cork.

double on 11 occasions between 1929 and 2009.

Instituted in 1925, the Irish National Football League is a competition organized, like the more prestigious All-Ireland Championships, at an inter-county level.

Kerry have won the League 19 times between 1928 and 2009, the **most National Irish Football League wins recorded by a single team**. Their most recent triumph came in 2009 over Derry.

Champions and award-winners

Canadian football		
Most Grey Cups (first awarded in 1909)	15	Toronto Argonauts (Canada)
	13	Edmonton Eskimos (Canada)
	10	Winnipeg Blue Bombers (Canada)
Grey Cup MVP awards (first awarded in 1959)	3	Sonny Wade (USA)
		Doug Flutie (USA)
		Damon Allen (USA)

Aussie rules		
Most VFL/AFL premiers (VFL first held in 1897; superseded by AFL in 1990)	16	Carlton (Australia), last in 1995
		Essendon (Australia), last in 2000
	15	Collingwood (Australia), last in 2010

Gaelic football		
Most Sam Maguire Cups (awarded to All-Ireland Championship winners since 1928)	36	Kerry (Ireland)
	23	Dublin (Ireland)
	9	Galway (Ireland)
Largest stadiums (by capacity)	82,300	Croke Park, Dublin (Ireland)
	53,500	Semple Stadium, Tipperary (Ireland)
	50,000	Gaelic Grounds, Limerick (Ireland)

Statistics correct as of 12 April 2012

Largest attendance

A crowd of 90,556 people saw Down beat Offaly at the All-Ireland final at Croke Park, Dublin in 1961.

Largest lesson

The largest Gaelic football lesson involved 528 participants at an event organized by St Joseph's Gaelic Athletic Club in Glenavy, Northern Ireland, UK, on 9 May 2010.

Most doubles

Kerry has won the All-Ireland Football Championship and the National Football League

Most Jock McHale Medals won consecutively

Jock McHale Medals are given to the coach of the winning Premiership team and two coaches have won three years in a row. Norm Smith won for Melbourne between 1955 and 1957, and Leigh Matthews (pictured), for Brisbane from 2001 to 2003.

Most AFL Grand Finals played

Michael Tuck (Australia) has competed in 11 Grand Finals – more than any other individual player. He joined Hawthorn in 1972 and made his record-breaking appearances between 1975 and his retirement as a player in 1991. He was made captain of the team in 1986.

Youngest female football referee

When Daisy Goldsmith (UK) celebrated her 14th birthday she also received her level-nine qualification from the Football Association, on 10 March 2010, in Puriton, Somerset, UK. She became the youngest of 25,502 qualified referees in the nation at the time of her appointment. Only 407 of her colleagues were also female.

then with Carlton in 2007. The Michael Tuck Medal is awarded to the player judged to be the best and fairest in the final of the AFL pre-season cup.

Most Leigh Matthews Trophies

Gary Ablett, Jr was awarded a record three Leigh Matthews Trophies in consecutive years while playing for Geelong from 2007 to 2009. The trophy is presented each year by the AFL Players Association to the league's most valuable player.

Most pre-season cups won

Hawthorn won four pre-season AFL cups, in 1988, 1991–92 and 1999 – a record matched by Essendon with wins in 1990, 1993–94 and 2000.

The AFL pre-season cup began in 1988. The 18 AFL clubs play four matches and the two teams with the best record play in the final.

AUSSIE RULES

Most consecutive Grand Final wins

The Brisbane Lions won the Australian Football League (AFL) Grand Final three times in a row in 2001–03. The team lost to Port Adelaide at its fourth consecutive Grand Final appearance in 2004.

Most consecutive matches kicking goals

Peter McKenna kicked at least one goal in each one of 120 consecutive matches playing for Collingwood from 1968 to 1974. He played for the team between 1965 and 1975.

Most goals kicked in a single Grand Final

Two players have managed to kick a record nine goals in an AFL Grand Final. Gordon Coventry set the record playing for Collingwood against Richmond in 1928, and Gary Ablett repeated the feat 61 years later, playing for Geelong against Hawthorn in 1989.

Most Michael Tuck Medals won

Nick Stevens has won a record two Michael Tuck Medals, first while playing for Port Adelaide in 2002 and

CANADIAN FOOTBALL

Most yards rushing

Mike Pringle (USA) rushed for a career record of 16,425 yards with the Edmonton Eskimos (Canada), Sacramento Gold Miners (USA), Baltimore Stallions (USA) and Montreal Alouettes (Canada) in 1992–2005.

Most kicks blocked

Barron Miles (USA) blocked 13 kicks in 1998–2009, playing in the CFL with the Montreal Alouettes and then the BC Lions (Canada).

Most points scored

Lui Passaglia (Canada) scored 3,991 points, a CFL career record. He played 408 games with BC Lions from 1976 to 2000, the **most games played in a regular CFL season**.

Most Champions League wins (female)

FFC Frankfurt (Germany) have won the premier competition in women's European club football three times, in 2002, 2006 and 2008. Formerly known as the UEFA Women's Cup, the competition was renamed the UEFA Women's Champions League in 2009–10 and has been running since 2001.

BALL FEATS

Longest duration spinning a basketball on a toothbrush

Thomas Connors (UK) kept a basketball spinning for a duration of 13.5 seconds while it was balanced on a toothbrush held in his mouth. Connors set the record in Cardiff Bay, Cardiff, UK, on 16 February 2012.

Most basketball circles around the waist in 30 seconds

Thaneswar Guragai (Nepal) passed a basketball around his own waist 56 times in 30 seconds, in Kathmandu, Nepal, on 4 April 2012. He overtook the previous record-holder by three circles.

Most baseballs held in a baseball glove

Ashrita Furman (USA) managed to hold 24 baseballs in one standard-size baseball glove. Furman grasped the record on 28 December 2011, in New York, New York, USA.

Football freestylers

John Farnworth (UK, left) has the record for the **most football touches with the toes in one minute**, with 109. He showed off his fleet feet on the BBC's *Match of the Day Kickabout* in London, UK, on 16 September 2011. Ash Randall (UK, right) completed the record for the **most football touches with the shin in one minute**, with 138, outside the Wales Millennium Centre in Cardiff, UK, on 16 February 2012. Ash is part of a collective of urban sports freestylers called SBX Entertainment. For both these records, the ball could not hit the ground.

SOCCER

First English Premier League goal

The very first goal scored in the English Premier League was by striker Brian Deane (England) for Sheffield United, which beat Manchester United 2–1 on 15 August 1992.

Most consecutive hat-tricks

Masashi Nakayama (Japan) scored hat-tricks in four consecutive games playing for Júbilo Iwata in the Japanese J League. He netted five goals against Cerezo Osaka at Nagai Stadium on 15 April 1998, four against Sanfrecce Hiroshima at Júbilo Iwata Stadium on 18 April 1998, another four against Avispa Fukuoka at Kumamoto City Stadium on 25 April 1998 and a hat-trick against Consadole Sapporo at Júbilo Iwata Stadium on 29 April 1998.

Most own goals in a domestic league football match

On 31 October 2002, in a league fixture in Madagascar, Stade Olympique l'Emyrne (SOE) lost 149–0 to AS Adema – with every goal an own goal! This unusual tactic was in protest against a refereeing decision that went against SOE in a previous play-off match.

Most UEFA Champions League goals

The most prolific goalscorer in the UEFA Champions League is Raúl González Blanco (Spain), who scored 71 times in 144 matches playing for Real Madrid (Spain) and Schalke 04 (Germany) from 1992 to the end of the 2011 season.

Largest tournament (by players)

Copa Telmex 2011 was contested by 181,909 players and a total of 10,799 teams. The competition was held in Mexico from 2 January to 11 December 2011.

Most goals in the FIFA World Cup (team)

Brazil has scored 210 goals at the FIFA World Cup finals.

Brazil is the only team to have qualified for all 19 World Cup tournaments since 1930, the **most appearances at the FIFA World Cup Finals**.

Most goals in a single FIFA World Cup (player)

Just Fontaine (France, b. Morocco) scored 13 goals in the 1958 World Cup in Sweden in just six matches.

Most goals in a single FIFA World Cup (team)

Runners-up Hungary netted 27 goals at the 1954 tournament in Switzerland.

Most clean sheets at the FIFA World Cup

Two goalkeepers have each kept 10 clean sheets (matches in which they have conceded no goals) in their World Cup finals career. Peter Shilton (England) achieved the feat playing for England between 1982 and 1990. Fabien Barthez equalled the record between 1998 and 2006 playing for France, with whom he won the 1998 World Cup.

Most appearances by a foreign player in the Premier League

The most appearances in the English Premier League by a foreign player is 468, by goalkeeper Mark Schwarzer (Australia) playing for Middlesbrough and Fulham between 1998 and the end of the 2011–12 season.

FACT: Schwarzer has played 94 times for Australia – more times than any of his countrymen.

Most goals in the FIFA World Cup Finals (player)

Ronaldo's namesake, the Brazilian striker Ronaldo Luís Nazário de Lima, scored 15 goals in World Cup Finals matches between 1998 and 2006.

Most expensive football player

A transfer fee of £80 million (€92.27 million; $131.86 million) was quoted for Cristiano Ronaldo's (Portugal) move to Real Madrid (Spain) from Manchester United (England) on 1 July 2009. Ronaldo also garnered the **highest combined transfer fees for an individual football player**: £92.2 million (€106.4 million; $152.1 million), for his moves from Sporting Lisbon (Portugal) to Manchester United and then Real Madrid.

Most Premier League appearances

Ryan Giggs (Wales) played 598 times for Manchester United in the English Premier League between 1992 and the end of the 2011–12 season. The remarkably enduring Giggs is the **only player to have appeared in every Premier League season** – 20 seasons in all – and the **only player to have scored in every Premier League season**. He has also won the **most Premier League winner's medals**, with 12.

Football's top tournaments

Most FIFA World Cups (first held 1930)	5	Brazil (1958, 1962, 1970, 1994, 2002)
	4	Italy (1934, 1938, 1982, 2006)
	3	Germany (1954, 1974, 1990)
Most European Championships (first held 1960)	3	Germany (1972, 1980, 1996)
	2	Spain (1964, 2008)
		France (1984, 2000)
Most European Cups (first held 1956; renamed in 1992 as the Champions League)	9	Real Madrid, Spain (1956, 1957, 1958, 1959, 1960, 1966, 1998, 2000, 2002)
	7	AC Milan, Italy (1963, 1969, 1989, 1990, 1994, 2003, 2007)
	5	Liverpool, England (1977, 1978, 1981, 1984, 2005)
Most Copa Américas (first held 1916)	15	Uruguay (1916, 1917, 1920, 1923, 1924, 1926, 1935, 1942, 1956, 1959, 1967, 1983, 1987, 1995, 2011)
	14	Argentina (1921, 1925, 1927, 1929, 1937, 1941, 1945, 1946, 1947, 1955, 1957, 1959, 1991, 1993)
	8	Brazil (1919, 1922, 1949, 1989, 1997, 1999, 2004, 2007)

Statistics correct as of 8 April 2012

Largest attendance at a World Cup match

A crowd of 174,000 watched the game between Uruguay and Brazil at the Maracanã Stadium in Rio de Janeiro, Brazil, on 16 July 1950. Uruguay won 2–1.

Most wins of the FIFA women's World Cup

Germany won the women's World Cup in 2003 and again in 2007. This equals the record achieved by the USA, who won the inaugural tournament in 1991 and triumphed for a second time in 1999.

Most goals scored in the FIFA women's World Cup

Birgit Prinz (Germany) has scored 14 goals in FIFA women's World Cup matches.

Her last goal was scored in the final at the Hongkou Stadium in Shanghai, China, on 30 September 2007.

The **most goals scored by an individual player in a women's World Cup tournament** is 10, by Michelle Akers (USA) in 1991.

Most times sent off in the FIFA World Cup

Two players have been sent off twice in World Cup matches. The record is shared by Rigobert Song (Cameroon), who was sent off in a game against Brazil in 1994 and then against Chile in 1998, and Zinedine Zidane (France), who first received his marching orders against Saudi Arabia in 1998, and then again in the final against Italy in 2006.

Most own goals in a FIFA World Cup match

There were two own goals in a World Cup match between the USA and Portugal in Suwon, South Korea, on 5 June 2002. The first was scored by Jorge Costa (Portugal), and the second by Jeff Agoos (USA). The USA won the match 3–2.

Most Olympic football titles

The greatest number of Olympic football titles won is three, by Great Britain in 1900 (unofficial competition), 1908 and 1912, and Hungary in 1952, 1964 and 1968.

Women's football was introduced to the Olympic Games in 1996. The **most women's Olympic football titles** is three, by the USA in 1996, 2004 and 2008.

Most goals in an Olympic match

The greatest number of goals scored in an Olympic football match by both teams is 18, in the game between France and Denmark in London, UK, on 22 October 1908. Denmark won the match 17–1.

The **most goals scored by an individual male player in an Olympic football tournament** is 12, by Ferenc Bene (Hungary) in 1964 in Tokyo, Japan. Hungary went on to win the title that year, beating Czechoslovakia 2–1.

The **most goals scored by an individual female player in an Olympic football tournament** is five, by Cristiane (Brazil) and Birgit Prinz (Germany) at the 2004 finals in Athens, Greece.

Most valuable team in sports

Manchester United (England) are worth $2.24 billion (£1.45 billion) according to Forbes, making them the most valuable sports team of any kind. The figure is based on enterprise value (equity plus debt) and revenue for 2010–11. Second is Real Madrid (Spain), worth $1.88 billion (£1.22 billion), and in third are baseball's New York Yankees and the NFL's Dallas Cowboys (both USA), and both at $1.85 billion (£1.20 billion).

Highest-paid footballer

David Beckham (England) remains the player to beat, with annual earnings of $40 million (£24.2 million) as of May 2011. *The Sunday Times* (UK) places his overall net worth at £135 million ($219 million).

FACT:
In March 2012, Messi's goal tally for FC Barcelona (Spain) hit 234, making him its all-time top scorer.

Most wins of the Ballon d'Or

On three occasions, diminutive South American dynamo Lionel Messi (Argentina) has been awarded the trophy for the most outstanding soccer player of the year. Johan Cruyff, Marco van Basten (both Netherlands) and Michel Platini (France) have matched this feat. Messi's wins have come in consecutive years, from 2009 to 2011. (The trophy was renamed the FIFA Ballon d'Or in 2010.)

Messi also scored the **most goals in a UEFA Champions League match**, when he notched up five goals in FC Barcelona's 7–1 demolition of Bayer Leverkusen (Germany) on 7 March 2012.

FACT:
On 2 May 2012, Messi scored his 68th goal of the 2011–12 season, the most goals in a European season.

RUGBY

Youngest World Cup final referee

Craig Joubert (South Africa, b. 8 November 1977) was 33 years 349 days old when refereeing the Rugby Union World Cup Final between New Zealand and France in Auckland, New Zealand, on 23 October 2011.

Australia in Sydney, Australia, on 15 July 2000. Winger Jonah Lomu sealed the win with a try.

Largest paying attendance at a club match

A crowd of 83,761 saw Harlequins beat Saracens 24–19 in the English Aviva Premiership, at Wembley Stadium, London, UK, on 31 March 2012.

Highest score

In Denmark, Comet beat Lindo by 194–0 on 17 November 1973. The highest British score is 177–3 by Norwich against Eccles and Attleborough in a Norfolk Cup match in 1996.

Most appearances in a Super Rugby career

Since his debut in 1999, Nathan Sharpe (Australia) has played 157 times for the Queensland Reds and Western Force, as of 9 May 2012.

Most British and Irish Lions tours as captain

Only one player has captained the British and Irish Lions rugby team on two separate tours: Martin Johnson (UK) in 1997 and 2001. In 1997, the Lions won 2–1 in South Africa, while in 2001 they lost to Australia 2–1. Johnson also toured with the Lions in 1993.

UNION

Biggest win in the World Cup

On 25 October 2003, Australia beat Namibia 142–0 in Adelaide, Australia. The Wallabies scored a World Cup record 22 tries, with full-back Chris Latham scoring five and wing Lote Tuqiri and fly-half Matt Giteau each scoring three. Mat Rogers kicked 16 conversions.

Longest drop goal

Gerald Hamilton "Gerry" Brand kicked a drop goal 77.7 m (255 ft) for South Africa vs England at Twickenham, UK, on 2 January 1932.

Largest paying attendance for an international

A crowd of 109,874 witnessed New Zealand's 39–35 victory over Australia at Stadium

Most Heineken Cup wins

The Heineken Cup is the premier European club competition, and Toulouse (France) have won it four times (1996, 2003, 2005 and 2010). On the last occasion, they beat Biarritz Olympique, France, 21–19 at the Stade de France in Paris.

Most points in a Heineken Cup final

The most points scored by a player in a Heineken Cup final is 30, by Diego Domínguez (Italy), playing for Stade Français against Leicester in Paris, France, on 19 May 2001.

Youngest World Cup try-scorer

George North (UK) was just 19 years 166 days old when he scored for Wales in a Rugby Union World Cup match against Namibia (right, North pictured second left) at New Plymouth in New Zealand on 26 September 2011. North is the third youngest player to play for Wales, making his international debut against South Africa on 13 November 2010 at the Millennium Stadium in Cardiff, Wales, aged 18 years 214 days.

LEAGUE

Fastest hat-trick

On 19 May 2002, Chris Thorman (UK) scored a hat-trick of tries just 6 min 54 sec after the start of a match. He was playing for Huddersfield Giants against Doncaster Dragons in the semi-final of the Buddies National League Cup at Doncaster, South Yorkshire, UK.

Highest score in an international match

France defeated Serbia and Montenegro 120–0 during the Mediterranean Cup at Beirut, Lebanon, on 22 October 2003.

Largest attendance

A crowd of 107,558 attended the National Rugby League Grand Final at Stadium Australia in Sydney, New South Wales, Australia, on 26 September 1999, to see Melbourne beat St George Illawarra 20–18.

Largest attendance for a World Cup final

On 24 October 1992, a total of 73,631 people attended the World Cup final between Australia and Great Britain at Wembley Stadium in London, UK.

Longest drop goal

On 25 March 1989, Joe Lydon (UK) scored from 56 m (183 ft 8 in) for Wigan against Warrington in a Challenge Cup semi-final at Maine Road in Manchester, UK.

Most appearances for the same club

The most appearances for one club is 774, by Jim Sullivan (UK) for Wigan, UK, from 1921 to 1946. He played a record 928 first-class games in all.

Most Australian premierships

South Sydney have won 20 premierships since 1908. The competition was known as the New South Wales Rugby League between 1908 and 1994, the Australian Rugby League between 1995 and 1997, and the National Rugby League (NRL) from 1998.

The Brisbane Broncos have won the **most NRL titles**, with three (1998, 2000, 2006), in addition to premiership wins in 1992, 1993 and 1997.

Most Australian top-flight appearances

Darren Lockyer (Australia) made 355 league appearances for the Brisbane Broncos from 1995 to 2011 in the Australian Rugby League, Super League and National Rugby League.

Most consecutive Super League titles

Leeds Rhinos achieved three Super League titles between 2007 and 2009. On each occasion, the Rhinos defeated St Helens in the final.

Most Four Nations titles

The most wins of the Four Nations is two, by Australia in 2009 and 2011. The competition is contested between Australia, England, New Zealand and one qualifier. It superseded the Tri-Nations (1999–2006), contested by Australia, Great Britain and New Zealand. Australia also holds the record for the **most Tri-Nations wins**, with three. New Zealand have won it once, in 2005.

Most international...

Rugby Union

Caps	139	George Gregan (Aus, 1994–2007)
	123	Brian O'Driscoll (Ire/Lions, 1999–)
	123	Ronan O'Gara (Ire/Lions, 2000–)
Points	1,250	Dan Carter (NZ, 2003–)
	1,246	Jonny Wilkinson (Eng/Lions, 1998–2011)
	1,090	Neil Jenkins (Wal/Lions, 1991–2002)
Tries	69	Daisuke Ohata (Jap, 1996–2006)
	64	David Campese (Aus, 1982–96)
	60	Shane Williams (Wal/Lions, 2000–11)

Rugby League

Caps	59	Darren Lockyer (Aus, 1998–2011)
	55	Ruben Wiki (NZ, 1994–2006)
	46	Mick Sullivan (UK, 1954–63)
		Garry Schofield (UK, 1984–94)
		Mal Meninga (Aus, 1982–94)
Points	278	Mal Meninga (Aus, 1982–94)
	228	Neil Fox (UK, 1959–69)
	204	Darren Lockyer (Aus, 1998–2011)
Tries	41	Mick Sullivan (UK, 1954–63)
	35	Darren Lockyer (Aus, 1998–2011)
	33	Ken Irvine (Aus, 1959–67)

Statistics correct as of 19 March 2012

Most points in an international (individual)

Hazem El Masri of Lebanon scored 48 points (16 goals, 4 tries) against Morocco in a World Cup qualifying match at Avignon, France, on 17 November 1999.

Most siblings to play in an international

Four Keinhorst brothers – James, Kristian, Markus and Nick – represented Germany against the Czech Republic in the European Rugby League Shield in Prague, Czech Republic, on 4 August 2007.

Most teams in a World Cup tournament

In all, 16 teams took part in the 2000 World Cup held at venues across the UK and France.

Oldest player in the Challenge Cup

Aged 52, Sid Miller (UK) appeared for Littleborough against Redhill in a first-round tie in December 1993.

BASEBALL

Highest paid player
On 13 December 2007, Alex Rodriguez (USA) signed a contract with the New York Yankees worth $275 million (£181 million) over 10 years, the largest in baseball history. According to money mavens Forbes in March 2012, Rodriguez's on- and off-field earnings in 2012 are expected to reach $32 million (£20 million), $5 million (£3 million) more than the next highest MLB earner, Joe Mauer (USA).

Oldest player to hit a home run
At 48 years 254 days, Julio Franco (Dominican Republic) became the oldest MLB player to hit a home run when he connected off Randy Johnson (USA) for a two-run home run to help lead the New York Mets to a 5–3 win over the Arizona Diamondbacks at Chase Field in Phoenix, Arizona, USA, on 4 May 2007.

Largest attendance
On 29 March 2008, a crowd of 115,300 turned out for an exhibition game between the Los Angeles Dodgers and the Boston Red Sox at the Los Angeles Memorial Coliseum in California, USA. The game was in celebration of the Dodgers' 50th anniversary in Los Angeles – previously the team had been based in Brooklyn, New York.

Largest television audience for a World Series
The highest average viewing figures per game for a World Series is 44,278,950 viewers for the 1978 event between the New York Yankees and LA Dodgers on 10–17 October 1978. Broadcast on NBC, the games averaged a 56% share of the TV audience and reached almost 24.5 million homes. The Yankees won the series 4–2.

Oldest diamond
Labatt Park in London, Ontario, Canada, was established in 1877 and is the oldest continually used diamond.

Highest batting average by a catcher
Joe Mauer's (USA) .365 batting average playing for the Minnesota Twins during the 2009 season was an MLB record for a catcher. It was Mauer's third batting title in four seasons.

FACT: Pujols has hit 30 or more home runs in every season since the start of his career in 2001.

Most grand-slam home runs in a game
The New York Yankees hit three grand-slam home runs in their 22–9 victory over the Oakland Athletics on 25 August 2011. The grand-slam home runs were hit by Robinson Canó (Dominican Republic), Russell Martin (Canada) and Curtis Granderson (USA, above). A grand-slam home run occurs when the bases are "loaded", each with a player, so the team scores four.

Most consecutive losing seasons
The Pittsburgh Pirates endured 19 MLB losing seasons from 1993 to 2011. Above, Ronnie Cedeno of the Pirates argues an umpire's call in another defeat: 9–1 to the St Louis Cardinals in 2010.

Career batting records
• Barry Bonds (USA) has the **most home runs** in the MLB, with 762 for the Pittsburgh Pirates and San Francisco Giants from 1986 to 2007. Henry Aaron is next on the list with 755 home runs and "Babe" Ruth is third with 714.

• Ty Cobb (USA) has the **highest batting average** – .367 for the Detroit Tigers and Philadelphia Athletics from 1905 to 1928. Rogers Hornsby is next with an average of .358 and Ed Delahanty is third with an average of .350.

Most hits in a World Series game
Two batters have recorded five hits in a World Series game: Paul Molitor (USA) for the Milwaukee Brewers in Game 1 of the 1982 World Series against the St Louis Cardinals on 12 October 1982 and Albert Pujols (Dominican Republic, left) for the St Louis Cardinals in Game 3 of the 2011 World Series against the Texas Rangers on 22 October 2011. In his game, Pujols also set the record for **most total bases in a World Series game**, with 14. He hit three home runs (12 total bases) and two singles (2 total bases).

MOST...

At-bats without recording a hit
Eugenio Vélez (Dominican Republic) of the Los Angeles Dodgers set a post-1900 MLB record for a non-pitcher by going hitless in 46 consecutive at-bats in 2010 and 2011. Vélez broke the record of 45 straight at-bats by Bill Bergen (USA) of the Brooklyn Superbas in 1909, Dave Campbell (USA) of the San Diego Padres and St Louis Cardinals in 1973, and Craig Counsell (USA) of the Milwaukee Brewers in 2011.

Most career runs batted in by a designated hitter

David Ortiz (Dominican Republic) has batted in 1,097 runs as a designated hitter playing for the Minnesota Twins and Boston Red Sox since 1997.

FACT: Ortiz also holds the record for **most home runs hit by a designated hitter in a career**, with 333.

York Yankees, Houston Astros and Washington Nationals since he made his MLB debut at age 19 on 20 June 1991.

Runs batted in (RBIs) in a single post-season

David Freese (USA) batted in 21 runs in the 2011 post-season for the St Louis Cardinals.

RBIs in an inning

Fernando Tatís (Dominican Republic) batted in eight runs playing for the St Louis Cardinals on 23 April 1999. Tatís hit a record two grand-slam home runs in the inning, both against Los Angeles Dodgers pitcher Chan Ho Park (South Korea).

Consecutive games

Cal Ripken, Jr played 2,632 MLB games for the Baltimore Orioles from 30 May 1982 to 19 September 1998.

Consecutive World Series victories

The New York Yankees won the World Series five times from 1949 to 1953.

Most saves for a rookie pitcher

Craig Kimbrel (USA) saved 46 games for the Atlanta Braves in 2011, his first full season in the MLB. He made such an impression that he was selected by San Francisco Giants manager Bruce Bochy for the 2011 All-Star Game.

Games won by a pitcher

Denton True "Cy" Young (USA) won 511 MLB games from 1890 to 1911 for the Cleveland Spiders, St Louis Cardinals, Boston Red Sox, Cleveland Indians and Boston Braves.

Cy Young Awards

Since 1956, the Cy Young Award has been given annually to the outstanding pitcher in the major leagues. Roger Clemens (USA) has won seven Cy Young Awards, playing for Boston Red Sox in 1986, 1987, 1991; Toronto Blue Jays in 1997–98; New York Yankees in 2001; and Houston Astros in 2004.

Wild pitches thrown in an inning

Several pitchers have thrown four wild pitches in an inning: R A Dickey (USA) is the most recent, playing for the Seattle Mariners on 17 August 2008.

Career pitching records

- Nolan Ryan (USA) has the **most strikeouts** with 5,714 from 1966 to 1993 for the New York Mets, California Angels, Houston Astros and Texas Rangers. Randy Johnson is next on the list with 4,875 and Roger Clemens third with 4,672.

- Ed Walsh (USA) has the **lowest earned run average**, with 1.82 for the Chicago White Sox and Boston Braves from 1904 to 1917. Addie Joss is next with an average of 1.89 and Mordecai Brown is third with 2.06.

Major League Baseball (MLB) records

Team		
Most World Series titles (first awarded in 1903)	27	New York Yankees
	11	St Louis Cardinals
	9	Philadelphia/Kansas City/Oakland Athletics
Largest current stadiums (by seating capacity)	56,000	Dodger Stadium (Los Angeles, California, USA), home of the Los Angeles Dodgers
	50,490	Coors Field (Denver, Colorado, USA), home of the Colorado Rockies
	50,291	Yankee Stadium (Bronx, New York, USA), home of the New York Yankees
Oldest clubs (year founded)	1870	Chicago Cubs
	1871	Boston/Milwaukee/Atlanta Braves
	1882	St Louis Cardinals
		Cincinnati Reds
		Pittsburgh Pirates
Individual		
Most MVP of the Year awards (first awarded in 1911)	7	Barry Bonds
	3	Jimmie Foxx, Joe DiMaggio, Stan Musial, Roy Campanella, Yogi Berra, Mickey Mantle, Mike Schmidt, Albert Pujols, Alex Rodriguez

Statistics correct as of the end of the 2011 season

Consecutive winless games by a starting pitcher

Three MLB starting pitchers have recorded 28 consecutive winless games: Jo-Jo Reyes (USA) for the Atlanta Braves and the Toronto Blue Jays from 2008 to 2011; Matt Keough (USA) for the Oakland Athletics in 1978–79; and Cliff Curtis (USA) for the Boston Braves in 1910–11.

Home runs hit in a post-season series

Nelson Cruz (Dominican Republic) hit six home runs while playing for the Texas Rangers against the Detroit Tigers in the 2011 American League Championship Series.

In this series, Cruz also set an MLB record for **most runs batted in (RBIs) in a post-season series**, with 13.

Hits by a short-stop

Derek Jeter (USA) has recorded 3,053 hits for the New York Yankees since 1995. He is the Yankees' all-time leader in hits.

Games played at short-stop

Omar Vizquel (Venezuela) played 2,699 MLB games as a short-stop for the Seattle Mariners, Cleveland Indians, San Francisco Giants, Texas Rangers and Chicago White Sox since 1989. Vizquel also has the record for **most seasons played at short-stop**, with 23.

Games played at catcher

Iván Rodríguez (Puerto Rico) has played 2,427 MLB games as a catcher while playing for the Texas Rangers, Florida Marlins, Detroit Tigers, New

Most games pitched with one team

Mariano Rivera (Panama) pitched 1,042 games for the New York Yankees from 1995 to the end of the 2011 season. Rivera also holds the record for **most career saves**, with 603. A save is credited when a relief pitcher holds on to a winning lead of three runs or fewer.

FACT: Rivera also holds the record for **most games finished in a career**, with 883.

CRICKET

Highest partnership in a Test match

Mahela Jayawardene and Kumar Sangakkara scored 624 together for Sri Lanka against South Africa in Colombo, Sri Lanka, on 27–29 July 2006. Jayawardene hit 374 – the fourth highest Test innings by an individual – and Sangakkara 287 as Sri Lanka scored 756 for 5 declared. Sri Lanka won the match by an innings and 153 runs.

Highest Test batting average

Sir Don Bradman (Australia) averaged 99.94 playing for Australia in 52 Tests between 1928 and 1948. He needed just four in his last innings against England at The Oval to attain a career average of 100, but he was out for a duck!

Highest score in a Test innings (team)

Sri Lanka scored 952 for 6 against India at Colombo in August 1997. This beat England's score of 903 for 7 against Australia at The Oval, London, UK, in August 1938.

Longest Test match

Before World War II, Test matches were often "timeless" – that is, played until one side won. The longest timeless Test was between England and South Africa at Durban, South Africa, on 3–14 March 1939. The total playing time was 43 hr 16 min and a record Test match aggregate of 1,981 runs were scored. Ironically, the match still did not have a positive result – it was abandoned after 10 days, with the eighth day rained off, because the ship taking the England team home was due to leave. The **shortest Test** was the rain-hit England-Australia match at Trent Bridge on 12 June 1926, which saw only 50 minutes of play.

Most Test series whitewashes

The country with the most Test series "whitewashes" is 19, by Australia between 1920 and the 4–0 thrashing of India in 2011–12 (above). This record includes series with a minimum of three matches.

Most consecutive wins in Test cricket

Australia recorded a run of 16 successive Test victories when they beat India by 10 wickets at Mumbai, India, in March 2001. Australia were all set to make it 17 against India at Eden Gardens, Kolkata, India, later that month – however, although they gained a first-innings lead of 274 runs and enforced the follow-on, India eventually won the match by 171 runs. This is the **greatest margin of victory after following-on**. Australia repeated its feat of 16 wins in a row from 26 December 2005 to 2 January 2008.

Lowest team score in a Test match innings

The lowest innings total in Test cricket is 26, by New Zealand versus England at Auckland on 28 March 1955.

Most runs scored in a Test match

Graham Gooch (England) scored 456 in total (333 in the first innings and 123 in the second) against India at Lords, London, England, between 26 and 31 July 1990. The **most runs scored by a female player in a Test match** was by Pakistan opener Kiran Baluch, who scored

Runs, wickets and World Cup wins		
Test cricket		
Most runs	15,470	Sachin Tendulkar (Ind, 1989–)
	13,288	Rahul Dravid (Ind, 1996–2012)
	13,200	Ricky Ponting (Aus, 1995–)
Most wickets	800	Muttiah Muralitharan (SL, 1992–2010)
	708	Shane Warne (Aus, 1992–2007)
	690	Anil Kumble (Ind, 1990–2008)
One-Day Internationals		
Most runs	18,342	Sachin Tendulkar (Ind, 1989–)
	13,704	Ricky Ponting (Aus, 1995–2012)
	13,430	Sanath Jayasuriya (SL,1989–2011)
Most wickets	534	Muttiah Muralitharan (SL, 1993–2011)
	502	Wasim Akram (Pak, 1984–2003)
	416	Waqar Younis (Pak, 1989–2003)
Most World Cup wins	4	Australia (1987, 1999, 2003, 2007)
	2	India (1983, 2011)
		West Indies (1975, 1979)
	1	Pakistan (1992)
		Sri Lanka (1996)

Statistics correct as of 1 April 2012

Highest individual score in an ODI

India captain and opener Virender Sehwag struck 219 runs from 149 balls against the West Indies at Holkar Cricket Stadium in Indore, India, on 8 December 2011. Sehwag's extraordinary innings, which lasted 208 minutes and included 25 fours and seven sixes, beat Sachin Tendulkar's (India) record ODI score of 200 not out. India scored 418 for five, their highest ODI score, and won the match by a whopping 158 runs.

FACT:
Gayle hit 6, 6 (off a no-ball), 4, 4, 6, 6, 4 – so with one run for the no-ball, 37 runs came off the over.

Most runs off an over in the IPL

Chris Gayle (Jamaica) of the Royal Challengers hit 37 off an over by Prasanth Parameswaran (India) of the Kochi Tuskers in Bangalore, India, on 8 May 2011.

Fastest players to 1,000 ODI runs

Three players have reached 1,000 ODI runs in only 21 innings – Viv Richards (West Indies) on 22 January 1980, Kevin Pietersen (England) on 31 March 2006 and Jonathan Trott (England, above), on 27 August 2009. Ironically, Trott scored a duck in his first ODI against Ireland in Belfast on 21 August 2009.

264 in total (242 in the first innings and 22 in the second) in the Test against West Indies at Karachi, Pakistan, on 15–18 March 2004.

Most dismissals in a Test match career

Mark Boucher (South Africa) has 555 Test dismissals in Tests (532 catches and 23 stumpings). Boucher also has the **most dismissals in international cricket**, with 998 (952 catches and 46 stumpings). All figures as of 24 April 2012.

Most sixes by a player in a first-class innings

Three batsmen have hit 16 sixes in a first-class innings: Andrew Symonds (Australia) for Gloucestershire against Glamorgan at Abergavenny, Wales, UK, on 24–25 August 1995; Graham Napier (UK) for Essex against Surrey, at Whitgift in Surrey, UK, on 19 May 2011; and Jesse Ryder (New Zealand) for New Zealand against Australia A at Brisbane, Australia, on 27 November 2011.

Highest partnership in an ODI

Rahul Dravid and Sachin Tendulkar hit 331 in a One-Day International (ODI) for India against New Zealand in Hyderabad, Andhra Pradesh, India, on 8 November 1999. Dravid made 153 and Tendulkar 186 not out in India's total of 376. India won by 174 runs.

Most ODI appearances (female)

Charlotte Edwards has played 155 matches for England in ODIs since 1997. She has scored 4,755 ODI runs with a top score of 173 not out.

Most sixes by a player in a Twenty20 international

In only his second Twenty20 international, Richard Levi hit 13 sixes for South Africa as he destroyed the New Zealand attack in Hamilton, New Zealand, on 19 February 2012. He scored 117 not out, equalling the **highest Twenty20 international individual score**, in South Africa's winning total of 174 for 2.

Most expensive IPL player

Gautam Gambhir (India) was bought for £1.54 million ($2.4 million) by the Kolkata Knight Riders in the Indian Premier League (IPL) Season 4 on 8 January 2011.

Most centuries in internationals

When he scored 114 against Bangladesh in an ODI on 16 March 2012, the "Little Master" Sachin Tendulkar (India) became the first player to score 100 international centuries.

FACT: Tendulkar has the **most runs overall (ODI, Test and Twenty20)** – 33,906 as of 25 April 2012.

Sachin's 100 hundreds

• Sachin's first international century was scored on 14 August 1990 at Old Trafford, Manchester, against England.

• Of his 100 hundreds, Sachin scored 51 in Test cricket and 49 in ODI cricket (the most in both forms of cricket).

• Australia are his favourite victims – he scored 20 of his 100 centuries against them.

• He hit his 99th century against South Africa on 12 March 2010, but had to wait 1 year 4 days for his 100th against Bangladesh. That was the second longest period between any of his centuries – the longest came after his first century.

Most ducks in Twenty20 internationals

The most scores of 0 recorded by an individual batsman in Twenty20 international matches is six, by Jean-Paul Duminy (South Africa, left), between 2007 and 2011. The record for the **most ducks in IPL Twenty20 cricket** is seven, held by Shane Warne (Australia) playing for Rajasthan Royals between 2008 and 2011.

ICE HOCKEY

Most overtime game winners

Joe Sakic (Canada) set the NHL record for the most overtime game-winning play-off goals, with eight, all scored for the Colorado Avalanche (USA) from 1996 to 2008.

Most Stanley Cup finals refereed

Bill McCreary (Canada) has skated as the referee in 44 career Stanley Cup finals games in the NHL. His 44th outing was Game 5 of the 2010 finals on 6 June, but it was with his 43rd, Game 3 of the 2010 finals on 3 June, that he surpassed the previous

record of 42, held by Bill Chadwick (USA). McCreary has refereed more than 1,600 games since making his debut in the 1984–85 season; his first Stanley Cup final series appearance was in 1994.

Fastest ice hockey shot

The hardest known ice hockey shot was a 177.5-km/h (110.3-mi/h) slapshot by Denis Kulyash (Russia) of Avangard Omsk, made in the Kontinental Hockey League's All-Star skills competition, held in St Petersburg, Russia, on 5 February 2011. Kulyash's shot has earned him the nickname "Tsar Cannon", after a 1586 cannon outside the Kremlin.

Kulyash's effort beat Zdeno Chára (Slovakia) of the Boston Bruins (USA), who hit a 170.4-km/h (105.9-mi/h) slapshot during the NHL All-Star SuperSkills competition in Raleigh, North Carolina, USA, on 29 January 2011.

NHL FIRSTS

• Marcus Vinnerborg (Sweden) became the **first European-trained referee in an NHL game**, overseeing a 2–1 win for the Dallas Stars over the visiting Anaheim Ducks (both USA) on 16 November 2010.

• Evgeni Nabokov (Russia) became **the first goalie to score a powerplay goal**, for the San Jose Sharks (USA) with a man advantage over the Vancouver Canucks (Canada), on 10 March 2002.

• It wouldn't be a list of firsts without an appearance from Martin Brodeur (Canada), the **first NHL goalie to win 600 career games**, hitting the mark when the New Jersey Devils defeated the Atlanta Thrashers (both USA), 3–0, on 6 April 2010.

FACT:
In 2011, Thomas made the **most saves in a single postseason**, with 798 in the Stanley Cup playoffs, and the **most saves in a single Stanley Cup final**, with 238 playing against the Vancouver Canucks.

Longest ice hockey marathon

Brent Saik (Canada) and friends really had to get their skates on when they played hockey for 242 hours at Saiker's Acres in Sherwood Park, Alberta, Canada, from 11 to 21 February 2011. The group of 40 was split into two teams called Blue and White. The Whites were the winners, with the final score standing at 2,067–2,005. It was the fourth attempt on the record by Saik and his associates, who were using the match to raise funds for cancer treatment.

Highest goalie save percentage

Tim Thomas (USA) saved 1,699 goals while playing for the Boston Bruins (USA) in the 2010–11 regular season and set a record NHL save percentage of .938. Fan favourite Thomas also set the record for the **highest save percentage by a goaltender in the NHL Stanley Cup finals**, with .967.

Most consecutive professional wins

The Cardiff Devils (UK) had a winning streak of 21 in the Elite Ice Hockey League (UK)

from 31 October 2010 to 15 January 2011. The Devils outscored opponents by a combined score of 111–38 during their perfect run.

Fewest wins in an NHL season

The fewest wins recorded by a team in a single NHL season – playing at least 70 games – is eight, by the Washington Capitals (USA) in 1974–75. The "Caps" notched up the **most consecutive losses in NHL history** that season, with 17.

Most consecutive seasons scoring over 100 points

The Detroit Red Wings (USA) topped 100 points in a record nine straight seasons from 1999–2000 to 2008–09.

GOAL-TENDERS

Oldest winner of the Conn Smythe Trophy

Tim Thomas (b. 15 April 1974) of the Boston Bruins was, at 37 years 62 days, the oldest player in National Hockey League history to win the Conn Smythe Trophy awarded to the Most Valuable Player of the Stanley Cup play-offs. He received the trophy on 15 June 2011.

Most regular season games played in an NHL career

By the end of the regular season on 7 April 2012, Martin Brodeur, goalie for the New Jersey Devils, had played the most career regular season games, with 1,191 since 1993–94.

Most goals scored in an NHL career by a US player

Mike Modano (USA) racked up an amazing 561 goals in his career for the Minnesota North Stars, Dallas Stars and Detroit Red Wings (all USA) from the 1989–90 season through to the end of the 2010–11 season. Only three other US-born players have scored 500 or more goals: Jeremy Roenick, Joe Mullen and Keith Tkachuk. Wayne Gretzky (Canada) has the **most goals in NHL history**, with 894.

FACT:
Modano is the highest-scoring US-born player in NHL history, with 1,374 career points – 561 goals and 813 assists.

Brodeur had also racked up the **most NHL career regular season minutes**, with 70,029. In the 2006–07 season, he had 48 wins, the **most matches won by a goaltender in a regular season**. Overall, he has 371 losses, the **most regular season NHL career losses**, yet has managed the **most regular season NHL career shutouts by a goalie**, with 119.

National Hockey League

Most Stanley Cup titles (first held 1893–94)	24	Montreal Canadiens (Canada)
	13	Toronto Maple Leafs (Canada)
Most regular season games	1,767	Gordon "Gordie" Howe (Canada)
	1,756	Mark Messier (Canada)
Most regular season goals	894	Wayne Gretzky (Canada)
	801	Gordon "Gordie" Howe (Canada)
Largest capacity arena	21,273	Bell Centre, Montreal (Montreal Canadiens)
	20,066	Joe Louis Arena, Detroit (Detroit Red Wings)

Statistics correct as of 5 April 2012

Most NHL shutouts in playoffs

Patrick Roy (Canada) recorded 23 shutouts in a career with the Montreal Canadiens (Canada) and Colorado Avalanche from 1985–86 to 2002–03. His shutouts have been equalled by Martin Brodeur in his career with the New Jersey Devils.

Most regular season goals allowed in a career

During the 1999–2000 season, Grant Fuhr (Canada) let in his 2,756th goal and – possibly not the most coveted title in the NHL – tied the record for most regular season goals conceded by a goaltender in a career. Fuhr played for the Edmonton Oilers, Toronto Maple Leafs (both Canada), Buffalo Sabres,

FACT: Mike Sillinger (Canada) played for a record 12 teams during his NHL career from 1990–91 to 2008–09.

Los Angeles Kings, St Louis Blues (all USA) and Calgary Flames (Canada) from 1981–82 to 1999–2000. The total was first reached by Gilles Meloche (Canada), who played between 1970–71 and 1987–88.

Youngest to record a shutout

At 18 years 65 days, Harry Lumley (Canada, 1926–98) became the youngest NHL netminder to record a shutout. Lumley was playing for the

Detroit Red Wings when he blanked the Toronto Maple Leafs (Canada) 3–0 on 14 January 1945. It turned out to be his only shutout of the 1944–45 season.

Lumley also holds the record for **youngest goalie to play in an NHL game**. He was 17 years 42 days old when he first took to the ice as a New York Rangers (USA) rookie in the 1943–44 season.

Most matches won in overtime in a career

Roberto Luongo (Canada) of the Vancouver Canucks set the NHL record for most overtime wins by a goaltender over the course of a career, with 49.

First NHL team to win three seven-game series in a postseason

During the 2011 NHL play-offs, the Boston Bruins became the first team in the league's history to win a Game 7 three times in the same postseason. The Bruins won a clinching Game 7 victory over the Montreal Canadiens (Canada) in the first round, the Tampa Bay Lightning (USA) in the Eastern Conference finals and Vancouver Canucks in the Stanley Cup finals.

Most saves by a goaltender in a career

The dazzling Martin Brodeur just can't help breaking goaltending records. By April 2012, he had set another in the NHL for the most regular season career saves by a goaltender, with 27,312. Brodeur, who has played with the New Jersey Devils (USA) for his entire career, reached the total playing from the 1993–94 season. He also holds the record for **most NHL regular season career wins by a goaltender**, with 656.

FACT: Brodeur has faced 28,919 shots since the 1993–94 season – another NHL career record for a goaltender.

TEAMS ROUND-UP

Most goals scored in a water polo international

Debbie Handley scored 13 goals to help Australia beat Canada 16–10 at the World Championship in Guayaquil, Ecuador, in 1982.

Netball, water polo and hockey victories

Netball

Most World Championships (first awarded in 1963, held every four years) *three-way tie	10	Australia (1963, 1971, 1975, 1979*, 1983, 1991, 1995, 1999, 2007, 2011)
	4	New Zealand (1967, 1979*, 1987, 2003)
	1	Trinidad and Tobago (1979*)

Water polo

Most men's Olympic golds (first awarded in 1900)	9	Hungary (1932, 1936, 1952, 1956, 1964, 1976, 2000, 2004, 2008)
	4	Great Britain (1900, 1908, 1912, 1920)
	3	Italy (1948, 1960, 1992)
Most women's Olympic golds (first awarded in 2000)	1	Australia (2000)
		Italy (2004)
		Netherlands (2008)

Hockey

Most men's World Cups (first awarded in 1971)	4	Pakistan (1971, 1978, 1982, 1994)
	3	Netherlands (1973, 1990, 1998)
	2	Germany (2002, 2006)
		Australia (1986, 2010)
Most women's World Cups (first awarded in 1974)	6	Netherlands (1974, 1978, 1983, 1986, 1990, 2006)
	2	Argentina (2002, 2010)
		Germany (1976, 1981)
		Australia (1994, 1998)
Most men's Olympics golds (first awarded in 1908)	8	India (1928, 1932, 1936, 1948, 1952, 1956, 1964, 1980)
	3	Germany (1972, 1992, 2008)
		Great Britain (1908, 1920, 1988)
Most women's Olympic golds (first awarded in 1980)	3	Australia (1988, 1996, 2000)
	2	Netherlands (1984, 2008)

Statistics correct as of 3 April 2012

NETBALL

Oldest club

The Poly Netball Club was founded in London, UK, in 1907 by a team from the Regent Street Polytechnic, and has been in continuous existence ever since. The club's first recorded match was a 40–4 victory over the Northampton Institute in January 1909.

Most points scored at a World Championships

Irene van Dyk (New Zealand, b. South Africa) scored 543 points in the 1995 World Championships, the most for a single tournament. She also holds the record for the **most international appearances**, with 202 as of 20 April 2012. These comprise 72 caps for South Africa and 130 caps for New Zealand (van Dyk moved to New Zealand in 2000 and became a citizen in 2005).

Longest game

Netball Alberta organized a match between Team Rockers and Team Rollers that lasted 61 hours at the South Fish Creek recreation complex in Calgary, Alberta, Canada, on 16–19 September 2011. Team Rockers won 2,759–1,405.

Most World Series wins

New Zealand have won the World Series twice, in 2009 and 2010.

Most Champions League handball wins

The European Handball Federation (EHF) Champions League, started in 1956, is Europe's premier club handball competition. FC Barcelona's (Spain) handball team have won the Champions League eight times, in 1991, 1996–2000, 2005 and 2011. In 2011, Barca beat BM Ciudad Real (Spain) 27–24 in Cologne, Germany, on 29 May, under the captaincy of László Nagy (kissing the trophy, above). VfL Gummersbach (Germany) are the second most successful team, with five wins.

BEACH VOLLEYBALL

Highest earnings for a player (female)

Misty May-Treanor (USA) has earned $2,078,083 (£1,287,780) in professional beach volleyball earnings up to April 2012. She took $1,062,945 (£658,705) from international matches and $1,015,138 (£629,079) from domestic matches. She also holds the record for the **most** career tournament victories with 110 – 69 domestic and 41 international wins.

Oldest person to win a title

Aged 44 years 284 days, Karch Kiraly (USA) won the Huntington Beach Open in California, USA, on 13 August 2005.

Youngest person to win a title

At 17 years 99 days, Xue Chen (China) won the China Shanghai Jinshan Open in Shanghai, China, on 28 May 2006.

Most Netball Superleague wins

The Netball Superleague, held since 1996, is the premier netball club competition in Britain. Team Bath (left), which originates from the University of Bath, UK, have won the competition a record four times, in 2006–07 and 2009–10. The Hertfordshire Mavericks have won two titles, in 2008 and 2011.

FACT: Brazil's Leandro Vissotto Neves spikes the ball against Japan in the 2009 Grand Champions Cup.

Most Volleyball World Grand Champions Cup wins

Volleyball's World Grand Champions Cup, inaugurated in 1993, is held every four years between six teams: the host nation, four continental champions and one wild card. Brazil has won three times in the men's event, in 1997, 2005 and in 2009, the year they were the first team to defend the Cup.

In the women's event, also held since 1993, Cuba, Russia, China, Brazil and Italy all have one win.

KORFBALL

Most Europa Cup wins

Korfball, a mixed-gender sport with teams of four men and four women, is similar to netball and basketball and the Europa Cup has been held since 1967. The most wins of the Europa Cup is six, by PKC (Netherlands) in 1985, 1990, 1999–2000, 2002 and 2006.

Highest score in a Europa Cup final

The highest score recorded by a club team in a Europa Cup final is 33, by Koog Zaandijk (Netherlands) in Budapest, Hungary, on 22 January 2011. Koog Zaandijk beat Royal Scaldis SC (Belgium) 33–23 – this match's 56 points also represents the **highest total points in a Europa Cup final**.

HOCKEY

Highest score in international hockey (women)

England defeated France 23–0 in Merton, London, UK, on 3 February 1923.

Most men's EuroHockey Nations Championship wins

The EuroHockey Nations Championship, held since 1970, is the premier international hockey competition in Europe. Germany (formerly West Germany) won the Championship seven times between 1970 and 2011.

FLOORBALL

Most World Championships

Floorball is a type of indoor hockey and Sweden has won the men's World Championships six times, from 1996 to 2006. Finland is the only other winner (in 2008 and 2010). Sweden also holds the record for the **most women's World Championships**, with five from 1997 to 2011. Finland, in 1999 and 2001, and Switzerland, in 2005, are the only other winners.

HURLING

Most All-Ireland Championships wins

Hurling is a 15-a-side sport of Gaelic origin, in which players attempt to score points by hitting a ball with a stick, known as a hurley, into or over their opponent's goal. Kilkenny won 33 All-Ireland Championships between 1904 and 2011. Kilkenny's four Championships in 2006–09 is a record for the **most successive All-Ireland Championships**, equalling the achievement of Cork in 1941–44.

Most All-Ireland Camogie Championship wins as captain

Camogie is the women's version of hurling. The most wins of the Camogie Championship by a team captain is six, by Sophie Brack (Ireland, d. 1996) for Dublin between 1948 and 1955.

Dublin has won the **most All-Ireland Senior Camogie Championships** with 26 victories between 1932 and 1984.

Most men's handball Super Globe wins

The International Handball Federation Super Globe is a handball competition contested between the champion clubs from continental confederations. BM Ciudad Real (Spain) have the most Super Globes, with two, in 2007 and 2010. Above, BM Ciudad Real player Luc Abalo tries to score against Qatar's Al-Sadd in the 2010 tournament in Doha, Qatar.

LACROSSE

Most men's World Championships

USA has won nine of the 11 World Championships, in 1967, 1974, 1982, 1986, 1990, 1994, 1998, 2010 and 2011. Canada won the two other titles, in 1978 and 2006.

Most women's World Cups

USA has won six World Cups, in 1982, 1989, 1993, 1997, 2001 and 2009. Canada is the only other winner, in 1978 and 2006.

Fastest lacrosse shot

Paul Rabil (USA) recorded a lacrosse shot of 178 km/h (111 mi/h) at the Major League Lacrosse All-Star Game's Fastest Shot competition in Boston, Massachusetts, USA, on 8 July 2010, matching a shot he made in 2009. In the competition, each participant shoots 9 m (10 yards) away from the goal and only shots that enter the goal count.

Most water polo World League wins

Serbia have won the men's FINA Water Polo League six times, in 2005–08 and 2010–11. In the 2011 competition, they beat Italy 8–7 in a dramatic final in Florence, Italy, on 26 June, shown right.

The **most wins of the FINA Water Polo World League by a women's national team** is also six, by the USA in 2004, 2006–07 and 2009–11. The men's World League has been contested every year since 2002 and the women's event since 2004.

FACT: Serbia's Filip Filipovic (right) and Italy's Stefano Luongo compete in the 2011 World League final.

BASKETBALL

Most three-point field goals converted by an NBA team in a play-off

The Seattle SuperSonics converted 20 three-point field goals against the Houston Rockets on 6 May 1996, a feat matched by the Dallas Mavericks against the Los Angeles Lakers on 8 May 2011. The Mavericks' Peja Stojaković (Serbia) is shown (above right) with the Lakers' Derek Fisher (USA).

Largest attendance

A crowd of 108,713 watched the NBA All-Star Game at Cowboys Stadium in Dallas, Texas, USA, on 14 February 2010.

Most three-point field goals in a career

Ray Allen (USA) scored a three-point field goal for the 2,561st time in his career during the first quarter of a game playing for the Boston Celtics against the Los Angeles Lakers on 10 February 2011, surpassing the previous mark of 2,560 held by Reggie Miller (USA) of the Indiana Pacers. Allen, who has also played for the Milwaukee Bucks and Seattle SuperSonics since 1996, had scored a total of 2,718 three-point field goals as of 23 April 2012.

Allen holds the record for the **most career three-point field goals attempted by an individual**, with 6,788 as of 23 April 2012. He also scored eight three-point field goals for the Boston Celtics against the Los Angeles Lakers at the Staples Center in Los Angeles, California, USA, on 6 June 2010, the **most three-point field goals ever scored by an individual in an NBA Finals game**.

Finally, Allen scored the **most three-point field goals by an individual in an NBA Finals series**: 22, against the Los Angeles Lakers in 2008.

FACT: In 2006–07, Dirk was the first European to win the NBA's Most Valuable Player (MVP) award.

Most free throw conversions without a miss in an NBA play-off

Dirk Nowitzki (Germany) of the Dallas Mavericks set an NBA play-off record by converting 24 straight free throws during a 121–112 defeat of Oklahoma City Thunder in the first game of the Western Conference play-offs on 17 May 2011.

NBA

Highest percentage shooting three-point field goals in a career

Playing for six different teams from 1988–89 to 2002–03, Steve Kerr (USA, b. Lebanon) recorded a three-point field-goal percentage of .454. Kerr made 726 of 1,599 attempts.

Most championship titles won by a coach

Phil Jackson (USA) won 11 NBA championships. He picked up six titles as coach of the Chicago Bulls, in 1991–93 and 1996–98, and five more as coach of the Los Angeles Lakers, in 2000–02 and 2009–10.

Jackson also holds the record for **most NBA career play-off games by a coach**. His total of 333 was achieved as coach of the Chicago Bulls from 1989 to 1998 and the Los Angeles Lakers from 1999 to 2011. During the same period, he set a new record for the **most NBA play-off wins by a coach**. And his 229 victories out of 333 play-offs yielded a winning percentage of .688, the **highest winning percentage by a coach in NBA play-offs**.

Most wins in a season

The Chicago Bulls racked up 72 wins and just 10 losses in the 1995–96 season.

Most losses in a season

The Philadelphia 76ers had the least successful regular season of all time, with 73 losses and only nine wins in 1972–73. The **most consecutive losses by a team** stands at 26, made by the Cleveland Cavaliers between 20 December 2010 and 11 February 2011.

Youngest player

On 2 November 2005, Andrew Bynum (USA, b. 27 October 1987) was 18 years 6 days old when he played

Most seasons with the leading field-goal percentage

Shaquille O'Neal (USA) held the leading NBA field-goal percentage for a record 11 seasons. He achieved the feat while playing for the Orlando Magic in 1993–94, the Los Angeles Lakers from 1997–98 to 2003–04, the Miami Heat from 2004–05 to 2005–06 and the Phoenix Suns in 2008–09. He also achieved the NBA **highest career field-goal percentage**, with .582 between 1992 and 2011. O'Neal converted 11,330 of 19,457 attempts.

FACT: In 1996, O'Neal was named as one of the 50 greatest NBA players – after only four seasons!

Highest rebounds per game average (WNBA)

Tina Charles (USA, above right) has recorded an average of 11.4 rebounds per WNBA game playing for the Connecticut Sun since 2010. Charles also recorded a single-season record 398 rebounds in 34 games by the end of the 2011 season.

for the Los Angeles Lakers against the Denver Nuggets.

The **youngest winner of the NBA Most Valuable Player award** is Derrick Rose (USA) of the Chicago Bulls. Rose was aged just 22 when he received this accolade for his efforts in the 2010–11 season.

WNBA

Most games played in a career

Tangela Smith (USA) has played in 448 games during her Women's National Basketball Association (WNBA) career with the Sacramento Monarchs, Charlotte Sting, Phoenix Mercury and Indiana Fever since 1998.

Most field goals scored in a career

Tina Thompson (USA) has scored 2,385 field goals playing for the Houston Comets and Los Angeles Sparks from 1997 until the end of the 2011 season.

The prolific Thompson has played 14,561 minutes, the **most minutes played in a WNBA career**, and also shares the record for the **most minutes played per game in a WNBA career** – 33.6 – with Katie Smith (USA).

Katie Smith has scored the **most three-point field goals in a WNBA career**. Her 834 three-point field goals have come during her stints with the Minnesota Lynx, Detroit Shock, Washington Mystics and Seattle Storm from 1999 to the end of the 2011 season.

Most assists in a career

Since 1998, Ticha Penicheiro (Portugal) has made 2,560 assists in 435 games for the Sacramento Monarchs and Los Angeles Sparks. She also has **most assists per game**: 5.9.

Most double-doubles in a season

The greatest number of double-doubles (recording double-figures in points scored and rebounds in the same game) stands at 23, by Tina Charles playing for the Connecticut Sun in 2011.

Fewest points scored in a quarter by a team

The WNBA record for fewest points scored in a quarter is one, by the Chicago Sky in the fourth quarter of a 59–49 defeat to the New York Liberty on 4 August 2011.

Most consecutive losses by a team

The Tulsa Shock started the 2011 season by winning just one of their first 10 games. The coach and his interim successor were both replaced but the team ended the season with a record 20 straight losses.

All WNBA records are until the end of the 2011 season.

FACT: The NBA currently comprises 29 teams from the USA and one from Canada: the Toronto Raptors. The WNBA has 12 teams, all playing in the USA.

Most steals in a career

Tamika Catchings (USA) – who in 2011 was named as one of the top 15 players in WNBA history – has recorded 775 steals for the Indiana Fever in 313 games since 2002.

NBA at a glance

• Formed on 6 June 1946, the NBA is the world's premier basketball league. Its first game, on 1 November 1946, saw the New York Knickerbockers beat the Toronto Huskies 68–66.

• Players must be at least 19 during the year of the draft and one season must have passed since the player's year graduated high school.

• Two of the three highest-paid athletes in the world are NBA players. In 2011, according to Forbes, Kobe Bryant earned $53 million (£32 million); LeBron James took home $48 million (£29 million).

Highest three-point field-goal percentage in an NBA season

Kyle Korver (USA) achieved a .536 three-point field-goal percentage while playing for the Utah Jazz during the 2009–10 season. Korver converted 59 of 110 attempts.

FACT: Sharp-shooting must be in Korver's genes. His mother once netted 74 points in a high-school match.

FIBA, NBA and WNBA

FIBA (International Basketball Federation)

Most FIBA World Championships (first held in 1950)	5	Yugoslavia/Serbia
	4	USA
	3	Soviet Union
Most FIBA Women's World Championships (first held in 1953)	8	USA
	6	Soviet Union
	1	Australia

NBA (National Basketball Association)

Most NBA titles (first held in 1946–47)	17	Boston Celtics
	16	Minneapolis/Los Angeles Lakers
	6	Chicago Bulls
Most NBA career appearances	1,611	Robert Parish (USA)
	1,560	Kareem Abdul-Jabbar (USA)
	1,504	John Stockton (USA)
Most NBA career points	38,387	Kareem Abdul-Jabbar (USA)
	36,928	Karl Malone (USA)
	32,292	Michael Jordan (USA)

WNBA (Women's National Basketball Association)

Most WNBA titles (first held in 1997)	4	Houston Comets
	3	Detroit Shock
	2	Los Angeles Sparks
		Phoenix Mercury
		Seattle Storm
Most WNBA career appearances	448	Tangela Smith (USA)
	435	Ticha Penicheiro (Portugal)
	433	Tina Thompson (USA)
Most WNBA career points	6,751	Tina Thompson (USA)
	6,263	Lisa Leslie (USA)
	6,015	Katie Smith (USA)

Statistics correct as of 2 April 2012

ATHLETICS – MEN

Oldest athletics medallist

Tebbs Lloyd Johnson (UK, 1900–84) was aged 48 years 115 days when he came third in the 50,000 m walk at the 1948 Olympics in London, UK.

The **oldest athletics gold medallist** is Irish-born Patrick "Babe" McDonald (USA, 1878–1954), who was 42 years 26 days old when he won the 25.4-kg (56-lb) weight throw at Antwerp, Belgium, on 21 August 1920.

Most Olympic gold medals by an athlete

Paavo Nurmi (Finland) won nine golds at the 1,500 m, 3,000 m, 5,000 m, 10,000 m and cross-country events from 1920 to 1928. Carl Lewis (USA) repeated the feat with nine golds at the 100 m, 200 m, 4 x 100 m relay and long jump from 1984 to 1996.

Most gold medals, 1,500 m

Sebastian Coe (UK) won two medals in the men's 1,500 m event, in 1980 and 1984. He later led London's bid for the 2012 Olympics, taking on the role of chairman of the London Organizing Committee for the Olympic Games (LOCOG).

Longest triple jump

Jonathan Edwards (UK) hopped, skipped and jumped 18.29 m (60 ft 0.78 in) at the 1995 World Championships in Gothenburg, Sweden, on 7 August. He had already set the world record with an earlier jump of 18.16 m (59 ft 6.96 in). Edwards also jointly holds the record for the **most men's European Athlete of the Year trophies**, with two (1995 and 1998). Javelin thrower Jan Železný (Czech Republic, below) and triple jumper Christian Olsson (Sweden) have also won the trophy twice.

OLYMPICS

First to feature athletes from all continents

The first modern Olympics was held in Athens, Greece, in 1896 but it was not until the fifth Games in Stockholm, Sweden, in 1912 that the Games could finally boast athletes from every continent (excluding Antarctica). In making its Olympic debut, Japan became the first Asian nation to compete in the Games, represented by marathon runner Shizo Kanakuri and sprinter Yahiko Mishima.

Fastest 4 x 100 m

The Jamaican team of (from left, above) Nesta Carter, Michael Frater, Yohan Blake and Usain Bolt ran the 4 x 100 m relay in 37.04 seconds at the 2011 World Championships at Daegu, South Korea, on 4 September. They broke the record of 37.10 seconds set by Jamaica's 2008 Olympic team, which included Asafa Powell instead of Blake.

WORLD CHAMPIONSHIPS

Most appearances

Jesús Ángel García (Spain) appeared in walking events at 10 World Championships between 1991 and 2009.

Most gold medals

Carl Lewis and Michael Johnson (both USA) each won eight World Championship golds: Lewis in 1983–91 in the 100 m, 4 x 100 m and long jump; Johnson in 1991–99 in the 200 m, 400 m and 4 x 400 m.

Most 100 m wins

Carl Lewis and Maurice Greene (both USA) have each won the World Championship 100 m three times: Lewis in 1983, 1987 and 1991; Greene in 1997, 1999 and 2001.

Most 1,500 m wins

Hicham El Guerrouj (Morocco) – winner of the **most IAAF World Athlete of the Year trophies** (three in 2001–03) – has won the World Championship 1,500 m four times, in 1997, 1999, 2001 and 2003.

Most marathon wins

Three athletes have won the World Championship marathon twice: Abel Antón (Spain) in 1997 and 1999, Jaouad Gharib (Morocco) in 2003 and 2005, and Abel Kirui (Kenya) in 2009 and 2011.

Most Olympic javelin gold medals

Jan Železný (Czech Republic) won three golds at successive Olympics in 1992, 1996 and 2000. Železný also holds the record for **most wins of the men's javelin at the World Championships**, with three, in 1993, 1995 and 1997. He is also the only man to have thrown the new javelin, introduced in 1986, over 94 m (308 ft).

FACT:
Jan has the five top javelin performances of all time, with his best at 98.48 m (323 ft 1.16 in).

Outdoor track events

EVENT	TIME	NAME & NATIONALITY	LOCATION	DATE
100 m	9.58	Usain Bolt (Jamaica)	Berlin, Germany	16 Aug 2009
200 m	19.19	Usain Bolt (Jamaica)	Berlin, Germany	20 Aug 2009
400 m	43.18	Michael Johnson (USA)	Seville, Spain	26 Aug 1999
800 m	1:41.01	David Lekuta Rudisha (Kenya)	Rieti, Italy	29 Aug 2010
1,000 m	2:11.96	Noah Ngeny (Kenya)	Rieti, Italy	5 Sep 1999
1,500 m	3:26.00	Hicham El Guerrouj (Morocco)	Rome, Italy	14 Jul 1998
1 mile	3:43.13	Hicham El Guerrouj (Morocco)	Rome, Italy	7 Jul 1999
2,000 m	4:44.79	Hicham El Guerrouj (Morocco)	Berlin, Germany	7 Sep 1999
3,000 m	7:20.67	Daniel Komen (Kenya)	Rieti, Italy	1 Sep 1996
5,000 m	12:37.35	Kenenisa Bekele (Ethiopia)	Hengelo, Netherlands	31 May 2004
10,000 m	26:17.53	Kenenisa Bekele (Ethiopia)	Brussels, Belgium	26 Aug 2005
20,000 m	56:26.00	Haile Gebrselassie (Ethiopia)	Ostrava, Czech Republic	26 Jun 2007
25,000 m	1:12:25.4	Moses Cheruiyot Mosop (Kenya)	Eugene, Oregon, USA	3 Jun 2011
30,000 m	1:26:47.4	Moses Cheruiyot Mosop (Kenya)	Eugene, Oregon, USA	3 Jun 2011
3,000 m steeplechase	7:53.63	Saif Saaeed Shaheen (Qatar)	Brussels, Belgium	3 Sep 2004
110 m hurdles	12.87	Dayron Robles (Cuba)	Ostrava, Czech Republic	12 Jun 2008
400 m hurdles	46.78	Kevin Young (USA)	Barcelona, Spain	6 Aug 1992
4 x 100 m relay	37.04	Jamaica (Yohan Blake, Nesta Carter, Michael Frater, Usain Bolt)	Daegu, South Korea	4 Sep 2011
4 x 200 m relay	1:18.68	Santa Monica Track Club, USA (Michael Marsh, Leroy Burrell, Floyd Heard, Carl Lewis)	Walnut, USA	17 Apr 1994
4 x 400 m relay	2:54.29	USA (Andrew Valmon, Quincy Watts, Harry Reynolds, Michael Johnson)	Stuttgart, Germany	22 Aug 1993
4 x 800 m relay	7:02.43	Kenya (Joseph Mutua, William Yiampoy, Ismael Kombich, Wilfred Bungei)	Brussels, Belgium	25 Aug 2006
4 x 1,500 m relay	14:36.23	Kenya (Geoffrey Rono, Augustine Choge, William Tanui, Gideon Gathimba)	Brussels, Belgium	4 Sep 2009

Outdoor field events

EVENT	RECORD	NAME & NATIONALITY	LOCATION	DATE
High jump	2.45 m (8 ft 0.45 in)	Javier Sotomayor (Cuba)	Salamanca, Spain	27 Jul 1993
Pole vault	6.14 m (20 ft 1.73 in)	Sergei Bubka (Ukraine)	Sestriere, Italy	31 Jul 1994
Long jump	8.95 m (29 ft 4.36 in)	Mike Powell (USA)	Tokyo, Japan	30 Aug 1991
Triple jump	18.29 m (60 ft 0.78 in)	Jonathan Edwards (UK)	Gothenburg, Sweden	7 Aug 1995
Shot	23.12 m (75 ft 10.23 in)	Randy Barnes (USA)	Los Angeles, USA	20 May 1990
Discus	74.08 m (243 ft 0.53 in)	Jürgen Schult (Germany)	Neubrandenburg, Germany	6 Jun 1986
Hammer	86.74 m (284 ft 7 in)	Yuriy Sedykh (Russia)	Stuttgart, Germany	30 Aug 1986
Javelin	98.48 m (323 ft 1.16 in)	Jan Železný (Czech Republic)	Jena, Germany	25 May 1996
Decathlon	9,026 points	Roman Šebrle (Czech Republic)	Götzis, Austria	27 May 2001

Statistics correct as of 30 March 2012

Fastest 30,000 m

On 3 June 2011, Moses Cheruiyot Mosop (Kenya) ran the 30,000 m in 1 hr 26 min 47.4 sec in Eugene, Oregon, USA. En route to the 30,000 m finish, he also ran the **fastest 25,000 m**, taking 1 hr 12 min 25.4 sec. Japan's Toshihiko Seko had previously held both records after his run in Christchurch, New Zealand, on 22 March 1981 yielded times of 1 hr 13 min 55.8 sec for the 25,000 m and 1 hr 29 min 18.8 sec for the 30,000 m. Mosop was the first man in 30 years to break the records.

Most World Championship long jump wins

Two athletes have won the men's long jump at the World Championships four times – Iván Pedroso (Cuba) and Dwight Phillips (USA, below). Pedroso won his titles consecutively in 1995, 1997, 1999 and 2001; he also won three consecutive Pan American Games golds in 1995, 1999 and 2003.

Phillips won his World Championship golds in 2003, 2005, 2009 and 2011. In 2011, he was randomly assigned the bib number "1111". After winning, Phillips proudly pointed to the number which reflected his position in the four championships. He commented: "From the moment I saw the bib, I said this championship is mine."

Most European Cross Country Championship wins

Serhiy Lebid (Ukraine) won the European Cross Country Championships nine times from 1998 in Ferrara, Italy, to 2010 in Albufeira, Portugal.

FACT: Serhiy has competed in a record 18 European Cross Country Championships.

ATHLETICS – WOMEN

Most World Championship appearances

Susana Feitor (Portugal) competed in walking events in 11 World Championships between 1991 and 2011. In 2005, she won bronze in the 20 km walk.

silver and six bronze – in the 100 m, 200 m and 4 x 100 m relay. Merlene has also won the **most medals at the World Championships**, with 14. She won three gold, four silver and seven bronze from 1983 to 1997.

Youngest world record holder

When Wang Yan (China), at the age of 14 years 334 days, completed a 5,000 m walk in 21 min 33.8 sec in Jinan, China, on 9 March 1986, she became the world's youngest individual female athletics record holder.

Fastest half marathon

Mary Keitany (Kenya) smashed the half marathon world record at Ras Al-Khaimah in the UAE on 18 February 2011 with a time of 1 hr 5 min 50 sec. This took an incredible 35 seconds off Lornah Kiplagat's (Netherlands) 2007 record, set when winning the World Half Marathon Championships at Udine, Italy. During her half marathon, Keitany also ran the **fastest 20,000 m**, in 1 hr 2 min 36 sec.

Most European Cross Country Championships

Paula Radcliffe (UK) in 1998 and 2003, and Hayley Yelling (UK) in 2004 and 2009, have both won the European Cross Country Championship twice.

Fastest 20 km road walk

Vera Sokolova (Russia) completed the 20 km walk in 1 hr 25 min 8 sec at the Russian Winter Walking Championships in Sochi, Russia, on 26 February 2011. The 23-year-old former world junior champion smashed the previous mark of 1 hr 25 min 41 sec, set by her compatriot Olimpiada Ivanova at the 2005 World Championships in Helsinki, Finland.

Oldest female world record holder in athletics

Marina Stepanova (USSR) was aged 36 years 139 days when she set a world record of 52.94 seconds for the 400 m hurdles at Tashkent, USSR, on 17 September 1986.

OLYMPICS

Youngest athletics gold medallist

Aged just 15 years 123 days, Barbara Pearl Jones (USA) was a member of the winning 4 x 100 m relay team at the Olympics in Helsinki, Finland, on 27 July 1952. She also won gold in the 4 x 100 m at the 1960 Rome Games.

Most athletics medals

From 1980 to 2000, Merlene Ottey (Jamaica) won nine Olympic medals – three

WORLD CHAMPIONSHIPS

Most gold medals

From 2005 to 2011, Allyson Felix (USA) won eight World Championship golds, in the 200 m at Helsinki, Finland, in 2005; the 200 m, 4 x 100 m and 4 x 400 m at Osaka, Japan, in 2007; the 200 m and 4 x 400 m in Berlin, Germany, in 2009; 4 x 100 m and 4 x 400 m in Daegu, South Korea, in 2011.

Most 1,500 m wins

Two athletes have won the World Championship 1,500 m twice: Tatyana Tomashova (Russia) in 2003 and 2005, and Maryam Yusuf Jamal (Bahrain, born in Ethiopia) in 2007 and 2009.

Most javelin wins

Trine Hattestad (Norway) in 1993 and 1997, and Mirela Manjani (Greece) in 1999 and 2003, have both won the World Championship javelin twice.

Most high jump wins

Stefka Kostadinova (Bulgaria) in 1987 and 1995, Hestrie Cloete (South Africa) in 2001 and 2003, and Blanka Vlašić (Croatia) in 2007 and 2009 have both won the World Championship high jump event twice.

Fastest 3,000 m steeplechase

In winning the Olympic 3,000 m steeplechase gold medal at the 2008 Beijing Olympics, Gulnara Samitova-Galkina (Russia) achieved a new world record of 8 min 58.81 sec. Silver medallist Eunice Jepkorir (Kenya) finished a massive 8.6 seconds behind her.

FACT: Gulnara first broke the 3,000 m steeplechase record in 2003 with a time of 9 min 8.33 sec.

Outdoor track events

EVENT	TIME	NAME & NATIONALITY	LOCATION	DATE
100 m	10.49	Florence Griffith-Joyner (USA)	Indianapolis, USA	16 Jul 1988
200 m	21.34	Florence Griffith-Joyner (USA)	Seoul, South Korea	29 Sep 1988
400 m	47.60	Marita Koch (GDR)	Canberra, Australia	6 Oct 1985
800 m	1:53.28	Jarmila Kratochvílová (Czech Republic)	Munich, Germany	26 Jul 1983
1,000 m	2:28.98	Svetlana Masterkova (Russia)	Brussels, Belgium	23 Aug 1996
1,500 m	3:50.46	Qu Yunxia (China)	Beijing, China	11 Sep 1993
1 mile	4:12.56	Svetlana Masterkova (Russia)	Zurich, Switzerland	14 Aug 1996
2,000 m	5:25.36	Sonia O'Sullivan (Ireland)	Edinburgh, UK	8 Jul 1994
3,000 m	8:06.11	Wang Junxia (China)	Beijing, China	13 Sep 1993
5,000 m	14:11.15	Tirunesh Dibaba (Ethiopia)	Oslo, Norway	6 Jun 2008
10,000 m	29:31.78	Wang Junxia (China)	Beijing, China	8 Sep 1993
20,000 m	1:02.36	Mary Keitany (Kenya)	Ras Al-Khaimah, UAE	18 Feb 2011
25,000 m	1:27:05.90	Tegla Loroupe (Kenya)	Mengerskirchen, Germany	21 Sep 2002
30,000 m	1:45:50.00	Tegla Loroupe (Kenya)	Warstein, Germany	6 Jun 2003
3,000 m steeplechase	8:58.81	Gulnara Samitova-Galkina (Russia)	Beijing, China	17 Aug 2008
100 m hurdles	12.21	Yordanka Donkova (Bulgaria)	Stara Zagora, Bulgaria	20 Aug 1988
400 m hurdles	52.34	Yuliya Pechonkina (Russia)	Tula, Russia	8 Aug 2003
4 x 100 m relay	41.37	GDR (Silke Gladisch, Sabine Rieger, Ingrid Auerswald, Marlies Göhr)	Canberra, Australia	6 Oct 1985
4 x 200 m relay	1:27.46	United States "Blue" (LaTasha Jenkins, LaTasha Colander-Richardson, Nanceen Perry, Marion Jones)	Philadelphia, USA	29 Apr 2000
4 x 400 m relay	3:15.17	USSR (Tatyana Ledovskaya, Olga Nazarova, Maria Pinigina, Olga Bryzgina)	Seoul, South Korea	1 Oct 1988
4 x 800 m relay	7:50.17	USSR (Nadezhda Olizarenko, Lyubov Gurina, Lyudmila Borisova, Irina Podyalovskaya)	Moscow, Russia	5 Aug 1984

Outdoor field events

EVENT	RECORD	NAME & NATIONALITY	LOCATION	DATE
High jump	2.09 m (6 ft 10.28 in)	Stefka Kostadinova (Bulgaria)	Rome, Italy	30 Aug 1987
Pole vault	5.06 m (16 ft 7.21 in)	Yelena Isinbayeva (Russia)	Zurich, Switzerland	28 Aug 2009
Long jump	7.52 m (24 ft 8.06 in)	Galina Chistyakova (USSR)	St Petersburg, Russia	11 Jun 1988
Triple jump	15.50 m (50 ft 10.23 in)	Inessa Kravets (Ukraine)	Gothenburg, Sweden	10 Aug 1995
Shot	22.63 m (74 ft 2.94 in)	Natalya Lisovskaya (USSR)	Moscow, Russia	7 Jun 1987
Discus	76.80 m (252 ft)	Gabriele Reinsch (GDR)	Neubrandenburg, Germany	9 Jul 1988
Hammer	79.42 m (260 ft 6.76 in)	Betty Heidler (Germany)	Halle, Germany	25 May 2011
Javelin	72.28 m (253 ft 6 in)	Barbora Špotáková (Czech Republic)	Stuttgart, Germany	13 Sep 2008
Heptathlon	7,291 points	Jackie Joyner-Kersee (USA)	Seoul, South Korea	24 Sep 1988
Decathlon	8,358 points	Austra Skujyteité (Lithuania)	Columbia, USA	15 Apr 2005

Statistics correct as of 30 March 2012

Most World Championship long jump wins

Three athletes have won the World Championships twice: Jackie Joyner-Kersee (USA) in 1987 and 1991; Fiona May (Italy) in 1995 and 2001; and Brittney Reese (USA), above, in 2009 and 2011. Reese also has two World Indoor Championship golds, won in Doha, Qatar, in 2010 and Istanbul, Turkey, in 2012.

WORLD CUP

Most points scored

Marita Koch (East Germany) was representing Europe when she scored 46 points in the 200 m and 400 m between 1979 and 1985. In each World Cup, at least eight teams took part – five continental and three national (occasionally the host nation would also compete, making it nine entrants). The event was renamed the Continental Cup in 2010 and limited to four teams: Africa, the Americas, Asia/Pacific and Europe.

The **most points scored in a single event** is 33, by Maria Mutola (Mozambique) in the 800 m between 1992 and 2002. The only person to have scored more is Javier Sotomayor (Cuba), with 35 points in the men's high jump between 1985 and 1998.

Most wins by a team

The most World Cup wins by a female team stands at four, by the East Germans in consecutive World Cups held in 1979, 1981, 1985 and 1989.

Greatest span of appearances

The longest time between first and final appearances in World Cup competitions is 15 years, by Tessa Sanderson (UK), representing Europe in the javelin between 1977 and 1992. Sanderson has the greatest span for any athlete, beating the men's record of 14 years held by pole-vaulter Okkert Brits (South Africa).

FACT: The first woman to throw the hammer over 70 m was Olga Kuzenkova (Russia) in 1997.

Farthest hammer throw

Betty Heidler (Germany) threw the hammer 79.42 m (260 ft 6.76 in) in Halle, Germany, on 25 May 2011. Heidler, who won the World Championships in 2007, eclipsed the previous mark of 78.30 m (256 ft 10.67 in) set by the 2009 world champion Anita Wlodarczyk of Poland in Bydgoszcz, Poland.

TO SEE HOW FAST HUMANS CAN RUN, HOT-FOOT IT TO P.232

MARATHONS

FACT: Makau celebrates his 2011 Berlin Marathon win, his second in a row, in front of the Brandenburg Gate.

Oldest marathon

The Boston Marathon (USA) is the oldest continuously run annual marathon. It was first held on 19 April 1897 over 39 km (24 miles 1,232 yards), rather than today's official distance of 42.195 km (26 miles 385 yards). Although he had run on a shortened course, the 1897 winner, John J McDermott (USA), recorded a time of 2 hr 55 min 10 sec, over 50 minutes short of today's world record (see left)!

Most marathons in a calendar year (male)

R Laurence Macon (USA) completed 113 marathons from 1 January to 31 December 2011, while Yolanda Holder (USA) has the record for the **most marathons run in a calendar year (female)**, with 106 between 1 January and 31 December 2010. Holder, nicknamed "Walking Diva", estimated her attempt cost $25,000 (£16,000) in travel, accommodation and entry fees.

Fastest marathon (female)

Paula Radcliffe (UK) won the London Marathon, UK, on 13 April 2003 in a record time of 2 hr 15 min 25 sec. She also holds the two other fastest times, one set when she won the 2002 Chicago Marathon and one in the 2005 London Marathon. Paula also ran the **fastest 10 km (road)**, in 30 min 21 sec at the 2003 World's Best 10K, in San Juan, Puerto Rico.

Most marathons run on consecutive days (male)

Akinori Kusuda (Japan) ran 52 marathons on 52 days in Besshonuma Park, Saitama, Japan, from 30 January to 22 March 2009. And when Cristina Borra (Italy) completed 13 marathons between

16–28 February 2010, all run in Ruffini Park, Turin, Italy, she achieved the record for the **most marathons run on consecutive days (female)**.

Fastest marathon (male)

On 25 September 2011, Patrick Makau (Kenya) ran the 38th Berlin Marathon, Germany, in 2 hr 3 min 38 sec. Previous record-holder Haile Gebrselassie (Ethiopia) was also in the race, but Makau left him behind shortly after the halfway point before shattering his record by 21 seconds. In doing so, he also ran the **fastest 30 km (road)** in 1 hr 27 min 38 sec.

2012 VIRGIN LONDON MARATHON: NEW WORLD RECORDS

While marathon running is a serious business for elite athletes, such as those featured above, for others it is a great excuse to have some fun on the run – and where better to have it than at the world's premier marathon event: the London Marathon?

Tallest costume
David Lawrenson's Blackpool Tower measured 7.976 m (26 ft 2 in)
7 hr 19 sec

Fastest on stilts
George and Charley Phillips (brother and sister)
6 hr 50 min 2 sec

Fastest run by a parent and child
Jeff and Russell Whittington
5 hr 42 min 1 sec

Fastest dribbling a football
Tony Barrance
5 hr 36 min 24 sec

Fastest hula hooping
Sasha Kenney
5 hr 5 min 57 sec

Fastest in a two-person pantomime costume
Billy and Tom Casserley (brothers)
4 hr 49 min 18 sec

Fastest dressed as a star
Ian Gear
4 hr 33 min 10 sec

Fastest dressed as a mascot (female)
Wendy Shaw running as Alfie (of Guide Dogs for the Blind, UK)
4 hr 6 min 6 sec

Fastest dressed as a vegetable (female)
Helen Juckes as a carrot
3 hr 47 min 15 sec

Fastest dressed as a monk
Gavin Long
3 hr 45 min 14 sec

Fastest in a wedding dress
Naomi Garrick
3 hr 41 min 40 sec

Fastest dressed as a book character (female)
Julie Donald dressed as Wally's friend Wenda
3 hr 39 min 49 sec

Fastest dressed as a dairy product (male)
Chris Atkins as a tub of ice-cream
3 hr 37 min 22 sec

Fastest dressed in school uniform (male)
Tony Audenshaw
3 hr 36 min 51 sec

Hottest marathon

The Badwater Ultramarathon, held every July on a 217-km (135-mile) course from Death Valley to Mt Whitney in California, USA, registers temperatures of up to 55°C. The finish is 2,530 m (8,000 ft) above sea level.

recorded the fastest time of 3 hr 36 min 10 sec in 2007. Cathrine Due (Denmark) is the fastest woman, with a time of 5 hr 37 min 14 sec in 2008.

Lowest marathon

The finish of the Dead Sea Marathon, held every April, is located 400 m (1,312 ft) below sea level at Amman, Jordan.

Most consecutive days running an ultramarathon

Enzo Caporaso (Italy) ran seven ultramarathons in seven consecutive days from 13 to 19 June 2010. All the races started in Turin, Italy, and covered 100 km (62.14 miles). Caporaso ran the first in 11 hr 28 min 43 sec, but slowed to 19 hr 23 min 11 sec by his last.

Most finishers in a marathon

A total of 47,323 runners out of 47,763 starters finished the New York Marathon, New York, USA, on 6 November 2011.

Most money raised by a marathon runner

At the London Marathon on 17 April 2011, Steve Chalke (UK) raised £2,330,159.38 ($3,795,581.14) for Oasis UK, a charity that helps vulnerable young people.

Most runners linked to complete a marathon

Organized by Robin Gohsman (USA), 62 runners, linked by ropes, finished the Milwaukee Lakefront Marathon in Milwaukee, Wisconsin, USA, on 2 October 2011.

Most northerly marathon

The North Pole Marathon has been held annually since 2003, on a course certified by the Association of International Marathons and Distance Races. Thomas Maguire (Ireland)

Greatest distance run barefoot in 24 hr

Abhijeet Baruah (India), a 22-year-old police constable, ran 156.2 km (97 miles) barefoot in Jorhat, Assam, in north-east India, on 30–31 January 2012.

Most wins of World Marathon Major races (female)

The Majors consist of the annual marathons in London (UK), New York, Boston, Chicago (all USA) and Berlin (Germany) plus the Olympic and the World Championship marathons. Grete Waitz (Norway) won 12 Majors between 1978 and 1987, comprising nine in New York, two in London and one World Championship marathon. Bill Rodgers has the **most wins (male)**, with eight from 1975 to 1980, comprising four in Boston and four in New York.

Youngest runner to complete 100 marathons (female)

Melanie Johnstone (UK, b. 7 December 1974) was aged 34 years 279 days when she completed her 100th marathon, the 2009 Moray Marathon, in Elgin, Scotland, UK, on 13 September 2009. Melanie's first marathon was the 2003 London Marathon.

Fastest dressed in school uniform (female)
Amy Tanner
3 hr 33 min 52 sec

Fastest dressed as an insect (female)
Magdalene Bennett as a bee
3 hr 32 min 30 sec

Fastest dressed as a videogame character
Joint holders: Dan McCormack as Luigi and Nash Pradhan as Mario
3 hr 29 min 41 sec

Fastest wearing a gas mask
Andy McMahon
3 hr 28 min 38 sec

Fastest dressed as a lifeguard
Hamish Khayat
3 hr 26 min 35 sec

Fastest in an animal costume (female)
Susannah Gill as a peacock
3 hr 18 min 9 sec

Fastest dressed as a nun
Kevin Day
3 hr 17 min 58 sec

Fastest dressed as a baby
Michael Brigham
3 hr 11 min 53 sec

Fastest dressed as a golfer (male)
Simon Le Mare
3 hr 10 min 4 sec

Fastest dressed as a jester
Alexander Scherz
3 hr 1 min 56 sec

Fastest dressed as a vegetable (male)
Edward Lumley as a carrot
2 hr 59 min 33 sec

Fastest dressed as a Roman soldier
David Tomlin
2 hr 57 min

Fastest dressed in a nurse's uniform (male)
Kevin Harvey
2 hr 51 min 37 sec

Fastest dressed as a fairy
Martin Hulbert
2 hr 49 min 44 sec

Fastest dressed as a book character (male)
David Mark Stone as Dracula
2 hr 42 min 17 sec

CYCLING

Most participants in a Furnace Creek 508

The Furnace Creek 508 race in California, USA, attracted 217 participants on 8–10 October 2011. Billing itself as "The toughest 48 hours in sport", the race is 817.5 km (508 miles) long, from Santa Clarita (just north of Los Angeles) to Twentynine Palms via the Mojave Desert, Death Valley and 10 mountain passes.

Most Vélo d'Or awards

Awarded annually since 1992 by *Vélo Magazine* (France) to the best rider of the year, the Vélo d'Or (Golden Bicycle) is widely regarded as the most prestigious accolade in cycle racing. Lance Armstrong (USA) won five Vélo d'Or awards in 1999–2001 and 2003–04.

Fastest women's team 3 km, standing start

On 5 April 2012, Laura Trott, Danielle King and Joanna Rowsell completed the 3 km team pursuit in 3 min 15.720 sec to take gold for GB at the World Championships in Melbourne, Australia.

Fastest men's team 750 m, unpaced standing start

René Enders, Maximillian Levy and Stefan Nimke (all Germany) cycled the three-lap 750 m track in 42.914 seconds at Cali, Colombia, on 1 December 2011.

Tour de France wins

Most Tour de France wins (Tour first held in 1903; yellow jersey, for overall winner, first formally awarded in 1919)	7	Lance Armstrong (USA)
	5	Jacques Anquetil (France)
		Bernard Hinault (France)
		Miguel Indurain (Spain)
		Eddy Merckx (Belgium)
	3	Louison Bobet (France)
		Greg LeMond (USA)
		Philippe Thys (Belgium)
Most Tour de France green jerseys (best sprinter, first awarded in 1953)	6	Erik Zabel (Germany)
	4	Sean Kelly (Ireland)
	3	Jan Janssen (Netherlands)
		Eddy Merckx (Belgium)
		Freddy Maertens (Belgium)
		Djamolidine Abdoujaparov (Uzbekistan)
		Robbie McEwen (Australia)
Most Tour de France red polka-dot jerseys (King of the Mountains, first awarded in 1933)	7	Richard Virenque (France)
	6	Federico Bahamontes (Spain)
		Lucien Van Impe (Belgium)
	3	Julio Jiménez (Spain)

Giro d'Italia wins

Most Giro d'Italias	5	Alfredo Binda (Italy)
		Fausto Coppi (Italy)
		Eddy Merckx (Belgium)
	3	Giovanni Brunero (Italy)
		Gino Bartali (Italy)
		Fiorenzo Magni (Italy)
		Felice Gimondi (Italy)
		Bernard Hinault (France)
	2	11 cyclists

Statistics correct as of 2 April 2012

Fastest 3 km, unpaced standing start (female)

Sarah Hammer (USA) cycled the 3 km unpaced from a standing start in 3 min 22.269 sec at the Pan American Championships in Aguascalientes, Mexico, on 11 May 2010.

Fastest time to cycle 10,000 km

Guus Moonen (Netherlands) cycled 10,000 km (6,213 miles) in 22 days 15 hr 34 min 9 sec around three circuits of the village of Oisterwijk, Netherlands, from 5 to 28 June 2010.

Fastest 500 m, unpaced flying start (female)

Olga Streltsova (Russia) completed the 500 m unpaced flying start in 29.481 seconds in Moscow, Russia, on 29 May 2011.

Greatest distance cycled in 48 hours on a mountain bike

Dave Buchanan (UK) cycled 571 km (354.8 miles) on an off-road trail between Cardiff and Caernarfon in Wales, UK, from 13 to 15 May 2011.

Greatest distance cycled in a year

Thomas Godwin (UK) cycled 120,805 km (75,065 miles) in 1939, an average of 330.97 km (205.65 miles) per day. He then went on to clock up a total of 160,934 km (100,000 miles) in the 500 days to 14 May 1940. His feat was completed on a four-gear steel bike weighing in excess of 13.5 kg (30 lb).

Longest static cycling marathon

Patrizio Sciroli (Italy) cycled for an epic 224 hr 24 min 24 sec from 6 to 15 May 2011 on a static bike in Teramo, Abruzzo, Italy. In order to achieve the record, Patrizio had to maintain a speed of at least 20 km/h (12 mi/h).

Fastest men's team pursuit (4 km)

On 4 April 2012 at the Hisense Arena in Melbourne, Australia, GB's Ed Clancy, Peter Kennaugh, Steven Burke and Geraint Thomas struck gold at the World Championships in 3 min 53.295 sec. They broke the record of 3 min 53.31 sec that the GB team (Ed Clancy, Bradley Wiggins, Paul Manning and Geraint Thomas) had set winning gold at the 2008 Beijing Olympics in China.

In the men's team pursuit, two teams ride against each other, starting on opposite sides of the velodrome. The object is to catch the other team or record the fastest time, determined by the time of the third rider.

Fastest 200 m unpaced flying start (female)

On 5 April 2012, Anna Meares (Australia) cycled the flying 200 m in 10.782 seconds in the first round of qualifying at the World Championships at the Hisense Arena in Melbourne, Australia.

Most cyclo-cross World Cups

Sven Nys (Belgium) won six cyclo-cross World Cups between 1999 and 2009. Cyclo-cross consists of many laps of a short course – typically 2.5–3.5 km (1.5–2 miles) – featuring short, steep hills, sharp corners and obstacles that require the rider to carry the bike. The terrain varies throughout and can include tarmac, hardpack dirt, grass, mud and sand. Daphny van den Brand (Netherlands, right) has won the **most women's cyclo-cross World Cups**, with three victories between 2005 and 2012.

TOUR DE FRANCE

Fastest average speed

Lance Armstrong (USA) finished first in the 2005 Tour with an average speed of 41.654 km/h (25.882 mi/h). He finished the 3,607-km-long (2,241-mile) Tour in 86 hr 15 min 2 sec. Armstrong announced his retirement after this race, but he returned to cycling in 2009 and finished third in the Tour that year.

Longest solo escape

Breaking away from the *peloton* (field) is risky, as you have no chance of slipstreaming (or "drafting") other riders. The longest solo escape was 253 km (157.2 miles) by Albert Bourlon (France) in 1947 to win the 14th stage between Carcassonne and Luchon.

Largest victory margin

Fausto Coppi (Italy) finished 28 min 27 sec in front of Stan Ockers (Belgium) in 1952.

Youngest winner

Henri Cornet (France) was 19 years 350 days when he won the second ever Tour, in 1904. Cornet had actually finished the race in 5th position, but was awarded the victory after the first four riders – Maurice Garin, Lucien Pothier, César Garin, and Hippolyte Aucouturier (all France) – were disqualified. In this controversial tour, riders were attacked to stop them, and nails were thrown over the road to cause punctures. Riders were also alleged to have used cars for lifts.

Oldest winner

Firmin Lambot (Belgium) won the Tour de France aged 36 years 4 months in 1922.

Longest Tour de France

Today, the Tour de France covers around 3,200 km (2,000 miles), but in 1926 the race totalled 5,745 km (3,569.77 miles) – farther than the distance between Paris and Moscow and back again. The race was won by Lucien Buysse (Belgium).

Most Tours completed

Hendrik "Joop" Zoetemelk (Netherlands) finished 16 Tours in 1970–73 and 1975–86. Over the 16 races, Joop recorded one Tour win, in 1980, and six second-place finishes. In 1985, aged 38, he also won the World Road Championship.

Fastest women's team sprint (500 m)

On 4 April 2012 at the Hisense Arena in Melbourne, Australia, Germany's Miriam Welte and Kristina Vogel clocked a time of 32.549 seconds to beat Australians Anna Meares and Kaarle McCulloch in the final of the World Championship women's team sprint. Welte and Vogel had already set a world record earlier in the day of 32.630 seconds in qualifying against Lithuania.

In the women's team sprint, the two riders race for two laps – one rider leads off while the other follows, centimetres behind, in her slipstream. On the second lap, the second rider sprints to the finish by herself.

RACING SPORTS

SKIING

Fastest speed
Simone Origone (Italy) skied at a speed of 252.40 km/h (156.83 mi/h) at Les Arcs, France, on 20 April 2006.

The **fastest speed by a female skier** is 242.59 km/h (150.73 mi/h), by Sanna Tidstrand (Sweden), also at Les Arcs, on 20 April 2006.

Youngest Alpine skier to win Olympic gold
On 16 February 1992, Kjetil André Aamodt (Norway) won the first of his four golds in Albertville, France, aged 20 years 167 days.

Ktejil is also **the oldest Alpine skier to win Olympic gold**. He won his fourth gold at the super giant slalom in Turin, Italy, on 18 February 2006, aged 34 years 169 days.

Longest race
The Vasaloppet Nordic ski race is 90 km (56 miles) long and is held annually every March in north-west Dalarna, Sweden. The fastest finish time is 3 hr 38 min 41 sec by Jörgen Brink (Sweden) in 2012. By contrast, the first winner in 1922, Ernst Alm (Sweden), took 7 hr 32 min 49 sec!

Fastest row, single sculls, lightweight
On 24 July 2011, Jeremie Azou (France) finished the single sculls (i.e., using two oars) in 6 min 46.93 sec at the World Rowing Under-23 Championships in Amsterdam, Netherlands.

Longest downhill race
The annual "Schlag das ASSinger", organized by the municipality of Nassfeld Hermagor (Austria), is 25.6 km (15.91 miles) long. The race starts at Gartenkofel and finishes at Tröpolach.

Longest marathon ski
The longest time spent skiing non-stop is 202 hr 1 min by Nick Willey (Australia) at Thredbo, a ski resort in New South Wales, Australia, on 2–10 September 2005.

BOBSLEIGH

Most Olympic golds
Three competitors have won three Olympic bobsleigh golds. Meinhard Nehmer and Bernhard Germeshausen (both GDR, now Germany) won theirs in the 1976 two-man and the 1976 and 1980 four-man races, while André Lange, also of Germany, won gold in the 2006 two-man and the 2002 and 2006 four-man races.

Oldest Olympic champion
Jay O'Brien (USA) was 47 years 357 days old when he won the gold medal with the four-man bobsleigh team during the 1932 Winter Olympics held at Lake Placid in New York, USA.

LUGE

Most doubles World Cup wins
The luge World Cup has been held annually since 1977 and Hansjörg Raffl and Norbert Huber (both Italy) have won the doubles at the event eight times, from 1983 to 1993. In the luge, competitors ride feet-first and face-up on the sled.

Most women's World Cup wins
The most overall wins of the women's luge World Cup is five, by Silke Kraushaar-Pielach (Germany) between 1998 and 2007.

SKELETON

Fastest speed
In the skeleton, the racer rides head-first, face-down on the sled. Alexander Tretyakov (Russia) and Sandro Stielicke (Germany) both hit speeds of 146.4 km/h (90.96 mi/h) in the Winter Olympics at Whistler in British Columbia, Canada, on 19 February 2010. On the same day, the **fastest speed for an individual female on a bobsleigh skeleton** was recorded by Marion Trott (Germany), who reached 144.5 km/h (89.78 mi/h).

Oldest competitor at the Winter Olympics
James Coates (GB) competed in the skeleton at the 1948 Olympics in St Moritz, Switzerland, aged 53 years 328 days. Coates finished seventh in the final, 5.4 seconds behind the winner.

Largest triathlon race
The most participants in a single triathlon race of international distance was 4,546 at the Nation's Triathlon in Washington, DC, USA, on 12 September 2010. International, or Olympic, distance triathlons consist of a 1.5-km (0.93-mile) swim, 40-km (24.85-mile) bicycle ride, and 10-km (6.21-mile) run. The event raised more than $3 million (£1.95 million) for the Leukaemia and Lymphoma Society.

SPEED SKATING

Fastest short-track 5,000-m relay (men)
Jon Eley, Richard Shoebridge, Paul Stanley and Jack Whelbourne (GB) completed the 5,000-m relay in 6 min 37.877 sec at the ISU Short Track Speed Skating World Cup in Dresden, Germany, on 20 February 2011. The short-track event is 111 m, compared with the 400-m long track.

Most Olympic golds (men)
Two men have won five gold medals at speed skating: Clas Thunberg (Finland) in 1924 and 1928; and Eric Arthur Heiden (USA) at one Games at Lake Placid in New York, USA, in 1980.

STAIR CLIMBING

Most Empire State Run-Up wins (men)
The Empire State Building Run-Up is a foot race up 1,576 steps from ground level to the 86th-floor observation deck. It has been held annually since 1978 and the most wins is seven, by Thomas Dold (Germany), consecutively from 2006 to 2012. Cyclist Paul Crake (Australia) has

FACT: Barzalona celebrated his 2012 win by standing up in his stirrups and waving his whip before the finish.

Richest horse race
The largest prize fund for a single horse race is $10 million (£6.71 million) for the Dubai World Cup, held at Meydan Racecourse in Dubai, United Arab Emirates. The 2012 race, held on 31 March, was won by 20/1 outsider Monterosso, ridden by the 20-year-old Mickael Barzalona (France).

FACT: At the 2011 World Championships, Sun Yang also won gold in the 800 m freestyle.

Fastest 1,500 m long-course freestyle swim

At the FINA World Championships on 31 July 2011, Sun Yang (China) won gold at the 1,500 m freestyle in 14 min 34.14 sec at the Oriental Sports Center in Shanghai, China. In doing so, Yang beat the longest-standing men's swimming world record of 14 min 34.56 sec set by Grant Hackett (Australia) at the 2001 World Championships in Fukuoka, Japan. (Long-course records take place in 50-m long pools.)

the **fastest time for the Run-Up** – 9 min 33 sec achieved in 2003. Crake is the only man to do it under 10 minutes. The last four of his five wins from 1999 to 2003 were all under 10 minutes.

Most Empire State Run-Up wins (female)

Cindy Moll-Harris (USA) has won the women's Run-Up four times, in 1998, 2000–01 and 2003. In 2006, Andrea Mayr (Austria) set the **fastest female time for the Run-Up** – completing in 11 min 23 sec.

ROWING

Most World Coach of the Year Awards

Richard Tonks (New Zealand), in 2005 and 2010, and Gianni Postiglione (Greece) in 2006 and 2011, have both won the World Rowing Coach of the Year Award twice.

Most World Rowing Cup wins

The World Rowing Cup has been held annually since 1997 and is won by the country that picks up the most points from three regattas. Germany has won the Cup 10 times, between 1998 and 2011. Great Britain has won it four times, consecutively from 2007 to 2010. Switzerland won the inaugural competition.

Most Olympic golds

One man and two women have five rowing golds. Steven Redgrave (GB) won golds at consecutive Olympics from 1984 to 2000. Elisabeta Lipă (Romania) won golds in 1984, 1992, 1996, 2000 and 2004; and Georgeta Damian (Romania) won two in 2000, two in 2004 and one in 2008.

Fastest 40,075 km (Equator) indoor row

David Holby (UK) rowed 40,075 km (24,901 miles) – the equivalent of the length of the Equator – in 2 years 6 months 20 days at The Malls shopping centre in Basingstoke, Hampshire, UK. Holby, who became known as "Dave the Rower" to the shoppers, rowed on average 300.34 km (186.62 miles) a week from May 2008 to December 2010.

Longest open-sea race

The Indian Rowing Race covers 3,140 nautical miles (5,820 km; 3,615 miles) from Geraldton, Western Australia, to Port Louis, Mauritius. It has been held twice, in 2009 and 2011.

Fabulous Phelps

• Michael Phelps (USA) is the most successful swimmer of all time. He took up the sport aged seven and qualified for the 2000 Sydney Olympics at 15, where he finished fifth in the final of the 200 m butterfly.

• At the 2004 Athens Olympics, while still a teenager, he won eight medals – six gold and two bronze – equalling the record for **most medals won at a single Olympics**.

• Michael won eight medals again at the 2008 Olympics – this time, though, they were all gold, so he broke the record for the **most golds at a single Olympics**. His tally comprised five individual records and three as part of relay teams.

• He has won the **most World Championships swimming golds** – one in 2001, four in 2003, five in 2005, seven in 2007, five in 2009, and four in 2011 – a total of 26.

• He also holds the record for the **most World Swimmer of the Year Awards**, with six, won in 2003–04 and 2006–09.

SWIMMING

Fastest 200 m short-course backstroke (female)

Melissa "Missy" Franklin (USA) – the 2011 FINA female Swimmer of the Year – swam the short-course 200 m backstroke at the 2011 World Cup in Berlin, Germany, on 22 October in a time of 2 min 0.03 sec. Six weeks later, on 16 December, the 16-year-old and her Team USA colleagues swam the **fastest 4 x 100 m short-course medley relay** at the Duel in the Pool in Atlanta, Georgia, USA, with a time of 3 min 45.56 sec.

Fastest 200 m long-course medley (male)

Ryan Lochte (USA) swam the 200 m long-course medley in 1 min 54.00 sec in Shanghai, China, on 28 July 2011.

Most Classic Luge World Cup wins

Road luge involves riding a wheeled board down an inclined paved road or course. The riders negotiate bends by leaning, and brake by using their feet on the road. Between 2007 and 2011, Michael Serek (Austria) won five International Gravity Sports Association (IGSA) Classic Luge World Cups.

Most wins in men's luge World Cup
Two men have secured 10 overall wins of the men's luge World Cup: Markus Prock (Austria) between 1987 and 2002, and Armin Zöggeler (Italy, right) between 1999 and 2011.

FACT: The IGSA World Cup has two events: Classic uses a board similar to a skateboard; Street uses a board similar to a luge.

FACT: In 2011, Serek was IGSA Classic European Champion, World Champion and World Cup Champion!

FACT: Zöggeler won gold in the single luge in the 2002 and 2006 Winter Olympics.

POWER SPORTS

Heaviest over-105 kg snatch (male)

Behdad Salimikordasiabi (Iran) lifted 214 kg in the men's over-105 kg snatch category at the 2011 World Weightlifting Championships in Paris, France, on 13 November. He broke the previous record of 213 kg, lifted by Salimikordasiabi's fellow Iranian and two-time Olympic champion Hossein Rezazadeh in 2003.

FACT:
Behdad won an Asian Games gold in 2010 despite being affected by swine flu and collapsing during one lift.

BOXING

Longest reigning world champion
Joe Louis (USA) was undefeated heavyweight champion for 11 years 252 days, from 22 June 1937 when he beat Jim Braddock (USA) to when he retired on 1 March 1949. Floyd Mayweather, Jr (USA) first became world champion on 3 October 1998 and, up to his win against Miguel Cotto (Puerto Rico) on 5 May 2012, was undefeated for 13 years 214 days. However, Floyd retired for a period during that time.

Most professional bouts (female)
Stephanie M Dobbs (USA) fought 62 professional bouts between her first fight on 2 March 2002 and 5 June 2010.

Oldest active boxer
Steve Ward (UK) was aged 55 years 219 days at the time of his most recent bout on 19 March 2011 in Chesterfield, Derbyshire, UK. Ward boxed as an amateur from the age of 11 to 21 before embarking on a 10-year professional career. He retired for 23 years from 1987 to 2010, before returning to fight three times in 2010 and 2011, with all fights sanctioned by the European Boxing Federation.

Oldest winner of a major world championship

At 46 years 126 days, Bernard "The Executioner" Hopkins (USA) defeated Jean Pascal (Canada, b. Haiti) in Montreal, Canada, on 21 May 2011 to capture the WBC, IBO and The Ring light heavyweight belts.

Heaviest heavyweight world champion

Nikolay Valuev (Russia) weighed in at a massive 148.7 kg (328 lb) for his WBA heavyweight title fight with Monte Barrett (USA) at Allstate Arena, Rosemont, Illinois, USA, on 7 October 2007. Valuev won the bout via technical knockout in round 11.

Most Fighter of the Year Awards

Muhammad Ali (USA) won five Fighter of the Year Awards, given by *The Ring* magazine, in 1963, 1972, 1974–75 and 1978.

Most Trainer of the Year Awards

Freddie Roach (USA) has won five Trainer of the Year Awards, in 2003, 2006 and 2008–10.

Most judo World Championship titles

Teddy Riner (France) won six judo World Championship golds from 2007 to 2011 – four at heavyweight (over-100 kg), one at openweight and one in men's teams. Riner also has a silver in openweight so shares the record for **most medals won at the World Championships** with seven, along with Naoya Ogawa (Japan), with four gold and three bronze from 1987 to 1995, and Robert Van de Walle (Belgium), with two silver and five bronze from 1979 to 1989.

FACT:
Riner was the **youngest to win a World Championship.** He was 18 years 192 days old when he took the heavyweight gold in 2007.

WRESTLING

Most men's Freestyle Wrestling World Championships
Two competitors have won the men's Freestyle Wrestling World Championships seven times: Aleksandr Medved (Belarus) in the 97 kg, over-97 kg and over-100 kg classes between 1962 and 1971; and Valentin Jordanov (Bulgaria) in the 52 kg class between 1983 and 1995.

Most Olympic golds
Five wrestlers have won three Olympic titles: Carl Westergren (Sweden) in 1920, 1924 and 1932; Ivar Johansson (Sweden) in 1932 (two) and 1936; Aleksandr Medved (Belarus) in 1964, 1968 and 1972; Aleksandr Karelin (Russia) in 1988, 1992 and 1996; and Buvaysar Saytiev (Russia) in 1996, 2004 and 2008.

Heaviest 63 kg snatch (female)

Svetlana Tsarukaeva (Russia) lifted 117 kg in the 63 kg weight category of the snatch competition at the 2011 World Weightlifting Championships in Paris, France, on 8 November 2011. Here, Svetlana is shown at the 2011 World Championships in the clean and jerk, where the bar is first lifted to the collar bone. In the snatch, the bar is lifted in one smooth, continuous movement.

Longest women's wrestling winning streak

Saori Yoshida (Japan) won 119 consecutive matches between 2002 and 2008. Yoshida eventually lost her unbeaten record in a match against Marcie Van Dusen (USA) in a Team World Cup event in Beijing, China, on 20 January 2008. Above, Saori is shown competing against Tonya Verbeek (Canada) on her way to gold in the 55 kg weight class at the 2008 Beijing Olympics.

Weightlifting records set in 2011

Men
105 kg clean and jerk
238 kg, by David Bejanyan (Russia) in Belgorod, Russia, on 17 December 2011.

Women
53 kg clean and jerk
130 kg, by Zulfiya Chinshanlo (Kazakhstan) in Paris, France, on 6 November 2011.

75 kg clean and jerk
163 kg, by Nadazda Evstyukhina (Russia) in Paris, France, on 10 November 2011.

75 kg total
296 kg, by Natalya Zabolotnaya (Russia) in Belgorod, Russia, on 17 November 2011.

Over-75 kg snatch
148 kg, by Tatiana Kashirina (Russia) in Belgorod, Russia, on 18 December 2011.

Over-75 kg total
328 kg, by Zhou Lulu (China) in Paris, France, on 13 November 2011.

Most consecutive UFC fight wins

Anderson "The Spider" Silva (Brazil) won 15 UFC fights between 2006 and 2011. His 15th victory was against Yushin Okami (Japan) on 27 August 2011 – after flooring Okami with a short right hook, Silva finished him off with a brutal ground-and-pound.

SUMO

Most bouts won in a calendar year
In 2009, *Yokozuna* Hakuhō Shō (Mongolia, birth name Mönkhbatyn Davaajargal) won 86 out of the 90 regulation bouts that a top *rikishi* (sumo wrestler) fights annually.

Heaviest wrestler
Samoan-American Saleva'a Fuauli Atisano'e (aka Konishiki), weighed in at 267 kg (589 lb) at Tokyo's Ryōgoku Kokugikan on 3 January 1994. He put his massive weight down to eating a high-protein stew called *chankonabe*.

Most top-division wins
The most *makuuchi*, or top division, wins in sumo wrestling by a *rikishi* is 815, by Kaiō Hiroyuki (Japan, birth name Hiroyuki Koga) from 1993 to 2010. There are 42 wrestlers in the *makuuchi*, ordered into five ranks.

TAEKWONDO

Most World Championship finweight titles won
Yeon-Ho Choi (South Korea) has won four finweight World Championship gold medals, in 2001, 2003, 2007 and 2009.

JUDO

Most women's World Championships medals
Ingrid Berghmans (Belgium) won 11 medals – comprising six gold, four silver and one bronze – at the World Championships between 1980 and 1989.

Youngest female judo world champion
Ryoko Tani (née Tamura, Japan) was 18 years 27 days when she won the under-48 kg title at the World Championships in Hamilton, Canada, in 1993.

A man of Manny talents

• In May 2010, Manny was elected congressman for Sarangani on the Philippine island of Mindanao. He is the first professional boxer to hold national public office while active in the ring.

• Manny has starred in films, including the boxing superhero movie *Wapakman* (2009), an entry in the Metro Manila Film Festival.

• Manny is also a keen singer. His albums include *Pac-Man Punch* (2007) for MCA Records, and his 2011 duet with singer-songwriter Dan Hill, "Sometimes When We Touch", reached No.19 on the US *Billboard* Adult Contemporary Top 20 list.

Most boxing world titles in different weight divisions

Manny Pacquiao (Philippines) won his eighth world title at different weights when he defeated Antonio Margarito (USA) to win the WBC super welterweight title on 13 November 2010. He has also held sanctioned belts in the WBC flyweight, super featherweight (which he won against Mexico's Juan Manuel Márquez, left) and lightweight divisions, plus The Ring featherweight, IBF super bantamweight, IBO and The Ring light welterweight, and WBO welterweight.

GOLF

Farthest golf shot

Flight Engineer Mikhail Tyurin (Russia), assisted by caddy Commander Michael Lopez-Alegria (USA), teed off during a spacewalk outside the *International Space Station* on 23 February 2006. NASA estimated the ball would orbit for three days and travel 2.02 million km (1.26 million miles) before burning up in the atmosphere.

The **longest golf shot at an altitude below 1,000 m** is 373.07 m (408 yd), by Karl Woodward (UK) at Golf del Sur, Tenerife, Spain, on 30 June 1999.

Highest-altitude golf course

The Yak golf course, part of an Indian Army base, is 3,970 m (13,025 ft) above sea level in Kupup, East Sikkim, India. Natural ponds and mountain streams provide hazards.

Largest golf range

The SKY72 Golf Club Dream Golf Range in Jung-gu, Incheon, South Korea, has 300 individual bays.

Largest golf facility

Mission Hills Golf Club in Shenzhen, China, has 12 fully operational 18-hole courses.

Largest bunker

The Hell's Half Acre bunker on the 535-m (585-yd) seventh hole of the Pine Valley course, Clementon, New Jersey, USA, starts 265 m (280 yd) from the tee and extends another 137 m (150 yd) up the fairway.

Longest hole

The seventh hole (par 7) of the Satsuki golf course in Sano, Japan, measures 881 m (964 yd).

Longest holed putt in a top-flight tournament

Jack Nicklaus (USA), in the 1964 Tournament of Champions, and Nick Price (Zimbabwe) in the 1992 United States PGA, both sank putts of 33.5 m (110 ft). Bob Cook (USA) holed a putt measured at 42.74 m (140 ft 2.75 in) on the 18th at St Andrews, Scotland, in the International Fourball Pro Am Tournament on 1 October 1976.

Lowest score to par after 72 holes in a top-flight tournament

Chapchai Nirat (Thailand) hit 32 under par at the 2009 SAIL Open (on the Asian Tour) at the Classic Golf Resort, Gurgaon, India, on 21 March 2009.

FACT:
Rory was 16 years 42 days when he won the 2005 Irish Amateur Close Championship.

Most European Tour event wins

The most event wins on golf's European Tour is 50, including five Majors, by Severiano "Seve" Ballesteros (Spain, 1957–2011) between 1976 and 1995. Seve also holds the record for the **most consecutive years with at least one event win on the European Tour** – 17 years from 1976 to 1992.

Most consecutive birdies in a PGA Tour event

Mark Calcavecchia (USA) hit nine birdies in the third round of the Canadian Open at Oakville in Ontario, Canada, on 25 July 2009. All nine of Calcavecchia's putts were within 4.72 m (15 ft) of the hole. Despite his amazing start, he ended the third round with a score of 71 (one under par).

Longest individual unbeaten streak in the Ryder Cup

Lee Westwood (UK) from 2002 to 2008, and Arnold Palmer (USA) from 1965 to 1971, both went 12 matches unbeaten in the Ryder Cup. Westwood lost two matches at the end of the 2008 Ryder Cup, but stormed back in the 2010 event, winning three matches and halving one, to help Europe regain the trophy.

Most consecutive Major wins

Tiger Woods (USA) claimed four consecutive Major titles in 2000–01, winning the US Open, the British Open and the PGA Championship in 2000 and the US Masters in 2001. This achievement has been dubbed the "Tiger Slam" – a true Grand Slam involves winning all the Majors in one calendar year.

Highest prize money for a golf tournament

The Players Championship, contested at Sawgrass, Florida,

Lowest total score in the US Open

Rory McIlroy (UK) won the US Open at Congressional Country Club in Bethesda, Maryland, USA, on 16–19 June 2011 with a score of only 268 (65-66-68-69). This score, 16 under par, was also the **lowest score to par in a US Open**. The win was Rory's first Major and, at the age of 22 years 46 days, he became the youngest US Open champion since Bobby Jones (USA) in 1923 and the youngest Major winner since Tiger Woods (USA) won the US Masters in 1997.

Oldest winner on European Tour

Des Smyth (Ireland) was aged 48 years 34 days when he won the Madeira Island Open at Santo da Serra, Portugal, on 17 March 2001. He hit a round of 270, 18 under par, to win by two strokes.

Most wins, highest earnings, lowest rounds

Most Majors *British Open, US Masters, US Open and US PGA Championship*	18	Jack Nicklaus (USA), 1962–86
	14	Tiger Woods (USA), 1997–2008
	11	Walter Hagen (USA), 1914–29
Highest career earnings – US Tour	$95,516,542	Tiger Woods (USA)
	$65,944,204	Vijay Singh (Fiji)
	$65,286,308	Phil Mickelson (USA)
Highest career earnings – European Tour	€26,985,651	Lee Westwood (UK)
	€26,472,392	Ernie Els (South Africa)
	€24,387,862	Colin Montgomerie (UK)
Lowest rounds – major tours only	58 (-12)	Ryo Ishikawa (Japan) The Crowns tournament, 2010, Japan Golf Tour
	59 (-13)	Al Geiberger (USA) Danny Thomas Memphis Classic, 1977, US PGA Tour
	59 (-13)	Chip Beck (USA) Las Vegas Invitational, 1991, US PGA Tour

Statistics correct as of 19 March 2012

FACT:
In 2009, Matteo became the youngest winner of the Silver Medal for best amateur at the British Open.

US Tour

The US Tour was the pioneer of the tour system and offers the most prize money.

• Tiger Woods and Jack Nicklaus (both USA) have been the **most frequent leading money winners**, and both finished first a record eight times. Ben Hogan and Tom Watson (both USA) come equal third, topping the list five times.

• Luke Donald (UK) became the first Brit to be the leading money-winner when he topped the list in 2011. The only other non-Americans to top the list are: Greg Norman (Australia) in 1986, 1990, and 1995; Nick Price (Zimbabwe) in 1993 and 1994; Gary Player (South Africa) in 1961; and Vijay Singh (Fiji) in 2003, 2004 and 2008.

• The **most US Tour tournament wins in a year** is 18, by Byron Nelson (USA) in 1945. The **most wins in a year in the modern era** (since the tour adopted the name PGA in 1975) is nine, achieved by Tiger Woods in 2000 and Vijay Singh in 2004.

USA, has a total prize pool of $9,500,000 (£5,906,672), with $1,710,000 (£1,063,201) going to the winner. K J Choi (South Korea) won the event in 2011.

Highest season's earnings on the Ladies' European Tour

Laura Davies (England) earned 471,727 euros (£354,644; $698,084) on the 2006 European Tour.

Highest season's earnings on the Ladies' US Tour

In 2007, Lorena Ochoa (Mexico) earned $4,364,994 (£3,198,973) on the US Ladies' PGA Tour.

Most consecutive US Opens started

Jack Nicklaus (USA) started all 44 US Opens from 1957 to 2000.

Most holes of golf played in one year

Richard Lewis (USA) played 11,000 holes, all at the Four Seasons Resort and Club in Irving, Texas, USA, from 1 January to 31 December 2010. Lewis played 611 full rounds of golf, plus an additional two holes, averaging more than 30 holes played per day!

Most British Opens hosted

The Royal and Ancient Golf Club of St Andrews – established in Fife, Scotland, UK, in 1754 and patronized by King William IV in 1834 – has hosted the Open golf championships a record 28 times between 1873 and 2010.

Most wins of the women's British Open

Karrie Webb (Australia) and Sherri Steinhauer (USA) have both won the British Open a record three times – Webb in 1995, 1997 and 2002; Steinhauer in 1998, 1999 and 2006.

Highest career earnings on the Asian Tour

Thongchai Jaidee (Thailand) earned $4,472,290 (£2.7 million) on golf's Asian Tour from 1999 to 19 March 2012. Jaidee has also recorded the **most event wins on the Asian Tour** with 13, the first being the Kolon Korea Open in 2000.

Youngest female to play in the Curtis Cup

Michelle Wie (USA) was aged 14 years 244 days when she competed in the Curtis Cup at Formby Golf Club in Merseyside, UK, on 11–12 June 2004. The Curtis Cup is the best-known team trophy for women amateur golfers – it has been played between the USA and Great Britain & Ireland since 1932.

Youngest winner on the European Tour

At the age of 17 years 188 days, Matteo Manassero (Italy) won his first European Tour event – the Castello Masters at Club de Campo del Mediterraneo in Costa del Azahar, Spain – on 24 October 2010. He soon proved this victory was not a fluke. On 17 April 2011, he won his second European Tour event – the Malaysian Open at the Kuala Lumpur Golf & Country Club – aged 17 years 363 days, to become the only golfer to win two European Tour events before turning 18.

FACT:
In 2006, Thongchai became the first Thai to compete in all four Majors.

RACKET SPORTS

Most men's wheelchair World Championships

Between 1995 and 2004, David Hall (Australia) won six International Tennis Federation men's wheelchair singles World Championships, awarded on performances throughout the year. David had to have both legs amputated after being hit by a car at the age of 16 on 11 October 1986. In 1987, he started playing wheelchair tennis and, by 1992, he was representing Australia at the Paralympics.

First tennis player to achieve the "golden" Grand Slam

In 1988, Steffi Graf (Germany) won the four Grand Slams – the Australian Open, the French Open, Wimbledon and the US Open – as well as the Olympic gold medal to complete the "golden" Grand Slam. She is the only person to have achieved this feat in singles in a calendar year. Two other players – Andre Agassi (USA) and Rafael Nadal (Spain) – have completed a "golden" Grand Slam over their careers.

Fastest serve

Ivo Karlović (Croatia), who stands 2.08 m (6 ft 10 in) tall, served a ball at 251 km/h (156 mi/h) in a doubles match against Germany in the Davis Cup on 5 March 2011.

The **fastest serve by a woman** is 209 km/h (130 mi/h), by Brenda Schultz-McCarthy (Netherlands) during the first round of the Western & Southern Financial Group Women's Open on 15 July 2006. This was matched by Venus Williams (USA) at the 2008 final of the Zurich Open.

Highest attendance

A crowd of 35,681 saw Kim Clijsters (Belgium) defeat Serena Williams (USA) 6–3, 6–2 in Brussels, Belgium, on 8 July 2010 in an exhibition match. The figure beat the "Battle of the Sexes" match between Billie Jean King and Bobby Riggs (both USA), which drew 30,472 people to the Astrodome in Houston, Texas, USA, on 20 September 1973.

Largest Grand Slam fine

Serena Williams (USA) was fined $82,500 (£53,000) for verbal abuse during the 2009 US Open semi-final at Flushing Meadows, New York, USA, on 12 September 2009. Williams's outburst occurred on match point against her, after she was called for a foot-fault. She was given a one-point penalty, which meant her opponent, Kim Clijsters, was awarded the match.

Most men's doubles wins at the badminton World Championships

The most wins of the men's doubles event by the same pair is four, by Cai Yun and Fu Haifeng (China) in 2006 and 2009–11. Their victory in the 2011 final came in straight sets against Ko Sung-Hyun and Yoo Yeon-Seong (both South Korea).

Longest professional match

The 2010 first-round match at Wimbledon between John Isner (USA) and Nicolas Mahut (France) lasted 11 hr 5 min and stretched over three days. After playing 183 games, Isner finally defeated Mahut 70–68 in the final set. Ironically, the pair were drawn against each other at the 2011 Wimbledon – this time, Isner won in straight sets in only 34 games.

Longest rally

Identical twins Ettore and Angelo A Rossetti (USA) played a 25,944-stroke rally at North Haven Health & Racquet in North Haven, Connecticut, USA, on 9 August 2008. The attempt lasted 15 hours.

TENNIS

Most consecutive weeks at No.1 (male)

Roger Federer (Switzerland) spent 231 weeks at the top of the singles rankings, from 2 February 2004 to 7 July 2008. He lost the top spot to Rafael Nadal (Spain) after falling to the Spaniard in a five-set Wimbledon final. The previous best was 160 weeks by Jimmy Connors (USA), from 29 July 1974 to 22 August 1977.

FACT:
In 2010, Nadal became the seventh player in history to win all four Grand Slams.

Longest men's tennis Grand Slam final

Rafael Nadal (Spain, left) and Novak Djokovic (Serbia, right) played for 5 hr 53 min in the Australian Open final at Melbourne, Australia, on 29 January 2012, a record for the Open era. Djokovic won the match, widely regarded

Most Grand Slam titles won by a mother

Kim Clijsters (Belgium, left), from 2009 to 2011, and Margaret Court (Australia) in 1973, have both won three Grand Slam singles titles after giving birth.

BADMINTON

Fastest hit

When testing Yonex rackets, Tan Boon Heong (Malaysia) hit a shuttlecock at 421 km/h (261.6 mi/h) at the Tokyo Metropolitan Gymnasium in Tokyo, Japan, on 26 September 2009. The **fastest hit recorded in competition** is 332 km/h (206 mi/h), by Fu Haifeng (China) in the 2005 Sudirman Cup.

Longest match

The men's singles final at the 1997 World Championships at Glasgow, UK, on 1 June lasted 124 minutes, with Peter Rasmussen (Denmark) overcoming Sun Jun (China) 16–17, 18–13, 15–10.

Most World Championship wins (men's singles)

Lin Dan (China) has won four World Championships – in 2006, 2007, 2009 and 2011.

Most World Championship wins (mixed doubles)

Two mixed pairs have won the World Championships twice: Park Joo-Bong and Chung Myung-Hee (South Korea) in 1989 and 1991, and Nova Widianto and Lilyana Natsir (Indonesia) in 2005 and 2007.

Most World Championship wins (women's doubles)

Gao Ling and Huang Sui (China) have won the World Championships three times – in 2001, 2003 and 2006.

Most consecutive women's squash World Opens

Nicol David (Malaysia, above right) won four women's World Opens in a row from 2008 to 2011. She claimed the 2011 title by beating Jenny Duncalf (England, b. Netherlands) in the final in straight sets (above). David also holds the **most women's World Opens** in total, with six, having also won in 2005 and 2006. She also has the **most Women's International Squash Players Association Player of the Year awards**, with six from 2005 to 2010.

Tennis, squash and table tennis

Tennis

Most Grand Slam singles – men	16	Roger Federer (Switzerland)
	14	Pete Sampras (USA)
	12	Roy Emerson (Australia)
Most Grand Slam singles – women	24	Margaret Court (Australia)
	22	Steffi Graf (Germany)
	19	Helen Wills Moody (USA)
Largest stadium capacity – ATP Tour and Grand Slams	23,200	Arthur Ashe Stadium, New York, USA (used for US Open)
	17,500	O2 Arena, London, UK (used for ATP World Tour Finals)
	16,100	Indian Wells Tennis Garden, California, USA (used for Indian Wells Masters)

Squash

Most British Opens – men (first held in 1930)	10	Jahangir Khan (Pakistan)
	8	Geoff Hunt (Australia)
	7	Hashim Khan (Pakistan)
Most British Opens – women (first held in 1922)	16	Heather McKay (Australia)
	10	Janet Morgan (England)
	8	Susan Devoy (New Zealand)
Most World Opens – men (first held in 1976)	8	Jansher Khan (Pakistan)
	6	Jahangir Khan (Pakistan)
	4	Geoff Hunt (Australia)
Most World Opens – women (first held in 1979)	6	Nicol David (Malaysia)
	5	Sarah Fitz-Gerald (Australia)
	4	Susan Devoy (New Zealand)

Table Tennis

Most World Championship singles – men (first held in 1926)	6	Viktor Barna (Hungary)
	4	Richard Bergmann (England, b. Austria)
	3	Zhuang Zedong (China)
		Wang Liqin (China)
Most World Championship singles – women (first held in 1926)	6	Angelica Rozeanu (Romania)
	5	Mária Mednyánszky (Hungary)
	3	Gizella Farkas (Hungary)
		Deng Yaping (China)
		Wang Nan (China)

Correct as of 27 March 2012

TABLE TENNIS

Longest rally

Brian and Steve Seibel (USA) played a rally lasting 8 hr 15 min 1 sec at the Christown YMCA in Phoenix, Arizona, USA, on 14 August 2004.

The **longest rally in a competition** was in a 1936 Swaythling Cup match in Prague between Alojzy "Alex" Ehrlich (Poland) and Paneth Farkas (Romania). The 2-hr 12-min rally was the first of the match.

SQUASH

Most World Championship wins (team, women)

The women's title has been won nine times by Australia, in 1981, 1983, 1992, 1994, 1996, 1998, 2002, 2004 and 2010.

Longest recorded competitive match

Jahangir Khan (Pakistan) took 2 hr 45 min to beat Gamal Awad (Egypt) 9–10, 9–5, 9–7, 9–2 in the final of the Patrick International Festival at Chichester, West Sussex, UK, on 30 March 1983. The first game alone lasted a record 1 hr 11 min.

as one of the greatest finals of all time, 5–7, 6–4, 6–2, 6–7, 7–5. Nadal had lost to Djokovic in the previous two Grand Slam finals (Wimbledon and the US Open) and so set an unwanted record of three for the **most consecutive tennis Grand Slam final losses in the Open era**. (The Open era began in 1968, when professional players were first allowed to enter Grand Slam tournaments – with the first being the French that year.)

TARGET SPORTS

Most Mosconi Cup appearances

Johnny Archer (USA) has appeared in the nine-ball Mosconi Cup pool tournament – the "Ryder Cup of Pool" – 15 times, playing for the USA between 1997 and 2011. He shares the record with Ralf "The Kaiser" Souquet (Germany), who has also notched up 15 appearances, for the European team.

ARCHERY

Highest FITA 24-hour score by a team of two
Sergeants Martin Phair and Jamie Fowler (both UK) scored 37,359 points shooting FITA (International Archery Federation) 18-m rounds at the Royal Air Force Benson gymnasium in Benson, Oxfordshire, UK, on 17–18 June 2009. Phair even managed to shoot a rare "Robin Hood" – firing one arrow directly into the back of another.

Largest archery tournament
On 4 August 2010, 1,024 participants took part in an archery contest organized by the People's Government of Xiwuzhumuqin County, in Balaga'ergaole, Inner Mongolia Autonomous Region, China. The tournament was carried out under standard Mongolian archery rules.

Farthest accurate distance (men's)
Under regulated FITA conditions, Peter Terry shot an arrow 200 m (656 ft 2 in), at the Kalamunda Governor Stirling Archers club in Perth, Western Australia, on 15 December 2005. Terry's feathered feat was accomplished using a compound bow, and he hit two out of six on a FITA 122-cm (48-in) target.

Highest score, indoor (18-m)
On 6 March 2011, compound archer Christopher Perkins (Canada) broke the junior and senior indoor 18-m archery records with a score of 599 at the Canadian Indoor Championships.

DARTS

Most 180s in a Premier League Darts match
Gary Anderson (UK) hit a total of 11 maximum scores of 180 while playing Simon Whitlock (Australia) on 21 April 2011. Anderson's sharp-shooting dartsmanship took place during a Premier League Darts match at the National Indoor Arena in Birmingham, UK.

Longest singles marathon
Ryne Du Shane and Dylan Smith (both USA) played a marathon darts game lasting 41 hours at the Itty Bitty Bar in Holland, Michigan, USA, from 16 to 18 May 2011. The duo played a variant of darts called "Cricket", with Du Shane winning 105 to 66.

Most Weber Cup appearances

The Weber Cup is a tenpin bowling contest played between Europe and the USA since 2000. Tim Mack has represented the USA in 10 Weber Cups between 2000 and 2010 – the largest number of appearances.

Mack won the Cup six times between 2000 and 2008, the **most wins of the Weber Cup by an individual**. The **most team wins of the Weber Cup** is seven, by the USA, in 2000–02, 2006–08 and 2011.

Fewest darts to score 1,000,001
On 21–23 August 2010, a team of eight men – Mickey Mansell, Mickey Taggart, Felix McBrearty, Daryl Gurney, Campbell Jackson, Ronan McMahon, Eamonn McGovern and Thomas Stoga (all UK) – threw 35,698 darts in more than 46 hours to reach a score of 1,000,001 at The Weigh Inn bar in Omagh, County Tyrone, UK.

Farthest thrown bull's-eye
Cricket star Andrew "Freddie" Flintoff (UK) scored a darts bull's-eye from 5.05 m (16 ft 6.8 in) as part of his BT Sport Relief Challenge, Flintoff's Record Breakers, in London, UK, on 19 March 2012.

Most archery wins in men's recurve

Brady Ellison (USA) has won two men's titles using a recurve bow in the FITA World Cup, in 2010 and 2011. The other category in the World Cup, which began in 2006, features the compound bow, and the record for **most wins in the men's compound World Cup** is also two, by Sergio Pagni (Italy) in 2009 and 2010.

Highest darts score in an hour (men's team)
Martin Cotter, Damian O'Driscoll, Steven Coveney, John O'Shea, Craig Sproat, Jason Kavanagh, Kevin McDonnell and James Corcoran (all Ireland) of the Cork Darts Organisation scored 35,087 in an hour at St Vincent's GAA Club in County Cork, Ireland, on 20 March 2010.

POOL

Most wins of the World Cup of Pool

The World Cup of Pool – a nine-ball competition for doubles – has been won twice by two countries. The Philippines, represented by Efren Reyes and Francisco Bustamante, took the honours in 2006 and 2009. China – Li Hewen and Fu Jianbo – triumphed in 2007 and 2010.

Largest tournament

The eight-ball division of the 2010 American Poolplayers Association National Team Championships recorded the largest ever pool contest when 5,361 participants played in Las Vegas, Nevada, USA, from 19 to 28 August 2010.

Longest singles marathon

Colin Pilcher and Marc Murray (both UK) cued up for 72 hr 2 min – a charity marathon

record achieved at the Stateside sports bar in Consett, County Durham, UK, from 31 July to 3 August 2011.

Youngest pool world champion

Wu Chia-Ching (Chinese Taipei, b. 9 February 1989) won the pool world championships at the age of 16 years 121 days old. The championship was staged at Kaohsiung, Chinese Taipei, on 10 June 2005.

SNOOKER

Youngest professional to score a break of 147

Thanawat Thirapongpaiboon (Thailand) was 16 years 312 days old when he potted a maximum break at the Euro Players Tour Championship in Rüsselsheim, Germany, on 22 October 2010.

The record for the **youngest player to score a maximum score of 147 in a televised snooker match** was

set by Ding Junhui (China), aged 19 years 288 days while playing at the Masters tournament at Wembley, UK, on 14 January 2007.

Longest singles marathon

Gerry Cunningham and Gary McDonald (both UK) set the record for the longest singles snooker marathon when they played for 50 hours at the Chatham Pool & Snooker Club in Chatham, Kent, UK between 27 February and 1 March 2009. McDonald had only stepped in after Cunningham's original partner fell ill.

TENPIN BOWLING

Most strikes in a minute

Colin Champion (USA) made eight tenpin bowling strikes in a minute at the Kegel Training Center in Lake Wales, Florida, USA, on 24 January 2011. Champion, a member

The art of darts

- Dartboards measure 45.7 cm (18 in) in diameter and are divided into 20 sections, scoring from 1 to 20. Each number has double and triple segments.

- The bull's-eye scores 50 and is placed 1.73 m (5 ft 8 in) above the floor. (The outer bull scores 25.)

- The "oche" – the line behind which players stand to throw the darts – is 2.37 m (7 ft 9.25 in) from the board.

- In competition, players usually start at 501 and must reduce their score to zero. The final dart – known as "the check-out" – must be a bull's-eye or a double.

FACT: Phil has won the **most World Matchplay darts titles**, with 12 victories between 1995 and 2011.

Most Premier League darts appearances

Premier League Darts is played weekly from February to May across the UK. Darts sensation Phil Taylor (UK) is the only player to take part in all eight editions of the competition since its inception in 2005. As of 23 April 2012, he has won the title five times, the **most Premier League Darts titles held**. He also has the **most wins of the darts World Grand Prix**, with 10 from 1998 to 2011. The World Grand Prix is held in Dublin, Ireland, every October.

of the Webber International University bowling team, required 10 throws to complete his record attempt.

Longest marathon

Charity fundraiser Stephen Shanabrook (USA) bowled for 134 hr 57 min (more than five days!) at Plano Super Bowl in Plano, Texas, USA, from 14 to 19 June 2010. In the course of his record tenpin session, Shanabrook completed 643 full games.

Youngest bowling world champion

Paeng Nepomuceno (Philippines, b. 30 January 1957) won the 1976 Bowling World Cup in Tehran, Iran, aged 19 years 292 days. Nepomuceno – named the "International Bowling Athlete of the Millennium" – also holds the record for winning the **most tenpin bowling World Cups** (four times, in 1976, 1980, 1992 and 1996) and the **most bowling titles** in a career (124).

Snooker and darts championships

Snooker		
Most WPBSA World Snooker Championships (first held in 1969)	7	Stephen Hendry (UK)
	6	Ray Reardon (UK)
		Steve Davis (UK)
Most UK Snooker Championships (first held in 1977)	6	Steve Davis (UK)
	5	Stephen Hendry (UK)
	4	Ronnie O'Sullivan (UK)
Darts		
Most Men's World Darts Championships (British Darts Organisation and Professional Darts Corporation)	15	Phil Taylor (UK)
	5	Eric Bristow (UK)
		Raymond van Barneveld (Netherlands)
Most Women's World Darts Championships (British Darts Organisation, first held in 2001)	9	Trina Gulliver (UK)
	2	Anastasia Dobromyslova (Russia)
	1	Francis Hoenselaar (Netherlands)

Statistics correct as of 1 April 2012

Most snooker Premier League titles

Ronnie O'Sullivan (UK) won the Snooker Premier League title on a record 10 occasions between 1997 and 2011. The round-robin competition was originally known as the Matchroom League from its debut in 1987 to 1998. Stephen Hendry (UK) is O'Sullivan's nearest rival with six wins (1987–2004).

O'Sullivan has also recorded the **most competitive 147 breaks in snooker**, with 11 in total. Hendry equalled his record, with a 147 against Stuart Bingham (UK) in the first round of the 2012 World Championship.

HIGH FLYERS

FACT:
The first canopy-piloting competitions were organized in the USA in 1996.

Fastest speed on a 70-m canopy-piloting course (female)

Canopy piloting, also known as swooping, involves a skydiver deploying the parachute (canopy) at 1,525 m (5,000 ft), then entering a steep rotating dive, before levelling out and completing a course. On 31 July 2011, Jessica Edgeington (USA, above) flew the 70-m course in 2.301 seconds in Longmont, Colorado, USA. This equates to an average speed of 109.55 km/h (68.07 mi/h).

The **fastest time to complete a 70-m course by a male canopy pilot** is 2.093 seconds, by Greg Windmiller (USA) in Johannesburg, South Africa, on 5 December 2009. This equates to an average speed of 120.38 km/h (74.8 mi/h).

• **Out-and-return distance** (two straight-line legs, one turn point): 2,247.6 km (1,396.5 miles) by Klaus Ohlmann (Germany) from Chapelco, Argentina, on 2 December 2003.
• **Overall distance** (with at least one, but not more than three, turn points): 3,009 km (1,869.7 miles) by Klaus Ohlmann (Germany) from Chapelco, Argentina, on 21 January 2003.

Highest speed

The highest speed in a glider to set an official Fédération Aéronautique Internationale (FAI) record is 306.8 km/h (190.6 mi/h), over an out-and-return course of 500 km (310 miles), by Klaus Ohlmann (Germany) on 22 December 2006 at Zapala, Argentina. He flew a Schempp-Hirth Nimbus-4DM.

The **highest average speed achieved in a glider by a woman** when setting an official FAI world record is 227.8 km/h (141.54 mi/h), by Ghislaine Facon (France) at Chos Malal, Argentina, on 22 November 2005.

Fastest speed (out-and-return course)

On 26 December 2009, pilots Jean-Marie Clement (France) and Bruce Cooper (UK) set the world record for speed on an out-and-return course when they flew their Schempp-Hirth Nimbus-4DM at an average speed of 208.19 km/h (129.36 mi/h) over a distance of 1,000 km (620 miles). The duo began and finished their flight at Bariloche, Argentina.

First World Air Games

The inaugural World Air Games took place on 15–21 September 1997, at six different sites in Turkey. Events included parachuting, air racing, aerobatics, aeromodelling, microlight, hang-gliding, paragliding and ballooning. The Games are staged every four years, and were held in 2001 in Spain, and 2009 in Italy; the 2005 Games were cancelled because of organizational difficulties.

HANG-GLIDING

Most consecutive loops

Chad Elchin (USA) performed 95 loops consecutively at the Highland Aerosports flight park at Ridgely in Maryland, USA, on 16 July 2001. Elchin was towed to 4,846 m (15,900 ft) and looped his Aeros Stealth Combat non-stop down to 213 m (700 ft), at speeds of 28–128 km/h (18–80 mi/h).

Most World Championships

The men's World Hang-Gliding Championships were first held in 1976. The most individual wins is three, by Tomas Suchanek (Czech Republic) in 1991, 1993 and 1995; and Manfred Ruhmer (Austria) in 1999, 2001 and 2003.

The **most individual wins of the women's World Hang-Gliding Championships** is four, by Corinna Schwiegershausen (Germany) in 1998, 2004, 2006 and 2008. The competition was inaugurated in 1987.

MICROLIGHT

Fastest speed

Pavel Skarytka (Czech Republic) achieved an average speed of 194.2 km/h (120.67 mi/h) in a B-612 microlight aircraft over a 15-km (9.3-mile) course near Bubovice, Czech Republic, on 11 October 2003.

Highest altitude

The highest altitude achieved in a microlight is 9,720 m (31,890 ft), by Serge Zin (France) over Saint-Auban, France on 18 September 1994.

Most microlights airborne at once

A group of 30 microlights completed two circuits (anti-clockwise) within a 3.7-km (2.2-mile) radius above the Wrekin hill in Shropshire, UK. The event was organized on 6 May 2000 by Shropshire Microlight Flying School and Telford Business Club (both UK) to raise money for charity.

AEROBATICS

Most consecutive rolls by an aircraft

Zoltán Veres (Hungary) performed a head-spinning 408 consecutive rolls in an aeroplane during the Al Ain Aerobatic Show in Al Ain, UAE, on 29 January 2007.

Longest inverted flight

The longest flight sustained with the aircraft upside down lasted 4 hr 38 min 10 sec and was performed by Joann Osterud (Canada), flying from Vancouver to Vanderhoof, Canada, on 24 July 1991.

GLIDING

Farthest distances

• **Free distance** (one straight-line leg): 2,192.9 km (1,362.6 miles) by Terence Delore (New Zealand) at El Calafate, Argentina, on 4 December 2004.

BASE basics

• BASE jumpers perform daredevil leaps from fixed structures (rather than aircraft), gliding to earth with a parachute.

• "BASE" stands for "Buildings, Aerials, Spans and Earth". "Spans" denotes bridges; "Earth" denotes cliffs or rock faces. BASE jumpers leap from all of them, often illegally.

• Unlike parachutists, BASE jumpers do not carry a second 'chute – mainly because their jumps are relatively low and there's no time to deploy it.

• In freefall, a BASE jumper reaches a speed of around 190 km/h (120 mi/h).

• It's dangerous! A 2008 study concluded that 1 in 60 BASE jumps ends in death.

• The most common cause of death is "offheading" – flying in an unintended direction and hitting a solid object.

YOU'LL FIND MORE ACTS OF EPIC ENDEAVOUR ON P.122

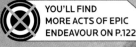

PARACHUTING

Fastest freefall style

In the freefall style discipline, skydivers must compete a pre-determined set of manoeuvres in the quickest time. The fastest time for the men's parachuting freefall style is 5.18 seconds by Marco Pflueger (Germany) over Eisenach, Germany, on 15 September 2007.

The **fastest women's parachuting freefall style** is 6.10 seconds, by Tatiana Osipova (Russia) over Békéscsaba, Hungary, on 19 September 1996.

Farthest non-stop flight by a powered parachute

The official FAI record for the longest distance flown in one hop by powered parachute is 1,105 km (686 miles), by Juan Ramón Morillas Salmerón (Spain) from Jerez in Cadiz to Lanzarote in the Canary Islands, Spain, on 23 April 2007.

Largest canopy formation

The largest canopy formation consisted of 100 parachutes and was formed by an international team over Lake Wales in Florida, USA, on 21 November 2007.

Most tandem jumps in 24 hours

On 10 July 2011, a total of 130 tandem parachute jumps took place in an event organized by Khalsa Aid and Skydive Hibaldstow (both UK) at Hibaldstow Airfield in Lincolnshire, UK.

The record for the **most tandem parachute jumps by an individual in 24 hours** is 105 and is shared by Luther Kurtz and Angela Bishop (both USA) at Harbor Springs Airport in Harbor Springs, Michigan, USA, on 29–30 June 2010. Kurtz served as the instructor on all jumps, with Bishop (his sister) as his tandem traveller.

PARAGLIDING

Farthest out-and-return distance

The greatest out-and-return distance achieved by a paraglider is 259.7 km (161.3 miles), by Aljaz Valic (Slovenia) at Soriska Planina, Slovenia, on 20 July 2006.

On 19 August 2009, Nicole Fedele (Italy) covered 164.6 km (102.2 miles) from Sorica, Slovenia, to Piombada, Italy, in a paraglider, the **farthest out-and-return distance by a female paraglider**.

Farthest flight in a tandem paraglider

Richard Westgate and Phillip Bibby (both UK) flew 356.2 km (221.3 miles) without landing from Vosburg to Krompoort Farm, South Africa, on 7 December 2006.

Greatest altitude

The greatest height gain in a paraglider is 4,526 m (14,849 ft), by Robbie Whittall (UK) at Brandvlei, South Africa, on 6 January 1993. By way of comparison, Boeing 747s normally cruise at 10,000 m (35,000 ft).

The **greatest altitude gained in a paraglider by a female** is 4,325 m (14,189 ft), by Kat Thurston (UK) over Kuruman, South Africa, on 1 January 1996.

Most loops

Raúl Rodríguez (Spain) carried out 108 continuous loops in his paraglider above Passy Plaine-Joux, France, on 15 June 2006.

SKYDIVING

Fastest speed

Switzerland's Christian Labhart reached a speed of 526.93 km/h (327.41 mi/h) in Utti, Finland, at the International Speed Skydiving Association (ISSA) World Cup on 4–6 June 2010.

The **highest speed achieved by a woman in a speed skydiving competition** is 442.73 km/h (275.09 mi/h), by Clare Murphy (UK) in Utti, Finland, at the ISSA World Cup on 15–17 June 2007.

Largest wingsuit formation

On 16 November 2009, 68 wingsuited skydivers jumped from four aircraft over Lake Elsinore, California, USA. They formed a complex diamond pattern for 3.2 km (2 miles) at an average speed of 160 km/h (100 mi/h). This is the largest formation recognized by the United States Parachute Association (USPA).

Longest banzai skydive

On 2 September 2000, over Davis, California, USA, Yasuhiro Kubo (Japan) jumped from a plane at an altitude of 3,000 m (9,842 ft) without a parachute. In 50 seconds, he hooked on to a parachute that had been thrown out prior to his jump!

Most Paragliding World Cups

Competitors in the Paragliding World Cup must negotiate a number of different courses at various sites worldwide. Each course has set turning points and a finishing line; the winner is the paraglider who is fastest to the line. Christian Maurer (Switzerland, right) has won three Paragliding World Cups, in 2005–07.

FACT: Skydivers generally carry out between 200 and 500 jumps before they try flying in a wingsuit.

Fastest speed in a wingsuit

On 28 May 2011, in the skies above Yolo County, California, USA, Shinichi Ito (Japan) reached a speed of 363 km/h (225.6 mi/h). He also travelled 23.1 km (14.35 miles), the **greatest horizontal distance in a wingsuit**.

Most World BASE Race victories

The annual World BASE Race has been held at Innfjorden in Rauma, Norway, since August 2008. Dressed in wingsuits, competitors leap from a mountainside and glide 760 m (2,500 ft) downwards. The winner is the BASE racer who reaches the ground most quickly – and, of course, without fatal injury. Frode Johannessen (Norway, above left) has won the World BASE Race twice, in 2009 and 2011.

FACT: Wingsuit flyers typically descend at a speed of 80–100 km/h (50–60 mi/h).

BOARD SKILLS

SKATEBOARD

Most Summer X Games medals

The greatest number of ESPN Summer X Games skateboard medals won to date is 19, by Andy Macdonald (USA). He won his first medal in 1999.

Highest hippy jump

A "hippy jump" is a trick in which the rider jumps off the skateboard and over an obstacle while the skateboard rides on underneath it. The highest skateboard hippy jump is 102.87 cm (40.5 in), and was achieved by Patrick Neal Rushing (USA) at Fish Creek Park in Arlington, Texas, USA, on 12 November 2011.

Most consecutive kickflips

The greatest number of consecutive kickflips performed on a skateboard is 1,546, by Zach Kral (USA) at 4 Seasons Skate Park in Milwaukee, Wisconsin, USA, on 30 November 2008.

Longest board slide

Rob Dyrdek (USA) produced a 30.62-m (100-ft 5.75-in) board slide on MTV's *Rob & Big* show in Los Angeles, California, USA, on 17 September 2007.

Fastest time to slalom 50 cones

On 28 August 2011, Janis Kuzmins (Latvia) slalomed through 50 cones in just 10.02 seconds at the Nike Riga Run in Mežaparks, Riga, Latvia.

FACT:
The ollie was originally known as a "no-hands aerial"...

Most consecutive ollies

Eric Carlin (USA) carried out 242 consecutive skateboard ollies at Mount Laurel in New Jersey, USA, on 16 July 2011. Carlin had three failed attempts (of 55, 122 and 20 consecutive ollies) before breaking the record on his fourth attempt of the day.

Most shove-its in 30 seconds

In a "shove-it", the skateboarder keeps the lead foot on the board while propelling his or her board with the other foot. The greatest number of skateboard shove-its executed in 30 seconds is 26, by Nicholas Hunter Heath (USA) in Ocoee, Florida, USA, on 4 September 2011.

Most tricks invented

Widely regarded as the most influential skater of all time, freestyler Rodney "The Mutt" Mullen (USA) invented at least 30 skateboard tricks between 1997 and 2008.

SNOWBOARD

Most Winter X Games gold medals

As of January 2012, Shaun White (USA) had won a record 12 Winter X Games golds. White won his 12th gold at Winter X Games 16 in 2012, when he scored the **first perfect 100 in the snowboard superpipe**. All of his gold medals came in snowboard superpipe and snowboard slopestyle. White has won 17 medals in all, the **most X Games medals won by an individual**.

Shaun, a two-time Olympic gold medallist, also holds the snowboard record for the **highest air on a superpipe**, reaching 7 m (23 ft) at Winter X Games 14 in Aspen, Colorado, USA, in 2010.

Most men's TTR World Snowboard Tour titles

Peetu Piiroinen (Finland) won three consecutive TTR World Snowboard Tour titles, from 2008/09 to 2010/11.

Most women's TTR World Snowboard Tour titles

To date, Jamie Anderson (USA) has picked up two Ticket To Ride (TTR) World Snowboard Tour titles, in 2007–08 and 2010–11.

Most World Snowboarding Championships

The greatest number of World Snowboarding Championship titles won (including Olympic titles) is seven, by Karine Ruby (France, 1978–2009). She won giant slalom in 1996, snowboard cross in 1997, Olympic gold in 1998, giant slalom, parallel slalom and snowboard cross in 2001, and snowboard cross in 2003.

Ruby also won the **most Fédération Internationale de Ski (FIS) Snowboard World Cups**, with 20 victories in the following categories: overall (1996–98, 2001–03); slalom/parallel slalom (1996–98, 2002); giant slalom (1995–98, 2001); snowboard cross (1997, 2001, 2003–04); and big air (2004).

The **most men's FIS Snowboard World Cups won** is six, by Mathieu Bozzetto (France), with victories in the overall (1999–2000) and slalom/parallel slalom (1999–2002) categories.

Fastest speed

The greatest speed achieved by a snowboarder is 201.907 km/h (125.459 mi/h), by Darren Powell (Australia) at Les Arcs in Savoie, France, on 2 May 1999.

Snowboard shortcuts

• The forerunner of the modern snowboard was called the "Snurfer" (a reference to snow and surf). It was created in 1965 by Sherman Poppen (USA).

• Having grown in popularity from its birth in the 1960s, snowboarding finally became an Olympic sport in 1998.

• The sport of snowboarding is part of the Fédération Internationale de Ski (FIS).

• The Snowboard World Cup series began in 1995. The sport's World Championships were inaugurated the following year.

Highest skateboarding ollie

An "ollie" involves raising all four wheels of the board off flat ground simultaneously. The highest ollie measured 114.3 cm (45 in) and was achieved by Aldrin Garcia (USA) at the Maloof High Ollie Challenge in Las Vegas, Nevada, USA, on 15 February 2011. Garcia was required to ollie over a rigid high bar without it making contact with any part of his body or board.

The ollie has a special place in the skate hall of fame: it was the **first skateboard trick** ever performed – by Alan Gelfand (USA) in 1976.

Fastest speed standing on a skateboard

The fastest skateboard speed from a standing position was 113 km/h (70.21 mi/h), by Douglas da Silva (Brazil) at Teutonia, Rio Grande do Sul, Brazil, on 20 October 2007.

FACT:
The WWS began in 2006 and ranks competitors based on their performance at a set of events worldwide.

(43.1 miles) on the Panama Canal on 19 March 2011 – the **longest wave surfed**. Saavedra followed a wave-creating boat for 3 hr 55 min 2 sec during the event, also breaking the record for the **longest time to surf a wave**.

Longest marathon
Kurtis Loftus (USA) surfed for 29 hr 1 min at Jacksonville Beach, Florida, USA, on 26–27 October 2011. The 50-year-old Loftus surfed 313 waves during his time in the ocean, using the same board throughout.

Oldest big-wave competition
The inaugural Eddie Aikau Memorial took place in Hawaii, USA, in 1984. The first event was staged at Sunset Beach on Oahu's North Shore, before moving the following year to its current location in Waimea Bay. The event has only been held eight times because of the precondition that the ocean swell must reach 20 m (66 ft).

Two boarders share the record for the **most women's world championships**. Tara Hamilton (USA) won the title in 1998 and 2002; Maeghan Major (USA) won in 1999 and 2000.

Most inverts in a minute
On 30 August 1999, Julz Heaney (UK) achieved 15 inverts (somersaults) in a minute on a wakeboard at the John Battleday Water Ski centre in Chertsey, Surrey, UK.

Story of the X Games
• The first "Extreme Games" were staged from 24 June to 1 July 1995. In 1996, they were re-christened "X Games".

• The Winter X Games debuted on 30 January 1997.

• Winter X Games 8 in 2004 was the first to be televised live; the 2011 Summer X Games were watched by an estimated 37 million television viewers!

Most Wakeboarding World Series wins

Phillip Soven (USA) won the Wakeboarding World Series (WWS) four times, consecutively, between 2007 and 2010. In 2011, he just missed out and finished second.

Longest rail grind
Calum Paton (UK) performed a rail grind measuring 78.7 m (258 ft 2.4 in) at the Milton Keynes Xscape in Buckinghamshire, UK, on 2 December 2011. The record was broken at an event organized by *Whitelines* snowboarding magazine, which saw professional and amateur riders attempt to break the record. No one matched the previous record until the very end of the event, when it was bettered by more than 10 m (32 ft 9.7 in).

SURFING

Most wins of the ASP longboard world championship
Nat Young (Australia) has won the Association of Surfing Professionals (ASP) Men's Longboard World Championship four times, in 1986 and 1988–90.

The **most wins of the ASP women's Longboard World Championship** is two, by Jennifer Smith (USA) in 2007 and 2009.

Largest wave surfed (unlimited)
On 1 November 2011, Garrett McNamara (USA) surfed a wave measuring 23.77 m (78 ft), trough to crest, off Praia do Norte, Nazaré, Portugal. The term "unlimited" denotes that the surfer is towed to the wave, enabling him or her to catch waves that would be too strong to be caught by paddling in.
Gary Saavedra (Panama) surfed a wave for 66.47 km

WAKEBOARD

Most world titles
Wakeboarding involves riding a board over water, usually pulled by boat, and employs water-skiing, snowboarding and surfing techniques. The World Wakeboard Association (WWA) World Championships were first held in 1994 and Darin Shapiro (USA) has won the men's title the most: three times in 1999, 2001 and 2002.

FACT:
To date, Gagnon has won 16 X Games medals – seven of which are gold.

Most X Games skateboard vert wins (men)

Pierre-Luc Gagnon (Canada) won the skateboarding vert competition (riding on a vertical ramp) at the Summer X Games five times from 2002 to 2010.

Longest rail slide
The longest wakeboard rail slide measured 46.87 m (153 ft 9.2 in), and was achieved by Borij Levski (Slovenia) in Ptuj, Slovenia, on 2 July 2011. Borij used a cablelift (similar to a ski lift) to tow him.

Longest ramp jump
Jérôme Macquart (France) performed a 15-m (49-ft 2-in) ramp jump on a wakeboard on the set of *L'Été De Tous Les Records* in Argelés-Gazost, France, on 14 July 2004.
The **longest ramp jump on a wakeboard by a woman** is 13 m (42 ft 2 in), by Sandrine Beslot (France) on the same TV show, and at the same location, on 7 July 2005.

Most ASP world titles (men)

Kelly Slater (USA) has won the men's ASP world title 11 times, in 1992, 1994–98, 2005–06, 2008 and 2010–11.

He has also recorded the **most consecutive wins of the men's ASP world title**, with five wins in 1994–98.

The **most ASP world titles won by a woman** is seven, by Layne Beachley (Australia), in 1998–2003 and 2006.

Highest career earnings for a pro surfer
Kelly Slater (USA) had won $3,062,005 (£1,931,274) by the end of the 2011 season. He also recorded the **highest season earnings** in surfing: $260,100 (£190,619) in 2008.

PREFER WEB SURFING? TRY SOCIAL MEDIA, P.164

WATER SPORTS

Youngest world champion

Fu Mingxia (China, b. 16 August 1978) won the women's world title for 10 m platform diving at Perth, Western Australia, on 4 January 1991, at the age of 12 years 141 days. The following year, aged 13, she won the same event at the Barcelona Olympics.

Most wins of the Diving World Series 3 m springboard (men)

Qin Kai (China) has won the Fédération Internationale de Natation (FINA/Midea) Diving World Series men's 3 m springboard event four times, in 2007 and consecutively in 2009–11.

Longest-distance underwater swim with one breath

Carlos Coste (Venezuela) swam 150 m (492 ft) in the Dos Ojos cave system in Quintana Roo, Mexico, on 3 November 2010. Coste's swim, which lasted 2 min 32 sec, is the longest with one breath in open water.

AQUABIKING

Most Pro Offshore World Championship wins (men)

Cyrille Lemoine (France) has won the Union Internationale Motonautique (UIM) men's Pro Offshore World Championship three times, in 2006, 2008 and 2010.

DIVING

Most wins of the Diving World Series 3 m springboard (women)

The most wins of the FINA Diving World Series women's 3 m springboard event is three, by He Zi (China), in 2009–11.

Most World Series 10 m Platform wins (men)

Qui Bo (China) notched up three consecutive wins in the FINA Diving World Series men's 10 m platform event in 2009–11.

First "perfect 10" in the World Championships

The first award of a score of 10 to a diver in the World Aquatic Championships was achieved by Greg Louganis (USA) at Guayaquil, Ecuador, on 5 August 1982. Louganis won gold medals in both the 3 m springboard and 10 m platform competitions.

Most World Championships

Guo Jingjing (China) won 10 FINA diving world titles, in the women's 3 m springboard, individual and synchronized events, five times: 2001, 2003, 2005, 2007 and 2009.

KITE SURFING

Youngest world champion (female)

Gisela Pulido (Spain, b. 14 January 1994) won her first Kiteboard Pro World Tour (KPWT) world championship on 4 November 2004, aged 10 years 294 days. She went on to win her first Professional Kiteboard Riders Association (PKRA) championship on 26 August 2007, aged just 13 years 224 days.

Fastest speed kite surfing (male)

Rob Douglas (USA) reached 55.65 knots (103 km/h; 64 mi/h), at the 2010 Lüderitz Speed Challenge in Lüderitz, Namibia, on 28 October 2010. The **fastest speed kite surfing by a woman** was 50.43 knots

(93 km/h; 58 mi/h), by Charlotte Consorti (France) at the 2010 Lüderitz Speed Challenge, in the same location on the same day.

Longest distance covered in 24 hours

Rimas Kinka (Lithuania) kite surfed for 504.8 km (313.6 miles) off the coast of Islamorada, Florida, USA, on 13 November 2011.

WATERSKIING

Longest jump

The farthest waterski jump by a male is 75.2 m (246 ft 8 in), by Freddy Krueger (USA) at Seffner in Florida, USA, on 2 November 2008. The **longest waterski jump by a woman** measured 57.1 m (187 ft 4 in), by June Fladborg (Denmark) in Lincoln, UK, on 24 August 2010.

Most flips (30 seconds)

Nicolas Le Forestier (France) completed 16 full 360° flips on one waterski in 30 seconds on the set of *L'Été De Tous Les Records* in Lac de Biscarrosse, France, on 5 August 2003. The **most waterski flips by a woman (30 seconds)** is eight and was achieved by Duan Zhenkun and Han Qiu (both China) in Xichang City, Sichuan Province, China, on 17 November 2011.

Barefoot slalom

Skiing on his bare feet, Keith St Onge (USA) performed 20.6 crossings of the wake in 30 seconds at the Gauteng North Barefoot Waterski Championships in Bronkhorstspruit, South Africa, on 6 January 2006. The **most barefoot crossings of the wake by a female waterskier in 30 seconds** is 17, by Nadine De Villiers (South Africa) on 5 January 2001 in Wolwekrans, South Africa.

Most wins of the women's aquabike World Championship

Julie Bulteau (France) has won the Union Internationale Motonautique (UIM) women's Pro Ski World Championship three times, consecutively, in 2009–11.

WHEEL SKILLS

Highest trials motorcycle wall climb

On 21 January 2009, Jordi Pascuet and Marcel Justribó (both Spain) each climbed a vertical wall on to a platform at a height of 3.22 m (10 ft 6.38 in) on the set of *Guinness World Records*, in Madrid, Spain.

Longest reverse ride

Hou Xiaobin (China) rode a motorcycle backwards for 150 km (93.21 miles) in Binzhou City, China, on 4 October 2006.

FACT: *Bad Habit* weighs 4,626.6 kg (10,200 lb). Each tyre is 167.6 cm (66 in) wide.

Longest ramp jump in a monster truck

Joe Sylvester (USA) carried out a 63.58-m (208-ft) ramp jump in his professional monster truck *Bad Habit* at the 10th Annual Cornfield 500 in Columbus, Pennsylvania, USA, on 5 September 2010. He made three attempts overall. During the first attempt the truck landed on its nose, shattering the front suspension.

Longest nose wheelie on a motocross bike

Riding a Kawasaki KX250T8F, Gary Harding (USA) maintained a nose wheelie for 86.2 m (282 ft) at Mason Dixon Dragway in Boonsboro, Maryland, USA, on 22 August 2010. Immediately after the attempt, Harding proposed to his girlfriend on the very same track. She quickly accepted!

BMX

Highest vertical air

Mat Hoffman (USA) carried out an 8.07-m (26-ft 6-in) air on a BMX bicycle from a 7.31-m-tall (24-ft) quarterpipe ramp on 20 March 2001, in Oklahoma City, Oklahoma, USA. He was towed by a motorcycle in the run-up to the jump.

The **highest air on a halfpipe** is 5.8 m (19 ft), by Dave Mirra (USA), off a 5.4-m-tall (18-ft) ramp in San Diego, California, USA, in January 2001.

Most backflips (single leap)

On 28 May 2011, Jed Mildon (New Zealand) performed three backflips on a bicycle in a single leap at the Unit T3 Mindtricks BMX Jam at Spa Park in Taupo, New Zealand. Mildon first rode his BMX bike down a 45° ramp from a height of 20 m (65 ft 7 in) before taking off from the up ramp.

Most gyrator spins in one minute

Takahiro Ikeda (Japan) carried out 59 gyrator spins in a minute on the set of *100 Handsome Men and Beautiful Women*, at the Kojimachi NTV studio in Tokyo, Japan, on 13 November 2011.

MOTORCYCLE

Longest front flip

On 17 November 2008, Jim DeChamp (USA) performed a 14.52-m-long (47-ft 8-in) motorcycle front flip at Godfrey Trucking/ Rocky Mountain Raceway in Salt Lake City, Utah, USA, for the MTV show *Nitro Circus*. This was the first time anyone has successfully front flipped a motorcycle.

First double backflip

Travis Pastrana (USA) made the first successful double backflip on a motorcycle at ESPN X Games 12 in Los Angeles, California, USA, on 4 August 2006.

Highest tightrope crossing

On 16 October 2010, in Benidorm, Spain, the aptly named Mustafa Danger (Morocco) motorcycled across a 666.1-m-long (2,185-ft) tightrope set at a height of 130 m (426 ft).

FACT: Born in Trieste, Italy, Tanja Romano began skating when she was just five years old.

Most World Roller Figure Skating Championships

Tanja Romano (Italy) won nine World Roller Figure Skating Championships at the women's combined event from 2002 to 2010. The most **World Roller Figure Skating Championships at the men's combined** is five, by Karl-Heinz Losch (Germany), from 1958 to 1966, and Sandro Guerra (Italy), from 1987 to 1992.

WHEELCHAIR

First landed backflip

Aaron Fotheringham (USA) landed the first wheelchair backflip at Doc Romeo skate park in Las Vegas, Nevada, USA, on 25 October 2008.

Longest stationary manual

A "stationary manual" is a position in which the wheelchair is held balanced on its rear wheels alone. Hermann van Heerden (South Africa) held this position for 10 hr 1 sec in Bloemfontein, South Africa, on 11 October 2011.

Longest wheelie

Eliza McIntosh (USA) sustained a continuous rear-wheel wheelie for 19.93 km (12.39 miles) at the East High School athletics track in Salt Lake City, Utah, USA, on 8 October 2011.

She completed 48 laps of the athletics track without the front wheels of the wheelchair touching the ground.

Most manual spins

On 23 February 2011, Gulshan Kumar (India) carried out a dizzying 63 manual wheelchair spins in one minute on the set of *Guinness World Records – Ab India Todega* in Mumbai, India.

AUTOSPORTS

Most F1 pole positions in a season

Sebastian Vettel (Germany), driving for Red Bull-Renault (UK/Austria), secured 15 Formula One pole positions from the 19 races in the 2011 season. Vettel won 11 grand prix races in the season (nine from pole position) and won the Drivers' Championship with 392 points, the **most points won in a F1 season**.

CARS

Most points scored by an F1 driver

Michael Schumacher (Germany) scored 1,517 points between 25 August 1991 and the end of the 2011 season.

Most consecutive F1 grand prix victories by a constructor

McLaren (UK) won 11 grands prix in a row in the 1988 season. Ayrton Senna (Brazil, 1960–94) won seven of the races and his fellow McLaren driver and arch-rival Alain Prost (France) won four. Senna went on to win the World Drivers' Championship, pipping Prost by three points.

Fastest lap of Le Mans

Loïc Duval (France) was driving a Peugeot 908 HDi FAP in the Le Mans 24-hour race when he recorded a lap of 3 min 19.07 sec, on 12 June 2010.

Closest finish in NASCAR racing

There are two instances of a NASCAR race being won by just 0.002 seconds. Ricky Craven beat Kurt Busch (both USA) by 0.002 seconds at Darlington Raceway in Darlington, South Carolina, USA, on 16 March 2003. Jimmie Johnson beat Clint Bowyer (both USA) by the same margin to win the 2011 Aaron's 499 race at Talladega Superspeedway, in Talladega, Alabama, USA, on 17 April.

Most NASCAR titles by a car make

Chevrolet (USA) has provided the car for the NASCAR champion 35 times between 1957 and 2011, including every year since 2003.

Most MotoGP Manufacturers' Championships

Yamaha (Japan) have won five Moto Grand Prix Manufacturers' Championships, in 2004–05 and 2008–10. Honda have won four championships (2003–04, 2006 and 2011) and Ducati one (2007).

Fastest speed in NHRA drag racing, top fuel

Top-fuel cars are the fastest drag racers – they have the engine at the back and a sleek "rail" design. The highest terminal velocity at the end of a 402-m (440-yd) run by a top-fuel car is 543.16 km/h (337.58 mi/h), by Tony Schumacher (USA) in Brainerd, Minnesota, USA, on 13 August 2005 in his US Army dragster.

Fastest speed in NHRA drag racing, funny car

"Funny cars" have the engine in the front and bodywork similar to a normal production car. Mike Ashley (USA) reached a terminal velocity of 538.04 km/h (334.32 mi/h) from a standing start over 402 m (440 yd) in a Dodge Charger in Las Vegas, Nevada, USA, on 13 April 2007.

First female IndyCar winner

Danica Patrick (USA) won the Indy Japan 300 in Motegi, Japan, on 20 April 2008. Danica began her career in kart racing and Formula Ford.

Most Supersport World Championships

Sébastien Charpentier (France) has won two Supersport World Championships (SWC), in 2005–06. In the SWC, the riders use models of motorcycles available to the public.

Most championship wins

Formula One		
Most World Drivers' Championships (first awarded in 1950)	7	Michael Schumacher (Germany, 1994–95, 2000–04)
	5	Juan Manuel Fangio (Argentina, 1951, 1954–57)
	4	Alain Prost (France, 1985–86, 1989, 1993)
Most World Constructors' Championships (first awarded in 1958)	16	Ferrari (Italy, 1961, 1964, 1975–76, 1977, 1979, 1982–83, 1999–2004, 2007–08)
	9	Williams (UK, 1980–81, 1986–87, 1992–94, 1996–97)
	8	McLaren (UK, 1974, 1984–85, 1988–91, 1998)

NASCAR (National Association for Stock Car Auto Racing)		
Most Sprint Cup Series Drivers' Championships (first awarded in 1949)	7	Richard Petty (USA, 1964, 1967, 1971–72, 1974–75, 1979)
		Dale Earnhardt (USA, 1980, 1986–87, 1990–91, 1993–94)
	5	Jimmie Johnson (USA, 2006–10)
	4	Jeff Gordon (USA, 1995, 1997–98, 2001)

Rallying		
Most World Rally Championships (first awarded in 1977)	8	Sébastien Loeb (France, 2004–11)
	4	Juha Kankkunen (Finland, 1986–87, 1991, 1993)
		Tommi Mäkinen (Finland, 1996–99)
	2	Walter Röhrl (Germany, 1980, 1982)
		Miki Biasion (Italy, 1988–89)
		Carlos Sainz (Spain, 1990, 1992)
		Marcus Grönholm (Finland, 2000, 2002)

Statistics correct as of 3 April 2012

BIKES

Most AMA Superbike Championships (manufacturer)

Suzuki (Japan) won 13 AMA (American Motorcyclist Association) Superbike titles between 1979 and 2009.

Most Superbike World Championships (manufacturer)

Ducati has won 17 Superbike World Championships, in 1991–96, 1998–2004, 2006, 2008–09 and 2011.

Fastest speed in NHRA drag racing, pro stock

Pro-stock bikes cannot use artificial induction such as turbocharging, supercharging, or nitrous oxide. The highest terminal velocity for a pro-stock motorcycle is 318.08 km/h (197.65 mi/h), by Michael Phillips (USA) in Baton Rouge, Louisiana, USA, on 18 July 2010.

Most F1 wins, manufacturer

The most Formula One grand prix wins by a manufacturer is 216, achieved by Italian constructor Ferrari between 1961 and 2011. Ferrari also has the **most starts in F1**: 830 from 1950 to 2011.

Most Motocross des Nations wins

Motocross takes place on off-road circuits and the Motocross des Nations, also known as the "Olympics of Motocross", has been contested annually between national teams since 1947. The USA has won the competition 22 times. Great Britain is second with 16, and Belgium is third with 14.

Longest motorcycle race circuit

The 60.72-km (37.73-mile) "Mountain" circuit on the Isle of Man, over which the principal TT (Tourist Trophy) races have been run since 1911 (with minor amendments in 1920), has 264 curves and corners.

FACT:
Jeff's 85 wins put him third in the list of all-time NASCAR wins. Richard Petty (USA) is top with 200.

Most wins in the modern era of NASCAR

The NASCAR Sprint Cup Series has been awarded since 1949, but the modern NASCAR era is usually dated from 1972, when the season was shortened from 48 races (including two on dirt tracks) to 31. Jeff Gordon (USA) has the most NASCAR wins in the modern era, with 85. He won his 85th race (pictured) at the AdvoCare 500 Race at Atlanta Motor Speedway, in Hampton, Georgia, USA, on 6 September 2011.

Most wins at the Isle of Man TT festival

Ian Hutchinson (UK) won all five solo races at the Isle of Man TT festival in 2010.

Fastest lap at the Isle of Man TT

John McGuinness (UK), riding a Honda in 2009, completed the "Mountain Circuit" in 17 min 12.30 sec. His average speed on the lap was 211.754 km/h (131.578 mi/h).

First female in the British Superbike Championship

In 2011, Jenny Tinmouth (UK) competed in the British Superbike Championship for the Splitlath Motorsport team.

Youngest and oldest

• The **youngest F1 grand prix winner** was Sebastian Vettel (Germany), who won the Italian Grand Prix at Monza on 14 September 2008, aged 21 years 73 days. In this race, Vettel was also the **youngest F1 grand prix driver to attain pole position**.

• The **oldest F1 grand prix winner** is Tazio Nuvolari (Italy), who won the Albi Grand Prix at Albi, France, on 14 July 1946, aged 53 years 240 days.

• Troy Ruttman (USA) is the **youngest winner of the Indianapolis 500** – he won the race at the age of 22 years 80 days on 30 May 1952.

• At 19 years 93 days old, Graham Rahal (USA) became the **youngest winner in major open-wheel racing history** when he won the IndyCar Honda Grand Prix of St Petersburg in Florida, USA, on 6 April 2008.

Open-wheel racing cars have wheels outside the car's main body (and often just one seat) so they include Formula One vehicles.

Most consecutive World Rally Championships

The most consecutive World Rally Championship (WRC) titles is eight, won by Sébastien Loeb (France) between 2004 and 2011. The next highest is four, by Tommi Mäkinen (Finland) between 1996 and 1999. Loeb won all eight titles in a Citroën, which is a record for **most consecutive World Rally Championship titles won by a manufacturer**.

FACT:
Loeb, above, leaps forward in the WRC rally in Portugal on 25 March 2011.

FACT vs FICTION

How did you get on with our sci-fi ships quiz on p.205? Here are the answers:

USS *Enterprise* (Star Trek)

Serenity (Firefly/Serenity)

Vigilant (Farscape)

Battlestar *Galactica* (Battlestar Galactica)

Nostromo (Alien)

Millennium Falcon (Star Wars)

Bird of Prey (Star Trek)

Tripod (War of the Worlds)

Station V (2001: A Space Odyssey)

ACKNOWLEDGEMENTS

Guinness World Records would like to thank the following for their help in compiling this year's edition:

Actors' Equity Association; Ruth Adams and Smokey; Dr John Andrews, OBE; Ascent Media; Eric Atkins; Back-to-back worldwide competition; Nigel Baker (Boxing Monthly); Josh Balber; Patrick Barrie (English Tiddlywinks Association); BBC Sport Relief; Sarah Bebbington; Dr George Beccaloni (Natural History Museum; Bender Helper Impact; Morty Berger (NYC Swim); Justin Bieber; Dr Janet Birkett; Bleeding Cool; Chelsea Bloxsome; Bolina; Boneau/Bryan-Brown; Bonhams; Michael Borowski; Catherine Bowell; The British Library; Broadway League; Lindsey Brown; Matt Burrows; Karumi Bustos (Zone Diet); Ronald "Ron" Byrd Akana; Cameron Mackintosh Limited; Hayley Campbell; The Cartoon Museum (London); Jennifer Cartwright; CCTV China (Guo Tong, Liu Ming, Wang Wei, Lin Feng, Liu Peng); Alan Cassidy, OBE (British Aerobatic Association); Clara and Camille Chambers; Georgina Charles; David Checkley (British Cave Research Association); Leland Chee; Mark Chisnall; Simone Ciancotti; City Montessori School; CITVC China (Wang Qiao); Joyce Cohen; Collaboration (Mr Suzuki, Miho, Masumi); Adam Cloke; Comic Connect; Connection Cars (Rob and Tracey Dunkerley); Don Coulson; Council on Tall Buildings and Urban Habitat; Kenneth and Tatiana Crutchlow; Andrew Currie; Dr Patrick Darling; Anastassia Davidzenka; Walter Day (Twin Galaxies); DC Thomson; Denmaur Independent Papers Limited; Mrs M. E. Dimery; The Dock Museum, Barrow-in-Furness; Joshua Dowling; Helen Doyle; Europroduzione/Veralia (Marco, Stefano, Gabriel, Renato, Carlo); Toby and Amelia Ewen; Eyeworks Germany (Kaethe, Andi, Michael, Oliver, Martin); Eyeworks Australia and New Zealand (Julie, Alison); F J T Logistics Limited (Ray Harper, Gavin Hennessy); Benjamin Fall; Rebecca Fall; Joanna Fells; Rebecca Fells; Simon Fells; Hannah Finch (Virgin London Marathon); Noah Fleisher; Patrik Folco; Esteve Font Canadell; Formulation Inc (Marcus, Ayako, Kei); Justin Garvanovic (Editor-in-Chief, European Coaster Club); Gerontology Research Group; Gerosa Group; Stewart Gillies; Sean Glover; Paul Gravett; Jackie Green; Martin Green; Victoria Grimsell; Alyson Hagert; Megan Hailshield; Kristin Mie Hamada; Hampshire Sports and Prestige Cars (Richard Johnston); Carmen Alfonzo de Hannah; Stuart Hendry; Heritage Auctions; High Noon Entertainment (Pam, Jim, Andrew, Fred, Peter, Rachel); HighestBridges.com; Graham Hill (Aerobatics); Deb Hoffmann; Hal Holbrook; Marsh K Hoover; Alan Howard (Archives Director, International Jugglers Association); Dora Howard; Matilda Howard; Katherine Howells; Colin Hughes; Paul Ibell; ICM (Michael and Greg); INP Media (Bryn Downing); Integrated Colour Editions Europe (Roger Hawkins, Susie Hawkins, Clare Merryfield); International Planetarium Society; Amy Isobel; Itonic (Lisa Bamford and Keren Turner); Nicolas Janberg (Structurae); Melanie Johnson; Roger Johnson (The Sherlock Holmes Journal); Rich Johnston; Barbara Jones (Lloyds Register Reference Library); Eberhard

Jurgalski (8000ers.com); Mark Karges; Yuriko Katsumata; Alex Keeler; Iryna Kennedy (Irish Long Distance Swimming Association); Siobhan Kenney (Protected Areas Programme, UNEP-WCMC); Anne B Kerr; Erik Kessels; Keys; Rishi Khanna; Christopher Knee (International Association of Department Stores); Dr Jennifer Krup; Siddharth Lama; Orla Langton; Thea Langton; The Library of Congress; Martin Lindsay; Ashley Fleur Linklater; Lion Television; Nickie Lister (Shiver Productions); Ashley Lodge; David Lotz; Peter Lowell; Dave McAleer; Sean Macaulay; Ewen Macdonald (Sea Vision UK); Eshani Malde; Albert, Stan and Sami Mangold; Steve Marchant; Duane Marden (Roller Coaster Database); Clodomiro Marecos; Mike Margeson; Missy Matilda; Clare "Babes" McLean (Flawless Files); Alex Meloy; Metropolis Collectibles, Inc. & ComicConnect.com); Miditech (Niret, Nivedith, Tarun, Alphi, Nikita); Jerry Mika (Asian Trekking); Mark Millar; Tamsin Mitchell; Harriet Molloy; Sophie and Joshua Molloy; Anikó Németh Móra (International Weightlifting Federation); Mark Muir (GRG); Steven Munatones (Open Water Source); Simon Murgatroyd; Kevin Murphy (Channel Swimming and Piloting Federation); National Maritime Museum (Claire Hyde, Sheryl Twigg, Rosie Linton); Captain Dexter Nelson (Oklahoma City Police Department); Forrest Nelson (Catalina Channel Swimming); Gemma Nelson; New Jersey Performing Arts Center; Jessica Nichols; Greg O'Connor (The Boston Light Swim Association); Nicola Oakey (Virgin London Marathon); Ralph Oates (boxing); Shaun Opperman (Battersea Dog Refuge); Michael Oram; Rubén Darío Orué Melgarejo; Tiffany Osborne (Virgin London Marathon); Peace One Day; Andrew and Charlotte Peacock; Daniel Phillips; Dr Clara Piccirillo; Elena Polubochko; Sarah Prior; Dr Robert Pullar; Shawn Purdy; Miriam Randall; Lauren Randolph; Dr Donald Rau; Simon Raw; Robert Reardon; Amnon Rechter; Dr Ofra Rechter; Re:fine Group; John Reed (WSSR Council); Rachel Reiner; Brian Reinert; Tom Richards; Fran Ridler (Virgin London Marathon); Jenny Robb (Curator and Assistant Professor at Billy Ireland Cartoon Library & Museum, Ohio State University); Gus and Dan Robertson; Jennifer Robson; Royal Shakespeare Company; Rosy Runciman; Richard Salisbury (The Himalayan Database); Tore Sand; Santa Barbara Channel Swimming Association (Scott Zornig and Evan Morrison); Schleich; Shaun Scarfe (Four One Four Ltd [BMX]); The Shakespeare Guild; Sean Shannon; Bill Sharp (Billabong XXL Global Big Wave Awards); Ang Tshering Sherpa; Apa Sherpa; Dawa Sherpa; Elisa Shevitz; Samantha Shutts (Columbus Zoo and Aquarium); Richard Sisson; Tom Sjogren (ExplorersWeb); Lottie, Jemima and Emma Skala; SLATE PR; Ben Smith; Society of London Theatres (SOLT); Maria Somma; Lyle Spatz; Spectratek Technologies, Inc (Mike Foster, Mike Wanless); Square Four; Peter Stanbury; Jennifer Stewart (The Broadway League); Stora Enso Veitsiluoto; Storyvault Films (Olivia Lichtenstein, Kieran Carruthers, Georgia Cheales); Strongman Champions League (Ilkka Kinnune and Marcel Mostert); Tej Sundher; Amy Taday; Emily Taday; Daina Taimina; Charlie, Daisy and Holly

Taylor; John Taylor (Skyhawk Aerobatics); Theatrical Management Association (TMA), London; Themed Entertainment Association; Spencer Thrower; TNR; Julian Townsend; truTV (Marissa, Adam, Angel, Marc, Stephen, Michael); UIM (Union Internationale Motonautique); V&A Theatre & Performance Enquiry Service; Alex Valerio; Pedro Vázquez; Lorenzo Veltri; Gabriela Ventura; Viacom18 (Sandhya, Romil); Anneka Wahlhaus; Charley Wainwright; Adam West; Beverley Williams; Adam Wilson; Stewart Wolpin; Lydia Wood; Dan Woods; World Planetarium database – APLF (France); Tobias Hugh Wylie-Deacon; X-Leisure and West India Quay; Nada Zakula; Cherry Zhu; Zippy Production (Mitsue); Zodiak Rights; Eric Zuerndorfer; Vincent Zurzolo. Plus the children and staff at St Thomas' Hospital, and all of our incredible record holders

STOP PRESS

Most Jaffa Cakes eaten in a minute

Peter Czerwinski (Canada, above) scoffed 13 Jaffa Cakes in just one minute in London, UK, on 1 May 2012. Stijn Vermaut (Belgium) matched Peter's feat in Vichte, Belgium, on 6 May 2012.

Highest altitude driven by car

Gonzalo Bravo and Eduardo Canales (both Chile) drove a 1986 modified Suzuki Samurai car to an altitude of 6,688 m (21,942 ft) on the slopes of Chile's Ojos Del Salado volcano on 21 April 2007.

First woman to climb all 8,000-m peaks without oxygen

Gerlinde Kaltenbrunner (Austria) summitted K2 on 23 August 2011 – her 14th "8,000-er" (a peak situated beyond 8,000 m, or 26,247 ft, above sea level) climbed without supplemental oxygen.

Heaviest mantle of bees

On 6 May 2012, Ruan Liangming (China) covered himself in a 62.1-kg (136-lb 14.51-oz) mantle of bees in Jiangxi Province, China.

Longest duration wing-suit flight

Jhonathan Florez (Colombia) was airborne in a wing suit for 9 min 6 sec above La Guajira, Colombia, on 20 April 2012.

The following day, he flew the **greatest horizontal distance in a wing suit** – 26.25 km (16.31 miles), again above La Guajira. He flew 28.91 km (17.52 miles) that day – the **greatest absolute distance flown in a wing suit**.

Longest literary work in Pilish

"Pilish" is a style of English writing in which the lengths of successive words correspond to the digits of π (pi, or 3.14159...). The longest text written in Standard Pilish is *Not a Wake* by Michael Keith (USA), following the first 10,000 digits of the mathematical constant. The opening lines run: "Now I fall, a tired suburban in liquid under the trees/Drifting alongside forests simmering red in the twilight over Europe", representing the digits 3.14159265358979323846...

Most calorific burger commercially available

The Heart Attack Grill in Las Vegas, Nevada, USA, offers the 1.4-kg (3-lb 2.9-oz) Quadruple Bypass burger, packing 9,982 calories, or 6.91 calories per g (195.95 calories per oz). In April 2012, the burger sold for $16.63 (£10.50) – bacon included, sales tax excluded.

Oldest company to supply Olympic medals

The Royal Mint (UK), which produced the medals for the 2012 Summer Olympics, was instituted in AD 886, which makes it more than 1,100 years old.

Sotheby's

Highest price for an artwork

The Scream, an 1895 pastel by Edvard Munch (Norway), was sold to an anonymous buyer for $119.9 million (£74 million) at Sotheby's in New York City, USA, on 2 May 2012. The price included the buyer's premium.

Oldest Eurovision Song Contest entrant (male)

Engelbert Humperdinck (UK, b. Arnold Dorsey, India, 2 May 1936) represented the UK at the 2012 Eurovision Song Contest aged 76 years 24 days. Humperdinck performed the track "Love Will Set You Free" at the 57th annual contest, which took place in Baku, Azerbaijan, on 26 May 2012.

Oldest pig

Born on 20 December 1990, Peeper (also known as "Pete") lived with his owners Ed and Denise Stottmann (USA) in Louisville, Kentucky, USA, until the age of 21 years 30 days.

Oldest woman to climb Mount Everest

Tamae Watanabe (Japan, b. 21 November 1938) summitted the 8,848-m-high (29,029-ft) peak of Everest for the second time on 19 May 2012 – aged 73 years 180 days.

Oldest female tandem paraglider

Margaret "Peggy" Mackenzie McAlpine (UK) was 104 years 5 months 16 days old when she completed a tandem paraglide in northern Cyprus on 14 April 2012. The feat saw her regain the title, which she had held aged 100.

Longest taxi ride

Leigh Purnell, Paul Archer and Johno Ellison (all UK) left Covent Garden in London, UK, by taxi on 17 February 2011 and travelled 69,716.12 km (43,319.5 miles) around the globe, arriving back at their starting point on 11 May 2012. The journey, in *Hannah* the taxi – a 1992 LTI Fairway FX4 London black taxi cab – clocked up £79,006.80 ($127,530) on the meter.

Largest sneaker collection

It all began back in 1999, when Jordy Geller (USA) started selling footwear on eBay. Jordy now has 2,388 pairs of sneakers in his "ShoeZeum" in San Diego, California, USA. All but six of those pairs are made by Nike.

FASTEST...

Completion of *Teamwork Temple, Wii Party* (Wii)

Francisco Franco Pêgo and Sofia Franco Ruivo (both Portugal) completed *Teamwork Temple, Wii Party* (Wii) in 60 seconds in Coimbra, Portugal, on 4 May 2012.

Mile hula hooped (male)

On 24 March 2012, Ashrita Furman (USA) covered a mile while hula hooping in 11 min 21.06 sec in New York City, USA.

LARGEST...

Chess piece

The Chess Club and Scholastic Center of Saint Louis and the World Chess Hall of Fame (both USA) created a "king" chess piece measuring 4.46 m (14 ft 7 in) tall and 1.83 m (6 ft) in diameter at its base. It was measured in St Louis, Missouri, USA, on 24 April 2012.

FACT:
Alex spent two whole years practising this feat. The record had not been broken for 16 years.

Chocolate sculpture

François Mellet (France/USA) created a chocolate sculpture weighing 8,273.3 kg (18,239 lb 8 oz) and measuring 1.8 m (6 ft) tall and 3.05 x 3.05 m (10 x 10 ft) at its base. It was presented in Irvine, California, USA, on 20 April 2012.

Most balls juggled

Juggler extraordinaire Alex Barron (UK) kept 11 balls in the air and achieved 23 consecutive catches in what is known as a "qualifying" juggling run. This feat was achieved at Roehampton Squash Club, London, UK, on 3 April 2012. He was 18 years old at the time.

Crocodile in captivity

Lolong, a saltwater crocodile (*Crocodylus porosus*), measured 6.17 m (20 ft 2.8 in) at Agusan del Sur province in Mindanao, the Philippines, on 9 November 2011. He weighed some 1,075 kg (2,370 lb).

Nappy sculpture

Huggies (Kimberly-Clark Argentina) created a diaper sculpture 5.14 m (16 ft 10 in) tall and measuring 13.2 m (43 ft 4 in) in diameter at the Golden Center, Buenos Aires, Argentina, on 14 April 2012.

Glow-in-the-dark painting

SZITIC Commercial Property (China) created a 104.18-m² (1,121.38-ft²) glow-in-the-dark painting in Shenzhen, China, on 29 March 2012.

Indoor Ferris Wheel

The government of Turkmenistan created an indoor Ferris Wheel with a diameter of 47.6 m (156 ft 2 in). It was measured in Ashgabat, Turkmenistan, on 30 April 2012.

Temporary straw bale maze

The MEGA MAZE, which measured 8,997.38 m² (96,847 ft²), was constructed by Garden Cents (USA) in Rupert, Idaho, USA, and was verified on 1 October 2011.

MOST...

Likes on a Facebook item

As of 21 May 2012, the most likes on a Facebook item is 1,045,272, in response to the announcement of Facebook founder Mark Zuckerberg's marriage to Priscilla Chan on 19 May 2012.

FACT:
Harry Feachen (UK) set the **longest diabolo grind** record at the 2011 Edinburgh Book Festival with a time of 1 min 35.6 sec.

First person to skate a 1080

Tom Schaar (USA) performed a "1080" (three full rotations while airborne) on a skateboard using a "mega ramp" at Woodward West in Tehachapi, California, USA, on 26 March 2012. Above, Tom receives his certificate from GWR's Kevin Lynch.

People dressed as chefs

A group of 2,111 people dressed up as chefs on 2 May 2012, in an event organized by the World Association of Chefs Societies (WACS) and Daejeon Metropolitan City Government in Daejeon, South Korea.

People dressed as leprechauns

A total of 1,263 leprechauns – each boasting the prerequisite green top hat and waistcoat, red beard and black buckled shoes – filled the streets of Bandon in County Cork, Ireland, on 17 March 2012.

People in one pair of underpants

A total of 169 participants squeezed themselves into a single pair of oversized underpants at an event organized by Dr Pepper (UK) at Thorpe Park in Chertsey, Surrey, UK, on 24 March 2012.

GUINNESS WORLD RECORDS

WANT MORE?

Take Guinness World Records with you wherever you go with the ebook editions of the 2013 book and the 2013 Gamer's Edition. Available for your device from your digital retailer.

GUINNESS WORLD RECORDS 2013

GAMER'S EDITION

Want a bonus chapter?

We're giving our readers a free digital bonus chapter from the Guinness World Records 2013 edition!

Read more incredible behind-the-scenes facts and trivia about this year's record-breakers by downloading the free bonus chapter now!

GUINNESSWORLDRECORDS.COM/ BONUSCHAPTER

Got what it takes to break a world record?

Have you always dreamed of being a Guinness World Records title holder?

Upload your video and you could join the league of amazing record-breakers!

GUINNESSWORLDRECORDS.COM/ CHALLENGERS

Love videogames?

If you're a fan of Guinness Worlds Records and addicted to videogames, look out for the 2013 Guinness World Records Gamer's Edition – coming soon in print and digital versions.

GUINNESSWORLDRECORDS.COM/ GAMERS

FOLLOW US TO GET EXCLUSIVE UPDATES ON THE WORLD OF RECORD-BREAKING AND MEET THE RECORD HOLDERS